VB & VBA
IN A NUTSHELL

The Language

The Language

Paul Lomax

O'REILLY®

Beijing · Cambridge · Köln · Paris · Sebastopol · Taipei · Tokyo

VB & VBA in a Nutshell: The Language

by Paul Lomax

Copyright © 1998 O'Reilly & Associates, Inc. All rights reserved.
Printed in the United States of America.

Published by O'Reilly & Associates, Inc., 101 Morris Street, Sebastopol, CA 95472.

Editor: Ron Petrusha

Production Editor: Mary Anne Weeks Mayo

Printing History:

   October 1998:   First Edition.

This book is printed on acid-free paper with 85% recycled content, 15% post-consumer waste. O'Reilly & Associates is committed to using paper with the highest recycled content available consistent with high quality.

ISBN: 1-56592-358-8   [4/99]

Table of Contents

Preface

Before we go any further, let's just clarify one fundamental point. Visual Basic for Applications (VBA) is the language used to program in Visual Basic (VB). VB itself is a development environment; the language element of that environment is VBA. Similarly, VBA is the language used to program all the applications in the Microsoft Office suite except Outlook, as well as a whole host of third-party applications. The VBA language (with a very few minor exceptions) is the same whether you're programming within VB or creating an application in a hosted VBA environment such as Word or Excel. Unless specifically noted, the language elements described in this book can be used exactly the same in both the retail version of VB and the hosted VBA environment; consequently throughout the book I often interchange the terms VB and VBA.

While it's important to emphasize that this book is a reference to a language component that's shared by VB and by applications that host VBA, it's also important to emphasize that it is *not* any of the following:

- A reference guide to VB controls and to their properties, events, and methods. These belong to the Visual Basic environment and aren't part of VBA at all. They are, however, documented in the forthcoming *Visual Basic Controls in a Nutshell*, written by Evan S. Dictor and published by O'Reilly & Associates.

- A reference guide to UserForms and their controls, all of which are defined by one or another version of the Microsoft Forms Library. Very much like VB controls, these belong to the hosted VBA IDE and aren't part of the language proper.

- A reference guide to the individual object models of the Office suite. By accessing its host application's object model VBA can automate the application. Nevertheless, both conceptually and practically, VBA code and object model code are distinct components. Some of the object models, however, are documented in the *Programming the...Object Model* series, published by

O'Reilly & Associates. These include *Programming the Access/DAO Object Models*, by Helen Feddema, and *Programming the Word Object Model*, by Julianne Sharer and Arthur Einhorn.

Why Another VB Book?

VBA is the single most important language for any developer to learn and master. The large numbers of people beginning VB and VBA programming, as well as the enormous number of current VB programmers who wish to deepen their knowledge and programming skills, is attested to by the wealth of published material about VB. Yet, there still is a desperate need for a detailed, professional reference of the VBA language.

There are literally hundreds of books lining the shelves about how to program using Visual Basic or how to use VBA to automate Office applications—seemingly each one promising to teach you more quickly than the rest. But if you're new to VB, you won't learn it overnight, or even in a few short weeks; VBA is a large and detailed language, with hundreds of different functions, statements, and language elements. Furthermore, because the Basic language has been developed over many years (portions even having their origin in Basic and QBasic), and each new version has to accommodate code written using the previous version, you will find that most tasks can be achieved in a number of different ways. There may be the really old function, the not-so-old function, and the brand-new function, all of which achieve a similar result—but which is the old one and which is the new one? Which one should you use? Is the new one really that much better than the old one? This depth of information is where the experience of using a language for many years, through all versions of VB and VBA, comes into play, and it is this experience that I hope to impart through this book.

What's Wrong with the Online Help?

In a word, nothing. The online help accompanying VB and VBA is an indispensable resource and one that most developers depend on. What this book does is take up where the help section leaves off, to give you the full picture. Contained within these pages are the experiences of professional VB developers who have used the VBA language in both VB and as a hosted language in Office applications all day, every day, over many years, to create complex mission-critical applications. It's these experiences that you can benefit from. Whether you have come to VB recently or have been using VB for years, there are always new tricks to learn. And it's always important to find out about the gotchas that'll getcha!

For the most part, the documentation with VB and VBA isn't bad; it just doesn't have the depth of information you need when you need it. Most of us can get by day to day without even opening the help section. But when you need to open the help section, it's probably because you've either hit an unexpected problem or need to know what the consequences of coding a particular procedure in a particular way will be. However, the help sections tend only to show you how a function should be included in your code. This is understandable; after all, the help sections for any language by their very nature must be created before that language goes into general use, but it is only general, everyday use in real-life situations that highlights how the language can best be used and what its problems and pitfalls are. Therefore, online help confines itself to the main facts: what the syntax is and, in a general way, how you should implement the particular function or statement.

A quick note here about the help section in VB6: Microsoft has decided to move the help section into MSDN and to convert it from WinHelp to HTML Help. During the prerelease stages, the new UI has come in for a lot of criticism for being slow, memory hungry, and unintuitive (to say the least!). I hope therefore that you'll read up on the new VB6 language features and then keep this book close to hand.

Who Should Read This Book?

This book is aimed at professional software developers. The VBA language is the most widely used rapid application development, or RAD, language in the world, and in addition to the millions of developers now using VBA, many more developers are coming into the VB arena from other languages, such as C++, not so much to replace those skills, but to augment their personal toolkit and to enhance their career opportunities.

This book is a reference work and not a tutorial, so, for example, I won't explain the concept of a For...Next loop; as a professional developer, you already know this, so you don't want someone like me insulting your intelligence. But I will detail how a For...Next loop works in VB, how it works in practice, what the alternatives to it are, how it can be used to the best advantage, and what pitfalls it has and how to get round them.

I also hope this book will be the main reference for experienced VB developers who are upgrading to VB6. I have spent several months working with VB6 in order to become familiar with and fully document the important new language elements and object models within it. Here again, though, if you're a VB developer upgrading to VB6, you don't want to be led by the hand like a newbie through the additional functions and object models; you know that your familiarity with the VBA language means that you can pick up the new features of VB6 quickly. You just need to know how this stuff works in the real world, and you'll be off and running.

An Emphasis on Professional VB Development

Because the VBA language is increasingly important for creating mission-critical applications, I have concentrated where appropriate on using language elements in a multiuser environment, detailing points of particular note for when you are programming components destined for an n-tier application model and for use within environments such as DCOM and Microsoft Transaction Server. In the same vein, I have also noted any differences found using language elements in NT and Windows 95.

Another pet peeve of mine is the readability and maintainability of VB code. Most corporate VB applications are now created by development teams rather than an individual programmer. It's therefore important to ensure that any member of the team can get up to speed quickly when maintaining your code, and of course that *you* can understand what it was you where trying to do when you wrote the code several months earlier! With this in mind, I have also noted—where necessary—tips to improve the readability and self-documenting character of your VB code.

How This Book Should Be Used

Well, to get here you've obviously passed the first hurdle, which is turning the pages; now all you need to do is read the words!

If You're a Developer New to VB

If you are new to the VBA language, then this book assumes that VBA is your second or subsequent language. The first half of the book leads you through the important areas of programming VB and VBA style, which, while very different from most other languages, are straightforward and easily mastered. I suggest therefore that you read these chapters in order while referring to Chapter 7 when necessary.

If You're a VB or VBA Developer

As an experienced developer, you can dip into the book to get the lowdown on a language element that interests you. Appendix A details all the functions, statements, and object models by category to help you find the relevant section in Chapter 7 more easily.

If You're a VB or VBA Developer New to VB6

Appendix D is a good place to start; it lists the new and amended language features and language-related object models in VB6. Work your way through this list, referring to the relevant sections in Chapter 7. While VB6 isn't the major leap forward that VB4 and VB5 were, you'll find some powerful additions that enhance both the speed at which you can develop an application and the quality of your applications. Note that because this book is specifically about the language, new VB6 nonlanguage features such as dynamic control addition aren't included.

How This Book Is Structured

This book is divided into three parts. The first part of the book, *The Basics*, is an introduction to the main features and concepts of Visual Basic programming. Even seasoned VB professionals should find items of interest here. If you're new to VB, this part of the book is essential reading. It's divided into the following chapters:

Chapter 1, Introduction
> In this chapter, you'll find information on what the VBA language is and how it fits in to the family of VB products. There's also a short discussion of the history of VBA.

Chapter 2, Program Structure
> This chapter details how you create the basic program structures in VB and VBA; how you implement procedures, functions, and properties; and how you start and stop VB and VBA programs.

Chapter 3, VBA Variables and Data Types
> This chapter looks at all the VBA data types and how to use them. There is also an in-depth look at the variant, a data type unique to the VBA language.

Chapter 4, Class Modules
> The introduction of the class module in Version 4 was probably the single most important innovation in VB since the introduction of VB itself; certainly, it has directly contributed to the success VB is now enjoying in the corporate world. In this chapter, you'll find out how to create and use class modules within VB and VBA applications.

Chapter 5, Automation
> Automation—the process by which a client accesses the functionality of a server application and drives it remotely—is one of the more powerful technologies supported by VB. This chapter describes how OLE automation is handled using VBA, detailing how to create and manipulate instances of ActiveX-enabled applications.

Chapter 6, Error Handling
> On the assumption that we all strive to create robust applications, this chapter shows how to include error handling in your VB or VBA application and how error handling is different when you're creating an ActiveX application.

The second part of the book, *The Reference*, consists of one large chapter, Chapter 7, *The Language Reference*, which thoroughly details all the functions, statements, and object models that make up the VBA language. The emphasis here is on the language elements found in VB4, 5, and 6. Also included (but with a lesser emphasis) for backward compatibility and completeness are the language elements still present in VB but that predate VB4; where these have been superseded by later additions to the language, this is noted.

The third and final section consists of the following appendixes:

Appendix A, Language Elements by Category
> A listing of all VBA functions, statements and major keywords by category.

Appendix B, Language Constants
> The constants built into the VBA language and available at all times.

Appendix C, Operators
> A list of the operators supported by VB, along with a slightly more detailed treatment of Boolean and bitwise operators.

Appendix D, What's New in VB6?
> A summary of the new language features and object models included in the latest version of Visual Basic.

The Format of the Language Reference

The following template has been used for all functions and statements that appear in Chapter 7:

Syntax
> This section uses standard conventions (detailed in the following section) to give a synopsis of the syntax used for the language item. It also lists parame-

ters and replaceable items, indicates whether they're optional or not, lists their data types, and provides a brief description.

Return Value

Where applicable, this section provides a brief description of the value or data type returned by the function or property.

Description

A short description of what the language element does, and when and why it should be used.

Rules at a Glance

This section describes the main points of how to use the function. The dos and don'ts are presented in the form of a bulleted list to enable you to quickly scan through the list of rules. In the vast majority of cases, this section goes well beyond the basic details found in the VB documentation.

Example

It's not uncommon for documentation to excel at providing bad examples. How often do we encounter code fragments like the following:

```
' Illustrate conversion from Integer to Long!
Dim iVar1 As Integer
Dim lVar2 as Long
iVar1 = 3
lVar2 = CLng(iVar1)
Msgbox "The value of lVar2 is: " & lVar2
```

So you won't find the gratuitous use of examples in this book. I see little point in including a one- or two-line code snippet that basically reiterates the syntax section. Therefore, I've only included examples that enhance the understanding of the use of a language element or demonstrate a poorly documented feature of a language element.

Programming Tips & Gotchas

This is the most valuable section of Chapter 7, gained from years of experience using the VBA language in many different circumstances. The information included here will save you countless hours of head scratching and experimentation. Mostly, this is the stuff Microsoft doesn't tell you!

See Also

A simple cross-reference list of related or complimentary functions.

Conventions Used in This Book

Throughout this book, we've used the following typographic conventions:

`Constant width`

Constant width in body text indicates a language construct such as a VBA statement (like `For` or `Set`), an intrinsic or user-defined constant, a user-defined type, or an expression (like `dElapTime = Timer()—dStartTime`). Code fragments and code examples appear exclusively in constant-width text. In syntax statements and prototypes, text in constant width indicates such language elements as the function or procedure name and any invariable elements required by the syntax. Constant width is also used for operators, statements, and code fragments.

Constant width italic

Constant width italic in body text indicates parameter and variable names. In syntax statements or prototypes, constant width italic indicates replaceable parameters.

Italic

Italicized words in the text indicate intrinsic or user-defined functions and procedure names. Many system elements such as paths and filenames are also italicized. Finally, italics are used to denote a term that's used for the first time.

How to Contact Us

We have tested and verified all the information in this book to the best of our ability, but you may find that features have changed (or even that we have made mistakes). Please let us know about any errors you find, as well as your suggestions for future editions, by writing to:

O'Reilly & Associates, Inc.
101 Morris Street
Sebastopol, CA 95472
1-800-998-9938 (in the United States or Canada)
1-707-829-0515 (international/local)
1-707-829-0104 (fax)

You can also send messages electronically. To be put on our mailing list or to request a catalog, send email to:

nuts@oreilly.com

To ask technical questions or comment on the book, send email to:

bookquestions@oreilly.com

Call for Additions and Amendments

It's our hope that, as the Visual Basic language continues to evolve, so too will *VB & VBA in a Nutshell: The Language,* and that the book will come to be seen by VB and VBA developers as the official (so to speak) unofficial documentation on the VBA language. To do that, we need your help. If you see errors here, we'd like to hear about them. If you're looking for information on some VBA language feature and can't find it in this book, we'd like to hear about that, too. And finally, if you would like to contribute your favorite programming tip and gotcha, we'll do our best to include it in the next edition of this book. You can request these fixes, additions, and amendments to the book at our website, *http://www.oreilly.com/ catalog/vbanut.*

Acknowledgments

This is my second book for O'Reilly & Associates, and I am proud to have been asked back. My sincere thanks go to my editor, Ron Petrusha, an accomplished author and Visual Basic programmer who has again contributed so much to this book, steering me in the right direction, crossing the Ts and dotting the Is, helping to nurture and develop this work, and adding that special quality that sets O'Reilly books apart from the rest.

My thanks also go to Tim O'Reilly for again having the faith to let me loose on his printing press! I would also like to thank the rest of the team at O'Reilly & Associates—Troy Mott, Katie Gardner, and all the other people within O'Reilly without whom this book would not have been possible. Thanks to Cheryl Smith-John for her hard work as technical editor, as well as to Dr. Steven Roman and Chris Burge for their technical reviews, which have (I hope) helped to make this a better book.

During the course of writing this book, I've been developing a client server application for Allied Carpets Group plc in the United Kingdom. I'd like to thank the VB development team there for their help and support—namely (but in no particular order) Gary Atkinson, Rachel Adams, James Cullen, and Ian Fremaux. My thanks also go to my agent, Nicky Properjohn at HG Resources.

Writing takes not just the dedication of the author, but a huge amount of support and understanding from the family. I count myself lucky to have such a devoted family—as always my strength and motivation Deb, Russel, and Victoria.

PART I

The Basics

This section serves as a general introduction to Visual Basic for Applications, the programming language that is common to both Visual Basic and to a range of host applications, including most of the applications in the Microsoft Office suite. Taken together, these chapters form an extremely fast-paced introduction to the most critical VBA programming topics. If you're an experienced programmer who is learning VBA as a second (or additional) programming language, this material should help to familiarize you with VBA in as short a time as possible. If you have some experience with VBA programming, you'll want to read Chapters 4 and 5 on class modules and automation, since they discuss two of the newer and most significant technologies incorporated into the VBA language.

In addition to its role as a tutorial, Chapter 3 is an essential reference to the data types supported by VBA.

Part I consists of the following chapters:

- Chapter 1, *Introduction*
- Chapter 2, *Program Structure*
- Chapter 3, *VBA Variables and Data Types*
- Chapter 4, *Class Modules*
- Chapter 5, *Automation*
- Chapter 6, *Error Handling*

CHAPTER 1

Introduction

To applications developers, end users, corporate buyers, and software vendors, Visual Basic for Applications (VBA) is becoming an increasingly important language. But VBA is more than just another software language; VBA is a unique conceptual method of creating professional business-oriented solutions.

VBA is the same language whether you are using it to create a Visual Basic application or to automate some task within Word or Excel. When you fire up your copy of the retail version of Visual Basic, the vast majority of language elements you use actually come from *VBAx.DLL*, the VBA library. Just look in the Object Browser to see how dependent on VBA Visual Basic actually is. Consequently, this book concentrates on the core VBA language regardless of its context.

What Is VBA?

Visual Basic for Applications is a hosted language and part of the Visual Basic family of development tools. Although VBA can be thought of as sitting below the retail version of VB and above VBScript in the VB hierarchy, VBA is actually an essential element of the retail version of VB, providing the vast majority of language elements used in VB. When hosted in VB, VBA provides language support and an interface for forms, controls, objects, modules, and data-access technologies. When hosted in other applications such as Word or Excel, VBA, using a technology called *automation*, provides the means of interacting with and accessing the host application's object model, as well as the object models of other applications and components.

In order to customize complex applications such as Excel, Word, Access, and a growing number of other applications from Microsoft and other vendors, VBA allows the developer to provide solutions that take advantage of sophisticated components that have been tried and tested. VBA is a glue language: a language that interfaces with the various objects that make up an application via the host application's object model. VBA is the means by which applications can become extensible, and it's ActiveX (or OLE automation) that provides the interface between VBA and its host application. It's this support for OLE automation that makes VBA an outstanding tool for rapidly developing robust Windows applications.

Until the launch of VBA 5.0 in early 1997, the language had no development environment; very much like VBScript today, VBA was simply a language interpreter. VBA 5.0 marked the start of an exciting new chapter for VBA; it now has its own integrated development and debugging environment running within the process space of the host application.

VBA itself becomes more object-oriented with each release, but the latest release (Version 6.0) adds relatively few functions and keywords to the VBA language. Instead, extra functionality has been incorporated into VB6 using new object models, and again it's the VBA language that allows you to integrate these object models into your application.

How Does VBA Differ from VB?

VBA is a programming language common to Microsoft Visual Basic, Microsoft Office, Microsoft Project, Visio, and a whole host of other applications. Although the particular "flavor" of VBA you use depends on the environment that hosts VBA, the core VBA language is basically identical regardless of the environment that hosts it. In other words, VB, the Microsoft Office suite, and a number of other applications share a common programming language named VBA that is identical across its various hosts.

Having made this generalization, we should introduce two qualifications. First, there are some differences that depend on the time at which the product hosting VBA was released. For example, although VB5 and Office 97 both indicate that they include version 5.00 of the VBA language, VBA for VB5 supports a number of language elements (like the `addressof` operator) that are not supported by VBA for Office 97. This is because VB5 was released somewhat after Office 97, which left more time to incorporate some new features in the former implementation that were omitted from the latter.

Second, there are some major differences that focus more on usage than on language elements. This is because VB is a complete RAD environment that features a range of user interface components and relies on VBA as its programming language:

- VBA programs and the VBA development environment itself both execute in the same process space as the host application, whereas VB programs can be compiled into executables and run in their own process space, independent of the host (i.e., Visual Basic) environment.

- Related to this, VB applications can be compiled into native code executables, whereas VBA applications are always interpreted.

- VB applications can be complied into ActiveX components and used within other applications.

- Unlike the retail version of VB, VBA allows code to be written for multiple platforms. Versions of VBA are currently available for Windows 95 and Windows NT on Intel; for NT on MIPS, Power PC, and Alpha RISC; and for Macintosh/Power PC.

• VBA as a hosted programming language and VBA in VB are typically used differently in developing applications. With VB, you normally use VBA to write code that references controls, procedures, and functions that are part of the program itself. With VBA, the vast amount of code is related to referencing the methods, properties, and functions that make up the object model of the host application. This is the overriding difference between VB and VBA, although the two are beginning to converge in this area as VBA is increasingly used in VB to control the ever-expanding list of VB's own object models, VB class modules, and in-process and out-of-process servers.

• The programs created by the two products are typically used for different purposes. VB creates standalone applications. VBA, though it can be used to create "applications" that act as intermediaries between the user and the host application (like Word or Excel) typically provides some essential service or adds some enhancement to its host application.

How Does VBA Differ from VBScript?

VBScript was born of VBA.* VBA supports OLE automation; that is, you can create instances of objects, call their methods, and set and return object properties. This functionality was left out of VBScript, since it was thought too risky for the web scripting environment. However, when used at the server side with Active Server Pages, VBScript has almost the same OLE (ActiveX) functionality as VBA.† In addition, VBScript is simply an interpreted language component; it has no design environment apart from the ActiveX Control Pad. In contrast, from Version 5 onward, VBA has its own integrated development environment, including an integrated debugging window, a Properties window, and many of the standard features that were originally found in the VB IDE.

How Does a VBA Program Differ from a Macro?

VBA takes over where macro languages left off. Macro languages are used to simply automate repetitive tasks in an application. Because VBA replaced the macro languages found in Office applications, there is still a common misconception that VBA is a macro language. However, referring to VBA as a macro language is like referring to a Ferrari as a means of getting from A to B. While it's basically a true statement, it hardly does justice to the product or to the sophistication of the technology involved. With VBA, like the Ferrari, you'll get from A to B faster and more stylishly, and you'll be in demand! (Unlike a Ferrari, though, VBA isn't red.)

---

* For a fast-paced introduction to VBScript, see *Learning VBScript*, by Paul Lomax, published by O'Reilly & Associates.

† It's able to do this because the ASP Server object, rather than VBScript, instantiates objects and provides support for automation. See *Active Server Pages in a Nutshell*, by Keyton Weissinger, due from O'Reilly & Associates in early 1999.

Let's look at how VBA has become the first almost universally accepted application customization language.

A Brief History of VBA

The incredible popularity of Visual Basic shortly after its launch prompted Microsoft to wonder if a "cut down" version of the product could replace the many different macro languages lurking behind its range of business applications. Bill Gates talked for many years—since the days of DOS—of a universal batch language. This goal is now coming to fruition in the shape of VBA. However, as the following chronology shows, this goal wasn't achieved overnight:

1993—VBA launched with Microsoft Excel
VBA first saw the light of day as a replacement for the macro language in Microsoft Excel. Its power and sophistication in comparison to the original macro languages made it an instant success with those developers creating custom solutions with Excel.

1994—VBA included with Microsoft Project
Perhaps because Microsoft Project had to be customized in many situations to satisfy the wide and varied needs of project managers, Project was next on the list of applications to be VBA-enabled.

1995—Included with Microsoft Access, replacing Access Basic
Perhaps the biggest boost to VBA came when Access Basic (a subset of VBA written specifically for Access) was replaced with the full version of VBA. Many of today's VB programmers apprenticed on VBA in Access, cutting their teeth on custom applications using VBA and Access. Many Access developers have moved on to the full version of Visual Basic to create full three-tier client server applications.

1996—VBA becomes the language element of Visual Basic
1996 saw the launch of Visual Basic 4.0, a massive leap forward and almost a totally different product from VB3. Written in C++, Version 4 was a ground-up rewrite of VB, whose previous versions were written in assembler. With VB4, VB became object-oriented; VB could be used to create class models and DLLs, as well as to easily reference external object libraries. Part of the componentization of Visual Basic was the use of a separate language library, VBA. Some intrinsic language elements remained in the VB and VB runtime libraries for backward compatibility, but most were transferred to the VBA library, and many were completely rewritten.

1996—Included with Word, replacing Word Basic
Many people were surprised that Word Basic was the last of the Microsoft macro languages to hit the dust. This appears to have happened partly because the demand for customized word processor applications is much smaller than for customized applications using the other components of the Office suite, and because the core of Word developers were initially opposed to a change to VBA.

1997—VBA 5.0 launched, covering the complete range of Office 97 products

With the inclusion of VBA in PowerPoint, all the members of Office 97 (with the exception of Outlook, which is VBScript-enabled) now include VBA as their programming language.

1997—Microsoft licenses VBA for use with other software

Over 50 major software vendors licensed VBA within the first few weeks of Microsoft's announcement. The fact that so many leading companies have chosen to license VBA bodes well for the future. In learning VBA now, you are building a skill set that will be in demand for a long time to come.

1998—VB and VBA Version 6 launched

The language continues to expand, although not at the same rate as previously. Interestingly, with the exception of two functions, the new functions in VBA have come from VBScript. The rest of the new functionality available to VB/VBA developers comes in the form of several new object models, which is likely to be the way VB and VBA will expand in the future.

What Can You Do with VBA?

VBA contains all the functions and statements necessary to create robust Windows applications, whether this is done using Visual Basic or a host application. The tasks you can perform with VBA include (but are not limited to):

- Creating instances of OLE (ActiveX) objects within your code
- Creating classes (reusable custom software objects)
- Linking to ODBC databases like Access and SQL Server
- Integrating with the messaging API (MAPI) to create Exchange/Mail applications
- Integrating with Internet and intranet solutions
- Creating custom dialog boxes and forms
- Storing and retrieving data from the Windows registry
- Detecting and handling errors
- Incorporating ActiveX controls into the application interface
- Passing data between VBA-enabled applications with a minimum of programming and fuss
- Driving a second VBA-enabled application from within a first VBA-enabled application
- Controlling the Office applications; in theory, 100% of the functionality of Office products is exposed as objects/properties/methods, which means that, with occasional exceptions, there isn't anything you can't do programmatically that you can do from the application's interface.
- Automating anything that can be done from the keyboard, mouse, or menus

There is also one thing you *can't* do directly with the VBA language: you can't output to a printer. So how do you print from a VBA application? When hosted in an application, VBA can control the application's own printing functionality; when used within VB, VBA can control the VB Printer object.

Customizing and Creating Applications with VBA

Off-the-shelf—or "shrink-wrapped"—software products don't always provide the specialized features most corporate and many private users need, which means that some kind of customization is often needed to create the desired solution. Software vendors include features within their products that will appeal to as large an audience as possible. They quite rightly have to balance the cost of development with the potential extra sales for any new feature they add to their product. There is such an infinite range of different and unique business problems that it would be impossible for any off-the-shelf package to be versatile enough to fulfill every need.

Let's say you need an application that links to the company's main database and presents data in such a way that managers can readily understand and work with it, create charts from it, reformat it, etc. You could either spend the next 12 months developing and debugging your very own spreadsheet application, or you could supply a custom application written with VBA using Excel as the host. This applies, of course, not only to Excel, but to the other applications in Microsoft Office as well, which means that as a developer, you can also program interoperability between all the applications in the Microsoft Office suite.

The traditional home of VBA has been in Microsoft products. However, since Microsoft has now stamped VBA's passport by licensing it to other major software vendors, you will find VBA venturing further afield into territory that was once off limits. VBA skills will become more and more in demand as a wider range of software becomes VBA-enabled. This also means that for the first time, developers across a wide range of products have a common programming interface.

Of course, a software developer can always start from scratch to create a solution to a business problem, and the most popular tool for creating business applications is Visual Basic. A mark of Visual Basic's maturity is that for the first time, Microsoft's own developers have used Visual Basic to write parts of the Visual Studio 6 development suite. The most sophisticated business solutions using the latest technologies can be created with Visual Basic, and corporations, large and small, around the world are now looking to Visual Basic to provide mission critical enterprise-wide applications. The speed and relative ease with which a Visual Basic application can be created and maintained results in major cost savings for corporations. When you add to this the ease with which a Visual Basic application can be ported to a web environment, you can see why Visual Basic is the world's most popular RAD tool.

Object Models: The Power of Programming with VBA

VBA is a single language, although when comparing code taken from a VBA program written for Word with one written for Access or Visual Basic, you could be forgiven for thinking you are reading code from two very different languages. This is because VBA interfaces with an application's object model, and much of the time the code you write references objects that are unique to the host application. To demonstrate this, in the VBA code fragments shown in Examples 1-1 through 1-4, generic VBA code is shown in a normal typeface, object code that is unique to the application is shown in bold, and variables are shown in italics.

Example 1-1: A Code Snippet from an Excel VBA Program

```
For Each c In Worksheets("Sheet1").Range("C4:C17").Cells
    If c.Value = iCond Then
        tempTot = tempTot + c.Offset(0, 1).Value
    End If
Next c
```

Example 1-2: A Code Snippet from a Word VBA Program

```
Set myRange = ActiveDocument.Range( _
    Start:=ActiveDocument.Paragraphs(2).Range.Start, _
            End:=ActiveDocument.Paragraphs(2).Range.End)
myRange.Select
myRange.Bold = True
```

Example 1-3: A Code Snippet from an Access VBA Program

```
Form_Form1.RecordSource = "SELECT Products.ProductCode, " _
  & " Products.BinLocation, Descriptions.Description" _
  & " FROM Products INNER JOIN Descriptions " _
  & " ON Products.ProductCode = Descriptions.ProductCode" _
  & " WHERE (((Descriptions.Language)=" _
  & iLangCode & "));"
Text0.ControlSource = "ProductCode"
Text2.ControlSource = "Descriptions.Description"
Text4.ControlSource = "BinLocation"
```

Example 1-4: A Code Snippet from a Visual Basic Program

```
Dim oADOComm     As ADODB.Command
Dim oADORecs     As ADODB.Recordset
Dim sSQL         As String

Set oADOComm = New ADODB.Command
    oADOComm.ActiveConnection = "LiveDSN"
    sSQL = "SELECT * FROM employees"
    oADOComm.CommandType = adCmdText
    oADOComm.CommandText = sSQL

    Set oADORecs = oADOComm.Execute
        If Not oADORecs.EOF And Not oADORecs.BOF Then
            Do While Not oADORecs.EOF
                cboEmployeeNames.AddItem _
                                oADORecs.Fields("Name").Value
                oADORecs.MoveNext
            Loop
        End If
    Set oADORecs = Nothing
Set oADOComm = Nothing
```

As you can see from these examples, the referenced object model plays an integral role in the creation of VBA-based programs. The object model describes the application and the features you can control. You then use VBA to access and change properties of the object model, handle events fired by objects in the model, and call the methods of the objects.

Once you're familiar with one object model, you will find great reductions in the time it takes to learn another object model. For example, about 50% of the Office 97 object models are shared. In short, if you can create applications using one object model, you can move to another host and develop custom applications there too, with a minimum amount of time spent learning the new object model.

Through the object model, the software vendor allows you to control the application, to set and retrieve properties, and to invoke methods. It's up to the software vendor to decide how much or how little of the application you have access to via its object model, and in the case of the Microsoft Office applications, 100% of their functionality is presumably exposed via the various object models. In addition to the object model, each host application has its own set of predefined (intrinsic) constants to speed development and make code easier to read and maintain.

So although they are conceptually distinct from the VBA language itself, object models are central to programming in VBA both within a host application, and—although to a lesser extent—in Visual Basic. The extensive reliance on individual object models, though, doesn't diminish the significance of VBA, even if it is only the "glue" that holds together a program's use of an object model (or, in the case of Visual Basic, a program's use of ActiveX controls).

As we've already seen throughout this chapter, the VBA language is the single most important development language in the business world and will continue to be so for some time to come. Becoming proficient in the VBA language is therefore important to many millions of professional developers across the world, because no other language presents the developer with so many opportunities—not just a promise but a real demand for skills right now. However, VBA is by its very nature a large language in terms of the number of functions, statements, and constructs that must be mastered. Once the language is mastered, the rest of the jigsaw falls into place, and you can easily and quickly move from one VBA-enabled development environment to another.

CHAPTER 2

Program Structure

In its simplest form, Visual Basic for Applications is a *glue* language. This means that as a VB or VBA developer, you concentrate on the interface of and interaction between the objects and controls within the application, gluing the various elements of the application together by writing procedures to perform programmatic tasks and by adding code to handle events. Visual Basic programs are primarily event-driven. Some event or other—such as the user clicking a button—triggers most of the procedures you will write.

From a developer's point of view, one of the most important characteristics of an event-driven application is that, for the most part, the various elements of the program are *not* interdependent. Sections of your program can be written in complete isolation from the rest. Procedures can be added, removed, or disabled without necessarily having an adverse effect on the whole application. This isn't to say that a Visual Basic application is unstructured; far from it. Before starting to write your VB application, you should have a clear plan of how the various elements of your application are going to interact.

Over the past few years, VB developers have been empowered with a rapidly expanding development environment that can now create custom controls and ActiveX DLLs and EXEs that run either as client-side servers or as remote servers. This movement towards a more object-based ethos has forced a change in the programming style of most VB developers. For the majority of professional VB developers, the days when you could sit in front of a blank form and begin programming without a written plan—altering the architecture of your application on the fly—are long gone.

In this chapter, you will see how to structure a VB program, from starting your program, through the various procedure types at your disposal, and then how you can eventually end your VB program.

Getting a VB Program to Run

Regardless of the type of application you're writing and the development tool (hosted VBA or the retail version of VB) you're using, there has to be a starting point or an entry point for your program. Here there is a major difference between VB and VBA: a VB application is launched as an application in its own right, whereas the VBA program has to be launched by the host application. But in either case, the starting point you choose is decided by the type of application you are writing, as well as by the facilities offered by your development environment for launching applications. In this section, we'll look at the methods available to you for starting your application.

Because VBA is now hosted in a wide range of different applications, each of which has its own ways of launching an application or routine, it's impossible to describe here how to start your program running in each. Instead, we'll focus on the two most popular applications for hosted VBA, Word and Excel.

 In discussing the launching of VBA programs in Word and Excel, I mention using the application's user interface to launch the program using a keyboard combination or a toolbar button. This can also be done programmatically. A discussion of how to do so, however, is beyond the scope of this book.

Running VBA Modules in Word

A Word/VBA program can take a multitude of forms, ranging from a small routine that accomplishes some utility function at one extreme to a complete application that handles every detail of the user's interaction with Word. Of course, you want the method that invokes your program to be consistent with its general purpose. Fortunately, Word provides several ways to launch a VBA application.

Storing your code

Whenever Word starts, it automatically loads the default global template file, *normal.dot*. It then loads all template (*.dot*) files in the Word startup directory, which (assuming the software is Word 97) is defined by the STARTUP-PATH value entry in the HKEY_CURRENT_USER\Software\Microsoft\Office\8.0\Word\ Options key in the registry and can be customized by selecting the File Locations tab from the Options dialog (Tools → Options) and modifying the Startup entry. These also become part of Word's global layer, as do Word add-in (*.wll*) files, which are loaded last. So if your application is to affect the Word environment or multiple Word documents, you should place your code in a template that is loaded into the global layer. If your program is to be distributed to other users, you should store your code in a global template file other than *normal.dot*, where you're likely to overwrite customizations the user has made.

A global template file loaded during Word startup is displayed in the Project window visible in the development environment, but isn't viewable. To edit the file, you must open it in the Word environment. Note that you may have to close and reopen Word in order for modifications to take effect. In some cases, even if the file is open, you still may not be able to edit its code in the VBA IDE. In that case, you'll have to make modifications to a copy of the file stored in another directory and synchronize the two copies.

If your application applies to a set of documents that are based on a template (which is typically stored in the Office Template directory or one of its subdirectories), you can place your code in the template file. Each document created using that template maintains a reference to the template. So even though the code remains in the template and isn't copied to the document, the VBA code in the template can be executed as long as the reference is valid.

If your application applies only to a particular document, you can store the code in the document itself. You don't have to work with the templates loaded into Word's global layer.

At startup

If you are developing an application or routine that is responsible for initializing the Word environment, that provides some service expected to be available throughout a Word session, or that implements a customized interface that mediates between the user and Word, you want to have Word launch your application whenever Word itself is launched. Word provides two methods of doing this. Both are remnants of WordBasic and both require that you store your macro in a global template:

- Add a procedure called *AutoExec* to any code module. In order to execute at startup, it must be a `Public` procedure.

- Create a new module named AutoExec and add a procedure to it called *Main*. Once again, *Main* must be declared as `Public` in order to run at startup.

There is also a converse scenario—running a procedure when Word is closing—that operates in exactly the same way as AutoExec. You simply name the procedure *AutoExit* or include an AutoExit module with a *Main* procedure.

When a document loads

In many cases, your application should launch whenever a particular document (or a set of documents, or even all documents) is opened. Once again, Word offers several methods of executing code when an existing document is opened or a new one is created. All of them require, though, that the code be located either in the current template or in the document itself. The methods are:

- Creating a procedure called *AutoOpen*, which is executed whenever an existing document containing a reference to *AutoOpen*'s template or containing the actual *AutoOpen* code is fired. Similarly, you can create a procedure called *AutoNew*, which is executed when a new document using the template containing the code is created. The procedures must be declared as `Public` to be visible. *AutoOpen* and *AutoNew* macros are a WordBasic, rather than a VBA, feature.

- Creating a code module named AutoOpen (or, for a new document, AutoNew) and defining a public *Main* procedure in it. AutoNew and AutoOpen code modules are a WordBasic, rather than a VBA, feature.

- Attaching code to the template's or document's Document_Open event, which fires when an existing document is opened, or to its Document_New event, which fires when a new document is created based on the template containing the Document.New event handler. This is the "official" VBA way to create self-executing macros when a document loads.

You can also designate a cleanup routine to execute when a document closes. WordBasic recognizes either an *AutoClose* procedure or a *Main* routine in a code module named AutoClose. VBA fires the Document.Close event when a document closes.

In response to direct user action

Frequently, VBA/Word code is less an "application" as we typically understand it than a "macro"—i.e., a small piece of self-contained code that performs some useful function. For macros to be useful, there has to be a way for the user to run them easily* from the Word interface. In this respect, Word provides a rich environment for the macro developer, since it supports so many ways of hooking a macro to the user interface. These include:

Intercepting Word's built-in commands

Most common Word operations are public procedures. This means that if you create a procedure of the same name and store it in a global template, in the current document's template, or in the active document itself, your procedure, rather than Word's built-in procedure, will execute. For example, when the user selects the Close option from the File menu, the *FileClose* procedure executes. Ordinarily, Word closes the active document. However, you can modify Word's behavior by substituting a *FileClose* routine like the following, which gives the user the option of closing all open documents:

```
Public Sub FileClose()

Dim lngResponse As Long
Dim objDoc As Document

If Documents.Count = 1 Then
    Application.ActiveDocument.Close
Else
```

---

* The most obvious method is one we won't discuss here. When the user selects Tools → Macro → Macros, Word displays the Macro dialog, which lists the names of all macros that are in scope (i.e., public macros in the global layer, macros in the current template, and macros in the current document).

```
        lngResponse = MsgBox("Close all open documents?", _
                             vbQuestion Or vbYesNoCancel, _
                             "File Close")
    Select Case lngResponse
       Case vbYes
          For Each objDoc In Documents
             objDoc.Close
          Next
       Case vbNo
             Application.ActiveDocument.Close
       Case vbCancel
             Exit Sub
    End Select
 End If

 End Sub
```

Assigning a macro to a toolbar button

You can add a button to a toolbar and assign a macro to it. To do this from Word's user interface, select the Customize option from the Tools menu, or right-click on any toolbar and select the Customize option. Word opens the Customize dialog. Make sure that the toolbar to which you add the button is checked in the Toolbars tab, then select the Commands tab. Select Macros in the Categories list box and the macro you want to add to the toolbar in the Commands list box. Then drag the macro object from the Commands list box, position it on the toolbar, and drop.

Assigning a macro to a key

To assign a macro to a keyboard combination, open the Customize dialog and click on the Keyboard button. Select Macros in the Categories list box, then select the macro to which you'd like to assign a key combination in the Commands list box. Move the cursor to the "Press new shortcut key" text box and select the key combination you'd like to activate your macro.

Running VBA Modules in Excel

An Excel/VBA application, like its Word counterpart, can be anything from a small routine that performs a useful service to a large application that completely shields the user from Excel's basic interface. Excel, like Word, provides a variety of ways to launch an application that's consistent with its overall purpose.

Storing your code

When Excel loads, it automatically loads all workbook (*.xls*) and add-in (*.xla*) files stored in the *XLStart* directory (and notably *Personal.xls*, a worksheet that can serve as a repository for code, and that Excel makes hidden by default) and in an alternate startup directory. *XLStart* is created by Excel during installation (it's typically a subdirectory of the Office directory) and can't be changed. The alternate startup directory, if one is defined, supplements the *XLStart* directory, and it's configurable. To define or change it, you can select the Options option from the Tools menu, click on the General tab of the Options dialog, and enter the path in the "Alternate startup file location" text box.

Typically, to store global macros, you'd want to create your own add-in file or your own worksheet, which can be hidden and stored in the *XLStart* folder. Particularly since *Personal.xls* is a frequent target of Excel macro viruses, it's best not to use it as a repository for your code. Excel actually loads each of these startup files; consequently, it's important that they remain hidden. While *Personal.xls* and all add-in files are hidden automatically, other files aren't. To hide them, select the Hide option from the workbook's Window menu.

Like Word, Excel also supports the creation of documents from templates, which also can contain code. So if your VBA code applies only to a particular kind of workbook (that is to say, to all workbooks created from the same template), you can store the code in the template (*.xlt*) file. Excel's behavior here, though, is somewhat different from Word's; whereas Word adds a reference to the template to the document, Excel actually embeds the template's code in a newly created workbook.

Finally, if VBA code applies only to a single document, the code can be added to the document, rather than to autoloaded workbooks, add-ins, or templates.

At startup

When Excel starts. it automatically loads all add-in and workbook files in its startup and alternate startup directories. Their Workbook.Open event is fired. Note that, although this is a document-level event (that is, it's fired by a workbook being opened, rather than by Excel starting), the fact that no document workbooks are open when the startup workbooks and add-ins are loaded makes these Workbook.Open event handlers functionally similar to the Word *AutoExec* procedure.

When a document loads

To execute code when a particular workbook is opened, that workbook must have been created using a template that included a Workbook.Open event handler, or a Workbook.Open event handler must have been added to the workbook itself. In fact, Excel workbooks support a rich event model; you can attach event handlers to such Workbook events as Activate, BeforeClose, Deactivate, NewSheet, and SheetActivate.

In response to direct user action

Like Word code, VBA code in Excel often consists of a set of macros. Sometimes, you can hook these to a Workbook event. But more commonly, you have to provide a way for the user to run your macro from the Excel interface. Although Excel lacks Word's ability to intercept basic procedures, it does offer two major options for "hooking" your macro into the Excel interface:

Assigning a macro to a toolbar button

You can add a button to a toolbar or submenu and assign a macro to it. To do this from Excel's user interface, select the Customize option from the Tools menu or right-click on any toolbar and select the Customize option. Excel opens the Customize dialog. Make sure that the toolbar to which you add the button is checked in the Toolbars tab, then select the Commands tab. Select

Macros in the Categories list box and either Custom Menu Item or Custom Button from the Commands list box, depending on how you will attach your macro to the interface. Next, drag the object from the Commands list box, position it on the toolbar, and drop. Finally, right-click on the new menu item or button, select the Assign Macro option from the context menu, and select the routine you want to assign to the menu item or toolbar button.

Assigning a macro to a key

To assign a macro to a keyboard combination, open the Macro dialog (Tools → Macro → Macros), and select the macro you want to assign to a key combination from the Macro Name list box. Next, click on the Options button to open the Macro Options dialog. Finally, select a shortcut key to use along with the Ctrl key to activate your macro. Note that Excel doesn't inform you if you've chosen a key assignment already in use; it simply overwrites the old assignment with the new one.

Running VB Executables

An application that is to be compiled into an executable file with the retail version of Visual Basic and that contains forms can be started by the Visual Basic runtime loading a form, or by running a specially named sub procedure called *Main*. An application that is to be compiled into an ActiveX EXE, DLL, or OCX can only be started using a Sub Main procedure. You specify the startup method for the project in the General tab of the Project Properties dialog box (you open it by selecting the <ProjectName> Properties option from the Project menu), where you select either a form name or Sub Main from the StartUp Object combo box.

Whether you specify a Form or a Sub Main procedure within a code module as the startup object for your program, the VB runtime module first loads into memory all Public or Global constants and variables in all code modules within the project. Therefore, you have instant access to these at startup. Beware, however, that publicly declared variables in form modules aren't loaded at startup time; they are only available while the form itself is loaded. This means that you can't assign a value to a Public variable in another form from that of your startup form or from a startup code module.

Using a Form at Startup

If you specify a form as the starting point for your project, the VB runtime module loads this form after loading project-level variables and constants but before executing any of your project code. When the form is loaded into memory, the form's Initialize event is fired, followed immediately by the Load event. Once the Form is displayed on screen, the Activate event is fired.

The Form Load and Initialize events

Until Version 4 of VB, the initialization code for a Form module was placed in the Form_Load event, and probably through habit—and possibly because it's still the default event—most VB developers continue to use the Form_Load event. However, in line with other object modules such as class modules, the Form module now contains an Initialize event, which is fired as the Form is loaded into memory. The Initialize event is immediately followed by the Form_Load event.

There is little operational difference between the Form's Load and Initialize events, and code to initialize the form—and the application if the form is the startup object—can be written in either. However, if you use both events to write initialization code, you may not always get the desired results. The reason for this is that controls contained on the form aren't completely loaded into memory when the Initialize event is fired. Therefore, any code in the Initialize event handler that references a control on the form forces the rest of the form to load, which then fires the Load event. The following example illustrates this problem:

```
Private Sub Form_Initialize()

    Text1.Width = 2000
    Text1.Text = "Hello "

End Sub

Private Sub Form_Load()

    Text1.Text = Text1.Text & "World"

End Sub
```

Given that the Initialize event fires before the Load event, you'd expect the code above to produce the tired old "Hello World" phrase in the text box. But you may be surprised to discover that when this form is run, only the word "Hello" appears. This is because when the Width property is set to 2000, execution branches to the Form Load event, and the string "World" is placed in the text box. Execution then passes back to the Initialize event and the string "Hello" is assigned to the text property, thereby overwriting the word "World."

Both the Form's Load and Initialize events are executed only once, each time the form is loaded into memory. Hiding the form and then reshowing it doesn't re-execute either event. However, another event, the Activate event, is executed in this situation. You shouldn't use the Activate event to write application initialization code because it executes every time the form regains the focus.

Using a Code Module at Startup

The preferred method of starting any Visual Basic application is to use a Sub Main procedure.

The Sub Main procedure

To create a Sub Main, you need to include a code module in your project. Then simply type the following:

```
Sub Main()
```

Visual Basic automatically adds an **End Sub** line for you. You can have only one Sub Main procedure in your project. A scope keyword—such as Private or

Public—isn't required for the Sub Main procedure. While it's possible to call Sub Main from another procedure, it's definitely not recommended.

The Sub Main procedure doesn't necessarily have to contain any code. In fact, in projects such as ActiveX DLLs, EXEs, or OCXs, it's best not to write code in the Sub Main. If you are using a Sub Main to start up a project and require a form to be loaded on startup, you can use a Sub Main procedure similar to the following:

```
Sub Main()
    Dim oForm as frmStartUp
    Set oForm = New frmStartUp
        oForm.Show vbModal
    Set oForm = Nothing
End Sub
```

Here, an object variable is declared. A reference to a new instance of a Form object called frmStartup is then assigned to that object variable. The object variable can now be used to call the form's Show method. The form is shown modally, which means that the rest of the code in this procedure can't be executed until the form has completed its processing and is either hidden or unloaded. Finally, the object variable is set to Nothing, thereby unloading the form from memory. Using a Sub Main procedure in this way is now the recommended alternative to specifying a Startup form, since it allows you greater flexibility when initializing the application.

The Structure of a VB Program

Any VB program—whether a hosted VBA application or a VB executable—is a collection of modules containing code, graphical user interface objects, and classes. This book concentrates on the language elements of VBA as they relate to both hosted VBA and the retail version of VB. The VBA and VB user interfaces—whether Word, Excel, Project, or a VB form—all fire events that are handled by the code you create using the VBA language. Therefore the code modules within your program are of greatest concern to us here.

Visual Basic code can be split into three categories:

- Code you write to handle events such as a button being clicked by the user; these procedures are called *event handlers*

- *Custom procedures*, where you create the main functionality of your application

- *Property procedures*, used in form and class modules

All Visual Basic language elements work equally well in all three types of procedure. For example, there are no restrictions placed on the type of code you can write within a particular type of procedure. It's left to you as the developer to decide what code goes where.

Events: The Starting Point

An event is always the starting point for your procedure. It can be a system-generated event, such as the Form Load event or a Timer control event, or it can be a user-generated event, such as the Click event on a command button.

To code an event handler for a control event, open the form's code window and select the control from the drop-down list of the available objects. Next, select the required event from the drop-down list of available events for that control. The Event handler definition is then automatically placed in the code window, and you can start coding the event handler.

If you are writing a small and simple application, you could program the whole thing within event handlers. However, the more complex your program becomes, the more you find yourself repeating code within these event handlers, and at this point you should start moving related blocks of code into their own separate functions.

Use Event Handlers to Call Functions and Methods

I would recommend that you keep the code in your event handlers to an absolute minimum, using them simply to call methods within a class or to call functions within the project. You will find that your code becomes easier to follow, code reuse is maximized, and maintenance time for the project is reduced.

The following Click event from a command button called cmdSave demonstrates this minimalist approach to event handling:

```
Private Sub cmdSave_Click()

    On Error GoTo cmdSave_Click_Err

        If SaveDetails() Then
            MsgBox "Details Saved OK", vbInformation
        Else
            MsgBox "Details have not been saved", vbCritical
        End If

        Exit Sub
cmdSave_Click_Err:
    MsgBox Err.Description & vbCrLf & Err.Number

    End Sub
```

Because all the code to actually save the details is held within the *SaveDetails* function, this function can be called from anywhere in the form or project.

The move towards removing functional code from the user interface has been spawned by the n-tier client-server model, in which the user interface is purely a graphical device for displaying information and collecting user input. The middle tier or tiers enforce business rules and provide the main functionality of the application. Here's another example of the same Click event, this time using a SaveDetails method stored in a class module:

```
Private Sub cmdSave_Click()

On Error GoTo cmdSave_Click_Err

Dim oObj As Business.BusinessObj
Set oObj = New Business.BusinessObj
```

```
        If oObj.SaveDetails() Then
            MsgBox "Details Saved OK", vbInformation
        Else
            MsgBox "Details have not been saved", vbCritical
        End If
    Set oObj = Nothing

    Exit Sub

    cmdSave_Click_Err:
        MsgBox Err.Description & vbCrLf & Err.Number & vbCrLf _
               & Err.Source

End Sub
```

The following snippet, which provides the same functionality, demonstrates the power of reducing UI code to a minimum:

```
Function doSave()

    Set oObj = CreateObject("Business.BusinessObj")
        If oObj.SaveDetails() Then
            doSave = "Details Saved OK"
        Else
            doSave = "Details have not been saved"
        End If
    Set oObj = Nothing

End Function
```

So what's so special about this function? Well, this function is calling exactly the same method as the previous Click event, only this code has been taken from an Active Server Page used in a corporate intranet. Because the vast majority of code has been moved away from the front end of the application, the task of porting the application to an HTML/ASP user interface is made extremely easy. In this simple example, the SaveDetails method could care less who or what has called it; it doesn't matter whether it was a Win32 application or an ASP web server application—or both!

Writing Custom Procedures

Custom procedures can be written in any type of VB module. As a general rule, form modules should only contain procedures that need to refer to properties of the controls contained within the Form. Therefore, a procedure that doesn't refer to any form control properties should be placed in a code module.

To create a new procedure, you can use either the Add Procedure dialog, which is accessed from the Add Procedure option of the Tools menu, or you can move to the bottom of the code window and start typing the Function or Sub definition.

There are three types of custom procedures in Visual Basic:

- Functions
- Sub procedures
- Property procedures

Functions

A *function* is a collection of related statements and expressions that perform a particular task. When it completes execution, the function returns a value to the calling statement. If you don't specify an explicit return value for the function, the default value of the return data type is returned. If you write a custom function in a class module and declare it as `Public`, it becomes a method of the class.

Here's a quick example of a function that's used to provide a minimum number:

```
Private Function MinNumber(ByVal iNumber As Integer) _
                As Integer
    If iNumber <= 500 Then
        MinNumber = iNumber
    Else
        MinNumber = 500
    End If

End Function
```

Because functions return a value, you can use them as part of an expression in place of a value. In the following snippet, the string passed to the VB *Instr* function is a custom function that returns a customer name given a customers code:

```
If InStr(1, GetCustomerName(sCustCode), "P") > 0 Then
```

For full details on the syntax and use of functions, see the `Private`, `Public`, and `Friend` statements in Chapter 7, *The Language Reference*. For details of how to pass values into a function, see Chapter 3, *VBA Variables and Data Types*.

Sub procedures

A *sub procedure* is used exactly the same way as a function, the only difference being that it doesn't return a value and therefore can't be used as part of an argument. Sub procedures are used by Visual Basic to provide event handling.

In general you should use functions rather than subs to create custom procedures. Functions allow you to return a value, which at a minimum could be a Boolean `True` or `False` to inform the calling statement that the function has succeeded or failed. I have done some testing to determine whether there is a performance hit for using a function instead of a sub, and there is no appreciable difference between the two, even though the function has to return a value to the calling statement, and a sub procedure doesn't.

Like a function, if you write a custom sub in a class module and declare it as `Public`, it becomes a method of the class.

For full details of the syntax and use of Sub procedures, see the `Private`, `Public`, and `Friend` statements in Chapter 7. For details of how to pass values into a sub procedure, see Chapter 3.

Property procedures

Property procedures are specialized procedures that assign and retrieve values of custom properties. They can be included only within object modules such as form or class modules. There are three types of property procedures:

```
Property Let
```
Assigns a value to a property

```
Property Get
```
Retrieves the value of a property

```
Property Set
```
Assigns an object reference to a property

For a more in-depth look at using properties and property procedures, see Chapter 4, *Class Modules*.

Controlling Execution Flow

So you've got your event handlers that spring into life when the user clicks a button, or a form loads, or a Timer control fires its Timer event. You've written some neat functions to do all the work behind the scenes. How do you link the two?

Calling sub and function procedures

Sub procedures can be called in one of two ways. First, you can use the `Call` statement, like this:

```
Call DoSomething(sSomeString, iSomeInteger)
```

If you use the `Call` statement, you must enclose the argument list in parentheses. The other method of calling a sub is by simply using its name, but if you don't use the `Call` statement, don't put parentheses around the argument list:

```
DoSomething sSomeString, iSomeInteger
```

If you aren't going to use the return value of a function, you can use either of the above methods to call the function. Otherwise, use the function name as part of an expression. For example:

```
If GetItNow(sSomeStuff) = 10 Then
```

Like the `Call` statement, when you use a function call as part of an expression, the argument list must be enclosed within parentheses.

For more information, see the entry for the `Call` statement in Chapter 7.

Explicitly calling event procedures

It's also possible to call an event handler from within your code. For example, to replicate the user clicking on a button called **cmdOne**, you can use the code:

```
Call cmdOne_Click()
```

Because event handlers are private to the form in which they are defined, you can only explicitly call an event handler from code within the same form.

Ending Your VB Program

At some stage, most users want to exit from a program. OK, yours might be a really great program, but unfortunately the user may want to go off and do something else—like go home! You have to allow your application to both exit and tidy up before it ends. One advantage you have when building an application in a VBA-hosted environment is that you don't have to worry too much about finishing the program; the majority of the work is taken care of by the host application. You just have to ensure that any object references are cleaned up, and all database connections closed. You can place this type of code in the Close event. VB developers writing executables have to take care of unloading the application themselves, but in most cases this is no more onerous a task than in VBA; this section shows you how.

How to End Your Program

If you specified a form as the startup object, then you must unload this form to close the application. You can do this by including the following statement somewhere in the form, usually in the event handler of an Exit menu option or Exit command button:

```
Unload Me
```

If you specified a Sub Main procedure as the startup object, the program terminates when the Sub Main procedure is completed. For example, here's the Sub Main you saw earlier in this chapter:

```
Sub Main()
    Dim oForm as frmStartUp
    Set oForm = New frmStartUp
        oForm.Show vbModal
    Set oForm = Nothing
End Sub
```

Because the form is shown modally, the Sub Main procedure doesn't continue until the form is either hidden—using the statement Me.Hide—or unloaded. Once this happens, program execution is handed back to the Sub Main procedure, which destroys the form object it created by setting the reference to Nothing. When the End Sub statement is executed, the whole application terminates.

If you are writing an ActiveX DLL or EXE, things are slightly different: you shouldn't place any code in your application to terminate the application. The termination should be handled by the operating system. Basically, when all references to your ActiveX component are set to Nothing, your component is unloaded from memory. You should, however, write code to destroy dependent objects in the Terminate event handler of any of your classes that have created dependent objects. You can find further information about this in Chapter 4.

How a Form Unloads

When a form is unloaded from memory, the following chain of events is triggered:

QueryUnload
    Allows you to cancel the unloading of a form. For example, you could use this event to check whether data in the form has been saved and, if it hasn't, prevent the form from unloading. The QueryUnload event passes a ByRef argument named Cancel to the event handler; if you set this to True, the

unloading of the form is cancelled. This event is ideal for catching those users who insist on closing an application using the Close Window button—the one at the right of the titlebar—instead of using the nice Exit button or the menu option that you provided.

Deactivate

This event is fired as the form loses focus to another form. You have to be careful not to place termination code here, since this event being fired doesn't necessarily mean that the form is being unloaded from memory. If you have an application in which multiple forms are displayed at the same time and any can be selected, the Deactivate event is fired as you move away from one form to another.

Unload

This is the point of no return. From here on, your application is on its way out. Until Version 4 of VB, this was the end of the road. However, in the same way that the Form Load event is now preceded by an Activate event, so the Form Unload event is followed by a Terminate event.

Terminate

This event brings form modules into line with Class modules, and should be used in place of the Unload event. As with the Form Load and Initialize events, you should only use either the form's Unload event or the Terminate event, not both. Use either the Unload or Terminate events to destroy any dependent objects you created during the lifetime of the form.

The End Statement

Visual Basic still supports an **End** statement, but this is purely for backward compatibility. In general, its use should be discouraged. In particular, its use in class modules and object-based VB applications is highly undesirable, since it has no concept of object cleanup. If you follow the previous procedure, you'll never need the **End** statement.

CHAPTER 3

VBA Variables and Data Types

The VBA language offers a full set of the usual data types, plus a smart data type called a *Variant*, which is the chameleon of the programming world, adapting itself seamlessly to hold any type of data. This chapter lists the data types available in VBA and discusses a complete range of issues related to data types, including variable scope and lifetime, the character of the variant, and performance issues that arise in using particular data types.

Visual Basic Data Types

Visual Basic and Visual Basic for Applications support the following data types:

Boolean
   Indicates the presence of logical data that can contain either of two values, True or False. The keywords True and False are constants that are predefined in VBA, so you can make use of them in your code when you want to assign a value to a Boolean variable, as the following code fragment shows:

```
var1 = True
var2 = False
```

Many of the properties of ActiveX controls have possible values of True or False. In addition, within programs, Boolean variables often serve as flags to control program flow, as the following example, which toggles (or reverses) the value of *myBool* within the If...Else...End If construct, shows:

```
If myBool = False Then
  myVar = 4
  myBool = True
Else
  myVar = 5
  myBool = False
End If
```

Storage required
   Two bytes

Range
   True or False

Default value
   False

Byte

The smallest numeric subtype available in VBA. Because only one byte holds a number ranging from 0 to 255 (or 00 to FF in hexadecimal), there is no room for the sign, and so only positive numbers can be held in a Byte data type. Attempting to assign a negative number or a number greater than 255 to byte data results in a runtime error.

Storage required
   One byte

Range
   0 to 255

Default value
   0

Currency

Provides a special numeric format for storing monetary values.

Storage required
   Eight bytes

Range
   −922,337,203,685,477.5808 to 922,337,203,685,477.5807

Default value
   0

Date

Contains a specially formatted number that represents the date or time.

Storage Required
   Eight bytes

Range
   1 January 100 to 31 December 9999

Default value
   00:00:00

Decimal

A variant subtype (and not a separate data type) that contains decimal numbers scaled by a power of 10. Variants of subtype Decimal can only be created by the *CDec* conversion function.

Storage required
   14 bytes

Range
   With no decimal point: +/− 79,228,162,514,264,337,593,543,950,335

With up to 28 decimal places: +/− 7.9228162514264337593543950335

Default value
0

Double

Stores a double precision floating point number; basically, it's the industrial strength version of the Single data type.

Storage required
Eight bytes

Range
Negative values: −1.79769313486232E308 to −4.94065645841247E-324

Positive values: 1.79769313486232E308 to 4.94065645841247E-324

Default value
0

Integer

A whole number that ranges from −32,768 to 32,767. One bit represents the sign (either positive or negative). Attempting to assign a value outside its range results in a runtime error.

Storage required
two bytes

Range
−32,768 to 32,767

Default value
0

Long

A signed integer stored in four bytes of memory. One bit represents the sign.

Storage required
Four bytes

Range
−2,147,483,648 to 2,147,486,647

Default value
0

Object

Contains a reference to (i.e., the address of) an object. The object can be an OLE automation object such as an ActiveX component, or it can be a class object within your project. When you use the generic Object data type, rather than a more specific object type, you automatically use late binding. For more information about using the Object data type, see Chapter 4, *Class Modules*.

Storage required
Four bytes

Range
Any object reference

Default value
>Nothing*

Single
A single precision number that represents fractional numbers, numbers with decimal places, or exponential numbers.

Storage required
>Four bytes

Range
>Negative values: −3.402823E38 to −1.401298E-45

>Positive values: 1.401298E-45 to 3.402823E38

Default value
>0

String (fixed length)
Popular in VB applications when memory and disk storage was at a premium and programmers had to spend most of their time optimizing the size of applications, fixed-length strings are now rarely used. To declare a fixed-length string, use the syntax:

```
Dim|Private|Public varname As String * stringlength
```

Storage required
>Length of string

Range
>1 to 65,400 characters

Default value
>A number of spaces equal to the length of the string

String (variable length)
String data type that expands and contracts dynamically to store as many characters as required, up to somewhere in the neighborhood of two billion. To declare a variable-length string, simply use the **String** keyword:

```
Dim variablename As String
```

VBA includes many useful intrinsic functions for handling and manipulating string data. The list of string functions has been expanded in VB6, as many of the string-manipulation functions introduced into VBScript have now made their way into the full language.

Storage required
>10 + length of the string

Range
>0 to 2 billion characters

Default value
>Zero-length string ("")

---

* Nothing and Empty are special Variant data subtypes and do not have the same meaning. For more information, see the section about the Variant data type later in this chapter.

User-defined type

A user-defined type allows you to create a single data type consisting of a combination of intrinsic VB data types, arrays, objects, or other user-defined types. User-defined types are created using the **Type** statement. The following snippet shows how to declare a user-defined type:

```
Type udtCustomer
    Name As String
    Code As Long
    Orders(20) As udtOrders
    RenewalDate As Date
End Type
```

User-defined types are important data structures in VB and are often essential when interfacing with the Windows API. For more information on user-defined types, see the section "User-Defined Types" later in this chapter and the entry for the **Type** statement in Chapter 7, *The Language Reference.*

Storage required

Sum of storage size of the individual elements

Range

Same range as data type of individual elements

Default value

The default value of the individual elements

Variant (character)

The variant string subtype is very much like a variable-length string data type. All VB string functions can accept variant strings, and many have two versions that return either a strongly typed string data type or a variant string subtype. For example, the *Left* function—which returns the leftmost *n* characters of a string—has two variations, *Left$* (which returns a string data type) and *Left* (which returns a variant of subtype string).

Storage required

22 bytes + length of string

Range

Same as variable length string

Default value

Empty*

Variant (numeric)

The variant numeric subtype holds any numeric value. As with all variant data, memory allocation changes dynamically to accommodate the numeric value. The variant also includes a special Decimal subtype that doesn't have an intrinsic equivalent, and allows you to hold very large numbers in a variety of formats.

Storage required

16 bytes

---

* Nothing and Empty are special Variant data subtypes and don't have the same meaning. For more information, see the section about the Variant data type later in this chapter.

Range
Same as Double

Default Value
Empty*

Type Conversion

VBA provides two sets of built-in conversion functions. The first set, which includes *Int* and *Str*, is from the early versions of VB and is simply left in for backwards compatibility. The functions of the second set all start with the letter "C" and are the more recent conversion functions. Microsoft recommends that you use this latter set of functions, since they are locale-aware; that is, they take account of international date, time, and number settings on the host system.

The syntax for each of the latter conversion functions is basically the same. For example:

```
CBool(variablename)
```

where *variablename* is either the name of a variable, a constant, or an expression (like *x–y*) that evaluates to a particular data type. Regardless of the particular function you use, the data type being converted is immaterial; what matters is the data type to which you want to convert a particular value.

The conversion functions supported by VBA are:

CBool
Converts *variablename* to a Boolean data type. *variablename* can contain any numeric data type or any string capable of being converted into a number. If *variablename* is 0 or "0", *CBool* returns False; otherwise, it returns True (-1).

CByte
Converts *variablename* to a Byte data type. *variablename* can contain any numeric data or string data capable of conversion into a number that is greater than or equal to 0 and less than or equal to 255. If *variablename* is out of range, VBA displays an Overflow error message. If *variablename* is a floating point number, it's rounded to the nearest integer before being converted to byte data.

CDec
Converts *variablename* to a Decimal data subtype. The function accepts any numeric data within the limits of the Decimal data subtype or any string data that can be converted to a number within the range of the Decimal data subtype. This conversion function provides the only method of creating a Decimal data subtype.

CDate
Converts *variablename* to a Date/Time data type. *CDate* accepts numeric and string data that appears to be a date and converts it to the format specified by

---

* Nothing and Empty are special Variant data subtypes and do not have the same meaning. For more information, see the section about the Variant data type later in this chapter.

the locale information on the host computer. For example, on a machine set to the American date format mm/dd/yy, if you enter a date in the British date format dd/mm/yy in a text box and use the *CDate* function on the contents of the text box, *CDate* converts it to the American mm/dd/yy format.

CCur

Converts *variablename* to a Currency data type. *CCur* accepts any numeric or string data that can be expressed as a currency value. The function recognizes the decimal and thousands separators based on locale information on the host computer. It, as well as the currency variant subtype, is recognized by VBA only.

CDbl

Converts *variablename* to a double precision data type. The function accepts any numeric data within the limits of the Double data type or any string data that can be converted to a number within the range of the double data type.

CInt

Converts *variablename* to an Integer data type. *CInt* accepts any numeric data within the limits of the integer data type or any string data that can be converted to a number and is within the limits of the integer data type.

CLng

Converts *variablename* to a Long data type. The function accepts any numeric data within the limits of the long integer data type or any string data that can be converted to a number whose value lies within the range of a long integer.

CSng

Converts *variablename* to a Single data type. The function accepts any numeric data within the limits of the single data type or any string data that can be converted to a number within the range of the Single data type.

CStr

Converts *variablename* to a String data type. *CStr* accepts any kind of data.

CVar

Converts *variablename* to a Variant data type. *CVar* accepts any kind of data.

Implicit Type Conversion in VB

It's worth mentioning that Visual Basic handles a lot of data type conversion for you in the background. For example, the Text property of a VB text box is quite clearly a String data type, not a Variant, and the Prompt property of a message box is also a string. Given this, you might not expect the following code to run successfully without generating a runtime type mismatch error:

```
Private Sub Command1_Click()

    Dim iValue As Integer
```

```
iValue = txtTextBox.Text
MsgBox Prompt:=iValue
```

```
End Sub
```

But assuming that a number is entered in the text box, there is no error; instead, you can see from this example that VB allows you to assign a string representation of a number to an Integer data type, then assign this integer to the Prompt property of a message box. VB handles the conversion of data types without your having to do it explicitly.

The Variant

VBA contains a special data type, the Variant. Internally, the Variant is highly complex, but it's also extremely easy to use. The Variant is the default data type of VBA, so the following code casts myVar as a variant:

```
Dim myVar
```

The Variant data type allows you to use a variable with any of the intrinsic VBA data types, automatically working out what is the closest data type to the value you are assigning. When you consider the amount of processing required to determine what data type should be used for an abstract value, it's a testament to the VB development team at Microsoft that the Variant is as quick as it is. However, there is a slight performance hit when using both variant data and functions that return variant data, which we discuss later in this chapter.

Another drawback to using variant data is that your code becomes at best horrible to read, and at worst unreadable! To illustrate, consider two versions of the same function, the first written exclusively with variants, the second using strong typing:

```
Private Function GoodStuff(vAnything, vSomething, _
                           vSomethingElse)

If vAnything > 1 And vSomething > "" Then
   GoodStuff = vAnything * vSomethingElse
Else
   GoodStuff = vAnything + 10
End If

End Function

Private Function GoodStuff(iAnything As Integer, _
                           sSomething As String, _
                           iSomethingElse As Integer) _
                           As Integer
If iAnything > 1 And sSomething > "" Then
   GoodStuff = iAnything * iSomethingElse
Else
   GoodStuff = iAnything + 10
End If

End Function
```

I know which one I'd rather maintain!

So how do you use variant data? Well, at the simplest level, you can ignore the fact that there are such things as data types (or, to be more precise, when using variants, you can ignore data subtypes). But to be a proficient VB programmer, if you use variants at all, it's best to be aware that every item of variant data has a subtype (like Integer, Long, or String) that corresponds to one of the major data types. And Decimal data is something of an exception: it's only available as a subtype of the Variant data type.

Special Variant Data Subtypes

In addition to all the intrinsic data types detailed above, the variant also supports the following special data types:

Empty

> The Empty subtype is automatically assigned to new Variant variables when you declare them, but before you explicitly assign a value to them. For instance, in the code fragment:
>
> ```
> Dim var1, var2
> var2 = 0
> ```
>
> the subtype of *var1* is Empty, whereas *var2* is only Empty for the brief period of time between the execution of the Dim statement on the first line and the assignment statement on the second line. In addition, a variable's subtype is Empty if it has been explicitly assigned a value of Empty, as in the following code fragment:
>
> ```
> Dim var1
> var1 = Empty
> ```

Null

> Null is a special data subtype that indicates a variable doesn't contain any valid data. Usually, a variable is assigned a null value to indicate that an error condition exists. In order for its subtype to be Null, a variable must have a Null value assigned to it explicitly, as in the following line of code:
>
> ```
> var1 = Null
> ```
>
> A Null value also results from any operation in which the value of one or more of the expressions is Null, as the following code fragment shows:
>
> ```
> dim myVarOne, myVarTwo, myVarThree  'All three variables are EMPTY now
> myVarOne = 9
> myVarTwo=NULL                        'We've made this variable NULL
> myVarThree = myVarOne + myVarTwo     'The result is NULL
> ```

Error

> The Error subtype is used to store an error number. Error numbers are generated automatically by VBA, and can then be used by your error handling routine. Error-handling routines are discussed in Chapter 6, *Error Handling*.

Determining the Variant Subtype

Having the variant data type take care of your data typing is all well and good, but what happens when you need to know exactly what type of data is stored to a variable? VBA provides two functions: *VarType*, which returns a number that indicates the type of data stored to a variable; and *TypeName*, which returns a string containing the name of the data type.

VarType

The syntax of *VarType* is:

```
VarType(variablename)
```

where **variablename** is the name of the variable whose subtype you want to determine. You can provide the name of only a single variable at a time. The following table details the possible values returned by *VarType* and the data subtypes they represent. For purposes of reference, the table also lists the VBA constants you can use in your code to compare with the values returned by the *VarType* function.

Value	Data Subtype	VBA Constant
0	Empty	vbEmpty
1	Null	vbNull
2	Integer	vbInteger
3	Long Integer	vbLong
4	Single	vbSingle
5	Double	vbDouble
6	Currency	vbCurrency
7	Date	vbDate
8	String	vbString
9	OLE Automation Object	vbObject
10	Error	vbError
11	Boolean	vbBoolean
12	Array of Variant	vbVariant
13	Data access object	vbDataObject
14	Decimal	vbDecimal
17	Byte	vbByte
36	User-defined Type	vbUserDefinedType
8192	Array	vbArray

Actually, the *VarType* function never returns 8192, as shown in the table; this is only a base figure indicating the presence of an array. When passed an array, *VarType* returns 8192 plus the value of the array's underlying data type. For example, if you pass the variable name of an array of string to *VarType*, the return value is 8200 (8192 + 8).

TypeName

The *TypeName* function allows you to write more readable, self-documenting code by returning the name of the data subtype rather than a more abstract number. The syntax for *TypeName* is:

```
result = TypeName(variable)
```

Like the *VarType* function, *TypeName* is read-only; you can use it to determine the subtype of a variable, but you can't use it to explicitly set the type of a variable. To do this, you must use the conversion functions discussed in the previous section. The following table shows the string that the *TypeName* function returns for each data subtype.

Return Value	Data Subtype
<object type>	Actual type name of an object
Boolean	Boolean value: True or False
Byte	Byte value
Currency	Currency value
Date	Date or time value
Decimal	Decimal (single-precision) value
Double	Double-precision floating-point value
Empty	Uninitialized
Error	Error
Integer	Integer value
Long	Long integer value
Nothing	Object variable that doesn't yet refer to an object instance
Null	No valid data
Object	Generic object
Single	Single-precision floating-point value
String	Character string value
Variant()	Variant array
Unknown	Unknown object type

If you pass an array of a particular data type to *TypeName*, the same return string is used for the underlying data type of the array, suffixed with "()" to denote an array. Therefore if you pass the variable name of an array of strings to *TypeName*, the return value is "String()".

As for making your code more readable and easier to maintain, just look at this snippet:

```
If TypeName(x) = "Double" Then
```

Now you've no excuse for getting those nasty "type mismatch" errors!

Variant and Strongly Typed Data

The Variant might appear to be the answer to all your data type needs, but there's a price to pay. The variant is more than a data type, it's a program within itself. It takes a lot of processing to determine the data type of an abstract value. In tests I've carried out, an expression consisting of only variant data executes about 30% slower than the same expression using the correct intrinsic data types.

Variant and Strongly Typed Functions

The VBA language includes a number of string-handling functions that have two versions, one that returns a variant and the other that returns a string. The latter are suffixed with the old string-specifying character $ (for example, *Left$*), while the former simply include the name of the function (for example, *Left*).

I have put the two versions through some performance testing to determine if there is a significant difference in their performance. To simplify matters, I tested both *Left* and *Left$* and *Mid* and *Mid$*. When using the strongly typed versions, I assigned the result to a string data type and passed string data types as parameters; when using the variant versions, I assigned the result to a variant and passed variant data types as parameters.

For example, here is a variant version of a sample code fragment that illustrates the performance tests:

```
Dim sString
Dim sPartString

sString = "ABCDEFGH"

sPartString = Mid(sString, 1, 2)
```

and here is the String version:

```
Dim sString As String
Dim sPartString As String

sString = "ABCDEFGH"

sPartString = Mid$(sString, 1, 2)
```

I found that the variant version of each function executed about 50% slower than its string counterpart. This obviously is a significant difference, and it suggests that we should use the typed versions of all functions whenever they are available.

Declaring Variables and Constants

As was mentioned earlier, VBA supports a default data type, which means that, unlike many other programming languages, VBA allows the implicit declaration of variables. As soon as you use a variable or constant name within your code, VBA does all the necessary work of allocating memory space, etc., and the variable is considered to be declared.

However, it's good programming practice (and one that will save you endless hours of grief) to explicitly declare any variables and constants you want to use by using the Dim, Private, or Public statements. Their syntax is:

```
Dim VariableName As datatype
Private VariableName As datatype
Public VariableName As datatype
```

If you have a number of variables to declare, you can do this on a single line by separating them with commas, as in the following Dim statement:

```
Dim iRefNo As Integer, iAnyVar As Integer
```

By explicitly declaring variables in this manner, you can reduce the number of bugs in your code caused by spelling errors, perhaps the most common of programming errors. Once declared, a variable name is available to you in the IntelliSense statement completion drop-down list, which means that you should never have a misspelled variable again!

For full details of how to use the Dim, Private, and Public statements, see their entries in Chapter 7. There is further discussion later in this chapter about how the declaration of variables affects their scope and lifetime.

Option Explicit

Using the Option Explicit statement is good programming practice. It forces us to declare all variables and constants. You can automatically have VB add this to new modules as they are created by checking the Require Variable Declaration option, which can be found on the Editor tab of the Options dialog. (Select the Options option from the Tools menu to open the dialog.)

When the Option Explicit statement is used, VB generates a compile-time error if it encounters a variable that has not been declared.

A Whole Load of Nothing

An important element of any programming language is its ability to detect and to handle nothing. By nothing, I actually mean "no valid data." Because there are several different types of "nothingness," the VBA language has developed a number of ways to allow you to determine or to assign empty or null values to a variable. An understanding of the differences is important, since each has its own uses and, in the main, they aren't interchangeable.

vbNull

Used with the *VarType* function to determine if a variable contains Null. For example:

```
varValue = Null
If VarType(varValue) = vbNull Then
```

Note that you can't use the constant to assign a Null value. If you assign vbNull to a variable, you actually assign a value of 1 (or "1", if the variable is a string), and the *IsNull* test will fail.

vbNullChar

Assigns or tests for a null character (as distinct from a Null value); a null character has a value of *Chr(0)*. In other words, vbNullChar is simply the equivalent of assigning *Chr(0)* to a variable and can test a variable to determine whether its value is a null character.

This constant is useful when passing strings to external libraries that expect a null-terminated string. For example:

```
sMyString & vbNullChar
```

vbNullString

Assigns or tests for a zero-length (empty) string. For example, the statement:

```
strVar1 = vbNullString
```

is equivalent to:

```
strVar1 = ""
```

Null keyword

Assigns a Null value to a variant variable. You can then test the variable for a null value by calling the *IsNull* function. Note that the code fragment:

```
varValue = Null
if varValue = Null
```

returns False, since a Null is False and therefore causes any expression containing Null to return False. The following code fragment shows how to use, and how not to use, the Null keyword:

```
Dim i As Variant

i = Null

If i = Null Then
    MsgBox "It's null" 'this fails
End If

If IsNull(i) Then
    MsgBox "It's null" 'this works
End If
```

Also note that the Null keyword can't be used to assign a Null value to a strongly typed variable; instead, it generates an "Invalid use of Null" error.

vbEmpty

Determines whether a variant has been initialized. For example:

```
If IsEmpty(varValue) Then
```

is identical to:

```
If varValue = vbEmpty then
```

However, you shouldn't use vbEmpty to assign an empty value to a variant. If you do, you actually assign 0 (or "0" if the variable is a string), and an *IsEmpty* function call will fail.

Nothing keyword

Used only with object variables to determine either if a variable has a valid object reference, as in:

```
If objVar Is Not Nothing Then
```

or to destroy a current object reference, as in:

```
Set objvar = Nothing
```

Array Variables

Before we look at the types of arrays at our disposal, let's quickly cover some of the terminology used when talking about arrays. Creating an array is called *dimensioning* the array (i.e., defining its size). The individual data items within the array are known as *elements*, and the number used to access an element is known as an *index*. The lowest and highest index numbers are known as *bounds* or *boundaries*. In VBA, there are four types of arrays: arrays can be either *fixed* or *dynamic*, and arrays can also be either *one-dimensional* or *multidimensional*.

Fixed Arrays

Most of the time, we know how many values we need to store in an array in advance. We can therefore dimension it to the appropriate size, or number of elements, prior to accessing it by using a `Dim` statement like the following:

```
Dim myArray(5) As Integer
```

This line of code creates an array, named `myArray`, with six elements. Why six? All VBA arrays start with location 0, so this `Dim` statement creates an array whose locations range from `myArray(0)` to `myArray(5)`.

Populating Arrays: The Array Function

If you want to populate an array with a series of values, use the *Array* function. The function allows you to quickly assign a range of comma-delimited values to an array. For instance:

```
myArray = Array(12,3,13,64,245,75)
```

To use the *Array* function, simply declare a variant variable, then assign the values of the array to the variable using the *Array* function. Any data type (even mixed data types) can be used with the *Array* function. Another point to remember about arrays built using the *Array* function is that they are always based at 0, regardless of the `Option Base` setting, which is used to define the lower boundary of an array.

But what happens if you try to access an element greater than five or less than zero? You get an error message, "Subscript out of range." In the next section you'll see how to check the size of the array before attempting to access a given element.

Dynamic Arrays

Fixed arrays are fine when we know in advance how many values or elements we need. But there are many cases where we do not have prior knowledge of this, and we need a way to expand our array should we have to. For example, one convenient use of an array is to store input from the user and allow the user to input as many items of data as he or she likes. Our application therefore has no way of knowing how to dimension the array beforehand. We can handle this situation by declaring and using a *dynamic array*. Dynamic arrays allow you to expand the number of array elements using the `ReDim` statement to redimension the array while the program is running.

A dynamic array is declared by leaving out its number of elements, like this:

```
Dim iDynamicArray() As Integer
```

When you need to resize the array, use the ReDim keyword:

```
ReDim iDynamicArray(10)
```

You can also declare a dynamic array and specify the initial number of elements at the same time by using ReDim:

```
ReDim anyDynamicArray(4) As Integer
```

There is no limit to the number of times you can redimension a dynamic array, but obviously, messing around with variables in this way carries an element of risk. As soon as you redimension an array, the data contained within it is lost. Don't panic; if you need to keep the data, use the **Preserve** keyword:

```
ReDim Preserve myDynamicArray(10)
```

In fact, ReDim creates a new array (hence its emptiness). **Preserve** copies the data from the old array to the new array. Another important point to note is that if you resize an array by contracting it, you *always* lose the data in the deleted array elements.

Note that while you can resize an array by modifying its upper bound, you can't resize the lower bound of an array; this generates runtime error 9, "Subscript out of range."

ReDim Preserve's Performance

As you have seen, dynamic arrays are resized using the **Preserve** keyword by creating a new array in memory and copying the contents of the old array into the new. This can obviously have an adverse affect on application performance. The larger and more complex the array becomes, the longer it takes to resize. Wherever possible, you should use fixed size arrays. And if you do choose to use dynamic arrays, you should avoid resizing the array each time you want to add an element; instead, you should add an arbitrary number of elements at a single time, as the following code fragment illustrates:

```
If lngCurPtr > UBound(varArray) Then
    ReDim Preserve varArray(UBound(varArray) + 10)
End If
```

In this case, we add 10 elements each time we redimension **varArray**. Depending on the expected size of the array, we could select any number greater than one, or we could even double the size of the array as long as we were reasonably certain that the array would remain fairly small (geometric progression has a habit of consuming memory very rapidly).

The following snippet shows how to use a dynamic array to save multiple inputs from the user. When the user clicks on the cmdButton1 button, the contents of the text box are added to sMyArray, an array that is dynamically resized beforehand:

```
Option Explicit              'require variable declaration
ReDim sMyArray(0) As String 'create a 1-element dynamic array
Dim iIndex As Integer       'variable to track array index
iIndex = 0                   'assign the first index number

Sub cmdButton1_OnClick
   'Store the user input in the array
   sMyArray(intIndex) = txtText1.Text
   'increment the array counter by one
   iIndex = iIndex + 1
  'increase the size of the array
   ReDim Preserve sMyArray(iIndex)
   txtText1.Text = ""          'Empty the text box again
End Sub
```

The above example is fine as it stands, except that, as you can see from the source code, we have to keep track of the size of the array by using the *intIndex* variable. But VBA allows a much cleaner approach to the problem of finding out how many elements there are in the array.

Determining array boundaries

The *UBound* and *LBound* functions can find the upper index and the lower index, respectively, of an array.

The syntax for *UBound* is:

```
x = UBound(arrayname)
```

UBound returns the highest index number of an array. The actual number of elements in the array depends upon the starting point of the array. If the default lower boundary of 0 has been used, then *UBound* is one less than the actual number of elements in the array. For example, if sMyArray has 10 elements and a lower boundary of 0, Ubound(sMyArray) returns the number 9. So we would determine the total number of elements in an array as follows:

```
iArraySize = UBound(array) + 1
```

If, however, the lower boundary has been set to 1, *UBound* returns the actual number of elements is the array. It therefore makes sense to use the *LBound* function in conjunction with the *UBound* function to determine the actual number of elements in the array, as follows:

```
iArraySize = UBound(array) - LBound(array) + 1
```

The *UBound* function is especially useful when dealing with dynamic arrays, as this snippet demonstrates:

```
Option Explicit

Private sValues() As String
```

```
Private Sub Form_Load()
    ReDim sValues(0)
End Sub

Private Sub Command1_Click()

    sValues(UBound(sValues)) = txtTextBox.Text
    ReDim Preserve sValues(UBound(sValues) + 1)

End Sub
```

Note that using the *UBound* function on an uninitialized array generates a Subscript Out of Range error; therefore, the Form_Load event is used to redimension the array to 0 to insure that the array has one element.

Setting the lower boundary

By default, VBA arrays start with element 0. However, you can change this on a per-module basis by using the **Option Base** statement in the declarations section of your module. For example:

```
Option Base 1
```

generates arrays starting with element 1. The **Option Base** statement must be used in the module before any variable declarations.

Another method used to set the lower boundary is to specify both the lower and upper boundaries when the array is dimensioned, as the following syntax shows:

```
Dim arrayname(lowerboundary To upperboundary) As datatype
```

Multidimensional Arrays

The arrays we have looked at so far are single-dimension arrays; they hold one element of data in each index location, which is fine for most needs. However, sometimes you need a full set of data for each element; this is called a *multidimensional array*.

In a single-dimension array, the data held within has no structure; it's accessed sequentially, and there is one piece of data for each element. When you need to store more than this one piece of data for each logical element, you should use either a multidimensional array or a user-defined type (which is discussed in the next section).

A multidimensional array allows you to have a separate array of data for each element of your array. Therefore, each element of the array in turn contains an array. The structure of a multidimensional array resembles that of a database table. The rows (or records) of the table represent the first dimension, and the columns (or fields) represent by the second dimension, as the following table illustrates.

	Field 1	*Field 2*	*Field 3*
Record 1	Array Element (0,0)		Array Element (0,2)
Record 2		Array Element(1,1)	

	Field 1	*Field 2*	*Field 3*
Record 3			
Record 4	Array Element (3,0)		Array Element (3,2)

 Multidimensional arrays can contain up to 60 dimensions, though it's extremely rare to use more than two or three dimensions.

To define a multidimensional array, use the following syntax:

```
Dim arrayname(upperboundDimension1, _
              upperboundDimension2, ....) As Datatype
```

As with single-dimension arrays, you can also specify the lower boundary within the array definition, and you can specify different lower boundaries for each element. For example:

```
Private myArray(1 To 20, 0 To 50) As String
```

Dynamic multidimensional arrays

Like single-dimension arrays, multidimensional arrays can be dynamic, and the rules for redimensioning them are similar. But since you have more than one dimension to think about, you have to take care how you use and redimension your array. The rules for using a dynamic multidimensional array are:

- You can ReDim a multidimensional array to change both the number of dimensions and the size of each dimension. This is illustrated by the following, where the *myArray* dynamic array is originally defined as a two-dimensional array with 11 elements in the first dimension and 6 in the second, but is then redimensioned into a three-dimensional array with 5 elements in the first dimension, 11 in the second, and 3 in the third.

```
Private myArray() As Integer
Private Sub  cmdButtonOne_OnClick
    ReDim myArray(10,5)
End Sub
Private Sub cmdButtonTwo_OnClick
    ReDim myArray(4,10,2)
End Sub
```

- If you use the Preserve keyword, you can only resize the last array dimension, and you can't change the number of dimensions at all. For example:

```
...
ReDim myArray(10,5,2)
...
ReDim Preserve myArray(10,5,4)
...
```

Using UBound and LBound with multidimensional arrays

As you saw earlier, the *UBound* function returns the highest subscript (element number) in an array—that is, its *Upper Bound*ary. You can also use *UBound* with a multidimensional array, except that to find the largest element of a multidimensional array, you need to also specify a dimension:

```
largestElement = UBound(arrayname, dimensionNo)
```

The same is true of the *LBound* function:

```
smallestElement = LBound(arrayname, dimensionNo)
```

User-Defined Types

One major limitation of the multidimensional array is that all the dimensions within the array must be of the same data type. The user-defined type (UDT), which combines multiple data types into a single new data type, overcomes this limitation.

Since VB 4.0, UDTs have gone out of fashion somewhat, this fall from favor having resulted from the introduction of the Collection object, which on the surface operates like an infinitely flexible UDT. However, VB6 has given the humble UDT a new lease on life by allowing UDTs to be passed as property values and to be used in public function declarations. This is good news, as the UDT is far more efficient than a Collection object.

So what is a user-defined type? Simply put, it's a pseudo-data type constructed from other data types. One of its common applications is the replication of a data record in memory. For example, let's say you want to create a local array to hold the data of your customer records. Because each of the fields within the record is of a different data type, a multidimensional array can't be used. A UDT, on the other hand, is ideal in this situation. The following snippet defines a simple UDT:

```
Private Type custRecord
    custAccNo As Long
    custName As String
    RenewalDate As Date
End Type

Private custArray(10) As custRecord
```

The last line of code creates a local array of the UDT.

You can also use other UDTs within a UDT, as the following example demonstrates:

```
Private Type custOrders
    OrderNo As Long
    OrderDate As Long
End Type

Private Type custRecord
    custAccNo As Long
    custName As String
    RenewalDate As Date
```

```
    orders(10) As custOrders
End Type

Private custArray(10) As custRecord
```

Here, a user-defined type, custOrders, is defined to hold the OrderNo and OrderDate fields; then, within the custRecord UDT, an array of type custRecord is defined.

Here are two simple lines of code that access the data within these UDTs:

```
Text1.Text = custArray(iCust).custName
Text2.Text = custArray(iCust).orders(iOrder).OrderNo
```

Variable Scope and Lifetime

Sometimes you need a variable to be seen by all the procedures within your project, while other variables should only be available within a particular procedure. The visibility of a variable is known as its *scope*. Closely related to a variable's scope is its *lifetime*, or the period of program execution when the variable is live and available for use. Precisely where you declare a variable or constant in a program determines its scope and its lifetime.

In a nutshell, variables declared in the declarations section of a module using the Private keyword can be accessed by all the procedures within the module. Variables declared in the declaration section of a code module using the Public keyword can be accessed by the whole project. Variables declared in the declaration section of a class module using the Public keyword can be accessed by the whole project once an object reference has been made to the class. And variables declared using the Dim statement within a subroutine or function can only be accessed in the procedure in which they've been declared.

Procedure-Level Scope

A variable that is declared within an individual procedure (that is, within a subroutine or a function) can only be used within that procedure, and is therefore said to have *procedure-level scope*. You can therefore define different variables that use the same name in different procedures (like the simple *x* variable commonly used in the For...Next loop). You can even use the same variable names in a calling procedure and in a procedure that it calls, and they will be treated as two separate variables.

The lifetime of a procedure-level variable ends when the End Sub or End Function statement is executed. As soon as the procedure is complete, references to the variables defined within that procedure are erased from the computer's memory. This makes procedure-level variables ideal for temporary, localized storage of information.

There is also a special type of variable that has procedure-level scope, called a *static* variable. A static variable is defined within a procedure, and although it has procedure-level scope, it has module-level lifetime. In practice, this means that you can only use the variable within the procedure in which it's defined, but its value is maintained between calls to the procedure. To declare a static variable, you use the `Static` keyword in a procedure; for example:

```
Static lngExecuted As Long
```

You can also declare a procedure as *Static*, in which case all variables declared within the procedure are treated as static, and their values are preserved between calls to the procedure. For example:

```
Static Procedure MyProcedure()
    Dim iCtr As Integer
```

Declaring a variable within a procedure must be done using the `Dim` or `Static` statement; you can't declare a variable or constant as `Public`, `Private`, or `Friend` within a procedure.

Module-Level or Private Scope

A variable has *module-level scope* when it can be accessed by all the subroutines and functions contained in a particular module. Variables and constants that have module-level scope also reside in memory for the lifetime of the module. That is to say, as long as the module remains in memory, its module-level variables and constants also remain in memory. To create a variable with module-level scope, you must declare it in the module's Declarations section (that is to say, outside of any subroutine or function) by using either the `Dim` or `Private` statement.

Friend Scope

The `Friend` keyword can only be used for variables and procedure declarations within an object module, such as a class or a form module. Friend scope gives other object modules within the project access to the variable or method without requiring that it be declared as `Public`, which would include it in the class type library, thereby making it accessible by software objects outside the project.

Public Scope

Used outside of a procedure in place of the `Dim` statement, `Public` allows a variable to be seen by all procedures in all modules in the current project. If used in the context of a Class module, its scope is extended beyond the boundaries of the current project. The automatic creation of a COM interface for any public procedure or property means that it can be called by other software components as a method or property of the class in which it's defined.

Object Variables and Binding

Although Object variables are in many ways no different from other types of variables, the fact that they are references to other software components rather than simple values warrants special attention. While objects, classes, and binding are discussed in greater depth in Chapter 4, a short introduction to the subject is nevertheless worthwhile.

Declaring Object Variables

Object variables are declared in much the same way as other variables. There are three ways to declare an object variable:

```
Dim myObject As LibName.ClassName
Dim myObject As New LibName.ClassName
Dim myObject As Object
```

In each of the methods shown above, a `Private` or `Public` statement can replace the `Dim` statement, and the same scope rules apply as for other variables.

In the first declaration, the object variable is referenced to the class type library, but no instance of the class is assigned to the variable. At this stage, `myObject` is set to `Nothing`. To reference the class in this manner, you must have used the References dialog to add a reference to the class to your project. To assign a reference to a real instance of the class, you must use the `Set` statement prior to using the variable; for example:

```
Set myObject = LibName.ClassName
```

This produces an early bound reference to the object.

In the second declaration, a reference to a new instance of the class is assigned to the object variable, which is now ready to use immediately. Again, to reference the class in this manner, you must have first used the References dialog to add a reference to the class to your project. This second method also produces an early bound reference to the object; however, the object isn't actually created until the object variable is used.

In the third declaration, the object variable has been declared as a generic Object data type. This is useful when you don't know beforehand what type of object you will be creating. At this stage, the object variable also has a value of `Nothing`; to assign an object reference to it, you must use either the *CreateObject* or *GetObject* functions. An object variable declared in this manner is said to be late bound.

Early and Late Binding: Performance Comparisons

Whenever you read about when and why to use early binding and late binding, the choice always seems unambiguous: late binding is less efficient than early binding. But this isn't always the case; there are a number of factors to consider when choosing a method of object binding.

First, does the object to which you are binding execute within the same process as the client, or does it run in its own process? Will it be running on the same machine or on a remote server? In general terms, late binding is slightly more efficient for out-of-process ActiveX EXEs, and early binding is vastly more efficient for in-process DLLs.

A second factor that affects the relative performance of late and early binding is the operating system. The differences between late and early binding appear to be magnified on Windows 95, whereas they are less noticeable under Windows NT 4.0. You may also find variations if your DLL is running through Microsoft Transaction Server.

In short, you should always bear in mind that efficient communication between software components takes careful planning and testing. You should be prepared to create test projects to experiment with the various options and to assess their performance.

In the same way that you should carefully consider how to handle your Object variables, the same performance considerations come into play when you are deciding how to pass variables between procedures and software components.

The Collection Object

VBA features one generic object type, the Collection object, which is simply a container for data. Although typically its members are other objects, it can in fact hold data of any type, including other collection objects. The collection object is therefore an object-oriented version of the Visual Basic array. It supports the following four methods:

Add

    Adds an item to the collection. Along with the data itself, you can specify a key value by which the member can be retrieved from the collection.

Count

    Returns the number of items in the collection.

Item

    Retrieves a member from the collection either by its index (or ordinal position in the collection) or by its key (assuming that one was provided when the item was added to the collection).

Remove

    Deletes a member from the collection either by its index or its key.

For example, the following code fragment defines a collection object, *colStates*, to hold U.S. state information, and adds two members to it that can later be accessed by their key, which in this case happens to be their two-letter state code:

```
Dim colStates As New Collection
colStates.Add "New York", "NY"
colStates.Add "Michigan", "MI"
```

As we've noted, collection objects, like arrays, are containers for data. Like the elements in arrays, the members of collections can be iterated using the For Each...Next construct. And like arrays, they are accessible by their index value, although the lower bound of a collection object's index is always 1, and can't be set otherwise in code. But given the similarity to arrays, why use collection objects, rather than arrays, in your code? The major reason is ease of access and ease of maintenance:

- Members can be added before or after an existing member based on the latter's key value as well as its index value.

- Members can be retrieved based on either their key value or their index value.

- Members can be deleted based on either their key value or their index value. Multiple deletions based on an index value, however, should be done backwards, from higher index values to lower ones, since the collection is reindexed after each deletion.

Passing Parameters

There are numerous occasions when you need to call a custom function or subroutine from another function or subroutine, and a variable you are using in the calling procedure is needed in the called procedure. You therefore pass the variable as a parameter to the called procedure. Whether the called procedure is in the same module, the same project, or is a method within a class on a remote server, passing variables from one procedure to the other is always the same.

The called procedure, and not the calling procedure, determines how the variable is passed from the calling to the called procedure. As the user of a called procedure, you have no control over how Visual Basic treats the passed parameters. As the author of a called procedure, it's up to you to decide how best to bring in variables from calling procedures.

Visual Basic allows you to pass variables between procedures and components in two ways. Within the function or subroutine definition, you specify either **ByRef** or **ByVal** for each of the variables in the argument list.

ByRef

This is the default method for passing variables between procedures in Visual Basic; that is, if you specify neither **ByVal** nor **ByRef**, VB treats the variable as though it had been specified as **ByRef**.

ByRef means that the variable is passed *by reference*. In other words, only a reference to the original variable is passed to the called procedure. The called procedure doesn't get its own copy of the variable; it simply references the original variable. This is very similar in concept to the pointers you find in C and C++. The result is that if you make a change to the variable in the called procedure, that change is reflected in the variable in the calling procedure, because they are actually the same variable.

The code fragment below demonstrates passing a variable by reference. It also demonstrates how to circumvent the problem that a function can only return one value. For example, if the *GetValue* function you are calling returns an input from the user, how do you determine if the user wants to cancel the input altogether? You can't necessarily do this by using the return value of the function, since it may be a valid input from the user. You therefore pass a Boolean variable by reference and test its value on return from the function:

```
Private Sub Command1_Click()

    Dim blnCancel As Boolean
    Dim lReturn As Long

    lReturn = GetValue(blnCancel)
    If blnCancel Then
        Exit Sub
```

```
        Else
            MsgBox lReturn
        End If

End Sub

Private Function GetValue(ByRef Cancel As Boolean) As Long

    Dim sResponse As String
    Dim iResponse As Integer

    Cancel = False

    sResponse = InputBox(Prompt:="Enter a value", _
                         Title:="Input Required", _
                         Default:=0)

    'an inputbox returns a zero length string if _
     the Cancel button was clicked
    If sResponse = "" Then
        Cancel = True
    Else
        If IsNumeric(sResponse) Then
            GetValue = CLng(sResponse)
        End If
    End If

End Function
```

As you can see, **ByRef** arguments can be extremely useful. For example, you can use a **ByRef** argument to "return" a value from a subroutine that normally can't return a value. This can be used to great effect to obtain return values from an event handler. And as demonstrated above, you can also use **ByRef** arguments to return more than the one return value from a function.

ByVal

If you pass a variable by value using the **ByVal** keyword, the called procedure obtains its own separate copy of the variable. You can therefore change the value of the variable in the called procedure without affecting the original value of the variable in the calling procedure.

ByRef and ByVal: Performance

When passing variables to procedures that are either in the same project or that are methods of an in-process ActiveX component, **ByRef** is much faster than **ByVal**. This is because the memory reference gives the called procedure almost instantaneous access to the variable's value.

However, when passing variables to a method in an out-of-process server, **ByVal** has the performance advantage. This is because a procedure in a different process can't use the reference supplied by **ByRef**. Since they don't share memory, the called procedure has to obtain a copy of the variable's value. But since parameters are usually passed by reference to permit called routines to change their value, the value of the `ByRef` argument is copied back to the calling procedure, and the original variable is updated with this value.

Optional Arguments

The `Optional` keyword can be used in the argument list of a procedure declaration to denote that a particular argument doesn't always have to be passed. This allows you the flexibility to have different calling procedures passing different argument lists. One restriction is that all arguments after the first optional argument must also be optional.

The `Optional` keyword was introduced in VB4, and at that time optional arguments could only be declared as type Variant. However, VB5 extended its functionality by allowing any intrinsic data type to be used as an optional argument.

To test if a variant optional argument has been passed into your procedure, use the *IsMissing* function. Other data types will have their default values if they have not been explicitly passed as arguments; this, however, may be confusing. If an optional integer value isn't passed as a parameter, for example, its value in the procedure is 0. But did the calling procedure actually pass in 0, or is its value 0 because the argument is missing?

ParamArray

The `ParamArray` keyword (short for Parameter Array) allows you to accept a variable number of arguments into a procedure. The `ParamArray` must be the last argument in the list, and it can't be used in the same argument list as an `Optional` argument.

The `ParamArray` is an optional variant array. That is, the array can be empty, or it can contain any number of variant elements. To see how this operates, here's a quick example:

```
Private Sub cmdCallDoStuff_Click()

    Dim blnOK As Boolean

    blnOK = DoStuff("Wednesday", 1234, _
            CDate("04/12/1999"), 123.444)

End Sub

Private Sub cmdCallDoOtherStuff_Click()

    Dim blnOK As Boolean
    Dim oTest As testEXE.txtClass
    Set oTest = New testEXE.txtClass
      blnOK = DoStuff(123, 9999999.99, "Hello World", _
              oTest)
    Set oTest = Nothing

End Sub
```

```
Private Function DoStuff(ParamArray anyArgs()) As Boolean

    Dim i As Integer
    For i = 0 To UBound(anyArgs)
        MsgBox anyArgs(i) & vbCrLf & TypeName(anyArgs(i))
    Next i

End Function
```

As you can see from this simple example, a **ParamArray** gives you incredible flexibility, allowing the calling program to pass any data type—including objects—in any order to a procedure or function. However, this flexibility is often a drawback. Imagine yourself as the programmer of the calling procedure. What arguments is the function looking for? What data types are they supposed to be? I would recommend that you not get too excited at the flexibility offered by **ParamArray**, and that you think instead about the wider benefits of type-safe functions that are both easy to use and easy to maintain.

One last word of caution about **ParamArrays**. I have found in the past (and particularly with early releases of Windows NT 4.0) that **ParamArrays** within remote server applications often displayed unstable and inexplicable behavior.

Intrinsic Constants

In addition to allowing you to define your own constants using the Const keyword, VBA includes a number of built-in or intrinsic constants whose values are predefined by VBA. Along with saving you from having to define these values as constants, the major advantage of using intrinsic constants is that they enhance the readability of your code. So, for instance, instead of having to write code like this:

```
If myObject.ForeColor = &hFFFF Then
```

you can write:

```
If myObject.ForeColor = vbYellow Then
```

Intrinsic constants are now available for most operations. The best place to find information about the available intrinsic constants is in the VB object browser, which you can open by selecting Object Browser from the View menu or by pressing F2. In many cases, though, a list of available constants for a particular operation will pop up as you are entering the code. Appendix B, *Language Constants*, also lists constants available in VB and VBA.

CHAPTER 4

Class Modules

To some degree, class modules can be seen as "replacements" for code modules—that is, class modules are repositories for shared variables as well as for shared code, just as code modules are. So why have class modules? What's wrong with normal code modules? Basically, there is nothing wrong with them. But code modules allow you to share procedures only within the project in which they reside. For example, you can call a public function from another code module in a project, but you can't call that function from another project. To do that, you have to add the code module to your project or, even worse, create a second copy of the code module.

Class modules have (without wanting to sound too evangelistic) revolutionized VB. The whole style of writing VB programs has changed since version 4.0 of VB was launched, bringing the VB/VBA language closer than ever to being a true object-oriented language. In fact, much of VB's current success in the corporate marketplace can be directly attributed to the ability to create ActiveX components, the cornerstone of which is the class module.

When you create a class module, you are creating a COM interface. Therefore, class modules allow you to describe your application to the outside world via a programmable interface that consists of properties, methods, and events in a way that allows you to retain control over the application. Using class modules, you can break an application into logical sections, each having its own class. This is the concept of *encapsulation*—everything having to do with a particular thing held within one wrapper—which is critical to object-oriented programming.

Finally, we have all heard and read loads about the "Holy Grail" of code reuse. OK, anyone can reuse any code; simply copy and paste a procedure from your last project, or create a *.bas* file containing a library of useful stuff you simply include in every project (VB3 programmers will remember *constant.bas*). The problem with this approach is that the source code has to be included in the project each time. What happens if you find a new, more efficient way to perform a particular function? You have to revisit each project to change all of the instances of the same code. However, if you'd used a class to create your library, you could simply add a reference to your class to any new project. This gives you the advantage of not allowing the source code to be seen (or changed) in the current project, and of only having to make a change to a procedure in one place. Class modules therefore allow you to reuse code in a structured manner in your own projects, and others can use them in their classes without having access to your source code.

Properties

An important element of any class is its properties. These are the equivalent of global or public variables in code modules. However, a property has the added advantages that you can both validate a value and execute other code every time a value is assigned to the property. In addition, properties declared within class modules can be accessed from outside the current project. Properties help eliminate the clutter of global variables that plagued almost every large-scale VB3 application I've seen, and that made both the development and maintenance of VB3 applications a nightmare.

Implementing Properties

Properties allow users and other programmers (including yourself) to safely access data. In many ways, properties are simply variables that hold a particular value or object. But with careful planning and a professional approach, you can turn these simple variables into powerful tools.

Take, for example, a class that is acting as a wrapper for a collection object. You may have a read-only property within your class called Count that returns the number of records held within the collection. Your Count property would simply pass on the Count property of the collection object. However, you could write code within your class's Count property procedure that checks if the value of the collection object's Count property is zero and, if it's zero, calls a procedure that populates the collection. In this way, the user of your class could populate the collection automatically by returning the Count property, as the following snippet demonstrates:

```
Public Property Get Count() As Long
    If mcolAnyColl.Count = 0 Then
        Call PopulateCollection()
```

```
      End If
      Count = mcolAnyColl.Count
   End Property
```

A major use of property procedures is to validate data. Without class modules and properties, validation is typically performed at the form level; for example, the Change or LostFocus event handler of a TextBox control determines if the data entered in the text box is acceptable. It often happens, though, that this value is referenced on many different forms, so that each reference has to be accompanied by the data validation code. If a programmer gets the validation code wrong, or simply ignores or forgets the validation altogether, you risk accepting invalid data into your database. If the validation rules change, you have to visit each form that contains a reference to the data item and change the validation code.

Now contrast this scenario with validation within a property procedure. The form can attempt to assign a nonvalidated value to the property, and the property procedure will validate the data and accept or reject it. The validation for this data item is thereby centralized. Any form can use the property, and you can be certain that only validated data is accepted into the database. Furthermore, if a change to the validation is required, you only have to change the validation logic in one place, thereby reducing the risk of error.

The following snippet demonstrates using a Property procedure to implement business rules to validate incoming data:

```
Public Property Let ClaimDate(dVal as Date)
    'business rule: a claim cannot be more than 10 days old
    If dVal < DateAdd("d",-10,Now) Then
        Err.Raise vbObjectError + 700001, "", _
                 "Cannot be more than 10 days ago"
    Else
        mdClaimDate = dVal
    End If
End Property
```

A property can be of any intrinsic data type or any user-defined object. As of VB6, you also can create a property whose data type is a user-defined type, although the implementation of this is somewhat different than that for a normal property; for details, see the section "Implementing a User-Defined Type Property" later in this chapter.

Properties can also be defined in Form modules, and can remove the need for global or public variables to pass state from one module to another in a project. For example, if you need to set a value for a form to use as it loads, the traditional method is to assign the value to a public variable, which is then accessible to the form. The problem with this method is that before long, a large project includes truckloads of global variables and keeping track of them is a nightmare. Instead, you should create a property in the form's code module; then, from outside the form, you can assign a value to this property, as the following code snippet shows:

```
Dim oFrm As frmEmpForm
Set oFrm = New frmEmpForm
oFrm.CurrentEmployeeCode = "0123"
```

```
oFrm.Show vbModal
Set oFrm = Nothing
```

You can create properties that return other objects, thereby building a hierarchy of objects. For example, consider an application that deals with employees. The individual employee's record could be held in a collection wrapper class called Employee, and the code to save and retrieve an employee's record that's common to all employees could be held in a class called Employees. You could then place a property procedure called Employee in the Employees class that returns an Employee class object, similar to the following:

```
Public Property Get Employee(sEmployeeCode As String) _
                            As Employee
    Set Employee = mcolEmployees.Item(sEmployeeCode)
End Property
```

You could then access a particular employee's record from the client application using the code:

```
TxtEmployeeName.Text = Employees.Employee("0123").Name
```

Having examined the vital role that property procedures can play in ActiveX object creation, let's look at the separate procedures you need to employ within your class to successfully implement a robust property.

The Anatomy of a Property

A properly defined read-and-write property consists of three components:

*   A `Private` member variable to hold the actual data
*   A `Property Let` procedure to validate and accept the incoming value
*   A `Property Get` procedure to pass the value of the private member variable to the calling program, or optionally a `Property Set` procedure when dealing with object references

Private member variable

The `Private` member variable holds the property's actual value or object reference. By declaring the variable `Private`, you protect it from the outside world; from outside its module, it's accessible by the `Property Let`, `Get`, or `Set` procedures.

 It's possible to create a property within a class module by simply dimensioning a `Public` variable. However, its value can be modified from any other module in your project by a simple assignment statement. This isn't recommended, since it fails to take advantage of the benefits associated with property procedures.

When creating a property for a user-defined type, the type declaration must be declared as Public. See the next section, "Implementing a User-Defined Type Property," for details.

The name of this variable should differ from that of the property to which it's attached. This is usually achieved using standard VB naming conventions and prefixing the name with a lowercase "m" to denote a member variable. For example:

```
Private msForeName As String
Private miNumber   As Integer
```

The Property Let procedure

A Property Let procedure assigns a value to a property. You can perform all your data validation within the Property Let procedure before assigning the incoming value to your Private member variable. (For full details, see the entry for the Property Let statement in Chapter 7, *The Language Reference*.) In its simplest form, a Property Let procedure looks something like this:

```
Public Property Let ForeName(sVal As String)
    msForeName = sVal
End Property
```

The data type of the property's argument must be the same as that of the private member variable to which its value is assigned.

A Property Let procedure doesn't return a value. Therefore, to reject a value within your data validation code, you should use the Err.Raise method to generate a trappable error in the client application.

A tricky issue is that of generating a warning, rather than an error. Let's say that part of your validation code checks the value of a data item and, if it's above a certain amount, warns the user that the amount appears high. You don't want to reject the value out of hand, because there could be a valid reason for the high value. Now, if you coded the warning as follows, you would never get past the warning if the value was above 10,000:

```
Public Property Let ClaimValue(dVal As Double)
    If dVal > 10000 Then
        Err.Raise vbObjectError + 40000, "", _
                "The Claim Value appears high"
    Else
        mdClaimValue = dVal
    End If
End Property
```

The way to get around this is to raise an event in the client. Events are covered later in the chapter, and we'll come back to this example in that section.

The Property Get procedure

The `Property Get` procedure is much like a function: just as you assign a value to the name of the function to define its return value, you assign the value of the `Private` member variable to the name of the `Property Get` procedure and thereby return the property value. (For full details, see the entry for the `Property Get` procedure in Chapter 7.)

In its simplest form, a `Property Get` procedure looks something like this:

```
Public Property Get ForeName() As String
    ForeName = msForeName
End Property
```

The data type returned by the `Property Get` procedure must be the same as that of the `Private` member variable.

If the data type of the property is an object reference, you must use the `Set` statement to return its value, like this:

```
Public Property Get Employee(sEmployeeCode As String) _
                    As Employee
    Set Employee = mcolEmployees.Item(sEmployeeCode)
End Property
```

Property scope

The keyword you employ to declare a property procedure determines where the property can be used:

`Private`
> Restricts the visibility of the property to the class module within which the method is defined. This is pointless, since you achieve identical results with a private variable.

`Friend`
> Restricts the visibility of the property to those modules contained within the same project as the property definition. `Friend` properties appear in the IntelliSense drop-down list for the class and are made available for statement completion in other modules within the same project.

`Public`
> Allows the property to be called from within the class module, from other modules in the project, and from outside the project. Defining a property as `Public` adds the property declaration to the Type Library for the class. When a reference is made to the class from another project, Public properties appear in the IntelliSense drop-down list for the class and are made available for statement completion.

Implementing a User-Defined Type Property

Visual Basic 6 adds the user-defined type (UDT) to the list of data types a property can represent. However, its use isn't intuitive. Here are the steps needed to create a UDT property in VB6:

1. Declare a **Public** user-defined type definition.

2. Declare a **Private** member variable whose data type is that of the user-defined type.

3. Declare a **Public Property Get** procedure whose data type is that of the user-defined type.

4. The assignation within the **Property Get** procedure should be the **Private** member variable.

5. Declare a **Public Property Let** procedure. The data type of the value parameter is that of the user-defined type.

In addition, client applications using the UDT property can do so only by using early binding. See the section "Using ActiveX Components in a Project" later in this chapter for information about early binding.

Here's a quick example:

Server code:

```
Public Type udtTestType
    EmployeeNo As Integer
    EmployeeName As String
End Type

Private mudtTestType As udtTestType

Public Property Get TestType() As udtTestType
    TestType = mudtTestType
End Property

Public Property Let TestType(udtVal As udtTestType)
    mudtTestType = udtVal
End Property
```

Client code:

```
Dim oServer As Server.ServerClass
Dim oRemUDT As Server.udtTestType

Set oServer = New Server.ServerClass

oRemUDT = oServer.TestType

oRemUDT.EmployeeName = "Tim"
oRemUDT.EmployeeNo = 1

oServer.TestType = oRemUDT

Set oServer = Nothing
```

To use remote user-defined types in this manner, you need a computer with NT4 and NT Service Pack 4 or above.

Implementing a Read-Only Property

To define a property as read-only, you should implement the following:

- A **Private** member variable to hold the actual data
- A **Property Get** procedure to pass the value of the private member variable to the calling program

In this way, the "outside world" can't change the value of the property, because there is no **Property Let** procedure. You have complete control over the value of the property within the class.

Using Properties in the Client Application

Within a procedure, you shouldn't make more than one call to a particular property. Each time you call a property, there is overhead, which can result in a massive performance hit on your application. This code snippet shows how *not* to use a property:

```
Dim oEmps as Employees
Set oEmps = New Employees
If oEmps.EmployeeNo <> sExcludedEmpNo Then
    TxtEmpNo.Text = oEmps.EmployeeNo
    Call BuildSomeCombo(oEmps.EmployeeNo)
    MsgBox "Found Employee No" & oEmps.EmployeeNo
End If
Set oEmps = Nothing
```

In this simple example, there are four calls to the EmployeeNo property. That's four times the client application has to navigate to the **Property Get** procedure, and four times the **Property Get** procedure has to execute. You can optimize this code by accessing the property once and storing its value in a local variable, as the following code fragment illustrates:

```
Dim oEmps as Employees
Dim sEmpNo as String
Set oEmps = New Employees
sEmpsNo = oEmps.EmployeeNo
Set oEmps = Nothing

If sEmpNo <> sExcludedEmpNo Then
    TxtEmpNo.Text = sEmpNo
    Call BuildSomeCombo(sEmpNo)
    MsgBox "Found Employee No" & sEmpNo
End If
```

You may have noticed another important benefit we've managed to gain in the reworked code. The object reference is destroyed at a much earlier stage, which means that the object is used only for a short period of time. This is a major consideration as far as scalability is concerned when designing large client-server applications.

Using a Mass Assignation Function in Collection Classes

What's a mass assignation function? Let's say you have a collection class that contains 20 properties, which you populate by reading data from a database. You have a procedure that opens the database, creates a recordset, and then assigns the values from the recordset to each of the relevant properties in the class, something like this:

```
oClass.EmployeeNo = rsRecordset!EmpNo
oClass.FirstName = rsRecordset!FirstName
Etc...
```

Using this method, you are calling the **Property Let** procedure of each property. If there is validation code within the **Property Let** procedure, this must execute too, most likely on data that has been validated before being saved in the database. A more efficient method of population is to create a function within the collection class, like this:

```
Friend Function Initialize(sEmpNo as String, _
              sFirstName as String ...etc) As Boolean
msEmpNo = sEmpNo
msFirstName = sFirstName
...Etc...
```

This single function assigns all the values for the object in one go by assigning the values directly to the local variables, thus bypassing the **Property Let** procedures and the redundant validation code. You can therefore pass all the values to populate the object at once:

```
If oClass.Initialise( rsRecordset!EmpNo, _
              rsRecordset!FirstName, _
              etc...) Then
```

Of course, you should only use this method within a class module—never from outside—and you should only employ this against data you are certain has already been validated.

Enumerated Constants

Constants, as you know, are useful for improving the readability and maintainability of code by making it self-documenting. However, you can't define a public constant (using the **Public Const** statement) within a class module. How do you make some constants available both to yourself and possibly to other users of your class? The answer lies in the use of enumerated constants.

Enumerated constants allow you to create a set of constants that become intrinsic to your application or class, very much like the intrinsic constants, such as **vbCrLf** and vbRightButton, within VB itself. By using enumerated constants within your class, you can associate a constant name and its value with the class, in the process providing the user of the class with a set of meaningful constants that are instantly available from the IntelliSense drop-down list for statement completion.

Using Enumerated Constants

To create a set of enumerated constants, you use the Enum statement, which defines the name of the set of constant values, the names of the individual constants within the set, and the individual values of these constants. You place the Enum statement in the declarations section of your class module. For example:

```
Public Enum empTypes
    empTypeOne = 1
    empTypeTwo = 2
    empTypeThree = 3
End Enum
```

The major drawback with enumerated constants is that their values can be numeric only. In other words, you can't declare an enumerated constant that represents a string.

Once you have created a reference to your class from the client application using the references dialog or automatically if the class module in which empTypes is defined is a part of your project, you have access to the enumerated constants via the IntelliSense drop-down list. For example, you could access the constants shown in the example above by typing emp, then pressing the Ctrl key and spacebar together; in the list of available items, you would see all three of the constants and the empTypes Enum type. This means that you can use either of the following syntactical forms:

```
If iType = empTypes.empTypeOne Then
If iType = empTypeOne Then
```

Note that to use the enumerated constants from within a class, you don't have to have instantiated an object variable of that class as you do to access a property within a class. This is an important point and worth repeating. Accessing a property within a class requires you to declare an object variable of that class, then use the variable and dot notation to get to the property; for example:

```
Dim oVar As Employee
Set oVar = New Employee
OVar.Name = "Peter"
```

However, as soon as a class module containing an enumerated constant is included in your project or a reference to its class is added to your project, you can use those constants within your code.

For more information on the Enum statement, see its entry in Chapter 7.

Class Module Events

Unlike normal code modules, class modules support two events that are automatically defined when you add a class module to your project. These two standard events, the Initialize and Terminate events, are analogous to the class constructor and destructor in an object-oriented programming language like C++; they are fired automatically when a class is instantiated and destroyed, respectively.

An *event handler* is the code attached to a particular event. When the event is fired, the event handler is executed automatically. Like all event handlers, writing code to handle the Initialize and Terminate events is optional, but it's at the heart of sound VB programming. So let's look at some of the uses you can put these event handlers to and some of the rules relating to these two events.

The Initialize Event

Let's begin by examining precisely when the Initialize event is fired, then look at some possible applications for the Initialize event handler.

When is the Initialize event fired?

The firing of the Initialize event depends on how the class object is instantiated. If you use the combined method of declaring a New instance of an object:

```
Dim oVar As New svrObject
```

the Initialize event is fired when the first reference is made to a member of the class, and not when the class is declared as New. For example:

```
Dim oVar As New svrObject ' Initialize event not called
oVar.AnyProp = sAnyVal    ' Initialize event fired _
                   immediately prior to the Property Let
```

However, if you use the Set statement to instantiate an object, the Initialize event is fired when the Set statement is executed. For example:

```
Dim oVar As svrObject
Set oVar = New svrObject   ' Initialize event fired here
```

Using the Initialize event

The Initialize event can be used for any of the following:

- To create new collection objects that are used within the class. For example:

```
Set mcolx = New Collection
```

- To include conditional debugging code to determine when the class has been initialized. For example:

```
#If ccDebug Then
    Debug.Print "xyz Class Initialized"
#End If
```

- To create and instantiate dependent objects. For example:

```
Set moDepObj = New clsDependant
```

The Terminate Event

As with the Initialize event, the precise time the Terminate event is fired has created some confusion. Once again, we'll examine when the Terminate event is fired before looking at some applications of the Terminate event handler.

When is the Terminate event fired?

The simple answer is that the Terminate event is fired when all references to the object are set to Nothing. However, life's never that simple. You may assume that because you have placed a `Set objVar = Nothing` statement in your program that the `objVar`'s Terminate event will be fired, and in the vast majority of cases it will be. However, having a live reference to another object in the `objVar` class prevents `objVar` from terminating. This occurs, for example, if your class contains a collection that contains a reference to another object, and you fail to destroy the collection. Similarly, if your class contains a dependent object whose reference was not released, your class may not terminate cleanly.

To prevent this from happening, use debugging code within both the Initialize and Terminate event handlers to ensure that all objects are destroyed cleanly when you think they should be destroyed. In addition, get into the habit of using the following template when handling object variables:

```
Dim objectVariable As Class
Set objectVariable = New Class
    'indent code then it's easy to see the start and
    'end of an object reference
Set objectVariable = Nothing
```

I actually go as far as writing my `Set objectVariable = Nothing` statement before I write the code between the two `Set` statements. This makes me approach the two `Set` statements as if they formed a code block, like an `If...Then...End If` block.

Using the Terminate event

The Terminate event can be used to provide "clean up" code for your class:

- To destroy collection objects used within the class being terminated. For example:

  ```
  Set mcolx = Nothing
  ```

- To include conditional debugging code to determine when the Terminate event has fired. For example:

  ```
  #If ccDebug Then
      Debug.Print "xyz Class Terminated"
  #End If
  ```

- To destroy dependent objects of the class being terminated. For example:

  ```
  Set moDepObj = Nothing
  ```

Implementing Custom Events

In the early versions of VB, programmers were limited to working with the built-in events. In VB5, however, three simple keywords—Event, RaiseEvent, and WithEvents—were added to the language to allow the programmer to define custom events or to trap events in external objects that would otherwise be inaccessible.

Custom events applications

Custom events can be used for any of the following:

- To report the progress of an asynchronous task back to the client application from an out-of-process ActiveX EXE component.

- To pass through events fired by the underlying control in an ActiveX custom control.

- As a central part of a real-time multiuser application in an *n*-tier client-server application. (Incidentally, events can't be fired from within a Microsoft Transaction Server Context.)

- To receive notification of events fired in automation servers.

- To query the user and receive further input.

Custom event rules

The following are some of the rules and "gotchas" for defining custom events:

- Events can be declared and fired only from within object modules (i.e., Form, User Control, and Class modules). You can't declare and fire events from a standard code module.

- Events can be handled or intercepted only from within object modules. You can't handle any type of event from within a code module. This isn't really a limitation because you can simply include a call to a function or sub within a code module from within your event handler, to pass program control to a code module—just like you would write code in form and control event handlers.

- The event declaration must be Public so that it's visible outside the object module; it can't be declared as Friend or Private.

- You can't declare an object variable as WithEvents if the object doesn't have any events.

- To allow the client application to handle the event being fired, the object variable must be declared using the WithEvents keyword.

- VB custom events don't return a value; however, you can use a ByRef argument to return a value, as you will see in the next section, "Creating a custom event."

- If your class is one of many held inside a collection, the event isn't fired to the "outside world"—unless you have a live object variable referencing the particular instance of the class raising the event.

Creating a custom event

To raise an event from within an object module, you first of all must declare the event in the declarations section of the object module that will raise the event. You do this with the **Event** statement using the following syntax:

```
[Public] Event eventname [(arglist)]
```

For example:

```
Public Event DetailsChanged(sField As String)
```

In the appropriate place in your code, you need to fire the event using the **RaiseEvent** statement. For example:

```
RaiseEvent DetailsChanged("Employee Name")
```

That is all you need to do within the object module. Simply declare an event using **Event**, and fire it using **RaiseEvent**.

The client code is just as simple. You declare an object variable using the **WithEvents** keyword to alert VB that you wish to be informed when an event is fired in the object. For example:

```
Private WithEvents oEmployee As Employee
```

This declaration should be placed in the Declarations section of the module. VB automatically places an entry for the object variable name in the Object drop-down list at the top left of your code window. When you select this, note that the events declared in the object are available to you in the Procedure drop-down list at the top right of your code window. You can then select the relevant event and its event handler. For example:

```
Private Sub oEmployee_DetailsChanged(sField As String)
    MsgBox sField & " has been changed"
End Sub
```

In the earlier section "The Property Let procedure," we mentioned using a custom event to fire a warning to the client as part of a data-validation procedure. Unfortunately, though, events don't return a value. However, if you define one of the parameters of your event to be **ByRef**, you can examine the value of the variable once the event has been handled to determine the outcome of the event handling within the client application. Here's a simple example:

Server code:

```
Public Event Warning(sMsg As String, ByRef Cancel As Boolean)

Public Property Let ClaimValue(dVal As Double)

    Dim blnCancel As Boolean

    If dVal > 10000 Then
        RaiseEvent Warning("The Claim Value appears high", _
                        blnCancel)
        If blnCancel Then
            Exit Property
        End If
```

```
        End If

        mdClaimValue = dVal

    End Property
```

Client code:

```
    Private WithEvents oServer As clsServer

    Private Sub oServer_Warning(sMsg As String, _
                           Cancel As Boolean)
        Dim iResponse As Integer
        iResponse = MsgBox(sMsg & " is this OK?", _
                      vbQuestion + vbYesNo, _
                      "Warning")
        If iResponse = vbNo Then
            Cancel = True
        Else
            Cancel = False
        End If

    End Sub
```

As you can see, this is a powerful technology. However, it also demonstrates another aspect of custom events that may not be desirable in certain circumstances: RaiseEvent is *not* asynchronous. In other words, when you call the RaiseEvent statement in your class code, your class code won't continue executing until the event has been either handled by the client or ignored. (If the client has not created an object reference using the WithEvents keyword, then it isn't handling the events raised by the class, and any events raised will be ignored by that client.) This can have undesirable side effects, and you should bear it mind when planning your application.

For more information on the custom event statements, see the entries for the Event, Friend, Private, Public, RaiseEvent, and WithEvents statements in Chapter 7.

Implementing Custom Class Methods

Class methods are implemented by creating subroutines (also known as sub procedures) and functions within the class. There is no practical difference between creating a subroutine or function in a class module or creating it in a code or form module. If you're used to programming in another language such as C or C++, the concept of a subroutine will be new to you, although it's analogous to a void function.

VB functions and subroutines differ only in the ability of a function to return a value to the calling procedure, and thus a function call can be placed on the right side of an assignment statement. However, I always recommend that modules consist only of functions, not of subroutines. Why? Since they are identical *except* that functions return a value, you can use functions to improve the robustness of your application by always returning at least a Boolean value indicating whether the function has succeeded or failed. The calling procedure isn't forced to handle the return value. Look at the two code snippets below:

```
Call OpenFile(sFileName)

If OpenFile(sFileName) Then
```

The first line of code calls a function to open a particular file. Since the return value is discarded, the function has to assume that the file was opened successfully. The function call in the second line of code returns a Boolean True or False value that is handled in the code, letting you know whether or not the call to the *OpenFile* function was successful.

The Scope of Custom Methods

As with variables and properties, the scope or visibility of a class method is determined by the scope statement you use when defining the method. These are:

Private
> Restricts the visibility of the method to the class module in which the method is defined.

Friend
> Restricts the visibility of the method to modules in the same project as the method definition. Friend class methods appear in the IntelliSense drop-down list for the class and are made available for statement completion in other modules within the same project.

Public
> Allows the method to be called from within the class module, from any other module in the project, and from outside the project. Specifying a method as public adds the method declaration to the Type Library for the class. When a reference is made to the class from another project, public class methods appear in the IntelliSense drop-down list for the class and are made available for statement completion.

Passing Arguments to Custom Methods

Although the way you pass arguments to methods is the same as passing arguments to other functions or subroutines, you should consider whether the class will be running in or out of the calling application's process.

If the method and calling statement are in the same process, generally you should pass arguments by reference, using the ByRef keyword. Within the same process, ByRef simply passes a reference to the variable, which in the main is more efficient that passing a copy of the variable's value, as ByVal does.

However, if there is a process boundary to be crossed, ByRef actually makes a copy of the value that it passes to the called procedure. When the called procedure terminates, it also makes a copy of the value to pass back to the calling procedure. The calling procedure then copies the returned value into the original value's address in memory. This means that if you are passing arguments across process boundaries, passing arguments by value with the ByVal keyword is more efficient.

Creating ActiveX Components

In the Professional and Enterprise editions of Visual Basic, you can use class modules to create ActiveX components and compile them as either ActiveX DLLs or ActiveX EXEs. The choice you are faced with, effectively, is whether you require an in-process or an out-of-process component.

In-Process Components

An ActiveX DLL is an in-process component. But why is it called "in-process"?

In 16-bit Windows, a DLL effectively became part of the operating system, and all running processes had access to the DLL. A handle to the DLL could be obtained centrally from the operating system, and the operating system knew at any given time how many (if any) handles to a particular DLL had been issued. In 32-bit Windows, a DLL doesn't become part of the operating system. It becomes part of the process space of the application that calls the DLL. A call to a DLL forces the operating system to create a file mapping object for the DLL. This object is then mapped into the process space of the client or calling process. Hence the term *in process.*

Out-of-Process Components

When you create an ActiveX EXE, you are creating an out-of-process component. An ActiveX EXE runs as a separate process with its own threads. This also means that calling a function within an ActiveX EXE is asynchronous; in other words, the calling application doesn't have to wait for a response from the function before continuing. By calling an out-of-process method, you have effectively created a multithreaded application.

While asynchronous function calls have tremendous benefits, they do require special handling. For example, you need to know when a function call has completed its task. This is typically done by raising an event from the out-of-process component.

Class Module Properties

Depending on the type of project in which the class module (*.cls*) file is included, class modules support the following properties that control their precise behavior:

Instancing
> Only available when a class is part of an ActiveX project, the instancing property defines how instances of the class are created. Its values are:

> *GlobalMultiUse*
>> The class becomes global to the project in which it's defined; references are not necessary. For example, most VB language objects are global; as soon as you load the environment, they are available to be used. Use this property setting to create class modules containing enumerated constants for your object model.

MultiUse

> The class has scope (i.e., it's visible) outside the project in which it's defined, and it can't be instantiated using the New keyword or the *CreateObject* function. Use this for top-level objects in a hierarchy or object model.

PublicNotCreateable

> Although the class has scope (i.e., it's visible) outside of the project in which it's defined, it can't be instantiated from outside the project using the New keyword or the *CreateObject* function. Use this for child objects that can be created by accessing a function or property of a higher-level object.

Private

> The class can't be "seen" outside the project in which it's defined.

SingleUse

> Every call by a client to create the object using either the New keyword or the *CreateObject* function creates a completely new instance of the object. Only available in ActiveX EXE projects.

GlobalSingleUse

> As with the SingleUse property value, every call by a client to create the object using either the New keyword or the *CreateObject* function creates a completely new instance of the object. However, GlobalSingleUse allows methods and properties to be seen as part of VB. Only available in ActiveX EXE projects.

DataSourceBehavior

> (VB6 only) This property, which isn't available when the class is part of an ActiveX EXE project, defines the ability of the class to serve as a data source for other objects. Values are:

vbNone

> The class doesn't expose a bindable data interface.

vbDataSource

> The class can act as a data source for other objects.

vbOLEDBProvider

> The class can act as an OLE DB Simple Provider.

DataBindingBehavior

> (VB6 only) This property controls the behavior of the class when it's bound to an external data source. Values are:

vbNone

> The class can't be bound to external data sources.

vbSimpleBound

> The class can be to bound to a single data field in an external data source.

vbComplexBound

> The class can be bound to a row of data in an external data source.

MTSTransactionMode

(VB6 only) Only available when the class is part of an ActiveX DLL project; you should set this property whenever the class is registered within Microsoft Transaction Server. This property automatically sets the Transaction Support property for the object when it is registered in MTS, thereby giving the developer control over how the component is used by MTS. Values are:

NotAnMTSObject
NoTransactions

Sets the Transaction Support property to "Does not support Transactions."

RequiresTransactions

Sets the Transaction Support property to "Requires a Transaction."

UsesTransactions

Sets the Transaction Support property to "Supports Transactions."

RequiresNewTransaction

Sets the Transaction Support property to "Requires a new Transaction."

Persistable

(VB6 only) Only available when a class is part of an ActiveX project, this property determines whether the class can be saved to disk. Values are:

NotPersistable

The class properties can't be saved.

Persistable

The class property values can be saved to a property bag.

Component Creation Hints and Tips

What follows are an assortment of topics, many of them frequently overlooked, to consider when building your own ActiveX components.

Including user interfaces in ActiveX components

There is nothing to stop you from including form modules within your ActiveX EXEs and DLLs. However, you should distinguish between an ActiveX component that is designed to run on the client machine and one that will be a remote server.

The rule is that ActiveX remote server components shouldn't contain any UI whatsoever—not only no forms, but no message boxes either. The reason for this is that the UI appears on the remote machine, not on the client machine. You can imagine the uselessness of a message box popping up on some remote application server stuck away in a locked machine room, waiting for someone to click OK!

Allowing clients to use the For Each...Next statement

Most of the time, we take the `For Each...Next` loop for granted as it iterates the members of an array or a collection. It's the fastest, most efficient method of visiting all the members of the collection or array, and we could care less that, by enumerating the members of the collection, the unseen code is actually generating new references to members of the collection with each iteration of the loop. However, as the provider of a collection class, it's up to you to provide an interface that the For Each...Next statement can work with.

This may sound a little daunting, but you'll be pleasantly surprised by how easy it is to implement a property that enumerates members of the collection within your class. First of all, you must create a Property Get procedure called *NewEnum* with the type of IUnknown. Its syntax is always the same:

```
Public Property Get NewEnum() As IUnknown
    Set NewEnum = mCol.[_NewEnum]
End Property
```

where mCol is the name of your private collection object variable.

Second, set the Procedure ID for this Property Get procedure to –4. To do this, select the Procedure Attributes option from the Tools menu, then click the Advanced button on the Procedure Attributes dialog. Enter a Procedure ID of –4. You should also check the "Hide this member" option to prevent the property from appearing in the IntelliSense drop-down list.

For more information about using the For Each...Next statement in a client application, see its entry in Chapter 7.

Error handling

More care and thought than normal needs to go into handling errors within a class module. In general you shouldn't do more than pass on the error to the client with the Err.Raise method. However, if your error handling code is going to pass the error number back to the client, you need to decide if the error number should have the vbObjectError constant added to it or not. (vbObjectError is a constant that allows a referencing object to determine that the error was generated in a VB class object.) Another consideration is whether or not and how the Err.Source property is passed back to the client.

A full discussion of error handling and the Err object, including class module error handling, can be found in Chapter 6, *Error Handling*.

One last point to note is that you should *never* use the End statement within a class module.

Use Dictionary objects rather than Collection objects

When you're creating object models, many of your ActiveX server components will be based upon collections of other objects. Ever since VB4, developers have become accustomed to writing these classes based on the Collection object (in effect, creating a wrapper for the Collection object), taking for granted the fact that the Collection object is slow and expensive in terms of overhead, but also knowing that there was no real alternative. However, if you're using VB6 to create collection classes, I strongly recommend that you use a Dictionary object in place of the Collection object. The Dictionary object is fast in comparison to the Collection, and it has more functionality. For a complete explanation of the Dictionary object, see the Dictionary Object entry in Chapter 7.

Creating ActiveX Components 73

Provide your own Exists property in collection classes

Collection objects are neat for quickly accessing values and objects given a key value. You can add items to the collection, retrieve a given item from the collection, find out how many items are in the collection, and remove an item from the collection. For example, this simple code retrieves an object from a collection using its key:

```
Public Property myClass(vVal as Variant) As myClass
    Set myClass = mCol.Item(vVal)
End Property
```

However, if the key *vVal* doesn't exist in the collection, you're faced with a runtime error. The gap in the usability of the Collection object is that there is no Exists property. But you can easily plug this gap and provide a way to add a missing property to the collection as follows:

```
Public Property Exists(sVal as String) As Boolean
    On Error Goto myClass_Err
    Dim oTest As myClass
    Set oTest = mCol.Item(sVal)
    Set oTest = Nothing
    Exists = True
    Exit Property
TryToGetIt:
    If getItemforCollection(sVal) Then
        Exists = True
    Else
        Exists = False
    End If
    Exit Property
MyClass_Err:
    If Err.Number = 5 Then
        Resume TryToGetIt
    Else
        'over-simplified error handler!
        Err.Raise Err.Number + vbObjectError
    End If
End Property
```

Quite simply, you attempt to assign the collection to a test object. If the assignment works, return **True**; otherwise, handle the error by calling a function, *getItemforCollection*, that adds the new item to the collection. If *getItemforCollection* returns **False**, however, this means that the item doesn't exist, and the Exists property must return **False**. Using the Exists property, you can preface each call to get an object with a conditional statement like the following:

```
Set oMyClasses = New myClasses
    If oMyClasses.Exists("xyz") Then
        Set oMyClass = oMyClasses.MyClass("xyz")
    Else
        MsgBox "Sorry it doesn't exist!"
    End if
Set oMyClass = Nothing
```

When is an in-process component out-of-process?

Until recently, you could say with certainty that an ActiveX EXE would run out-of-process, whereas an ActiveX DLL would run in-process. However, if you were now asked if a particular component was in-process or out-of-process, you would have to respond with the question, "Whose process?"

Technically, ActiveX DLLs will always be in-process, but traditionally (if you can call a couple of years a tradition!) the "process" referred to is that of the client application—but not any more! This shift in thinking has come about because of new technologies such as Distributed COM (DCOM), Microsoft Transaction Server (MTS), and Microsoft Distributed Transaction Coordinator (MDTC), which are blurring the traditional process boundaries.

For example, an ActiveX DLL running in MTS is running within the MTS's process, but it's running outside of the client application's process. In fact, boundaries are becoming blurred to such an extent that to the user of the client application, the old boundaries are for the most part completely invisible. During the development of a client-server application recently, I was aware that one of my DLLs was executing, only I wasn't quite sure which one of three machines it was executing on!

Using ActiveX Components in a Project

If the ActiveX object you need to reference provides a type library and is registered on your computer, you can create a reference to the component using the References dialog. This includes the component's properties, methods, and events in the Intellisense drop-down list and provides statement completion for its properties, methods, and events. Furthermore, this enables you to early bind to the component's classes.

If the ActiveX object either doesn't provide a type library, or you don't know at design time which classes of a component you will need, you should use late binding.

Manually Registering and Unregistering ActiveX Components

There are occasions when you need to use an ActiveX component in your project, and the DLL is available on your machine, but it isn't registered. In this situation, you must manually register the component before you can use it. Fortunately, ActiveX components are designed to be self-registering: every ActiveX DLL contains information about itself that Windows can write to the registry using a program called *RegSvr32.exe*. For example, to register a DLL called *myServer.DLL*:

1. Click the Windows Start button and select Run.

2. Type `RegSvr32 c:\windows\system32\myserver.dll`, or the precise path of the DLL. If you don't know where the DLL is stored, you can locate it using Explorer, type `RegSvr32` in the Run dialog, then select the DLL and drag it to the text box in the Run dialog; the complete path (with no spelling mistakes!) is entered into the Run dialog for you.

3. Click OK.

4. A dialog box should then be displayed informing you of the success or failure of the component registration.

There are also occasions, particularly when you are developing remote server applications, when you need to unregister components on your local machine. The procedure is almost the same as that to register a component, the only difference being that you add the –U switch (for unregister). For example:

```
RegSvr32 -U c:\windows\system32\myserver.dll
```

Early Binding

Early binding is the most efficient method of accessing an ActiveX component. This is because the reference to the Type Library for the component can be compiled into your project, giving your project an almost instant navigational path to the properties, methods, and events of the component, and allowing memory to be allocated based on the type library. To provide early binding for a component, you must use the References dialog to add a reference to the object to your project. You can then use either of two methods of instantiating the object:

```
Dim oObjVar As New myClass
```

or:

```
Dim oObjVar As myClass
Set oObjVar = New myClass
```

Late Binding

Late binding is flexible in terms of coding but is much less efficient at runtime because references to objects have to be resolved on the fly. To implement a late bound object, you should declare an object variable as an Object or a generic object, and then use the *CreateObject* function to assign a reference to the object variable:

```
Dim oObjVar As Object
Set oObjVar = CreateObject("myComponent.myClass")
```

or, in VB6:

```
Set oObjVar = CreateObject("myComponent.myClass", "DEVSVR1")
```

As you can see, late binding allows you to specify the name of the class (and in VB6, the name of the server where the component resides). However, late bound component properties, methods, and events are not available for statement completion, because your project knows nothing about the structure of the classes at design time.

For more information about using object references, see the entries for the *CreateObject* function, the Dim statement, the Friend statement, the *GetObject* function, the Private statement, the Public statement, and the Set statement in Chapter 7.

CHAPTER 5

Automation

In this chapter, you will see how VB can take advantage of the power of OLE automation to extend the capabilities of any VB application. While you will see Microsoft Office applications acting as OLE automation servers, this technology isn't restricted to Microsoft Office applications; there are now hundreds of applications that can be used in this way, allowing you either to program within the application itself using its VBA development environment or to use a VB/VBA program to control the OLE automation application from outside.

The key to controlling an OLE automation application is a firm understanding of the application's object model. Each application's object model is different, and the amount of control you have over the application varies considerably. Microsoft now claims that every function of every application in the Office suite is available to the developer via the application's object model.

The object model is a hierarchy of objects that contain the methods, properties, and events that control the application. It acts to describe the application to you, the developer. Once you have become familiar with one or two object models, you will find that, in general, you can quickly pick up the basics of other object models you come across.

Creating Object Model References

Before you can use the properties, methods, and events of an object model, you must first create a programmatic reference to the class containing the properties, methods, or events you wish to use. You do this by declaring a local object variable to hold a reference to the object. You then assign a reference to the object to the local variable. There are two methods, detailed next, for doing this in VB.

Generic Object References and Late Binding

In situations in which the object you are instantiating doesn't provide a type library, or when you are unsure at design time precisely which object you need to reference, you can use a local variable dimensioned as the generic type of Object. Then you use the *CreateObject* or *GetObject* function to return an object reference to assign to the local generic object variable. For example:

```
Dim oObjVar As Object
Set oObjVar = CreateObject("myComponent.myClass")
```

VB6 has also added to the functionality of the *CreateObject* function by allowing you to pass the server machine name as a string parameter. (For details on how to use *CreateObject* and *GetObject* see Chapter 7, *The Language Reference*.)

If You Haven't Set It, You Can't Use It!

To assign an object reference to a local object variable, you must use the Set statement. The sole exception is the For Each...Next loop, which can iterate the object members of a collection. It generates an object reference automatically for each object that it iterates.

This method of creating an object reference produces a late bound interface; your application has no way of knowing in advance (that is, at design time) what the makeup of the object interface is. Only at runtime does your application get to bind to the interface; hence the term *late binding*. Because of this, you won't be given any help from VB's IntelliSense statement completion feature when writing your code; see the section "Reading the Object Model."

Early Binding

The other—and now most common—method of adding an object reference to your project is by using the References dialog, which is shown in Figure 5-1. You can access the References Dialog by selecting the References option from the Project Menu. All OLE Automation Servers registered on your machine are shown in the list. To create a reference to one of them, check the box and click OK.

Once you have added a reference to your project in this manner, you can create an early bound interface to the object by using the Private, Public, Friend, or Dim statement to declare an object variable of the exact type. Then use the Set statement to assign an object reference to the local variable. (For details on how to use the Private, Public, Friend, Dim, and Set statements, see their entries in Chapter 7.) For example:

```
Dim objDoc as Document
Set objDoc = Word.Application.ActiveDocument
```

You can also use the New keyword with the Private, Public, Friend, or Dim statement, as in the following example:

```
Dim objDoc As New Document
```

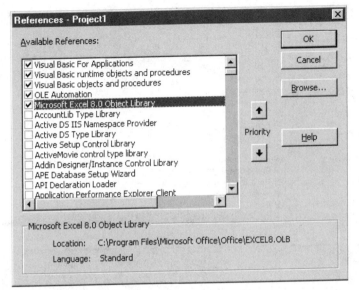

Figure 5-1: The References dialog

Because your project has a reference to the object's type library, binding to the object can take place at compile time, which makes your application more efficient and allows you to get help in your coding from IntelliSense.

Reading the Object Model

The object model of an OLE Automation server is a hierarchy of classes, each containing methods, properties, and events. These methods, properties, and events determine how you can control the application. First of all, though, you need to know what methods, properties, and events are available to you. The first port of call should be the documentation (if any) available from the producer of the OLE Automation server. In addition, once you've created a project-level reference to the application, you can find out a lot about the application's object model from within the VB development environment.

Using the Object Browser

You can use the Object Browser to explore the contents of each class and to find out, for example, what data types are returned by various methods and properties, or what parameters a particular method is expecting. To open the Object Browser, which is shown in Figure 5-2, do any of the following:

- Click the Object Browser button on the toolbar.
- Select the Object Browser option from the View menu.
- Press F2.

The Object Browser is divided into three panes. The left pane displays the classes contained within the selected library; the right pane displays the properties,

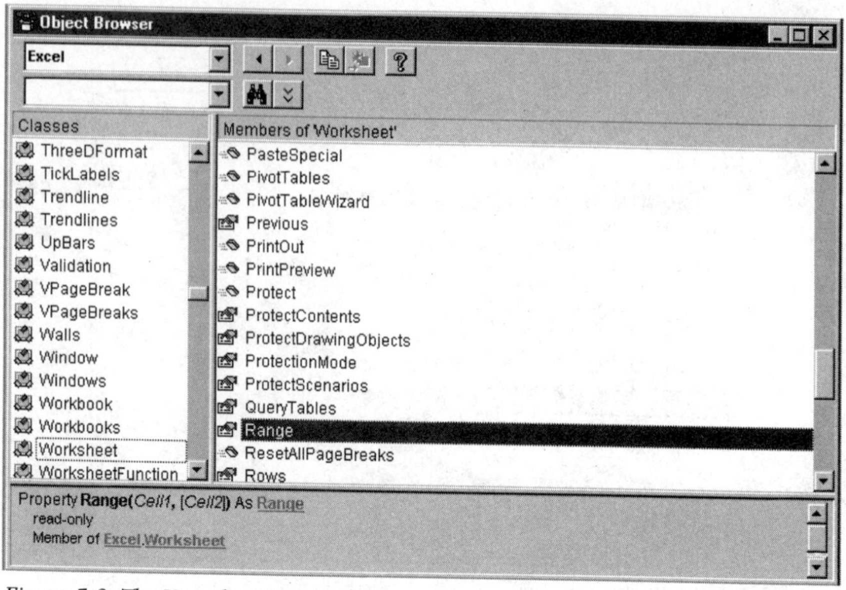

Figure 5-2: The Visual Basic Object Browser

methods, events, and constants of the selected class; and the bottom pane displays details about the selected method, property, event, or constant, such as its data type or its parameters. There is a fourth pane that can be opened to show the results of a library search.

IntelliSense and Statement Completion

Both the retail version of VB and the VBA development environment make use of Microsoft's IntelliSense technology. Statement Completion not only helps to speed the development of VB applications, but it acts as a guide, leading you through the object's hierarchy as you are coding by displaying only those objects, methods, properties, and events that are available for the code you are currently writing, as Figure 5-3 shows.

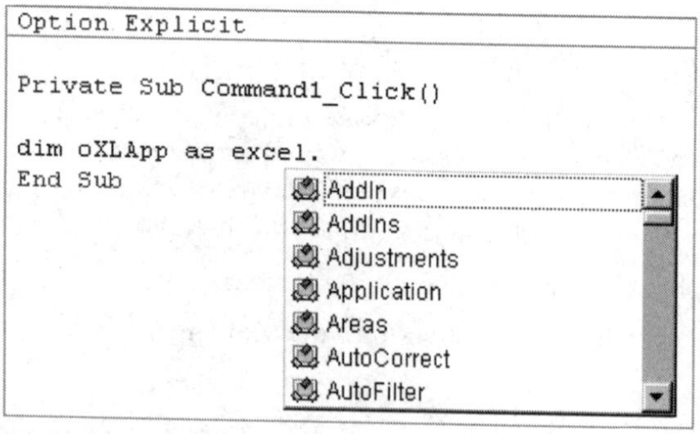

Figure 5-3: Statement Completion

By adding an object reference to your project, you expose the class's type library to the VB development environment, allowing the details of its class hierarchy to be displayed as you enter your code. The main features of IntelliSense and Statement Completion are:

- Available properties, events, and methods are shown in a drop-down list when you press the dot key.

- Pressing the Ctrl key and spacebar combination when partway through an object or procedure name either completes the name or displays a list of possible names.

- Where a property or method takes an argument list, a template of the argument list is shown as a tool tip above or below the line of code. Such a template is shown in Figure 5-4.

When coding object references and calls to methods and properties, you soon find that the number of keystrokes is dramatically reduced by IntelliSense.

```
Option Explicit

Private Sub Command1_Click()

Dim oXLApp As Excel.Application
Set oXLApp = New Excel.Application

oXLApp.GetOpenFilename |
        GetOpenFilename([FileFilter], [FilterIndex], [Title], [ButtonText], [MultiSelect])
End Sub
```

Figure 5-4: Microsoft IntelliSense

Working with the Object Model

Regardless of the particular object model with which you're working and the application you're developing, the same issues tend to arise: how to create a new instance of an object, how to navigate downward from a parent to a child object, and how to move up the object hierarchy from a child to its parent object. In this section, we'll take a look at these and other issues.

Externally Createable Objects

Before you can start to work with your OLE automation server application, you must first create an instance of it. To do this, you must first know at what level the objects within the application can be created—that is, which objects allow the use of the New keyword.

Many OLE automation servers only allow you to use the New keyword with the top-level object, like Word.Application. However, other OLE automation servers, such as Microsoft Active Data Objects (ADO), allow you to create instances of objects much further down the object hierarchy. The statement-completion feature of Visual Basic helps you here. After you have typed the New keyword, a drop down list is displayed containing only those objects that are *externally createable*.

So if you can't directly create an instance of the required object, how do you obtain a reference to it? First, create an instance of an externally createable object higher up the hierarchy; then use the prescribed method or property to create an instance of the required object. For example:

```
Dim oXLapp As Excel.Application
Dim oXLwsh As Excel.Worksheet
Dim oXLhyp As Excel.Hyperlinks

Set oXLapp = New Excel.Application
Set oXLwsh = oXLapp.Worksheets.Add
Set oXLhyp = oXLwsh.Hyperlinks.Add
```

In the above snippet, your goal is to create a reference to an Excel Hyperlink object. However, you can't simply create a new Hyperlink object. You have to create the Application object first, then a Worksheet object, then finally the Hyperlink object.

 For details of how you can restrict the creation of your own classes written in VB, see the section "Class Module Properties—Instancing" in Chapter 4, *Class Modules*.

Navigating Through the Object Model

You can think of the object model as a road map. To get from town A to town B, you can't simply drive across fields, through forests and rivers to get to your destination. You must take designated highways, and you leave the highway at the most convenient interchange and take a minor road to the place you are going. The same is true of an object hierarchy. You must use the paths laid down by the designer of the object model to navigate from one level of the hierarchy to the next, and so on. And just like a road system, there is often more than one route to get to the same place, but one may be quicker and more efficient than another.

Objects returned by properties

One of the most common ways to obtain a reference to an object on the next level down in an object model hierarchy is through a property that returns an object. For example, a property of Excel's Worksheet object is Cells, which in fact returns a Range object. You must therefore understand what type of object is returned by a particular property or method in order to declare a local object variable of the correct type. For example:

```
Dim oXLapp As Excel.Application
Dim oXLwsh As Excel.Worksheet
Dim oXLrng As Excel.Range

Set oXLapp = New Excel.Application
Set oXLwsh = oXLapp.Worksheets.Add
Set oXLrng = oXLwsh.Cells
```

Navigating up through the object model

There are many occasions when you are working with a particular object and need to call a method or property belonging to an object directly above it in the hierarchy. For this purpose, most object hierarchies provide you with a means of navigating back up the object model. This not only saves time when coding, but it's much more efficient at runtime. While the implementation is different in each object model, you should be on the lookout for properties called Parent, Window, Application, or Top. These are the properties that return a reference to objects further up the hierarchy.

Collection Objects

Many of the classes that make up an object model are in fact collections of other classes or objects. You will find that these classes have several generic methods and properties, such as Add, Item, and Count. The Add method creates a new member of the collection stored against a unique key, the Item method returns a member of the collection given a unique key or index value, and the Count method returns the number of members in the collection.

You may find, however, that the collection object's standard Item method has been wrapped within a property, the name of which is the same as the name of the class held by the collection. A call to this property returns an object of the type of the class held by the collection. For example, an Employees collection object may implement an Employee property that returns an Employee object, like this:

```
Public Property Get Employee(vEmpCode As Variant) As Employee
    Set Employee = McolEmployees.Item(vEmpCode)
End Property
```

Collections within object models are most commonly at the top of an object hierarchy or at the top of a branch of an object hierarchy, and are most likely createable with the New keyword or the *CreateObject* function. Access to individual objects is gained through the collection. For example, the Worksheets object spawns a Worksheet object; a Cells object spawns a Cell object.

Referencing by Name or Number

A correctly implemented collection object allows you to access the members of the collection either by key name or by ordinal position in the collection. This is handled by the Item method, which accepts a variant as its single parameter. If the parameter is a string value, Item tries to match the parameter with a key in the collection. On the other hand, if the parameter is numeric (including the string representation of a number), the Item method uses this number to return the item in that ordinal position. This is demonstrated by the following snippets:

```
sEmployeeName = adoRecordset.Fields.Item(1)
```

or:

```
sEmployeeName = adoRecordset.Fields(1)
```

or:

```
sEmployeeName = adoRecordset.Fields("Empname")
```

You will also note from the above snippets that because Item is the default method of the collection object, it can be called implicitly.

For Each...Next

You can iterate through a collection by obtaining its Count property value, which returns the number of items in the collection, and executing a `For...Next` loop, each time setting an object variable to the new collection member, as follows:

```
For i = 1 To oColl.Count
    Set oCollMember = oColl.Item(i)
        'do some stuff with oCollMember
    Set oCollMember = Nothing
Next i
```

However, VB provides a more efficient method: the `For Each...Next` loop. The `For Each...Next` loop iterates through the collection, automatically assigning a reference to the current member of the collection, then exiting once the end of the collection has been reached, as this rewritten snippet shows:

```
For Each oCollMember in oColl
    'do some stuff with oCollMember
Next
```

Using `For Each...Next` is also safer because collection members can be automatically reindexed by the actions of another part of the program—for example, if a member is removed from the collection—which means that stored index numbers shouldn't relied upon.

For more information about the Collection object and the `For Each...Next` statement, see their entries in Chapter 7.

Trapping an Automation Server's Events

Most objects raise events, which can be used to great effect in your VB application and add a further dimension to OLE automation. Rather than the usual one-way conversation, in which your application is forever telling the server what to do or asking it to provide information about its properties, making use of the server's events is like giving the server a "voice," allowing it to report back to your application. You might, for example, receive an event notification from the server when certain tasks are about to be or have been completed.

You enable your application to listen for these event notifications by using the WithEvents keyword. Use of the WithEvents keyword is restricted to variables defined in the declarations section of your module. Only object modules—that is, class and form modules—can contain variables declared using the WithEvents keyword. Once a module-level variable is declared as WithEvents, you can program against this event, enabling your application to respond to the changing state of the OLE automation server.

One word of warning when using the `WithEvents` keyword: if you are building a client-server system using a `WithEvents` object reference, you must ensure that the client machine gives permission for the server machine to create processes on it. Otherwise, even though the client can create instances of the object on the server, the server won't be able to call back to the client with event notifications. In fact your application won't even launch before a Permission Denied or similar error is generated. You can alter the permissions on the client using the DCOM Config utility.

For more information about the `WithEvents` keyword see the entries for the `Dim`, `Friend`, `Private`, and `Public` statements in Chapter 7.

Automation Examples

So let's bring together all you've seen in this chapter with a few sample implementations of OLE automation servers.

Using Word as a Report Writer from VB

This first application demonstrates how you can seamlessly use Microsoft Word to print output from your VB program without the user knowing that you have actually used Microsoft Word:

```
Private Sub cmdWordDoc_Click()

    'create an error handler
    On Error GoTo cmdWordDoc_Err

        'create the local Early Bound object variables
    Dim oWord            As Word.Application
    Dim oWordActiveDoc   As Word.Document
    Dim oWordSel         As Word.Selection

    'Create a new instance of Word
    Set oWord = New Word.Application
    'Create a new document object
    Set oWordActiveDoc = oWord.Documents.Add
    Set oWordSel = oWord.Selection

        'Do some work with the Selection object
    oWordSel.TypeText "This is some text from the VB app."
    oWordSel.WholeStory
    oWordSel.Font.Name = "Arial"
    oWordSel.Font.Size = 12
    oWordSel.Font.Bold = wdToggle

        'Now print out the doc
    oWordActiveDoc.PrintOut
```

```
    'always tidy up before you leave
    Set oWordSel = Nothing
    Set oWordActiveDoc = Nothing

    Set oWord = Nothing

    Exit Sub

cmdWordDoc_Err:
    MsgBox Err.Number & vbCrLf & Err.Description & vbCrLf _
           & Err.Source

    End Sub
```

Because this example uses early binding, you'll have to use the References dialog to add a project reference to the Word 8 Object Model.

 Note that this application appears seamless because the application's Visible property is False by default. If you wanted to show the Word application window in operation (which may be required while debugging), simply set the property to True.

Using Email Within VB

This application demonstrates how you can work with a late bound object. The OLE server in this instance is Windows MAPI. Using MAPI in this way uses Outlook sort of through the back door; you don't actually create an instance of Outlook, but this sample demonstrates how closely tied MAPI and Outlook are. In fact, the mail side of Outlook isn't much more than a nice GUI to the Windows MAPI. If you are connected to an Exchange server when this simple application runs, the mail is sent automatically; otherwise, the mail is placed in Outlook's outbox, ready for you to send. You may also have to change the profile name to match that on your own system.

The sample function shown below is called from a form containing a text box (txtDomain) that holds the domain name of the recipients, and a list box (lstEmails) that holds the individual addresses of the recipients. This example is in fact part of a working application used several times a day to send test messages to new email accounts:

```
    Private Function SendReturnEMail() As Boolean

    ' create an error handler
    On Error GoTo SendReturnEMail_Err

        'set the default return value
        SendReturnEMail = False

        'we're using late binding for this app
        Dim objSession    As Object
        Dim objMessage    As Object
```

```
Dim objRecipient As Object

'declare some other utility variables
Dim i              As Integer
Dim sSubject       As String
Dim sText          As String
Dim sName          As String

'set up the email message text
sText = "This is an automatic test message, " & _
        vbCrLf & _
        "Please reply to the sender confirming receipt."
'and the subject
sSubject = "Test Message"

'start with the top of the mapi hierarchy --
'the session object
Set objSession = CreateObject("mapi.session")
    'use the local Outlook default profile
    objSession.LogOn profilename:="Microsoft Outlook"

    'this application will send a number of test messages
    'to the members of a particular domain
    For i = 0 To lstEmails.ListCount - 1
        'build the addresses from the names in the list
        'and the given domain name
        sName = Trim(lstEmails.List(i)) & "@" & _
                Trim(txtDomain.Text)
        'now create a new message object
        Set objMessage = objSession.outbox.messages.Add
            'feed in the required property values for the
            'message
            objMessage.subject = sSubject
            objMessage.Text = sText
            'create a new recipient for this message
            Set objRecipient = objMessage.Recipients.Add
                'and set it's properties
                objRecipient.Name = sName
                objRecipient.Type = 1
                'make sure the email address is resolved
                objRecipient.resolve
                'now send the message
                objMessage.Send showdialog:=False
                'tidy up this message
            Set objRecipient = Nothing
        Set objMessage = Nothing
        'and go round again for the next one
    Next i
    'all done so off we go
    objSession.logoff
'tidying up as always
Set objSession = Nothing
'set the success return value
SendReturnEMail = True
```

```
        Exit Function

SendReturnEMail_Err:
    MsgBox Err.Number & vbCrLf & Err.Description & vbCrLf _
        & Err.Source

End Function
```

Output from VB to Excel

To finish with, here's an easy little application that places values from a VB application into an Excel spreadsheet. There are project-level (early bound) references created to both Excel and the ADODB 2.0 Reference Library. An ADO recordset has already been created and is passed as a parameter to the *OutputToExcel* function. The function creates an instance of a new Excel workbook and worksheet, then copies the values from the ADO recordset into the worksheet. Excel's functionality is used to perform a simple calculation on the data, the worksheet is saved, Excel is closed down, and all references are tidied up.

This example illustrates the power of a glue language such as Visual Basic. Here VB is acting as the glue between ADO, which is an ActiveX server, and Excel—controlling both to produce a simple yet patently powerful and seamless application:

```
    Private Function OutputToExcel(oADORec As ADODB.Recordset) _
            As Boolean

On Error GoTo cmdExcel_Err

    'set up the default return value
    OutputToExcel = False

    ' Declare the Excel object variables
    Dim oXLApp  As Excel.Application
    Dim oXLWBook As Excel.Workbook
    Dim oXLWSheet As Excel.Worksheet

    'start at the top of the model
    Set oXLApp = New Excel.Application
        'and work your way down
        Set oXLWBook = oXLApp.Workbooks.Add
            'until you get to the worksheet
            Set oXLWSheet = oXLWBook.Worksheets.Add

                oXLWSheet.Cells(1, 1).Value = oADORec!FirstValue
                oXLWSheet.Cells(2, 1).Value = oADORec!SecondValue

                ' do some stuff in Excel with the values
                oXLWSheet.Cells(3, 1).Formula = "=R1C1 + R2C1"

                ' save your work
                oXLWSheet.SaveAs "vb2XL.xls"

                'quit Excel
```

```
oXLApp.Quit

        ' always remember to tidy up before you leave
        Set oXLWSheet = Nothing
    Set oXLWBook = Nothing
Set oXLApp = Nothing

OutputToExcel = True

Exit Function

cmdExcel_Err:
    MsgBox Err.Description & vbCrLf & Err.Number & _
        vbCrLf & Err.Source

End Function
```

Automation Performance Tips

Because automation involves the remote control of a server application by a client application, performance is always an issue. What follows are some basic tips to help you optimize your application's performance when using automation.

Use early binding wherever possible

Because an early bound reference to an object can be resolved at compile time, by the VB or VBA IDE, rather than at design time, by the runtime module, the result of early binding is significantly better performance. It isn't always possible to use early binding, but you should always try to use it if you can.

Use as few "dots" as possible

Every dot that you place in your code represents at least one (and possibly many) procedure calls that have to be executed in the background. Both the For Each...Next loop and the With statement can be used to improve performance. But what can really help is locally caching object references. For example, you should store references to the upper levels of an object model in local object variables, then use these references to create other objects further down the hierarchy. For example, to reference a cell in an Excel spreadsheet, you could use this code:

```
Dim oExcel As Excel.Application
Set oExcel = New Excel.Application
For i = 1 to 10
    oExcel.Workbooks(1).Worksheets(1).Cells(1,i).Value _
        = "Something"
Next i
```

The following code, though, would be far more efficient, because the calls to obtain references to the Workbook and Worksheet object would only be made once, whereas above they are being made 10 times:

```
Dim oExcel As Excel.Application
Dim oWorkBk As Excel.WorkBook
Dim oWorkSht As Excel.WorkSheet
```

```
Set oExcel = New Excel.Application
Set oWorkBk = oExcel.Workbooks(1)
Set oWorkSht = oWorkBk.WorkSheets(1)

For i = 1 to 10
    oWorkSht.Cells(1,i).Value = "Something"
Next i
```

Improve your own performance: use the macro recorders

If the application you are programming against has a built-in macro recorder, you should try to use it whenever possible. (In the Office applications that support it, you can access the macro recorder by selecting the Macro → Record New Macro submenus from the Tools menu.) For example, the basic code for the sample Excel and Word applications used earlier in this chapter was written using their respective macro recorders. You can save yourself hours of valuable programming time by letting the application tell you what method and property calls you need to make to achieve a particular result. You can then focus on optimizing its code to achieve the best possible performance.

CHAPTER 6

Error Handling

Who was Murphy? I don't know, but I know his law well enough: "Whatever can go wrong will." As application developers, we quickly learn that assumption and complacency lead to disaster. It's no good telling users that you didn't expect them to enter the word Four instead of the number 4, or that you didn't know that one part of the system entered a Null value into a database field that you were trying to read. Neither users nor MIS managers want excuses; they want applications that work—and by work I mean applications that don't curl up in the corner and die at the first sign of trouble. Sure, errors and situations beyond your control—such as a database server that unexpectedly goes off-line—are going to happen, but that shouldn't kill your application. At the very least, you should be in a position to report back to the user what the problem is without generating a runtime error that will bring down your application.

This chapter hasn't been written as an exhaustive reference of all the statements, objects, methods, and properties involved in VB error handling, but rather as a guide to help you plan your error handling. It lays out the error-handling template for you, and also sets out some of the ground rules involved in resolving the everyday and not so everyday exceptions that can be thrown at your program.

We'll assume that you have set the Option Explicit statement at the start of each module (so there can't be any variable name typos),* and that you have started your program with a full compile (CTRL+F5) so that you won't encounter any syntax errors.

---

* Option Explicit requires that all variables used in your program be declared in advance. It's an option I highly recommend. Aside from the fact that variable declaration is a critical technique for professional programming, it helps to prevent and diagnose typos, which are the most common programming error. To require variable declaration, select the Options option from the Tools menu, select the Editor tab, and check the Require Variable Declaration box.

For a complete description of each of the statements, objects, methods, and properties mentioned in this section, refer to the relevant entries in Chapter 7, *The Language Reference*.

So, before we get into the nitty-gritty of error handling, here are a few pointers to help make your application more robust.

Building a Robust Application

There are two approaches to error handling. The first is to let the error occur, then do something about it; the second is to prevent the error from occurring. Each has its own merits. Supporters of the first approach argue that most errors occur very infrequently. For example, users of a computer system are by and large well trained and make few data entry errors. Therefore, the extra processing to prevalidate such things as numeric values is a waste of processing time and power; it's more efficient to execute an error-handling routine occasionally than to invoke a validation routine for every entry. On the other hand, supporters of the second approach argue that it's not good practice to allow errors to be generated and that if there are techniques available that prevent an error from occurring, they should be used. A remote server that's offline, for example, could take several minutes to generate an error due to network timeouts, whereas a correctly written validation function could report this in seconds. Furthermore, error-handling routines themselves can be the source of further errors.

I think that each argument has merits. You have to judge for yourself whether to use a "belts and braces" approach within a given procedure or whether the likelihood of an error is so remote that a simple error-handling routine will suffice. Don't forget that adding functionality to a program costs time, which is money. Here, though, is a list of simple error prevention measures you can add to any application without ballooning the development time:

Check data types

In situations where you accept a numeric value from the user to use within a vital function (like the index of an array, for example), you should first check that a numeric item has been entered using the *IsNumeric* function, and then check that it's within bounds.

Check that objects have been created

Before you rush into using an object variable, first check that an object reference has actually been assigned to it. If not, the object variable will contain a special value, Nothing. However, you can't use the equality operator (=) when querying an object variable; instead, you need to use the Is operator. For example, the following code checks that the object variable *myObject* isn't Nothing—i.e., that it is something!

```
If Not myObject Is Nothing Then
... continue what you where doing
Else
... you have a problem
End If
```

Trap Null data

When you are assigning column values from a recordset, you should ensure that the column value doesn't contain Null. This is quite a common occurrence with database recordsets, and often catches the unwary developer by surprise. Even if you don't expect to have any Null values, there may be occasions when one is recorded in the database. The next time you access that record, your program screams out with an "Invalid Use of Null" error.

There are two quick solutions for this. First, you can test the value using the *IsNull* function, as follows:

```
If IsNull(rsRecordset!FieldName) Then
```

Second, you can catch Null string values using the *Format* function with no parameters other than the field value. This returns a zero-length string and is the quickest and easiest method:

```
sProperty = Format(rsRecordset!FieldName)
```

Check array boundaries

Applications are quicker and easier to maintain if you keep literal values and constants to a minimum by making use of functions. One prime example of this is the boundary function to determine the lower and upper boundaries of an array. Imagine a situation where you regularly iterate through an entire array in many different places within the program. You know that there are 10 elements in the array, and that there always have been, so you write the function thus:

```
For i = 0 to 9
    cboList.AddItem myArray(i)
Next i
```

One day, someone comes along and adds a new element to the array. You're now faced with the task of finding all the instances where the program references the maximum element of the array and increasing it by one. However, if you had written the code with future maintenance in mind, it would look like this:

```
For i = LBound(myArray) to UBound(myArray)
    cboList.additem myArray(i)
Next i
```

Test for the presence of a remote server

VB developers are increasingly in the front line of client-server application development, which means that sooner rather than later you'll be called on to reference a remote ActiveX component from your client application. Regardless of the connection between client machine and the remote server, there will also come a time (again, usually sooner rather than later!) when the connection between the two machines is broken. When this happens, your client application will sit twiddling its thumbs waiting for the operating system to connect to the server, eventually the operation will time out, and to make matters worse, the only error message displayed will indicate that the ActiveX component couldn't be created—which could be caused by any number of things. An added complication to this little problem is DCOM; as the client application developer, you may not know where the server component is going to execute (and even if you do when writing your application, this may change over time).

The solution is to add a reference to a system DLL, *RacReg.DLL*, that contains a function you can use to return information about the remote server component you are trying to reach. Armed with this information, you can use any number of quick and easy tests to determine if the remote server is online. This could be as complex as writing a C++ program to access Net functionality or ping the server, to something as simple as using the *Dir* function on the root of the server.

For more information on using the RacReg DLL, see the *GetAutoServerSettings* entry in Chapter 7.

Use functions instead of sub procedures

Apart from their use for event handlers, I have yet to see a convincing argument for having custom Sub procedures in Visual Basic. In contrast, the use of functions in place of subroutines can improve the stability of your application. To demonstrate, let's compare two versions of the same program, the first of which uses a simple subroutine. In this example, we are going to call a subroutine to open a disk file, then use the contents of the file:

```
Private Sub Command1_Click()

    On Error GoTo Command1_Err

    Dim iFile As Integer
    Dim sContents As String

    iFile = FreeFile

    Call FileOpener(File1.filename, iFile)

    Get #iFile, , sContents

    Text1.Text = sContents

    Exit Sub 'don't forget to exit or the error
             'handler will be executed!

Command1_Err:
    MsgBox Err.Description & vbCrLf & Err.Number
End Sub

Private Sub FileOpener(sFileName As String, _
                    iFileNo As Integer)

    On Error GoTo FileOpener_Err

    Open sFileName For Input As #iFileNo

    Exit Sub

FileOpener_Err:
```

```
    MsgBox Err.Description & vbCrLf & Err.Number
End Sub
```

As you can see, if the attempt to open the file fails, an error is raised in the subroutine, and a message displayed to the user. However, the code following the call to *FileOpener* is still executed, causing another error.

Now look how much smoother the operation is when using a function that returns **True** if the file is successfully opened and **False** if an error occurs:

```
Private Sub Command1_Click()

    On Error GoTo Command1_Err

    Dim iFile As Integer
    Dim sContents As String

    iFile = FreeFile

    If FileOpener(File1.filename, iFile) = True Then
        Get #iFile, , sContents
        Text1.Text = sContents
    End If

    Exit Sub

Command1_Err:
    MsgBox Err.Description & vbCrLf & Err.Number
End Sub

Private Function FileOpener(sFileName As String, _
                    iFileNo As Integer) As Boolean

    On Error GoTo FileOpener_Err

    Open sFileName For Input As #iFileNo

    FileOpener = True

    Exit Function

FileOpener_Err:
    MsgBox Err.Description & vbCrLf & Err.Number
End Function
```

In this second version, should an error occur within the *FileOpener* function, the function returns its default value of **False**, and the code to access the file's contents isn't executed. There are numerous places within an application where this style of programming can make the code both easier to read and more stable in execution.

Error Handling in Procedures

Even while building as robust an application as possible, errors inevitably occur, and your application is expected to handle them elegantly. In this section, we examine how to use VB and VBA's error-handling features to do just that, first by examining error handling in subroutines and functions within standard modules (i.e., code modules and form modules that make up a standard EXE or a standard VBA program), and then by examining error handling in code or class modules that are used in an ActiveX DLL, EXE, or OCX project. The reason for making this distinction will become clear as you read through these sections.

To begin, let's look at a couple of templates you can use to add error handling to your procedures:

```
Private Sub Command1_Click()

    On Error GoTo Command1_Err

    Exit Sub

Command1_Err:
    MsgBox Err.Number & vbCrLf & Err.Description, _
        vbCritical, "Error!"

End Sub
```

This is error handling at its simplest; when an error occurs, an error message is displayed, and the routine in which the error occurred terminates. The second template is a variation on the same theme, but this time the Resume statement resumes program execution at the Command1_Exit label:

```
Private Sub Command1_Click()

    On Error GoTo Command1_Err

    . . .

Command1_Exit:
    Exit Sub

Command1_Err:
    MsgBox Err.Number & vbCrLf & Err.Description, _
        vbCritical, "Error!"
    Resume Command1_Exit
End Sub
```

Finally, here is a slightly more sophisticated error-handling device that automatically reexecutes a bunch of code a given number of times—ideal for situations where a connection may be temporarily unavailable:

```
Private Sub Command1_Click()

    On Error GoTo Command1_Err

    Dim iRetries As Integer

    '...your code goes here

Do_Retry:
```

```
     '...your code goes here

     Exit Sub

Command1_Err:
     If Err.Number = 12345 And iRetries < 5 Then
          iRetries = iRetries + 1
          Resume Do_Retry
     Else
          MsgBox Err.Number & vbCrLf & Err.Description, _
               vbCritical, "Error!"
     End If
End Sub
```

The On Error Statement

The basic structure of error handling in VB begins with the On Error statement. It diverts program execution in the event of an error, or it switches off error handling in the given procedure.

The On Error statement remains valid while the procedure in which it's defined is in scope, or until another On Error statement is encountered. To explain, let's break this down.

First of all, a procedure is within scope until either an end or exit procedure statement is executed. This means that a procedure is still in scope even when a call is made to another procedure. This has important implications for the On Error statement. For example, let's say you define an error handler in one procedure, and you then call another procedure that doesn't contain an error handler. If an error occurs in the called procedure, the first procedure (and its error handler) is still in scope, so the error is handled by the calling procedure.

The following snippet demonstrates how this works. In this example, an error handler is defined in the Command1 button's Click event handler. A call is made to the *FunWithNumbers* sub, and the value 0 is passed to it as a parameter. Unfortunately, *FunWithNumbers* uses this value as the divisor and, since it's illegal to divide by zero, a runtime error is generated. The fun has just gone out of *FunWithNumbers*, and the function has no error handler to handle the error. However, the Command1_Click event handler is still in scope, so the error is handled by the Command1_Click_Err error handler:

```
Private Sub Command1_Click()

     On Error GoTo Command1_Click_Err
          FunWithNumbers 0
          MsgBox "all ok"
          Exit Sub

Command1_Click_Err:
     MsgBox Err.Number & vbCrLf & Err.Description

End Sub

Private Sub FunWithNumbers(iVal As Integer)
```

```
    Dim i As Integer
    i = 1
    txtResult.Text = CStr(i / iVal)

End Sub
```

To locate an error handler, the VB call stack is used. Each time a call is made from a procedure, it's added onto the end of the call stack. If an error occurs in a procedure that doesn't have an error handler, VB looks at the previous procedure in the stack, until it finds an error handler. If no error handler is found, a terminal runtime error is generated, and your program hits the dust.

A word of warning: you should take care when using On Error Resume and Resume Next within a procedure that calls another procedure. If the called procedure—like *FunWithNumbers*—doesn't contain any error handling, execution resumes with the line of code containing (in the case of Resume) or the line of code immediately following (in the case of Resume Next) the call to the procedure in the original calling routine that contains the error handler. This is illustrated in the following code fragment:

```
Private Sub Command1_Click()

    On Error Resume Next

    FunWithNumbers 0
    MsgBox "All OK"
    Exit Sub

End Sub

Private Sub FunWithNumbers(iVal As Integer)

    Dim i As Integer
    i = 1
    txtResult.Text = CStr(i / iVal)

End Sub
```

The user would assume that the procedure has worked correctly because all he sees is the "All OK" message; *FunWithNumbers* hasn't updated the *txtResult* text box with a value because control didn't return to *FunWithNumbers* after the error.

An On Error statement, then, remains in effect until the next On Error statement, which can be in the same procedure or in a called procedure. For instance, in the example above, if *FunWithNumbers* had implemented an error handler, it would have handled the error rather than passing it back up the call stack to the command button's error handler. The following is an example of a procedure that uses multiple On Error statements. In this example, an error handler is defined and immediately activated. However, later in the procedure, a For Each...Next statement is used in a way that most likely will cause an error in normal operation (as would happen, for instance, if a control in the Controls collection doesn't have a Text property), so the original On Error statement is replaced by an On Error Resume Next statement that basically skips past any errors. Once this section of the procedure is complete, the original error handler is switched back on, canceling On Error Resume Next:

```
Private Function ResetControls() As Boolean

    On Error GoTo ResetControls_Err
    Dim oControl As Control

    If Not blnSaved Then
        Call ShowWarningMsg
        Exit Function
    End If

    On Error Resume Next
    For Each oControl In Controls
        oControl.Text = ""
    Next

    On Error GoTo ResetControls_Err

    Call DisplayDefaultValues
    Exit Function

ResetControls_Err:
    MsgBox Err.Number & vbCrLf & Err.Description
End Function
```

Note that if an error is generated within an error handler, the error is terminal; Visual Basic doesn't look back up the call stack for another enabled error handler.

The options for error handling within a VB procedure are set using the On Error statement as follows:

On Error 0
> Switches off error handling until the next On Error statement (a procedure can contain any number of On Error statements).

On Error Resume
> Take care with this one! Program execution continues with the line that caused the error; using it may not be the smartest thing you ever did!

On Error Resume Next
> Basically, the error is ignored, and program execution continues with the line following the line containing the error.

On Error Goto *label*
> *label* is the beginning of your error-handling routine within the procedure. A label is a subroutine name followed by a full colon (:).

The Exit Sub Statement

The Exit Sub statement typically isn't considered an error-handling statement, though it's present in virtually every error handler. As the templates above illustrate, if you forget to include it before the error handler, program execution always falls through to the error handler, whether or not an error has occurred.

The Err Object

The Err object has the following properties:

Description
> A string containing a standard description of the last error.

Number
> The system or custom number of the last error.

Source
> A string containing the application or ActiveX server name in which the error was generated.

LastDLLErr
> About as much use as an ashtray on a motorbike. This supposedly contains the error number from a called DLL—supposedly. And if you actually get it to work, you must remember that the Err object's Description property isn't updated with a description of a DLL error.

HelpFile
> A string containing the full path to the help file for this application (if one is available).

HelpContext
> A string containing the context ID of the help section relating to this error (if available).

Here are its methods:

Raise
> Generates an error. Use this to pass errors back to the client from OLE servers.

Clear
> Resets the Err object to default values.

The Resume Statement

Resume as a standalone statement, when not combined with the On Error statement, terminates the error handler and indicates where program flow should return. The Resume statement resets the Err object's properties to their default values, then resumes normal program execution at the point specified by the argument included with the Resume statement. If no arguments are included—i.e., the Resume statement is used on its own—execution recommences with the line of code that generated the error. The valid arguments are:

Next
> Normal program execution recommences with the line immediately following the line of code in which the error occurred.

label
> Normal program execution recommences at the specified subroutine label.

Error Handling in ActiveX Servers

While the basic error-handling concepts are the same, errors within an ActiveX server class have to be handled slightly differently than errors in a client application. Some of the important differences include:

Don't display the error

Unlike a client application, in which you might display a message box to the user detailing the problem, you should remember that with a server-side application, there might be no one there to click OK! Instead, you should write an entry into an event log. (The following section, "Reporting Errors," details how to write an event log.) If you have a large application that already has many *MsgBox* calls, and you don't want to spend ages rewriting this code, simply go to the project properties dialog and select the Unattended Execution option. This forces all *MsgBox* calls to be written to an event log.

Use Err.Raise

Once you've logged the error in your server class, you need some way of informing the user that an error occurred. The simplest method of doing this is to raise an error using the Err.Raise method. This error will be picked up by the client's error handler, and the relevant message displayed. This simple client and server code demonstrates the Err.Raise method:

Client code:

```
Private Sub Command3_Click()

    On Error GoTo Command3_Err

    Dim oTest As TestErrors.DoStuff
    Set oTest = New TestErrors.DoStuff
        oTest.SomeStuff
    Set oTest = Nothing
Command3_Err:
    MsgBox Err.Description & vbCrLf & Err.Number & _
            vbCrLf & Err.Source

End Sub
```

Server code:

```
Public Function SomeStuff() As Boolean

    On Error GoTo SomeStuff_Err

    Dim i As Integer
    i = 100
    i = i / 0

    Exit Function

SomeStuff_Err:
    App.LogEvent Err.Description & " in " & _
                "TestErrors::SomeStuff", _
                vbLogEventTypeError
```

```
        Err.Raise vbObjectError + Err.Number, _
                "TestErrors::SomeStuff", Err.Description
End Function
```

As you can see from the server code, an illegal operation takes place—you can't divide by zero. The error handler logs the event and then uses the Err.Raise method to pass this error on to the client.

You can also use the Err.Raise method to trap incorrect user input. Look at *MoreStuff*, the following modified version of the server *SomeStuff* function:

```
Public Function MoreStuff(iVal As Integer) As Integer

    On Error GoTo MoreStuff_Err

    If iVal > 50 Then
        Err.Raise 23456, "TestErrors::MoreStuff", _
                "Can't have a figure greater than 50"
    End If

    iVal = iVal / 0

    Exit Function

MoreStuff_Err:
    App.LogEvent Err.Description & " in " & _
                "TestErrors::MoreStuff", _
                vbLogEventTypeError
    Err.Raise vbObjectError + Err.Number, _
                "TestErrors::MoreStuff", Err.Description

End Function
```

This time, the Err.Raise method passes back a custom error code and description alerting the user of the invalid input.

Use the vbObjectError constant

Errors generated in OLE objects start at –2147221504. (Actually, OLE automation errors aren't negative numbers; they are unsigned long integers. But because VB doesn't support unsigned longs, they appear as a negative.) VB provides **vbObjectError**, an intrinsic constant for this value that you should add to both custom error codes and system error codes. However, if you add **vbObjectError** to an error code that is already of greater negative magnitude than –262144, you generate an "Overflow" error that masks the real error that occurred in the procedure. Because of this, it's best if your error handler adds **vbObjectError** only to positive numbers, as this snippet demonstrates:

```
SomeStuff_Err:
    App.LogEvent Err.Description & " in " & _
                "TestErrors::SomeStuff", _
                vbLogEventTypeError
    If Err.Number < 0 Then
        Err.Raise Err.Number, "TestErrors::SomeStuff", _
                Err.Description
    Else
        Err.Raise vbObjectError + Err.Number, _
```

```
            "TestErrors::SomeStuff", Err.Description
    End If
```

Where did the error occur?

Passing back the source of the error to the client application is very important. However, unless you take care writing your error handler, you can report the source as the last procedure to handle the error, rather than the one in which the error occurred. This example shows how this can happen:

```
Public Function SomeStuff() As Boolean

    On Error GoTo SomeStuff_Err

    Dim i As Integer
    i = 100
    i = MoreStuff(i)

    Exit Function

SomeStuff_Err:
    App.LogEvent Err.Description & " in " & _
                "TestErrors::SomeStuff", _
                vbLogEventTypeError
    If Err.Number < 0 Then
       Err.Raise Err.Number, _
                "TestErrors::SomeStuff", Err.Description
    Else
       Err.Raise vbObjectError + Err.Number, _
                "TestErrors::SomeStuff", Err.Description
    End If
End Function

Private Function MoreStuff(iVal As Integer) As Integer

    On Error GoTo MoreStuff_Err

    iVal = iVal / 0

    Exit Function

MoreStuff_Err:
    Err.Raise vbObjectError + Err.Number, _
                "TestErrors::MoreStuff", Err.Description

End Function
```

In this example, *SomeStuff* has called *MoreStuff*, in which an error is raised. The error is first handled by the error handler in *MoreStuff*, which reports the source of the error correctly. The error is then handled by *SomeStuff*'s error handler, which overwrites the original Source argument and reports it as being *SomeStuff*. You would wrongly assume that your problem was with the *SomeStuff* function.

If a system-generated error occurs, the source property of the Err object is set to the same value as the App.Title property. So you know that if the

Err.Source property is the same as App.Title, the error has been generated in the current procedure, and you can safely use your own custom Source string. However, if the Err.Source property differs from the application title, the current Err.Source property should be passed on, as this snippet shows:

```
Dim ErrSrc As String
If Err.Source <> App.Title Then
    ErrSrc = Err.Source
Else
    Err.Src = App.Title & "::SomeStuff"
End If
```

Don't forget to clean up before you leave

If your procedure exits unexpectedly, you run the risk of leaving objects that have been used in the procedure live. To prevent this, you should get into the habit of adding code to the beginning of your error handler to set all object variables that are declared in the procedure to **Nothing**. This way, whenever an error occurs, you will be sure that all objects are safely destroyed.

Reporting Errors

Information about errors is vital to allow you as the developer to track down the source of the error and to take steps to prevent it from happening again. The traditional method of reporting an error is to simply display a message box, but you can also create a log on the user's machine.

Reporting to the User

Include enough information both to inform the user that an error has occurred, and to aid the developer to get to the real root of the problem. Your error message should report:

- The name of the module
- The name of the procedure
- The error number
- The error description
- The error source

It's entirely up to you how you style your message box. Figures 6-1 and 6-2 illustrate two very different methods. You will probably find that nontechnical users can assimilate—and therefore both remember and recount—the information in the style of Figure 6-1 much more readily than the impersonal style of Figure 6-2.

Adding Help

The *MsgBox* function from Version 5 of Visual Basic on includes the option to display a Help button on the message box dialog, as shown in Figure 6-3. By including the **vbMsgBoxHelpButton** constant for the *Button* parameter, VB automatically displays the Help button. If your application provides context-sensitive help, you can specify the help filename and a context ID as parameters, which allows the user to navigate directly to the particular help section for the error:

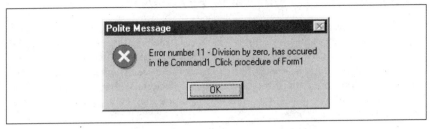

Figure 6-1: A conversational style message box

Functional Message

Error No: 11
Description: Division by zero
Module: Form1
Procedure: Command1_Click

OK

Figure 6-2: A bare-facts message box

```
MsgBox prompt:="Error Number: " & Err.Number & vbCrLf _
       & Err.Description, _
       buttons:=vbCritical + vbMsgBoxHelpButton, _
       Title:="Error!", _
       HelpFile:=Err.HelpFile, _
       context:=Err.HelpContext
```

Polite Message

Error number 11 - Division by zero, has occured
in the Command1_Click procedure of Form1

OK   Help

Figure 6-3: Context-sensitive Help button on the Message Box dialog

One word of warning here, though. If your users are nontechnical, I would
suggest that you make the display of the Help button conditional on the error
number. The reason for this is that internal VB errors try to display the VB help
section, which probably won't be loaded on an end user's machine. Therefore,
only display the Help button for your own error codes when you have written a
specific section about the error in your application's help file.

Silent Reporting: Logging the Error Event

Your efforts to resolve issues within an application are often frustrated by users not reporting errors. The user simply clicks past the message box reporting the error and continues. Either they forget or can't be bothered to contact the MIS department or the software developer to report the issue. There is a way you can store information about the error on the user's machine without having to go to the trouble of coding a file open/write/close routine that itself could cause a fatal error within the error handler.

The App object includes a method called LogEvent whose operation depends on the operating system being used. On NT the LogEvent method writes to the machine's event log, whereas in Windows 9x a log file is created or an existing log file appended to. Logging only takes place in compiled VB applications.

You can specify an event log file using the StartLogging method, which takes two parameters, the log filename and the log mode. (The App object's LogPath and LogMode properties, which you would expect to set before beginning logging, are read-only and can only be set by calling the StartLogging method.)

 Note that the log mode constants were missing from Version 5 of VB, so you either have to enter their literal values, or you have to define your own constants.

In Windows NT, if you call the StartLogging method but don't specify a log file, or in Windows 95, if you don't call the StartLogging method at all, VB creates a file called *vbevents.log*, which is placed in the Windows directory. To use event logging, you don't necessarily need to use the StartLogging method.

The LogEvent method itself takes two parameters. The first is a string containing all the detail you wish to store about the error or event. The second is an Event-Type constant, which denotes an error, information, or a warning. In NT, this event type value displays the correct icon in the event log, whereas in Windows 95, the word "Error," "Information," or "Warning" appears at the start of the item in the event log file.

 In a previous section, "Error Handling in ActiveX Servers," you saw how to force *MsgBox* prompts to be automatically written to an event log by selecting the Unattended Application option. But which event log? The *MsgBox* function doesn't take a parameter to specify an optional event log, so VB will write the string contained within the Prompt parameter to the default *vbevents.log* in Windows 9x or to the application event log in Windows NT. However, you can place a call to the app object's *StartLogging* method in the class's Initialize event, thereby specifying a log file for all *Msgbox* and *LogEvent* calls.

Once you have an event log for your application, you can look back through the history of the application any time you choose. If you are networked to the user's machine, you can open the user's event log from your machine and detect problems without even leaving your desk.

PART II

Reference

This section consists of only a single very long chapter, Chapter 7, *The Language Reference*, which contains an alphabetic reference to VBA language elements. It doesn't document the properties, methods, and events of Visual Basic forms and controls or of VBA UserForms.

The chapter does document the following:

- Statements, like Dim or For Each.

- Functions, like *Format* or *InStr*.

- The object models, like the File System object model or the Data Binding object model, that have been introduced with VB6. Here you'll find complete documentation of all of the objects, along with their properties and methods.

When you're looking for a particular language element but don't quite remember what it's called, an alphabetic reference is of little value. For this reason, I've included Appendix A, *Language Elements by Category*.

Finally, except for Like, VBA operators aren't included in this section. Instead, you'll find them discussed in Appendix C, *Operators*.

CHAPTER 7

The Language Reference

VBA is a high-level language and, like all high-level languages, it is, by its very nature, a large yet rich language. While this means that it takes time for new users to understand the intricacies of the many and varied functions and statements available to them, at the same time the language's syntax is straightforward, logical, and therefore easy to understand.

Perhaps the biggest obstacle to overcome is deciding which one of a number of functions and statements available to perform roughly the same task should be used. This situation has come about as the language has evolved over a number of years, and older statements have been left in the language to provide backward compatibility. If you always bear in mind that the language was originally made up of statements, that later versions introduced functions, and that only recently have object models been provided, then you can pinpoint the latest functionality within the language.

To help speed the process of finding the right function or statement to perform a particular task, you can use Appendix A, *Language Elements by Category*, to determine what language elements are available for the purpose you require. You can also make use of the VB or VBA Object Browser to search or browse the VBA library.

As I've stated several times already, this book concentrates on the VBA language, and therefore doesn't include the following components, which don't form a part of the VBA language:

- The methods, properties, and events associated with VB forms and controls

- The methods, properties, and events associated with VBA UserForms and the VBA controls available from the Microsoft Forms library

- The objects, as well as their associated properties, methods, and events, that are provided by each application that hosts VBA

You will, however, come across some (but thankfully very few) language elements that relate only to VB or only to VBA. There are two reasons for this:

- The VBA DLL that provides VB with its language is slightly different than that used in the hosted version of VBA, since they were released at different times.

- VB includes several unique functions to support its ability to create stand-alone applications as either EXEs, DLLs, or OCXs.

The elements of the VBA language can be broken into four main areas: statements, functions, operators, and object models.

Statements

Statements form the cornerstone of the language. You'll notice from Appendix A that the largest concentration of statements is in the program structure section. Statements are mainly used for such tasks as declaring variables or declaring procedures.

There is another large concentration of statements in the file manipulation section of VB. Again, these statements predate object programming in VB. It's likely that the new File System object model released with VB6 will replace the intrinsic VBA file statements.

Some statements in VB are quite old, having their roots back in (and before) Version 1 of VB. (Remember that Version 1 of VB itself represented a graphical interface design program grafted onto the Basic language.) In some cases, statements have been replaced by newer and more flexible functions, but the statement remains in the language for compatibility. That said, there are literally only one or two instances where both a statement and function of the same name exist.

Most statements don't accept named arguments, since this concept didn't exist in the early days of VB. In the main, statements don't return a value. Therefore, you are often well-advised to wrap these statements in a custom function that can return a value you can use to determine if a task was successful or not.

Some newer statements are in fact methods of VBA class libraries. For example the `DeleteSetting` statement is a method of the VBA.Interaction class.

Functions

Functions are relatively new additions to the language, most dating back to the Version 4 rewrite of VB and VBA. In the main, functions return a value, although, as with any function, you can choose to ignore the return value.

In addition to returning a value, there are other important benefits of functions over statements:

- You can view most functions in the VB Object Browser, whereas most statements don't appear.

- Most functions accept *named arguments*. This means that you can improve the readability of your code by using the name of an argument and the special argument assignment operator ":=", as this code fragment shows:

```
Dim iReturnVal As Integer
iReturnVal = MsgBox(Prompt:="Click OK", Title:="Test")
```

Operators

An operator connects or performs some operation upon one or more language elements to form a single expression. For example, in the code fragment:

```
strResult = 16 + int(lngVar1)
```

the addition operator (+) combines 16 and the value returned by int(lngVar1) into a single expression whose value is assigned to the variable *strResult*.

Object models

Object models are increasingly used to provide additional functionality in the VBA language. This is an ideal way of extending the language, since VBA itself is adept at handling object models.

Interestingly, the VBA language is itself implemented as an object model, although very rarely is it used as such. Since it's a flat model (that is, it doesn't define a class hierarchy), it isn't actually thought of as an object model. Nevertheless, if you use the object browser to examine the VBA component, you'll see that it's an external library containing various classes.

Some of the latest additions to VBA have used object models. For example, the Scripting Runtime provides us with the File System object model and the Dictionary object. VB6 also includes the Data Binding and Data Formatting objects. As time goes by we'll find more and more object models augmenting and replacing statements and functions in VBA.

Because of their importance to VB6, I've included full descriptions of the File System, Dictionary, Data Binding, and Data Formatting object models in this language section. Note that as long as the object libraries are available and are registered in the system registry, their objects are available to all 32-bit VB and VBA applications and macros developed in the current version, as well as earlier versions of VB and VBA-hosted applications.

#Const Directive

Named Arguments

No

Syntax

```
#Const constantname = expression
constantname
```
    Use: Required

    Data Type: Variant (String)

    Name of the constant.

```
expression
```
    Use: Required

Data Type: Literal

Any combination of literal values, other conditional compilation constants defined with the #Const directive, and arithmetic or logical operators except Is.

Description

Defines a conditional compiler constant. By using compiler constants to create code blocks that are included in the compiled application only when a particular condition is met, you can create more than one version of the application using the same source code. This is a two-step process:

- Defining the conditional compiler constant. This step is optional; conditional compiler constants that aren't explicitly defined by the #Const directive but that are referenced in code default to a value of 0 or False.

- Evaluating the constant in the conditional compiler #If...Then statement block.

A conditional compiler constant can be assigned any string, numeric, or logical value returned by an expression. However, the expression itself can consist only of literals, operators other than Is, and another conditional compiler constant.

When the constant is evaluated, the code within the conditional compiler #If...Then block is compiled as part of the application only when the conditional compiler constant evaluates to True.

You may wonder why you should bother having code that is compiled only when a certain condition is met, when a simple If...Then statement could do the same job. The reasons are:

- You may have code that contains early bound references to objects that are present only in a particular version of the application. You'd want that code compiled only when you know it wouldn't create an error.

- You may wish to include code that executes only during the debugging phase of the application. It's often wise to leave this code in the application even after the application has been released, so that you can check back over a procedure if an issue arises. However, you don't want the code to be executed in the final application. The answer is to wrap your debugging code in a conditional statement. You can then provide a conditional constant that acts as a switch to turn debugging code on or off, as the example below demonstrates.

- Although most operations performed with conditional compilation can be replicated with normal If...Then code blocks, conditional compilation reduces the size of the compiled application and thereby the amount of memory required for the application, making for a more efficient application.

Rules at a Glance

- Conditional compiler constants are evaluated by the conditional compiler #If...Then statement block.

- You can use any arithmetic or logical operator in the expression except Is.

- You can't use other constants defined with the standard Const statement in the expression.

- According to the documentation, you can't use intrinsic functions in the expression; e.g., #Const MY_CONST = Chr(13) is illegal. In most cases, VBA displays a "Compile error : Variable not found" message if you try this. But there are numerous exceptions. For example, the use of the *Int* function in the following code fragment doesn't produce a compiler error, and in fact, successfully defines a constant ccDefInt whose value is 3:

```
#Const ccDefFloat = 3.1417
#Const ccDefInt = Int(ccDefFloat)
```

- When using #Const, you can't use variables to assign the conditional constant a value.

- Constants defined with #Const can be used only in conditional code blocks.

- Constants defined with #Const have scope only within the module in which they are defined; i.e., they are private.

- You can place the #Const directive anywhere within a module.

- You can't use the #Const directive to define the same constant more than once within a module. Attempting to do so produces a "Compile Error: Duplicate Definition" error message.

- Interestingly, you can define the same constant both through the VB or VBA interface (see the second item in the "Programming Tips & Gotchas" section) and using the #Const directive. In this case, the constant defined through the interface is visible throughout the application, except in the routine in which the #Const directive is used, where the private constant is visible.

- The #Const directive must be the first statement on a line of code. It can be followed only by a comment. Note that the colon, which combines two complete sets of statements onto a single line, can't be used on lines that contain #Const.

Example

```
#Const ccDebug = 1 'evaluates to true

Function testValue(sValue as String)

sValue = UCase(sValue)
testValue = sValue

#If ccDebug Then
    'this code only executes if ccDebug evaluates to true
    Debug.Print sValue
#End If

End Function
```

Programming Tips & Gotchas

- Conditional compiler constants help you debug your code, as well as provide a way to create more than one version of your application. You can include code that operates only when run in debug mode. The code can be left in your final version and won't compile unless running in the debugger. Therefore, you don't need to keep adding and removing debugging code.

- You can also define conditional constants outside of the application's code. In the VBA Editor, enter the conditional compiler constant into the Conditional Compilation Arguments text box on the General tab of the Project Properties dialog. You can reach it by selecting the *Project* Properties option (where *Project* is the name that you've assigned to the project) from the Tools menu. In Visual Basic, the Conditional Compilation Arguments text box is found on the Make property sheet of the Project Properties dialog. It can be accessed by selecting the *Project* Properties option (again, where *Project* is the name that you've assigned to the project) from the Project menu. In Access, the Conditional Compilation Arguments text box is found on the Advanced property sheet of the Options dialog, which can be accessed by selecting the Options item from the Tools menu. Conditional compiler constants defined in this way are public to the project.

Constants Defined Through the VB/VBA Interface

The rules for defining constants in the Conditional Compilation Arguments text box are somewhat different than for constants defined in code using the #Const statement. The value assigned through the VB/VBA interface must be an integer literal; it can't be an expression formed by using multiple literals or conditional constants, along with one or more operators, nor can it be a Boolean value (i.e., True or False). If multiple conditional constants are assigned through the user interface, they are separated from one another by a colon. For instance, the following fragment defines three constants, ccFlag1, ccFlag2, and ccFlag3:

```
ccFlag1 = 1 : ccFlag2 = 0 : ccFlag3 = 1
```

- In many cases, failing to properly define a constant doesn't produce an error message. When this happens (as it does, for instance, when you attempt to assign a variable's value to a constant), the default value of the constant is False. As a result, attempting to assign the value resulting from an invalid expression to a constant can lead to the inclusion of the wrong block of code in the compiled application.

- Although it may be obvious, it's important to remember that the constant defined by #Const is evaluated at compile time, and therefore doesn't return information about the system on which the application is running. For example, the intent of the following code fragment is to test for a sound card and, if one is present, to include code taking advantage of the system's enhanced sound capabilities:

```
If waveOutGetNumDevs > 0 Then
    #Const ccSoundEnabled = True
Endif
. . .
```

```
#If ccSoundEnabled Then
    ' Include code for sound-enabled systems
#Else
    ' Include code for systems without a sound card
#End If
```

However, the code doesn't work as expected, since it includes or excludes the code supporting a sound card based on the state of the development machine, rather than the machine on which the application is running.

See Also

#If...Then...#Else Directive

#If...Then...#Else Directive

Named Arguments

No

Syntax

```
#If expression Then
    statements
[#ElseIf furtherexpression Then
    [elseifstatements]]
[#Else
    [elsestatements]]
#End If
```

expression
> Use: Required

> An expression made up of operators and conditional compiler constants that evaluate to True or False.

statements
> Use: Required

> One or more lines of code that are executed if *expression* evaluates to True.

furtherexpression
> Use: Optional

> An expression made up of operators and conditional compiler constants that evaluates to True or False. *furtherexpression* is evaluated only if the preceding expression evaluates to False.

elseifstatements
> Use: Optional

> One or more lines of code that are executed if *furtherexpression* evaluates to True.

elsestatements
> Use: Optional

One or more lines of code that are executed if *expression* or *further-expression* evaluates to False.

Description

Defines a block or blocks of code that are included in the compiled application only when a particular condition is met, allowing you to create more than one version of the application using the same source code. Conditionally including a block of code is a two-step process:

* Using the #Const directive to assign a value to a conditional compiler constant

* Evaluating the conditional compiler constant using #If...Then...#End If statement block.

As with the standard If...Then statement, only expressions that evaluate to True are executed directly after the statement. You can use the #Else statement to execute code when the #If...Then expression has evaluated to False. You can also use an #ElseIf statement to evaluate more expressions in the event that previous expressions in the same block have evaluated to False.

Some uses of conditional compilation code are:

* To provide blocks of debugging code that can be left within the source code and switched on and off using a conditional constant.

* To provide blocks of code that can perform different functions based on the build required by the developer. For example, you may have a sample version of your application that offers less functionality than the full product. This can be achieved using the same source code and wrapping the code for menu options, etc., within conditional compiler directives.

* To provide blocks of code that reference different ActiveX servers depending on the build criteria of the application.

#If...Then and Platform

In Visual Basic 4.0, which included both 16- and 32-bit versions, the major application of the #If...Then compiler directive was to generate separate executables for the 16- and 32-bit Windows platforms. For this purpose, VBA included two conditional compiler constants, Win16 and Win32; if one was True, the other was automatically set to False. Visual Basic 5.0 and VBA 5.0 onwards, however, support only the 32-bit Windows platforms. Consequently, the Win16 and Win32 constants are no longer supported.

Rules at a Glance

* According to the documentation, only operators (other than Is) and conditional compiler constants can be used in the expression to be evaluated. In fact, you can draw on a considerably broader range of the VBA language to

---

evaluate a conditional compiler expression. In addition to these, you can use literals, variables, and some functions.

- Unlike the normal `If...Then` statement, you can't use a single-line version of the `#If...Then` statement.

- All conditional compiler constants used in conditional compiler expressions must be defined; otherwise, they evaluate to `Empty`. This, in turn, means that the conditional compiler expression evaluates to `False`.

Example

```
#Const ccVersion = 2.5
Private oTest as Object

Sub GetCorrectObject()

#If ccVersion = 2.5 Then
    Set oTest = New MyObject.MyClass
#Else
    Set oTest = New MyOtherObject.MyClass
#End If

End Sub
```

Programming Tips & Gotchas

- You can negate the evaluation of the expression in the `#If...Then` or `#ElseIf...Then` statements by placing the `Not` operator before the expression. For example, `#If Not ccVersion = 5 Then` forces the code after this line to be compiled in all situations where `ccVersion` doesn't equal 5.

- Conditional compilation helps you debug your code, as well as provide a way to create more than one version of your application. You can include code that operates only when run in debug mode. The code can be left in your final version and won't compile unless running in the debugger; therefore, you don't need to keep adding and removing code.

- That you can use a wider range of language elements without generating a compiler error doesn't necessarily mean that you should use them or that using them produces the result that you want. This applies to the use of variables in particular; the distinguishing feature of a variable (and the reason for its name) is that its value is allowed to vary at runtime. The evaluation of conditional expressions, however, occurs at compile time.

See Also

#Const Directive, Debug.Print Method, If...Then Statement

Abs Function

Named Arguments

No

Syntax

```
result = Abs(number)
number
```

  Use: Required

  Data Type: Any valid numeric expression

  The number whose absolute value is to be returned.

Return Value

The absolute value of *number*. The data type is the same as that passed to the function.

Description

Returns the absolute value of a number (i.e., its unsigned magnitude). For example, `Abs(-1)` and `Abs(1)` both return 1. If *number* contains `Null`, `Null` is returned; if it's an uninitialized variable, zero is returned.

Rules at a Glance

Only numeric values can be passed to the *Abs* function.

Example

In this example, the *LineLength* function determines the length of a line on the screen. If the line runs from left to right, *X1* is less than *X2*, and the equation (*X2-X1*) returns the length of the line. If, however, the line runs from right to left, *X1* is greater than *X2*, and a negative line length is returned. As you know, in most circumstances, it doesn't matter which way a line is pointing; all you want to know is how long it is. Using the *Abs* function allows you to return the same figure whether the underlying figure is negative or positive.

```
Function LineLength(X2 as Integer) as Integer

    Dim X1 As Integer

    X1 = 100
    LineLength = Abs(X2 - X1)

End Function
```

Programming Tips & Gotchas

Because the *Abs* function accepts only numeric values, you may want to check the value you pass to *Abs* using the *IsNumeric* function to prevent generating an error. This is illustrated in the following code snippet:

```
If IsNumeric(vExtent) Then
    Abs(vExtent)
    ...
End If
```

See Also

IsNumeric Function

AddressOf Operator

Named Arguments

No

Syntax

```
AddressOf procedurename
procedurename
```

Use: Required

The name of an API procedure.

Description

Passes the address of a procedure to an API function. There are some API functions that require the address of a *callback function* as a parameter. (A callback function is a routine in your code that is invoked by the routine that your program is calling: it calls back into your code.) These callback functions are passed to the API function as pointers to a memory address. In the past, calling functions that required callbacks posed a unique problem to VB, since, unlike C or C++, it lacks a concept of pointers. However, the AddressOf operator allows you to pass such a pointer in the form of a long integer to the API function, thereby allowing the API function to call back to the procedure.

Rules at a Glance

- The callback function must be stored in a code module; attempting to store it in a class or a form module generates a compile-time error, "Invalid use of AddressOf operator."

- The AddressOf operator must be followed by the name of a user-defined function, procedure, or property.

- The data type of the corresponding argument in the API function's Declare statement must be As Any or As Long.

- The AddressOf operator can't call one VB procedure from another.

Example

The following example uses the *EnumWindows* and *GetWindowText* API calls to return a list of currently open windows. *EnumWindows* requires the address of a callback function as its first parameter. A custom function, *EnumCallBackProc*, is the callback function that populates the `lstWindowTitles` list box.

When the *cmdListWindows* command button is clicked, the list box is cleared, and a call to the *EnumWindows* API function is made, passing the AddressOf the *EnumCallBackProc* function and a reference to the list box control. *EnumWindows* then calls back to *EnumCallBackProc*, passing it the window handle of an open window and the reference to the list box. *EnumCallBackProc* then uses the *GetWindowText* API function to return the text in the titlebar of the window, passing it the window handle, a string buffer, and the length of that buffer. *EnumCallBackProc* is called by the API function as many times as is required, depending upon the number of open windows. The first portion of the example

Reference

code must be stored in a code module, while the cmdListWindows_Click event handler can be stored in the form module containing the *cmdListWindows* button.

```
Option Explicit

Public Declare Function EnumWindows Lib "User32" _
                        (ByVal lpEnumFunc As Any, _
                        ByVal lParam As Any) As Long

Public Declare Function GetWindowText Lib "User32" _
                        Alias "GetWindowTextA" _
                        (ByVal hWnd As Long, _
                        ByVal lpString As String, _
                        ByVal cch As Long) As Long

Function EnumCallBackProc(ByVal hWnd As Long, _
                        ByVal lParam As ListBox) As Long

    On Error Resume Next

    Dim sWindowTitle As String
    Dim lReturn As Long

    sWindowTitle = String(512, 0)

    lReturn = GetWindowText(hWnd, sWindowTitle, 512)

    If lReturn > 0 Then
        lParam.AddItem sWindowTitle
    End If

    EnumCallBackProc = 1

End Function

Private Sub cmdListWindows_Click()

    Dim lReturn As Long

    lstWindowTitles.Clear
    lReturn = EnumWindows(AddressOf EnumCallBackProc, _
                        lstWindowTitles)

End Sub
```

Programming Tips & Gotchas

- Debugging calls containing AddressOf is at best very difficult and most of the time downright impossible.

- It's possible to pass an AddressOf pointer from one VB procedure to another by creating a wrapper for the callback function. To do this, however, you must declare the pointer as either Long or Any. The following snippet shows how you could add such a wrapper function to the example used above:

```
Private Sub cmdListWindows_Click()

Dim lReturn As Long

lReturn = DoWindowTitles(AddressOf EnumCallBackProc, _
                         lstWindowTitles)
End Sub

Private Function DoWindowTitles(CallBackAddr As Long, _
                         lstBox As ListBox) As Long

    'other stuff here
    lstBox.Clear
    DoWindowTitles = EnumWindows(CallBackAddr, lstBox)

End Function
```

- Because you can't pass an error back to the calling Windows API function from within your VB callback function, you should use the **On Error Resume Next** statement at the start of your VB callback function.

See Also

Declare Statement

AppActivate Statement

Named Arguments

Yes

Syntax

AppActivate *title* [, *wait*]

title

> Use: Required
>
> Data Type: Variant
>
> The name of the application as currently shown in the application window titlebar. Can also be the task ID returned from the *Shell* function.

wait

> Use: Optional
>
> Data Type: Boolean
>
> If set to **True**, the calling application must itself wait to obtain the focus before activating the called application. If set to **False** (its default value), the application specified in *title* is activated immediately.

Description

Sets the focus to the application with a titlebar caption matching *title*. The application title passed to **AppActivate** isn't necessarily the name of the program file of the application; it's the name currently displayed in the application's titlebar.

Reference

Rules at a Glance

- *title* isn't case sensitive.

- The title of each running application is compared against *title*.

- If the application designated by *title* isn't running, AppActivate doesn't launch it.

- If no title matching *title* is found, an application whose title starts with *title* is matched. For example, the *title* "Microsoft Word" matches "Microsoft Word—MyDocument.doc".

- If more than one instance of an application is found, AppActivate passes the focus to one of the instances purely at random.

- The window state (Maximized, Minimized, or Normal) of the activated application isn't affected by AppActivate.

- If a matching application can't be found, runtime error 5, "Invalid procedure call or argument," is generated.

- AppActivate can be used with both standard windows and console mode or DOS applications. In the latter case, *title* must correspond to the window caption Windows assigns the console window.

Example

```
Private Sub CommandButton2_Click()

    Dim bVoid As Boolean
    bVoid = ActivateAnApp("Microsoft Excel")

End Sub

Function ActivateAnApp(vAppTitle As Variant) As Boolean

    On Error GoTo Activate_Err

    ActivateAnApp = False
    AppActivate vAppTitle
    ActivateAnApp = True

Activate_Exit:
    Exit Function

Activate_Err:
    MsgBox "Application " & vAppTitle & _
           " could not be activated"
    Resume Activate_Exit

End Function
```

Programming Tips & Gotchas

- You can also use the task ID returned by the *Shell* function with the AppActivate statement, as this simple example demonstrates:

```
Option Explicit
Private vAppID

Private Sub Command1_Click()
    vAppID = Shell("C:\Program Files\Internet\IEXPLORE.EXE")
End Sub
Private Sub Command2_Click()
    AppActivate vAppID
End Sub
```

- `AppActivate` is difficult to use with applications whose application titles change to reflect the state or context of the application. Microsoft Outlook furnishes an excellent illustration of this problem. If the user has Outlook in the Calendar section, the titlebar reads "Calendar—Microsoft Outlook," whereas in the Inbox section, the titlebar reads "Inbox—Microsoft Outlook."

- Due to the uncertain nature of attempting to activate an application over which you have little or no programmatic control, you are strongly advised to wrap the `appActivate` statement within stout error handling.

- Wherever possible, it's preferable to manipulate the other application using its COM interface—i.e., to create an instance of the application object.

- `AppActivate` is often used to give a particular window the focus before sending keystrokes to it using the `SendKeys` statement, which acts only upon the active window.

- All high-level languages by their very nature have limitations. After all, if we wanted a language that could do everything possible, we'd all be using assembler. To my mind the `AppActivate` and the *Shell* functions highlight the limitations of VB in 32-bit Windows, and especially Windows NT. To make a long story short, if you want to manipulate other applications with your application, you should either be using a technology, such as OLE automation, that focuses on controlling an application remotely, or you should be programming those parts of your application in C++—and that doesn't mean MFC! (Even MFC is too high-level for some of the low-level windows functionality you need to do the job right.)

See Also

Shell Function

Array Function

Syntax

```
Array([element1], [elementN],....)
element
```
    Use: Required

    Data Type: Any

    The data to be assigned to the first array element

```
elementN
```
    Use: Optional

Data Type: Any

Any number of data items you wish to add to the array.

Return Value

A variant array consisting of the arguments passed into the function.

Description

Returns a variant array containing the elements whose values are passed to the function as arguments.

The code fragment:

```
Dim vaMyArray
vaMyArray = Array("Mr", "Mrs", "Miss", "Ms")
```

is the equivalent to writing:

```
Dim vaMyArray(3)
vaMyArray(0) = "Mr"
vaMyArray(1) = "Mrs"
vaMyArray(2) = "Miss"
vaMyArray(3) = "Ms"
```

Because *Array* creates a variant array, you can pass any data type, including user-defined types and objects, to the *Array* function. You can also pass the values returned by calls to other *Array* functions to create multidimensional arrays (but see the comment on multidimensional arrays in the "Programming Tips & Gotchas" section).

Rules at a Glance

- You can assign the array returned by the *Array* function only to a Variant.

- Although the array you create with the *Array* function is a variant data type, the individual elements of the array can be a mixture of different data types.

- The initial size of the array you create is the number of arguments you place in the argument list and pass to the *Array* function.

- The lower bound of the array created by the *Array* function is determined by the Option Base directive; if there is no Option Base statement, the lower bound of the array is 0.

- The array returned by the *Array* function is a dynamic rather than static array. Once created, you can redimension the array using Redim, Redim Preserve, or another call to the *Array* function.

- If you don't pass any arguments to the *Array* function, an empty array is created. Although this may appear to be the same as declaring an array in the conventional manner with the statement:

```
Dim myArray()
```

the difference is that you can then use the empty array with the *Array* function again later in your code.

Programming Tips & Gotchas

- You can effectively use the *Array* function only in situations where you know in advance the number of elements you will need. It's not possible to write the function statement with a variable number of elements.

- You can't assign the return value of *Array* to a variable previously declared as an array variable. Therefore, *don't* declare the variant variable as an array using the normal syntax:

```
Dim MyArray()
```

Instead, simply declare a variant variable, such as:

```
Dim MyArray as Variant
```

- *Array* can also be invoked as a method within the VBA object model* by using the syntax:

```
VBA.Array()
```

In this case, **Option Base** has no effect on the base element number of the array; the first element is always 0. Try this example:

```
Option Base 1
Private Sub CommandButton1_Click()

Dim vaListOne As Variant
vaListOne = VBA.Array("One", 2, "Three", 4)
MsgBox vaListOne(1)

Dim vaListTwo As Variant
vaListTwo = Array("One", 2, "Three", 4)
MsgBox vaListTwo(1)

End Sub
```

- The *Array* function is ideal for saving space and time and writing more efficient code when creating a fixed array of known elements, for example:

```
Dim Titles as Variant
Title = Array("Mr", "Mrs", "Miss", "Ms")
```

- You can use the *Array* function to create multidimensional arrays. However, accessing the elements of the array needs a little more thought. The following code fragment creates a simple two-dimensional array with three elements in the first dimension and four elements in the second:

```
Dim vaListOne As Variant

vaListOne = Array(Array(1, 2, 3, 4), _
                  Array(5, 6, 7, 8), _
                  Array(9, 10, 11, 12))
```

---

* If you use the Object Browser to locate the **Array** method within the VBA object, though, you won't be able to find it, since, as a member of the **_HiddenModule** module, it's hidden from view, although it remains accessible.

Surprisingly, the code you'd expect to use to access the array returns a "Subscript out of range" error:

```
'This line generates a Subscript out of range error
MsgBox vaListOne(1, 2)
```

You can overcome this limitation by declaring a second variant and assigning to it the element from the first dimension, then accessing the second dimension element in the normal way, like this:

```
Dim vaListTwo As Variant
vaListTwo = vaListOne(1)

MsgBox vaListTwo(2)
```

- You can also use the *Array* function to populate the ActiveX (Microsoft Forms 2.0) ListBox or ComboBox controls, as the following example shows:

```
Private Sub CommandButton2_Click()

ComboBox1.Clear
ComboBox1.List = Array("Mr", "Mrs", "Miss", "Ms")
ComboBox1.ListIndex = 0

End Sub
```

Note that this doesn't work with the standard Visual Basic ListBox or ComboBox controls; it produces an "Argument not optional" compiler error. Our performance comparisons, however, indicate that the conventional technique of calling the control's AddItem method to add an item is between 5 and 25% faster than calling the *Array* function.

- Here's another neat trick you can use with the *Array* function: you can even create your own "on-demand" control array (of existing controls) by simply listing a group of existing controls in the argument list to pass to the *Array* function. You can then use the array element the same way you'd use an object variable, as the following code demonstrates:

```
Dim vaTest as Variant

vaTest = Array(CommandButton1, CommandButton2, _
               CommandButton3)

MsgBox vaTest(1).Caption
```

- Because you declare the variant variable to hold the array as a simple variant, rather than an array, and can then make repeated calls to *Array*, the function can create dynamic arrays. For example, the following code fragment dimensions a variant to hold the array, calls *Array* to create a variant array, then calls *Array* again to replace the original variant array with a larger variant array:

```
Dim varArray As Variant
varArray = Array(10,20,30,40,50)
...
varArray = Array(10,20,30,40,50,60)
```

The major disadvantage of using this method is that, while it makes it easy to replace an array with a different array, it doesn't allow you to easily expand or contract an existing array.

See Also

Dim Statement, LBound Function, Option Base Statement, ReDim Statement, Ubound Function

---

Asc, AscB, AscW Functions

Named Arguments

No

Syntax

```
Asc(string)
AscB(string)
AscW(string)
string
```

      Use: Required

      Data Type: String

      Any expression that evaluates to a string.

Return Value

An integer that represents the character code of the first character of the string. The range for the returned value is 0–255 on non-DBCS systems, but –32768–32767 on DBCS systems.

Description

Returns the ANSI or Unicode character code that represents the first character of the string passed to it. All other characters in the string are ignored. Use *AscB* with Byte data and *AscW* on Unicode (DBCS) systems.

Rules at a Glance

- The string expression passed to the function must contain at least one character, or a runtime error (either "Invalid use of Null" or "Invalid procedure call or argument") is generated.
- Only the first character of the string is evaluated by *Asc*, *AscB*, and *AscW*.
- Use the *AscW* function to return the Unicode character of the first character of a string.
- Use the *AscB* function to return the first byte of a string containing byte data.

Example

```
Dim sChars As String
Dim iCharCode As Integer

sChars = TextBox1.Text
If Len(sChars) > 0 Then
```

Reference

```
    iCharCode = Asc(sChars)
    If iCharCode >= 97 And iChar <= 122 Then
        MsgBox "The first character must be uppercase"
    End If
End If
```

Programming Tips & Gotchas

- Always check that the string you are passing to the function contains at least one character using the *Len* function, as the following example shows:

```
If Len(sMyString) > 0 Then
    iCharCode = Asc(sMyString)
Else
    MsgBox "Cannot process a zero-length string"
End If
```

- On platforms which don't support Unicode, the *AscW* function performs exactly the same as *Asc*.

- Surprisingly, although the VB Object Browser clearly shows that the data type of the parameter passed to the *Asc* function is String, it can actually be any data type. Evidently the *Asc* routine converts incoming values to strings before extracting their first character.

- Use *Asc* within your data validation routines to determine such conditions as whether the first character is upper- or lowercase and whether it's alphabetic or numeric, as the following example demonstrates:

```
Private Sub CommandButton1_Click()

Dim sTest As String
Dim iChar As Integer

sTest = TextBox1.Text

If Len(sTest) > 0 Then
    iChar = Asc(sTest)
    If iChar >= 65 And iChar <= 90 Then
        MsgBox "The first character is UPPERCASE"
    ElseIf iChar >= 97 And iChar <= 122 Then
        MsgBox "The first character is lowercase"
    Else
        MsgBox "The first character isn't alphabetical"
    End If
Else
    MsgBox "Please enter something in the text box"
End If

End Sub
```

- Use the *Asc* function and its converse, *Chr*, to create rudimentary encryption methods. Once you have obtained the character code for a particular character, you can perform calculations on this code to come up with a different number and then convert this to a character using the *Chr* function. To decrypt your string, simply reverse the calculation. Be sure, though, that your calculation doesn't generate character codes less than 20, since these are special nonprinting characters, which, if displayed or printed, can cause undesirable effects.

```
Private Sub CommandButton2_Click()

Dim MyName As String, MyEncryptedString As String
Dim MyDecryptedString As String
Dim i As Integer

MyName = "Paul Lomax"

For i = 1 To Len(MyName)
   MyEncryptedString = MyEncryptedString & _
                       Chr(Asc(Mid(MyName, i, 1)) + 25)
Next i

MsgBox "Hello, my name is " & MyEncryptedString

For i = 1 To Len(MyName)
   MyDecryptedString = MyDecryptedString & _
   Chr(Asc(Mid(MyEncryptedString, i, 1)) - 25)
Next i

MsgBox "Hello, my name is " & MyDecryptedString

End Sub
```

Unicode Characters and AscB, AscW, ChrB, and ChrW

The Unicode character set was developed to support software internationalization and the consequent need for many more characters than the original ASCII character set could provide. Unicode characters are represented by two bytes and can therefore represent up to 65,536 characters, whereas ANSI's one-byte representation can cope only with 256. Today, both Windows NT and OLE 2.0 are entirely Unicode, and since Version 4, Visual Basic has represented strings in Unicode internally.

Because of the way VB handles strings internally, the operation of certain functions (such as *Chr*) has changed when compared to VB's early versions. For example, assigning the return value of *Chr* to a string data type results in a string one byte in length under Windows 95, a non-Unicode system; this is the traditional behavior of *Chr*. But under Windows NT, a Unicode system, it results in a string two bytes in length. To cope with the extra demands of Unicode, VB4 introduced a number of new functions, including *AscB*, *AscW*, *ChrB*, and *ChrW*. The "W"-suffixed functions handle the two bytes of Unicode characters. The "B"-suffixed functions work with Byte data, but, like the *Asc* and *Chr* functions, handle only the first byte of the byte string passed to them.

Reference

See Also

Chr, ChrB, ChrW Functions

Atn Function

Named Arguments

No

Syntax

```
Atn(number)
```
number

Use: Required

Data Type: Numeric

Any numeric expression, representing the ratio of two sides of a right angle triangle.

Return Value

The return value is a Double data type representing the arctangent of *number*, in the range –pi/2 to pi/2 radians.

Description

Takes the ratio of two sides of a right triangle (*number*) and returns the corresponding angle in radians. The ratio is the length of the side opposite the angle divided by the length of the side adjacent to the angle.

Rules at a Glance

- If no number is specified, a runtime error is generated.

- The return value of *Atn* is in radians, not degrees.

Example

```
Private Sub CommandButton1_Click()

    Dim dblSideAdj As Double
    Dim dblSideOpp As Double
    Dim dblRatio As Double
    Dim dblAtangent As Double

    dblSideAdj = 50.25
    dblSideOpp = 75.5

    dblRatio = dblSideOpp / dblSideAdj
    dblAtangent = Atn(dblRatio)
    'convert from radians to degrees
    dblDegrees = dblAtangent * (180 / 3.142)
    MsgBox dblDegrees & " Degrees"

End Sub
```

Programming Tips & Gotchas

- To convert degrees to radians, multiply degrees by pi/180.

- To convert radians to degrees, multiply radians by 180/pi.

- Don't confuse *Atn* with the cotangent. *Atn* is the inverse *trigonometric* function of *Tan*, as opposed to the simple inverse of *Tan*.

See Also

Tan Function

Beep Statement

Syntax

```
Beep
```

Description

Sounds a tone through the computer's speaker.

Example

```
Private Sub CommandButton2_Click()

    iVoid = DoSomeLongFunction()
    Beep
    MsgBox "Finished!"

End Sub
```

Programming Tips & Gotchas

- The frequency and duration of the tone depends on the computer's hardware. Bear in mind that on some systems, a mouse click is louder than the beep.

- Overuse of the **Beep** statement won't endear you to your users.

- Thoughtful use at the end of a long possibly unattended process may be appropriate.

- Since the successful operation of the **Beep** statement doesn't require the presence of any multimedia hardware (like a sound board, for example), it can be used when a system isn't configured to support sound. For example, if the following is defined in the declarations section of a code module:

```
Declare Function waveOutGetNumDevs Lib "winmm.dll" () As Long
Declare Function PlaySound Lib "winmm.dll" _
        Alias "PlaySoundA" (ByVal lpszName As String, _
        ByVal hModule As Long, ByVal dwFlags As Long) _
        As Long

Public Const SND_APPLICATION = &H80
Public Const SND_ASYNC = &H1
Public Const SND_FILENAME = &H20000
Public Const SND_NODEFAULT = &H2
```

Reference

```
Public HasSound As Boolean

Public Function IsSoundSupported() As Boolean
    If (waveOutGetNumDevs > 0) Then _
        IsSoundSupported = True
End Function
```

then the procedure

```
Private Sub Form_Load()
    Dim intCtr As Integer
    HasSound = IsSoundSupported()
    If HasSound Then
        Call PlaySound("c:\windows\media\tada.wav", 0, _
                    SND_FILENAME Or SND_NODEFAULT)
    Else
        For intCtr = 0 To 3
            Beep
        Next
    End If
End Sub
```

BindingCollection Object (VB6)

Description

The BindingCollection object—as the name suggests—is a collection of Binding objects. The BindingCollection object plays a central role in the new data-binding technology in VB6, allowing you to automatically map data fields to standard form controls and to specify formatting for those data. Your application can have any number of BindingCollection objects, each referring to a distinct data member provided by a data source such as an ADO recordset or a VB data source class. The Binding objects held within the class represent the individual mapping of consumer control property to data provider field, a relationship created using the BindingCollections Add method.

The relationship between the various data binding elements is shown in Figure 7-1.

For an overview of data-binding objects, including the library reference needed to access the object model, see the Data Binding Objects entry.

Createable

Yes

BindingCollection Properties

Count

Data Type: Long

The number of Binding objects in the collection.

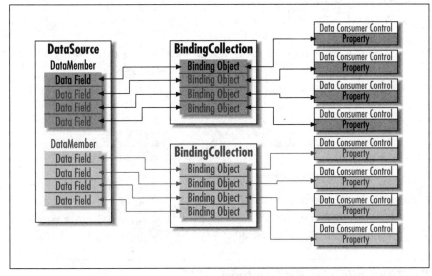

Figure 7-1: How data-binding elements relate to each other

DataMember

Type: DataMember

An optional string specifying the data member to use from the data source. This is useful where the source provides more than one data member. A DataSource application can provide many data members; you need to create a BindingCollection object for each data member to which you wish to bind.

DataSource

Data Type: DataSource

A valid data source object such as an ADO recordset or a VB class object set to **vbDataSource**. The DataSource is distinct from the DataMember; the DataSource is the application providing the data, whereas the Data-Member is a discrete recordset within the DataSource.

Item

Data Type: Binding Object

Returns a Binding object. If you use a key string in the Add method, you can also access the Binding object by key, as in:

```
obcAuthors.Item("fname")
```

UpdateMode

Type: UpdateMode enumerated constant (see below)

Specifies at what stage the data source is updated. However, if you open a recordset as read-only, no update occurs.

Reference

UpdateMode Constants

`vbUpdateWhenPropertyChanges`
> Value: 1

> Don't use this constant when dealing with VB class data sources. I found it disabled the Binding object's DataChanged property.

`vbUpdateWhenRowChanges`
> Value: 2

> The recordset is updated.

`vbUsePropertyAttributes`
> Value: 0

> Not relevant to class data sources.

BindingCollection Methods

The BindingCollection object supports the Add. Clear, and Remove collection object methods. For details, see the entries for each method.

BindingCollection.Add Method (VB6)

Named Arguments

Yes

Syntax

```
oBindingColl.Add Object, PropertyName, DataField[, _
                 DataFormat[, Key]]
```

`oBindingColl`
> Use: Required

> Data Type: BindingCollection object

> An object reference that returns a BindingCollection object.

`Object`
> Use: Required

> Data Type: Object

> The data consumer object. Either a form, control, or VB data bound class.

`PropertyName`
> Use: Required

> Data Type: String

> The property of the consumer object to be bound to *DataField*

`DataField`
> Use: Required

> Data Type: String

> The field of the recordset to be bound to *PropertyName*.

`DataFormat`
> Use: Optional

Data Type: StdDataFormat object

An object reference to a stdDataFormat object; see the Data Format Objects entry for additional detail.

Key

Use: Optional

Data Type: String

A unique string value to allow direct access to the Binding object.

Description

You use the Add method to create the link between a field in the data provider object and a field in the data consumer object.

The Add method of the BindingCollection object is identical in concept to any other collection's Add method. The BindingCollection object uses the Add method to assign various properties and to create a new Binding object in the collection.

Rules at a Glance

Object must be a data consumer object. It can be any form, control, form object, or even a VB class.

Programming Tips & Gotchas

* The data provider object is assigned to the BindingCollection by assigning an object reference to the DataSource property. Both the DataSource and DataMember properties should be assigned before adding Binding objects to the collection using the Add method.

* The Binding object provides simple binding, where each field of the data provider is mapped to an individual property of a data consumer. Don't use the Add method to bind complex controls or a complex bound data consumer class. (In complex binding, the data consumer is bound to a complete row of a recordset.)

* Many VB programmers now select property names from the IntelliSense dropdown lists or use statement completion. But these features (i.e., IntelliSense and statement completion) don't apply to the *PropertyName* parameter, which is a string value. This allows greater flexibility in runtime code, but creates a greater chance of typo errors creeping into your code.

* Although *key* is optional, it's recommended that you provide a meaningful key for your Binding object. This key allows you to directly reference the Binding object in the BindingCollection later in your application.

* If the purpose of the format object defined by *DataFormat* is incompatible with the control being bound, the Add method generates an error.

Example

```
obcAuthors.DataMember = "Authors"

Set obcAuthors.DataSource = oSource

obcAuthors.Add txtFirstName, "Text", "au_fname", fmtF1, _
```

Reference

```
                      "fname"
    obcAuthors.Add txtLastName, "Text", "au_lname", fmtF1, _
                      "lname"
```

See Also

Binding Object

BindingCollection.Clear Method (VB6)

Syntax

```
oBindingColl.Clear
oBindingColl
```
Use: Required

Data Type: BindingCollection object

An object reference that returns a BindingCollection object.

Description

Removes all previously added Binding objects from the BindingCollection object.

Programming Tips & Gotchas

It's not necessary to use the Clear method before setting the BindingCollection object to Nothing. If all references to Binding objects within the collection have been set to Nothing when the BindingCollection is set to Nothing, the object is destroyed cleanly.

BindingCollection Remove.Method (VB6)

Named Arguments

Yes

Syntax

```
oBindingColl.Remove(Binding)
oBindingColl
```
Use: Required

Data Type: BindingCollection object

An object reference that returns a BindingCollection object.

Binding
Use: Required

Data Type: Binding object

A reference to a binding object in the BindingCollection.

Description

Removes a previously added Binding object from the BindingCollection object.

Programming Tips & Gotchas

Unlike most other Remove methods attached to collections in VBA, the Binding-Collection's Remove method's parameter is a reference to the object being removed from the collection.

Example

In this short snippet, we access the Item method using the key assigned to the Binding object we want to remove. The method call assigns a reference to the Binding object to be removed to our local *oBind* object variable, which can then be passed to the Remove method. We then set the *Bind* object variable to Nothing afterwards. The For Each...Next statement proves that the object has been removed.

```
Set oBind = obcAuthors.Item("address")
   obcAuthors.Remove oBind
Set oBind = Nothing

For Each oBind In obcAuthors
   Debug.Print oBind.Key
Next
```

Binding Object (VB6)

Description

The binding object represents the binding of one property of one form control (or another data consumer) to a data source. The data consumer represented by the Binding object's Object property can be a form control—or the form itself, or a VB class with its DataBindingBehavior set to either vbSimpleBound or vbComplex-Bound. The data consumer's property that is updated by the data source is represented by the string assigned to the PropertyName property. The data source can be any valid data source, such as an ADO recordset or a VB class with its DataSouceBehavior property set to vbDataSource

For an overview of data binding objects, including the library reference needed to access the object model, see the Data Binding Objects entry. See the BindingCollection object for more detail about data binding and an example demonstrating the use of the Binding object.

Createable

Yes

Properties

DataChanged
Data Type: Boolean

A True or False flag that indicates if the user has changed the data value. If the data value is the same as the recordset, the DataChanged property is **False**; if not, the value is **True**. Note that changing the property value by navigating through the recordset doesn't change the DataChanged property.

DataField

Data Type: String

The name of the field in the recordset held by the data source that is bound to the property in the data consumer control.

DataFormat

Data Type: StdDataFormat

A stdDataFormat object that specifies the type of formatting to apply to the data.

Key

Data Type: String

An optional key to quickly reference an individual binding object from within the collection.

Object

Data Type: Object

The data consumer object, either a form, a control, or a VB class with its DataBindingBehavior property set to **vbSimpleBound** or **vbComplex-Bound**.

PropertyName

Data Type: String

The name of the property in the data consumer object that is assigned the value from the DataField property.

Calendar Property

Syntax

```
Calendar = calendarconstant
```

calendarconstant can be either of the following constants:

Constant	Value	Description
vbCalGreg	0	Application uses the Gregorian calendar (default)
vbCalHijri	1	Application uses the Hijri calendar

Description

Returns or sets a value specifying the type of calendar to use with your project. The Gregorian calendar year of 1998 (which is based on the birth of Christ) is roughly equivalent to the Hijri year of 1418 (which is based on the birth of Mohammed). Note that the new year of each calendar is different, and the Hijri calendar, being based more accurately on the cycles of the moon, is 11 days shorter than the Gregorian calendar.

Example

```
Calendar = vbCalHijri
MsgBox Format(Now, "dd-mm-yyyy")
```

Programming Tips & Gotchas

Unless you are writing applications that will be used by or for users living or working in certain Muslim countries that use the Hijri calendar (for example, Saudi Arabia), you shouldn't need to set the Calendar property.

Call Statement

Syntax

```
[Call] procedurename [argumentlist]
Call
```

> Use: Optional

procedurename

> Use: Required

> Data Type: n/a

> The name of the subroutine being called.

argumentlist

> Use: Optional

> Data Type: Any

> A comma-delimited list of parameters to pass to the subroutine being called.

Description

Passes execution control to a procedure, function, or dynamic-link library (DLL) procedure.

Rules at a Glance

*   Components of *argumentlist* may include the keywords ByVal or ByRef to describe how the arguments are treated by the called procedure. However, ByVal and ByRef can be used with Call only when calling a DLL procedure defined with the Declare statement. ByRef indicates that the variable's address in memory, rather than its value, is to be passed to the external routine; this means that, should the external routine modify the variable's value, this change is reflected in the variable's value when the external DLL routine returns control to the calling procedure. ByVal, on the other hand, indicates that the parameter is passed to the DLL routine *by value*; in other words, a copy of the value, rather than its location in memory, is passed to the external library routine. This means that, if the parameter is a variable, the external routine can't modify its value. (An exception is a string expression that's passed by value to a DLL routine. All strings are passed by reference to external DLLs; however, a string passed using the ByVal keyword is passed by reference as a C string; whereas a string passed using the ByRef keyword is passed by reference as a Visual Basic string.)

- You aren't required to use the `Call` keyword when calling a procedure. However, if you use the `Call` keyword to call a procedure that requires arguments, `argumentlist` must be enclosed in parentheses. If you omit the `Call` keyword from the procedure call, you must also omit the parentheses around `argumentlist`.

- If you use either `Call` syntax to call any intrinsic or user-defined function, the function's return value is discarded.

Example

```
Call myProcedure(True, iMyInt)

Sub myProcedure(blnFlag as Boolean, iNumber as Integer)
...
End Sub
```

Programming Tips & Gotchas

- To pass a whole array to a procedure, use the array name followed by empty parentheses.

- Your code will be easier to read and understand if you explicitly use the `Call` keyword.

See Also

Sub Statement, Function Statement

CallByName Function (VB6)

Named Arguments

No

Syntax

```
CallByName(object, procedurename, calltype, _
           [argument1,..., argumentn])
```

object
> Use: Required
>
> Data Type: Object
>
> A reference to the object containing the procedure being called.

procedurename
> Use: Required
>
> Data Type: String
>
> The name of the procedure to call.

calltype
> Use: Required
>
> Data Type: vbCallType constant
>
> A constant that indicates the type of procedure being called. vbCallType constants are listed in the next table.

---

arguments

Use: Optional

Data Type: Variant

Any number of variant arguments, depending on the argument list of the procedure to call.

Constant	Value	Description
vbGet	2	The called procedure is a **Property Get**
vbLet	4	The called procedure is a **Property Let**
vbMethod	1	The called procedure is a method; this can be a Sub or a Function within *object*
vbSet	8	The called procedure is a **Property Set**

Return Value

Depends on the return value (if any) of the called procedure.

Description

Provides a flexible method for calling a public procedure in a VB object module. Since *procedurename* is a string expression, rather than the hard-coded name of a routine, it's possible to call routines dynamically at runtime with a minimum of coding.

Rules at a Glance

* The return type of *CallByName* is the return type of the called procedure.

* *procedurename* isn't case sensitive.

Programming Tips & Gotchas

* At last, VB allows you to create a call to a procedure using a string. This means that the call can be flexible at runtime.

* The only drawback to the current implementation of *CallByName* is that the parameters to pass to the called function must be entered individually. This means that, when coding the *CallByName* function, you need to know in advance how many parameters are needed. You could work around this by coding your functions to accept only Variant arrays so that you only need to pass a single parameter.

* Late binding is necessarily used to instantiate objects whose procedures are invoked by the *CallByName* function. Consequently, the performance of *CallByName* is inferior to that of method invocations in early bound objects. This degradation of performance is especially acute if *CallByName* is invoked repeatedly inside a looping structure.

Example

The following example takes *CallByName* and the amendments to *CreateObject* to their logical conclusion: a variable procedure call to a variable ActiveX server in a variable location. In this example, the SQL Server *pubs* database is used as the

Reference

source of the data. Two ActiveX objects on two separate machines are used to create two different recordsets: one from the Authors table, the other from the Titles table. However, nowhere in the program are the names of the ActiveX DLLs, the procedures, or the remote servers mentioned.

The middle tier of this application uses the registry to store these names, allowing fast alteration of the application without touching a single line of code or creating incompatibilities between components. The repercussions of this approach to enterprise-wide programming are wide-reaching, and the prospects very exciting.

Only when dealing with the user interface of the client component are the names of the required datasets and fields specified. The Form_Load event calls a standard function to populate combo box controls with the required data:

```
Private Sub Form_Load()


    PopulateCombo cboAuthors, "Authors", "au_lname"
    PopulateCombo cboTitles, "Titles", "title"


End Sub
```

The *PopulateCombo* function calls a *GetRecordset* function in the first middle tier of the model, passing in the recordset name required (either Authors or Titles in this case) and a search criteria string that is concatenated into the embedded SQL script to refine the recordset. *GetRecordset* returns an ADO recordset that populates the desired combo box:

```
Private Function PopulateCombo(oCombo As ComboBox, _
                    sRecords As String, _
                    sField As String) As Boolean

    Dim adorRecords As ADODB.Recordset
    Dim sSearch As String

    If sRecords = "Authors" Then
        sSearch = "contract = 1 AND state = 'CA'"
    Else
        sSearch = ""
    End If

    Set adorRecords = oAdmin.GetRecordset(sRecords, sSearch)

    Do While Not adorRecords.EOF
        oCombo.AddItem adorRecords(sField)
        adorRecords.MoveNext
    Loop

    adorRecords.Close
    Set adorRecords = Nothing

End Function
```

The GetRecordset method that sits on a central machine interrogates the registry (using the *GetSetting* function) to determine the names of the ActiveX server, the machine, and the procedure to call. I've also coded an alternative method of obtaining these names using a `Select Case` statement (which is commented out in the code sample). Finally, the *CreateObject* function obtains a reference to the appropriate ActiveX server on the appropriate machine and a call is made to the function in that server to obtain the correct recordset:

```
Public Function GetRecordset(sRecords As String, _
                             sCriteria As String _
                             ) As ADODB.Recordset

    Dim sServer     As String
    Dim sLocation   As String
    Dim sMethod     As String

    Dim oServer     As Object

    sServer = GetSetting(App.Title, sRecords, "Server")
    sLocation = GetSetting(App.Title, sRecords, "Location")
    sMethod = GetSetting(App.Title, sRecords, "GetMethod")

' An alternative method of obtaining the names of the
' elements of the remote procedure call is to hard-code
' them into the application as follows:
'     Select Case sRecords
'         Case Is = "Titles"
'             sServer = "TestDLL.Titles"
'             sLocation = "NTSERV1"
'             sMethod = "GetTitles"
'         Case Is = "Authors"
'             sServer = "Test2DLL.Authors"
'             sLocation = "NTWS2"
'             sMethod = "getAuthors"
'         Case Else
'             Set GetRecordset = Nothing
'             Exit Function
'     End Select

    Set oServer = CreateObject(sServer, sLocation)

    Set GetRecordset = CallByName(oServer, _
                                  sMethod, _
                                  VbMethod, _
                                  sCriteria)

End Function
```

The code to create the recordsets in `TestDLL.Titles` and `Test2DLL.Authors` isn't shown here, as it's straightforward database access code.

Now, imagine for a moment that the organization using this application wanted a minor alteration in the way the Authors recordset was presented to the client (a different sort order, for example). You can now make a change to the procedure, calling it *getAuthorsRev*; compile a completely new ActiveX server; and place it on the remote server. Then with two quick edits of the registry, all the clients in the organization would instantly access the new procedure with a minimum of fuss, no loss of component compatibility, zero downtime, and an almost seamless transition.

See Also

Call Statement

CBool Function

Named Arguments

No

Syntax

```
CBool(expression)
```
expression

    Use: Required

    Data Type: String or Numeric

    Any numeric expression or a string representation of a numeric value.

Return Value

expression converted to Boolean data type (`True` or `False`).

Description

Casts *expression* as a Boolean data type. Expressions that evaluate to 0 are converted to `False` (0), and expressions that evaluate to nonzero values are converted to `True` (−1).

Rules at a Glance

If the expression to be converted is a string, the string must be capable of being treated as a number. Therefore, `CBool("ONE")` results in a type mismatch error, yet `CBool("1")` converts to `True`.

Programming Tips & Gotchas

- You can check the validity of the expression prior to using the *CBool* function by using the *IsNumeric* function.

- When you convert an expression to a Boolean, an expression that evaluates to 0 is converted to `False` (0), and any nonzero number is converted to `True` (−1). Therefore, a Boolean `False` can be converted back to its original value (i.e., 0), but the original value of the `True` expression can't be restored unless it was originally −1.

See Also

IsNumeric Function

CByte Function

Named Arguments

No

Syntax

```
CByte(expression)
expression
```
> Use: Required
>
> Data Type: Numeric or String
>
> A string or numeric expression that evaluates to between 0 and 255.

Return Value

expression converted to Byte data type.

Description

Converts *expression* to a Byte data type. The byte data type is the smallest data storage device in VBA. Being only one byte in length, it can store unsigned numbers between 0 and 255.

Rules at a Glance

- If *expression* is a string, the string must be capable of being treated as a number.
- If *expression* evaluates to less than 0 or more than 255, an overflow error is generated.
- If *expression* isn't a whole number, *CByte* rounds the number prior to conversion.

Example

```
If IsNumeric(sMyNumber) Then
    If val(sMyNumber) >= 0 and val(sMyNumber) <= 255 Then
        BytMyNumber = Cbyte(sMyNumber)
    End If
End If
```

Programming Tips & Gotchas

- Check that the value you pass to *CByte* is neither negative nor greater than 255.
- Use *IsNumeric* to insure the value passed to *CByte* can be converted to a numeric expression.
- When using *CByte* to convert floating point numbers, fractional values up to but not including .5 are rounded down, while values of .5 and above are rounded up.

See Also

IsNumeric Function, Chapter 3

Reference

CCur Function

Named Arguments

No

Syntax

```
CCur(expression)
expression
```
> Use: Required
>
> Data Type: Numeric or String
>
> A string or numeric expression that evaluates to a number between –922,337,203,685,477.5808 and 922,337,203,685,477.5807.

Return Value

expression converted to a currency data type.

Description

Converts an expression into a currency data type. The currency data type is stored in eight bytes, with a precision to four decimal places.

Rules at a Glance

- If the expression passed to the function is outside the range of the Currency data type, an overflow error occurs.

- Expressions containing more than four decimal places are rounded to four decimal places.

- The only localized information included in the value returned by *CCur* is the decimal symbol.

Example

```
If IsNumeric(sMyNumber) Then
    curMyNumber = CCur(sMyNumber)
End If
```

Programming Tips & Gotchas

- It's often tempting to use the *Val* function to return a numeric data type from a string. However, you should always use the correct data type function, which takes account of the computer's regional settings. In particular, *CCur* can successfully handle currency symbols and thousands separators embedded in a currency string, whereas *Val* can't. This means, for example, that if the user inputs a string value of $1,200.68, the *CCur* function can successfully convert it to a currency value of 1200.68, whereas *Val* returns a value of 0.

- *CCur* doesn't prepend or append a currency symbol; for this, you need to use the *Format* function or (in VB6) the new *FormatCurrency* function. *CCur* does, however, correctly convert strings that include a localized currency symbol. For instance, if a user enters the string "$ 1234.68" into a text box whose

Text property is passed as a parameter to the *CCur* function, *CCur* correctly returns a currency value of 1234.68.

- *CCur* doesn't include the thousands separator; for this, you need to use the *Format* function or (in VB6) the new *FormatCurrency* function. *CCur* does, however, correctly convert currency strings that include localized thousands separators. For instance, if a user enters the string "1,234.68" into a text box whose Text property is passed as a parameter to the *CCur* function, *CCur* correctly converts it to a currency value of 1234.68.

See Also

Format Function, FormatCurrency Function, FormatNumber Function, Chapter 3

CDate Function

Named Arguments

No

Syntax

```
CDate(expression)
expression
```
   Use: Required

   Data Type: String or Numeric

   Any valid date expression.

Return Value

expression converted into a Date data type.

Description

Converts *expression* to a Date data type. The format of *expression*—the order of day, month, and year—is determined by the locale setting of your computer. To be certain of a date being recognized correctly by *CDate*, the month, day, and year elements of *expression* must be in the same sequence as your computer's regional settings; otherwise the *CDate* function has no idea that 4 is supposed to be the 4th of the month, not the month of April.

CDate also converts numbers to a date. The precise behavior of the function, however, depends on the value of *expression*:

- If *expression* is less than or equal to 23 and includes a fractional component less than 60, the integer is interpreted as the number of hours since midnight, and the fraction is interpreted as the number of seconds.

- In all other cases, the integer portion of *expression* is converted to a date that interprets the integer as the number of days before (in the case of negative numbers) or after December 31, 1899, and its fractional part is converted to the time of day, with every .01 representing 864 seconds (14 minutes 24 seconds) after midnight.

Reference

Rules at a Glance

- *CDate* accepts both numerical date expressions and string literals. You can pass month names into *CDate* in either complete or abbreviated form; for example, "31 Dec 1997" is correctly recognized.

- You can use any of the date delimiters specified in your computer's regional settings; for most systems, this includes ",", "/", "-", and " ".

- The oldest date that can be handled by the Date data type is 01/01/100, which in VBA terms equates to the number –657434. Therefore, if you try to convert a number of greater magnitude than –657434 with *CDate*, an error ("Type mismatch") is generated.

- The furthest date into the future that can be handled by the Date data type is 31/12/9999, which in VBA terms equates to the number 2958465. Therefore, if you try to convert a number higher than 2958465 with *CDate*, an error ("Type mismatch") is generated.

- A "Type mismatch" error is generated if the values supplied in **expresssion** are invalid. However, *CDate* tries to treat a month value greater than 12 as a day value.

Programming Tips & Gotchas

- Use the *IsDate* function to determine if **expression** can be converted to a date or time.

- A common error is to pass an uninitialized variable to *CDate*, in which case 31 December 1899 is returned.

- A modicum of intelligence has been built into the *CDate* function. It can determine the day and month from a string regardless of their position, but only where the day number is larger than 12, which automatically distinguishes it from the number of the month. For example, if the string "30/12/97" were passed into the *CDate* function on a system expecting a date format of mm/dd/yy, *CDate* sees that 30 is obviously too large for a month number and treats it as the day. It's patently impossible for *CDate* to second guess what you mean by "12/5/97"—is it the 12th of May, or 5th of December? In this situation, *CDate* relies on the regional settings of the computer to distinguish between day and month. This can also lead to problems, as you may have increased a month value to more than 12 inadvertently in an earlier routine, thereby forcing *CDate* to treat it as the day value. If your real day value is 12 or less, no error is generated, and a valid, albeit incorrect, date is returned.

- If you pass a two-digit year into *CDate*, how does it know which century you are referring to? Is "10/20/97" 20 October 1997 or 20 October 2097? The answer is that two-year digits less than 30 are treated as being in the 21st Century (i.e., 29 = 2029), and two-year digits of 30 and over are treated as being in the 20th Century (i.e., 30 = 1930).

- Don't follow a day number with "st", "nd", "rd", or "th", since this generates a type mismatch error.

- If you don't specify a year, the *CDate* function uses the year from the current date on your computer.

- A *CVDate* function is also provided for compatibility with earlier versions of Visual Basic. The syntax of the *CVDate* function is identical to the *CDate* function. However, *CVDate* returns a Variant whose subtype is Date instead of an actual Date type. Since there is now an intrinsic Date type, there is no further need for *CVDate*.

- The Date data type is basically a Double data type. You can therefore return the underlying date number (i.e., the number of days after or before 31 December 1899) by converting the date variable to a double. For example:

```
Dim dtDate as Date
Dim dblDate as Double
Dim sDate as string
SDate = "31/12/97"
DtDate = Cdate(sDate)
DblDate = CDbl(DtDate) 'returns 35795
```

This can be useful for converting back and forth between Unix dates, which have a starting point of 1 January 1970 (VB date number 25569), and are based as number of seconds, as this snippet demonstrates:

```
Dim dblDate As Double
Dim dblUnix As Double

dblDate = CDbl(dtDate)
dblUnix = (dblDate - 25569) * 86400
```

- All date functions, including *CDate*, are affected by the application's Calendar property setting. For example, if the Calendar property has been set to **vbCalHijri**, the underlying date number is increased by 206362.

See Also

CVDate Function, Calendar Property, Format Function, FormatDateTime Function

---

CDbl Function

Named Arguments

No

Syntax

CDbl(*expression*)

expression

Use: Required

Data Type: Numeric or String

$-1.79769313486232E308$ to $-4.94065645841247E-324$ for negative values; $4.94065645841247E-324$ to $1.79769313486232E308$ for positive values.

Return Value

expression cast as a Double data type.

Description

Converts *expression* to a Double data type.

Rules at a Glance

- If the value of *expression* is outside the range of the double data type, an overflow error is generated.

- Expression must evaluate to a numeric value; otherwise, a type mismatch error is generated.

Example

```
Dim dblMyNumber as Double
If IsNumeric(sMyNumber) then
    dblMyNumber = CDbl(sMyNumber)
End If
```

Programming Tips & Gotchas

- When converting a string representation of a number to a numeric, you should use the data type conversion functions—such as *CDbl*—instead of *Val*, because the data type conversion functions take account of the system's regional settings. While *CDbl* recognizes and handles the thousands separator, the *Val* function can't. If a user inputs a value of 6,231,532.11, for example, *CDbl* correctly converts it to a double with a value of 6231532.11, while *Val* returns a value of 6.

- Use *IsNumeric* to test whether *expression* evaluates to a number.

See Also

FormatNumberFunction, IsNumeric Function, Val Function

CDec Function

Named Arguments

No

Syntax

```
CDec(expression)
```
expression

> Use: Required

> Data Type: Numeric or String

> The range is +/–79,228,162,514,264,337,593,543,950,335 for numbers with no decimal places. For numbers with up to 28 decimal places, the range is +/–7.9228162514264337593543950335. The smallest possible nonzero number is 0.0000000000000000000000000001.

Return Value

expression cast as a Variant Decimal subtype.

Description

As there is no intrinsic Decimal data type in Visual Basic, *CDec* actually casts expression as a variant of subtype Decimal.

Rules at a Glance

- If the value of **expression** is outside the range of the double data type, an overflow error is generated.

- **Expression** must evaluate to a numeric value; otherwise a type-mismatch error is generated. To prevent this, it can be tested beforehand with the *IsNumeric* function.

Example

```
Dim decMyNumber
If IsNumeric(sMyNumber) then
    decMyNumber = CDec(sMyNumber)
End If
```

Programming Tips & Gotchas

- Use the Decimal variant subtype for very large, very small, or very high precision numbers.

- Use *IsNumeric* to test whether **expression** evaluates to a number.

- When converting a string representation of a number to a numeric, you should use the data type conversion functions—such as *CDec*—instead of *Val*, because the data type conversion function takes account of the system's regional settings. In particular, the *CDec* function recognizes the thousands separator if it's encountered in the string representation of a number. For example, if the user inputs the value 1,827,209.6654, *CDec* converts it to the decimal value 1827209.6654, while *Val* converts it to a double value of 1.

See Also

CVar Function, FormatNumber Function, Val Function

ChDir Statement

Named Arguments

No

Syntax

```
ChDir path
path
```
Use: Required

Data Type: String

The path of the directory to set as the new default directory.

Description

Changes the current working (default) directory.

Reference

Rules at a Glance

- *Path* can be an absolute or relative reference.
- On Windows systems, changing the default directory doesn't change the default drive; it changes only a particular drive's default directory.

Example

```
sNewDir = "c:\program files\my folder\"
ChDir sNewDir
...
ChDir ".." 'c:\program files is now the default directory.
```

Programming Tips & Gotchas

- Remember that on the Apple Power Macintosh, the relative notation "::" moves to the next higher folder, whereas on Windows 95 and NT, the notation is "..".
- On Windows systems, the relative notation "." represents the current directory.
- On Windows systems, the relative notation ".." represents the parent of the current directory. If the root directory is the current directory, the statement:

```
ChDir ".."
```

doesn't change the current directory and doesn't produce a syntax error.

- On the Apple Power Macintosh, ChDir changes both the default directory and the default drive.
- On Windows systems, the current drive is unaffected by ChDir. For instance, if the current drive is *C:* and you issue the statement:

```
ChDir "D:\MyFolder"
```

the current directory on drive D: is changed to *D:\MyFolder*, but the current drive is still *C:*.

- If *path* isn't found, a trappable error, 76, "Path not found," is generated. However, if *path* refers to another machine on the network, error 75, "Path/File access error," is generated.
- Although you can use a network path such as *\\NTSERV1\d$\TestDir* to change the current directory on the network admin share *\\NTSERV1\d$*, you can't access this drive using ChDrive without having the drive mapped to a drive letter, which makes using network paths with ChDir a little pointless!
- Use *CurDir* to determine the current default directory for a particular drive.
- If you are using VB6, you will find that the new File System objects offer much more flexibility than the intrinsic drive and directory statements.

See Also

ChDrive Statement, CurDir Function, MkDir Statement, Name Statement, RmDir Statement, File System Objects

ChDrive Statement

Named Arguments

No

Syntax

```
ChDrive driveletter
driveletter
```
> Use: Required
>
> Data Type: String
>
> The letter of the drive (A–Z) to set as the new default drive.

Description

Changes the current working (default) disk drive.

Rules at a Glance

- If a zero-length string is supplied, the drive isn't changed.

- If *driveletter* consists of more than one character, only the first character determines the drive.

Example

The following example demonstrates a utility function that uses ChDrive to determine if a given drive is available. By centralizing the test, the function reduces the amount of coding required each time you need to use ChDrive:

```
Private Function IsAvailableDrive(sDrive As String) _
                As Boolean

    'if an error occurs goto to the next line of code
    On Error Resume Next

    Dim sCurDrv As String

    'get the letter of the current drive
    sCurDrv = Left$(CurDir$, 1)
    'attempt to change the drive
    ChDrive sDrive
    'did an error occur?
    If Err.Number = 0 Then
        'no - this drive is OK to use
        IsAvailableDrive = True
    Else
        'yes - don't use this drive
        IsAvailableDrive = False
    End If
    'set the drive back to what it was
    ChDrive sCurDrv

End Function
```

The following snippet shows how this function could be implemented within your application:

```
If IsAvailableDrive(sDrv) Then
    ChDrive sDrv
Else
    MsgBox "Cannot use Drive " & sDrv & ":\"
End If
```

Programming Tips & Gotchas

- On the Macintosh, ChDrive changes the current folder to the root folder of the specified drive. On Windows systems, the default directory is unaffected by the ChDrive statement.

- As ChDrive processes only the first letter of the *driveletter* string, it isn't possible to supply a piped name network drive name (e.g., *//NTServer/*); instead, the machine your program is running on must have a drive letter mapped to the network resource using Explorer or other network commands. If *driveLetter* is specified as a UNC path, the function raises error number 5, "Invalid procedure call or argument."

- If *driveLetter* is invalid, the function returns error number 68, "Device unavailable."

- If you are using VB6, you will find that the new File System Objects offer much more flexibility than the intrinsic drive and directory statements, especially when it comes to dealing with network drives.

See Also

ChDir Statement, File System Objects

Choose Function

Named Arguments

No

Syntax

```
Choose(index, item1[, item2, ...[,itemn]])
```
index

    Use: Required

    Data Type: Single

    An expression that evaluates to the number of the item to choose from the list.

item1 – n

    Use: Required

    Data Type: Variant

    A comma-delimited list of values from which to choose.

Return Value

A variant data type item chosen from the list; the data subtype is that of the chosen item.

Description

Programmatically selects an item from a predefined list of values (which are passed as parameters to the function) based on its ordinal position in the list. Using *Choose* is a simpler alternative to populating an array with fixed values.

Rules at a Glance

- The list of items is based from 1, rather than the more usual VB default base of 0.

- Because the list of values is a variant parameter array, you can mix data subtypes within the list; you aren't forced to use the same data subtype for each item in the list. For example, *item1* can be a variant string, *item2* a long integer, and *item3* a floating point number.

- The list of values can't be expanded or contracted programmatically, but the items within the list can be generated dynamically by including the return value of a function call. For example:

```
vChosenOption = Choose(iOption, vFunction1(), _
                vFunction2(), vFunction3())
```

Example

Choose is useful for returning some result based on an option button selection. This is most straightforward with Visual Basic, which supports control arrays. For example:

```
Private Sub Option1_Click(Index As Integer)

Form1.BackColor = Choose(Index + 1, &HFF&, _
                  &HFF00&, &HFF0000)

End Sub
```

Within Office/VBA (which doesn't support control arrays), using the *Choose* function to handle the an option button selection is still useful:

```
Private Sub SetBackgroundColor(Index As Integer)

    UserForm1.BackColor = Choose(Index, &HFF&, &HFF00&, _
                          &HFF0000)

End Sub

Private Sub OptionButton1_Click()
   SetBackgroundColor 1
End Sub

Private Sub OptionButton2_Click()
   SetBackgroundColor 2
End Sub
```

Reference

```
Private Sub OptionButton3_Click()
    SetBackgroundColor 3
End Sub
```

Programming Tips & Gotchas

- Passing an index value that is either negative, zero, or greater than the number of items in the list returns a variant data subtype of Null without generating an error. Because the return value is a variant, you should check for it by calling the *IsNull* function, as shown below; otherwise, you'll generate an "Invalid use of Null" error when you try to use the result:

```
Dim z As Variant
z = Choose(0, "Eany", "Meany", "Miney", "Mo")
If IsNull(z) Then
    MsgBox "bad choice"
Else
    MsgBox z
End If
```

- Strangely, the data type of *index* is Single, and not an Integer as you may have expected (though it's hard to believe anyone would hand-code a list of more than 32,767 items to warrant a Long!). Does this mean you can choose the 1.234th item in the list? No, of course not; the index number is automatically rounded down to a whole number prior to being used to select an item.

- One word of warning when using the return value of functions to populate the *Choose* list: All items in the list are evaluated. This means that every call to the *Choose* function generates calls to each of the functions listed, which in turn means that you must be sure that each function has the ability to be successfully executed without causing undesirable side effects each time you call the *Choose* function.

- You can save memory and create more efficient and self documenting code by using the *Choose* function in preference to creating an array and populating it with fixed values each time the program executes. As the following example illustrates, you can turn several lines of code into one:

```
Dim vMyArray(3)
vMyArray(1) = "This"
vMyarray(2) = "That"
vMyArray(3) = "The Other"
...
Sub chooseFromArray(iIndex as Integer)
    vResult = vMyArray(iIndex)
End Sub

Sub chooseFromChoose(sglIndex as Single)
    vResult = Choose(sglIndex, "This", "That", "The Other")
End Sub
```

See Also

IIf Function, Select Case Statement, Switch Statement

Chr, Chr$, ChrB, ChrB$, ChrW Functions

Named Arguments

No

Syntax

```
Chr(charactercode)
Chr$(charactercode)
ChrB(charactercode)
ChrB$(charactercode)
ChrW(charactercode)
charactercode
```

> Use: Required
>
> Data Type: Long
>
> An expression that evaluates to either an ASCII or DBCS character code.

Return Value

Chr, *ChrB*, and *ChrW* return a variant of the string subtype that contains the character represented by *charactercode*.

Chr$* and *ChrB$ return a string containing the character represented by *charactercode*.

Description

Returns the character represented by *charactercode*.

Rules at a Glance

- *Chr* and *Chr$* return the character associated with an ASCII or ANSI character code.

- *ChrB* and *ChrB$* return a one-byte string variant or a one-byte string, respectively.

- *ChrW* returns a Unicode character; however, on systems that don't support the Unicode character set, the function behaves identically to the *Chr* function.

Programming Tips & Gotchas

- Use `Chr(34)` to embed quotation marks inside a string, as shown in the following example:

```
sSQL = "SELECT * FROM myTable _
        where myColumn = " & Chr(34) & sValue & Chr(34)
```

- It's up to you as the programmer to decide which variation of the function to use—that is, whether to use the string or variant version of the function. The String versions, *Chr$* and *ChrB$* use less memory than their variant counterparts; however, you may find the variant versions more flexible, since they convert data types automatically and handle Null values more cleanly.

- You can use the *ChrB* function to assign binary values to String variables. Try this little demonstration of outputting a Unicode character (Unicode characters are two bytes in length; for example, "F" is represented by binary 70 and binary 0):

```
Dim sBinVar As String
sBinVar = ChrB(70) & ChrB(0)
Debug.Print sBinVar
```

- You can use the *ChrW* function to return Unicode characters, but for the most part these are difficult to see in VB, as the immediate window, label, and text-box know how to display only the Unicode equivalent of ANSI characters! However, try this code to produce a Unicode "G":

```
Dim sBinVar As String
sBinVar = ChrW(AscW("G"))
Debug.Print sBinVar
```

Well, wasn't that exciting: a "G" was displayed in the immediate window! The difference is that the character displayed is a Unicode "G". I wouldn't, however, recommend that you try to convert all ANSI characters in this way; it's better to use the *StrConv* function.

- The following table lists some of the more commonly used character codes that are supplied in the call to the *Chr* function:

Code	Value	Description
0	NULL	For C/C++ string functions, the null character required to terminate standard strings; equivalent to the **vbNullChar** constant.
8	BS	Equivalent to the **vbBack** constant.
9	TAB	Equivalent to the **vbTab** constant.
10	CR	Equivalent to the **vbCr** and **vbCrLf** constants.
13	LF	Equivalent to the **vbLf** and **vbCrLf** constants.
34	"	Quotation mark. Useful to embed quotation marks within a literal string, especially when forming SQL query strings.

See Also

Asc Function, CStr Function, Str Function

CInt Function

Named Arguments

No

Syntax

```
CInt(expression)
```

expression

> Use: Required

> Data Type: Numeric or String

> The range of expression is –32,768 to 32,767; fractions are rounded.

Return Value

expression cast as an Integer.

Description

Converts *expression* to an integer; any fractional portion of *expression* is rounded.

Rules at a Glance

- *expression* must evaluate to a numeric value; otherwise a type mismatch error is generated.
- If the value of *expression* is outside the range of the Integer data type, an overflow error is generated.
- When the fractional part of *expression* is exactly 0.5, *CInt* always rounds it to the nearest even number. For example, 0.5 rounds to 0, and 1.5 rounds to 2.

Example

```
Dim iMyNumber as Integer
If IsNumeric(sMyNumber) then
    iMyNumber = CInt(sMyNumber)
End If
```

Programming Tips & Gotchas

- When converting a string representation of a number to a numeric, you should use the data type conversion functions—such as *CInt*—instead of *Val*, because the data type conversion functions take account of the system's regional settings. In particular, *CInt* recognizes the thousands separator if it's present in *expression*, whereas *Val* doesn't. For example, if *expression* is 1,234, *CInt* successfully converts it to the integer value 1234, while *Val* converts it to 1.
- Use *IsNumeric* to test whether *expression* evaluates to a number before performing the conversion.
- *CInt* differs from the *Fix* and *Int* functions, which truncate, rather than round, the fractional part of a number. Also, *Fix* and *Int* always return a value of the same type as was passed in.

See Also

Fix Function, FormatNumber Function, Int Function, IsNumeric Function

CLng Function

Named Arguments

No

Syntax

```
CLng(expression)
expression
    Use: Required
```

Data Type: Numeric or String

The range of *expression* is −2,147,483,648 to 2,147,483,647; fractions are rounded.

Return Value

expression cast as a Long data type.

Description

Converts *expression* to an long integer; any fractional element of *expression* is rounded.

Rules at a Glance

- *expression* must evaluate to a numeric value; otherwise, a type mismatch error is generated.

- If the value of *expression* is outside the range of the long data type, an overflow error is generated.

- When the fractional part is exactly 0.5, *CLng* always rounds it to the nearest even number. For example, 0.5 rounds to 0, and 1.5 rounds to 2.

Example

```
Dim lngMyNumber as Long
If IsNumeric(sMyNumber) then
    lngMyNumber = CLng(sMyNumber)
End If
```

Programming Tips & Gotchas

- When converting a string representation of a number to a numeric, you should use the data type conversion functions—such as *CLng*—instead of *Val*, because the data type conversion function takes account of the system's regional settings. In particular, *CLng* recognizes the thousands separator if it's included in *expression*, while *Val* can't. For example, if a user enters a value of 1,098,234 into a text box, *CLng* converts it to the long integer 1098234, but *Val* converts it to a value of 1.

- Use *IsNumeric* to test whether *expression* evaluates to a number.

- *CLng* differs from the *Fix* and *Int* functions, which truncate, rather than round, the fractional part of a number. Also, *Fix* and *Int* always return a value of the same type as was passed in.

See Also

Fix Function, FormatNumber Function, Int Function, IsNumeric Function, Val Function

---

Close Statement

Named Arguments

No

Syntax

```
Close [filenumber]
filenumber
```
    Use: Optional

    Data Type: Integer

    The file number used when opening the file in the Open statement.

Description

Closes a file opened with the Open statement.

Rules at a Glance

- If *filenumber* is omitted, all open files are closed.

- If the file you are closing was opened for output or append, the remaining data in the I/O buffer is written to the file. The memory buffer is then reclaimed.

- When the Close statement is executed, the file number used is freed for further use.

- The hash (#) sign in front of the file number is optional.

- *filenumber* can either be a numeric constant (e.g., #1) or a numeric variable.

Example

```
Dim intFileNo as Integer
intFileNo = FreeFile()
Open sFileNameString For Output As #intFileNo
Write #intFileNo, sOutputString
Close #intFileNo
```

Programming Tips & Gotchas

- You can close more than one file at once with the Close method, by specifying the file numbers as a comma-delimited list, as shown below:

```
Close #1, #3, #4
```

- The Close statement doesn't check first to see if there is a file associated with the given file number. Therefore, no error occurs if you use the Close statement with a nonexistent file number. The drawback to this is that you may think you have closed a file inadvertently when in fact you haven't, thereby leaving the file open, as this snippet demonstrates:

```
Dim sFilename As String
sFilename = "testtext.txt"

Open sFilename For Output As #1
Write #1, sFilename
Close #2
'just to prove the file is still open
Write #1, sFilename
```

See Also

Open Statement, File System Objects

Collection Object

Syntax

```
Dim objectvariable As [New] Collection
Set objectvariable = [New] Collection
objectvariable
    Use: Required

    Data Type: Collection

    The name of the Collection object.
```

Description

A Collection object allows you to store members of any data type, object, control, class, or another collection, and to retrieve them using a unique key. You can therefore create a structured collection object containing referential data. The real power of a collection comes by using collections with user-defined classes. (You can find details of creating and using class modules in Chapter 4, *Class Modules*.)

The collection is an intrinsic VBA object. VBA offers two method of creating a collection. The first uses the **New** keyword in the collection declaration; for example:

```
Dim obj As New Collection
Obj.Add Item:="Hello" Key:="Greeting"
```

Using the **New** keyword within the **Dim** statement forces an implied **Set** statement, which causes the Collection object to be instantiated at that point. The second syntax is:

```
Dim obj As Collection
Set obj = New Collection
Obj.Add Item:="Hello" Key:="Greeting"
```

In this second method, a **Set** statement is required to instantiate the collection, and is preferable in situations where the creation of the object is the result of a conditional statement, because if the condition fails, the collection isn't instantiated, and memory is saved. (Memory is still reserved for the collection, but there isn't the overhead involved in creating the collection.) In contrast, using the first syntax, the collection resides in memory, perhaps needlessly, regardless of the result of the conditional statement. The following code fragment, for instance, illustrates the use of the **Dim** and **Set** statements to conditionally create a Collection object:

```
Dim obj As Collection

If x = 10 then
    Set obj = New Collection
    Obj.Add Item:="Hello", Key:="Greeting"
Else
    Exit Sub
End If
```

The New keyword is required to create an instance of a collection that has not been instantiated.

You can add only one piece of data, object, or another collection to a particular "position" within a collection. This may at first glance seem somewhat limited. However, the important point to note is that you can add a collection to a collection; in fact, there is no limit to nesting collections within collections.

Rules at a Glance

- You can use a Collection object to store any data type, control, object, or another collection.

- Only one piece of data, etc. (known as a *member*) can be stored in each collection location (see the Collection.Add method).

- Members of a collection can be accessed either by using their ordinal number or by referring to the member's Key, assuming that one was assigned at the time that the member was added to the collection (see the Collection.Item method).

- Use the Count method to return the number of members in the collection.

- The first member in a collection is stored at ordinal position 1 (not at 0, as is the default for an array).

Example

This example shows how you can nest one collection within another. Basically, 10 instances of *colSubCollection* are created, each containing two integer values. These 10 *colSubCollection* objects are stored within *colMainCollection*. The code also shows how to read back the values of *colMainCollection* and *colSubCollection*:

```
Sub testCollection()
    'declare objects for the main and sub collections
    'creating a new instance of the main collection
    'in the process
    Dim colMainCollection As New Collection
    Dim colSubCollection As Collection

    For i = 1 To 10
        'create a new instance of the sub collection object
        Set colSubCollection = New Collection
        'populate the sub collection with two integer values
        colSubCollection.Add Item:=i + 6, _
                        Key:="MySixPlusVal"
        colSubCollection.Add Item:=i + 3, _
                        Key:="MyThreePlusVal"
        'now add the sub collection to the main collection
        'using the count converted to a string as the key
        colMainCollection.Add Item:=colSubCollection, _
                        Key:=CStr(i)
        'destroy the reference the sub collection
        Set colSubCollection = Nothing
    Next i
```

```
MsgBox colMainCollection.Count

For i = 1 To colMainCollection.Count
    'use the Item method to obtain a reference to the
    'subcollection
    Set colSubCollection = _
                    colMainCollection.Item(CStr(i))
    'display the values held in the sub collection.
    Debug.Print "6 + " & i & " = " & _
            colSubCollection.Item("MySixPlusVal")
    Debug.Print "3 + " & i & " = " & _
            colSubCollection.Item("MyThreePlusVal")
    'destroy the reference to the sub collection
    Set colSubCollection = Nothing
Next i

End Sub
```

Programming Tips & Gotchas

- A highly efficient method of enumerating the members of a collection uses the **For Each...Next** loop, as the following example shows:

```
Dim colMyCollection As New Collection
Dim colSubCollection As Collection

For i = 1 To 10
    Set colSubCollection = New Collection
    colSubCollection.Add Item:=i + 6, _
                    Key:="MySixPlusVal"
    colSubCollection.Add Item:=i + 3, _
                    Key:="MyThreePlusVal"
    colMyCollection.Add Item:=colSubCollection, _
                    Key:=CStr(i)
    Set colSubCollection = Nothing
Next i

For Each colSubCollection In colMyCollection
    MsgBox colSubCollection.Item("MySixPlusVal")
Next
```

- The recommended three-character code convention for the collection object is "col".

- If you are using VB6, you should also take a look at the Dictionary object, which is similar to the Collection object but operates faster and provides more built-in functionality.

See Also

Collection.Add Method, Collection.Count Property, Collection.Item Method, Collection.Remove Method, Dictionary Object, Dim Statement, For Each...Next Statement, Set Statement

Collection.Add Method

Named Arguments

Yes

Syntax

```
objectvariable.Add item [, key, before, after]
objectvariable
```
> Use: Required
>
> Data Type: Collection object
>
> The name of the Collection object to which an item is to be added.

```
item
```
> Use: Required
>
> Data Type: Any
>
> An expression of any type that specifies the member to add to the collection.

```
key
```
> Use: Optional
>
> Data Type: String
>
> A unique string expression that specifies a key string that can be used instead of a positional index to access a member of the collection.

```
before
```
> Use: Optional
>
> Data Type: String or Numeric
>
> An expression that specifies a relative position in the collection. The member to be added is placed in the collection before the member identified by the *before* argument.

```
after
```
> Key: Optional
>
> Data Type: String or Numeric
>
> An expression that specifies a relative position in the collection. The member to be added is placed in the collection after the member identified by the *after* argument.

Description

Adds a data item to a collection.

Rules at a Glance

- If you don't specify a *before* or *after* value, the member is appended to the end of the collection.

- If you don't specify a *key* value, you can't then access this member using a *key*, but instead must access it either by using its ordinal number or by enu-

Reference

merating all the members of the collection with the **For Each. . .Next** construct.

- Whether the *before* or *after* argument is a string expression or a numeric expression, it must refer to an existing member of the collection, or an error (runtime error 5, "Invalid procedure call or argument") occurs. If it's a string value, the key must exist; if numeric it must be between 1 and the maximum number of items.

- Key values must be unique or an error (runtime error 457, "This key is already associated with an element of this collection") is generated.

- You can specify a *before* or an *after* position, but not both.

Example

```
colMyCollection.Add Item:="Paul Lomax" Key:="Name"
```

Programming Tips & Gotchas

- Using named parameters helps to self-document your code:

```
colMyCollection.Add Item:="VB and VBA in a Nutshell"_
                    Key:="Title"
```

- If your key parameter is a value being brought in from outside your program, you must ensure that each value is always unique. One method for doing this is illustrated in the entry for the Collection.Item method.

See Also

Collection Object, Collection.Count Property, Collection.Item Method, Collection.Remove Method

---

Collection.Count Property

Syntax

```
objectvariable.Count
objectvariable
```

> Use: Required
>
> Data Type: Collection object
>
> Object variable referring to a Collection object.

Description

Returns the number of members in the collection.

Rules at a Glance

Collections are 1-based; that is, the index of the first element of a collection is 1. In contrast, arrays are 0-based; by default, the index of the first element of an array is 0.

Example

```
For i = 1 To colMyCollection.Count
    Set colSubCollection = colMyCollection.Item(CStr(i))
    MsgBox colSubCollection.Item("Name")
```

```
      Set colSubCollection = Nothing
   Next i
```

Programming Tips & Gotchas

Because collections are 1-based, you can iterate the members of a collection by using index values ranging from 1 to the value of *objectvariable*.Count.

See Also

Collection Object, Collection.Add Method, Collection.Count Property, Collection.Item Method

---

Collection.Item Method

Named Arguments

Yes

Syntax

```
objectvariable.Item(index)
objectvariable
```
> Use: Required

> Data Type: Collection object

> An object variable of type Collection.

```
index
```
> Use: Required

> Data Type: Numeric or String

> If a string, *index* is the key; if numeric, *index* is the ordinal position.

Description

Returns the member of the collection whose key or ordinal position corresponds to *index*.

Rules at a Glance

- If *index* is a string, it's taken to be the key, and the member of the collection with the key of *index* is returned.

- If *index* is a number, it's taken to be the *index* number and the member in the ordinal position *index* is returned.

- If *index* is a string and the key doesn't exist in the collection, an error (runtime error 5, "Invalid procedure call or argument") is generated.

- If *index* is numeric, it must be between 1 and the maximum number of items in the collection, or an error (runtime error 9, "Subscript out of range") is generated.

Programming Tips & Gotchas

- When writing wrapper classes for collections, you can make your object model more readable by making the name of the property that wraps the

Item method the same as the name of the object being obtained from the collection. For example, if your collection class is called Employees and is a collection of Employee records, your object model reads much better with an Employee **Property Get** procedure, as follows:

```
Public Property Get Employee(vEmpCode as Variant) _
                As Boolean
    Employee = mcolEmployees.Item(vEmpCode)
End Property
```

- Note that in the above **Property Get** procedure, the parameter is passed as a variant. This is because a Collection item can be extracted by its key (a string) or by its ordinal number (integer or long). Therefore, by passing a variant, your **Property Get** procedure can accept a number or a string, and the Item method determines whether to access the collection by its key or its ordinal number. There is, however, one little glitch here: what happens if you have used the string representation of a number for the key? For example:

```
iKey  = 10
mcol.Add Item:="Somestuff" Key:=CStr(iKey)
```

In this case, passing a string representation of the number as a variant doesn't work; the Item method is passed a number and assumes you want the item at that ordinal position.

- Unlike the Dictionary object in VB6, there is no Exists method in the Collection object, so you can't find out in advance if a particular key exists within the Collection. However, you can create an "Exists" function by calling the Item method with a given key and returning **True** if an item is returned or **False** if an error is generated, as the following code shows:

```
Public Function Exists(vKey As Variant) As Boolean

    On Error Resume Next

    msValue = mcolMyCollection.Item(vKey)

    If Err.Number = 0 Then
        Exists = True
    Else
        Exists = False
    End If

End Function
```

- When I create wrapper classes for collections, I always include an Exists function like the one shown above, but with a little extra—if the Item requested by the client doesn't exist, I attempt to load it into the collection, as this code demonstrates:

```
Public Function Exists(sEmpCode As String) As Boolean

On Error Goto Exists_Err
    'declare an object variable to hold the test object
    Dim oTest as Employee
    'attempt to get the Employee object from
```

```
     'the Employees collection
     oTest = mcolEmpoyees.Item(sEmpCode)
     'if the code gets here then we know all is well
     'clean up and leave
     Set oTest = Nothing
     Exists = True
     Exit Function
Exists_Err:
     'was the error because the Employee object did not
     'exist in the collection?
     If Err.Number = 5 Then
         'attempt to get the Employee object
         If GetEmployee(sEmpCode) then
             'we got the employee record and added it to
             'the collection
             Exists = True
         Else
             'the employee code does not exist so we
             'couldn't get the record
             Exists = False
         End If
     Else
         Exists = False
     End If

End Function
```

With this function in place, I can always ensure that the client-side code operates smoothly:

```
Dim oEmployees As New Employees
Dim oEmployees As Employee

If oEmployees.Exists(sEmpCode) Then
     Set oEmployee = oEmployees.Employee(sEmpCode)
Else
     MsgBox "This Employee Code could not be found"
End if
```

- The Item method is the default member of the Collection object. This means that, when retrieving a member of a collection, you don't have to actually include an explicit call to the Item method. The following two statements, for example, are identical to one another:

```
set objMember = objCollection.Item(6)
set objMember = objCollection(6)
```

See Also

Collection Object, Collection.Add Method, Collection.Count Property, Collection.Remove Method

Collection.Remove Method

Named Arguments

Yes

Syntax

```
objectvariable.Remove index
objectvariable
```
   Use: Required

   Data Type: Collection object

   An object variable of the Collection type.

index
   Use: Required

   Data Type: Numeric or String

   If a string, *index* is interpreted as the key; if numeric, *index* is treated as the ordinal position.

Description

Removes a member from a collection.

Rules at a Glance

- If *index* is a string data type or a variant of the string data subtype, *index* is taken to be the key, and the member whose key corresponds to *index* is removed.

- If *index* is a numerical data type or a variant of a numeric data subtype, *index* is taken to be the index number, and the member in the *index* ordinal position is removed.

- If *index* is a string and the key doesn't exist in the collection, an error (run-time error 5, "Invalid procedure call or argument") is generated.

- If *index* is numeric and at least one member has been added to the collection, its value must be between 1 and the maximum number of items in the collection or an error (runtime error 9, "Subscript out of range") is generated.

Example

```
colMyCollection.Remove "Name"
```

Programming Tips & Gotchas

- Members of the collection that follow the removed member are automatically moved downward by one position; therefore, no gaps are left in the collection.

- Because the collection is reindexed after each deletion, you should be sure not to delete a member of the collection based on a stored numeric value of *index*, since this value is capable of changing. Instead, you should either delete the member by key or retrieve the index value immediately before calling the Remove method.

- If you are deleting multiple members of a collection by numeric index value, you should delete them backwards, from highest index value to lowest, because the collection is reindexed after each deletion.

- If you are using a collection as the basis for a class module, or if you are using functions in your application to wrap and enhance the limited functionality of a collection, you can include a Clear method to remove all the members in your collection. The method should be written to remove the member in position 1 until no members are left, as the following code demonstrates:

```
Public Sub Clear()

    Dim i As Integer

    For i = 1 To mcolMyCollection.Count
        mcolMyCollection.Remove 1
    Next i

End Sub
```

- Alternately, you could do the same thing by working from the end of the collection forward, as the following code illustrates:

```
Dim intCtr As Integer

For intCtr = objCollec.Count To 1 Step -1
    objCollec.Remove intCtr
Next
```

See Also

Collection Object, Collection.Add Method, Collection.Count Property, Collection.Item Method

---

Command Function

Named Arguments

No

Syntax

```
Command
```

Description

Returns the arguments used when launching VB or an application created with VB.

Rules at a Glance

- For applications created with VB and compiled into an EXE, *Command* returns a string containing everything entered after the name of the executable file.

- This function isn't implemented in hosted versions of VBA. Regardless of any command line that may be passed to the host application, *Command* returns a null string.

Example

The following example demonstrates how to parse command-line arguments to set up a series of options in your executable. This example (which is bereft of all error handling) looks for a hyphen or a forward slash in the command line arguments and assumes that the following character is a command line switch. Given the command-line arguments:

```
-d:50 -f -g -k
```

the program displays the following in the Immediate window:

```
Got option d
Option d Parameter = 50
Got option f
Got option g
Got option k
```

The source code is as follows:

```
Private Sub ParseCommandLine()

Dim i As Integer
Dim s As String
Dim iParam As Integer

For i = 1 To Len(Command)
    If Mid$(Command, i, 1) Like "[-/]" Then
        s = Mid$(Command, i + 1, 1)
        Select Case s
            Case Is = "d"
                Debug.Print "Got option d"
                iParam = Int(Mid$(Command, i + 3, 2))
                Debug.Print "Option d Parameter = " & _
                            CStr(iParam)
            Case Is = "f"
                Debug.Print "Got option f"
            Case Is = "g"
                Debug.Print "Got option g"
            Case Is = "k"
                Debug.Print "Got option k"
            Case Is = "l"
                Debug.Print "Got option l"
        End Select
    End If
Next i

End Sub
```

Programming Tips & Gotchas

- During the development phase, you can pass arguments to your program using the Command Line Arguments text box, which can be found by selecting Properties from the Project menu and clicking the Make tab of the Project Properties dialog.

- To handle command-line arguments, you have to write a routine similar to that shown above to parse the string returned by *Command*, since the function returns only a single string containing all input after the name of the executable file.

- Command-line arguments are ideal for specifying various options on unattended applications.

Const Statement

Named Arguments

No

Syntax

```
[Public|Private] Const constantname = constantvalue
constantname
```
> Use: Required
>
> The name of the constant.

```
constantvalue
```
> Use: Required
>
> Data Type: Numeric or String
>
> A constant value, and optionally, arithmetic operators. Unlike variables, constants must be initialized.

Description

Declares a constant value: i.e., its value can't be changed throughout the life of the program or routine. One of the ideas of declaring constants is to make code easier to both write and read; it allows you to simply replace a value with a recognizable word.

Rules at a Glance

- The rules for *constantname* are the same as those of any variable: the name can be up to 255 characters in length and can contain any alphanumeric character, although it must start with an alphabetic character. In addition, the name can include almost any other character except a period or any of the data type definition characters $, &, %, !.

- The *constantvalue* expression can't include any of the built-in functions or objects, although it can be a combination of absolute values and operators. The expression can also include previously defined constants. For example:

```
Private Const CONST_ONE = 1
Private Const CONST_TWO = 2
Private Const CONST_THREE = CONST_ONE + CONST_TWO
```

- The **Private** keyword restricts the use of the constant to the module in which it's defined, whereas the **Public** keyword allows the constant to be used in all modules within the project. If neither Public nor Private is declared, the constant has private scope by default. The Public keyword can be used only with a Const in the declarations section of a code module.

Example

```
Private Const  MY_CONSTANT = 3.1417
```

Programming Tips & Gotchas

- You can't declare a Public Const in a class module. For ways in which you can work around this limitation, see Chapter 4.

- Although the new Enum (Enumerated Constants) keyword, which was introduced as part of Visual Basic Version 5, appears in the Microsoft documentation for VBA, the statement causes a compile-time error and isn't part of VBA. Enum, however, does work as documented with Visual Basic 5.0 and up.

- The recognized coding convention for constants is that the name is in uppercase letters, and multiple-word names are separated with underscores. For example, MY_CONSTANT is a constant name that adheres to this coding convention.

- One of the benefits of long variable and constant names (of up to 255 characters) in VBA is that you can make your constant names as meaningful as possible while using abbreviations sparingly. After all, you may know what abbreviations mean, but will others?

- The older scope syntax of Global is still legal, although the more meaningful Public declaration statement has superseded it.

- If you are building a large application with many different modules, you will find your code easier to maintain if you create a single separate code module to hold your Public constants.

See Also

#Const Directive, Private Statement, Public Statement

Cos Function

Named Arguments

No

Syntax

```
Cos (number)
number
```

> Use: Required
>
> Data Type: Double or numeric expression
>
> An angle in radians.

Return Value

A Double data type denoting the cosine of an angle.

Description

Takes an angle specified in radians and returns a ratio representing the length of the side adjacent to the angle divided by the length of the hypotenuse.

Rules at a Glance

The cosine returned by the function is between –1 and 1.

Example

```
Dim dblCosine as Double
dblCosine = Cos(dblRadians)
```

Programming Tips & Gotchas

- To convert degrees to radians, multiply degrees by pi/180.

- To convert radians to degrees, multiply radians by 180/pi.

See Also

Atn Function, Sin Function, Tan Function

CreateObject Function

Named Arguments

No

Syntax

```
Set objectvariable = CreateObject("library.object"[, servername])
```
objectvariable

Use: Required

Data Type: Object

A variable to hold the reference to the instantiated object.

library

Use: Required

Data Type: String

The name of the application or library containing the object.

object

Use: Required

Data Type: String

The type or class of object to create.

servername

Use: Optional (Available in VB6 only)

Data Type: String

The name of the server on which the object resides.

Reference

Return Value

A reference to an ActiveX object.

Description

Creates an instance of an OLE Automation (ActiveX) object. Prior to calling the methods, functions, or properties of an object, you are required to create an instance of that object. Once an object is created, you reference it in code using the object variable you defined.

Rules at a Glance

- If your project doesn't include a reference to the object, you must declare the object variable type as Object; this allows the variable to reference any type of object.

- If an instance of the ActiveX object is already running, *CreateObject* may start a new instance when it creates an object of the required type.

Example

The following routine defines a generic Object variable, as well as an Excel application object. It then uses the *Timer* function to compare the performance of the code fragment that uses late binding to instantiate the Excel application object with the one that uses early binding. (For a discussion of late and early binding, see the first item in the "Programming Tips & Gotchas" section.)

```
Private Sub TestBinding()

Dim dblTime As Double
Dim strMsg As String

' Calculate time for late binding
dblTime = Timer()
Dim objExcelLate As Object
Set objExcelLate = CreateObject("excel.application")
Set objExcelLate = Nothing
strMsg = strMsg & "Late Bound: " & Timer() - dblTime
strMsg = strMsg & vbCrLf

' Calculate time for early binding
dblTime = Timer()
Dim objExcelEarly As Excel.Application
Set objExcelEarly = Excel.Application
Set objExcelEarly = Nothing
strMsg = strMsg & "Early Bound: " & Timer() - dblTime

MsgBox strMsg, vbOKOnly, "Late and Early Binding"

End Sub
```

Programming Tips & Gotchas

- The Object data type is the most generic of Visual Basic objects. When an object variable has been defined as type Object, *CreateObject* performs what is termed *late binding*. This means that because the precise object type is unknown at design time the object can't be bound into your program when it's compiled. Instead, this binding occurs only at runtime, when the program is run on the target system and the *CreateObject* function is executed. This need to determine the precise object type by referencing the relevant interfaces at runtime is necessarily time-consuming, and therefore results in poor performance. You can vastly improve performance by using *early binding*. Early binding necessitates your adding a reference to the required object to your project. You do this in VB by selecting the References option from the Project menu and then selecting the required object from the References dialog. For example, to use the Microsoft Remote Data Objects (RDO) 2.0 library in your project, simply open the References dialog and check the Microsoft Remote Data Object 2.0 option. Then you can create explicit object variables directly, as the following snippet shows:

```
Dim rcMyConnection As rdoConnection
Dim rsMyResults As rdoResultset
Dim sSQL As String

sSQL = "SELECT * FROM testtable"

Set rcMyConnection = _
    rdoEnvironments(0).OpenConnection("TestServ")
Set rsMyResults = rcMyConnection.OpenResultset(sSQL)
```

Because your project has a direct reference to the object, it can create the object at the compilation stage. Your program is therefore able to bind references to the object and its OLE interfaces before the object is needed (hence the term early binding), thus improving the performance of the application. If you are unsure of the available objects, methods, events, and properties, you can get complete information from the Object Browser.

• With the advent of DCOM, the ActiveX object doesn't need to necessarily reside on the computer on which your program is running, although it must always be registered on the computer on which your program is running.

• VB6 takes the *CreateObject* function one step further by adding a new parameter, **servername**. You can now specify the name of the server on which the ActiveX object is registered. This means that you could even specify different servers depending upon prevailing circumstances, as this short example demonstrates:

```
Dim sMainServer As String
Dim sBackUpServer As String

sMainServer = "NTPROD1"
sBackUpServer = "NTPROD2"

If IsOnline(sMainServer) Then
    CreateObject("Sales.Customer",sMainServer)
Else
    CreateObject("Sales.Customer",sBackUpServer)
End If
```

Reference

- To use a current instance of an already running ActiveX object, use the *Get-Object* function.

- If an object is registered as a single-instance object (i.e., an out-of-process ActiveX EXE), only one instance of the object can be created; regardless of the number of times *CreateObject* is executed, you will obtain a reference to the same instance of the object.

- It's considered good programming practice (and often a necessity) to tidy up after you have finished using an object by setting *objectvariable* to Nothing. This has the effect of freeing the memory taken up by the instance of the object, and, if there are no other "live" references to the object, shutting it down. For example:

```
Set objectvariable = Nothing
```

- For a more in-depth look at creating objects and using them within your application, see Chapter 4.

See Also

GetObject Function, Set Statement, Chapter 4

CSng Function

Named Arguments

No

Syntax

```
CSng(expression)
expression
```
Use: Required

Data Type: Numeric or String

The range of *expression* is –3.402823E38 to –1.401298E-45 for negative values, 1.401298E-45 to 3.402823E38 for positive values.

Return Value

expression cast as a Single data type.

Description

Returns a single-precision number.

Rules at a Glance

- *expression* must evaluate to a numeric value; otherwise, a type mismatch error is generated.

- If the value of *expression* is outside the range of the double data type, an overflow error is generated.

Example

```
Dim sngMyNumber as Single
If IsNumeric(sMyNumber) then
```

```
        sngMyNumber = CSng(sMyNumber)
    End If
```

Programming Tips & Gotchas

- Test that *expression* evaluates to a number by using the *IsNumeric* function.

- When converting a string representation of a number to a numeric, you should use the data-type conversion functions—such as *CSngl*—instead of *Val*, because the data type conversion functions take account of the computer's regional settings. The thousands separator is the most important of these regional settings. For example, if the value of *expression* is the string 1,234.987, *CSng* converts it to 1234.987, while *Val* incorrectly converts it to 1.

See Also

FormatNumber Function, IsNumeric Function, Val Function

CStr Function

Named Arguments

No

Syntax

```
CStr(expression)
  expression
      Use: Required
      Data Type: Any
      Any expression that evaluates to a string.
```

Return Value

expression converted to a string.

Description

Returns a string representation of *expression*.

Rules at a Glance

- Almost any data can be passed to *CStr* to be converted to a string.

- *CStr* is equivalent to the older *Str* function.

Example

```
Dim sMyString as String
SMyString = CStr(100)
```

Programming Tips & Gotchas

- The string representation of Boolean values is either **True** or **False**, as opposed to their underlying values of 0 and –1.

- Uninitialized numeric data types passed to *CStr* return "0".

- An uninitialized date variable passed to *CStr* returns "12:00:00AM."

See Also

Format Function, Str Function, Chapter 3

CurDir, CurDir$ Functions

Named Arguments

No

Syntax

```
CurDir[(drive)]
drive
```
> Use: Optional
>
> Data Type: String
>
> The name of the drive.

Return Value

The current path.

Description

Returns a Variant of subtype String representing the current path.

Rules at a Glance

*   If no drive is specified or if **drive** is a zero-length string (""), *CurDir* returns the path for the current drive.

*   **drive** can be the single-letter drive name with or without a colon (i.e., both "C" and "C:" are valid values for **drive**).

*   If **drive** is invalid, the function generates runtime error 68, "Device unavailable."

*   Because *CurDir* can accept only a single character string, you can't use network drive names, share names, or UNC drive names.

See Also

ChDir Statement, ChDrive Statement, MkDir Statement, Name Statement, RmDir Statement

---

CVar Function

Named Arguments

No

Syntax

```
CVar(expression)
expression
```
> Use: Required

Data Type: Numeric or String

Same range as Double for numerics. Same range as String for non-numerics.

Return Value

expression cast as a Variant.

Description

Returns *expression* as a Variant data type; the data subtype is automatically selected by the *CVar* routine.

Rules at a Glance

There really aren't any rules: you can literally throw anything at *CVar*, and a variant of the appropriate data subtype is returned.

Programming Tips & Gotchas

Use *CVar* only in situations where you are confident that the data type you pass into the function isn't ambiguous; in other words, where you can be sure of the data subtype that *CVar* selects. If you need data of a particular data type, use the appropriate conversion function.

CVDate Function

The *CVDate* function is provided only for compatibility with previous versions of VBA. *CVDate* returns a variant of subtype Date. However, because there is now an intrinsic data type of Date as of VB 5.0, you should use the *CDate* function, which returns a Date data type and whose syntax is identical to *CVDate*.

See Also

CDate Function

CVErr Function

Named Arguments

No

Syntax

```
CVErr(errornumber)
```
errornumber

Use: Required

Data Type: Long

Any valid number.

Return Value

A Variant of subtype Error containing an application-defined error number.

Description

Creates user-defined errors in user-created procedures. For example, you can use *CVErr* to pass back error codes from a function, which allows you to handle exceptions in the data rather than going to the full extent of raising an error and invoking full error-handling routines. While the difference may appear subtle, in practice the *CVErr* function offers a much more gentle approach to handling exceptions that aren't threatening to the stability of the application.

Rules at a Glance

The code `CVErr(8001)` returns "Error 8001."

Example

```
Public Function GetValue(strText As String) As Variant

If IsNumeric(strText) Then
    GetValue = strText
    If GetValue <= 0 Then
        GetValue = CVErr(10001)
    End If
Else
    GetValue = CVErr(10001)
End If

End Function

Private Sub Command1_Click()

Dim varNumber As Variant
Dim lngNumber As Long

varNumber = GetValue(Text1.Text)
If TypeName(varNumber) = "Error" Then
    lngNumber = 0
    MsgBox "Please enter a positive integer in the text box."
Else
    lngNumber = varNumber
End If

End Sub
```

Programming Tips & Gotchas

- Although the return value from *CVErr* may appear to be a string, it is in fact a Variant of subtype Error. Take care, therefore, not to directly assign the return value of *CVErr* to a string variable, or to any other strongly typed variable. For example, the following seemingly straightforward code generates a runtime "Type Mismatch" error:

```
Function MyFunc(iValue as Integer) As String
    If iValue > 0 Then
        MyFunc = "Correct"
    Else
```

```
     MyFunc = CVErr(80001)
  End If
End Function
```

The way you should handle this is to explicitly convert the return value to a string data type using the *CStr* function. Alternately, you can assign the return value to a variant and determine whether its data subtype is Error when the function returns.

- *CVErr* isn't the same as *Err.Raise*. *Err.Raise* invokes error handlers and assigns values to the Err object, whereas *CVErr* doesn't.

- Typically, you use inline code to handle an error raised by *CVErr*.

See Also

CStr Function, Err.Raise Method

Data Binding Objects (VB6)

Library to Reference

Microsoft Data Binding Collection (*../SYSTEM32/MSBIND.DLL*)

Description

Apparently, when Microsoft was planning the new release of Visual Basic, they researched how professional developers were using the language. One result which seems to have taken the VB development team by surprise was that very few professional developers use the Data control and data bound controls. The reason for this is quite easy to understand: rightly or wrongly, professional VB developers see the Data control and data bound controls as inflexible and an encroachment on their control over the database. Furthermore, as more and more VB applications follow the *n*-tier paradigm, in which database access is performed on a remote server, with only properties passed to (or requested by) the client, the usefulness of a Data control was diminishing rapidly.

With this in mind, Microsoft introduced a new object model to give developers control over data mapping without sacrificing the rapid development time offered by more or less central data binding. The binding objects sit between standard form controls and your recordset (which can be wrapped within a class in an ActiveX server), automatically updating the form control as the user navigates through the recordset. Therefore, any form control can now be bound to a database field.

The Binding object model, which is shown in Figure 7-2, consists of a top-level collection to which you add Binding objects, these being the physical binding of data column to form control. The Binding object offers a flexibility that should satisfy most needs. For example, you can bind data to any property on a control, and you can specify at what point the data binding should be updated. A major enhancement over previous data binding technologies is the ability to bind the controls on a form to a VB class object. This can be achieved in both directions; that is to say, a VB class module can now be a data source, or it can be a data consumer.

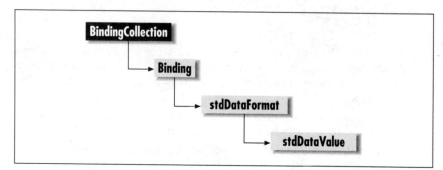

Figure 7-2: The Data Binding object model

Example

To introduce the objects involved in both data binding and data formatting, this example demonstrates how the objects can bind data from an ActiveX OLE server to standard VB form controls without using a Data control. This example uses the sample SQL Server *pubs* database, but it can be easily modified to use an Access database or even the computer's own file system as a source of data. What's important is the relationship between the different objects in the Data Binding and Data Formatting object model.

In this example, an ActiveX DLL class object performs the database access and exposes itself as a data source. The form creates a BindingCollection object that binds various controls on the form to database fields in two different recordsets held in the class. The example shows how to:

- Expose a VB class as a data source.
- Create a BindingCollection object.
- Specify the VB class as the data source for the BindingCollection object.
- Add individual Binding objects to the collection, thereby binding controls to database fields held within the data provider class object.
- Create DataFormat objects to perform formatting functions on the incoming and outgoing data.
- Navigate through the recordset.
- Perform simple validation and confirmation before updating the database.

Data Consumer Form Code

The form includes the following object references, which are selected from the References dialog:

- Microsoft Data Binding Collection
- Microsoft Data Formatting Object Library

In addition, if the data source class isn't in the same project as the data consumer form, a reference to the data source class needs to be added.

The form contains the following controls:

Control Name	Control Type
chkContract	Checkbox
cmdMoveNext	Command button
cmdMovePrevious	Command button
txtAddress	Text box
txtContract	Text box
txtFirstName	Text box
txtlastName	Text box
txtPubDate1	Text box
txtTitle1	Text box

```
Option Explicit
'declare object variables for the BindingCollection
'objects we'll need and a single Binding object.
Private obcAuthors As BindingCollection
Private obcTitles  As BindingCollection
Private oBind      As Binding

'declare an object variable referencing our
'BindingSource class
Private oSource    As BindingSource

'declare object variables for the DataFormat objects
Private WithEvents fmtF1 As StdDataFormat
Private WithEvents fmtF2 As StdDataFormat
Private WithEvents fmtF3 As StdDataFormat
Private WithEvents fmtF4 As StdDataFormat

Private Sub Form_Load()

    'create new instances of the required objects
    'our source class
    Set oSource = New BindingSource
    'and the two BindingCollections
    Set obcAuthors = New BindingCollection
    Set obcTitles = New BindingCollection

    'Set up the required Format Objects
    'first to show a short message and automatically
    'handle NULL database values
    Set fmtF1 = New StdDataFormat
    fmtF1.Type = fmtCustom
    fmtF1.NullValue = "No Data Found"

    'second to handle 0 and 1 values in the database
    'displaying a string in the text box instead
    Set fmtF2 = New StdDataFormat
    fmtF2.Type = fmtBoolean
```

```
         fmtF2.FalseValue = "No Contract"
         fmtF2.TrueValue = "Contract Signed"

         'third to switch a checkbox on or off automatically
         'depending on the database value of 0 or 1
         Set fmtF3 = New StdDataFormat
         fmtF3.Type = fmtCheckbox

         'last one to format a date field
         Set fmtF4 = New StdDataFormat
         fmtF4.Type = fmtGeneral
         fmtF4.Format = "long date"

         'instruct the BindingCollection not to perform
         'an update until the user moves to the next record
         obcAuthors.UpdateMode = vbUpdateWhenRowChanges
         'set the DataMember to the required value - this
         'will be passed to the class to obtain a reference
         'to the correct recordset
         obcAuthors.DataMember = "Authors"

         'now assign our source class as the datasource for
         'the authors bindings collection
         Set obcAuthors.DataSource = oSource
         'use the add method to create the binding between
         'form controls and database fields
         obcAuthors.Add txtFirstName, "Text", "au_fname", _
                     fmtF1, "fname"
         obcAuthors.Add txtLastName, "Text", "au_lname", _
                     fmtF1, "lname"
         obcAuthors.Add txtContract, "Text", "contract", _
                     fmtF2, "contract"
         obcAuthors.Add chkContract, "Value", "contract", _
                     fmtF3, "chkCont"
         obcAuthors.Add txtAddress, "Text", "address", _
                     fmtF1, "address"

         'now do the same for the Titles recordset
         obcTitles.UpdateMode = vbUpdateWhenRowChanges
         obcTitles.DataMember = "Titles"
         Set obcTitles.DataSource = oSource
         obcTitles.Add txtTitle1, "Text", "title", _
                     fmtF1, "title"
         obcTitles.Add txtPubDate1, "Text", "pubdate", _
                     fmtF4, "pubdate"

End Sub

Private Sub fmtF1_Format(ByVal DataValue As _
                     StdFormat.StdDataValue)

         'the format event is called when a custom type
         'is about to be formatted. Just for fun let's set
         'the firstname field to uppercase and the
```

```
        'lastname field to lowercase
    If DataValue.TargetObject.Name = "txtFirstName" Then
        fmtF1.Format = ">"
    Else
        fmtF1.Format = "<"
    End If

End Sub

Private Sub fmtF1_UnFormat(ByVal DataValue As _
                           StdFormat.StdDataValue)

    'the unformat event is only called for custom type
    'formats that are just about to be written back to
    'the database - so lets convert them back to proper
    'case
    DataValue.Value = StrConv(DataValue.Value, _
                              vbProperCase)

End Sub

Private Sub cmdMoveNext_Click()

    'the user has finished with the record and wants
    'the next one.

    'just check this out first..
    Call CheckForUpdate

    'ok now we'll give them the next record by calling
    'the MoveNext method in our source class.
    oSource.MoveNext
    'we need to rebind the titles recordset because
    'it's dynamically built
    Set obcTitles.DataSource = oSource

End Sub

Private Sub cmdMovePrev_Click()

    Call CheckForUpdate
    'call the MoveBack method in our source class
    oSource.MoveBack

End Sub

Private Function CheckForUpdate() As Boolean

    Dim iResponse As Integer

    'before we give them the next record - let's just
    'check whether they made any amendments to the
    'current record.
    'iterate through the Binding objects
```

Reference

```
      For Each oBind In obcAuthors
         'see if any values have been changed by the user
         If oBind.DataChanged Then
            'indeed they did--was it intentional though?
            iResponse = MsgBox("The data has changed" _
                              & vbCrLf & _
                              "do you wish to update?", _
                              vbYesNo + vbQuestion)
            If iResponse = vbNo Then
               'obviously not - so cancel the update from
               ' being written back to the database
               oBind.DataChanged = False
            End If
            'no point in looking any further...
            Exit For
         End If
      Next

   End Function
```

Notes

- This form is set as the project's startup object.

- In the Form_Load event, a reference to the data source class is assigned to the BindingCollection.DataSource property, firing the data source class's GetData-Member event. The GetDataMember event handler assigns a reference to the recordset specified in the BindingCollection.DataMember property to the BindingCollection.

- The Binding object's DataChanged property gives you control first, to interrogate the binding and determine if the value has been changed by the user, and second, to prevent the update from being written back to the database.

- See the Data Format Objects entry for more information about the stdDataFormat object.

Data Source Class Code

The class references the Microsoft ActiveX Data Objects 2.0 Library, selected from the References dialog. The class also has its DataSourceBehavior property set to **vbDataSource**.

```
Option Explicit
'declare the ADO objects
Private cn As ADODB.Connection
Private WithEvents rsAuthors As ADODB.Recordset
Private WithEvents rsTitles As ADODB.Recordset

Private Sub Class_GetDataMember(DataMember As String, _
                                Data As Object)
   'this event is called as the datasource is assigned
   'to the BindingCollection object.
   If DataMember = "Authors" Then
      'this class provides two data members
      'the first is authors, the other is titles
```

```
                  'assign the required recordset back to the
                  'BindingCollection object
                  Set Data = rsAuthors
          Else
                  Set Data = rsTitles
          End If
End Sub

Private Sub Class_Initialize()
      Dim sSQL

          'create an instance of the ADO Recordset to use
          'for the Titles recordset later
          Set rsTitles = New ADODB.Recordset

          'create the connection object
          Set cn = New ADODB.Connection
              'there is a DNS called Test on this machine
              'pointing to the Pubs database
              cn.ConnectionString = "Test"
              cn.Open

          'peform the query to return the data from Authors
          sSQL = "SELECT * FROM authors"
          Set rsAuthors = New ADODB.Recordset
          rsAuthors.Open sSQL, cn, adOpenKeyset, adLockOptimistic

          'force the Titles recordset to be created
          rsAuthors.MoveFirst

End Sub

Public Sub MoveNext()
      'move to the next record
      rsAuthors.MoveNext
      If rsAuthors.EOF Then
          rsAuthors.MoveFirst
      End If
End Sub

Public Sub MoveBack()
      'move to the previous record
      rsAuthors.MovePrevious
      If rsAuthors.BOF Then
          rsAuthors.MoveLast
      End If
End Sub

Private Sub rsAuthors_MoveComplete(ByVal adReason As _
                      ADODB.EventReasonEnum, _
                      ByVal pError As ADODB.Error, _
                      adStatus As ADODB.EventStatusEnum, _
                      ByVal pRecordset As ADODB.Recordset)
```

```
'Move_Complete is an event from the ADO Recordset
'This code allows us to keep the two recordsets
'in synch.
Dim sSQL As String

sSQL = "SELECT titles.title, titles.pubdate" & vbCrLf _
    & "  FROM titles, titleauthor" & vbCrLf _
    & " WHERE titleauthor.au_id = '" _
    & rsAuthors("au_id") & "'" & vbCrLf _
    & "   AND titles.title_id = titleauthor.title_id"

If rsTitles.State = adStateOpen Then
    rsTitles.Close
End If

'you'll need to rebind this recordset - see code in form
rsTitles.Open sSQL, cn, adOpenKeyset, adLockOptimistic

End Sub
```

Notes

- The Class_GetDataMember event handler is automatically placed in the class for you when you set the class's DataSourceBehavior property to **vbData-Source**.

- By declaring the ADO recordset object as **WithEvents**, you can access all the events in the recordset object (such as WillChangeField, which allows you to perform validation and cancellation prior to updating, if you wish).

See Also

BindingCollection Object, Binding Object

Data Format Objects (VB6)

Library to Reference

Microsoft Data Formatting Object Library (*../SYSTEM32/MSSTDFMT.DLL*)

Description

The Data Format objects can be used only in conjunction with the Data Binding objects, although their use isn't mandatory. They allow you to perform complex formatting operations with a minimum of code. For example, formatting null data or mapping a data field to a checkbox are common operations you had to code manually in almost all database applications. Now these operations can be handled with just a few lines of code.

The object model, which is shown in Figure 7-3, consists of a collection object, a format object, and a value object. For most applications, you want to create a formats collection object to hold the various format objects you use in the application, but you can also simply create a format object without using the collection. The value object isn't createable and is available only when it's passed to the format object's Format or Unformat events.

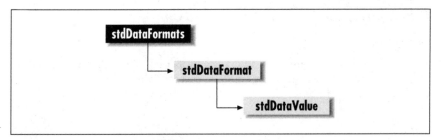

Figure 7-3: The Data Format object model

When you bind a data source to a control using the bindings collection, you can specify a Format object to bind with them. As data is read from the source, it's formatted and displayed automatically. When data is read from the control and written back to the data source, it's unformatted automatically. For complex formatting operations, you can use the Format and Unformat events to code the formatting and unformatting of data.

See Also

stdDataFormat Object, stdDataFormats Object

DataBindingBehavior Property (VB6 only)

Description

This property is one of the new VB6 class properties, and determines the behavior of the class when it's bound to an external data source. That is, the class is to act as a Data Consumer. This property is available only at design time.

Values

vbNone
> The class can't be bound to external data sources.

vbSimpleBound
> The class can be bound to a single data field in an external data source.

vbComplexBound
> The class can be bound to a row of data in an external data source.

Programming Tips & Gotchas

When the property is set to vbSimpleBound, two procedures—the Property-Changed event and the CanPropertyChange method—are automatically added to the class module.

See Also

DataBinding Object, Chapter 4

DataSourceBehavior Property (VB6 only)

Description

This property is one of the new VB6 class properties, although it isn't available when the class is part of an ActiveX EXE project. It defines the ability of the class to serve as a data source for other objects. This property is available only at design time.

Values

vbNone

> The class doesn't expose a bindable data interface and therefore can't act as a data source.

vbDataSource

> The class can act as a data source for other objects.

vbOLEDBProvider

> The class can act as an OLE DB Simple Provider.

Programming Tips & Gotchas

- When the property is set to **vbDataSource** or **vbOLEDBProvider**, the Get-DataMember event procedure is automatically added to the class module.

- The property may be set to **vbOLEDBProvider** only if the class is public.

- If the property is set to **vbOLEDBProvider**, the OnDataConnection event procedure is added automatically to the class module.

See Also

DataBinding Object, Chapter 4

Date, Date$ Functions

Syntax

```
Date
```

Return Value

Date returns a Variant of subtype Date; *Date$* returns a String data type.

Description

Returns the current system date.

Rules at a Glance

They don't come any easier than this!

Programming Tips & Gotchas

- Although *Date* returns a Variant, you can assign the return value of *Date* to a variable declared as a Date data type.

- To return both the current date and time in one variable, use the *Now* function.

- You can set the system date by using the `Date` statement.

See Also

Date Statement, IsDate Function, Now Function

Date Statement

Named Arguments

No

Syntax

```
Date = newdate
newdate
```
  Use: Required

  Date Type: String, Date, or Date Variant

  Any valid date value.

Description

Sets the current system date.

Rules at a Glance

- If you are setting the system date with numbers, as opposed to spelling the month, the sequence of Day, Month, and Year must be in the same sequence as the computer's regional settings.

- If you are running under Microsoft Windows, the earliest system date you can set is January 1, 1980; the latest system date you can set is December 31, 2099.

- For Microsoft Windows NT, the earliest and latest system dates are January 1, 1980 and December 31, 2079, respectively.

Example

```
Date = "31 January 1998"
```

Programming Tips & Gotchas

- It's good programming practice to synchronize the dates across the machines in a multiuser environment, most commonly from the date on a server. This can be done at the operating-system level within the logon script or at application level using the *Date* and *Time* statements.

- To bulletproof your application from curious users who want to see what happens if they change the regional settings to Danish, your application from being installed on a new system on which the system administrator forgets to change the regional settings to your locale, and a host of other ways in which the computer your application is running on has regional settings different from those you expect, you should never take a date for granted. Wherever possible, use the *Format* function to explicitly set the date format you require prior to using a date value.

- Modern windows systems are more reliant on the system date than ever before. A single machine can have literally hundreds of different applications installed, many of which will use dates in one way or another. You should respect the machine on which your application is running and only in very exceptional circumstances should you change the system date programmatically.

See Also

Date Function, IsDate Function

DateAdd Function

Named Arguments

Yes

Syntax

```
DateAdd(interval, number, date)
interval
```
>   Use: Required

>   Data Type: String

>   An expression denoting the interval of time you need to add or subtract (see the table "Interval Settings").

`number`
>   Use: Required

>   Data Type: Numeric

>   An expression denoting the number of time intervals you want to add or subtract.

`date`
>   Use: Required

>   Data Type: Date Variant

>   A Variant of subtype Date or a literal denoting the date on which to base the *DateAdd* calculation.

Interval Settings

Setting	Description
yyyy	Year
q	Quarter
m	Month
y	Day of year
d	Day
w	Weekday

Setting	Description
ww	Week
h	Hour
n	Minute
s	Second

Return Value

A Variant of subtype Date.

Description

Returns a variant of subtype Date representing the result of adding or subtracting a given number of time periods to or from a given date. For instance, you can calculate the date 178 months before today's date, or the date and time 12,789 minutes from now.

Rules at a Glance

- Specify the interval value as a string enclosed in quotation marks (i.e., **"ww"**).

- If *number* is positive, the result is in the future; if *number* is negative, the result is in the past. (The meaning of "future" and "past" here is relative to *date*.)

- The *DateAdd* function has a built-in calendar algorithm to prevent it returning an invalid date. For example, you can add 10 minutes to 31 December 1999 23:55, and *DateAdd* automatically recalculates all elements of the date to return a valid date, in this case, 1 January 2000 00:05. This includes leap years: the calendar algorithm takes the presence of 29 February into account for leap years.

Example

```
Dim lNoOfIntervals as Long
lNoOfIntervals = 100
Msgbox DateAdd("d", lNoOfIntervals, Now)
```

Programming Tips & Gotchas

- When working with dates, always check that a date is valid using the *IsDate* function prior to passing it as a parameter to the function.

- To add a number of days to *date*, use either the day of the year **"y"**, the day **"d"**, or the weekday **"w"**.

- Both the Date data type and the Variant date subtype can handle dates only as far back as 100 A.D. *DateAdd* generates an error (runtime error number 5, "Invalid procedure call or argument") if the result precedes the year 100.

- Both the Date data type and the Variant date subtype can handle dates as far into the future as 9999 A.D.—from a practical application standpoint, a virtual infinity. If the result of *DateAdd* is a year beyond 9999 A.D., the function generates runtime error number 5, "Invalid procedure call or argument."

- If *number* contains a fractional value, it's rounded to the nearest whole number before being used in the calculation.

See Also

DateDiff Function, DatePart Function, DateSerial Function, IsDate Function

---

DateDiff Function

Named Arguments

Yes

Syntax

```
DateDiff(interval, date1, date2[, firstdayofweek[,
        firstweekofyear]])
```

interval
> Use: Required
>
> Data Type: String
>
> The units of time used to express the result of the difference between *date1* and *date2* (see the table "Interval Settings").

date1
> Use: Required
>
> Data Type: Variant (Date)
>
> The first date you want to use in the differential calculation.

date2
> Use: Required
>
> Data Type: Variant (Date)
>
> The second date you want to use in the differential calculation.

firstdayofweek
> Use: Optional
>
> Data Type: Numeric constant
>
> A numeric constant that defines the first day of the week. If not specified, Sunday is assumed (see the table "First Day of Week Constants").

firstweekofyear
> Use: Optional
>
> Data Type: Numeric constant
>
> A numeric constant that defines the first week of the year. If not specified, the first week is assumed to be the week in which January 1 occurs (see the table "First Week of Year Constants").

Interval Settings

Setting	Description
yyyy	Year
q	Quarter
m	Month
y	Day of year
d	Day
w	Weekday
ww	Week
h	Hour
n	Minute
s	Second

First Day of Week Constants

Constant	Value	Description
vbUseSystem	0	Use the NLS API setting
vbSunday	1	Sunday (default)
vbMonday	2	Monday
vbTuesday	3	Tuesday
vbWednesday	4	Wednesday
vbThursday	5	Thursday
vbFriday	6	Friday
vbSaturday	7	Saturday

First Week of Year Constants

Constant	Value	Description
vbUseSystem	0	Use the NLS API setting.
vbFirstJan1	1	Start with the week in which January 1 occurs (default).
vbFirstFourDays	2	Start with the first week that has at least four days in the new year.
vbFirstFullWeek	3	Start with first full week of the year.

Reference

Return Value

Variant (Long).

Description

Returns a variant of subtype long specifying the number of time intervals between two specified dates.

The *DateDiff* function calculates the number of time intervals between two dates. For example, you can use the function to determine how many days there are between 1 January 1980 and 31 May 1998.

Rules at a Glance

* The calculation performed by *DateDiff* is always **date2–date1**. Therefore, if **date1** chronologically precedes **date2**, the value returned by the function is negative.

* If **interval** is Weekday "w", *DateDiff* returns the number of weeks between **date1** and **date2**. *DateDiff* totals the occurrences of the day on which **date1** falls, up to and including **date2**, but not including **date1**. Note that an **interval** of "w" doesn't return the number of weekdays between two dates, as you might expect.

* If **interval** is Week "ww", *DateDiff* returns the number of calendar weeks between **date1** and **date2**. To achieve this, *DateDiff* counts the number of Sundays (or whichever other day is defined to be the first day of the week by the **firstdayofweek** argument) between **date1** and **date2**. If **date2** falls on a Sunday, it's counted, but **date1** isn't counted even if it falls on a Sunday.

* The **firstdayofweek** argument affects only calculations that use the "ww" (week) interval values.

Example

```
Dim dtNow As Date
Dim dtThen As Date
Dim sInterval As String
Dim lNoOfIntervals As Long

dtNow = Date
dtThen = "01/01/1990"
sInterval = "m"

lNoOfIntervals = DateDiff(sInterval, dtThen, dtNow)

MsgBox lNoOfIntervals
```

Programming Tips & Gotchas

* When working with dates, always check that a date is valid using the *IsDate* function prior to passing it as a function parameter.

* When comparing the number of years between December 31 of one year to January 1 of the following year, *DateDiff* returns 1 although in reality, the difference is only one day.

* *DateDiff* considers the four quarters of the year to be January 1–March 31, April 1–June 30, July 1–September 30, and October 1–December 31. Consequently, when determining the number of quarters between March 31 and April 1 of the same year, for example, *DateDiff* returns 1, even though the latter date is only one day after the former.

* If **interval** is "m", *DateDiff* simply counts the difference in the months on which the respective dates fall. For example, when determining the number

of months between January 31 and February 1 of the same year, *DateDiff* returns 1, even though the latter date is only one day after the former.

- To calculate the number of days between *date1* and *date2*, you can use either Day of year "y" or Day "d".

- In calculating the number of hours, minutes, or seconds between two dates, if an explicit time isn't specified, *DateDiff* provides a default value of midnight (00:00:00).

- If you specify *date1* or *date2* as strings within quotation marks (" ") and omit the year, the year is assumed to be the current year, as taken from the computer's date. This allows the same code to be used in different years.

See Also

DateAdd Function, DatePart Function, IsDate Function

DatePart Function

Named Arguments

Yes

Syntax

```
DatePart(interval, date[,firstdayofweek[, _
        firstweekofyear]])
```

interval

Use: Required

Data Type: String

The unit of time to extract from within *date* (see the table "Interval Settings").

date

Use: Required

Data Type: Variant (Date)

The Date value that you want to evaluate.

firstdayofweek

Use: Optional

Data Type: Numeric constant

A numeric constant that defines the first day of the week. If not specified, Sunday is assumed (see the table "First Day of Week Constants").

firstweekofyear

Use: Optional

Data Type: Numeric constant

A numeric constant that defines the first week of the year. If not specified, the first week is assumed to be the week in which January 1 occurs (see the table "First Week of Year Constants").

Reference

Interval Settings

Setting	Description
yyyy	Year
q	Quarter
m	Month
y	Day of year
d	Day
w	Weekday
ww	Week
h	Hour
n	Minute
s	Second

First Day of the Week Constants

Constant	Value	Description
vbUseSystem	0	Use the NLS API setting
vbSunday	1	Sunday (default)
vbMonday	2	Monday
vbTuesday	3	Tuesday
vbWednesday	4	Wednesday
vbThursday	5	Thursday
vbFriday	6	Friday
vbSaturday	7	Saturday

First Week of Year Constants

Constant	Value	Description
vbUseSystem	0	Use the NLS API setting.
vbFirstJan1	1	Start with week in which January 1 occurs (default).
vbFirstFourDays	2	Start with the first week that has at least four days in the new year.
vbFirstFullWeek	3	Start with first full week of the year.

Return Value

Variant (Integer)

Description

Extracts an individual component of the date or time (like the month or the second) from a date/time value. It returns a Variant (Integer) containing the specified portion of the given date. *DatePart* is a single function encapsulating the individual *Year, Month, Day, Hour, Minute,* and *Second* functions.

Rules at a Glance

The *firstdayofweek* argument affects only calculations that use either the "w" or "ww" interval values.

Example

```
Dim sTimeInterval As String
Dim dtNow As Date

sTimeInterval = "n" 'minutes
dtNow = Now

MsgBox DatePart(sTimeInterval, dtNow)
```

Programming Tips & Gotchas

- When working with dates, always check that a date is valid using the *IsDate* function prior to passing it as a function parameter.

- If you specify *date* within quotation marks (" ") omitting the year, the year is assumed to be the current year taken from the computer's date.

- If you attempt to extract either the hours, the minutes, or the seconds, but *date1* doesn't contain the necessary time element, the function assumes a time of midnight (0:00:00).

See Also

DateSerial Function, Day Function, Month Function, Year Function, Minute Function, Hour Function, Second Function

---

DateSerial Function

Named Arguments

Yes

Syntax

```
DateSerial(year, month, day)
```
year

    Use: Required

    Data Type: Integer

    Number between 100 and 9999, inclusive, or a numeric expression.

month

    Use: Required

    Data Type: Integer

    Any numeric expression to express the month between 1 and 12.

day

    Use: Required

Data Type: Integer

Any numeric expression to express the day between 1 and 31.

Return Value

Variant (Date).

Description

Returns a Variant 7 data subtype (a date) from the three date components (year, month, and day). For the function to succeed, all three components must be present, and all must be numeric values. The value returned by the function takes the short date format defined by the Regional Settings applet in the Control Panel of the client machine.

Rules at a Glance

*   If the value of a particular element exceeds its normal limits, *DateSerial* adjusts the date accordingly. For example, if you tried DateSerial (96,2,31)—February 31, 1996—*DateSerial* returns March 2, 1996.

*   You can specify expressions or formulas that evaluate to individual date components as parameters to *DateSerial*. For example, DateSerial (98,10+9,23) returns 23 March 1999. This makes it easier to use *DateSerial* to form dates whose individual elements are unknown at design-time or that are created on the fly as a result of user input.

Example

```
Dim iYear As Integer
Dim iMonth As Integer
Dim iday As Integer

iYear = 1987
iMonth = 3 + 11
iday = 16

MsgBox DateSerial(iYear, iMonth, iday)
```

Programming Tips & Gotchas

*   If any of the parameters exceed the range of the Integer data type (-32,768 to 32,767), an error (runtime error 6, "Overflow") is generated.

*   The Microsoft documentation for this function incorrectly states, "For the year argument, values between 0 and 99, inclusive, are interpreted as the years 1900–1999." In fact, *DateSerial* handles two-digit years in the same way as other Visual Basic date functions. A year argument between 0 and 29 is taken to be in the 21st Century (2000 to 2029), year arguments between 30 and 99 are taken to be in the 20th Century (1930 to 1999). Of course, the safest way to specify a year is to use the full four digits.

See Also

DateAdd Function

DateValue Function

Named Arguments

No

Syntax

```
DateValue(stringexpression)
stringexpression
    Use: Required
    Data Type: String
    Any of the date formats recognized by IsDate.
```

Return Value

Variant (Date).

Description

Returns a date variant (variant type 7) containing the date represented by *stringexpression*. The date value is formatted according to the short date setting defined by the Regional Settings applet in the Control Panel. *DateValue* can successfully recognize a *stringexpression* in any of the date formats recognized by *IsDate*. *DateValue* doesn't return time values in a date/time string; they are simply dropped. However, if *stringexpression* includes a valid date value but an invalid time value, a runtime error results.

Rules at a Glance

- The order of the day, the month, and the year within *stringexpression* must be the same as the sequence defined by the computer's regional settings.

- Only those date separators recognized by *IsDate* can be used.

- If you don't specify a year in your date expression, *DateValue* uses the current year from the computer's system date.

Example

```
Dim sDateExpression As String

sDateExpression = 10 & "/" & "March" & "/" & 1998

If IsDate(sDateExpression) Then
    Debug.Print DateValue(sDateExpression)
Else
    Debug.Print "invalid date"
End If
```

Programming Tips & Gotchas

- When working with dates, always check that a date is valid using the *IsDate* function prior to passing it as a function parameter.

- If *stringexpression* includes time information as well as date information, the time information is ignored; however, if only time information is passed to *DateValue*, an error is generated.

- *DateValue* handles two-digit years in the following manner: year arguments between 0 and 29 are taken to be in the 21st Century (2000 to 2029), while year arguments between 30 and 99 are taken to be in the 20th Century (1930 to 1999). Of course, the safest way to specify a year is to use the full four digits.

- The current formats being used for dates are easier to discover on Windows NT than on Windows 95. On Windows NT, the date formats are held as string values in the following registry keys:

  Date Separator
  HKEY_CURRENT_USER\Control Panel\International, sDate value entry

  Long Date
  HKEY_CURRENT_USER\Control Panel\International, sLongDate value
  entry

  Short Date
  HKEY_CURRENT_USER\Control Panel\International, sShortDate value
  entry

- The more common approach to date conversion is to use the *CDate* function. Microsoft also recommends using the C... conversion functions due to their enhanced capabilities and their locale awareness.

Returning the Current Date Formats in Windows NT

The example shows how to use the Windows API to return the current long and short date formats on Windows NT 4.0 machines. Unfortunately, Windows 95 exposes only the Locale ID in the registry unless individual elements have been changed individually, and there are a thousand and one API constants and function calls required to retrieve the settings. Such deep API work is really outside the scope of this book.

Example

```
Option Explicit

'declare the API Functions and constants required
Private Const HKEY_CURRENT_USER = &H80000001
Private Const KEY_ACCESS = &H3F
Declare Function RegOpenKeyEx Lib "advapi32.dll" Alias _
    "RegOpenKeyExA" (ByVal hKey As Long, _
    ByVal lpSubKey As String, ByVal ulOptions As Long, _
    ByVal samDesired As Long, phkResult As Long) _
    As Long
Declare Function RegQueryValueExNULL _
```

```
      Lib "advapi32.dll" Alias "RegQueryValueExA" _
      (ByVal hKey As Long, ByVal lpValueName As String, _
      ByVal lpReserved As Long, lpType As Long, _
      ByVal lpData As Long, lpcbData As Long) As Long
Declare Function RegQueryValueExString _
      Lib "advapi32.dll" Alias "RegQueryValueExA" _
      (ByVal hKey As Long, ByVal lpValueName As String, _
      ByVal lpReserved As Long, lpType As Long, _
      ByVal lpData As String, lpcbData As Long) As Long
Declare Function RegCloseKey Lib "advapi32.dll" _
      (ByVal hKey As Long) As Long

Public Function CurrentDateFormat(sType As String) _
   As String

   CurrentDateFormat = _
      QueryDateFormat("Control Panel\International", _
                      "s" & sType & "Date")
End Function

Private Function QueryDateFormat(sKeyName As String, _
               sValueName As String) As String

   On Error GoTo QueryDateFormat_Err

   Dim lReturn As Long             'API Call return value

   Dim lhKey As Long               'handle of opened key
   Dim sValueSetting As String     'date format setting
   Dim lCCh         As Long
   Dim lType        As Long
   Dim lValue       As Long

   'open the registry key
   lReturn = RegOpenKeyEx(HKEY_CURRENT_USER, sKeyName, _
                          0, KEY_ACCESS, lhKey)
   'get the legnth of the setting
   lReturn = RegQueryValueExNULL(lhKey, sValueName, _
                          0&, lType, 0&, lCCh)

   If lReturn <> 0 Then
      Err.Raise 40000, App.Title, _
               "Can't get registry key value"
   Else
      'pad a string to the legnth of the setting
      sValueSetting = String(lCCh, 0)
      'query the setting
      lReturn = RegQueryValueExString(lhKey, sValueName, _
            0&, lType, sValueSetting, lCCh)
      If lReturn = 0 Then
         QueryDateFormat = Left$(sValueSetting, lCCh)
      Else
         QueryDateFormat = ""
      End If
```

```
        End If
        'close the registry key
        RegCloseKey (lhKey)

        Exit Function

QueryDateFormat_Err:
    MsgBox Err.Description
End Function
```
...which can be accessed simply from the client like this...
```
Option Explicit

Private Sub Command1_Click()
    MsgBox CurrentDateFormat("Long")
End Sub
Private Sub Command2_Click()
    MsgBox CurrentDateFormat("Short")
End Sub
```

See Also

CDate Function, DateSerial Function, IsDate Function

Day Function

Named Arguments

No

Syntax

Day(*dateexpression*)
dateexpression
    Use: Required

    Data Type: Any valid date expression

    The path of the directory to set as the new default directory.

Return Value

Variant of subtype Integer.

Description

Returns a variant integer data subtype that can take on a value ranging from 1 to 31, representing the day of the month of *dateexpression*. *dateexpression*, the argument passed to the *Day* function, must be a valid date/time or time value.

Rules at a Glance

- *dateexpression* can be any variant, numeric expression, or string expression that represents a valid date.
- The range of *dateexpression* is 1/1/0000 to 12/31/9999.
- If *dateexpression* is Null, Null is returned.

Example

```
Debug.Print Day(Now)
```

Programming Tips & Gotchas

- When working with dates, always check that a date is valid using the *IsDate* function prior to passing it as a function parameter.

- If *dateexpression* omits the year, *Day* still returns a valid day.

- If the day portion of *dateexpression* is outside its valid range, the function generates runtime error 13, "Type mismatch." This is also true if the day and month portion of *dateexpression* is 2/29 for a nonleap year.

- To return the day of the week, use the *WeekDay* function.

See Also

DatePart Function, WeekDay Function, WeekDayName Function, Month Function, Year Function

---

DDB Function

Syntax

```
DDB(cost, salvage, life, period[, factor])
```

cost

> Use: Required
>
> Data Type: Double
>
> The initial cost of the asset.

salvage

> Use: Required
>
> Data Type: Double
>
> The value of the asset at the end of *life*.

life

> Use: Required
>
> Data Type: Double
>
> Length of life of the asset.

period

> Use: Required
>
> Data Type: Double
>
> Period for which the depreciation is to be calculated.

factor

> Use: Optional
>
> Data Type: Variant
>
> The rate at which the asset balance declines. If omitted, 2 (double-declining method) is assumed. However, the documentation doesn't mention what other values are supported or what they mean.

Reference

Return Value

Double representing the depreciation of an asset.

Description

Returns a Double representing the depreciation of an asset for a specific time period using the double-declining balance method or another method you specify using the *factor* argument. The double-declining balance calculates depreciation at an differential rate that varies inversely with the age of the asset. Depreciation is highest at the beginning of the life of an asset and declines over time.

Rules at a Glance

- *life* and *period* must be specified in the same time units. In other words, both must be expressed in units of months, or both must be years.

- All arguments must be positive numbers.

Example

```
Dim dblInitialCost As Double
Dim dblSalvageValue As Double
Dim dblUsefulLife As Double
Dim dblPeriod As Double
Dim dblThisPeriodDepr As Double
Dim dblTotDepreciation As Double

dblInitialCost = 2000
dblSalvageValue = 50
dblUsefulLife = 12
dblTotDepreciation = 0

For dblPeriod = 1 To 12
    dblThisPeriodDepr = DDB(dblInitialCost, _
                dblSalvageValue, dblUsefulLife, dblPeriod)
    dblTotDepreciation = dblTotDepreciation + _
                    dblThisPeriodDepr
    Debug.Print "Month " & dblPeriod & ": " & _
            dblThisPeriodDepr
Next dblPeriod

Debug.Print "TOTAL: " & dblTotDepreciation
```

Programming Tips & Gotchas

- The double-declining balance depreciation method calculates depreciation at a higher rate in the initial period and decreases in subsequent periods.

- The *DDB* function uses the following formula to calculate depreciation for a given period:

```
Depreciation / period = ((cost - salvage) * factor) / life
```

See Also

A psychiatrist!

Debug Object

In both Visual Basic and VBA, the Debug Object is a relatively inaccessible object that is responsible for sending output to the Immediate window.

Debug Object Methods

Method	Description
Assert	Conditionally suspends execution and transfers control to the Immediate window; available in Visual Basic, but not in VBA.
Print	Displays output in the Immediate window.

Debug.Assert Method

Syntax

```
object.Assert booleanexpression
object
```
   Use: Required

   Data Type: Debug object

   Always evaluates to the Debug object.

```
booleanexpression
```
   Use: Required

   Data Type: Boolean

   Expression that evaluates to a Boolean value.

Return Value

None.

Description

Conditionally suspends program execution and transfers control to the Immediate window if the value of *booleanexpression* is `False`.

Rules at a Glance

- *booleanexpression* must evaluate to a Boolean value.

- If *booleanexpression* is `False`, program execution is suspended and control transfers to the Immediate window.

- Program execution can be resumed by pressing the Continue button on either the Standard or Debug toolbars.

Programming Tips & Gotchas

- The Assert method is available only in Visual Basic; the Debug object in the VBA development environment doesn't support the Assert method.

- *Assert* is typically used when debugging to test an expression that should evaluate to True. If it doesn't, the Immediate window can be used to investigate why the test failed.

- *Debug.Assert* executes only when an application is run in the design-time environment; the statement has no effect in a compiled application. This means that *Debug.Assert* never produces a runtime error if the call to it is inappropriate, nor does it suspend program execution outside of the VB IDE. Because of this, you don't have to remove *Debug.Assert* statements from finished code or separate them with conditional #If...Then statements.

Debug.Print Method

Syntax

```
object.Print [outputlist]
object
```
Use: Required

Data Type: Debug object

Always evaluates to the Debug object.

```
outputlist
```
Use: Optional

Data Type: String

Expression or list of expressions to print. If omitted, a blank line is printed (for details, see the following table).

Output Syntax

```
{Spc(n) | Tab(n)} expression charpos
Spc(n)
```
Use: Optional

Inserts *n* space characters in the output string.

```
Tab(n)
```
Use: Optional

Inserts a Tab character at position *n*.

```
expression
```
Use: Optional

Numeric or string expression to print in the Immediate window.

```
charpos
```
Use: Optional

Determines the position of the next character.

Description

Prints text in the Immediate pane of the Debug window in the design-time environment.

Rules at a Glance

- *expression* can include literal, numeric, string, and variant data.

- If *charpos* is a semicolon (;), the next character immediately follows the last character of *expression*. For example:

```
Debug.Print sFileName; iFileNo
```

- The Tab(*n*) argument doesn't actually insert any tab characters (Chr(9)); it fills the space from the end of the last expression to column *n* (or to the start of the next print zone) with space characters.

- You can also use Tab(*n*) as the *charpos* argument to position the next character at an absolute column number.

- If *charpos* is omitted, a carriage return is appended to *expression*, and the next character is printed on the next line.

- Use the & concatenation character to create an output string from several elements.

- The Debug.Print method uses the locale settings of the current system to format dates, times, and numbers using the correct separators.

Example

```
#Const ccDebug = 1
...
#If ccDebug  Then
    Debug.Print "Value of dblx: " & dblx
#End if
```

Programming Tips & Gotchas

- The Debug.Print method examines the values of variables or traces program flow in a programming running within the VB or VBA design-time environment. It allows you to gather information about your program without interrupting its execution, as you would if you set breakpoints or used the *MsgBox* function to display debugging messages or the values of program variables.

- Unlike the retail version of VB, the Debug object in the VBA development environment doesn't include an Assert method.

- Certain data types may not behave as you'd expect, as this table shows:

Output Data Type	Formatted Output to Immediate Window
Boolean	True or False
Date	Short Format Date as per system locale settings
Error	Error followed by the corresponding error code
Null (Variant)	Null

- In Visual Basic applications, *Debug.Print* executes only when an application is run in the design-time environment; the statement has no effect in a compiled application. Similarly, in Microsoft Office, *Debug.Print* executes only when the Visual Basic editor window is open and the Immediate window is displayed. This means that *Debug.Print* never produces a runtime error if the call to it is inappropriate, and that you don't have to remove *Debug.Print* from finished code or separate it with conditional #If...Then statements.

See Also

#Const Directive, #If...Then...#Else Statement

Declare Statement

Named Arguments

No

Syntax

Syntax for subroutines

```
[Public | Private] Declare Sub name Lib "libname" _
     [Alias "aliasname"] [([arglist])]
```

Syntax for functions

```
[Public | Private] Declare Function name Lib "libname"
     [Alias "aliasname"] [([arglist])] [As type]
Public
```

Use: Optional

Keyword used to declare a procedure that has scope in all procedures in all modules in the application.

Private

Use: Optional

Keyword used to declare a procedure that has scope only within the module in which it's declared.

Sub

Use: Optional

Keyword indicating that the procedure doesn't return a value. Mutually exclusive with Function.

Function

Use: Optional

Indicates that the procedure returns a value. Mutually exclusive with Sub.

name

Use: Required

Data Type: String

Any valid procedure name within the DLL or code library. If the *aliasname* argument is used, *name* represents the name the function or procedure is called in your code, while *aliasname* represents the name of the routine as found in the external library.

`Lib`

> Use: Required
>
> Keyword indicating that the procedure is contained within a DLL or other code library.

libname

> Use: Required
>
> Data Type: String
>
> The name of the DLL or other code library that contains the declared procedure.

`Alias`

> Use: Optional
>
> Keyword whose presence indicates that *name* is different from the procedure's real name within the DLL or other code library.

aliasname

> Use: Optional
>
> Data Type: String
>
> The real name of the procedure within the DLL or code library.

arglist

> Use: Optional
>
> Data Type: Any
>
> A list of variables representing the arguments that are passed to the procedure when it's called. (For details of the *arglist* syntax and elements, see the entries for the Sub statement or Function statement.)

type

> Use: Optional
>
> Data type of the value returned by a function. (For further details see the Function statement entry.)

Description

Used at module level to declare references to external procedures in a dynamic-link library (DLL).

Rules at a Glance

- You can place a Declare statement within a code module, in which case it can be public or private, or within the declarations section of a form or class module, in which case it must be private.

- Leaving the parentheses empty and not supplying an *arglist* indicates that the Sub or Function procedure has no arguments.

- The number and type of arguments included in *arglist* are checked each time the procedure is called.

- The data type you use in the As clause following *arglist* must match that returned by the function.

Example

```
Option Explicit

Declare Function GetVersion Lib "kernel32"() As Long

Public Function WhereAmI() As Boolean

    Dim lWinVersion As Long
    Dim lWinMajVer As Long
    Dim lWinMinVer As Long
    Dim sSys As String

    lWinVersion = GetVersion()

    lWinMajVer = lWinVersion And 255
    lWinMinVer = (lWinVersion And 65280) / 256

    If lWinVersion And &H80000000 Then
        sSys = "Windows 95"
    Else
        sSys = "Windows NT"
    End If

    Msgbox "Platform: " & sSys & vbCrLf & _
            "Version: " & lWinMajVer & "." & lWinMinVer
```

Programming Tips & Gotchas

- If you don't specify a Public or Private keyword, the visibility of the external procedure is public by default. However, if the routine is declared in the declarations section of a form or a class module, a compiler error ("Constants, fixed length strings, arrays, and Declare statements not allowed as Public members of object modules") results.

- Using an alias is useful when the name of an external procedure would conflict with a Visual Basic keyword or with the name of a procedure within your project, or when the name of the procedure in the code library isn't allowed by the Visual Basic DLL naming convention. In addition, *aliasname* is frequently used in the case of functions in the Win32 API that have string parameters, where the "official" documented name of the function is used in code to call either of two "real" functions, one an ANSI and the other a Unicode version. For example:

```
Declare Function ExpandEnvironmentStrings _
    Lib "kernel32" Alias "ExpandEnvironmentStringsA" _
    (ByVal lpSrc As String, ByVal lpDst As String, _
    ByVal nSize As Long) As Long
```

defines the documented Win32 function *ExpandEnvironmentStrings* to a VB application. However, although calls to the function take the form:

```
lngBytes = ExpandEnvironmentStrings(strOriginal, _
            strCopy, len(strCopy)
```

the actual name of the function as it exists in *Kernel32.dll* is *ExpandEnviron-mentStringsA*. (Windows API functions ending in A are the ANSI string versions, and those ending in W (for Wide) are the Unicode string versions.)

- You can use the # symbol at the beginning of *aliasname* to denote that *aliasname* is in fact the ordinal number of a procedure within the DLL or code library. In this case, all characters following the # sign that compose the *aliasname* argument must be numeric. For example:

```
Declare Function GetForegroundWindow Lib "user32" _
        Alias "#237" () As Long
```

- Remember that DLL entry points are case sensitive. In other words, either *name* or, if it's present and doesn't represent a routine's ordinal position, *aliasname* must correspond in case exactly to the routine as it's defined in the external DLL. Otherwise, VB displays runtime error 453, "Specified DLL function not found." If you aren't sure how the routine name appears in the DLL, use QuickView to browse the DLL and scan for its export table.

- *libname* can include an optional path that identifies precisely where the external library is located. If the path isn't included along with the library name, VB by default searches the current directory, the Windows directory, the Windows system directory, and the directories in the path, in that order.

- If the external library is one of the major Windows system DLLs (like *Kernel32.dll* or *Advapi32.dll*), *libname* can consist of only the root filename, rather than the complete filename and extension.

- In some cases, a single parameter to an API function can accept one of several data types as arguments. This is particularly common when a function accepts a pointer to a string buffer if an argument is to be supplied and a null pointer if it doesn't; the former is expressed in Visual Basic by a string argument and the latter by a 0 passed to the function by value. It's also the case whenever an API function designates a parameter's data type as LPVOID, which indicates a pointer to any data type. To handle this, you can define separate versions of the DECLARE statement, one for each data type to be passed to the function. (In this case, *name* designates the name by which a particular API function is referenced in your program, while the ALIAS clause designates the name of the routine as it exists in the DLL.) A second alternative, rather than having to "strongly type" a parameter in *arglist*, is to designate its data type as As Any, indicating that the routine accepts an argument of any data type. While this provides you with a flexible way of partly overcoming the mismatch between VB and C data types, you should use it with caution, since it suspends Visual Basic's normal type checking for that argument.

- Windows NT was built from the ground up using Unicode (two-byte) strings; however, it also supports ANSI strings. OLE 2.0 was built to use Unicode strings exclusively. Visual Basic from Version 4 onwards uses Unicode strings internally, but passes ANSI strings into your program. What does all this mean for you? Well, Windows NT and OLE 2.0 API calls that have string parameters require them to be passed as Unicode strings. Unfortunately, although Visual Basic uses Unicode strings internally, it converts strings passed to these DLLs back into ANSI. The remedy is to use a dynamic array of type Byte. Passing and receiving arrays of bytes circumvents Visual Basic's Unicode-ANSI conversion.

To pass a string to a Unicode API function, declare a dynamic byte array, assign your string to the array, and concatenate a terminating null character (vbNullChar) to the end of the string, then pass the first byte of the array (at element 0) to the function, as the following simple snippet shows:

```
Dim bArray() As Byte
bArray() = "My String" & vbNullChar
someApiCall(bArray(0))
```

- One of the most common uses of the Declare statement is to make routines in the Win32 API accessible to your programs. For more information on calling the Win32 API from Visual Basic, see Dan Appleman's *The Visual Basic Programmer's Guide to the Win32 API,* published by Ziff-Davis Press.

See Also

Sub Statement, Function Statement, StrConv Function

Def... Statement

Syntax

```
DefBool letterrange[, letterrange]
DefByte letterrange [, letterrange]
DefInt letterrange [, letterrange]
DefLng letterrange [, letterrange]
DefCur letterrange [, letterrange]
DefSng letterrange [, letterrange]
DefDbl letterrange [, letterrange]
DefDec letterrange [, letterrange]
DefDate letterrange [, letterrange]
DefStr letterrange [, letterrange]
DefObj letterrange [, letterrange]
DefVar letterrange [, letterrange]
```

letterrange

    Use: Required

    Data Type: String

    Use the syntax *Letter1[-Letter2]*.

 Unless you are using a strict code convention, this way of declaring variables is a way to become extremely confused with the data types used in your application in as short a time as possible.

Description

Used at module level to define a default data type for variables, arguments passed to procedures, and the return type for Function and Property Get procedures whose names start with the specified characters. For example, the statement DefStr s tells your program that *every* variable, function, and argument beginning with the letter "s" is a string data type.

Rules at a Glance

- The statement name determines the data type:

Statement	Data Type
DefBool	Boolean
DefByte	Byte
DefInt	Integer
DefLng	Long
DefCur	Currency
DefSng	Single
DefDbl	Double
DefDec	Decimal
DefDate	Date
DefStr	String
DefObj	Object
DefVar	Variant

- You can override the default data types defined with `Def...` by using the `Dim` statement.

- `Def...` statements have scope only within the module in which they appear. There is no such thing as a public or global `Def...` statement for the project.

Example

```
DefStr s
DefDbl d
DefInt i

. . .

iMyInteger = 100
dMyDouble = 122345.899
sMyString = "Hello World"
```

Programming Tips & Gotchas

- Elements of user-defined types aren't affected by `Def...` statements because the elements must be explicitly declared.

- `Def...` statements must appear before all other declarations within the declarations section of a module.

- If your code includes the `Option Explicit` statement, which indicates that your application relies on strong variable typing, `Def...` statements for the most part are rendered superfluous, since the `Dim` statement is still required to declare each variable. However, in this case, the `Def...` statement defines the data type of variables whose `Dim` statements don't specify a specific data type. For example, in the code fragment:

```
Option Explicit
DefStr s

Public strMyVar1
```

strMyVar1 has been defined as a string by the DefStr statement.

See Also

Dim Statement

DeleteSetting Statement

Named Arguments

Yes

Syntax

```
DeleteSetting appname[, section[, key]]
appname
```
> Use: Required

> Data Type: String

> The name of the application. This must be a subkey of the HKEY_
> CURRENT_USER\Software\VB and VBA Program Settings registry key.

```
section
```
> Use: Optional

> Data Type: String

> The name of the application key's subkey that is to be deleted. *section* can be a single key or a registry path separated with backslashes.

```
key
```
> Use: Optional

> Data Type: String

> The name of the value entry to delete.

Description

Deletes a complete application key, one of its subkeys, or a single value entry from the Windows registry.

Rules at a Glance

- *section* can contain a relative path (similar to that used to describe the folders on a hard drive) to navigate from the application key to the subkey to be deleted. For example, to delete the value entry named TestKey in the registry key HKEY_CURRENT_USER\Software\VB and VBA Program Settings\ RegTester\BranchOne\BranchTwo, you'd use:

```
DeleteSetting "RegTester", "BranchOne\BranchTwo", _
        "TestKey"
```

- You can't use DeleteSetting to delete entries from registry keys that aren't subkeys of HKEY_CURRENT_USER\Software\VB and VBA Program Settings.

- If *key* is supplied, only the value entry named *key* and its associated value are deleted.

- If *key* is omitted, the subkey named `section` is deleted.

- If `section` is omitted, the entire application key named *appname* is deleted.

Example

```
Sub TestTheReg()
    SaveSetting "MyRealGoodApp", _
        "TestBranch\SomeSection\AnotherSection", _
        " Testkey ", "10"
    MsgBox "Now look in RegEdit"
End Sub

Sub TestDelete()

    If GetSetting("MyRealGoodApp", _
                "TestBranch\SomeSection\AnotherSection", _
                "") = "" Then

        DeleteSetting "MyRealGoodApp", _
        "TestBranch\SomeSection\AnotherSection", _
        "TestKey"

        MsgBox "Look again!"
    End If
End Sub
```

Programming Tips & Gotchas

- `DeleteSetting` was designed to operate on initialization files on 16-bit platforms and on the registry on 32-bit platforms. But the terminology that describes the statement in the official documentation is based on initialization files, rather than on the registry. In particular, what is described as a *key* is a named key in an initialization file and a value entry in the registry.

- The behavior of the `DeleteSetting` statement differs under Windows 95 and Windows NT when it's used to remove a key from the registry. Under Windows 95, if the statement deletes either *appname* or *section*, all subkeys belonging to the key to be deleted are also deleted. Under Windows NT, on the other hand, the keys *appname* and *section* are deleted only if they contain no subkeys.

- `DeleteSetting` can't delete the default value (that is, the unnamed value entry) belonging to any key. If you're using only the VB registry functions, though, this isn't a serious limitation, since `SaveSetting` doesn't allow you to create a default value.

- Unless you are quite sure what you're doing, you should delete only registry settings that have been placed in the registry by your own code. Inadvertently deleting the wrong entries can have disastrous consequences. However, because this statement gives you access only to the subkeys of `HKEY_CURRENT_USER\Software\VB and VBA Program Settings`, the potential damage is minimized.

- Never assume that the key you want to delete is necessarily present in the registry. DeleteSetting deletes a user key (that is, a subkey of HKEY_ CURRENT_USER); except on Win95 systems that aren't configured to support multiple users, the user key is formed from a file that reflects only the present user's settings. This means that when one user runs an application, user settings are stored in his or her registry key. But when a second user runs the application for the first time, settings for that user aren't likely to be there. Attempting to delete a nonexistent key produces runtime error 5, "Invalid procedure call or argument." To prevent the error, you should first test for the presence of the registry key, as shown in the previous example.

- For full details of how to work properly with the registry, see *Inside the Windows 95 Registry*, written by Ron Petrusha, published by O'Reilly & Associates.

See Also

GetAllSettings Function, GetSetting Function, SaveSetting Statement

---

Dictionary Object (VB6)

Reference

Microsoft Scripting Runtime (../*SYSTEM32/SCRRUN.DLL*)

Description

The Dictionary object is another new feature of VB6 that has found its way into wider use from its humble beginnings in Version 2 of the VBScript scripting runtime. The Dictionary object is similar to a Collection object, except that it's loosely based on the Perl associative array. Like an array or a Collection object, the Dictionary object holds elements, which are called *items* or members, containing data. A Dictionary object can contain any data whatsoever, including objects and other Dictionary objects. You access the value of these dictionary items by using unique *keys* (or named values) that are stored along with the data, rather than by using an item's ordinal position, as you do with an array. This makes the Dictionary object ideal when you need to access data that is associated with a particular unique named value.

So if you're happily using Collection objects throughout your VB programs, why should you want to change? Here are some of the advantages afforded by the Dictionary object over a Collection object:

- A Dictionary object returns an array of all its keys using one simple method.

- A Dictionary object returns an array of all its members using one simple method.

- A Dictionary object lets you determine if a given key exists in the Dictionary.

- A Dictionary object gives you the ability to overwrite a member value.

- A Dictionary object lets you change a key value.

If that's not enough to convince you, what about performance? In the performance comparisons I've run, very much to my surprise, the Dictionary object ran about twice as fast as a Collection object when adding and reading back objects.

But when adding and reading back simple data types, the Dictionary object was up to three times faster than a Collection object. A clue to the excellent performance of the Dictionary object can be found when you interrogate the Dictionary object in the VB object browser and set the "Show Hidden Members" option.[*] A new hidden property called HashVal appears. It appears, therefore, that the Dictionary object uses a hash table and some advanced sorting and indexing algorithms to achieve this superior performance.

Most of the code written for the Collection object appears to work perfectly well with the Dictionary object, with several notable exceptions:

- You have to resort to some workarounds to use For Each...Next with a Dictionary object. Actually, until recently, it was generally believed that For Each...Next didn't work with the Dictionary object. But in fact, it does. However, rather than the _NewEnum function returning a reference to a member of the Dictionary (as it would with a Collection object), it returns a variant containing the key associated with the member. You then have to pass this key to the Item method to retrieve the member, as the following example shows:

```
Private Sub Command1_Click()

    Dim vKey As Variant
    Dim sItem As String
    Dim oDict As Dictionary

    Set oDict = New Dictionary
        oDict.Add "One", "Engine"
        oDict.Add "Two", "Wheel"
        oDict.Add "Three", "Tire"
        oDict.Add "Four", "Spanner"

    For Each vKey In oDict
        sItem = oDict.Item(vKey)
        Debug.Print sItem
    Next

    Set oDict = Nothing

End Sub
```

Note that even though the key is always a string, a variant must be used in this situation because the For Each variable must be either a variant or an object.

- You can't directly access a Dictionary object item by its ordinal position in the Dictionary. You can work around this easily by assigning the value returned by the Items method to a variant array and iterating through that by ordinal number. (For an example, see the code fragment for the Dictionary.Items

---

[*] To do this, click the right mouse button in either pane of the Object Browser. Then check the Show Hidden Members option on the context menu.

entry.) Even with this extra step, the Dictionary object is significantly faster than a Collection object.

• The syntax of the Dictionary object's Add method is:

```
Dictionary.Add( Key, Item)
```

The order of *Key* and *Item* are the reverse of that in the Collection object. Furthermore, the *Key* parameter isn't optional, and the Dictionary object doesn't support parameters to place an item *Before* or *After* another item, since the object doesn't support ordered access by any means other than a key value.

Note that the Word object model also includes a Dictionary object of rather a different kind. You can still use Dictionary objects in your Word VBA code, but you have to qualify the object library from which you wish to instantiate the Dictionary class. The following code fragment does that:

```
Dim objDict as New Scripting.Dictionary
```

Createable

Yes

Dictionary Object Properties

The Dictionary object includes the following four properties:

CompareMode	Item
Count	Key

Dictionary Object Methods

The Dictionary object supports the following six methods:

Add	Items	Remove
Exists	Keys	RemoveAll

Dictionary.Add Method (VB6)

Named Arguments

Yes

Syntax

```
dictionaryobject.Add key, item
dictionaryobject
```
    Use: Required

    Data Type: Dictionary object

    A reference to a Dictionary object.

key
    Use: Required

    Data Type: String

    A key value that's unique in the Dictionary object.

---

item
>   Use: Required
>
>   Data Type: String
>
>   The item to be added to the dictionary.

Description

Adds a key and its associated item to the specified Dictionary object.

Rules at a Glance

*   If the key isn't unique, runtime error 457, "This key is already associated with an element of this collection," is generated.

*   *item* can be of any data type, including objects and other Dictionary objects.

Example

```
Set oDict = New Dictionary
    iVal = 1
    Set oTest = New clsTest
        With oTest
            .Age = 10
            .Phone = "0112 31234"
            .TestName = "Russell"
        End With

        oDict.Add CStr(iVal), oTest
    Set oTest = Nothing
```

Dictionary.CompareMode Property (VB6)

Syntax

```
dictionaryobject.CompareMode [= CompareMethodConst]
dictionaryobject
```
>   Use: Required
>
>   Data Type: Dictionary object
>
>   A reference to a Dictionary object.

`CompareMethodConst`
>   Use: Optional when returning, required when setting
>
>   Data Type: Numeric constant
>
>   Acceptable values for CompareMode are **BinaryCompare** (0, Binary), **TextCompare** (1, Text), and **DatabaseCompare** (2, Database). Values greater than 2 refer to comparisons using specific locale IDs (LCIDs).

Property Data Type

Numeric enumeration (`CompareMethod` constant).

Description

Sets or returns the mode used to compare the keys in a Dictionary object. The CompareMode setting is used by *StrComp*, the string comparison function.

Rules at a Glance

- CompareMode can be set only on a dictionary that doesn't contain any data.

- You need to explicitly set the CompareMode property only if you don't wish to use the default binary comparison mode.

Dictionary.Count Property (VB6)

Syntax

```
dictionaryobject.Count
dictionaryobject
```
    Use: Required

       Data Type: Dictionary object

       A reference to a Dictionary object.

Property Data Type

Long.

Description

A read-only property that returns the number of key/item pairs in a Dictionary object.

Rules at a Glance

Unlike a Collection object, the Dictionary object is always 0-based.

Example

The following code fragment shows how you can use the Count property:

```
Dim vArray As Variant
vArray = DictObj.Items
For i = 0 to DictObj.Count -1
    Set oObj = vArray(i)
Next
```

Dictionary.Exists Method (VB6)

Named Arguments

Yes

Syntax

```
dictionaryobject.Exists(key)
dictionaryobject
```
    Use: Required

Data Type: Dictionary object

A reference to a Dictionary object.

key

Use: Required

Data Type: String

The key value being sought.

Return Value

Boolean.

Description

Determines if a given key is present in a Dictionary object.

Rules at a Glance

Returns `True` if the specified key exists in the Dictionary object; `False` if not.

Programming Tips & Gotchas

If you attempt to return the Item of a nonexistent key, or assign a new key to a nonexistent key, the nonexistent key is added to the dictionary, along with a blank item. To prevent this, you should use the Exists property to ensure that the Key is present in the dictionary before proceeding.

Example

```
If oDict.Exists(strOldKey) Then
    oDict.Key(strOldKey) = strNewKey
End If
```

Dictionary.Item Property (VB6)

Named Arguments

Yes

Syntax

The syntax for setting an item is:

```
dictionaryobject.Item(key) = item
```

The syntax for returning an item is:

```
value = dictionaryobject.Item(key)
dictionaryobject
```

Use: Required

Data Type: Dictionary object

A reference to a Dictionary object.

Reference

key

Use: Required

Data Type: String

A unique string key for this Dictionary object.

item

Use: Optional

Data Type: Any

The data associated with key.

Property Data Type

Any.

Description

Sets or returns the data item to be linked to a specified key in a Dictionary object.

Rules at a Glance

- The data type is that of the item being returned.

- If you try to set *item* to a nonexistent key, the key is added to the dictionary, and the item is linked to it, a sort of "implicit add."

Programming Tips & Gotchas

- Unlike the Collection object, the Dictionary object doesn't allow you to retrieve an item by its ordinal position.

- If you provide a nonexistent key when trying to retrieve an item, the dictionary exhibits rather strange behavior: it adds *key* to the Dictionary object along with a blank item. You should therefore use the Exists method prior to setting or returning an item, as the example shows.

- A major gripe of all programmers who use the Collection object is the difficulty involved in overwriting an existing Collection member—not so with the Dictionary object. Simply assign the value as you would with other properties.

Example

```
Dim sKey As String
Dim sName As String
sKey = "Name"
If oDictionary.Exists(sKey) Then
    sName = oDictionary.Item(sKey)
Else
    MsgBox "The Key " & sKey & " does not exist"
End If
```

This next example shows how to set or overwrite an item:

```
Dim sKey As String
Dim sName As String
sName = "Dick Shennary"
sKey = "Name"
If oDictionary.Exists(sKey) Then
```

```
     oDictionary.Item(sKey) = sName
Else
     MsgBox "The Key " & sKey & " does not exist"
End If
```

Dictionary.Items Method (VB6)

Named Arguments

Yes

Syntax

```
dictionaryobject.Items
dictionaryobject
```
>   Use: Required

>   Data Type: Dictionary object

>   A reference to a Dictionary object.

Return Value

A Variant array.

Description

Returns an array containing all the items in the specified Dictionary object.

Rules at a Glance

The returned array is always a zero-based variant array whose data subtype matches that of the items in the Dictionary object.

Programming Tips & Gotchas

- The only way to directly access members of the Dictionary is via their key values. However, using the Items method, you can "dump" the data from the Dictionary into a zero-based variant array. The data items can then be accessed like an array in the normal way, as the following code shows:

```
Dim vArray As Variant
vArray = DictObj.Items
For i = 0 to DictObj.Count -1
    Debug.Print vArray(i)
Next I
```

- The Items method retrieves only the items stored in a Dictionary object; you can retrieve all the Dictionary object's keys by calling its Keys method.

Dictionary.Key Property (VB6)

Data Type

String

Named Arguments

Yes

Syntax

The syntax for setting a new key is:

```
dictionaryobject.Key(key) = newkey
```

dictionaryobject
> Use: Required
>
> Data Type: Dictionary object
>
> A reference to a Dictionary object.

key
> Use: Required
>
> Data Type: String
>
> A unique string key for this Dictionary object.

newkey
> Use: Required
>
> Data Type: String
>
> A unique string key for this Dictionary object.

Property Data Type

A String.

Description

Returns the key or replaces an existing key with a new one.

Rules at a Glance

- As with the Item property, if a key that you are attempting to change doesn't exist, the new key is added to the dictionary and is linked to a blank item.

- A concept unknown to users of the Collection object is the ability to change the key associated with an item; however, this is easy with the Dictionary object, as the example demonstrates.

Example

```
Private Function ChangeKeyValue(sOldKey As String, _
                                sNewKey As String) _
                                As Boolean
    If oDictionary.Exists(sOldKey) Then
        oDictionary.Key(sOldKey) = sNewKey
        ChangeKeyValue = True
    Else
        ChangeKeyValue = False
    End If
End Function
```

Dictionary.Keys Method (VB6)

Named Arguments

Yes

Syntax

```
dictionaryobject.Keys
dictionaryobject
```
> Use: Required
>
> Data Type: Dictionary object
>
> A reference to a Dictionary object.

Return Value

A Variant array of subtype String.

Description

Returns an array containing all the Key values in the specified Dictionary object.

Rules at a Glance

The returned array is always a 0-based variant array whose data subtype is String.

Programming Tips & Gotchas

The Keys method retrieves only the keys stored in a Dictionary object; you can retrieve all the Dictionary object's items by calling its Items method.

Example

```
Dim vArray As Variant
vArray = DictObj.Keys
For i = 0 to DictObj.Count -1
    Debug.Print vArray(i)
Next
```

Dictionary.Remove Method (VB6)

Named Arguments

Yes

Syntax

```
dictionaryobject.Remove key
```

```
dictionaryobject
```
> Use: Required
>
> Data Type: Dictionary object
>
> A reference to a Dictionary object.

key

> Use: Required
>
> Data Type: String
>
> The key associated with the item to be removed.

Description

Removes both the specified key and its associated data (i.e., its item) from the dictionary.

Rules at a Glance

If *key* doesn't exist, runtime error 32811, "Method 'Remove' of object 'IDictionary' failed," occurs.

Dictionary.RemoveAll Method (VB6)

Named Arguments

Yes

Syntax

```
dictionaryobject.RemoveAll
dictionaryobject
```

> Use: Required
>
> Data Type: Dictionary Object
>
> A reference to a Dictionary Object.

Description

Clears out the dictionary; in other words, removes all keys and their associated data from the dictionary.

Programming Tips & Gotchas

Analogous to the Collection object's Clear method.

Dim Statement

Named Arguments

No

Syntax

```
Dim varname[([subscripts])] [As [New] type] [,
    varname[([subscripts])] [As [New] type]] . . .
varname
```

> Use: Required
>
> Your chosen name for the variable.

subscripts

    Use: Optional

    Dimensions of an array variable.

New

    Use: Optional

    Keyword that creates an instance of an object.

type

    Use: Optional

    The data type of *varname*.

Description

Declares and allocates storage space in memory for variables. The Dim statement is used either at the start of a procedure or the start of a module to declare a variable of a particular data type.

Rules at a Glance

- In addition to the Visual Basic data types listed in Chapter 3, *type* can be an Object, an object type, or a user-defined type. The default data type, when no type is explicitly declared, is Variant.

- Variable-length strings are declared using the syntax:

```
Dim variablename As String
```

Fixed-length strings, on the other hand, are declared using the syntax:

```
Dim variablename As String * length
```

- You can declare multiple variables in a single Dim statement, but each variable you declare must use a separate **As type** clause.

- Variables have the following values when they are first initialized with the Dim statement:

Data Type	Initial Value
Numeric	0
Variable-length string	Zero-length string ("")
Fixed-length string	Padded with zeros
Variant	Empty
Object	Nothing

- To use an object variable that has not been declared using the New keyword, the Set statement must assign an object to the variable before it can be used, as the following code fragment illustrates:

```
Dim oMySubObj As TestObject.SubObject
Set oMySubObj = oMyObj.SubObject
```

If, however, you use the New keyword, a new instance of the object is automatically created when you first reference the variable, as shown in the following code fragment:

```
Dim oMyObj As New TestObject
```

- To declare array variables, use the following syntax:

  Fixed length, single dimension
  ```
  Dim arrayname(lower To upper) As type
  ```
  Example: `Dim myArray(1 To 10) As Integer`

  Fixed length, multidimension
  ```
  Dim arrayname(lower To upper, lower To upper, ...)
  ```
  Example: `Dim MyArray(20,30) As Integer`

  Variable length, single or multidimension
  ```
  Dim arrayname()
  ```
  Example: `Dim myArray() As Integer`

- You can declare a multidimensional array with up to 60 dimensions.

- Variable-length arrays can be resized using the `ReDim` statement. Fixed-length arrays can't be resized.

- If you don't state *lower*, the index of the first element of the array is either the number indicated in the `Option Base` statement, or zero if `Option Base` hasn't been used.

Example

```
Public Sub Main()

Dim varArr As Variant
Dim intCtr As Integer

varArr = MakeArray()

For intCtr = 0 To UBound(varArr)
    Debug.Print intCtr & ": " & varArr(intCtr)
Next

End Sub


Private Function MakeArray() As Variant

Dim x As Variant

x = Array(5, 6, 7, 8)
MakeArray = x

End Function
```

Programming Tips & Gotchas

- It's accepted practice to place all the `Dim` statements to be used in a particular procedure at the beginning of that procedure.

- To declare a multidimensional array that can handle different types of data in each dimension, declare the array as a Variant.

- When you declare an object reference as `WithEvents`, that object's events can be handled within your application. Object variables must be declared `WithEvents` at the module level to allow you to provide an error handler. The reason for this is that if you declared the object variable `WithEvents` inside a procedure, the object variable would have scope and lifetime only within that procedure.

  When you declare an object variable as `WithEvents` in the declarations section of the module, the name of the object variable appears in the Object drop-down list at the top left of your code window. Select this, and note that the events exposed by the object are available in the Procedure drop-down list at the top right of the code window. You can then add code to these event procedures in the normal way, as shown below:

```
Private WithEvents oEmp As Employee

Private Sub oEmp_CanDataChange(EmployeeCode As String, Cancel
As Boolean)
    'event handling code goes here
End Sub

Private Sub oEmp_DataChanged(EmployeeCode As String)
    'event handling code goes here
End Sub
```

  For a fuller description and discussion of the uses of `WithEvents`, `Event`, and `RaiseEvent`, see the `Event`, `RaiseEvent`, and `WithEvents` entries, as well as Chapter 4.

- The way in which you declare an Object variable with the `Dim` statement dictates whether your application uses late binding or early binding. *Early binding* allows object references to be resolved at compile time and objects to be initialized as your program is loaded into memory; therefore, they are available for use within your program almost instantaneously. *Late binding*, on the other hand, resolves an object reference and initializes an object only when it's referenced in the code at runtime; therefore, your program can appear to "hang" in mid-air while you wait for the object to be created in memory. To optimize the performance of your application, you should use early binding whenever possible. For more information, see Chapter 4.

- Variables declared with `Dim` at the module level are available to all procedures within the module. At the procedure level, variables are available only within the procedure.

- If you are calling a function that returns an array, define the array variable as a simple variant. When the function returns, it's a variant array, as the previous example illustrates.

- Take care when dimensioning fixed-length strings; you can't use them to pass data to external DLLs that are expecting string arguments.

See Also

Const Statement, Def... Statement, Global Statement, Private Statement, Public Statement, ReDim Statement, Set Statement, Static Statement, Type Statement, Chapter 4

Dir, Dir$ Functions

Named Arguments

No

Syntax

```
Dir[(pathname[, attributes])]
```

pathname

Use: Optional

Data Type: String

A string expression that defines a path that may contain a drive name, a folder name, and a filename.

attributes

Use: Optional

Data Type: Numeric or Constant

A constant or numeric expression specifying the file attributes to be matched.

Return Value

Dir returns a variant of subtype string; *Dir$* returns a string data type.

Description

Returns the name of a single file or folder matching the pattern or attribute passed to the function.

Rules at a Glance

- A zero-length string ("") is returned if a matching file isn't found.
- Possible values for *attributes* are:

Constant	Value	Description
vbNormal	0	Normal (not hidden and not a system file)
vbHidden	2	Hidden
vbSystem	4	System file
vbVolume	8	Volume label; if specified, all other attributes are ignored
vbDirectory	16	Directory or folder

- The object browser and published documentation list several other constants that can be supplied as arguments to the *attributes* parameter. However, these either don't work on the Win9x/NT platforms (i.e., **vbAlias**, which is available only on the Macintosh) or have no effect on the operation of the function (**vbReadOnly**, **vbArchive**).

- The *attributes* constants can be added together to create combinations of attributes to match; e.g., **vbHidden** + **vbDirectory** matches hidden directories.

- If *attributes* isn't specified, files matching *pathname* are returned regardless of *attributes*.

- You can use the wildcard characters * and ? within *pathname* to return multiple files.

- Although *pathname* is optional, the first call you make to *Dir* must include *pathname*. *pathname* must also be specified if you are specifying *attributes*. In addition, once *Dir* returns a zero-length string, subsequent calls to *Dir* must specify pathname or runtime error 5 ("Invalid procedure call or argument") results.

Example

```
Private Sub CommandButton1_Click()

Dim sFileName As String
Dim sPath As String

sPath = "c:\windows\*.txt"
sFileName = Dir$(sPath)

Do While sFileName > ""
    ListBox1.AddItem sFileName
    sFileName = Dir$
Loop

End Sub
```

Programming Tips & Gotchas

- *Dir* can return only one filename at a time. To create a list of more than one file that matches *pathname*, you must first call the function using the required parameters, then make subsequent calls using no parameters. When there are no more files matching the initial specification, a zero-length string is returned. Once *Dir* has returned a zero-length string, you must specify a *pathname* in a subsequent call or an error is generated. The example for the *Dir* function shows how to do this in a VBA application using a UserForm with a command button and a list box control. (Note: to get the example to run under VB rather than VBA, the references to ListBox1 should simply be replaced with List1. Also note that the above example doesn't work with the **vbDirectory** attribute.)

- The *Dir* function is the only method of determining if a file exists without having to create elaborate error-handling routines. Quite simply, pass the function the name of the file you wish to check. If *Dir* returns a zero-length string, you know that the file doesn't exist, as the following example shows:

Reference

```
Public Function FileExists(sPath As String) As Boolean

    If Dir(sPath) > "" Then
        FileExists = True
    Else
        FileExists = False
    End If

End Function
```

- The *Dir* function returns filenames in the order in which they appear in the file allocation table. If you need the files in a particular order, you should first store the names in an array before sorting.

- The *Dir* function saves its state between invocations, which means that the function can't be called recursively. For example, if the function returns the name of the directory, you can't then call the *Dir* function to iterate the files in that directory and then return to the original directory.

- If *attributes* is set to vbDirectory only, the function behaves somewhat differently. If wildcard characters are used in *pathname*, the function returns only the first directory that matches the search criteria. Subsequent calls to the function without providing a new *pathname* argument return the names of ordinary files.

- If you are calling the *Dir* function to return the names of one or more files, you must provide an explicit file specification. In other words, if you want to retrieve the names of all files in the Windows directory, for instance, the function call:

```
strFile = Dir("C:\Windows", vbNormal)
```

necessarily fails. Instead, the *Dir* function must be called with the pathname defined as follows:

```
strFile = Dir("C:\Windows\*.*", vbNormal)
```

- A major limitation of the *Dir* and *Dir$* functions is that they return only the filename; they don't provide other information, such as the size, date and time stamp, or attributes of a file. These are most easily accessible by using the File object's Attributes property in the File System object model.

- Many difficulties with the *Dir* function result from not fully understanding how various *attributes* constants affect the file or files returned by the function. By default, *Dir* returns a "normal" file (i.e., a file whose hidden or system attributes aren't set). vbHidden returns a normal file or a hidden file, but not a system file and not a system file that is hidden. vbSystem returns a normal file or a system file, but not a hidden file, including a system file that is hidden. vbSystem + vbHidden returns any file, regardless of whether it's normal, hidden, system, or system and hidden.

- Using the new File System object model in VB6 overcomes all the limitations of *Dir* and *Dir$*.

See Also

CurDir Statement, File System Objects

Do...Loop Statement

Named Arguments

No

Syntax

```
Do [{While | Until} condition]
    [statements]
[Exit Do]
    [statements]
Loop
```

or:

```
Do
    [statements]
[Exit Do]
    [statements]
Loop [{While | Until} condition]
```

condition

> Use: Optional
>
> Data Type: Boolean expression
>
> An expression that evaluates to **True** or **False**.

statements

> Use: Optional
>
> Program statements that are repeatedly executed while, or until, *condition* is **True**.

Description

Repeatedly executes a block of code while or until a condition becomes **True**.

Rules at a Glance

- **Do...Loop** on its own repeatedly executes the code that is contained within its boundaries indefinitely. You therefore need to specify within the code under what conditions the loop is to stop repeating. In addition, if the loop executes more than once, the variable controlling loop execution must be modified inside of the loop. For example:

```
Do
    intCtr = intCtr + 1    ' Modify loop control variable
    MsgBox "Iteration " & intCtr & _
           " of the Do loop..."
    ' Compare to upper limit
    If intCtr = 10  Then Exit Do
Loop
```

  Failure to do this results in the creation of an endless loop.

- Adding the **Until** keyword after **Do** instructs your program to **Do** something **Until** the condition is **True**. Its syntax is:

```
Do Until condition
   'code to execute
Loop
```

If *condition* is **True** before your code gets to the **Do** statement, the code within the **Do...Loop** is ignored.

- Adding the **While** keyword after **Do** repeats the code while a particular condition is **True**. When the condition becomes **False**, the loop is automatically exited. The syntax of the **Do While** statement is:

```
Do While condition
   'code to execute
Loop
```

Again, the code within the **Do...Loop** construct is ignored if *condition* is **False** when the program arrives at the loop.

- In some cases, you may need to execute the loop at least once. You might, for example, evaluate the values held within an array and terminate the loop if a particular value is found. In that case, you'd need to execute the loop at least once. To do this, place the **Until** or **While** keyword along with the condition *after* the **Loop** statement. **Do...Loop Until** always executes the code in the loop at least once and continues to loop until the condition is **True**. Likewise, **Do...Loop While** always executes the code at least once, and continues to loop while the condition is **True**. The syntax of these two statements is as follows:

```
Do
   'code to execute
Loop Until condition
```

```
Do
   'code to execute
Loop While condition
```

- A **Null** *condition* is treated as **False**.
- Your code can exit the loop at any point by executing the **Exit Do** statement.

Programming Tips & Gotchas

You'll also encounter situations in which you intend to continually execute the loop while or until a condition is **True**, except in a particular case. This type of exception is handled using the **Exit Do** statement. You can place as many **Exit Do** statements within a **Do...Loop** structure as you require. As with any exit from a **Do...Loop**, whether it's exceptional or normal, the program continues execution on the line directly following the **Loop** statement. The following code fragment illustrates the use of **Exit Do**:

```
Do Until condition1
   'code to execute
      If condition2 Then
         Exit Do
      End if
   'more code to execute—only if condition2 is false
Loop
```

See Also

For...Next Statement, For Each...Next Statement, While...Wend Statement

DoEvents Function

Named Arguments

No

Syntax

```
DoEvents()
```

Return Value

In VBA, *DoEvents* returns 0; in the retail version of VB, it returns the number of open forms.

Description

Allows the operating system to process events and messages waiting in the message queue. For example, you can allow a user to click a Cancel button while a processor-intensive operation is executing. In this scenario, without *DoEvents*, the click event wouldn't be processed until after the operation had completed; with *DoEvents*, the Cancel button's Click event can be fired and its event handler executed even though the processor-intensive operation is still executing.

Rules at a Glance

Control is returned automatically to your program or the procedure that called *DoEvents* once the operating system has processed the message queue.

Example

The following example uses a UserForm with two command buttons to illustrate how *DoEvents* interrupts a running process:

```
Option Explicit
Private lngCtr As Long
Private blnFlag As Boolean

Private Sub CommandButton1_Click()

    blnFlag = True

    Do While blnFlag
        lngCtr = lngCtr + 1
        DoEvents
    Loop
    MsgBox "Loop interrupted after " & lngCtr & _
           " iterations."
End Sub

Private Sub CommandButton2_Click()
```

Reference

```
        blnFlag = False

End Sub
```

Programming Tips & Gotchas

*   You may consider using the retail version of VB to create standalone ActiveX
    EXEs that handle very intensive or long processes. These can then be called
    from your VBA code. This allows you to pass the responsibility of time slic-
    ing and multitasking to the operating system.

*   Make sure that during the time you have passed control to the operating sys-
    tem with *DoEvents*, the procedure calling *DoEvents* isn't called from another
    part of the application or from another application, since the return from
    DoEvents may be compromised. For the same reason, you must not use the
    DoEvents function within VB in-process ActiveX DLLs.

*   While *DoEvents* can be essential for increasing the responsiveness of your
    program, it should at the same time be used judiciously, since it entails an
    enormous performance penalty. For example, the following table compares
    the number of seconds required for a simple **For...Next** loop to iterate one
    million times when *DoEvents* isn't called, on the one hand, and when it's
    called on each iteration of the loop, on the other:

without *DoEvents*	0.3 seconds
with *DoEvents*	49.8 seconds

If most of a procedure's processing occurs inside a loop, one way of avoid-
ing far-too-frequent calls to *DoEvents* is to call it conditionally every hundred
or thousand iterations of the loop. For example:

```
Dim lngCtr As Long
For lngCtr = 0 To 1000000
    If lngCtr / 1000 = Int(lngCtr / 1000) Then
        DoEvents
    End If
Next
```

Drive Object (VB6)

Description

Interrogates the system properties of any drive connected to the current machine,
including network drives. The Drive object supports no methods. The RootFolder
property returns a Folder object representing a drive's root folder or directory;
from this you can obtain a Folders collection object containing the subfolders of
the root, and thus gain access to all parts of the drive.

See the File System object model entry for an overview, including the library reference needed to access it.

Createable

No

Returned by

FileSystemObject.Drives.Item property

Properties

All Drive object properties are read-only. In addition, removable media drives must be ready (i.e., have media inserted) for the Drive object to read certain properties.

AvailableSpace
> Data Type: Variant

> The number of bytes unused on the disk.

DriveLetter
> Data Type: String

> The drive letter used for this drive on the current machine (e.g., *C*).

DriveType
> Data Type: DriveType constant

> A Drive Type constant (see table) indicating the type of drive. Any remote drive is shown only as remote. For example, a shared CD-ROM or Zip drive that is both remote and removable is shown simply as remote on any machine other than the machine on which it's installed.

Constant	Value
CDROM	4
Fixed	2
RAM Disk	5
Remote	3
Removable	1
Unknown	0

FileSystem
> Data Type: String

> The installed filesystem; returns FAT, NTFS, or CDFS.

FreeSpace
> Data Type: Variant

> The number of bytes unused on the disk.

IsReady
> Data Type: Boolean

> For hard drives, this should always return **True**. For removable media drives, **True** is returned if media is in the drive; otherwise, **False** is returned.

Reference

Path

> Data Type: String

> The drive name followed by a colon (e.g., *C:*) This is the default property of the Drive object.

RootFolder

> Data Type: Folder object

> Gives you access to the rest of the filesystem by exposing a Folder object representing the root folder.

SerialNumber

> Data Type: Long

> The serial number of the drive.

ShareName

> Data Type: String

> For a network share, the machine name and share name (e.g., *NTSERV1*\ *TestWork*).

TotalSize

> Data Type: Variant

> The total size of the drive in bytes.

VolumeName

> Data Type: String

> The drive's volume name, if one is assigned (e.g., *DRIVE_C*).

Drives Collection Object (VB6)

Description

All drives connected to the current machine are included in the Drives collection, even those that aren't currently ready (like removable media drives with no media inserted in them). The Drives collection object is zero-based and is read-only.

See the File System object model entry for an overview, including the library reference needed to access it.

Createable

No

Returned by

FileSystemObject.Drives property

Properties

Count

> Data Type: Long

> Returns the number of Drive objects in the collection.

Item

Syntax: oDrives.Item(*key*)

Data Type: Drive object

Returns a Drive object whose key is *key*, the drive letter. This is an unusual collection, since the drive's index value (its ordinal position in the collection) can't be used; attempting to do so generates runtime error 5, "Invalid procedure call or argument." Since attempting to retrieve a Drive object for a drive that doesn't exists generates runtime error 68, it's a good idea to call the FileSystemObject object's DriveExists method beforehand.

Example

```
Dim ofsFileSys  As FileSystemObject
Dim ofsDrives As Drives
Dim ofsDrive As Drive

Set ofsFileSys = New FileSystemObject
    Set ofsDrives = ofsFileSys.Drives
        Set ofsDrive = ofsDrives.Item("C")
            MsgBox ofsDrive.DriveType
        Set ofsDrive = Nothing
    Set ofsDrives = Nothing
Set ofsFileSys = Nothing
```

See Also

Drive Object, FileSystemObject.Drives Property

End... Statement

Syntax

```
End Enum
End Function
End If
End Property
End Select
End Sub
End Type
End With
```

Description

Ends a procedure or a block of code.

Rules at a Glance

The **End** statement is used as follows:

Statement	Description
End	Terminates program execution.
End Enum	Marks the end of an enumerated type.
End Function	Marks the end of a **Function** procedure.

Statement	Description
End If	Marks the end of an If...Then...Else statement.
End Property	Marks the end of a Property Let, Property Get, or Property Set procedure.
End Select	Marks the end of a Select Case statement.
End Sub	Marks the end of a Sub procedure.
End Type	Marks the end of a user-defined type definition.
End With	Marks the end of a With statement.

Programming Tips & Gotchas

Although supported, the End statement used by itself to terminate the program shouldn't be used within a VBA application. Instead you should terminate execution of a procedure prematurely using the Exit... statement.

See Also

Exit... Statement

Enum Statement

Named Arguments

No

Syntax

```
[Public | Private] Enum name
membername [= constantexpression]
membername [= constantexpression]
. . .
End Enum
```

name
> Use: Required

> The name of the enumerated data type.

membername
> Use: Required

> The name of a member of the enumerated data type.

constantexpression
> Use: Optional

> Data Type: Long

> The value to be assigned to membername.

Description

Defines an enumerated data type. All the values of the data type are defined by the instances of membername.

Rules at a Glance

- The Enum statement can appear only at module level, in the declarations section of a form, code module, or class module.

- The Public keyword makes the enumerated data type visible throughout the project in which it's used; this is the default behavior. Note that adding a reference to a library containing public enumerated types to a project makes those types visible to the project. A class doesn't have to be instantiated to access these enumerated types.

- The Private keyword makes the enumerated data type visible only to the module in which it appears.

- *constantexpression* must evaluate to a Long. It can be either a negative or a positive number. It can also be another member of an enumerated data type or an expression that includes long integers and enumerated data types.

- If you assign a floating point value to *constantexpression*, it's rounded and converted to a long integer automatically.

- If *constantexpression* is omitted, the value assigned to *membername* is 0 if it's the first expression in the enumeration. Otherwise, its value is 1 greater than the value of the preceding *membername*.

- The values assigned to *membername* can't be modified at runtime.

Programming Tips & Gotchas

- When two enumerated data types in different libraries share the same name but different members or values, references to the enumerated type are resolved based on the library that has been assigned the highest priority in the References dialog. Because enumerated data types aren't members of a class (even though they are defined in a class's type library), a reference to a particular enumerated data type can't be qualified with a class name or library name.

- Once you define an enumerated type, you can use *name* as the return value of a function. For example, given the enumeration:

```
Public Enum enQuarter
    enQ1 = 1
    enQ2 = 2
    enQ3 = 3
    enQ4 = 4
End Enum
```

you can use it as the return value of a function, as illustrated by the following function declaration:

```
Public Function QuarterFromDate(datVar as Date) _
            As enQuarter
```

You can also use it in a procedure's parameter list when defining a parameter's data type, as in the following code fragment:

```
Public Function GetQuarterlySales(intQ As enQuarter) _
            As Double
```

- Individual values of an enumerated type can be used in your program just like normal constants.

- Enumerated types provide the advantage of allowing you to replace numeric values with more mnemonic labels, and of allowing you to select values using the Auto List Members feature in the VB and VBA IDEs. However, when you declare a parameter or function's return value to be an enumerated type, VBA provides no automatic type checking. Consequently, if your program needs to insure that the values passed to a routine are valid, your code is responsible for handling the validation.

- Remember that the members of an enumerated type must evaluate to a Long. This is a major limitation, and there is no workaround.

See Also

Const Statement, Select Case Statement

Environ, Environ$ Functions

Named Arguments

Yes

Syntax

```
Environ({envstring | number})
```
envstring
  Key: Optional

  Data Type: String

  The name of the required environment variable.

number
  Key: Optional

  Data Type: Numeric expression

  The ordinal number of the environment variable within the environment string table.

Return Value

Environ returns a string containing the text assigned to *envstring*.

Description

Returns the value assigned to an operating-system environment variable.

Rules at a Glance

- A zero-length string ("") is returned if *envstring* doesn't exist in the operating system's environment-string table, or if there is no environment string in the position specified by *number*.

- *envstring* and *number* are mutually exclusive; that is, you can specify one or the other, but not both.

Example

```
Private Type env
    strVarName As String
    strValue As String
End Type

Private Sub Form_Load()

Dim intCtr As Integer, intPos As Integer
Dim strRetVal As String
Dim udtEnv As env

intCtr = 1
Do
    strRetVal = Environ(intCtr)
    If strRetVal <> "" Then
        intPos = InStr(1, strRetVal, "=")
        udtEnv.strVarName = Left(strRetVal, intPos - 1)
        udtEnv.strValue = Mid(strRetVal, intPos + 1)
    Else
        Exit Do
    End If
    intCtr = intCtr + 1
Loop

End Sub
```

Programming Tips & Gotchas

- If you use *number* to specify the environment variable, both the name and the value of the variable are returned. An equals sign (=) separates them. For example, the function call *Environ(1)* might return the string TEMP=C:\WIN-DOWS\TEMP.

- If you retrieve environment variables and their values by ordinal position, the first variable is in position 1, not position 0.

- Due to the flexibility offered, it's now accepted and recommended practice to use the registry for variables needed by your application, rather than the environment string table.

- Environment variables can be defined in a variety of ways, including by the *AUTOEXEC.BAT* and *MSDOS.SYS* files, as well as by the HKEY_LOCAL_MACHINE\System\CurrentControlSet\Control\SessionManager\Environment and HKEY_CURRENT_USER\Environment keys in the registry. However, the *Environ* function doesn't recognize environment variables defined in the registry.

Reference

EOF Function

Named Arguments

No

Syntax

```
EOF (filenumber)
filenumber
```

Use: Required

Data: Integer

Any valid file number.

Return Value

An integer containing –1 (**True**), or 0 (**False**).

Description

Returns an integer evaluating to **True** (–1) when the end of a file has been reached; until the end of the file is reached, EOF returns **False** (0).

Rules at a Glance

• *filenumber* must be a valid number used in the **Open** statement to open either a random or sequential file.

• If you have opened the file using either random or binary access, a **Get** statement that can't read a complete record (i.e., an attempt to access a record past the last record in the file) causes *EOF* to return **True**.

Example

```
iFile = FreeFile
Open sFilename for Input as #iFile
Do While Not EOF(iFile)
    LineInput #iFile, sDataLine
    ...
Loop
Close #iFile
```

Programming Tips & Gotchas

• *EOF* allows you to test whether the end of a file has been reached without generating an error.

• Because *EOF* dates back to the times when VB didn't support an intrinsic Boolean data type, the function uses an integer data type to hold the 0 and –1 **False** and **True** values.

• Because you always write data to sequential files at the end of the file, the file marker is always at the end of the file, and *EOF* therefore always returns **True** when testing files opened with their modes set equal to either input or append.

• As Visual Basic is continually enhanced with new functions and new objects, there are more efficient and elegant alternatives to some of the VB language elements that have been with us since before "Visual" was even thought of! The following snippets compare methods of populating an array with data extracted from a comma-delimited text file. The first snippet uses a standard **Do...Loop** and *EOF* flag:

```
Dim sFilename As String
Dim sContents As String
Dim iFile      As Integer
Dim sArray()  As String

iFile = FreeFile
sFilename = "testinput.txt"
ReDim sArray(0)
Open sFilename For Input As #1
   Do While Not EOF(1)
      Input #1, sContents
      ReDim Preserve sArray(UBound(sArray) + 1)
      sArray(UBound(sArray)) = sContents
   Loop
Close #1
```

You can replace this with a single call to the *Input* function, passing to it the length of the text file, and, if you're using VB6, you can call the *Split* function to parse the comma-delimited string:

```
Dim sFilename As String
Dim sContents As String
Dim iFile      As Integer
Dim sArray()  As String

sFilename = "testinput.txt"
Open sFilename For Input As #iFile
    sContents = Input(LOF(iFile), iFile)
Close #iFile
sArray = Split(sContents, ",")
```

Again, for VB6 users only, there is the object-oriented way of extracting the data, again passing the resulting string to the *Split* function to be parsed. For this example to work, you have to create a project reference to the Microsoft Scripting Runtime Library, which gives you access to the File System Object:

```
Dim sFilename      As String
Dim sArray()       As String
Dim ofsFileSys     As New Scripting.FileSystemObject
Dim ofsTextStream As TextStream

sFilename = "testinput.txt"
Set ofsTextStream = _
                ofsFileSys.OpenTextFile(sFilename)
   sArray = Split(ofsTextStream.ReadAll, ",")
Set ofsTextStream = Nothing
```

- Don't confuse the *EOF* Function with the EOF property of the RDO, DAO, and ADO recordsets and result sets. The former is a function for testing the position of the file pointer in a file opened using the VBA **Open** statement; the latter is a property that indicates the state of the record pointer in a database or recordset opened using automation.

- The AtEndOfStream property is the TextStream object's equivalent to the EOF function.

See Also

File System Objects, Get Statement, Loc Function, LOF Function, Open Statement

---

Erase Statement

Syntax

```
Erase arraylist
arraylist
```
Use: Required

Data Type: String

A list of array variables to clear.

Description

Resets the elements of an array to their initial (unassigned) values. In short, **Erase** "clears out" or empties an array.

Rules at a Glance

- Specify more than one array to be erased by using commas to delimit *arraylist*.

- Fixed array variables remain dimensioned; on the other hand, all memory allocated to dynamic arrays is released.

- The following table describes how **Erase** reinitializes the elements of a fixed array.

Element Data Type	Element Reset to...
Numeric	Zero
Variable-length string	Zero-length string ("")
Fixed-length string	Zero
Boolean	False
Variant	Empty
User-defined type	Each member of the user-defined type is treated as a separate variable
Object	Nothing

Programming Tips & Gotchas

Once you use **Erase** to clear dynamic arrays, they must be redimensioned with **ReDim** before being used again. This is because **Erase** releases the memory storage used by the dynamic array back to the operating system, which sets the array to have no elements.

See Also

Dim Statement, ReDim Statement

Err Object

Description

The Err object contains properties and methods that allow you to obtain information about a single runtime error in a Visual Basic program. It also allows you to generate errors and to reset the error object. Because the Err object is an intrinsic object (which means that it's part of every VB project you create) with global scope, you don't need to create an instance of it within your code.

When an error is generated in your application—whether it's handled or not—the properties of the Err object are assigned values you can then access to gain information about the error that occurred. You can even generate your own errors explicitly using the *Err.Raise* method. You can also define your own errors to unify the error-handling process.

When your program reaches an **Exit Function**, **Exit Sub**, **Exit Property**, **Resume**, or **On Error** statement, the Err object is cleared and its properties reinitialized. This can also be achieved explicitly using the *Err.Clear* method.

Properties

Property Name	Description
Description	The string associated with the given error number.
HelpContext	A context ID within a VB Help file.
HelpFile	The path to a VB Help file.
LastDLLError	The last error code generated by a DLL; available only on 32-bit Windows systems.
Number	A long integer used to describe an error (i.e., an error code).
Source	Either the name of the current project or the class name of the application that generated the error.

Methods

Method Name	Description
Clear	Resets all the properties of the Err object.
Raise	Forces an error of a given number to be generated.

Programming Tips & Gotchas

- You may come across legacy code that has been written with either the *Err* function or the **Err** statement, both of which simply returned the error number. This code still runs because the Err object's default property is the Number property. As a result, simply using Err in your code (as you do when you call either the *Err* function or the **Err** statement) is the same as writing **Err.Number**.

- The Visual Basic Err object isn't a collection; it contains only information about the last error, if one occurred. You could, however, implement your

Reference

own error-collection class to store a number of errors by copying error information from the Err object into an application-defined error-collection object.

- The **Error** statement, which was used in earlier versions of VB to generate an error, is included only in the language for backward compatibility and shouldn't be used in new code. Use the Err.Raise method instead.

- An Err object can't be passed back from a class module to a standard code module.

- For a full description of error trapping and error handling, see Chapter 6, *Error Handling*.

See Also

Err.Clear Method, Err.Raise Method, On Error Statement, Resume Statement

---

Err.Clear Method

Syntax

```
object.Clear
object
```
> Use: Required
>
> Data Type: Error object
>
> An instance of the Err object.

Description

Explicitly resets all the properties of the Err object after an error has been handled.

Rules at a Glance

You need only to Clear the Err object if you need to reference its properties for another error within the same subroutine or before another **On Error** statement within the same subroutine.

Example

```
On Error Resume Next

i = oObjectOne.MyFunction(iVar)

If Err.Number <> 0 Then
    MsgBox "The Error : " & Err.Description & vbCrLf _
           & " was generated in " & Err.Source
    Err.Clear
End If

j = oObjectTwo.YourFunction(iVar)

If Err.Number <> 0 Then
    MsgBox "The Error : " & Err.Description & vbCrLf _
           & " was generated in " & Err.Source
    Err.Clear
End If
```

Programming Tips & Gotchas

- Resetting the Err object explicitly using the Clear method is necessary when you use On Error Resume Next and test the value of *Err.Number* repeatedly. Unless you reset the Err object, you run the very real risk of catching the previously handled error, the details of which are still lurking in the Err object's properties.

- The Err object is automatically reset when either a Resume, Exit Sub, Exit Function, Exit Property, or On Error statement is executed.

- You can achieve the same results by setting the *Err.Number* property to 0; however your code will be more self-documenting if you use the Clear method.

- When testing the value of *Err.Number*, don't forget that OLE servers often return "negative" numbers. Actually internally they're not really negative; they're unsigned longs, but VB has no unsigned long data type. The extra bit of the unsigned long type appears as a "-".

See Also

Err Object, Err.Raise Method, On Error Statement, Resume Statement

---

Err.Description Property

Syntax

To set the property:

```
Err.Description = string
```

To return the property value:

```
string = Err.Description
string
```
    Use: Required

    Data Type: String

    Any string expression.

Description

A read/write property containing a short string describing a runtime error.

Rules at a Glance

- When a runtime error occurs, the Description property is automatically assigned the standard description of the error.

- For application-defined errors, you must assign a string expression to the Description property or the error won't have an accompanying textual message.

- You can override the standard description by assigning your own description to the Err object for both VB errors and application-defined errors.

Reference

Programming Tips & Gotchas

- If an error occurs within a class module, an ActiveX DLL, or an EXE—regardless of whether it's running in or out of your application's process space—no error information from the component is available to your application unless you explicitly pass back an error code as part of the error-handling routine within the component. This is done using the Err.Raise method, which allows you to raise an error on the client, passing custom parameters for Number, Source, and Description.

- If you raise an error with the Err.Raise method and don't set the Description property, the Description property is automatically set to "Application Defined or Object Defined Error."

- You can also pass the Err.Description to a logging device such as a log file in Windows 95 or the application log in Windows NT by using the App.LogEvent method, as the following code fragment demonstrates:

```
EmployeesAdd_Err:
App.LogEvent "EmployeesAdd" & "; " & _
             Err.Description, vbLogEventTypeError
```

- The best way to set the Description property for your own application-defined errors is to use the named description argument with the Raise method, as the following code shows:

```
Sub TestErr()

On Error GoTo TestErr_Err

    Err.Raise Number := 65444, _
              Description := "Meaningful Error Description"

TestErr_Exit:
    Exit Sub

TestErr_Err:
    MsgBox Err.Description
    Resume TestErr_Exit

End Sub
```

See Also

Err.Object, Err.Number, Err.Raise Method

Err.HelpContext Property

Syntax

```
Err.HelpContext
```

Description

A read/write property that either sets or returns a long integer value containing the context ID of the appropriate topic within a Help file.

Rules at a Glance

- The Err object sets the HelpContext property automatically when an error is raised.

- If the error is user-defined, and you don't explicitly set the HelpContext property yourself, the Err object sets the value to 1000095, which corresponds to the "Application-defined or object-defined error" help topic in the VBA Help file. (The HelpContext property is set by the fifth parameter to the *Err.Raise* method.)

- HelpContext IDs are decided upon when writing and creating a Windows help file. Once the Help file has been compiled, the IDs can't be changed. Each ID points to a separate Help topic.

Example

```
Sub TestErr()

On Error GoTo TestErr_Err

    Dim i
    i = 8

    MsgBox (i / 0)

TestErr_Exit:
    Exit Sub

TestErr_Err:
    MsgBox Err.Description, vbMsgBoxHelpButton, "ErrorVille", _
        Err.HelpFile, Err.HelpContext
    Resume TestErr_Exit

End Sub
```

Programming Tips & Gotchas

- You can display a topic from the Visual Basic help file by using the *MsgBox* function with the **vbMsgBoxHelpButton** constant and passing *Err.HelpContext* as the *HelpContext* argument (as shown in the previous example). While this is a simple and effective way to add much more functionality to your applications, bear in mind that some of your users could find the explanations within the VB help file somewhat confusing. If time and budget allow, the best method is to create your own help file (for which you need the Help compiler and other Help file resources from the full version of VB), and pass both the HelpContext and HelpFileName to *MsgBox*.

- Another method of displaying the Help file is to call the Application.Help method, again passing both the Err.HelpFile and Err.HelpContext properties into the method, as follows:

```
If Err.Number > 0 then
    Application.Help Err.HelpFile, Err.HelpContext
End If
```

Reference

This method has the disadvantage that the help file page is shown immediately, without giving the user a chance to either recognize that an error has taken place or to skip viewing the Help file altogether.

- If you supply a HelpContext ID that can't be found in the Help file, the contents page for the Help file should be displayed. However, what actually happens is that a Windows Help error is generated, and a message box is displayed, which informs the user to contact their vendor.

- Some objects that you may use within your application have their own help files, which you can access using HelpContext to display highly focused help to your users.

- The Microsoft VBA Help Reference wrongly states that the Err.HelpContext property is a string data type. It is in fact a Long.

See Also

MsgBox Function, Err.HelpFile Property, Chapter 6

Err.HelpFile Property

Syntax

```
Err.HelpFile
```

Description

A read/write string property that contains the fully qualified path of a Windows Help file.

Rules at a Glance

- You can set a global Help file for the project in the project Properties dialog box, which can be accessed from the Tools menu in VB 4.0 and the Project menu in VB 5.0 and 6.0.

- The HelpFile property is automatically set by the Err object when an error is raised.

- The default help file is the Microsoft Visual Basic for Applications reference.

Example

See Err.HelpContext.

Programming Tips & Gotchas

- You can display a topic from the Visual Basic help file by using the *MsgBox* function with the **vbMsgBoxHelpButton** constant and passing Err.HelpFile as the HelpFile argument (as shown in the example for the Err.HelpContext property). While this is a simple and effective way to add more functionality to your applications, bear in mind that some of your users could find the explanations within the VB help file somewhat confusing. If time and budget allow, the best method is to create your own help file (for which you need the Help compiler and other Help file resources from the full version of VB), and pass both the HelpContext and HelpFileName to *MsgBox*.

- Another method of displaying the Help file is to call the Application.Help method, again passing both the Err.HelpFile and Err.HelpContext properties into the method, as follows:

```
If Err.Number > 0 then
    Application.Help Err.HelpFile, Err.HelpContext
End If
```

This has the disadvantage that the help file page is shown immediately, without giving the user a chance to either recognize that an error has taken place or to skip displaying the Help file altogether.

- Surprisingly, even if you have specified a Help file in the Project Properties dialog, the Err object defaults to the VBA help file. The only way to use another help file is to explicitly set the HelpFile property immediately prior to calling either the *MsgBox* function or the Application.Help method.

- Some objects you may use within your application have their own help files, which you can access using HelpFile to display highly focused help to your users.

- Remember that once the program encounters an Exit... statement or an On Error statement, all the properties of the Err object are reset; this includes the Help file. You must therefore set the Err.HelpFile property each time your application needs to access the help file.

See Also

Err.HelpContext Property, Err.Number Property, Chapter 6

Err.LastDLLError Property

Syntax

```
Err.LastDLLError
```

Description

A read-only property containing a long data type representing a system error produced within a DLL called from within a VB program.

Rules at a Glance

- Only direct calls to a Windows system DLL from VB code assign a value to LastDLLError.

- The value of the LastDLLError property depends upon the particular DLL being called. Your code must be able to handle the various codes that can be returned by the DLL you are calling.

- Don't forget that a failed DLL call doesn't itself raise an error within your VB program. As a result, the Err object's Number, Description, and Source properties aren't filled.

Reference

Programming Tips & Gotchas

- The LastDLLError property is used only by system DLLs, such as *kernel32.dll*, and therefore errors that occur within DLLs you may have created in VB won't be assigned.

- Obtaining accurate documentation about the return values of system DLLs can be a challenging experience. Most useful information can be found by studying the API documentation for Visual C++. However, you can use the Windows API *FormatMessage* to return the actual Windows error message string from within *Kernel32.DLL*, which incidentally is also in the correct language. The following is a brief example you can use in your applications to display the actual Windows error description:

```
Option Explicit
Declare Function FormatMessage Lib "kernel32" _
        Alias "FormatMessageA" _
        (ByVal dwFlags As Long, lpSource As Any, _
        ByVal dwMessageId As Long, _
        ByVal dwLanguageId As Long, _
        ByVal lpBuffer As String, ByVal nSize As Long, _
        Arguments As Long) As Long
Public Const FORMAT_MESSAGE_FROM_SYSTEM = &H1000
Public Const FORMAT_MESSAGE_IGNORE_INSERTS = &H200

Function apiErrDesc(lErrCode As Long) As String

    Dim sErrDesc As String
    Dim lReturnLen As Long
    Dim lpNotUsed As Long

    sErrDesc = String(256, 0)
  lReturnLen = FormatMessage(FORMAT_MESSAGE_FROM_SYSTEM _
               Or FORMAT_MESSAGE_IGNORE_INSERTS, _
               lpNotUsed, lErrCode, 0&, sErrDesc, _
               Len(sErrDesc), ByVal lpNotUsed)

    If lReturnLen > 0 Then
        apiErrDesc = Left$(sErrDesc, lReturnLen)
    End If

End Function
```

Here's a snippet demonstrating how you can use this utility function:

```
lReturn = SomeAPICall(someparams)
If lReturn  <> 0 then
    Err.Raise Err.LastDLLError & vbObjectError, _
            "MyApp:Kernel32.DLL", _
            apiErrDesc(Err.LastDLLError)
End If
```

Note that some API calls return 0 to denote a successful function call; others return 0 to denote an unsuccessful call. You should also note that some API functions don't appear to set the LastDLLError property. In most cases, these are functions that return an error code. You could therefore modify the snippet above to handle these cases:

```
lReturn = SomeAPICall(someparams)
If lReturn  <> 0 then
    If Err.LastDLLError <> 0 Then
        Err.Raise Err.LastDLLError & vbObjectError, _
                "MyApp:Kernel32.DLL", _
                apiErrDesc(Err.LastDLLError)
    Else
        Err.Raise lReturn  & vbObjectError, _
                "MyApp:Kernel32.DLL", _
                apiErrDesc(lReturn)
    End If
End If
```

See Also

Err Object, Chapter 6

Err.Number Property

Syntax

```
Err.Number
```

Description

A read-write property containing a long value that represents the error code for the last error generated.

Rules at a Glance

- When a runtime error is generated within the program, the error code is automatically assigned to Err.Number.

- The Number property is updated with an application-defined error whose code is passed as an argument to the Err.Raise method.

- When using the Err.Raise method in normal code, your user-defined error codes can't be greater than 65536 and less that 0. (For an explanation, see the final note in the "Programming Tips & Gotchas" section of the entry for the Err.Raise method.)

- VBA error numbers in the range of 1–1000 are for its own trappable errors. In addition, error numbers from 31001 to 31037 are also used for VBA trappable errors. In implementing a series of application-defined errors, your error handlers should either translate application errors into VBA trappable errors or, preferably, assign a unique range to application-defined errors.

- When using the Err.Raise method in ActiveX objects, add the **vbObjectError** constant. (–2147221504) to your user-defined error code to distinguish OLE errors from local application errors.

- When control returns to the local application after an error has been raised by the OLE server, the application can determine that the error originated in the

Reference

OLE server and extract the error number with a line of code like the following:

```
Dim lError as Long
If Err.Number And vbObjectError Then _
    lError = Err.Number XOr vbObjectError
```

Programming Tips & Gotchas

- An error code is a useful method of alerting your program that a function within an ActiveX or class object has failed. By returning a number based on the vbObjectError constant, you can easily determine that an error has occurred. By then subtracting vbObjectError from the value returned by the object's function, you can determine the actual error code:

```
If Err.Number < 0 then
    Err.Number = Err.Number - vbObjectError
End If
```

- You can create a sophisticated multiresult error-handling routine by using the Err.Number property as the Case statement within a Select Case block, taking a different course of action for different errors, as this snippet demonstrates:

```
Select Case Err.Number
    Case < 0
        'OLE Object Error
        Set oObject = Nothing
        Resume DisplayErrorAndExit
    Case 5
        'increment the retry counter and try again
        iTries = iTries + 1
        If iTries < 5 Then
            Resume RetryFunctionCall
        Else
            Resume DisplayErrorAndExit
        End If
    Case 20
        'we almost expected this one!
        Resume Next
    Case Else
        Resume DisplayErrorAndExit
End Select
```

See Also

Err Object, Err.Raise Property, Chapter 6

Err.Raise Method

Named Arguments

Yes

Syntax

```
object.Raise number, source, description, _
            helpfile, helpcontext
```

object
: Use: Required.

  Data Type: Err object

  The Err object.

number
: Use: Required.

  Data Type: Long integer

  A numeric identifier of the particular error.

source
: Use: Optional.

  Data Type: String

  The name of the object or application responsible for generating the error.

description
: Use: Optional.

  Data Type: String

  A useful description of the error.

helpfile
: Use: Optional.

  Data Type: String

  The fully qualified path of a Microsoft Windows Help file containing help or reference material about the error.

helpcontext
: Use: Optional.

  Data Type: Long

  The context ID within *helpfile*.

Description

Generates a runtime error.

Rules at a Glance

- To use the Raise method, you must specify an error number.
- If you supply any of the *number, source, description, helpfile*, and *helpcontext* arguments when you call the Err.Raise method, they are supplied as values to the Number, Source, Description, HelpFile, and HelpContext properties, respectively. Refer to the entries for the individual properties for full descriptions of and rules for each property.

Programming Tips & Gotchas

- The Err.Raise method replaces the older **Error** statement, which shouldn't be used in new code.

- The Raise method doesn't reinitialize the Err object prior to assigning the values you pass in as arguments. This can mean that if you Raise an error against an Err object that hasn't been cleared since the last error, any properties you don't specify values for still contain the values from the last error.

- As well as using Raise in a runtime scenario, you can put it to good use in the development stages of your program to test the viability of your error-handling routines under various circumstances.

- The fact that Err.Number accepts only numbers in the range 0–65536 may appear to be strange at first because the data type of the Error Number parameter in the Raise event is a Long; however deep in the recesses of the Err object, the error code must be declared as an unsigned integer, a data type not supported by VB.

See Also

Err Object, Err.Clear Method, Err.HelpContext Property, Err.Number Property, Chapter 6

Err.Source Property

Syntax

```
Err.Source
```

Description

A read-write string property containing the name of the application or the object that has generated the error.

Rules at a Glance

- When a runtime error occurs in your code, the Source property is automatically assigned the project name (that is, the string that is assigned to the project's Name property). Note that this isn't necessarily the filename of the project file.

- For clarity of your error messages, when you raise an error in a class module, the format of the source parameter should be *project.class*. You can use the App.Title property to obtain the project name.

Programming Tips & Gotchas

Knowing what type of error has occurred within a program is often of little use to you if you don't know where the error was generated. However, if you enhance the standard Source by adding the name of the procedure, your debugging time can be cut dramatically.

See Also

Err Object, Chapter 6

Error, Error$ Functions

Named Arguments

No

Syntax

```
Error[(errornumber)]
errornumber
       Use: Optional
       Data Type: Long
       Any valid error code.
```

Return Value

Error returns a variant of subtype string; *Error$* returns a String. Both return values are standard descriptions for the particular error code.

Description

Returns either the error description corresponding to the given error number or the description for the last error.

Rules at a Glance

*   If *errornumber* isn't passed to the function, *Error* returns the description for the last error to have occurred. If no errors have occurred, a zero-length string ("") is returned.

*   If *errornumber* isn't recognized as a VB error, the function returns the description "Application-defined or object-defined error."

*   If *errornumber* is outside the range of a valid error code, an overflow error is generated.

Example

```
x = Error(100)
```

Programming Tips & Gotchas

The *Error* and *Error$* functions are included for only backward compatibility. Instead, you should use the Description property of the Err object in all new code. The *Error$* function, however, is useful for obtaining an error description for any error code "after the event," when perhaps the Err object has been reinitialized.

See Also

Err.Description Property

Error Statement

Syntax

```
Error errornumber
```

Reference

errornumber

>Use: Optional

>Data Type: Long

>Any valid error code.

Description

Raises an error.

Rules at a Glance

The Error statement is included only for backward compatibility; instead, you should use the Err.Raise method in new code.

See Also

>Err.Raise Method

Event Statement

Named Arguments

No

Syntax

```
Public Event eventName [(arglist)]
```
eventName

>Use: Required

>Data Type: String

>The name of the event.

arglist

Optional; has the following syntax:

```
[ByVal | ByRef] varname[( )] [As type]
```
ByVal

>Use: Optional

>The argument is passed by value; that is, a local copy of the variable is assigned the value of the argument.

ByRef

>Use: Optional

>The argument is passed by reference; that is, the local variable is simply a reference to the argument being passed. All changes made to the local variable are reflected in the calling argument. ByRef is the default method of passing variables.

varname

>Use: Required

>The name of the local variable containing either the reference or value of the argument.

type

Use: Optional

The data type of the argument. Can be any data type.

Description

Defines a custom event that the object can raise at any time using the `RaiseEvent` statement.

Rules at a Glance

- The event declaration must be `Public` so that it's visible outside the object module; it can't be declared as `Friend` or `Private`.

- An `Event` statement can appear only in the Declarations section of an object module—that is, in a form or class module.

Example

The following snippet demonstrates how you can use an event to communicate a status message back to the client application. To take advantage of this functionality, the client must declare a reference to this class using the `WithEvents` keyword.

```
Public Event Status(Message As String)

Private Function UpdateRecords() as Boolean
...
    RaiseEvent Status "Opening the database..."
...
    RaiseEvent Status "Executing the query..."
...
    RaiseEvent Status "Records were updated..."
...
End Function
```

Programming Tips & Gotchas

- To allow the client application to handle the event being fired, the object variable must be declared using the `WithEvents` keyword.

- VB custom events don't return a value; however, you can use a `ByRef` argument in *arglist* to simulate a return value; for more details, see the `RaiseEvent` statement.

- Unlike parameter lists used with other procedures, `Event` parameters lists can't include `Optional` or `ParamArray` arguments or default values.

- If you use the `Event` statement in a standard interface class (i.e., a class in which only properties and methods are defined but no code is included in the procedures) for use with the `Implements` statement, the `Implements` statement doesn't recognize the "outgoing interfaces" used by events, and therefore the event is ignored.

- Events can't be raised from within a Microsoft Transaction Server context.

- For more information about implementing your own custom events, see the section, "Implementing Custom Events" in Chapter 4.

Reference

See Also

RaiseEvent Statement, WithEvents Keyword

Exit Statement

Syntax

```
Exit Do
Exit For
Exit Function
Exit Property
Exit Sub
```

Description

Prematurely exits a block of code.

Rules at a Glance

Exit Do

Exits a Do...Loop statement. If the current Do...Loop is within a nested Do...Loop, execution continues with the next Loop statement wrapped around the current one. If, however, the Do...Loop is standalone, program execution continues with the first line of code after the Loop statement.

Exit For

Exits a For...Next loop. If the current For...Next is within a nested For...Next loop, execution continues with the next Next statement wrapped around the current one. If, however, the For...Next loop is stand-alone, program execution continues with the first line of code after the Next statement.

Exit Function

Exits the current function. Program execution is passed to the line following the call to the function.

Exit Property

Exits the current property procedure. Program execution is passed to the line following the call to the property.

Exit Sub

Exits the current sub procedure. Program execution is passed to the line following the call to the procedure.

Programming Tips & Gotchas

Traditional programming theory recommends one entry point and one exit point for each procedure. However, you can improve the readability of long routines by using the Exit statement, as shown below. Using Exit Sub can save having to wrap almost an entire subroutine (which could be tens of lines long) within an If...Then statement.

With Exit Sub

```
Sub MyTestSub(iNumber As Integer)
    If iNumber = 10 Then
```

```
        Exit Sub
    End If
    ...'code
End Sub
```

Without Exit Sub

```
Sub MyTestSub(iNumber As Integer)
    If iNumber <> 10 Then
        ...'code
    End If
End Sub
```

See Also

Do...Loop Statement, For...Next Statement, For Each...Next Statement, Function Statement, Property Get Statement, Property Let Statement, Property Set Statement, Sub Statement

---

Exp Function

Named Arguments

No

Syntax

```
Exp(number)
number
```
> Use: Required
>
> Data Type: Numeric Variant
>
> Any valid numeric expression.

Return Value

A Double representing the antilogarithm of *number*.

Description

Returns the antilogarithm of a number; the antilogarithm is the base of natural logarithms, *e* (whose value is the constant 2.7182818), raised to a power.

Rules at a Glance

The maximum value for *number* is 709.782712893.

Programming Tips & Gotchas

Exp is the converse of the *Log* function.

See Also

Log Function

File Object (VB6)

Description

The File object represents a disk file that can be a file of any type and allows you to interrogate the properties of the file and to move upward in the file system hierarchy to interrogate the system on which the file resides. The process of creating a File object—for example, assigning a reference from the Files object's Item property to a local object variable—doesn't open the file.

The File object is part of the File System object model; for an overview of the model, including the library reference needed to access it, see the File System object model entry.

Createable

No

Returned by

Files.Item property

Properties

Attributes

 Data Type: FileAttribute constant

 See the "FileAttribute Constants" table in the Folder Object entry.

DateCreated

 Data Type: Date

 The date the file was created.

DateLastAccessed

 Data Type: Date

 If available from the operating system, the date the file was last accessed.

DateLastModified

 Data Type: Date

 The date the file was last modified.

Drive

 Data Type: Drive object

 Returns a Drive object representing the drive on which the file resides.

Name

 Data Type: String

 The name of the file.

ParentFolder

 Data Type: Folder object

 Returns a Folder object representing the folder in which the file resides.

Path

 Data Type: String

Returns the full path to the file from the current machine, including drive letter or network path/share name.

ShortName

    Data Type: String

    Returns a DOS 8.3 filename; may not work on an NTFS system.

ShortPath

    Data Type: String

    Returns a DOS 8.3 folder name; may not work on an NTFS system.

Size

    Data Type: Variant

    Returns the size of the file in bytes.

Type

    Data Type: String

    Returns a string containing the registered type description. This is the type string displayed for the file in the Windows Explorer. If a file doesn't have an extension, the type is simply "File." When a file's type isn't registered, the type appears as the extension and "File."

Methods

Copy	Move
Delete	OpenAsTextStream

File.Copy Method (VB6)

Named Arguments

Yes

Syntax

```
oFileObj.Copy Destination [, OverwriteFiles]
oFileObj
```
    Use: Required

    Data Type: File object

    Any object variable returning a File object.

`Destination`

    Use: Required

    Data Type: String

    The path and optionally the filename of the copied file.

`OverwriteFiles`

    Use: Optional

    Data Type: Boolean

Reference

True if the copy operation can overwrite an existing file; False otherwise.

Description

Copies the file represented by *oFileObj* to another location.

Rules at a Glance

Wildcard characters can't be used in *Destination.*

Programming Tips & Gotchas

- If the *Destination* path is set to read-only, the Copy method fails regardless of the *Overwrite* setting.

- If *OverwriteFiles* is False and the file exists in *Destination*, a trappable error, runtime error 58, "File Already Exists," is generated.

- If the user has adequate rights, *Destination* can be a network path or share name. For example:

```
Copy "\\NTSERV1\d$\RootTwo\"
Copy "\\NTSERV1\RootTest"
```

File.Delete Method (VB6)

Named Parameters

Yes

Syntax

```
oFileObj.Delete [Force]
oFileObj
```
    Use: Required

    Data Type: File object

    Any object variable returning a File object.

Force

    Use: Optional

    Data Type: Boolean

    If set to True, ignores the file's read-only flag (if it's on), and deletes the file.

Description

Removes the current file.

Rules at a Glance

- If the file is open, the method fails with a "Permission Denied" error.
- The default setting for *Force* is False.
- If *Force* is set to False, and the file is read-only, the method will fail.

Programming Tips & Gotchas

- Unlike the FileSystemObject object's DeleteFile method, which accepts wildcard characters in the path parameter and can therefore delete multiple files, the Delete method deletes only the single file represented by *oFileObj*.

- As a result of the Delete method, the Files collection object containing *oFileObj* is automatically updated, the deleted file is removed from the collection, and the collection count reduced by one. You shouldn't try to access the deleted file object again; instead, you should set *oFileObj* to Nothing.

See Also

FileSystemObject.DeleteFile Method, Kill Statement

File.Move Method (VB6)

Named Arguments

Yes

Syntax

```
oFileObj.Move destination
oFileObj
```
> Use: Required
>
> Data Type: File object
>
> Any object variable returning a File object.

```
destination
```
> Use: Required
>
> Data Type: String
>
> The path to the location where the file is to be moved.

Description

Moves a file from one folder to another.

Rules at a Glance

- Wildcard characters can't be used in *Destination*.
- *Destination* can be either an absolute or a relative path.

Programming Tips & Gotchas

- If a fatal system error occurs during the execution of this method (like a power failure), the worst that can happen is that the file is copied to the destination but not removed from the source. There are no rollback capabilities built into the File.Move method; however, because the copy part of this two-stage process is executed first, the file can't be lost.

- You can use the FileSystemObject's FileExists and GetAbsolutePath methods prior to calling the Move method to ensure its success.

Reference

- Unlike the FileSystemObject's MoveFile method, which accepts wildcard characters in the path parameter and can therefore move multiple files, the Move method moves only the single file represented by *oFileObj*.

- As a result of the Move method, the Files collection object containing *oFileObj* is automatically updated, the moved folder being removed and the collection count reduced by one. You shouldn't try to access the moved file object again in the same Folders collection object.

- If the user has adequate rights, *Destination* can be a network path or share name. For example:

```
oFile.Move "\\NTSERV1\d$\RootTwo\myfile.doc"
```

See Also

FileSystemObject.MoveFile Method

File.OpenAsTextStream Method (VB6)

Named Arguments

Yes

Syntax

```
oFileObj.OpenAsTextStream ([IOMode[, Format]])
```

oFileObj
> Use: Required
>
> Data Type: File object
>
> Any object variable returning a File object.

IOMode
> Use: Optional
>
> Data Type: IOMode constant
>
> A constant specifying the purpose for opening the file.

Format
> Use: Optional
>
> Data Type: Tristate constant
>
> A constant specifying ASCII or Unicode format.

Return Value

A TextStream object.

Description

Opens the referenced text file for reading or writing.

Rules at a Glance

- *IOMode* can be one of the following `IOMode` constants:

Constant	Value	Description
ForAppending	8	Opens the file in append mode; that is, the current contents of the file are protected, and new data written to the file is placed at the end of the file.
ForReading	1	Opens the file for reading; you can't write to a file that has been opened for reading.
ForWriting	2	Opens the file for writing; all previous file content is overwritten by new data.

- *Unicode* can be one of the following `Tristate` constants:

Constant	Value	Description
TristateUseDefault	–2	Open as System default
TristateTrue	–1	Open as Unicode
TristateFalse	0	Open as ASCII

- The default *IOMode* setting is ForReading (1).

- The default *Format* setting is ASCII (`False`).

- If another process has opened the file, the method fails with a "Permission Denied" error.

See Also

FileSystemObject: OpenTextFile Method, TextStream Object

File System Object Model (VB6)

Library to Reference

Microsoft Scripting Runtime (*../SYSTEM32/SCRRUN.DLL*)

Description

For years, VB developers have been using the VBA language to perform tasks such as opening, writing, and closing files, but with VB6, that's about to change. Of course, for backward compatibility, all the original file and directory manipulation statements and functions are still there, but now VB includes the File System object model, a rich object model for local and network file access.

The File System object model is itself not an intrinsic part of the VBA language, but is part of the Scripting Runtime library. Those of you familiar with VBScript may recognize the original components of the File System object model, a very basic version of which first appeared in Version 2 of the Scripting Runtime library, when the model simply contained a top-level object, the FileSystemObject object, and the TextStream object. Version 4 of the Scripting Runtime that ships with VB6

Reference

contains a full object model that represents all drives that are attached to the computer, including hard drives, floppy and removable media drives, RAM drives, CD-ROM drives, and drives on other machines. The File System object model allows you to interrogate, create, delete, and otherwise manipulate folders and text files. The depth of information that is provided within the object model would have forced you to resort to the Win32 API in previous versions of VB.

To access the File System object model, you must use the References dialog to add a reference to the Microsoft Scripting Runtime library to your project. You can then create an instance of the FileSystemObject object, the only externally createable object in the model. From there, you can navigate through the object model, as shown in the object hierarchy diagram in Figure 7-4.

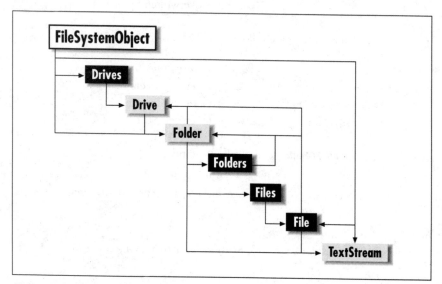

Figure 7-4: The File System object model

If you are dealing with random access files, the intrinsic VB language functions and statements are still the way to go, since the File System object only directly opens text files using the TextStream object.

See Also

File Object, Files Collection Object, FileSystemObject Object, Folder Object, Folders Collection, TextStream Object

---

FileAttr Function

Named Arguments

Yes

Syntax

```
FileAttr(filenumber, [returntype])
```

`filenumber`
> Use: Required
>
> Data Type: Integer
>
> Any valid file number.

`returntype`
> Use: Required
>
> Data Type: Integer
>
> An optional number specifying the information to return; if you omit the argument, its value defaults to 1.

Return Value

If you specify a `returntype` of 1, the file access mode is returned as a long integer, as shown in the following table:

Mode	Value
Input	1
Output	2
Random	4
Append	8
Binary	32

Description

Determines the file access mode for a file opened using the Open statement. When used on a 16-bit Windows system, *FileAttr* can also obtain an operating-system file handle.

Rules at a Glance

- Use a `returntype` of 1 to obtain a return value that indicates the mode in which the file was opened.

- On 16-bit Windows systems only, use a `returntype` of 2 to obtain an operating system file handle for the file.

Programming Tips & Gotchas

- *File handles*—the numbers by which files are identified by the operating system—are assigned by the operating system. In contrast, the application-defined file number used in the Open statement or returned by the *FreeFile* function is simply a pointer into an internal table of file handles maintained by Visual Basic. In other words, the file number that references a file in a 16-bit Visual Basic program is really a pseudo-handle that is local to the program. By calling the *FileAttr* function with a `returnvalue` of 2, you can obtain the systemwide file handle. This can then be used when calling MS-DOS functions (like the services provided by MS-DOS interrupts) that require the file handle but don't recognize the application-defined file number.

- Remember that a *returntype* of 2 can be used only on a 16-bit system; its use on a 32-bit system generates an error.

- For 32-bit systems, the *returntype* argument is superfluous, since the only legal value is the default value of 1. Supplying any other value generates runtime error 5, "Invalid procedure call or argument."

- The File System object model, new to VB6, includes a File object, one of whose properties is Attributes. The File object has many properties that can be queried to give far more information that the *FileAttr* function.

See Also

Open Statement, File System Object

FileCopy Statement

Named Arguments

Yes

Syntax

```
FileCopy source, destination
source
```
> Use: Required.
>
> Data Type: String
>
> The name of the source file to be copied.

```
destination
```
> Use: Required.
>
> Data Type: String
>
> The name and location of the file when copied.

Description

Copies a file.

Rules at a Glance

- The *source* and *destination* arguments may contain a drive name and a folder name, but they must *always* contain the filename.

- You can't copy a file that is currently in an open state.

Programming Tips & Gotchas

- If you don't specify a drive or folder in either the *source* or *destination*, the file is assumed to be in the current drive or folder.

- Unlike copying a file from one folder to another from outside VB, when using the FileCopy statement, it isn't sufficient to simply enter a path for *destination*. You must supply a filename, even if it's the same as the *source*; otherwise, runtime error 75, "Path/File access error" results.

- `FileCopy` is a statement and not a function; there is no return value. You therefore have to assume that if there are no errors generated from calling the `FileCopy` statement, the file has been successfully copied. So be sure to wrap `FileCopy` in robust error handling.

- Be aware that if the *destination* file already exists, it will be overwritten without warning.

- A number of functions allow you to use the copy operation to rename a file. (Typically, this is done by specifying the same path in the destination as in the source, along with a different filename.) The `FileCopy` statement, however, doesn't work in this way.

- In order for the copy operation to succeed, *source* must not be opened by another application; if it is, runtime error 70, "Permission denied," is generated. If *source* has already been opened by the application, the copy operation will still succeed if the file isn't locked (i.e., has been opened with the `Shared` keyword) or has been opened with a write lock only. If *source* has already been opened with either a read lock or a read-write lock, the *FileCopy* operation generates runtime error 70, "Permission denied."

- *destination* must not be open if the copy operation is to succeed. If it has been opened by another application, runtime error 70, "Permission denied," is generated. If it has already been opened by the application itself, runtime error 55, "File already open," is generated.

- VB6 introduces a new File System object, which has several methods that allow you to copy and move files and folders.

See Also

ChDir Statement, File System Object

FileDateTime Function

Named Arguments

No

Syntax

```
FileDateTime(pathname)
```
pathname

> Use: Required
>
> Data Type: String
>
> The filename, along with an optional drive and path.

Return Value

A Variant of subtype Date containing the date and time that the specified file was last modified.

Description

Obtains the date and time a particular file was last modified.

Rules at a Glance

If you don't specify a drive or folder with `filename`, the file is assumed to be in the current drive or folder.

Programming Tips & Gotchas

- Use the *Dir* function to determine that the file exists before calling *File-DateTime*. If `filename` doesn't exist, your application generates runtime error 53, "File not found."

- *FileDateTime* is a read-only: you can retrieve, but you can't set, the file's date and time property.

- If a file has not been modified, its creation date and last modified date are identical. However, if the file has been modified since its creation, the *File-DateTime* function returns only the date last modified. To obtain the file's creation date, you must use the Window's API. The *GetFileTime* API call returns not only the date last modified, but the file's creation date and last access date as well.

- You can also use *FileDateTime* on hidden files.

- The File System object model in VB6 allows you to reference a file using the File object. You can use it to obtain the date a file was created, last accessed, and last modified.

See Also

ChDir Statement, Dir Statement

FileLen Function

Named Arguments

No

Syntax

```
FileLen(pathname)
Pathname
```
>   Use: Required
>
>   Data Type: String
>
>   The filename, optionally along with its path and drive.

Return Value

A Long data type containing the length of the specified file in bytes.

Description

Indicates the length of a file.

Rules at a Glance

If you don't specify a drive or folder with `filename`, the file is assumed to be in the current drive or folder.

Programming Tips & Gotchas

- Use the *Dir* function to determine that the file exists before calling *FileDateTime*. If the file doesn't exist, *FileDateTime* generates runtime error 53, "File not found." Another method of determining that a file exists before referencing it comes from the new FileSystemObject object in VB6, which includes a FileExists method.

- Because *FileLen* returns the length of a file based on the file allocation table, the value returned by *FileLen* reflects the size of the file before it was opened. In the case of open files, you should instead use the *LOF* function to determine the open file's current length.

See Also

FileDateTime Function, LOF Function, File System Objects

Files Collection Object (VB6)

Description

The Files collection object is a container for File objects that is returned by the Files property of any Folder object. All files contained in the folder are included in the Files collection object. You can obtain a reference to an individual File object using the Files collection object's Item property; this takes the exact filename, including the file extension, as a parameter. To iterate through the collection, you can use the `For Each...Next` statement.

The Files collection object is one of the objects in the File System object model; for an overview of the model, including the library reference needed to access it, see the File System object model entry.

Createable

No

Returned by

Folder.Files property

Properties

Count

Data Type: Long

The number of File objects in the collection.

Item

Data Type: File Object

Takes the filename (including the file extension) as a parameter and returns the File object representing the file with that name. Individual File objects can't be accessed by their ordinal position in the collection. Item is the Files collection object's default property. The following code fragment uses the Item property to retrieve the *autoexec.bat* File object:

```
Dim ofsFileSys  As New FileSystemObject
Dim ofsFiles As Files
Dim ofsFile As File

Set ofsFiles = ofsFileSys.Drives("C").RootFolder.Files
   Set ofsFile = ofsFiles.Item("autoexec.bat")
      MsgBox ofsFile.DateCreated & vbCrLf & _
             ofsFile.DateLastModified & vbCrLf & _
             ofsFile.DateLastAccessed
   Set ofsFile = Nothing
Set ofsFiles = Nothing
Set ofsFileSys = Nothing
```

FileSystemObject Object (VB6)

Description

The FileSystemObject object is at the top level of the File System object model and is the only externally createable object in the hierarchy; that is, it's the only object you can use the **New** keyword with. For information about the FileSystemObject object's properties and methods, see the entry for each property and method.

See the File System object model entry for an overview, including the library reference needed to access it.

Createable

Yes

Properties

Drives (returns a Drives collection object)

Methods

BuildPath	FileExists	GetFileName
CopyFile	FolderExists	GetFolder
CopyFolder	GetAbsolutePathName	GetParentFolderName
CreateFolder	GetBaseName	GetSpecialFolderd
CreateTextFile	GetDrive	GetTempName
DeleteFile	GetDriveName	MoveFile
DeleteFolder	GetExtensionName	MoveFolder
DriveExists	GetFile	OpenTextFile

FileSystemObject.BuildPath Method (VB6)

Syntax

```
oFileSysObj.BuildPath(Path, Name)
```

oFileSysObj

    Use: Required

    Data Type: FileSystemObject object

    Any object variable returning a FileSystemObject object.

Path

    Use: Required

    Data Type: String

    A drive and/or folder path.

Name

    Use: Required

    Data Type: String

    The folder or file path to append to *path*.

Return Value

String

Description

Creates a string by concatenating the path parameter with the folder or filename, adding, where required, the correct path separator for the host system.

Rules at a Glance

- *Path* can be an absolute or relative path and doesn't have to include the drive name.

- Neither *Path* nor *Name* has to currently exist.

- BuildPath doesn't check the validity of the new folder or filename.

Programming Tips & Gotchas

The only advantage to using the *BuildPath* function as opposed to concatenating two strings manually is that the function selects the correct path separator.

FileSystemObject.CopyFile Method (VB6)

Named Arguments

Yes

Syntax

```
oFileSysObj.CopyFile Source, Destination [, OverwriteFiles]
oFileSysObj
```

    Use: Required

    Data Type: FileSystemObject object

    Any object variable returning a FileSystemObject object.

Reference

> ### Source
>> Use: Required
>>
>> Data Type: String
>>
>> The path and name of the file to be copied.
>
> ### Destination
>> Use: Required
>>
>> Data Type: String
>>
>> The path and optionally the filename of the copy to make.
>
> ### OverwriteFiles
>> Use: Optional
>>
>> Data Type: Boolean
>>
>> Flag indicating whether an existing file is to be overwritten (**True**) or not (**False**).

Description

Copies a file or files from one folder to another.

Rules at a Glance

* The default value for *OverwriteFiles* is **True**.
* The source path can be relative or absolute.
* The source filename can contain wildcard characters; the source path can't.
* Wildcard characters can't be included in *Destination*.

Programming Tips & Gotchas

* If the destination path or file is read-only, the CopyFile method fails, regardless of the value of *OverwriteFiles*.
* If *OverwriteFiles* is set to **False** and the file exists in Destination, a trappable error—runtime error 58, "File Already Exists"—is generated.
* If an error occurs while copying more than one file, the *CopyFile* function exits immediately, thereby leaving the rest of the files uncopied. There is no roll-back facility to undo copies made prior to the error.
* If the user has adequate rights, the source or destination can be a network path or share name. For example:

```
CopyFile "c:\Rootone\*.*", "\\NTSERV1\d$\RootTwo\"
CopyFile "\\NTSERV1\RootTest\test.txt", "c:\RootOne"
```

* The CopyFile method copies a file or files stored in a particular folder. If the folder itself has subfolders containing files, the method doesn't copy these; use the CopyFolder method.

See Also

FileSystemObject.CopyFolder Method, Folder.Copy Method

FileSystemObject.CopyFolder Method (VB6)

Named Arguments

Yes

Syntax

```
oFileSysObj.CopyFolder Source, Destination [, _
                         OverwriteFiles]
```

oFileSysObj

Use: Required

Data Type: FileSystemObject object

Any object variable returning a FileSystemObject object.

Source

Use: Required

Data Type: String

The path and name of the folder to be copied from.

Destination

Use: Required

Data Type: String

The path for the folder where the copy is to be made.

OverwriteFiles

Use: Optional

Data Type: Boolean

Flag indicating whether existing files are to be overwritten (**True**) or not (**False**).

Description

Copies the contents of a folder, including its subfolders, to another location.

Rules at a Glance

- *Source* must end with either a wildcard character or no path separator.

- Wildcard characters can be used in *Source*, but only for the last component.

- Wildcard characters can't be used in *Destination*.

- All subfolders and files contained within the source folder are copied to *Destination* unless disallowed by the wildcard characters. That is to say, the CopyFolder method is recursive.

- If *Destination* ends with a path separator, or *Source* ends with a wildcard, CopyFolder assumes that the folder stated in *Source* exists in *Destination* or should otherwise be created. For example, given the following folder structure:

```
C:\
    Rootone
```

```
            SubFolder1
            SubFolder2
        RootTwo
```

CopyFolder "c:\Rootone*", "C:\RootTwo" produces this folder structure:

```
C:\
    Rootone
        SubFolder1
        SubFolder2
    RootTwo
        SubFolder1
        SubFolder2
```

CopyFolder "c:\Rootone", "C:\RootTwo\" produces this folder structure:

```
C:\
    Rootone
        SubFolder1
        SubFolder2
    RootTwo
        Rootone
            SubFolder1
            SubFolder2
```

Programming Tips & Gotchas

- If the destination path or any of the files contained in *Destination* are set to read-only, the CopyFolder method fails, regardless of the value of *Overwrite*.

- If *OverwriteFiles* is set to *False*, and the source folder or any of the files contained in *Source* exists in *Destination*, a trappable error—runtime error 58, "File Already Exists"—is generated.

- If an error occurs while copying more than one file or folder, the *CopyFolder* function exits immediately, leaving the rest of the folders or files uncopied. There is also no roll-back facility to undo the copies prior to the error.

- If the user has adequate rights, both the source or destination can be a network path or share name. For example:

```
CopyFolder "c:\Rootone", "\\NTSERV1\d$\RootTwo\"
CopyFolder "\\NTSERV1\RootTest", "c:\RootOne"
```

See Also

Folder.Copy Method

FileSystemObject.CreateFolder Method (VB6)

Named Arguments

Yes

Syntax

```
oFileSysObj.CreateFolder(Path)
oFileSysObj
    Use: Required
```

Data Type: FileSystemObject object

Any object variable returning a FileSystemObject object.

Path

Use: Required

Data Type: String

An expression that returns the name of the new folder to create.

Return Value

A Folder object

Description

Creates a single new folder in the path specified and returns its Folder object.

Rules at a Glance

- Wildcard characters aren't allowed in *newfoldername*.

- *Path* can be a relative or absolute path.

- If no path is specified in *Path*, the current drive and directory are used.

Programming Tips & Gotchas

- If the *Path* path is read-only, the CreateFolder method fails.

- If *Path* already exists, the method generates runtime error 58, "File already exists."

- If the user has adequate rights, *Path* can be a network path or share name. For example:

```
CreateFolder "\\NTSERV1\d$\RootTwo\newFolder"
CreateFolder "\\NTSERV1\RootTest\newFolder"
```

- You must use the Set statement to assign the Folder object to an object variable. For example:

```
Dim oFileSys As New FileSystemObject
Dim oFolder As Folder
Set oFolder = oFileSys.CreateFolder("MyFolder")
```

See Also

Folders.Add Method

FileSystemObject.CreateTextFile Method (VB6)

Named Arguments

Yes

Syntax

```
oFileSysObj.CreateTextFile Filename [, Overwrite[, _
         Unicode]])
```

    oFileSysObj
        Use: Required

        Data Type: FileSystemObject object

        Any object variable returning a FileSystemObject object.

    Filename
        Use: Required

        Data Type: String

        Any valid filename, along with an optional path.

    Overwrite
        Use: Optional

        Data Type: Boolean

        Flag indicating if an existing file of the same name should be overwritten.

    Unicode
        Use: Optional

        Data Type: Boolean

        Flag indicating if *newfilename* is to be written in Unicode or ASCII.

Return Value

A TextStream object.

Description

Creates a new file and returns its TextStream object.

Rules at a Glance

- Wildcard characters aren't allowed in *Filename*.

- *Filename* can be a relative or absolute path.

- If no path is specified in *Filename*, the application's current drive and directory are used.

- If the path specified in *Filename* doesn't exist, the method fails.

- The default value for *Overwrite* is False.

- If *Unicode* is set to True, the file is created in Unicode; otherwise it's created as an ASCII text file. The default value for *Unicode* is False.

Programming Tips & Gotchas

- The newly created text file is automatically opened only for writing. If you subsequently wish to read from the file, you must first close it and reopen it in read mode.

- If the path referred to in *Filename* is set to read-only, the CreateTextFile method fails regardless of the value of *Overwrite*.

- If the user has adequate rights, *Filename* can contain a network path or share name. For example:

```
CreateTextFile "\\NTSERV1\RootTest\myFile.doc"
```

- You must use the Set statement to assign the TextStream object to your local object variable.

See Also

Folder.CreateTextFile Method

FileSystemObject.DeleteFile Method (VB6)

Named Arguments

Yes

Syntax

```
oFileSysObj.DeleteFile FileSpec [, Force]
oFileSysObj
```

> Use: Required
>
> Data Type: FileSystemObject object
>
> Any object variable returning a FileSystemObject object.

```
FileSpec
```

> Use: Required
>
> Data Type: String
>
> The name and path of the file or files to delete.

```
Force
```

> Use: Optional
>
> Data Type: Boolean
>
> If set to True, the read-only flag on a file is ignored and the file deleted.

Description

Permanently removes a given file or files.

Rules at a Glance

- *FileSpec* can contain wildcard characters as the final path component.
- *FileSpec* can be a relative or absolute path.
- If any of the files specified for deletion are open, the method fails with a Permission Denied error.
- The default setting for *Force* is False.
- If the specified file or files can't be found, the method fails.
- If only a filename is used in *FileSpec*, the application's current drive and directory is assumed.

Programming Tips & Gotchas

- If an error occurs while deleting more than one file, the DeleteFile method exits immediately, thereby leaving the rest of the files undeleted. There is also no roll-back facility to undo deletions prior to the error.

- If the user has adequate rights, the source or destination can be a network path or share name. For example:

  ```
  DeleteFile "\\NTSERV1\RootTest\myFile.doc"
  ```

- DeleteFile permanently deletes files; it doesn't move them to the Recycle Bin.

See Also

Kill Statement

FileSystemObject.DeleteFolder Method (VB6)

Named Arguments

Yes

Syntax

```
oFileSysObj.DeleteFolder FileSpec[, Force]
oFileSysObj
```

> Use: Required
>
> Data Type: FileSystemObject object
>
> Any object variable returning a FileSystemObject object.

```
FileSpec
```

> Use: Required
>
> Data Type: String
>
> The name and path of the folders to delete.

```
Force
```

> Use: Optional
>
> Data Type: Boolean
>
> If set to True, the read-only flag on a file is ignored and the file deleted.

Description

Removes a given folder and all its files and subfolders.

Rules at a Glance

- *FileSpec* can contain wildcard characters as the final path component.
- *FileSpec* can't end with a path separator.
- *FileSpec* can be a relative or absolute path.
- If any of the files within the specified folders are open, the method fails with a Permission Denied error.
- The DeleteFolder method deletes all contents of the given folder, including other folders and their contents.
- The default setting for *Force* is False.

- If *Force* is `False`, and any of the files in the folders are read-only, the method fails.

- If the specified folder can't be found, the method fails.

Programming Tips & Gotchas

- If an error occurs while deleting more than one file or folder, the Delete-Folder method exits immediately, thereby leaving the rest of the folders or files undeleted. There is also no roll-back facility to undo the deletions prior to the error.

- DeleteFolder permanently deletes folders and their contents; it doesn't move them to the Recycle Bin.

- If the user has adequate rights, the source or destination can be a network path or share name. For example:

```
DeleteFolder "\\NTSERV1\d$\RootTwo"
DeleteFolder "\\RootTest"
```

See Also

RmDir Statement

FileSystemObject.DriveExists Method (VB6)

Named Arguments

Yes

Syntax

```
oFileSysObj.DriveExists (DriveSpec)
```
oFileSysObj
  Use: Required

  Data Type: FileSystemObject object

  Any object variable returning a FileSystemObject object.

DriveSpec
  Use: Required

  Data Type: String

  A path or drive letter.

Return Value

Boolean (`True` or `False`).

Description

Determines if a given drive (of any type) exists on the local machine or on the network.

Rules at a Glance

- If *DriveSpec* is a Windows drive letter, it doesn't have to include the colon. For example, "C" works just as well as "C:".

- Returns `True` if the drive exists or is connected to the machine, `False` if not.

Programming Tips & Gotchas

- DriveExists doesn't note the current state of removable media drives; for this, you must use the IsReady property of the given drive.

- If the user has adequate rights, *DriveSpec* can be a network path or share name. For example:

```
If ofs.DriveExists("\\NTSERV1\d$") Then
```

- This method is ideal for detecting any current drive around the network before calling a function in a remote ActiveX server located on that drive.

FileSystemObject.Drives Property (VB6)

Syntax

```
oFileSysObj.Drives
oFileSysObj
```
Use: Required

Data Type: FileSystemObject object

Any object variable returning a FileSystemObject object.

Return Value

Drives collection object.

Description

Drives is a read-only property that returns the Drives collection; each member of the collection is a Drive object, representing a single drive available on the system. Using the collection object returned by the Drives property, you can iterate all the drives on the system using a `For...Next` loop, or you can retrieve an individual Drive object, which represents one drive on the system, by using the Drives collection's Item method.

See Also

Drive Object, Drives Collection Object

FileSystemObject.FileExists Method (VB6)

Named Arguments

Yes

Syntax

```
oFileSysObj.FileExists(FileSpec)
oFileSysObj
```
Use: Required

Data Type: FileSystemObject object

Any object variable returning a FileSystemObject object.

FileSpec
> Use: Required
>
> Data Type: String
>
> A complete path to the file.

Return Value

Boolean (`True` or `False`).

Description

Determines if a given file exists.

Rules at a Glance

- Returns `True` if the file exists or is connected to the machine, `False` if not.

- *FileSpec* can't contain wildcard characters.

Programming Tips & Gotchas

If the user has adequate rights, *FileSpec* can be a network path or share name. For example:

```
If ofs.FileExists("\\TestPath\Test.txt") Then
```

FileSystemObject.FolderExists Method (VB6)

Named Arguments

Yes

Syntax

```
oFileSysObj.FolderExists(FolderSpec)
oFileSysObj
```
> Use: Required
>
> Data Type: FileSystemObject object
>
> Any object variable returning a FileSystemObject object.

FolderSpec
> Use: Required
>
> Data Type: String
>
> The complete path to the folder.

Return Value

Boolean (`True` or `False`).

Description

Determines if a given folder exists.

Rules at a Glance

- *FolderSpec* can't contain wildcard characters.

Reference

- Returns `True` if the folder exists, `False` if not.

Programming Tips & Gotchas

If the user has adequate rights, *FolderSpec* can be a network path or share name. For example:

```
If ofs.FileExists("\\NTSERV1\d$\TestPath\") Then
```

FileSystemObject.GetAbsolutePathName Method (VB6)

Named Arguments

Yes

Syntax

```
oFileSysObj.GetAbsolutePathName(Path)
oFileSysObj
```
   Use: Required

   Data Type: FileSystemObject object

   Any object variable returning a FileSystemObject object.

`Path`
   Use: Required

   Data Type: String

   A path specifier.

Return Value

A string containing the absolute path of a given path specifier.

Description

Converts a relative path to a fully qualified path, including the drive letter.

Rules at a Glance

- "." returns the drive letter and complete path of the current folder.

- ".." returns the drive letter and path of the parent of the current folder.

- "*filename*" returns the drive letter and path up to and including filename within the current folder.

- All relative path names are assumed to originate at the current folder.

- If a drive isn't explicitly provided as part of *Path*, it's assumed to be the current drive.

- Wildcard characters can be included in *path* at any point.

Programming Tips & Gotchas

- For mapped network drives and shares, the method doesn't return the full network address. Rather, it returns the fully qualified local path and locally issued drive letter.

- GetAbsolutePathName doesn't verify that a given file or folder exists in the path specified.

FileSystemObject.GetBaseName Method (VB6)

Named Arguments

Yes

Syntax

```
oFileSysObj.GetBaseName(Path)
oFileSysObj
```
> Use: Required
>
> Data Type: FileSystemObject object
>
> Any object variable returning a FileSystemObject object.

```
Path
```
> Use: Required
>
> Data Type: String
>
> A path specifier.

Return Value

A string containing the last element in *Path.*

Description

Returns the name of the last path component, less any extension.

Rules at a Glance

The file extension of the last element in *Path* isn't included in the returned string.

Programming Tips & Gotchas

- GetBaseName doesn't verify that a given file or folder exists in *Path.*

- In stripping the "file extension" and returning the base name of *Path,* GetBaseName has no intelligence. That is, it doesn't know whether the last component of *Path* is a path or a filename. If the last component includes one or more dots, it simply removes the last one, along with any following text. Hence, GetBaseName returns a null string for a *Path* of "." and it returns "." for a *Path* of "..". It is, in other words, really a string manipulation function, rather than a file function.

Reference

FileSystemObject.GetDrive Method (VB6)

Syntax

```
oFileSysObj.GetDrive(drivespecifier)
oFileSysObj
```
> Use: Required

Data Type: FileSystemObject object

Any object variable returning a FileSystemObject object.

drivespecifier
Use: Required

Data Type: String

A drive name, share name, or network path.

Return Value

A Drive object.

Description

Obtains a reference to a Drive object for the specified drive.

Rules at a Glance

- If *drivespecifier* is a share name or network path, GetDrive ensures that it exists as part of the process of creating the Drive object; if it doesn't, the method generates runtime error 76, "Path not found."

- If the specified drive isn't connected or doesn't exist, runtime error 67, "Device unavailable," occurs.

Programming Tips & Gotchas

- If you are deriving the *drivespecifier* string from a path, you should first use GetAbsolutePathName to insure that a drive is present as part of the path; then you should use FolderExists to verify that the path is valid before calling GetDriveName to extract the drive from the fully qualified path. For example:

```
Dim oFileSys As New FileSystemObject
Dim oDrive As Drive

sPath = oFileSys.GetAbsolutePathName(sPath)
If oFileSys.FolderExists(sPath) Then
    Set oDrive = _
        oFileSys.GetDrive(oFileSys.GetDriveName(sPath))
End If
```

- If *drivespecifier* is a network drive or share, you should use the DriveExists method to confirm the required drive is available prior to calling the GetDrive method.

- You must use the Set statement to assign the Drive object to a local object variable.

See Also

Drives.Item Property

FileSystemObject.GetDriveName Method (VB6)

Named Arguments

Yes

Syntax

```
oFileSysObj.GetDriveName (Path)
oFileSysObj
```
    Use: Required

    Data Type: FileSystemObject object

    Any object variable returning a FileSystemObject object.

`Path`
    Use: Required

    Data Type: String

    A path specifier.

Return Value

A String.

Description

Returns the drive name of a given path.

Rules at a Glance

If the drive name can't be determined from the given path, a zero-length string ("")
is returned.

Programming Tips & Gotchas

- GetDriveName doesn't verify that a given drive exists in `Path`.

- `Path` can be a network drive or share.

FileSystemObject.GetExtensionName Method (VB6)

Named Arguments

Yes

Syntax

```
oFileSysObj.GetExtensionName(Path)
oFileSysObj
```
    Use: Required

    Data Type: FileSystemObject object

    Any object variable returning a FileSystemObject object.

`Path`
    Use: Required

Data Type: String

A path specifier.

Return Value

A String.

Description

Returns the extension of the file element of a given path.

Rules at a Glance

If the extension in *Path* can't be determined, a zero-length string ("") is returned.

Programming Tips & Gotchas

*   GetExtensionName doesn't verify that *Path* is valid.

*   *Path* can be a network drive or share.

*   GetExtensionName has no intelligence. It simply parses a string and returns the text that follows the last dot of the last element.

FileSystemObject.GetFile Method (VB6)

Syntax

```
oFileSysObj.GetFile(FilePath)
```
oFileSysObj

Use: Required

Data Type: FileSystemObject object

Any object variable returning a FileSystemObject object.

FilePath

Use: Required

Data Type: String

A path and filename.

Return Value

File object.

Description

Returns a reference to a File object.

Rules at a Glance

*   *FilePath* can be an absolute or a relative path.

*   If *FilePath* is a share name or network path, GetFile ensures that the drive or share exists as part of the process of creating the File object.

*   If any part of the path in *FilePath* can't be contacted or doesn't exist, an error occurs.

Programming Tips & Gotchas

- The object returned by GetFile is a File object, not a TextStream object. A File object isn't an open file; the point of the File object is to perform methods such as coping or moving files and interrogating a file's properties. Although you can't write to or read from a File object, you can use the File object's OpenAsTextStream method to obtain a TextStream object.

- You should first use GetAbsolutePathName to create the required *FilePath* string.

- If *FilePath* includes a network drive or share, you could use the DriveExists method to confirm the required drive is available prior to calling the GetFile method.

- Since GetFile generates an error if the file designated in *FilePath* doesn't exist, you should call the FileExists method before calling GetFile.

- You must use the Set statement to assign the File object reference to a local object variable.

See Also

Files.Item Property

FileSystemObject.GetFileName Method (VB6)

Named Arguments

Yes

Syntax

```
oFileSysObj.GetFileName (Path)
oFileSysObj
```
    Use: Required

    Data Type: FileSystemObject object

    Any object variable returning a FileSystemObject object.

Path

    Use: Required

    Data Type: String

    A path specifier.

Return Value

A String value.

Description

Returns the filename element of a given path.

Rules at a Glance

- If the filename can't be determined from the given *Path*, a zero-length string ("") is returned.

Reference

- *Path* can be a relative or an absolute reference.

Programming Tips & Gotchas

- GetFileName doesn't verify that a given file exists in *Path*.
- *Path* can be a network drive or share.
- GetFileName has no built-in intelligence; it assumes that the last element of the string that isn't part of a drive specifier is, in fact, a filename. As with all the Get*x*Name methods of the FileSystemObject object, the GetFileName method is more a string-manipulation routine than an object-related routine.

FileSystemObject.GetFolder Method (VB6)

Syntax

```
oFileSysObj.GetFolder(FolderPath)
```
oFileSysObj

    Use: Required

    Data Type: FileSystemObject object

    Any object variable returning a FileSystemObject object.

FolderPath

    Use: Required

    Data Type: String

    A path to the required folder.

Return Value

A Folder object.

Description

Returns a reference to a Folder object.

Rules at a Glance

- *FolderPath* can be an absolute or relative path.
- If *FolderPath* is a share name or network path, GetFolder ensures that the drive or share exists as part of the process of creating the Folder object.
- If any part of *path* can't be contacted or doesn't exist, an error occurs.

Programming Tips & Gotchas

- You should first use GetAbsolutePathName to create the required *path* string.
- If *FolderPath* includes a network drive or share, you could use the DriveExists method to confirm the required drive is available prior to calling the GetFolder method.
- Since GetFolder requires that *FolderPath* is the path to a valid folder, you should call the FolderExists method to verify that *FolderPath* exists.

- You must use the `Set` statement to assign the Folder object reference to a local object variable.

See Also

Folders.Item Property

FileSystemObject.GetParentFolderName Method (VB6)

Named Arguments

Yes

Syntax

```
oFileSysObj.GetParentFolderName(Path)
oFileSysObj
```
    Use: Required

    Data Type: FileSystemObject object

    Any object variable returning a FileSystemObject object.

```
Path
```
    Use: Required

    Data Type: String

    A path specifier.

Return Value

A String.

Description

Returns the folder name immediately preceding the last element of a given path.

Rules at a Glance

- If the parent folder name can't be determined from *Path*, a zero-length string ("") is returned.
- *Path* can be a relative or an absolute reference.

Programming Tips & Gotchas

- GetParentFolderName doesn't verify that any element of *Path* exists.
- *Path* can be a network drive or share.
- GetParentFolderName assumes that the last but one element of the string that isn't part of a drive specifier is the parent folder. It makes no other check than this. As with all the GetxName methods of the FileSystemObject object, the GetParentFolderName method is more a string parsing and manipulation routine than an object-related routine.

Reference

See Also

Folder.ParentFolder Property

FileSystemObject.GetSpecialFolder Method (VB6)

Syntax

```
oFileSysObj.GetSpecialFolder(SpecialFolder)
```
oFileSysObj
> Use: Required
>
> Data Type: FileSystemObject object
>
> Any object variable returning a FileSystemObject object.

SpecialFolder
> Use: Required
>
> Data Type: Special folder constant
>
> A value specifying one of three special system folders.

Return Value

A Folder object

Description

Returns a reference to a Folder object of one of the three special system folders: System, Temporary, and Windows.

Rules at a Glance

SpecialFolder can be one of the following special folder constants:

Constant	Value	Description
SystemFolder	1	The Windows system folder (*/windows/system* or */windows/system32*)
TemporaryFolder	2	The folder that stores temporary files (*../windows/temp*)
WindowsFolder	0	The root folder of the Windows system folder tree (*/windows* or */winnt*)

Programming Tips & Gotchas

- This method is a great boon for VB programmers who don't want to get involved with the Windows API, which, in the past, is how you had to determine a path to one of the special folders.

- You can use the Set statement to assign the Folder object reference to a local object variable. However, if you're interested only in retrieving the path to the special folder, you can do it with a statement like the following:

```
sPath = oFileSys.GetSpecialFolder(iFolderConst)
```

or:

```
sPath = oFileSys.GetSpecialFolder(iFolderConst).Path
```

The first statement works because the Path property is the Folder object's default property. Since the assignment isn't to an object variable, it's the default property's value, rather than the object reference, that is assigned to *sPath.*

FileSystemObject.GetTempName Method (VB6)

Syntax

```
oFileSysObj.GetTempName
oFileSysObj
```
Use: Required

Data Type: FileSystemObject object

Any object variable returning a FileSystemObject object.

Return Value

A String.

Description

Returns a system-generated temporary file or folder name.

Rules at a Glance

GetTempName doesn't create a temporary file or folder; it simply provides a name you can use with the CreateTextFile method.

Programming Tips & Gotchas

As a general rule, you shouldn't create your own temporary filenames. Windows provides an algorithm within the Windows API to generate the special temporary file and folder names so that it can recognize them later. The GetTempName nicely wraps this *GetTempFilename* API function.

FileSystemObject.MoveFile Method (VB6)

Named Arguments

Yes

Syntax

```
oFileSysObj.MoveFile source , destination
oFileSysObj
```
Use: Required

Data Type: FileSystemObject object

Any object variable returning a FileSystemObject object.

source
Use: Required

Data Type: String

The path to the file or files to be moved.

destination

Use: Required

Data Type: String

The path to the location where the file or files are to be moved.

Description

Moves a file from one folder to another.

Rules at a Glance

- If *source* contains wildcard characters or if **destination** ends in a path separator, **destination** is interpreted as a path; otherwise, its last component is interpreted as a filename.

- If the destination file exists, an error occurs.

- *source* can contain wildcard characters, but only in its last component.

- **destination** can't contain wildcard characters.

- Both *source* and **destination** can be either absolute or relative paths.

- Both *source* and **destination** can be network paths or share names.

Programming Tips & Gotchas

- MoveFile resolves both arguments before beginning the operation.

- Any single file move operation is atomic; that is, any file removed from *source* is copied to **destination**. However, if an error occurs while multiple files are being moved, the execution of the function terminates, but files already moved aren't moved back to their previous folder. If a fatal system error occurs during the execution of this method (like a power failure), the worst that can happen is that the affected file is copied to the destination but not removed from the source. There are no rollback capabilities built into the File.Move method, however, since, because the copy part of this two-stage process is executed first, the file can't be lost. But while there is no chance of losing data, particularly in multifile operations, it's more difficult to determine whether the move operations have succeeded or not. This is because an error at any time while files are being moved causes the MoveFile method to be aborted.

- You can use the GetAbsolutePath, FolderExists, and FileExists methods prior to calling the MoveFile method to ensure its success.

See Also

FileSystemObject.CopyFile Method, FileSystemObject.FileExists Method, FileSystemObject.GetAbsolutePath Method, File.Move Method

---

FileSystemObject.MoveFolder Method (VB6)

Named Arguments

Yes

Syntax

```
oFileSysObj.MoveFolder source , destination
oFileSysObj
```
    Use: Required

    Data Type: FileSystemObject object

    Any object variable returning a FileSystemObject object.

source

    Use: Required

    Data Type: String

    The path to the folder or folders to be moved.

destination

    Use: Required

    Data Type: String

    The path to the location where the folder or folders are to be moved.

Description

Moves a folder along with its files and subfolders from one location to another.

Rules at a Glance

- *source* must end with either a wildcard character or no path separator.

- Wildcard characters can be used in *source*, but only for the last component.

- Wildcard characters can't be used in *destination*.

- All subfolders and files contained within the source folder are copied to *destination* unless disallowed by the wildcard characters. That is to say, the MoveFolder method is recursive.

- If *destination* ends with a path separator or *Source* ends with a wildcard, MoveFolder assumes that the folder in *Source* exists in *Destination*. For example, given the following folder structure:

```
C:\
    Rootone
        SubFolder1
        SubFolder2
    RootTwo
```

MoveFolder "c:\Rootone*", "C:\RootTwo\" produces this folder structure:

```
C:\
    Rootone

    RootTwo
        SubFolder1
        SubFolder2
```

MoveFolder "c:\Rootone", "C:\RootTwo\" produces this folder structure:

```
C:\

    RootTwo
```

```
Rootone
   SubFolder1
   SubFolder2
```

- *source* and *destination* can be either absolute or relative paths.

- *source* and *destination* can be network paths or share names.

Programming Tips & Gotchas

- The MoveFolder method resolves both arguments before beginning the operation.

- If a fatal system error occurs during the execution of this method (like a power failure), the worst that can happen is that the file is copied to the destination but not removed from the source. There are no rollback capabilities built into the FileSystemObject.MoveFolder method, however, since, because the copy part of this two-stage process is executed first, the file can't be lost.

- Although there is no chance of actually losing data, it can be difficult to determine whether the operation has succeeded or failed in the event of an error when multiple folders are being moved. This is because an error in the middle of a multifile move operation causes the MoveFolder method to be abandoned and subsequent folder operations to be aborted.

- You can call the GetAbsolutePath and FolderExists methods before calling the MoveFile method to ensure its success.

- If the user has adequate rights, the source or destination can be a network path or share name. For example:

```
MoveFolder "c:\Rootone", "\\NTSERV1\d$\RootTwo\"
```

See Also

FileSystemObject.CopyFolder Method, FileSystemObject.FolderExists Method, FileSystemObject.GetAbsolutePath Method, Folder.Move Method

---

FileSystemObject.OpenTextFile Method (VB6)

Named Arguments

Yes

Syntax

```
oFileSysObj.OpenTextFile(FileName[, IOMode[, Create[, _
                         Format]]])
```

oFileSysObj
   Use: Required

   Data Type: FileSystemObject object

   Any object variable returning a FileSystemObject object.

FileName
   Use: Required

   Data Type: String

   The path and filename of the file to open.

IOMode
Use: Optional

Data Type: IOMode constant

A constant specifying the purpose for opening the file.

Create
Use: Optional

Data Type: Boolean

A Boolean flag denoting if the file should be created if it can't be found in the given path.

Format
Use: Optional

Data Type: Tristate constant

A constant specifying ASCII or Unicode format.

Return Value

A TextStream object.

Description

Opens (and optionally first creates) a text file for reading or writing.

Rules at a Glance

- File open (*IOMode*) constants are:

Constant	Value	Description
ForAppending	8	Opens the file for appending; that is, the current contents of the file are protected and new data written to the file is placed at the end of the file.
ForReading	1	Opens the file for reading; ForReading files are read-only.
ForWriting	2	Opens the file for writing; all previous file content is overwritten by new data.

- Tristate (*Format*) constants:

Constant	Value	Description
TristateUseDefault	−2	Open as System default
TristateTrue	−1	Open as Unicode
TristateFalse	0	Open as ASCII

- The path element of *FileName* can be relative or absolute.
- The default *IOMode* setting is ForReading (1).
- The default *Format* setting is ASCII (False).

- If another process has opened the file, the method fails with a Permission Denied error.

Programming Tips & Gotchas

- You can use the GetAbsolutePath and FileExists methods prior to calling the OpenTextFile method to ensure its success.

- The value of *IOMode* can be only that of a single constant. For example, a method call such as the following:

```
lMode = ForReading Or ForWriting
oFileSys.OpenTextStream(strFileName, lMode)   ' WRONG
```

generates runtime error 5, "Invalid procedure call or argument."

- If the user has adequate rights, path element of *FileName* can be a network path or share name. For example:

```
OpenTextFile "\\NTSERV1\d$\RootTwo\myFile.txt"
```

See Also

File.OpenAsTextStream Method, TextStream Object

Filter Function (VB6)

Named Arguments

No

Syntax

```
Filter(SourceArray, FilterString[, Switch[, Compare]])
```
SourceArray

    Use: Required

    Data Type: String or Variant

    An array containing values to be filtered.

FilterString

    Use: Required

    Data Type: String

    The string of characters to find in the source array.

Switch

    Use: Optional

    Data Type: Boolean

    A Boolean (**True** or **False**) value. If **True**, the default value, *Filter* includes all matching values in *result*; if **False**, *Filter* excludes all matching values (or, to put it another way, includes all nonmatching values).

Compare

    Use: Optional

    Type: Constant of **vbCompareMethod** Enumeration

An optional constant (possible values are **vbBinaryCompare**, **vbText-Compare**, **vbDatabaseCompare**) that indicates the type of string comparison to use. The default value is **vbBinaryCompare**.

Return Value

A String array of the elements filtered from *SourceArray*.

Description

Produces an array of matching values from an array of source values that either match or don't match a given filter string. In other words, individual elements are copied from a source array to a target array if they either match or don't match a filter string.

Rules at a Glance

* The default *Switch* value is **True**.

* The default *Compare* value is **vbBinaryCompare**.

* **vbBinaryCompare** is case sensitive; that is, *Filter* matches both character and case. In contrast, **vbTextCompare** is case insensitive, matching only character regardless of case.

* The returned array is always base 0, regardless of any **Option Base** setting.

Programming Tips & Gotchas

* The *Filter* function ignores zero-length strings ("") if *SourceArray* is a string array and ignores empty elements if *SourceArray* is a variant array.

* The array you declare to assign the return value of Filter must be a dynamic, single-dimension String array or a variant.

* Although the *Filter* function is primarily a string function, you can also filter numeric values. To do this, specify a *SourceArray* of type Variant and populate this array with numeric values. Although *FilterString* appears to be declared internally as a string parameter, a String, Variant, Long, or Integer can be passed to the function. Note, though, that the returned string contains string representations of the filtered numbers. For example:

```
Dim varSource As Variant, varResult As Variant
Dim strMatch As String

strMatch = CStr(2)
varSource = Array(10, 20, 30, 21, 22, 32)
varResult = Filter(varSource, strMatch, True, _
                vbBinaryCompare)
```

In this case, the resulting array contains four elements: 20, 21, 22, and 32.

* The *Filter* function is an ideal companion to the Dictionary object. The Dictionary object is a collection-like array of values, each of which is stored with a unique string key. The Keys method of the Dictionary object allows you to produce an array of these Key values, which you can then pass into the *Filter* function as a rapid method of filtering the members of your Dictionary, as the following example demonstrates.

Example

```
Dim sKeys()      As String
Dim sFiltered()  As String
Dim sMatch       As String
Dim blnSwitch    As Boolean
Dim oDict        As Dictionary

Set oDict = New Dictionary

oDict.Add "One Microsoft Way", "Microsoft"
oDict.Add "31 Harbour Drive", "AnyMicro Inc"
oDict.Add "The Plaza", "Landbor Data"
oDict.Add "999 Pleasant View", "Micron Co."

sKeys = oDict.Keys
sMatch = "micro"
blnSwitch = True
'find all keys that contain the string "micro" - any case
sFiltered() = Filter(sKeys, sMatch, blnSwitch, _
    vbTextCompare)
'now iterate through the resulting array
For i = 0 To UBound(sFiltered)
    Set oSupplier = oDict.Item(sFiltered(i))
        With oSupplier
            Debug.Print oSupplier.Address1
        End With
    Set oSupplier = Nothing
Next i
```

Fix Function

Named Arguments

No

Syntax

```
Fix(number)
```
number

> Use: Required

> Data Type: Numeric

> Any valid numeric expression.

Return Value

The same data type as passed to the function containing only the integer portion of *number*.

Description

Removes the fractional part of a number. Operates in a similar way to the *Int* function.

Rules at a Glance

* If *number* is Null, *Fix* returns Null.

* The operations of *Int* and *Fix* are identical when dealing with positive numbers: numbers are rounded down to the next lowest whole number. For example, both Int(3.14) and Fix(3.14) return 3.

* If *number* is negative, *Fix* removes its fractional part, thereby returning the next greater whole number. For example, Fix(-3.667) returns –3. This contrasts with *Int*, which returns the negative integer less than or equal to number (or –4, in the case of our example).

Example

```
Sub TestFix()

    Dim dblTest As Double
    Dim varTest  As Variant

    dblTest = -100.9353
    varTest = Fix(dblTest)
    ' returns -100
    Debug.Print varTest & " " & TypeName(varTest)

    dblTest = 100.9353
    varTest = Fix(dblTest)
    'returns 100
    Debug.Print varTest & " " & TypeName(varTest)

End Sub
```

Programming Tips & Gotchas

Fix doesn't round *number* to the nearest whole number; it simply removes the fractional part of *number*. Therefore, the integer returned by *Fix* is the nearest whole number less than (or greater than, if the number is negative) the number passed to the function.

See Also

Int Function, CInt Function, CLng Function

Folder Object (VB6)

Description

The Folder object allows you to interrogate the system properties of the folder and provides methods that allow you to copy, move, and delete the folder. You can also create a new text file within the folder.

The Folder object is unusual because with it, you can gain access to a Folders collection object. The more usual method is to extract a member of a collection to gain access to the individual object. However, because the Drive object exposes only a Folder object for the root folder, you have to extract a Folders collection object from a Folder object (the collection represents the subfolders of the root).

From this collection, you can navigate downward through the file system to extract other Folder objects and other Folders collections. A Boolean property, IsRoot-Folder, informs you whether or not the Folder object you are dealing with currently is the root of the Drive or not.

The Folder object is one of the objects in the File System object model; see the File System object model entry for an overview of the model, including the library reference needed to access it.

Createable

No

Returned by

Drive.RootFolder Property, Folder.SubFolders.Item Property

Properties

Attributes

Data Type: FileAttributes constant

A set of flags representing the folder's attributes. You can determine which flag is set by using logical AND along with the value returned by the property and the value of the constant you'd like to test. For example:

```
If oFolder.Attributes And ReadOnly Then
    ' Folder is read-only
```

The FileAttributes constants are:

Constant	Value
Alias	64
Archive	32
Compressed	2048
Directory	16
Hidden	2
Normal	0
ReadOnly	1
System	4
Volume	8

Date Created

Data Type: Date

The date the folder was created.

DateLastAccessed

Data Type: Date

If available from the operating system, the date the Folder was last accessed.

DateLastModified

Data Type: Date

The date the folder was last modified.

Drive

Data Type: Drive object

Returns a Drive object representing the drive on which this folder resides.

Files

Data Type: Files collection object

Returns a Files collection object representing all files in the current folder.

IsRootFolder

Data Type: Boolean

Returns **True** if the folder is the root folder of its drive.

Name

Data Type: String

Returns the name of the folder.

ParentFolder

Data Type: Folder object

Returns a folder object representing the folder that's the parent of the current folder; not available if the current object is the root folder of its drive.

Path

Data Type: String

Returns the complete path of the current folder, including its drive.

ShortName

Data Type: String

Returns a DOS 8.3 folder name. May not work on an NTFS system.

ShortPath

Data Type: String

Returns a DOS 8.3 folder name. May not work on an NTFS system.

Size

Data Type: Variant

Returns the complete size of all files, subfolders, and their contents in the folder structure, starting with the current folder.

SubFolders

Data Type: Folders collection object

Returns a Folders collection object representing all subfolders within the current folder.

Type

Data Type: String

Doesn't appear to be fully implemented; always returns "File Folder."

Methods

Copy	CreateTextFile
Delete	Move

Folder.Copy Method (VB6)

Named Arguments

Yes

Syntax

```
oFolderObj.Copy Destination [, OverwriteFiles]
oFolderObj
```
Use: Required

Data Type: Folder object

Any object variable returning a Folder object.

```
Destination
```
Use: Required

Data Type: String

The path and optionally the filename of the copy to be made.

```
OverwriteFiles
```
Use: Optional

Data Type: Boolean

Indicates whether existing files and folders should be overwritten (**True**) or not (**False**).

Description

Copies the current folder and its contents, including other folders, to another location.

Rules at a Glance

- Wildcard characters can't be used in `Destination`.

- The folder and all subfolders and files contained in the source folder are copied to `Destination`. That is to say, the Copy method is recursive.

- Unlike the FileSystemObject.CopyFolder method, there is no operational difference between ending `Destination` with a path separator or not.

Programming Tips & Gotchas

- If the destination path or any of the files contained in the `Destination` structure are set to read-only, the Copy method will fail regardless of the value of `OverwriteFiles`.

- If `OverwriteFiles` is set to **False**, and the source folder or any of the files contained in the `Destination` structure exists in the `Destination` structure, then trappable error 58, "File Already Exists," is generated.

- If an error occurs while copying more than one file, the Copy method exits immediately, leaving the rest of the files uncopied. There is also no roll-back facility to undo the copies prior to the error.

- If the user has adequate rights, *Destination* can be a network path or share name. For example:

```
oFolder.Copy "\\NTSERV1\d$\RootTwo\"
```

Folder.CreateTextFile Method (VB6)

Named Arguments

Yes

Syntax

```
oFolderObj.CreateTextFile FileName[, Overwrite[, _
          Unicode]])
```

oFolderObj

Use: Required

Data Type: Folder object

Any object variable returning a Folder object.

FileName

Use: Required

Data Type: String

Any valid filename and optional path.

Overwrite

Use: Optional

Data Type: Boolean

Flag to indicate if an existing file of the same name should be overwritten.

Unicode

Use: Optional

Data Type: Boolean

Flag to indicate if file is to be written in Unicode or ASCII.

Return Value

A TextStream object

Description

Creates a new file at the specified location and returns a TextStream object for that file.

Rules at a Glance

- Wildcard characters aren't allowed in *FileName*.

- The default value for *Overwrite* is *False*.

- If *Unicode* is set to **True**, a Unicode file is created; otherwise it's created as an ASCII text file.

- The default value for *Unicode* is **False**.

Programming Tips & Gotchas

- The newly created text file is automatically opened only for writing. If you subsequently wish to read from the file, you must first close it and reopen it in read mode.

- You must use the **Set** statement to assign the TextStream object to a local object variable.

- The CreateTextFile method in the Folder object is identical in operation to that in the FileSystemObject object.

See Also

FileSystemObject.CreateTextFile Method

Folder.Delete Method (VB6)

Named Arguments

Yes

Syntax

```
oFolderObj.Delete [Force]
oFolderObj
```
　　Use: Required

　　Data Type: Folder object

　　Any object variable returning a Folder object.

Force
　　Use: Optional

　　Data Type: Boolean

　　If set to **True**, any read-only flag on a file is ignored and the file deleted.

Description

Removes the current folder and all its files and subfolders.

Rules at a Glance

- If any of the files within the folder are open, the method fails with a "Permission Denied" error.

- The Delete method deletes all the contents of the given folder, including other folders and their contents.

- The default setting for *Force* is **False**.

- If *Force* is set to **False** and any of the files in the folders are set to read-only, the method fails.

Programming Tips & Gotchas

- If an error occurs while deleting more than one file or folder, the Delete method exits immediately, thereby leaving the rest of the folders or files undeleted. There is also no roll-back facility to undo the deletions prior to the error.

- Unlike the FileSystemObject's DeleteFolder method, which accepts wildcard characters in the path parameter and can therefore delete multiple folders, the Delete method deletes only the single folder represented by the Folder object.

- Immediately after the Delete method executes, the Folders collection object containing the Folder object is automatically updated. The deleted folder is removed from the collection, and the collection count reduced by one. You shouldn't try to access the deleted Folder object again, and you should set the local object variable to Nothing, as the following snippet demonstrates:

```
Set ofsSubFolder = ofsSubFolders.Item("roottwo")
    MsgBox ofsSubFolders.Count
    ofsSubFolder.Delete False
    MsgBox ofsSubFolders.Count
Set ofsSubFolder = Nothing
```

See Also

FileSystemObject.DeleteFolder Method, RmDir Statement

Folder.Move Method (VB6)

Named Arguments

Yes

Syntax

```
oFolderObj.Move destination
oFolderObj
```
> Use: Required
>
> Data Type: Folder object
>
> Any object variable returning a Folder object.

```
destination
```
> Use: Required
>
> Data Type: String
>
> The path to the location where the folder or folders are to be moved.

Description

Moves a folder structure from one location to another.

Rules at a Glance

- Wildcard characters can't be used in *Destination.*
- If any of the files within the folder being moved are open, an error is generated.

- All subfolders and files contained within the source folder are copied to *Destination*, unless disallowed by the wildcard characters. That is to say, the Move method is recursive.

- *Destination* can be either an absolute or a relative path.

Programming Tips & Gotchas

- If a fatal system error occurs during the execution of this method (like a power failure), the worst that can happen is that the folder is copied to the destination but not removed from the source. There are no roll-back capabilities built into the Folder.Move method, however, since, because the copy part of this two-stage process is executed first, the folder can't be lost.

- If an error occurs in the middle of a move operation, the operation is terminated immediately, and the remaining files and folders in the folder aren't moved.

- To ensure its success, you can use the FileSystemObject's FolderExists and GetAbsolutePath methods prior to calling the Move method.

- Unlike the FileSystemObject's MoveFolder method, which accepts wildcard characters in the *source* parameter and can therefore move multiple folders, the Move method moves only the single folder represented by the Folder object and its contents.

- Immediately after the Move method executes, the Folders collection object containing the Folder object is automatically updated, the moved folder is removed from the collection and the collection count is reduced by one. You shouldn't try to access the moved folder object again from the same Folders collection object.

- If the user has adequate rights, the destination can be a network path or share name. For example:

```
Move "\\NTSERV1\d$\RootTwo\"
```

See Also

FileSystemObject.MoveFolder Method

Folders Collection Object (VB6)

Description

The Folders collection object is a container for Folder objects. Normally, you expect to access a single object from the collection of that object; for example, you'd expect to access a Folder object from the Folders collection object. However, things are the other way round here: you access the Folders collection object from an instance of a Folder object. This is because the first Folder object you instantiate from the Drive object is a Root Folder object, and from it you instantiate a subfolders collection. You can then instantiate other Folder and subfolder objects to navigate through the drive's filesystem.

The Folders collection object is one of the objects in the File System object model; see the File System object model entry for an overview of the model, including the library reference needed to access it.

Createable

No

Returned by

Folder.SubFolders property

Properties

Item
> Data Type: Folder object
>
> Retrieves a particular Folder object from the Folders collection object. You can access an individual folder object by providing the exact name of the folder without its path. However, you can't access the item using its ordinal number. For example, the following statement returns the Folder object that represents the *roottwo* folder:
>
> ```
> Set ofsSubFolder = ofsSubFolders.Item("roottwo")
> ```

Count
> Data Type: Long
>
> The number of Folder objects contained in the Folders collection.

Methods

> Add

See Also

> Folders.Add Method, Folder Object

Folders.Add Method (VB6)

Syntax

```
oFoldersCollObj.Add newfoldername
oFoldersCollObj
```
> Use: Required
>
> Data Type: Folders collection object
>
> Any object variable returning a Folders collection object.

newfoldername
> Use: Required
>
> Data Type: String
>
> The name of the new folder.

Return Value

Folder object.

Reference

Description

Creates a new folder. The location of the new folder is determined by the parent to which the Folders collection object belongs. For example, if you are calling the Add method from a Folders collection object that is a child of the root Folder object, the new folder is created in the root (i.e., it's added to the root's subfolders collection). For example:

```
Dim oFileSys As New FileSystemObject
Dim oRoot As Folder, oChild As Folder
Dim oRootFolders As Folders

Set oRoot = oFileSys.Drives("C").RootFolder
Set oRootFolders = oRoot.SubFolders
Set oChild = oRootFolders.Add("Downloads")
```

Rules at a Glance

You can't use a path specifier in *newfoldername*; you can use only the name of the new folder.

See Also

FileSystemObject.CreateFolder Method

For...Next Statement

Named Arguments

No

Syntax

```
For counter = initial_value To maximum_value _
          [Step stepcounter]
   'code to execute on each iteration
    [Exit For]
Next [counter]
```

counter

Use: Required (optional with **Next** statement)

Data Type: Numeric Variant

Any valid numeric variable to be used as the loop counter.

initial_value

Use: Required

Data Type: Numeric Variant

Any valid numeric expression that specifies the loop counter's initial value.

maximum_value

Use: Required

Data Type: Numeric Variant

Any valid numeric expression that specifies the loop counter's maximum value.

stepcounter

Use: Optional (required if Step used)

Data Type: Numeric Variant

Any valid numeric expression that indicates how much the loop counter should be incremented with each new iteration of the loop.

Description

Defines a loop that executes a given number of times, as determined by a loop counter. To use the For...Next loop, you must assign a numeric value to a counter variable. This counter is either incremented or decremented automatically with each iteration of the loop. In the For statement, you specify the value that is to be assigned to the counter initially and the maximum value the counter will reach for the block of code to be executed. The Next statement marks the end of the block of code that is to execute repeatedly, and also serves as a kind of flag that indicates the counter variable is to be modified.

Rules at a Glance

- If *maximum_value* is greater than *initial_value*, and no Step keyword is used or the step counter is positive, the For...Next loop is ignored and execution commences with the first line of code immediately following the Next statement.

- If *initial_value* and *maximum_value* are equal and *stepcounter* is 1, the loop executes once.

- *counter* can't be a Boolean variable or an array element.

- *counter* is incremented by one with each iteration unless the Step keyword is used.

- The For...Next loop can contain any number of Exit For statements. When the Exit For statement is executed, program execution commences with the first line of code immediately following the Next statement.

- If the Step keyword is used, *stepcounter* specifies the amount *counter* is incremented if *stepcounter* is positive or decremented if it's negative.

- If the Step keyword is used, and *stepcounter* is negative, *initial_value* should be greater than *maximum_ value*. If this isn't the case, the loop doesn't execute.

Example

The following example demonstrates the use of a For...Next statement to iterate through the items in a combo box until an item in the combo box list matches a particular value:

```
For i = 0 to cboCombo.ListCount - 1
    If cboCombo.List(i) = sSought Then
        cboCombo.ListIndex = i
        Exit For
```

```
            End If
      Next i
```

The next example demonstrates how to iterate from the end to the start of an array of values:

```
For i = UBound(sArray) to LBound(sArray) Step - 1
     Debug.Print sArray(i)
Next i
```

This last example demonstrates how to select only every other value from an array of values:

```
For i = LBound(sArray) to UBound(sArray) Step 2
     Debug.Print sArray(i)
Next i
```

Programming Tips & Gotchas

- You can also nest For...Next loops, as shown below:

```
For iDay = 1 to 365
   For iHour = 1 to 23
      For iMinute = 1 to 59
            . . .
      Next iMinute
   Next iHour
Next iDay
```

- Although the counter following the Next keyword is optional, you will find your code is much easier to read if you use it, especially when nesting For...Next loops.

- You should avoid changing the value of *counter* in the code within the loop. Not only can this lead to unexpected results; it makes for code that's incredibly difficult to read and to understand.

- Once the loop has finished executing, the value of *counter* is officially undefined. That is, you shouldn't make any assumptions about its value outside of the For...Next loop, and you shouldn't use it unless you first reinitialize it.

See Also

For Each...Next Statement

For Each...Next Statement

Named Arguments

No

Syntax

```
For Each element In group
[statements]
[Exit For]
[statements]
Next [element]
```

element
> Use: Required
>
> Data Type: Variant or Object
>
> A variant or object variable to which the current element from the group is assigned.

group
> Use: Required
>
> A collection, object collection, or an array.

statements
> Use: Optional
>
> A line or lines of program code to execute within the loop.

Description

Loops through the items of a collection or the elements of an array.

Rules at a Glance

- The `For...Each` code block is executed only if *group* contains at least one element. If group is a dynamic array that has not yet been dimensioned or an empty collection, a syntax error (runtime error 92, "For loop not initialized," and 424, "Object required," respectively) results.

- All *statements* are executed for each *element* in *group* in turn until either there are no more elements in *group*, or the loop is exited prematurely using the `Exit For` statement. Program execution then continues with the line of code following `Next`.

- `For Each...Next` can't be used with an array of user-defined types, because you can't assign a user-defined type to a variant.

- `For Each...Next` can't be used with an array of fixed-length strings.

- `For Each...Next` loops can be nested, but each *element* must be unique. For example:

```
For Each myObj In AnObject
    For Each subObject In myObj
        SName = subObject.NameProperty
    Next
Next
```

uses a nested `For Each...Next` loop, but two different variables, *myObj* and *subObject*, represent *element*.

- Any number of `Exit For` statements can be placed with the `For Each...Next` loop to allow for conditional exit of the loop prematurely. On exiting the loop, execution of the program continues with the line immediately following the `Next` statement. For example, the following loop terminates once the program finds a name in the *myObj* collection that has fewer than 10 characters:

```
For Each subObject In myObj
    SName = subObject.NameProperty
```

Reference

```
        If Len(Sname) < 10 then
            Exit For
        End if
    Next
```

Programming Tips & Gotchas

- Each time the loop executes when iterating the objects in a collection, an implicit Set statement is executed. The following code reflects the "long-hand" method that is useful for explaining what is actually happening during each iteration of the For Each...Next loop:

```
For i = 1 to MyObject.Count
    Set myObjVar = MyObject.Item(i)
    Debug.Print myObjVar.NameProperty
Next i
```

- Because the elements of an array are assigned to *element* by value, element is a local copy of the array element, and not a reference to the array element itself. This means that you can't make changes to the array element using For Each...Next and expect them to be reflected in the array once the For Each...Next loop terminates, as the following example demonstrates:

```
strNameArray(0) = "Paul"
strNameArray(1) = "Bill"

For Each varName In strNameArray
    varName = "Changed"
    Debug.Print strNameArray(0)
Next
```

  If you run the code through the VB or VBA development environment, note that on the first loop, although *varName* has been changed from "Paul" to "Changed," the underlying array element, *strNameArray(0)*, still reports a value of "Paul." This proves that a referential link between the underlying array and object variable isn't present, and that, instead, the value of the array element is passed to *element* by value.

- The Microsoft VBA documentation for the For Each...Next loop contains an example which is confusing, misleading, and incorrect. The example states, "The following code loops through each element in an array and sets the value of each to the value of the index variable I":

```
Dim TestArray(10) As Integer, i As Variant
For Each i In TestArray
    TestArray(i) = i
Next i
```

  In fact, if you look at this code carefully, you'll see that on each loop, *i* has a value of 0. Therefore all this code does is assign a value of 0 to element 0 of the array 11 times! This example makes the mistake of combining the For Each...Next statement, which iterates each member of an array or collection in an arbitrary order, with the traditional For...Next statement, which iterates each member of an array in index order.

See Also

Exit Statement, For...Next Statement

Format, Format$ Functions

Named Arguments

No

Syntax

```
Format(expression[, format[, firstdayofweek[, _
    firstweekofyear]]])
```

expression
> Use: Required

> Data Type: String/Numeric

> Any valid string or numeric expression.

format
> Use: Optional

> A valid named or user-defined format expression.

firstdayofweek
> Use: Optional

> Data Type: Numeric

> A constant that specifies the first day of the week.

firstweekofyear
> Use: Optional

> Data Type: Numeric

> A constant that specifies the first week of the year.

Return Value

A variant of subtype string containing the formatted expression.

Description

Allows you to use either predefined or user-defined formats to create an infinite variety of ways to output string, numeric, and date/time data. It's possibly the most complex single function call in VB.

Rules at a Glance

- See *CDate* for an explanation of the *firstdayofweek* and *firstweekofyear* arguments.

- *format* can be either a predefined or a user-defined format.

- User-defined formats for numeric values are created with up to four sections. Each section is used for a different type of numeric value and is delimited with a semicolon. The four possible sections are shown in the following table:

Section	Applies to
1	All values, if used alone; positive values, if used with more than one section
2	Negative values
3	Zero values
4	Null values

- It's not necessary to include all four sections in the *format* clause. However, the number of sections present determines what types of numeric values each section defines, as the following table shows:

# of Sections	Applies to
1	All numeric values
2	Positive and zero values, negative values
3	Positive values, negative values, zero values
4	As shown in previous table

- If you leave a section blank, that section uses the same format as that defined for positive values. For example, the format string:

  `"#.00;;#,##"`

  means that negative values will appear in the same format as positive values.

- Only one section is allowed where one of the named formats is used.

- User-defined formats for string values can have two sections. The first is for all values, the second applies only to Null values or zero-length strings.

  The predefined date and time formats are:

  General Date
  > Example: `Format("01/06/98","General Date")`

  > Returns: 1/6/98

  Long Date
  > Example: `Format("01/06/98","Long Date")`

  > Returns: Tuesday, January 06, 1998

  Medium Date
  > Example: `Format("01/06/98","Medium Date")`

  > Returns: 06-Jan-98

  Short Date
  > Example: `Format("01/06/98","Short Date")`

  > Returns: 1/6/98

Long Time
    Example: `Format("17:08:06","Long Time")`

    Returns: 5:08:06 P.M.

Medium Time
    Example: `Format("01/06/98","Medium Time")`

    Returns: 05:08 P.M.

Short Time
    Example: `Format("01/06/98","Short Time")`

    Returns: 17:08

The predefined numeric formats are:

General Number
    Example: `Format(562486.2356, "General Number")`

    Returns: 562486.2356

Currency
    Example: `Format(562486.2356, "Currency")`

    Returns: $562,486.24

Fixed
    Example: `Format(0.2, "Fixed")`

    Returns: 0.20

Standard
    Example: `Format(562486.2356, "Standard")`

    Returns: 562,486.24

Percent
    Example: `Format(.7521, "Percent")`

    Returns: 75.21%

Scientific
    Example: `Format(562486.2356, "Scientific")`

    Returns: 5.62E+05

Yes/No
    Example #1: `Format(0,"Yes/No")`

    Returns: No

    Example #2: `Format(23,"Yes/No")`

    Returns: Yes

True/False
    Example #1: `Format(0," True/False")`

    Returns: False

    Example #2: `Format(23," True/False")`

    Returns: True

Reference

On/Off

Example #1: Format(0," On/Off")

Returns: Off

Example #2: Format(23," On/Off")

Returns: On

• Characters that create user-defined date and time formats are:

c   Element: Date

Display as: A date and/or time based on the short date and short time international settings of the current Windows system.

Example: Format("01/06/98 17:08:06", "c")

Returns: 1/6/98 5:08:06 PM

ddddd

Element: Date

Display as: A complete date based on the long date international setting of the current Windows system.

Example: Format("01/06/98", "ddddd")

Returns: Tuesday, January 06, 1998

(/) Element: Date separator

Display as: A date delimited with the specified character.

Example: Format("01/06/98", "mm-dd-yyyy")

Returns: 01-06-1998

d   Element: Day

Display as: A number (1–31) without a leading zero.

Example: Format("01/06/98", "d")

Returns: 6

dd Element: Day

Display as: A number (01–31) with a leading zero.

Example: Format("01/06/98", "dd")

Returns: 06

ddd

Element: Day

Display as: An abbreviation (Sun–Sat).

Example: Format("01/06/98", "ddd")

Returns: Tue

dddd

Element: Day

Display as: A full name (Sunday–Saturday).

Example: `Format("01/06/98", "dddd")`

Returns: Tuesday

ddddd

Element: Date

Display as: A date based on the short date section in the computer's Windows international settings.

Example: `Format("01/06/98", "ddddd")`

Returns: 1/6/98

h   Element: Hour

Display as: A number (0–23) without leading zeros.

Example: `Format("05:08:06", "h")`

Returns: 5

hh   Element: Hour

Display as: A number (00–23) with leading zeros.

Example: Format("05:08:06", "hh")

Returns: 05

n   Element: Minute

Display as: A number (0–59) without leading zeros.

Example: `Format("05:08:06", "n")`

Returns: 8

nn   Element: Minute

Display as: A number (00–59) with leading zeros.

Example: Format("05:08:06", "nn")

Returns: 08

m   Element: Month

Display as: A number (1–12) without a leading zero.

Example: Format("01/06/98", "m")

Returns: 1

mm   Element: Month

Display as: A number (01–12) with a leading zero.

Example: `Format("01/06/98", "mm")`

Returns: 01

mmm

Element: Month

Display as: An abbreviation (Jan–Dec).

Example: `Format("01/06/98", "mmm")`

Returns: Jan

mmmm
> Element: Month
>
> Display as: A full month name (January–December).
>
> Example: Format("01/06/98", "mmmm")
>
> Returns: January

q Element: Quarter

> Display as: A number (1–4)
>
> Example: Format("01/06/98", "q")
>
> Returns: 1

s Element: Second

> Display as: A number (0–59) without leading zeros.
>
> Example: Format("05:08:06", "s")
>
> Returns: 6

ss Element: Second

> Display as: A number (00–59) with leading zeros.
>
> Example: Format("05:08:06", "ss")
>
> Returns: 06

ttttt
> Element: Time
>
> Display as: A time based on the 12-hour clock, using the time separator and leading zeros specified in Windows locale settings.
>
> Example: Format("05:08:06", "ttttt")
>
> Returns: 5:08:06 AM

AM/PM
> Element: Time
>
> Display as: A 12-hour clock format using uppercase A.M. and P.M.
>
> Example: Format("17:08:06", "hh:mm:ss AM/PM")
>
> Returns: 05:08:06 PM

am/pm
> Element: Time
>
> Display as: A 12-hour clock format using lowercase a.m. and p.m.
>
> Example: Format("17:08:06", "hh:mm:ss am/pm")
>
> Returns: 05:08:06 pm

A/P Element: Time

> Display as: A 12-hour clock format using an uppercase "A" for A.M. and "P" for P.M.
>
> Example: Format("17:08:06", "hh:mm:ss A/P")
>
> Returns: 05:08:06 P

a/p Element: Time

Display as: A 12-hour clock format using a lowercase "a" for a.m. and "p" for p.m.

Example: Format("17:08:06", "hh:mm:ss a/p")

Returns: 05:08:06 p

(:) Element: Time separator

Display as: A time format using a nonstandard character.

Example: Format("17:08:06", "hh::mm::ss")

Returns: 17::08::06

ww Element: Week

Display as: A number (1–54).

Example: Format("01/06/98", "ww")

Returns: 2

w Element: Weekday

Display as: A number (1 for Sunday through 7 for Saturday).

Example: Format("01/06/98", "w")

Returns: 3

y Element: Day of Year

Display as: A number (1–366).

Example: Format("01/06/98", "y")

Returns: 6

yy Element: Year

Display as: A two-digit number (00–99).

Example: Format("01/06/98", "yy")

Returns: 98

yyyy

Element: Year

Display as: A 4-digit number (100–9999).

Example: Format("01/06/98", "yyyy")

Returns: 1998

- Characters that create user-defined number formats are as follows:

(0) Description: Digit Placeholder. If *expression* contains a digit in the appropriate position, the digit is displayed; otherwise, a 0 is displayed. The format definition dictates the number of digits after the decimal point, forcing the number held within an expression to be rounded to the given number of decimal places. It doesn't, however, affect the number of digits shown to the left of the decimal point.

Example #1: Format(23.675, "00.0000") returns 23.6750

Example #2: Format(23.675, "00.00") returns 23.68

Example #3: Format(2658, "00000") returns 02658

Example #4: Format(2658, "00.00") returns 2658.00

(#) Description: Digit placeholder. If *expression* contains a digit in the appropriate position, the digit is displayed; otherwise, nothing is displayed.

Example #1: Format(23.675, "##.##") returns 23.68

Example #2: Format(23.675, "##.####") returns 23.675

Example #3: Format(12345.25, "#,###.##") returns 12,345.25

(.) Description: Decimal placeholder. The actual character displayed as a decimal placeholder depends on the international settings of the local Windows system.

(%) Description: Percentage placeholder. Displays *expression* as a percentage by first multiplying the value of *expression* by 100.

Example: Format(0.25, "##.00%") returns 25.00%

(,) Description: Thousands separator. The actual character displayed as a thousands separator depends on the international settings of the local Windows system. You need to show only one thousands separator in your definition.

Example: Format(1000000, "#,###") returns 1,000,000

(E- E+ e- e+)

Description: Scientific format. If the format expression contains at least one digit placeholder (0 or #) to the right of "E-", "E+", "e-", or "e+", the number is displayed in scientific format, and the letter "E" or "e" that was used in the *format* expression is inserted between the number and its exponent. The number of digit placeholders to the right determines the number of digits displayed in the exponent. Use "E-" or "e-" to place a minus sign next to negative exponents. Use "E+" or "e+" to place a minus sign next to negative exponents and a plus sign next to positive exponents.

Example: Format(1.09837555, "######E-###") returns 109838E-5

- + $ ( )

Description: Displays a literal character

Example: Format(2345.25, "$#,###.##") returns $2,345.25

(\) Description: The character following the backslash is displayed as a literal character. Use the backslash to display a special formatting character as a literal.

Example: Format(0.25, "##.00\%") returns .25%

Note the difference between the result of this example and the result of the % formatting character.

- Characters that create user-defined string formats:

    @   Description: Character placeholder. If *expression* contains a character in the appropriate position, the character is displayed; otherwise, a space is displayed.

    Example: `Format("VBA", "\*@\*@@@@@")` returns * * VBA

    &   Description: Character placeholder. If *expression* contains a character in the appropriate position, the character is displayed; otherwise, nothing is displayed.

    Example: `Format("VBA", "\*&&\*&&&&")` returns **VBA

    <   Description: Displays all characters in lowercase.

    Example: `Format("VBA", "<")` returns vba

    >   Description: Displays all characters in uppercase.

    Example: `Format("vba", ">")` returns VBA

    !   Description: Processes placeholders from left to right (the default is to process from right to left).

Programming Tips & Gotchas

- A little-known and important use of the *Format* function is to prevent an Invalid Use of Null error from occurring when assigning values from a recordset to a variable within your program. For example, if a field within either a DAO or RDO recordset created from either an Access or SQL Server database contains a Null value, you can trap this and change its value to "" as follows:

```
If IsNull(rsMyRecordSet!myValue) Then
    sMyString = ""
Else
    sMyString = rsMyRecordSet!myValue
End If
```

However, assigning the value returned by the *Format* function that has been passed the recordset field can do away with this long and tedious coding, as the following line of code illustrates:

```
sMyString = Format(rsMyRecordSet!myValue)
```

- The *Format* function is a workaround when using the ! delimiter to assign the value of a field in an RDO recordset to an item of a collection. The following code shows the assignment of a recordset field to a collection element:

```
MyColl.Add rsMyRecordSet!myValue
```

When this recordset is closed, references to this item of this collection element results in an error. One of the simplest workarounds is to assign the return value of a *Format* function, like this:

```
MyColl.Add Format(rsMyRecordSet!myValue)
```

- If you are passing a date to SQL Server, what date format should you use? By default, SQL Server expects an American date format, mmddyy, but the database may have been altered to accept other date formats, or you could be passing data to a stored procedure that begins with a date time conversion statement (SET DATEFORMAT *dateformat*). The only sure way of passing a date into SQL Server is by using the ANSI standard date format `'yyyymmdd'`— including the single quotation marks.

- When passing a date to a Jet (Access) database, you should surround the date with hash characters (#); for example: #12/31/1999#.

- Formatting numbers using *Format* without a format definition is also preferable to simply using the *Str* function. Unlike *Str*, the *Format* function removes the leading space normally reserved for the sign from positive numbers.

- You can also use the *Format* function to scale numbers by 1000 by placing a thousands separator to the immediate left of the decimal point for each 1000 you wish the number to be scaled by. Thus:

```
' one separator divides the expression by 1000 = 1000
Format(1000000, "##0,.")
'two separators divides the expression by 1,000,000 = 1
Format(1000000, "##0,,.")
```

- Visual Basic Version 6 introduces the concept of *data binding*, where a field in a data recordset can be programmatically bound to a property of a form, control, or other data consumer. Part of this new technology is the Format Object, which automatically formats data coming from the recordset based on properties you set within the object. Modified data passed back to the recordset is automatically unformatted.

See Also

CStr Function, Data Format Objects, Str Function

FormatCurrency, FormatNumber, FormatPercent Functions (VB6)

Named Arguments

No

Syntax

```
FormatCurrency(number[,DecimalPlaces ][, _
    IncLeadingZero[,UseParenthesis[,GroupDigits]]]])
FormatNumber(number[,DecimalPlaces ][, _
    IncLeadingZero[,UseParenthesis[,GroupDigits]]]])
FormatPercent(number[,DecimalPlaces ][, _
    IncLeadingZero[,UseParenthesis[,GroupDigits]]]])
```
number
    Use: Required

    Data Type: Any numeric expression

    The number to be formatted.

DecimalPlaces
    Use: Optional

Data Type: Long

Number of digits the formatted string should contain after the decimal point.

IncLeadingZero
Use: Optional

Data Type: TriState constant

Indicates if the formatted string is to have a 0 before floating point numbers between 1 and –1.

UseParenthesis
Use: Optional

Data Type: TriState constant

Specifies whether parentheses should be placed around negative numbers.

GroupDigits
Use: Optional

Data Type: TriState constant

Determines whether digits in the returned string should be grouped using the delimiter specified in the computer's regional settings. For example, on English language systems, the value 1000000 is returned as 1,000,000 if *GroupDigits* is True.

Return Value

String

Description

The three functions are almost identical. They all take identical arguments, the only difference being that *FormatCurrency* returns a formatted number beginning with the currency symbol specified in the computer's regional settings, *Format-Number* returns just the formatted number, and *FormatPercent* returns the formatted number followed by a percentage sign (%).

Rules at a Glance

- If *DecimalPlaces* isn't specified, the value in the computer's regional settings is used.

- The Tristate constant values are `TristateTrue`, `TristateFalse`, and `TriStateUseDefault`.

Programming Tips & Gotchas

These three functions first appeared in VBScript version 2 as "light" alternatives to the *Format* function, which had originally been left out of VBScript due to its size. They are quick and easy to use, and make your code more self-documenting; you can instantly see what format is being applied to a number without having to decipher the format string.

See Also

Format Function

FormatDateTime Function (VB6)

Syntax

```
FormatDateTime(date[, format])
```

date

> Use: Required
>
> Data Type: Date or String
>
> Any expression that can be evaluated as a date.

format

> Use: Optional
>
> Data Type: vbDateTimeFormat constant
>
> Defines the format; see the list of constants in the section "Rules at a Glance."

Return Value

String

Description

Formats a date or time expression based on the computer's regional settings.

Rules at a Glance

- The intrinsic constants to use for the format argument are:

  vbGeneralDate

  > Value: 0
  >
  > Displays a date and/or time. If there is a date part, displays it as a short date. If there is a time part, displays it as a long time. If present, both parts are displayed.

  VbLongDate

  > Value: 1
  >
  > Uses the long date format specified in the client computer's regional settings.

  VbShortDate

  > Value; 2
  >
  > Uses the short date format specified in the client computer's regional settings.

  VbLongTime

  > Value: 3
  >
  > Uses the time format specified in the computer's regional settings.

  VbShortTime

  > Value: 4
  >
  > Uses a 24-hour format (hh:mm).

- The default date format is **vbGeneralDate**.

Programming Tips & Gotchas

- Remember that date and time formats obtained from the client computer are based on the client computer's regional settings. It's not uncommon for a single application to be used internationally, so that date formats can vary widely. Not only that, but you can never be sure that a user has not modified the regional settings on a computer. In short, never take a date coming in from a client machine for granted; ideally, you should always insure it's in the format you need prior to using it.

- It's hard to see why this new function has been added to VB6. There is no appreciable difference in either coding or performance between these two statements:

```
sDate = FormatDateTime(dDate, vbLongDate)
sDate = Format(dDate, "Long Date")
```

See Also

Format Function

FreeFile Function

Named Arguments

No

Syntax

```
FreeFile[(rangenumber)]
```
rangenumber

    Use: Optional

    Data Type: Variant

    Specifies the range of numbers from which the next available file number is selected.

Return Value

An integer representing a the next unused file number.

Description

Returns the next available file number for use in an **Open** statement.

Rules at a Glance

- You can change the range of numbers used by *FreeFile* by supplying a *rangenumber* argument, as follows:

rangenumber	File Number Range
0 (or None)	1–255
1	256–511

Programming Tips & Gotchas

Get into the habit of always using *FreeFile* to obtain a file number to use in the Open statement: you can't go wrong!

See Also

Open Statement

Function Statement

Named Arguments

No

Syntax

```
[Public | Private | Friend] [Static] Function name _
        [(arglist)] [As type][()]
    [statements]
    [name = expression]
    [Exit Function]
    [statements]
    [name = expression]
End Function
```

Public

> Use: Optional
>
> Type: Keyword
>
> Gives the function scope through all procedures in all modules in the project. If used within a createable class module, the function is also accessible from outside the project. Public, Private, and Friend are mutually exclusive.

Private

> Use: Optional
>
> Type: Keyword
>
> Restricts the scope of the function to those procedures within the same module. Public, Private, and Friend are mutually exclusive.

Friend

> Use: Optional
>
> Type: Keyword
>
> Only valid within a class module; gives the function scope to all modules within a project, but not to modules outside the project. Public, Private, and Friend are mutually exclusive.

Static

> Use: Optional
>
> Type: Keyword
>
> Preserves the value of variables declared inside the function between calls to the function.

name
> Use: Required

> The name of the function.

arglist
> Use: Optional

> A comma-delimited list of variables to be passed to the function as arguments from the calling procedure.

type
> Use: Optional

> The return data type of the function.

statements
> Use: Optional

> Program code to be executed within the function.

expression
> Use: Optional

> The value to return from the function to the calling procedure.

arglist uses the following syntax and parts:

```
[Optional] [ByVal | ByRef] [ParamArray] varname[( )] [As type]
[= defaultvalue]
```

Optional
> Use: Optional

> An optional argument is one that need not be supplied when calling the function. However, all arguments following an optional one must also be optional. A ParamArray argument can't be optional.

ByVal
> Use: Optional

> The argument is passed by value; that is, the local copy of the variable is assigned the value of the argument.

ByRef
> Use: Optional

> The argument is passed by reference; that is, the local variable is simply a reference to the argument being passed. All changes made to the local variable are also reflected in the calling argument. ByRef is the default method of passing variables.

ParamArray
> Use: Optional

> Indicates that the argument is an optional array of variants containing an arbitrary number of elements. It can be used only as the last element of the argument list, and it can't be used with the ByRef, ByVal, or Optional keywords.

varname
> Use: Required

> The name of the local variable containing either the reference or value of the argument.

type
> Use: Optional

> The data type of the argument.

defaultvalue
> Use: Optional

> For optional arguments, you can specify a constant default value.

Description

Defines a function procedure.

Rules at a Glance

- If you don't include one of the Public, Private, or Friend keywords, a function is Public by default.

- If you declare a function as Public within a module that contains an Option Private directive, the function is treated as Private.

- Any number of Exit Function statements can be placed within the function. Execution continues with the line of code immediately following the call to the function. If a value has not been assigned to the function when the Exit Function statement executes, the function returns the default initialization value of the data type specified for the return value of the function. If the data type of the function was an object reference, the exited function returns Nothing.

- The return value of a function is passed back to the calling procedure by assigning a value to the function name. This may be done more than once within the function.

- To return an object reference from a function, the object must be assigned to the function's return value using the Set statement. For example:

```
Private Function GetAnObject() As SomeObject
    Dim oTempObject As SomeObject
    Set oTempObject = New SomeObject
        Set GetAnObject = oTempObject
    Set oTempObject = Nothing
End Function
```

- Until Visual Basic Version 6, the return value of a function could not be an array of any data type. One of the major improvements in VB6 is that it allows you to return arrays of any type from a procedure. But to do this, there are two rules to follow. First, you must use parentheses after the data type—which is also mandatory—in the return value of the function declaration. Second, any array in the calling program that is assigned the return value of the function call must be of the same data type as the function.

Here's a quick example showing this in operation. Here, the *PopulateArray* function is called and is passed a string value. *PopulateArray* takes this value and concatenates the numbers 1 to 10 to it, assigns each value to an element of an array, then passes this array back to the calling procedure. Note that in the calling procedure, the array that accepts the array returned from the function is declared as a dynamic array. Its size is never explicitly defined in the calling routine; another new feature of VB6 is the ability to assign arrays of any type from one array variable to another in a single assignment statement—as long as the array on the left side of the expression is dynamic:

```
Private Sub Command3_Click()

    Dim i As Integer
    Dim sReturnedArray() As String

    sReturnedArray() = PopulateArray("A")

    For i = 1 To UBound(sReturnedArray)
        Debug.Print sReturnedArray(i)
    Next i

End Sub

Private Function PopulateArray(sVal As String) _
            As String()

    Dim sTempArray(10) As String
    Dim i As Integer

    For i = 1 To 10
        sTempArray(i) = sVal & CStr(i)
    Next i

    PopulateArray = sTempArray

End Function
```

- If you specify an optional parameter in your function declaration, you can also provide a default value for that parameter. For example:

```
Private Function ShowMessage(Optional sMsg _
                    As String = "Not given")
```

- If you're not using VB6, you can still return an array from a function. However, it can be only a variant containing an array. For example:

```
Private Function MakeArray() As Variant

   MakeArray = Array(1, 2, 3, 4)

End Function

Private Sub Form_Load()

    Dim varArray As Variant
```

```
     varArray = MakeArray()
     MsgBox UBound(varArray)

End Sub
```

- A function can't define a fixed-length string as an argument in *arglist*; this produces the design-time error, "Expected array."

- A calling program can pass a fixed-length string to a function. In most cases, however, this makes little sense, since the string as defined by the function prototype must be either a variable-length string or a variant string. This means that if another string is concatenated with the string, the "extra" portion of the string is lost when the function returns.

- A user-defined type can't be included in an argument list as an optional argument.

- Another addition to VB6 is the ability to pass a user-defined type (UDT) remotely; that is, you can add a UDT to the parameter list of a public function and as the return value of a public function or method. To enable a public class or code module to expose a UDT, you must declare its type as Public so that clients can "see" the UDT. Here's a simple example of passing a UDT remotely. The first part of the example is a class module in an ActiveX DLL; the second part is a standard EXE project that has a reference to the ActiveX DLL. First, the server code:

```
Option Explicit
'declare the public user defined type
Public Type RemUDT
    AuID As String
    LName As String
    FName As String
    Phone As String
End Type

'declare a local array variable to hold an
'array of the udt
Private muRemUDT(1 To 10) As RemUDT

Private Function getAuthors() As Boolean
    'this function simply populates the udt array
    'using the SQL Server pubs test database
    Dim adoConn As ADODB.Connection
    Dim adoRecs As ADODB.Recordset
    Dim i       As Integer
    Dim sSQL    As String
    'create instances of ADO objects
    Set adoConn = New ADODB.Connection
    Set adoRecs = New ADODB.Recordset
        'open the ado connection using a test DSN
        adoConn.Open "Test"
        'create a SQL query
        sSQL = "SELECT *" & vbCrLf _
            & "FROM authors" & vbCrLf _
        'open the recordset
        adoRecs.Open sSQL, adoConn, adOpenForwardOnly, _
```

```
            adLockReadOnly
      'populate 10 elements of the array
      For i = 1 To 10
         muRemUDT(i).AuID = adoRecs!au_id
         muRemUDT(i).LName = adoRecs!au_lname
         muRemUDT(i).FName = adoRecs!au_fname
         muRemUDT(i).Phone = adoRecs!Phone
      Next i
   'kill the ado recordset
   Set adoRecs = Nothing
End Function

Public Function AuthorUDTArray() As RemUDT()
     'pass back an array of the udt to the client
     AuthorUDTArray = muRemUDT
End Function

Public Function AuthorUDT(iVal As Integer) As RemUDT
     'pass back a single element of the
     'udt array to the client
     AuthorUDT = muRemUDT(iVal)
End Function
```

Here's the client code:

```
Option Explicit
'declare local array for udt
Private uUDTArray() As RemUDT
'declare local copy of udt
Private uUDT As RemUDT
'declare local udt class object
Private oUDT As UDTClass

Private Sub Form_Load()
   'instantiate the udt class object
   Set oUDT = New UDTClass
End Sub

Private Sub cmdUDTArray_Click()

   Dim i As Integer

   'call the remote array function and
   'assign the array to the local udt array
   uUDTArray = oUDT.AuthorUDTArray
   'iterate through the array
   For i = 1 To UBound(uUDTArray)
      With uUDTArray(i)
         Debug.Print .AuID
         Debug.Print .FName
         Debug.Print .LName
         Debug.Print .Phone
      End With
```

```
      Next i

  End Sub

  Private Sub cmdSingleUDT_Click()

      Dim sVal As String
      Dim i As Integer

      For i = 1 To 10
          'call the single udt function  & assign the result
          'to the local udt copy
          uUDT = oUDT.AuthorUDT(i)
          With uUDT
              Debug.Print .AuID
              Debug.Print .FName
              Debug.Print .LName
              Debug.Print .Phone
          End With
      Next i

  End Sub

  Private Sub Form_Unload(Cancel As Integer)
      'kill the udt class object reference
      Set oUDT = Nothing
  End Sub
```

- The default value for an optional object argument can be only **Nothing**.

Programming Tips & Gotchas

- There is often confusion between the **ByRef** and **ByVal** methods of assigning arguments to the function. **ByRef** assigns a reference to the variable in the calling procedure to the variable in the function; any changes made to the variable from within the function are in reality made to the variable in the calling procedure. On the other hand, **ByVal** assigns the value of the variable in the calling procedure to the variable in the function. Changes made to the variable in the function have no effect on the variable in the calling procedure. In general, **ByRef** arguments within class modules take longer to perform, since marshalling back and forth between function and calling module must take place; so unless you need to modify a variable's value explicitly within a function, it's best to pass parameters by value.

- Functions can return only one value, or can they? Look at the following code:

```
Sub testTheReturns()

    Dim iValOne As Integer

    iValOne = 10
    If testValues(iValOne) = True Then
        Debug.Print iValOne
```

```
    End If

End Sub

Function testValues(ByRef iVal As Integer) As Boolean

    iVal = iVal + 5
    testValues = True

End Function
```

Because the argument was passed **ByRef**, the function acted upon the underlying variable *iValOne*. This means you can use **ByRef** to obtain several "return" values (although they're not strictly return values) from a single function call. I would go so far as to say that your program can be made much more robust by returning only a Boolean from the actual function call, then testing its value prior to proceeding with the routine in hand.

- It's possible to pass an array as the return value for a function by assigning the array to the function in the usual manner—i.e., `myFunction = myArray()`. However, Microsoft recommends you not use this method for "performance reasons."

- What about a performance gain from returning arrays from functions? In many cases you will be simply shifting the creation of the array from one place to another, i.e., in the earlier example, assuming both procedures are within the same project, the performance gain is minimal, since the only benefit is that you are making one function call instead of 10 to populate an array. However when you start to investigate more complex uses for returning arrays, you start to see some substantial benefits.

For example, the following code demonstrates two methods of populating a combo box with the names of authors in the SQL Server sample database "pubs." An Authors object holds a collection of Author objects, which to keep things simple holds only the name of each author. Two methods are used. In the first, Command1_Click uses the traditional method of instantiating an Author object by calling the Authors.Author property for each Author object in the Authors collection and assigning the value of the AuthorName property to the combo box's list. In the second, Command2_Click calls a function, Authors.AuthorsNames, which returns an array of all the author names. Here's the code for the client application:

```
Option Explicit

Private moAuthors As Authors

Private Sub Command1_Click()

    cboAuthors.Clear
    Dim i As Integer
    Dim oAuthor As Author
    'the traditional method of obtaining the names
    For i = 1 To moAuthors.Count
        Set oAuthor = moAuthors.Author(i)
```

```
              cboAuthors.AddItem oAuthor.AuthorName
        Set oAuthor = Nothing
     Next i

End Sub

Private Sub Command2_Click()

   cboAuthors.Clear
   Dim i As Integer
   Dim sAuthors() As String
   'the new method of bringing in an array from
   'the object
   sAuthors() = moAuthors.AuthorNames
   For i = 1 To UBound(sAuthors)
      cboAuthors.AddItem sAuthors(i)
   Next i

End Sub
```

The code for the Authors object is shown below. Note that the Author object is prepopulated to save confusing the code here:

```
Option Explicit

Private mcolAuthors As Collection

Public Function AuthorNames() As String()
   Dim oAuthor As Author
   Dim sTempArray() As String
   Dim i As Integer

   ReDim sTempArray(1 To mcolAuthors.Count)
   For i = 1 To mcolAuthors.Count
      Set oAuthor = mcolAuthors.Item(i)
          sTempArray(i) = oAuthor.AuthorName
      Set oAuthor = Nothing
   Next i
   AuthorNames = sTempArray
End Function

Public Property Get Author(vVal As Variant) As Author
    Set Author = mcolAuthors.Item(vVal)
End Property

Public Property Get Count() As Long
    Count = mcolAuthors.Count
End Property
```

The two projects were then run as a standard client EXE and an ActiveX server DLL. When executed on the same machine, the time taken to populate the combo box is roughly the same, although the array method has a slight advantage. When the DLL was run via Microsoft Transaction Server on a remote machine, the difference in performance is astounding—though not entirely surprising. Below are the figures obtained from taking the average time required to populate the combo box 100 times using each method:

Method Used	Average Time (secs.)
Returned object	.4175
Returned array	.0455

- Another addition to VB6 goes hand in hand with returning arrays from functions: the ability to assign arrays of any type from one array variable to another in a single assignment expression. There is one condition: the array on the left side of the assignment statement must be dynamic.

- Using UDTs remotely—that is, passing a UDT from a DLL to a client or from an EXE to a client—requires you to upgrade OLE on both the client and server machine. If you are running NT5 or Windows 98, you should already have the required upgrade, as should an NT machine with Service Pack 4 applied. Otherwise you need to obtain the latest versions of *OLE32.DLL* and *RPCRT4.DLL.* For Windows 95 machines, you should install the latest version of DCOM95.

- Optional arguments afford you wonderful flexibility, allowing you to create generic functions that can be used in a variety of scenarios. Until version 5 of VBA, optional arguments could be only of the variant data type. Now, with the release of VB 5.0, almost any data type can be cast as an optional argument. However, I would still advocate the use of a variant for optional arguments. Why? The variant has a special state called *Missing* that makes it easy to check the value of an optional argument using the *IsMissing* function. If *IsMissing* returns True, you know immediately that the optional argument wasn't supplied in the function call. Checking to determine whether a strongly typed variable (an integer, for example) is missing is more difficult:

```
Sub testMissingInt()

    Dim iVal As Integer
    Dim iValTwo As Integer

    iVal = 10
    iValTwo = 0

    Debug.Print testFunc(iVal, iValTwo)

End Sub

Function testFunc(ByRef iVal As Integer, _
            Optional iValTwo As Integer) As Integer

    If iValTwo = 0 Then
        'perform this if iValTwo is missing
        testFunc = iVal + 10
    Else
        'perform this if iValTwo is present
        testFunc = iVal + iValTwo
```

```
    End If

End Function
```

A missing optional integer argument appears within the function as its initialized value, which is 0. But what happens when you want to pass the value 0 to the function? It's interpreted as being missing. In other words, in a case such as this, you have no way to tell if the argument is really missing.

- A **ParamArray** must be declared in the function as an array of type variant. However, the calling procedure doesn't pass the argument explicitly as an array; the individual elements are passed as a comma-delimited list of values or variables, as the following example shows:

```
Sub testParam()

    Debug.Print testFunc(10, 500, 60)

End Sub

Function testFunc(ParamArray someArgs() As Variant) _
                  As Integer
    Dim iArg As Integer
    Dim i As Integer
    Dim vArg As Variant

    For Each vArg In someArgs
        iResult = iResult + vArg
    Next

    testFunc = iResult

End Function
```

- For reasons I haven't quite fathomed yet, you can't use **ParamArrays** to pass arguments to functions in remote server applications. It's difficult to describe the results you obtain; suffice it to say they don't generate errors, but that, quite simply, the results are little more than garbage. However, you can pass an explicit variant array to a function in a remote server application. The enormous advantage of this is that you can change both the type and number of arguments passed into the function without changing the COM interface, thereby retaining compatibility with a previous version of the server application.

- One of the most useful additions to VB5 and VBA5 is the **Friend** keyword, which allows you to expose a property function or subroutine in a class module to the other modules within the same project, but at the same time prevent "the outside world" from having access to the interface. This can be seen as halfway between **Private**—which prevents the interface from being seen by any module—and **Public**—which exposes the interface both to modules in the same project and to modules outside the project.

- There are many occasions where you will run into the dreaded (by some!) *recursive* function call. Recursion occurs when you call a function from within itself. Recursion is a legitimate and often essential part of software development; for example, it's the only reliable method of enumerating or iterating a hierarchical structure. However, you must be aware that Microsoft—while never being specific on this point—indicates that recursion can lead to stack overflow. The extent to which you can get away with recursion really depends upon the complexity of the function concerned, the amount and type of data being passed in, and an infinite number of other variables and unknowns.

See Also

IsMissing Function, Option Private Statement, Sub Statement, Declare Statement

---

FV Function

Named Arguments

Yes

Syntax

```
FV(rate, nper, pmt[, pv [, due]])
```
rate

> Use: Required
>
> Data Type: Double
>
> The interest rate per period.

nper

> Use: Required
>
> Data Type: Integer
>
> The number of payment periods in the annuity.

pmt

> Use: Required
>
> Data Type: Double
>
> The payment made in each period.

pv

> Use: Optional
>
> Data Type: Variant
>
> The present value of the loan or annuity.

due

> Use: Optional
>
> Data Type: Variant
>
> Flag specifying whether payments are due at the start or the end of the period.

Return Value

A Double specifying the future value of an annuity.

Description

Calculates the future value of an annuity (either an investment or loan) based on a regular number of payments of a fixed value and a static interest rate over the period of the annuity.

Rules at a Glance

- The time units used for the number of payment periods, the rate of interest, and the payment amount must be the same. In other words, if you state the payment period in months, you must also express the interest rate as a monthly rate and the amount paid per month.

- The rate per period is stated as a fraction of 100. For example 10% is stated as .10. If you are calculating using monthly periods, you must also divide the rate per period by 12. Therefore, 10% per annum, for example, equates to a rate per period of .00833.

- The *pv* argument is most commonly used as the initial value of a loan. The default is 0.

- Payments made against a loan or added to the value of savings are expressed in negative numbers.

- The *due* argument indicates whether the payment is made at the start of a period (1) or at the end (0, which is the default value).

See Also

IPmt Function, NPer Function, Pmt Function, PPmt Function, PV Function, Rate Function

---

Get Statement

Named Arguments

No

Syntax

```
Get [#] filenumber, [recnumber], varname
filenumber
```
> Use: Required
>
> Data Type: Integer
>
> Any valid file number.

```
recnumber
```
> Use: Optional
>
> Data Type: Variant (Long)
>
> Record or byte number.

```
varname
```
> Use: Required
>
> Data Type: Any

The variable into which the data is read.

Description

Copies data from a file on disk into a program variable.

Rules at a Glance

- For files opened in random mode, *recnumber* refers to the record number in the file.

- For files opened in binary mode, *recnumber* refers to the byte number within the file.

- The number of bytes read by the Get statement is governed by the data type of *varname*.

- The position of the first record or byte within a file is always 1.

- Even if *recnumber* is omitted, you must use the delimiting commas (i.e., Get #1,,myVar).

- When a record or number of bytes is read from a file using Get, the file pointer automatically moves to the record or byte following the one just read. You can therefore read all data from a random or binary file sequentially by omitting *recnumber*, as this snippet shows:

```
Dim hFile as long
hFile = FreeFile()
Open sFileName For Random as #hFile
Do While Not EOF(1)
    Get #1,,myVar
Loop
Close #hFile
```

- Get is used most commonly to read data from files written with the Put statement.

Programming Tips & Gotchas

- If you are using a Len clause with the Open statement and reading data from a random access file with the Get statement, you must be aware of the total number of bytes that the Get statement reads for each data field. This isn't always straightforward, since many data types use descriptors to inform programs reading them how many bytes the data takes up on the disk. For example, when reading a variant of a numeric subtype, Get first reads a two-byte descriptor, then the length of the data type. Your Len clause must therefore take account of these descriptors. You can obtain a complete list of all descriptors for each data type in the explanation of the Open statement.

- It's usual practice to create a user-defined type to accept data from the file into your program. Your user-defined type must match both the data types and positions of the data in the file. You can then create an instance of your user-defined type to use as the variable, as the following example shows:

```
Option Explicit

Type MyType
```

Reference

```
            CustNo as Long
            CustName As String * 20
            CustPhone As String * 30
            CustZip As String * 10
      End Type

      Public CustDetails(10) As MyType

      Public Function ReadData() As Boolean

            Dim sFileName As String
            Dim i As Integer

            sFileName = "custData.dat"
            Open sFileName For Random As #1 Len = 64

            For i = 1 To 10
                Get #1, i, CustDetails(i)
            Next i
            Close #1

            MsgBox CustDetails(3).CustPhone

      End Function
```

- With the increase in the power, flexibility, and ease of use of modern DBMSs, the use of external standalone data files has fallen dramatically, which means that statements such as Get and Open are fast becoming redundant. Furthermore, any application or user-specific configuration data is best kept in the registry, again reducing the need for external files.

- If you use a Len clause in the Open statement, you should ensure that the value of Len matches the record length. It's possible to read records whose length is less than Len; however, you will then be unsure where the end of the record is, because the space between the length of Len and the end of the record will have been automatically padded with spurious characters.

See Also

Open Statement, Put Statement, Seek Function

GetAllSettings Function

Named Arguments

Yes

Syntax

```
GetAllSettings(appname, section)
```
appname

    Use: Required

    Data Type: String

    Name of the application.

---

section

> Use: Required
>
> Data Type: String
>
> Relative path from *appname* to the key containing the settings to retrieve.

Return Value

A Variant containing a two-dimensional array of strings.

Description

Returns the registry value entries and their corresponding values for the application.

Rules at a Glance

- *GetAllSettings* works exclusively with the subkeys of HKEY_CURRENT_USER\Software\VB and VBA Program Settings.

- The elements in the first dimension of the array returned by *GetAllSettings* contain the value entry names.

- The elements in the second dimension of the array returned by *GetAllSettings* contain the values for the respective value entries.

- The two-dimensional array returned by *GetAllSettings* is based at zero. Therefore, the first value entry name is referenced using (0,0).

- A call to *GetAllSettings* returns only the value entry names and data belonging to the final registry key specified by the *section* argument. If that key itself has one or more subkeys, their data isn't retrieved by the function.

- If an application has multiple nested subkeys, all their data can be retrieved by specifying the relative path from the application key to the desired key in the *section* parameter. For example, if Settings\Coordinates is the value of the *section* argument, the function attempts to retrieve all values from the subkey HKEY_CURRENT_USER\Software\VB and VBA Program Settings\appname\Settings\Coordinates.

- If *appname* or *section* doesn't exist, *GetAllSettings* returns an uninitialized Variant.

Programming Tips & Gotchas

- *GetAllSettings* is a function that was developed to retrieve data from initialization files in 16-bit environments and to retrieve data from the registry under Win9x and WinNT. The language of the documentation, however, reflects the language of initialization files. The arguments labeled *appname* and *section* are in fact registry keys; the argument labeled *key* is a registry value entry.

- The built-in registry manipulation functions allow you to create professional 32-bit applications that use the registry for holding application specific data, in the same way that *.INI* files were used in the 16-bit environment. You can, for example, store information about the user's desktop settings (i.e., the size and position for forms) the last time the program is run.

- Because the built-in registry functions in VB create only string type registry keys, *GetSetting* and *GetAllSettings* return string values. Therefore, before you use a numeric value returned from the registry, you should explicitly convert the value to a numeric data type.

- *GetAllSettings, SaveSettings,* and *GetSetting* allow you direct access to a limited section of the windows registry, that being a special branch created for your application (HKEY_CURRENT_USER\Software\VB and VBA Program Settings*yourappname*). You can't access or change other registry settings without using the Win32 API.

- Use the App object's EXEName property to pass your application's name to the *GetAllSetting* function.

- All the registry-manipulation functions in VB work equally well with both Windows NT and Windows 95. The same, however, can't be said of the Win32 API calls required to return and change other registry settings.

- Only those settings that are created using either the Win32 API or the *SaveSettings* function are returned. In other words, a VB application doesn't have a registry entry unless you create one explicitly.

- If the key read by *GetAllSettings* has a default value, that value isn't retrieved by the function. If you want to store and retrieve default values, you must call the Win32 API directly.

- Because *GetAllSettings* returns an uninitialized Variant when either **appname** or **section** doesn't exist, if you subsequently try to perform a *UBound* or *LBound* function on the variant, a Type Mismatch error is generated. You can test the validity of the returned variant using the *IsEmpty* function as follows:

```
Dim vRegSettings As Variant
Dim iSettings As Integer

vRegSettings = GetAllSettings(appname:=App.EXEname, _
                              section:="Startup")
If Not IsEmpty(vRegSettings) Then
   For iSettings = LBound(vRegSettings, 1) To _
                   UBound(vRegSettings, 1)
      Debug.Print vRegSettings(iSettings, 0) & "; " _
                  & vRegSettings(iSettings, 1)
   Next iSettings
End If
```

- Because *GetAllSettings* retrieves data from the user branch of the registry, and the physical file that forms the user branch of the registry may change (depending, of course, on who the user is and, in the case of Win9x systems, whether or not the system is configured to support multiple users), never assume that an application has already written data to the registry. In other words, even if you're sure your application's installation routine or the application itself has successfully stored values in the registry, never assume that a particular value entry exists and always be prepared to substitute a default value if it doesn't.

See Also

DeleteSetting Statement, GetSetting Function, SaveSetting Statement

GetAttr Function

Named Arguments

No

Syntax

```
GetAttr(pathname)
pathname
```
> Use: Required
>
> Data Type: String
>
> File and optional path name.

Return Value

An integer representing the attributes set for the file or folder, being the sum of the following constant values:

Constant	Value	Description
vbNormal	0	Normal
vbReadOnly	1	Read-only
vbHidden	2	Hidden
vbSystem	4	System
vbDirectory	16	Directory or folder
vbArchive	32	File has changed since last backup

Description

Determines which attributes have been set for a file, directory, or folder.

Rules at a Glance

- *pathname* may optionally include a directory or folder name and a drive letter, including a network drive. *pathname* can also follow the UNC format of //machine_name/drive.

- You can check if a particular attribute has been set by performing a bit-wise comparison of the *GetAttr* return value and the value of the attribute constant using the And operator. A nonzero result means that the particular attribute has been set; conversely, a zero value indicates that the attribute has not been set. For example:

```
If GetAttr(myfile.txt) And vbReadOnly = 0 then
    Msgbox "The file is Read-Write"
Else
    MsgBox "The file is Read-Only"
End If
```

Programming Tips & Gotchas

The file attribute constants are defined to be globally available for use within your projects.

GetAutoServerSettings Function

Syntax

```
object.GetAutoServerSettings([Progid], [Clsid])
object
```
> Use: Required
>
> Data Type: Object expression
>
> An object variable representing the RacReg library.

```
Progid
```
> Use: Optional
>
> Data Type: Variant
>
> The programmatic identifier (ProgID) for the component.

```
Clsid
```
> Use: Optional
>
> Data Type: Variant
>
> The class identifier (CLSID) for the component.

Return Value

A Variant containing an array of values, described in the following table:

Index	Description
1	1 if the ActiveX component is registered to execute remotely, 0 if registered to run locally
2	Remote machine name
3	RPC network protocol name
4	RPC authentication level

Description

Returns registration information for an ActiveX object.

Rules at a Glance

- Although both *ProgID* and *Clsid* are optional, one must be specified. They are also mutually exclusive.

- The variant array that is returned by *GetAutoServerSettings* is one-based.

- To access this function, you must reference the RacReg library in the References section of your project.

Example

```
Public Function tryCalling() As Boolean

    'create local variables
    Dim oMyObj As MyRemServer.ServClass
    Dim oRacReg As New RacReg.RegClass
    Dim vASS As Variant
```

```
Dim sTest As String

'get the settings of the ActiveX server
vASS = _
oRacReg.GetAutoServerSettings("MyRemServer.ServClass")

If Not (IsEmpty(vASS)) Then
    'check element 1 of the array - True if remote
    If vASS(1) Then
        'quick and dirty method of contacting the server
        'at least it'll still work with NT5!
        sTest = Dir("\\" & vASS(2) & "\c$\autoexec.bat")
        'test the return value of the Dir function
        If sTest = "autoexec.bat" Then
            'if ok then create the instance
            Set oMyObj = New MyRemServer.ServClass
                'do some stuff with the object here
        End If
    Else
        'the server is local  - no problem!
        Set oMyObj = New MyRemServer.ServClass
        'do some stuff with the object here
    End If
End If

tryCalling_Exit:
    'tidy up before you leave
    Set oMyObj = Nothing
    Set oRacReg = Nothing

tryCalling_Err:
    'catch the error thrown by the Dir function when it
    'times out because the LAN or WAN lines to the
    'remote server are down
    If Err.Number = 52 Then
        MsgBox "The server " & vASS(2) & _
               " can't be reached at this time"
    Else
        MsgBox Err.Description
    End If

    'a variation is to ask the user if they want to retry
    '& resume to a label just above the Dir function.
    Resume tryCalling_Exit

End Function
```

Programming Tips & Gotchas

- Be sure to test that the variant is not empty before trying to reference the array elements.

- This rather neat little function allows you to determine if an ActiveX component is registered to run locally or remotely via DCOM. That said, it doesn't allow you to change where the component is registered, nor is there any immediately perceptible benefit in knowing on which server it's to run. I suppose if you know that a particular server is switched off during certain times of the day you can bypass the call!

- The function allows you to build in some precall testing to check that the LAN or WAN lines to the server are operational. In other words, you could programmatically "ping" the server and, if successful, make your call to the ActiveX component. This is particularly beneficial when producing client-server applications that operate across a corporate WAN. An annoyance of trying maintain such systems is that the error returned when the "lines" are down is exactly the same as the one when a local DLL can't be instantiated. Therefore, being able to inform the user that a remote server can't be reached and to exit the program gracefully is of great benefit to both user and developer. A complete working example of this concept is shown in the previous example.

- RPC stands for Remote Procedure Call; DCOM for Distributed COM.

- If this book hits the streets before you upgrade to NT5, and you're having problems with DCOM on your NT4 boxes, make sure you've applied the now legendary Service Pack 3, since earlier builds and service packs had some fairly fundamental glitches in DCOM (i.e., it didn't work!). If you're running Windows 95, you don't automatically have DCOM; however, it's available as a free download from the Microsoft web site. As Windows 9x moves ever closer to NT, DCOM has been made an integral part of Windows 98.

- The example for *GetAutoServerSettings* in the VB5 help file contains an error; the name of the remote server is held at element 2 of the array, not element 1.

- The "registered to run remotely" flag held in element 1 of the array returns 1 or 0, not `True` or `False` (a subtle but important difference in VB).

GetObject Function

Named Arguments

Yes

Syntax

```
GetObject([pathname] [, class])
pathname
```
Use: Optional

Data Type: Variant (String)

The full path and name of the file containing the ActiveX object.

`class`
Use: Optional

Data Type: Variant (String)

The class of the object (see next list).

The `class` argument has these parts:

Appname
> Use: Required
>
> Data Type: Variant (String)
>
> The name of the application.

Objecttype
> Use: Required
>
> Data Type: Variant (String)
>
> The class of object to create, delimited from *Appname* by using a point (.). For example, `Appname.Objecttype`.

Return Value

Returns a reference to an ActiveX object.

Description

Accesses an ActiveX server held within a specified file.

Rules at a Glance

* Although both *pathname* and *class* are optional, at least one parameter must be supplied.

* In situations in which you can't create a project-level reference to an ActiveX object, you can use the *GetObject* function to assign an object reference from an external ActiveX object to an object variable.

* *GetObject* is used when there is a current instance of the ActiveX object; to create the instance, use the *CreateObject* function.

* If you specify *pathname* as a zero-length string, *GetObject* returns a new instance of the object—unless the object is registered as single instance, in which case the current instance is returned.

* If you omit the pathname, the current instance of the object is returned.

* An error is generated if *pathname* isn't specified, and no current instance of the object can be found.

* The object variable you use within your program to hold a reference to the ActiveX object is dimensioned as type Object. This causes the object to be late bound; that is, your program knows nothing of the type of object nor its interface until the object has been instantiated within your program. To assign the reference returned by *GetObject* to your object variable, you must use the Set statement:

```
Dim myObject As Object
Set myObject = GetObject("C:\OtherApp\Library.lib")
```

* The details of how you create different objects and classes are determined by how the server has been written; you need to read the documentation for the server to determine what you need to do to reference a particular part of the object. There are three ways you can access an ActiveX object:

- The overall object library. This is the highest level, and it gives you access to all public sections of the library and all its public classes:

  ```
  GetObject("C:\OtherApp\Library.lib")
  ```

- A section of the object library. To access a particular section of the library, use an exclamation mark (!) after the filename, followed by the name of the section:

  ```
  GetObject("C:\OtherApp\Library.lib!Section")
  ```

- A class within the object library. To access a class within the library, use the optional **Class** parameter:

  ```
  GetObject("C:\OtherApp\Library.lib", "App.Class")
  ```

Programming Tips & Gotchas

- Pay special attention to objects registered as single instance. As their type suggests, there can be only one instance of the object created at any one time. Calling *CreateObject* against a single-instance object more than once has no effect; you still return a reference to the same object. The same is true of using *GetObject* with a pathname of ""; rather than returning a reference to a new instance, you obtain a reference to the original instance of the object. In addition, you must use a pathname argument with single-instance objects (even if this is ""); otherwise an error is generated.

- You can't use *GetObject* to obtain a reference to a class created with Visual Basic.

- When possible, you should use early binding in your code. For more details on early and late binding, see Chapter 4. You can use *GetObject* in early binding, as in:

  ```
  Dim objExcel As Excel.Application
  Set objExcel = GetObject(, "Excel.Application")
  ```

The following table shows when to use *GetObject* and *CreateObject*:

Task	Use
Create a new instance of an OLE server	*CreateObject*
Create a subsequent instance of an already instantiated server (if the server isn't registered as single instance)	*CreateObject*
Obtain a further reference to an already instantiated server without launching a subsequent instance	*GetObject*
Launch an OLE server application and load an instance of a subobject	*GetObject*
Instantiate a class created with VB	*CreateObject*
Instantiate a class registered on a remote machine	*CreateObject*

See Also

CreateObject Function, Set Statement

GetSetting Function

Named Arguments

Yes

Syntax

```
GetSetting(appname, section, key[, default])
```

appname

    Use: Required

    Data Type: String

    The name of the application.

section

    Use: Required

    Data Type: String

    The path from the application key to the key containing the value entries.

key

    Use: Required

    Data Type: String

    The name of the value entry whose value is to be returned.

default

    Use: Optional

    Data Type: String

    The value to return if no value can be found.

Return Value

A string containing the value of the specified *key*; *default* if *key*, *section*, or *appname* aren't found.

Description

Returns a single value from a specified section of your application's entry in the HKEY_CURRENT_USER\Software\VB and VBA Program Settings\ branch of the registry.

Rules at a Glance

- If *appname*, *section*, or *key* isn't found in the registry, *GetSetting* returns *default*.

- If *default* is omitted, it's assumed to be a zero-length string ("").

- The function retrieves a value from a subkey of the KEY_CURRENT_ USER\Software\VB and VBA Program Settings key of the registry.

- *section* need not be an immediate subkey of *appname*; instead, *section* can be a fully qualified path to a nested subkey, with each subkey separated from its parent by a backslash. For example, a value of Settings\Coordinates for the *section* argument indicates that the value is to be retrieved from HKEY_

CURRENT_USER\Software\VB and VBA Program Settings\appname\Set-
tings\Coordinates.

Programming Tips & Gotchas

- *GetSetting* is a function that was developed to retrieve data from initialization files in 16-bit environments and to retrieve data from the registry under Win9x and WinNT. The language of the official documentation, however, reflects the language of initialization files. The arguments labeled *appname* and *section* are in fact registry keys; the argument labeled *key* is in fact a registry value entry.

- Because the built-in registry functions in VB create only string type registry value entries, *GetSetting* and *GetAllSettings* return string values. Therefore, before you use numeric values returned from the registry, you should convert the value to a numeric data type explicitly using the appropriate conversion function.

- Use the App object's EXEName property to pass your application's name to the *GetSetting* function as the value of the *appname* parameter both when reading and writing registry data.

- The built-in registry manipulation functions allow you to create professional 32-bit applications that use the registry for holding application-specific data, in the same way *.INI* files were used in the 16-bit environment. You can, for example, store information about the user's desktop settings (i.e., the size and position of forms) from the last time the program was run.

- *GetSetting*, *GetAllSettings*, and *SaveSettings* allow you direct access to only a limited section of the windows registry, that being a special branch created for your application (HKEY_CURRENT_USER\Software\VB and VBA Program Settings\yourappname). You can't access or change other registry settings without resorting to the Windows API.

- *GetSetting* doesn't allow you to retrieve the default value of a registry key. Attempting to do so produces runtime error 5, "Invalid procedure call or argument." This isn't as great a limitation as it may appear, since *SaveSetting* also can't write a default value to a registry key.

- Because *GetSetting* retrieves data from the user branch of the registry, and the physical file that forms the user branch of the registry may change (depending, of course, on who the user is and, in the case of Win9x systems, whether or not the system is configured to support multiple users), never assume that an application has already written data to the registry. In other words, even if you're sure your application's installation routine or the application itself has successfully stored values in the registry, always supply a meaningful value for the *default* argument.

- Only those settings that are created using the Windows API or the *SaveSetting* function are returned. In other words, a VB application doesn't have a registry entry unless you have create one explicitly.

- Although *GetSetting* writes string data only to the registry, you can use a variable of almost any data type to retrieve it. The *GetSetting* function automatically handles the conversion of string data to the data type of the variable to which the return value of *GetSetting* is assigned. The sole exceptions are user-defined data types and arrays of byte data.

See Also

DeleteSetting Statement, GetAllSettings Function, SaveSetting Statement

---

GoSub...Return Statement

Syntax

```
GoSub label
...
label:
...
Return
label
```

> Use: Required
>
> Subroutine name.

Description

Passes execution to and returns from a subroutine within a procedure.

Rules at a Glance

- GoSub and its counterpart, Return, must reside within the same procedure. This means you can't use GoSub to "call" a subroutine from within another procedure.

- A subroutine can contain any number of Return statements.

- Return causes execution to continue with the code immediately following the last executed GoSub.

Programming Tips & Gotchas

The only reason I've included this relic of the past here is to help if you have the misfortune of maintaining or updating legacy code (and by legacy, I mean VB1 or 2!). A program written in VB3 onward shouldn't contain a single GoSub. If you come across a GoSub, split the code into its own Sub procedures, or, better still, create a new function procedure containing the code within the GoSub. Even if you aren't going to use a return value now, cast the return value of the function as a Boolean; this is good programming practice and allows early error trapping within your code.

Old code

```
Private Sub Command1_Click()
    Dim iSomething As Integer
    Dim strOther As String
    GoSub AnOldGosub
    GoSub AnOlderGosub
    GoSub AnotherGosub
    Exit Sub
AnOldGosub:
```

Reference

```
        Dim x As Integer
        For x = 1 To 10
            iSomething = iSomething + 1
        Next x
        Return
    AnOlderGosub:
        Dim y As Integer
        For y = 1 To 10
            strOther = strOther & "="
        Next y
        Return
    AnotherGosub:
        Printer.Print strOther
        Printer.Print iSomething
        Printer.EndDoc
        Return
    End Sub
```

New code

```
    Private Sub Command2_Click()
        Printer.Print GetOther()
        Printer.Print GetSomething()
        Printer.EndDoc
    End Sub

    Private Function GetSomething() As Integer
        Dim x As Integer
        For x = 1 To 10
            iSomething = iSomething + 1
        Next x
        GetSomething = iSomething
    End Function

    Private Function GetOther() As String
        Dim y As Integer
        For y = 1 To 10
            strOther = strOther & "="
        Next y
        GetOther = strOther
    End Function
```

See Also

Goto Statement

Goto Statement

Syntax

```
    GoTo label
    label
```
> Use: Required

> Subroutine name.

Description

Passes execution to a subroutine within a procedure.

Rules at a Glance

label must be a subprocedure defined within the same procedure as `Goto`.

Programming Tips & Gotchas

- The only time a modern VB program should include a `Goto` statement is in an error handler, as in:

```
On Error Goto My_Sub_Err
```

- For more information on error handling, see Chapter 6.

See Also

GoSub...Return Statement, Chapter 6

Hex, Hex$ Functions

Named Arguments

No

Syntax

```
Hex(number)
number
```

> Use: Required
>
> Data Type: Numeric or String
>
> A valid numeric or string expression.

Return Value

String representing the hexadecimal value of *number*.

Description

Returns a string that represents the hexadecimal value of a number.

Rules at a Glance

- If *number* contains a fractional part, it's rounded automatically to the nearest whole number prior to processing.

- *number* must evaluate to a numeric expression that ranges from $-2{,}147{,}483{,}648$ to $2{,}147{,}483{,}647$. If the argument is outside this range, runtime error 6, "Overflow," results.

- The return value of *Hex* is dependent upon the value and type of *number*:

number	Return Value
Null	Null
Empty	Zero (0)
Any other number	Up to eight hexadecimal characters

Programming Tips & Gotchas

If the value of *number* is known beforehand and isn't the result of an expression, you can represent the number as a hexadecimal by simply affixing &H to *number*. Each of the following two statements assigns a hexadecimal value to a variable, for instance:

```
lngHexValue1 = &HFF                    ' Assigns 255
lngHexValue2 = "&H" & Len(dblNumber)   ' Assigns 8
```

See Also

Oct, Oct$ Functions

Hour Function

Named Arguments

No

Syntax

```
Hour(time)
time
```
> Use: Required
>
> Data Type: Any variant, numeric, or string expression
>
> Any valid time expression.

Return Value

A variant of data subtype Integer representing the hour of the day.

Description

Extracts the hour element from a time expression.

Rules at a Glance

* Regardless of the time format passed to *Hour*, the return value is a whole number between 0 and 23, representing the hour of a 24-hour clock.
* If *time* contains Null, Null is returned.

See Also

Minute Function, Now Function, Second Function

If...Then...Else Statement

Named Arguments

No

Syntax

```
If condition Then
    [statements]
```

```
[ElseIf condition-n Then
    [elseifstatements] ...
[Else
    [elsestatements]]
End If
```

Or, you can use the single-line syntax:

```
If condition Then [statements] [Else elsestatements]
condition
```
> Use: Required
>
> Data Type: Boolean
>
> An expression returning either True or False or an object type.

statements
> Use: Optional
>
> Program code to be executed if *condition* is True.

condition-n
> Use: Optional
>
> Same as *condition.*

elseifstatements
> Use: Optional
>
> Program code to be executed if the corresponding *condition-n* is True.

elsestatements
> Use: Optional
>
> Program code to be executed if the corresponding *condition* or *condition-n* is False.

Description

Executes a statement or block of statements based on the Boolean (True or False) value of an expression.

Rules at a Glance

- If *condition* is True, the statements following the If are executed.

- If *condition* is False and no Else or ElseIf statement is present, execution continues with the corresponding End If statement. If *condition* is False and ElseIf statements are present, the condition of the next ElseIf is tested. If *condition* is False, and an Else is present, the statements following the Else are executed.

- In the block form, each If statement must have a corresponding End If statement. ElseIf statements don't have their own End If. For example:

```
If condition Then
    statements
ElseIf condition Then
    statements
End If
```

- **ElseIf** and **Else** are optional, and any number of **ElseIf** and **Else** statements can appear in the block form. However, no **ElseIf** statements can appear after an **Else**.

- *condition* can be any statement that evaluates to **True** or **False**.

- If *condition* returns **Null**, it's treated as **False**.

- You can also use the **If** statement to determine object types by using the **TypeOf** and **Is** keywords, as follows:

  ```
  If TypeOf objectname Is objecttype Then
  ```

- *statements* are optional only in the block form of **If**. However, *statements* are required when using the single-line form of **If** in which there is no **Else** clause.

Programming Tips & Gotchas

- You can use the single-line form of the **If** statement to execute multiple statements, which you can specify by delimiting the statements using colons; however, single-line form **If** statements are hard to read and maintain, and should be avoided for all but the simplest of situations.

- In situations where you have many possible values to test, you will find the **Select Case** statement much more flexible, manageable, and readable than a bunch of nested **If** statements.

- You will come across situations in which very large blocks of code have to execute based one or more conditions. In these—and in all situations—you should try to make your code as readable as possible, not only for other programmers, but for yourself when you try to maintain the code several months down the line. Take a common scenario in which, at the beginning of a procedure, a check is made to see if the procedure should in fact be executed under the current circumstances. You have the choice of surrounding the whole code with an **If...Then...End If** construct, like this:

  ```
  If iSuccess Then
      ...
      ...
      ... 'x000 lines of code
  End If
  ```

  Or you can switch the result to look for a **False**, then exit the sub, like this:

  ```
  If Not iSuccess Then
      Exit Sub
  End If
  .... 'x000 lines of code
  ```

  The difference is that, with the second method, you don't have to scroll down screens worth of code looking for the matching **End If**.

- Indentation is important for the readability of **If**, and especially nested **If**, statements. The recommended indentation is four characters, which you will find is the Visual Basic editor's default tab value. The set of statements within each new **If...Else..EndIf** block should be indented. And here's a quick tip when using the VB5 or VBA development environment: you can select a block of code and press the Tab key to indent the complete selected block. The following example shows correctly indented code:

```
If x = y Then
    DoSomethingHere
    If y < z Then
        DoSomethingElseToo
    Else
        DoAnotherThing
        If z - 1 = 100 Then
            DoAThing
        End If
    End If
Else
    DoAlternative
End If
```

- Use of the If statement requires some understanding of the implicit and explicit use of **True** in Visual Basic. The following **If** statement uses an implicit **True**:

```
If iSuccess Then
```

Notice that you are allowing VB to evaluate the *iSuccess* variable to **True** or **False**. When this implicit form is used, any non-zero value evaluates to **True**, and conversely a zero value evaluates to **False**. For example, the following code evaluates *iSuccess* as **True** and prints the "OK" message box:

```
Dim iSuccess As Integer
iSuccess = 41
If iSuccess Then
    MsgBox "OK"
Else
    MsgBox "False"
End If
```

However, when you compare a variable to an explicit **True** or **False**, the value must be −1 to evaluate to **True**, and 0 for **False**. If you amend the above code fragment as follows:

```
iSuccess = 41
If iSuccess = True Then
```

iSuccess doesn't evaluate to VB's version of **True** (−1). As you can imagine, this can lead to some confusion, since a variable can evaluate to **True** when using an implicit comparison but not when using an explicit comparison. Actually, just to add to the confusion, you could get the explicit comparison to behave the same as the implicit one by converting *iSuccess* to a Boolean:

```
If CBool(iSuccess) = True Then
```

This isn't entirely recommended, but it does show that VB's built-in constants of **True** and **False** evaluate *only* −1 and 0, respectively.

- Logical comparison operators can be included in the *condition* expression, allowing you to make decisions based on the outcome of more than one individual element. The most common of these are And and Or. You can create conditions like:

```
If x = 1 And y = 3 Then
```

- Visual Basic always evaluates both sides of a logical comparison, unlike some languages that allow you to stop before each portion of a comparison has been evaluated. For example, in the following code, if x does equal 1, then the If condition has been met. Some languages would stop the evaluation here. But regardless of the value of *x,* Visual Basic still evaluates the comparison with *y.*

```
If x = 1 Or y = 3 Then
```

- The If statement is also used with objects to determine if an object has been successfully assigned to an object variable. (Actually, that's not completely accurate; you check to see if the object variable is still set to Nothing.) However, you can't use the equality operator (=) for this comparison. Instead, you must use the object comparison operator Is, as the following code shows:

```
If Not objectname Is Nothing Then
```

See Also

Choose Function, IIf Function, Select...Case Statement, Switch Function

---

IIf Function

Named Arguments

Yes

Syntax

```
IIf(expr, truepart, falsepart)
expr
```
    Use: Required

    Data Type: Boolean

    Expression to be evaluated.

truepart

    Use: Required

    Data Type: Any value or expression

    Expression or value to return if *expr* is True.

falsepart

    Use: Required

    Data Type: Any value or expression

    Expression or value to return if *expr* is False.

Return Value

The value or result of the expression indicated by *truepart* or *falsepart.*

Description

Returns one of two results, depending on whether *expr* evaluates to True or False.

Rules at a Glance

- *IIf* always evaluates both the *truepart* and *falsepart* expressions independently of the value of *expr*. You must therefore ensure that both expressions can be safely evaluated when the *IIf* function is called or an error is generated.

- The *IIf* function is the equivalent of:

```
If testexpression Then
    result = truereturn
Else
    result = falsereturn
End If
```

The only difference is that, in the corresponding If...Then...Else...End If statement, only one of either *truepart* or *falsepart* is evaluated, depending on the result of *expr*.

- *truepart* and *falsepart* can be any one variable, constant, literal, expression, or the return value of a function call.

Programming Tips & Gotchas

The *IIf* function is ideal for very simple tests resulting in single expressions. If you really feel the need, *IIf* function calls can be nested; however, your code can become difficult to read quickly. The following code fragment illustrates the use of a nested *IIf* function:

```
Dim x As Integer
x = CInt(Text1.Text)
MsgBox IIf(x < 10, "Less than ten", IIf(x < 20, _
          "Less than 20", "Greater than 20"))
```

See Also

Choose Function, If...Then...Else Statement, Select Case Statement, Switch Function

---

IMEStatus Function

Named Arguments

No

Syntax

```
IMEStatus()
```

Return Value

A Long representing the status of the *input method editor* (IME), as represented by the following constants for the Japanese, simplified Chinese, and traditional Chinese locales:

Reference

Constant	Value	Description
vbIMENoOP	0	IME not implemented.
vbIMEOn	1	IME is on.
vbIMEOff	2	IME is off.
vbIMEDisable	3	IME is disabled (Japanese locale only).
vbIMEHiragana	4	IME is using Hirgana double-byte characters (Japanese locale only).
vbIMEKatakanaDbl	5	IME is using Katakana double-byte characters (Japanese locale only).
vbIMEKatakanaSng	6	IME is using Katakana single-byte characters (Japanese locale only).
vbIMEAlphaDbl	7	IME is using an alphanumeric double-byte character set (Japanese locale only).
vbIMEAlphaSng	8	IME is using an alphanumeric single-byte character set (Japanese locale only).

For a Korean locale, the status of the IME is given by the five low-order bytes of the return value:

Byte	Value	Description
0	0	IME not installed
	1	IME installed
1	0	IME disabled
	1	IME enabled
2	0	IME English mode
	1	Hangeul mode
3	0	Banja mode (single-byte)
	1	Junja mode (double-byte)
4	0	Normal mode
	1	Hanja conversion mode

The status of any particular pair of attributes can therefore be accessed with a code fragment like the following:

```
If 2 And IMEStatus() Then
    Debug.Print "IME is enabled"
Else
    Debug.Print "IME Is disabled"
End If
```

Description

Indicates the state or character set of the IME, which is used in the Far Eastern editions of Windows to handle keyboard messages and to translate them into a local character set.

Rules at a Glance

In the case of non-Far Eastern versions of Windows, where IMEs aren't supported, a call to *IMEStatus* returns vbIMENoOP.

Implements Statement

Named Arguments

No

Syntax

```
Implements objVarName
objVarName
    Use: Required
    Type: Class
    The name of an object variable referencing a standard interface class.
```

Description

The Implements statement allows you to provide *polymorphism* within your object models. Polymorphism has the advantages of speed and flexibility over inheritance—though, unfortunately, we have neither the time nor space to explore these concepts in depth here. Polymorphism boils down to a set of guidelines or a framework the user works within to create a different end result (or implementation). Polymorphism is seen most obviously in nature. For example, a structure we all know well is a tree; its model states that it has a trunk, leaves, branches, and roots. An oak tree is one implementation of the tree "model," whereas a pine is a very different implementation of the same basic model. In Visual Basic, polymorphism is provided by standard interface (or abstract) classes and the Implements statement. The Implements statement informs VB that you are going to provide implementations for each of the Public methods and properties found in the referenced standard interface class.

The basic concept of standard interface classes is that it's the user of the class—not the interface class itself—that decides how a particular method or property should be implemented. For example, you could create a standard interface class that acts as a wrapper for a collection object. The standard interface could provide an *Exists* function, for example. However, the implementation of this procedure could be very different depending on the context in which the class implementing the standard interface is being used.

The following examples show a procedure prototype as it may appear within our example standard interface, followed by two different ways in which this procedure could be implemented. First, the standard (or abstract) procedure prototype:

```
Public Function Exists(vVal as Variant) As Boolean
End Function
```

One implementation of the *Exists* method might look like this:

```
Public Function Exists(vVal As Variant) As Boolean
```

```
        On Error Goto Exists_Err
            Dim oTest as TestObject
            Set oTest = m_col.Item(vVal)
            Set oTest = Nothing
            Exists = True
            Exit Function

    Exists_Err:
        Exists = False
    End Function
```

Another implementation of the *Exists* method might be as follows:

```
Public Function Exists(vVal As Variant) As Boolean

        On Error Goto Exists_Err
            Dim oTest as TestObject
            Set oTest = m_col.Item(vVal)
            Set oTest = Nothing
            Exists = True
            Exit Function
    Retry:
        If GetNewItem(vVal) = True Then
            Exists = True
        Else
            Exists = False
        End If
        Exit Function
    Exists_Err:
        If Err.Number = 5 Then
            Resume Retry
        End If
        Exists = False
    End Function
```

A standard interface class therefore is a class that contains only procedure declarations; there is no code in those procedures. It's up to the developer who uses this class interface to implement code for these procedures.

Rules at a Glance

- Within the module containing the Implements statement, you must create a procedure for each of the public procedures in the class being implemented.

- The Implements statement can be used only in Form and Class modules.

- A reference to the class *objVarName* must be added to the project using the References dialog.

- By convention, you should name your abstract or standard interface classes beginning with a capital I to denote them as interfaces (for example, Imy-Interface).

Programming Tips & Gotchas

- If you don't wish to support a procedure from the implemented class, you must still create a procedure declaration for the implemented procedure.

However, you can simply raise an error using the special error constant `Const E_NOTIMPL = &H80004001`.

- The `Implements` statement doesn't support events. Any events publicly declared in the standard interface class are ignored.

- Standard (or abstract) interfaces allow for greater coherence when developing in teams. For example, all developers could use a set of standard interfaces to produce controls and objects of a particular type without being constrained by implementation. That is, each developer would be free to implement a particular property or method in the way that he or she saw fit.

- The polymorphism model dictates that standard interface classes shouldn't change once they have been written and distributed. Any additional functionality required should be provided by defining additional interfaces.

- The use of the `Implements` statement provides an increasingly important method of adding extra functionality to VB. For example, the `Implements` statement with an object reference to the `OLEDBSimpleProvider` type library creates an OLEDB simple provider.

Initialize Event

Syntax

```
Private Sub object_Initialize()
```

Description

Use the Initialize event of an object or class to prepare the object or class for use, setting any references to subobjects or assigning values to module-level variables.

Rules at a Glance

- The Initialize event is triggered automatically when an object or class module is first used. The precise point at which the Initialize event is fired depends on how the object is created.

- The Initialize event isn't triggered by the declaration of a new object. It's not until the object is used for the first time that the Initialize event is called. For example, in the code fragment:

```
Dim MyObject As New MyClass
'some code
. . .
'initialize event called here
strName = MyObject.CustName
```

The assignment of the CustName property value generates the Initialize event, yet in the following code, the Set statement generates the Initialize event.

```
Dim MyObject As MyClass
'some code
. . .
'initialize event called here
Set MyObject = New MyClass
StrName = MyObject.CustName
```

- The Initialize event is only private and doesn't take any arguments.

Programming Tips & Gotchas

- While it's possible to explicitly call the Initialize event from within the object at any stage after the object has been created, it isn't recommended because the code in the Initialize event should be written to be "run once" code.

- Use the Initialize event of a class module to generate references to dependent objects. For example:

```
Option Explicit

Dim mcolMyCollection As Collection
Dim moSubObject As mySubObject

Private Sub Class_Initialize()

    Set mcolMyCollection = New Collection
    Set moSubObject = New mySubObject
    If glbInstance = 0 Then
        Set glbMainObj = Me
        glbInstance = 1
    End If

End Sub
```

- The Initialize event is triggered only once, when a new object is created. When an object variable is assigned a reference to an existing object, the Initialize event isn't invoked. For example, in the following code fragment, the Initialize event is invoked only once, when the Set objMine1 statement is executed:

```
Dim objMine1 As MyObj, objMine2 As MyObj
Set objMine1 = New MyObj
Set objMine2 = objMine1
```

- See Chapter 4 for an in-depth study using classes and objects in VB and VBA.

See Also

Set Statement, Terminate Event

Input, Input$, InputB, InputB$ Functions

Syntax

```
Input(number, [#] filenumber)
```
number
> Use: Required

> Data Type: Numeric

> Specifies the number of characters to return.

filenumber
> Use: Required

Data Type: Integer

Any valid file number.

Return Value

A string (in the case of *Input$* and *InputB$*) or a variant string (if *Input* or *InputB*) containing *number* characters.

Description

Accesses data from within a file opened in input or binary mode.

Rules at a Glance

*   *Input* should be used only once with files opened in input or binary mode.

*   The function begins reading characters from the current position of the file pointer.

*   *Input* returns all characters it reads, regardless of their type, returning the raw data of the file. This includes spaces, carriage returns, linefeeds, commas, end-of-file markers, unprintable characters, etc.

*   Once the function finishes reading *number* characters, it also advances the file pointer *number* characters.

*   The *InputB* and *InputB$* function variants of the *Input* function are used to read binary data from a file. In this case, *number* refers to the number of bytes to read, as opposed to the number of characters.

Programming Tips & Gotchas

*   *Input* reads data written to a file using either the `Print#` or `Put` statements.

*   *Input* always attempts to read precisely *number* characters from the file. If there aren't *number* characters from the position of the file pointer to the end of the file, *Input* attempts to read beyond the end of the file, thereby generating runtime error 62, "Input past end of file." To prevent this, you should use the *LOF* function after opening the file to insure that you don't attempt to read past the end-of-file marker.

See Also

Input# Statement, LOF Function, Open Statement, Print# Statement, Put Statement, Write# Statement

---

Input # Statement

Syntax

```
Input #filenumber, varlist
filenumber
```
Use: Required

Data Type: Integer

Any valid file number.

varlist

>Use: Required
>
>Data Type: Any
>
>Comma-delimited list of variables or user-defined types.

Description

Reads delimited data from a sequential file opened in input or binary mode.

Rules at a Glance

- Use Input# only with files opened in input or binary modes.

- Variables in *varlist* can't be array or object variables.

- Both the type and position of data items in the file must match the variables in *varlist*.

- If Input# expects to find a numeric value based on the type of a variable in *varlist*, and the data in the file isn't numeric, the variable is assigned a zero value. When reading the value of a variable, the function won't perform any data conversion. This means, for example, that if your program reads the string "10" and assigns it to a long integer variable named *lngVar*, the value of *lngVar* is 0.

- Input# strips off quotation marks ("") it finds around strings.

- After Input# reads *varlist*, it advances the file pointer to the first unread variable or, if the file contains no additional delimited data, to the end of the file.

- If the end of the file is reached during an Input#, an error is generated.

- Input# assigns string and numeric data to the relevant variable in *varlist* without modification; however, other types of data can be modified as shown in the following table.

Data	*Value Assigned to Variable*
Delimiting comma or blank line	Empty
#NULL#	Null
#TRUE# or #FALSE#	True or False
#yyyy-mm-dd hh:mm:ss#	Date and/or time
#ERROR errornumber#	Error number (variable is a variant of subtype error)

Programming Tips & Gotchas

- Use the *EOF* function to check that the end of the file has or hasn't been reached.

- You should use the Write# statement to write data to a file, since Write# delimits data fields correctly. This insures that the data can be read correctly with the Input# statement.

See Also

Input, InputB, Input$, InputB$ Functions; Write# Statement

InputBox Function

Named Arguments

Yes

Syntax

```
InputBox(prompt[, title] [, default] [, xpos] _
         [, ypos] [, helpfile, context])
```

prompt

Use: Required

Data Type: String

The message in the dialog box.

title

Use: Optional

Data Type: String

The titlebar of the dialog box.

default

Use: Optional

Data Type: String

String to be displayed in the text box on loading.

xpos

Use: Optional

Data Type: Numeric

The distance from the left side of the screen to the left side of the dialog box.

ypos

Use: Optional

Data Type: Numeric

The distance from the top of the screen to the top of the dialog box.

helpfile

Use: Optional

Data Type: String

Specifies the Help file to use if the user clicks the Help button on the dialog box.

context

Use: Optional

Data Type: Numeric

Specifies the context number to use within the Help file specified in `helpfile`.

Return Value

InputBox returns a variant string containing the contents of the text box from the *InputBox* dialog.

Description

Displays a dialog box containing a label, which prompts the user about the data you expect them to input, a text box for entering the data, an OK button, a Cancel button, and optionally a Help button. When the user clicks OK, the function returns the contents of the text box.

Rules at a Glance

- If the user clicks Cancel, a zero-length string ("") is returned.

- *prompt* can contain approximately 1,000 characters, including nonprinting characters like the intrinsic **vbCrLf** constant.

- If the *title* parameter is omitted, the name of the current application or project is displayed in the titlebar.

- If you don't use the *default* parameter to specify a default entry for the text box, the text box is shown empty; a zero-length string is returned if the user doesn't enter anything in the text box prior to clicking OK.

- *xpos* and *ypos* are specified in *twips*. A twip is a device-independent unit of measurement that equals 1/20 of a point or 1/1440 of an inch).

- If the *xpos* parameter is omitted, the dialog box is centered horizontally.

- If the *ypos* parameter is omitted, the top of the dialog box is positioned approximately one-third of the way down the screen.

- If the *helpfile* parameter is provided, the context parameter must also be provided, and vice versa.

- In VB5 and in VBA applications, when both *helpfile* and *context* are passed to the *InputBox* function, a Help button is automatically placed on the *InputBox* dialog, allowing the user to click and obtain context-sensitive help. In VB4, the user wasn't presented with a Help button and could access help only by pressing the F1 key.

Programming Tips & Gotchas

- If you are omitting one or more optional arguments and are using subsequent arguments, you must use a comma to signify the missing parameter. For example, the following code fragment displays a prompt, a default string in the text box, and the help button, but default values are used for the title and positioning.

```
sString = InputBox("Enter it now", , "Something", , _
        , "help.hlp", 321321)
```

- Note that when using *InputBox* with VBA in Office applications, the maximum length of the prompt string is 256 characters.

See Also

MsgBox Function

Instancing Property (VB only)

Description

Only available when a class is part of an ActiveX project. The Instancing property defines how instances of the class are created, and whether or not instances of the class can be created outside of the project. This property is available only at design time.

Values

GlobalMultiUse

> The class becomes global to the project in which it's defined; references aren't necessary. For example, most VB language objects are global; as soon as you load the environment, they can be used. Not available within ActiveX Control projects.

MultiUse

> The default property value for classes within ActiveX DLL or EXE projects. The class has scope (i.e., it's visible) outside the project in which it's defined, and it can be instantiated using the **New** keyword or the *CreateObject* function. Not available within ActiveX Control projects.

PublicNotCreateable

> The default property value for classes within ActiveX Control projects. Although the class has scope (i.e., it's visible) outside the project in which it's defined, it can't be instantiated from outside the project using the **New** keyword or the *CreateObject* function.

Private

> The default property value for classes within standard EXE projects. The class can't be "seen" outside of the project in which it's defined. Also, the only instancing property available in standard EXE projects.

SingleUse

> Every call by a client to create the object using either the **New** keyword or the *CreateObject* function creates a completely new instance of the object. Only available in ActiveX EXE projects.

GlobalSingleUse

> As with the SingleUse property value, every call by a client to create the object using either the **New** keyword or the *CreateObject* function creates a completely new instance of the object. However, GlobalSingleUse allows methods and properties to be seen as part of VB. Only available in ActiveX EXE projects.

Programming Tips & Gotchas

- Use the GlobalMultiUse property setting to create class modules containing enumerated constants for your object model.

- Use the MultiUse property setting for top-level objects in a hierarchy or object model.

- Use the PublicNotCreatable property setting for child objects created by accessing a function or property of a higher-level object.

- Use the Private property setting for objects that are used only within the project.

- With the GlobalSingleUse property value, an instance of the class is created automatically for you. It's therefore not necessary to explicitly create an instance of the class.

- If the class is part of an ActiveX control project and the control's Public property is set to `False`, the Instancing property is ignored.

See Also

Chapter 4

InStr, InStrB Functions

Named Arguments

No

Syntax

```
InStr([start, ]stringtosearch, stringtofind[, _
    comparemode])
```

start
   Use: Optional

   Data Type: Numeric

   The starting position for the search.

stringtosearch
   Use: Required

   Data Type: String

   The string being searched.

stringtofind
   Use: Required

   Data Type: String

   The string being sought.

comparemode
   Use: Optional

   Data Type: Integer

   The type of string comparison.

Return Value

A variant of subtype Long.

Description

Finds the starting position of one string within another.

Rules at a Glance

- The return value of *InStr* is influenced by the values of *stringtosearch* and *stringtofind*, as the following table details:

Condition	InStr Return Value
stringtosearch is zero-length	0
stringtosearch is Null	Null
stringtofind is zero-length	start
stringtofind is Null	Null
stringtofind is not found	0
stringtofind found within *stringtosearch*	Position at which the start of *stringtofind* is found
start > len(stringtofind)	0

- If the *start* argument is omitted, *InStr* commences the search with the first character of *stringtosearch.*
- If the *start* argument is Null, an error occurs.
- You must specify a *start* argument if you are specifying a *comparemode* argument.
- VB5 and VBA support intrinsic constants for *comparemode*, as follows:

Comparison Mode	Value	Constant
Binary (default)	0	vbBinaryCompare
Text—case insensitive	1	vbTextCompare
Database (Microsoft Access only)	2	vbDatabaseCompare

- If the *comparemode* argument contains Null, an error is generated.
- If *comparemode* is omitted, the type of comparison is determined by the Option Compare setting.

Programming Tips & Gotchas

You can use the *InStrB* function to compare byte data contained within a string. In this case *InStrB* returns the byte position of *stringtofind*, as opposed to the character position.

See Also

InStrRev Function, Left Function, Mid Function, Option Compare Statement, Right Function, StrComp Function

InstrRev Function (VB6)

Named Arguments

No

Syntax

```
InstrRev(sourcestring, soughtstring[, start[, compare]])
```
sourcestring
> Use: Required
>
> Data Type: String
>
> The string to be searched.

soughtstring
> Use: Required
>
> Data Type: String
>
> The substring to be found within *sourcestring*.

start
> Use: Optional
>
> Data Type: Numeric
>
> The starting position of the search. If no value is specified, *start* defaults to 1.

compare
> Use: Optional
>
> Type: **vbBinaryCompare** constant
>
> The method that compares *soughtstring* with *sourcestring*; its value can be **vbBinaryCompare**, **vbTextCompare**, or **vbDatabaseCompare**.

Return Value

Long

Description

Determines the starting position of a substring within a string by searching from the end of the string to its beginning.

Rules at a Glance

* While *InStr* searches a string from left to right, *InStrRev* searches a string from right to left.

* **vbBinaryCompare** is case sensitive; that is, *InstrRev* matches both character and case, whereas **vbTextCompare** is case insensitive, matching only character, regardless of case.

* The default value for *compare* is **vbBinaryCompare**.

* *start* designates the starting point of the search and is the number of characters from the start of the string.

- If *start* is omitted, the search begins from the last character in *source-string.*

- *sourcestring* is the complete string in which you want to find the starting position of a substring.

- If *soughtstring* isn't found, *InStrRev* returns 0.

- If *soughtstring* is found within *sourcestring,* the value returned by *InStr-Rev* is the position of *sourcestring* from the start of the string.

Programming Tips & Gotchas

The usefulness of a function that looks backward through a string for the occurrence of another string isn't immediately apparent.

Example

This example uses both *InStr* and *InStrRev* to highlight the different results produced by each. Using a *sourcestring* of "I like the functionality that *InStrRev* gives", *InStr* finds the first occurrence of "th" at character 8, while *InStrRev* finds the first occurrence of "th" at character 26.

```
Dim myString As String
Dim sSearch As String
myString = "I like the functionality that InsStrRev gives"
sSearch = "th"

Debug.Print InStr(myString, sSearch)
Debug.Print InStrRev(myString, sSearch)
```

See Also

InStr Function

Int Function

Named Arguments

No

Syntax

```
Int(number)
number
```
> Use: Required
>
> Data Type: Any valid numeric data type
>
> The number to be processed.

Return Value

Returns a value of the data type passed to it.

Description

Returns the integer portion of a number.

Rules at a Glance

- The fractional part of *number* is removed and the resulting integer value returned. *Int* doesn't round *number* to the nearest whole number; for example, Int(100.9) returns 100.

- If *number* is negative, *Int* returns the first negative integer less than or equal to *number*; for example, Int(-10.1) returns −11.

Programming Tips & Gotchas

- *Int* and *Fix* work identically with positive numbers. However, for negative numbers, *Fix* returns the first negative integer greater than *number*. For example, Int(-10.1) returns −10.

- Don't confuse the *Int* function with *CInt*. *CInt* casts the number passed to it as an Integer data type, whereas *Int* returns the same data type that was passed to it.

See Also

Fix Function

IPmt Function

Named Arguments

Yes

Syntax

```
IPmt(rate, per, nper, pv[, fv[, type]])
```

rate

    Use: Required

    Data Type: Double

    The interest rate per period.

per

    Use: Double

    Data Type: Any valid numeric expression

    The period for which a payment is to be computed.

nper

    Use: Double

    Data Type: Any valid numeric expression

    The total number of payment periods.

pv

    Use: Double

    Data Type: Any valid numeric expression

    The present value of a series of future payments.

fv

    Use: Optional

Data Type: Variant

The future value or cash balance after the final payment. If omitted, the default value is 0.

type

Use: Optional

Data Type: Variant

A value indicating when payments are due. 0 indicates that payments are due at the beginning of the payment period; 1 indicates that payments are due at the end of the period. If omitted, the default value is 0.

Return Value

A Double representing the interest payment.

Description

Computes the interest payment for a given period of an annuity based on periodic, fixed payments and a fixed interest rate. An annuity is a series of fixed cash payments made over a period of time. It can be either a loan payment or an investment.

Rules at a Glance

- The value of *per* can range from 1 to *nper*.

- If *pv* and *fv* represent liabilities, their value is negative; if assets, their value is positive.

Example

The *ComputeSchedule* function accepts a loan amount, an annual percentage rate, and a number of payment periods. It uses the *Pmt* function to calculate the payment per period, then returns a two-dimensional array in which each subarray contains the number of the period, the interest paid for that period, and the principal paid for that period.

```
Private Function ComputeSchedule(dblAmount As Double, _
               dblRate As Double, lngNPer As Long) _
               As Variant

Dim dblIPmt As Double, dblPmt As Double
Dim dblPrincipal As Double
Dim lngPer As Long
Dim strFmt As String
Dim varArray() As Variant
ReDim varArray(lngNPer, 2)

strFmt = "###,###,##0.00"
dblPmt = Pmt(dblRate / 12, lngNPer, -dblAmount, 0, 0)

For lngPer = 1 To lngNPer
    dblIPmt = IPmt(dblRate / 12, lngPer, lngNPer, -dblAmount)
    dblPrincipal = PPmt(dblRate / 12, lngPer, lngNPer, _
             -dblAmount)
```

```
        dblAmount = dblAmount - dblPrincipal
        varArray(lngPer, 0) = lngPer & "."
        varArray(lngPer, 1) = Format(dblIPmt, strFmt)
        varArray(lngPer, 2) = Format(dblPrincipal, strFmt)
    Next

    ComputeSchedule = varArray

    End Function
```

Programming Tips & Gotchas

- *rate* and *nper* must be expressed in the same time unit. That is, if *nper* reflects the number of monthly payments, *rate* must be the monthly interest rate.

- The interest rate is a percentage expressed as a decimal. For example, if *nper* is the total number of monthly payments, an annual percentage rate (APR) of 12% is equivalent to a monthly percentage rate of 1%. The value of *rate* is therefore .01.

See Also

NPer Function, Pmt Function, PPmt Function, Rate Function

IRR Function

Named Arguments

Yes

Syntax

```
IRR(values()[, guess])
values()
```
> Use: Required
>
> Data Type: Array of Double
>
> An array of cash flow values.

guess
> Use: Optional
>
> Data Type: Double
>
> Estimated value to be returned by the function.

Return Value

A Double representing the internal rate of return.

Description

Calculates the internal rate of return for a series of periodic cash flows (payments and receipts). The internal rate of return is the interest rate generated by an investment consisting of payments and receipts that occur at regular intervals. It's generally compared to a "hurdle rate," or a minimum return, to determine whether a particular investment should be made.

Rules at a Glance

- *values* must be a one-dimensional array that contains at least one negative value (a payment) and one positive value (a receipt).

- Individual members of *values* are interpreted sequentially; that is, *values(0)* is the first cash flow, *values(1)* is the second, etc.

- If *guess* is omitted, the default value of 0.1 is used.

- IRR begins with *guess* and uses iteration to derive an internal rate of return that is accurate to within 0.00001 percent. If *IRR* can't do this within 20 iterations, the function fails.

Programming Tips & Gotchas

- Each element of *values* represents a payment or a receipt that occurs at a regular time interval. If this isn't the case, *IRR* returns erroneous results.

- If the function fails if it can't calculate an accurate result in 20 iterations, try a different value for *guess*.

See Also

MIRR Function

IsArray Function

Named Arguments

No

Syntax

```
IsArray(varname)
varname
```
    Use: Required

    Data Type: Any

    The name of the variable to be checked.

Return Value

Boolean (**True** or **False**).

Description

Tests whether a variable is an array.

Rules at a Glance

If the variable passed to *IsArray* is an array or contains an array, **True** is returned; otherwise, *IsArray* returns **False**.

Programming Tips & Gotchas

Due to the nature of variants, it isn't always obvious if a variant variable contains an array, especially if you pass the variant to a function, and the function may or may not attach an array to the variant. Calling any of the array functions, such as

LBound or *UBound*, or trying to access an element in an array that doesn't exist will obviously generate an error. In these situations, you should first use the *IsArray* function to determine if you can safely process the array.

IsDate Function

Named Arguments

No

Syntax

```
IsDate(expression)
```
expression
> Use: Required

> Data Type: Variant

> Variable or expression containing a date or time.

Return Value

Boolean (**True** or **False**).

Description

Determines if a variable's value can be converted to a date.

Rules at a Glance

If the expression passed to *IsDate* is a valid date, **True** is returned; otherwise, *IsDate* returns **False**.

Programming Tips & Gotchas

- *IsDate* uses the locale settings of the current Windows system to determine if the value held within the variable is recognizable as a date. Therefore, what is a legal date format on one machine may fail on another.

- *IsDate* is particularly useful for validating data input. However, don't use *IsDate* in the VB text box control's Change event. The Change event is fired with every keystroke, which means that when the user starts to enter the date, the chances are that the date will be invalid until the point at which the user has completed the data entry.

IsEmpty Function

Named Arguments

No

Syntax

```
IsEmpty(varname)
```
varname
> Use: Required

Data Type: Variant

A numeric or string expression.

Return Value

Boolean (True or False).

Description

Determines if the variable has been initialized by having an initial value (other than Empty) assigned to it.

Rules at a Glance

- If the variant passed to *IsEmpty* has been initialized, True is returned; otherwise, *IsEmpty* returns False.

- *IsEmpty* works only with variants. You shouldn't use it with the primitive data types (such as Integer, String, etc.) because these data types are automatically initialized with default values and therefore are never empty.

- Although *IsEmpty* can take an expression as the value of varname, it always returns False if more than one variable is used in the expression. *IsEmpty* is therefore most commonly used with single variables.

Programming Tips & Gotchas

When dealing with uninitialized object variables, if a reference to an object variable has not been successfully set, the variable has a value of Nothing. However, to determine if an object variable has been set successfully, you must use the syntax:

```
If objvar is Nothing Then
...
End If
```

IsError Function

Named Arguments

No

Syntax

```
IsError(expression)
expression
```
  Use: Required

  Data Type: Variant

  Variable to be evaluated to determine if its subtype is vbError.

Return Value

Boolean (True or False).

Description

Determines whether *expression* is a valid error value.

Rules at a Glance

• Use *IsError* only with variants. (Strongly typed variables can also be passed to *IsError*, but that's pointless; only variants have a **vbError** subtype and therefore have a chance of returning **True**.)

• If the variant passed to *IsError* represents a valid error number, **True** is returned; otherwise, *IsError* returns **False**.

Example

In this example, the *SquarePositive* function squares the values of only positive integers; if an integer isn't positive, the function returns a variant of subtype **vbError**:

```
Private Function SquarePositive(lngVal As Long) As Variant

If lngVal > 0 Then
    SquarePositive = lngVal ^ 2
Else
    SquarePositive = CVErr(0)
End If

End Function

Private Sub cmdSquare_Click()

Dim varRetVal As Variant

If IsNumeric(txtNumber.Text) Then
    varRetVal = SquarePositive(CLng(txtNumber.Text))
    If IsError(varRetVal) Then
        MsgBox "Error: Enter a positive number!"
    Else
        txtNumber.Text = varRetVal
    End If
Else
    txtNumber.Text = ""
End If

End Sub
```

Programming Tips & Gotchas

• You can create an error value by converting a real number using the *CVErr* function.

• *IsError* evaluates the value returned by a function to determine whether the function executed without error, as the previous example shows.

See Also

CVErr Function

IsMissing Function

Named Arguments

No

Syntax

```
IsMissing(argname)
argname
```
> Use: Required
>
> Data Type: Variant
>
> The name of an optional procedure argument of type Variant.

Return Value

Boolean (**True** or **False**).

Description

Determines whether an argument has been passed to a procedure.

Rules at a Glance

- If the argument name passed to *IsMissing* has not been passed to the procedure, **True** is returned; otherwise, *IsMissing* returns **False**.

- **False** is returned if *IsMissing* is used on data types other than variants, which may lead to incorrect handling of optional arguments.

Programming Tips & Gotchas

- Always use *IsMissing* to detect a missing optional variant parameter.

- Version 5 of both VB and VBA for the first time allowed other data types to be used as optional arguments within procedure prototypes; previously, optional arguments had to be variants. However, if you use data types other than variants for optional arguments, you can't use the *IsMissing* function; instead, you must check for the uninitialized value of the data type. For example, if an integer argument is missing, its value is 0. This can cause confusion, because you have no way of knowing whether a 0 was a legal value passed to the procedure or whether the argument was not passed at all. The only safe way to use optional arguments is to continue to use variants and to check their validity using the *IsMissing* function.

- You can't use *IsMissing* on an optional **ParamArray** because the function always returns **False**. Instead, you should check for a missing or empty **ParamArray** by using *UBound* and *LBound* to compare the values of its upper and lower bounds; if the **ParamArray** is empty, the upper bound is less than the lower bound.

See Also

LBound Function, UBound Function

IsNull Function

Named Arguments

No

Syntax

```
IsNull(expression)
expression
```
> Use: Required
>
> Data Type: Variant
>
> An expression containing string or numeric data.

Return Value

Boolean (True or False).

Description

Determines whether *expression* contains any Null data.

Rules at a Glance

- If the expression passed to *IsNull* contains null data, True is returned; otherwise, *IsNull* returns False.

- All variables in *expression* are checked for null data. If null data is found in any one part of the expression, True is returned for the entire expression.

- Although any data type can be passed to the function, only a variant variable can be null. As a result, it makes little sense to pass nonvariant data to the function, since it must always return False.

Programming Tips & Gotchas

- *IsNull* is useful when returning data from a database. You should check field values in columns that allow Nulls against *IsNull* before assigning the value to a collection or other variable. This stops the common "Invalid Use of Null" error from occurring.

- *IsNull* is the only way to evaluate an expression containing a null. For example, the seemingly correct statement:

```
If varMyVar = Null Then
```

always evaluates to False, even if *varMyVar* is null. This occurs because the value of an expression containing Null is always Null and therefore False.

IsNumeric Function

Named Arguments

No

Syntax

```
IsNumeric(expression)
expression
```

> Use: Required
>
> Data Type: Any numeric or string expression
>
> A numeric or string expression.

Return Value

Boolean (**True** or **False**).

Description

Determines whether *expression* can be evaluated as a number.

Rules at a Glance

If the expression passed to *IsNumeric* evaluates to a number, **True** is returned; otherwise, *IsNumeric* returns **False**.

Programming Tips & Gotchas

- If *expression* is a date or time, *IsNumeric* evaluates to **False**.

- If *expression* is a currency value, including a string that includes the currency symbol defined by the Control Panel's Regional Settings applet, *IsNumeric* evaluates to **True**.

IsObject Function

Named Arguments

No

Syntax

```
IsObject(varname)
varname
```

> Use: Required
>
> Data Type: Any
>
> Name of the variable to be evaluated.

Return Value

Boolean (**True** or **False**).

Description

Indicates if a variable contains a reference to an object—in other words, if it's an object variable.

Rules at a Glance

If the variable passed to *IsObject* references or has referenced an object, even if its value is **Is Nothing**, **True** is returned; otherwise, *IsObject* returns **False**.

Programming Tips & Gotchas

- *IsObject* doesn't validate the reference being held by an object variable; it simply determines if the variable has been declared as an object or as an instance of a valid class. To insure that an object reference is valid, you can use the syntax Is Nothing, as shown in this code snippet:

```
If objVar is Nothing Then
    ...
End if
```

- *IsObject* is simply a "convenience" function that is roughly equivalent to the following Visual Basic user-defined function:

```
Private Function IsObject(varObj As Variant) As Boolean

If VarType(varObj) = vbObject Then
    IsObject = True
Else
    IsObject = False
End If

End Function
```

Join Function (VB6)

Named Arguments

No

Syntax

```
result = Join(sourcearray, [delimiter])
```
sourcearray
> Use: Required

> Data Type: String or Variant

> Array whose elements are to be concatenated.

delimiter
> Use: Optional

> Data Type: String

> Character used to delimit the individual values in the string.

Return Value

A String.

Description

Concatenates an array of values into a delimited string using a specified delimiter.

Rules at a Glance

- If no delimiter is specified, the space character is used as a delimiter.

- If you use numeric values in *sourcearray*, use a Variant array, don't specify a numeric data type for *sourcearray*; otherwise, the function raises runtime error 5, "Invalid procedure call or argument."

- *sourcearray* can have any lower bound; that is, *Join* operates equally well with 0- or 1-based arrays.

- When a delimiter is specified, unused *sourcearray* elements are noted in the return string by the use of the delimiter. For example, if you specify a delimiter of "," and a source array with a lower bound of 1 and an upper bound of 10 in which only the first two elements are used, *Join* returns a string similar to the following:

  ```
  "a,b,,,,,,,,"
  ```

Programming Tips & Gotchas

The *Join* function is ideal for quickly and efficiently writing out a comma-delimited text file from an array of values.

Kill Statement

Named Arguments

No

Syntax

```
Kill pathname
pathname
```
>   Use: Required
>
>   Data Type: String
>
>   The file or files to be deleted.

Description

Deletes a file from disk.

Rules at a Glance

- If *pathname* doesn't include a drive letter, the folder and file are assumed to be on the current drive.

- If *pathname* doesn't include a folder name, the file is assumed to be in the current folder.

- You can use the multiple-character (*) and single-character (?) wildcards to specify multiple files to delete.

- If the file is open or is set to read-only, an error is generated.

Programming Tips & Gotchas

- Note that in the Windows 95 and NT environments, the deleted file isn't placed in the Recycle Bin. However, the following code demonstrates how to use the *FileOperation* API found in *Shell32.DLL* to move a file to the Windows 95 Recycle Bin or the NT4 Recycler:

```
Option Explicit

'declare the file operation structure
Type SHFILEOPSTRUCT
    hWnd As Long
    wFunction As Long
    pFrom As String
    pTo As String
    fFlags As Integer
    fAborted As Boolean
    hNameMaps As Long
    sProgress As String
End Type

'declare two constants needed for the delete operation
Private Const FO_DELETE = &H3
Private Const FO_FLAG_ALLOWUNDO = &H40

'declare the API call function
Declare Function SHFileOperation Lib "shell32.dll" _
        Alias "SHFileOperationA" _
        (lpFileOp As SHFILEOPSTRUCT) As Long


Public Function WinDelete(sFileName As String) As Long
    'create a copy of the file operation structure
    Dim SHFileOp As SHFILEOPSTRUCT

    'need a Null terminating string
    sFileName = sFileName & vbNullChar

    'assign relevant values to structure
    With SHFileOp
        .wFunction = FO_DELETE
        .pFrom = sFileName
        .fFlags = FO_FLAG_ALLOWUNDO
    End With

    'pass the structure to the API function
    WinDelete = SHFileOperation(SHFileOp)

End Function
```

- Use the **RmDir** statement to delete folders.

See Also

RmDir Statement

LBound Function

Syntax

```
LBound(arrayname[, dimension])
```

`arrayname`
> Use: Required
>
> Data Type: Any
>
> The name of the array.

`dimension`
> Use: Optional
>
> Data Type: Variant (Long)
>
> A number specifying the dimension of the array.

Return Value

A Long integer.

Description

Determines the lower limit of a specified dimension of an array. The lower boundary is the smallest subscript you can access within the specified array.

Rules at a Glance

* If `dimension` isn't specified, 1 is assumed. To determine the lower limit of the first dimension of an array, set `dimension` to 1, 2 for the second, and so on.

* The lower bound of an array dimension can be set using To, Dim, Private, Public, Redim, and Static, and can be set to any integer value.

Programming Tips & Gotchas

* The Option Base statement sets the default lower bound of an array to either 1 or 0.

* An array created with the *Array* function always has a lower bound of zero.

* The *LBound* function can't determine the lower limit of a control array. Instead, in both Visual Basic and Visual Basic for Applications, you can use the control array's LBound property to determine its lower limit.

See Also

Array Function, Option Base Statement, UBound Function

LCase, LCase$ Functions

Named Arguments

No

Syntax

`LCase(string)`
`string`
> Use: Required
>
> Data Type: String
>
> A valid string expression.

Return Value

LCase$ returns a String, and *LCase* returns a variant of subtype String.

Description

Converts a string to lowercase.

Rules at a Glance

- *LCase* affects only uppercase letters; all other characters in **string** are unaffected.

- *LCase* returns Null if **string** contains a Null.

Programming Tips & Gotchas

As with all string functions for which two variations are available (one suffixed with the $ sign and one without a $), the $ version returns a String data type, while the plain version returns a variant of subtype String.

See Also

UCase Function

Left, Left$, LeftB, LeftB$ Functions

Named Arguments

Yes

Syntax

```
Left(string, length)
```
string
> Use: Required

> Data Type: String

> The string to be processed.

length
> Use: Required

> Data Type: Variant (Long)

> The number of characters to return from the left of the string.

Return Value

Left$* and *LeftB$ return a String, and *Left* and *LeftB* return a variant of subtype String.

Description

Returns a string containing the leftmost **length** characters of **string**.

Rules at a Glance

- If **length** is 0, a zero-length string ("") is returned.

- If **length** is greater than the length of **string**, **string** is returned.

- If *length* is less than 0 or Null, the function generates runtime error 5, "Invalid procedure call or argument," and runtime error 94, "Invalid use of Null," respectively.

- If *string* contains Null, *Left* returns Null.

- *Left* and *Left$* process strings of characters; *LeftB* and *LeftB$* process binary data.

Programming Tips & Gotchas

- Use the *Len* function to determine the overall length of *string*.

- When you use the *LeftB* function with byte data, *length* specifies the number of bytes to return.

See Also

Len Function, Mid Functions, Right Function

Len, LenB Functions

Syntax

Len(*string* | *varname*)

string
> Use: Required
>
> Data Type: String
>
> A valid string expression.

varname
> Use: Required
>
> Data Type: Any except object
>
> A valid variable name.

Return Value

A Long integer

Description

Counts the number of characters within a string or the size of a given variable. Use *LenB* to determine the actual number of bytes required to hold a given variable in memory.

Rules at a Glance

- *string* and *varname* are mutually exclusive; that is, you must specify either *string* or *varname*, but not both.

- If either *string* or *varname* contains Null, *Len* returns Null.

- *Len* returns the size (number of characters) that a user-defined type occupies when written to a file.

- *LenB* returns the actual size of a user-defined type in memory.

- When you use *LenB* with byte data or a Unicode string, *LenB* returns the number of bytes that represent the data or the string.

- You can't use *Len* with an object variable.

- If **varname** is an array, you must also specify a valid subscript. In other words, *Len* can't determine the total number of elements in or the total size of an array.

Programming Tips & Gotchas

- When you use a random access file to store data and a user-defined type to handle that data within your application, you can use *Len* to determine the value of the Len = clause of the file's Open statement. However, if you have used variable length strings within your user-defined type, *Len* may not accurately determine the actual storage requirement of the user-defined type. For this purpose, fixed-length strings that are set equal to the maximum size of the string field should be used instead. The following example shows how to use the *Len* function to specify the buffer length when opening a random access file:

```
Option Explicit

Type udtTest
    FName As String * 20
    LName As String * 25
    Age   As Integer
End Type

Public udtRec(1 To 10) As udtTest

Public Function RandomFileSave() As Boolean

    Dim sFile  As String
    Dim iFile  As Integer
    Dim i      As Integer

    sFile = "test.dat"
    iFile = FreeFile

    Open sFile For Random As #iFile Len = Len(udtRec(1))
        For i = 1 To 10
            Put #iFile, i, udtRec(i)
        Next i
    Close #iFile

End Function
```

- Variants are treated the same as a string variables, and *Len* returns the actual number of characters stored to the variable. But this can lead to unexpected results. Take the following snippet as an example:

```
Dim vVar
vVar = 100

MsgBox Len(vVar)
```

You may expect the *Len* function to return 2 because *iVar* is obviously a variant of subtype integer. In fact, *Len* returns 3—the number of characters contained within the variant.

- When used with a strongly typed variable, *Len* returns the number of bytes required to store that variable. The length of a Long, for instance, is 4.

- Because Visual Basic uses Unicode strings (which store each character in two bytes) internally, different return values are obtained from *Len* and *LenB* when string variables are passed. For example, a string of four characters returns 4 from *Len*, but returns 8 from *LenB*.

- Just in case you had any doubt about the efficiency of explicitly declaring data types wherever possible, you can try this quick example with the *LenB* function:

```
Dim lVar As Long
Dim vVar

lVar = 10000000
vVar = 10000000

MsgBox "The Long version uses " & LenB(lVar) & _
       " bytes of memory" & vbCrLf & _
       "The Variant version uses " & LenB(vVar)
```

The conclusion is clear: variants consume significantly more memory than strongly typed variables.

Like Operator

Syntax

```
result = string Like pattern
result
```
    Use: Required

    Data Type: Boolean

    If *string* matches *pattern*, *result* is True; otherwise, *result* is False.

string
    Use: Required

    Data Type: String

    The string to be tested against *pattern.*

pattern
    Use: Required

    Data Type: String

    A series of characters used by the Like operator to determine if *string* and *pattern* match.

Description

Determines if a string matches a given pattern.

Rules at a Glance

- If either *string* or *pattern* is Null, then *result* is Null.

- The default comparison method for the Like operator is binary. This can be overridden using the Option Compare statement.

- Binary comparison is based on comparing the internal binary number representing each character; this produces a case-sensitive comparison.

- Text comparison, the alternative to binary comparison, is case insensitive; therefore, A = a.

- The sort order is based on the code page currently being used, as determined by the Windows regional settings.

- The following table describes the special characters to use when creating pattern; all other characters match themselves:

Character	Meaning
?	Any single character
*	Zero or more characters
#	Any single digit (0–9)
[list]	Any single character in list
[!list]	Any single character not in list
[]	A zero-length string ("")

- *list* matches a group of characters in **pattern** to a single character in *string* and can contain almost all available characters, including digits.

- Use a hyphen (-) in *list* to create a range of characters to match a character in *string*; for example [A-D] matches A,B,C, or D in that character position in *string*.

- Multiple ranges of characters can be included in *list* without the use of a delimiter. For example, [A-D J-L].

- Ranges of characters should appear in sort order; for example, [c-k].

- Use the hyphen at the start or end of *list* to match to itself. For example, [- A-G] matches a hyphen or any character from A to G.

- The exclamation mark in pattern matching is similar to the negation operator in C. Use an exclamation mark before a character or range of characters in *list* to match all but that character. For example, [!A-G] matches all characters apart from the characters from A to G.

- The exclamation mark outside of the bracket matches itself.

- To use any special character as a matching character, enclose the special character in brackets. For example, to match to a question mark, use [?].

Example

The following example displays OK if the text entered into Text1 starts with either V or A, followed by any characters and ends with "in a Nutshell." Therefore "Paul in a Nutshell" returns Wrong, whereas either "ASP in a Nutshell" or "VB & VBA in a Nutshell" is OK.

```
Private Sub Command1_Click()
    Dim sTitle As String, sPattern As String
    sTitle = "in a Nutshell"
    sPattern = "[V A]* " & sTitle
    If Text1.Text Like sPattern Then
        MsgBox "OK"
    Else
        MsgBox "Wrong"
    End If
End Sub
```

Programming Tips & Gotchas

Different languages place different priority on particular characters with relation to sort order. Therefore, the same program using the same data may yield different results when run on machines in different parts of the world, depending upon the locale settings of the systems.

See Also

Option Compare Statement

Line Input# Statement

Syntax

```
Line Input #filenumber, varname
```

filenumber

Use: Required

Data Type: Integer

Any valid file number.

varname

Use: Required

Data Type: String or Variant

The name of a string or variant variable.

Description

Assigns a single line from a sequential file opened with the For Input method to a string or variant variable.

Rules at a Glance

- Data is read into a buffer one character at a time until a line feed or carriage return sequence (either Chr(13) or Chr(13)+Chr(10)) is encountered.

When this happens, all characters in the buffer are assigned to **varname** as a single string, without the carriage return sequence, and the buffer is cleared.

- After reading a line, the file pointer advances to the first character after the end of the line or to the end-of-file marker.

Example

```
Dim intLine As Integer, hFile As Integer
Dim strBuffer As String

hFile = FreeFile
Open "lineinp.txt" For Input As #hFile
Do While Not EOF(hFile)
    intLine = intLine + 1
    Line Input #hFile, strBuffer
    List1.AddItem strBuffer
Loop

Close #hFile
```

Programming Tips & Gotchas

You use the **Line Input** statement to read data from unstructured sequential data files. To write data back to this type of file, use the **Print #** statement.

Load Statement

Syntax

```
Load object
object
```

> Use: Required
>
> Data Type: A Form or Control object
>
> An expression that evaluates to a form or control.

Description

Loads a form or control into memory.

Rules at a Glance

- When a control or form is first loaded using the **Load** statement, it's resident in memory, but it isn't visible on the screen. To make a form visible, use the form's Show method. To make a control visible, set its Visible property to **True**.

- You can explicitly create a control only with the **Load** statement as part of a control array. See following sidebar "Creating a Dynamic Control Array."

Programming Tips & Gotchas

- Use the **Unload** statement to remove from memory the form or control you've loaded with the **Load** statement.

Creating a Dynamic Control Array

To create a *dynamic control array*—that is, an array of controls you can add to at runtime—you must first place a control of the required type on the form and set its index property to 0. You can then use the **Load** statement to create new controls based on the control whose Index is 0. The new controls inherit all the properties of the original control, including its size and position. This means you must set the Left and Top properties for the new controls; otherwise, all your controls will sit on top of each other! These newly loaded controls are also hidden, so you must also set their Visible property to **True** once you have sized and positioned them. The following example creates a control array containing five command buttons that appear horizontally across a form:

```
Private Sub Form_Load()
    Dim intCtrlCtr As Integer
    Dim varCtrl As Variant

    For intCtrlCtr = 1 To 4
        Load cmdArray(intCtrlCtr)
        cmdArray(intCtrlCtr).Caption = "Button #" _
                        & intCtrlCtr + 1
        cmdArray(intCtrlCtr).Top = cmdArray(0).Top
        cmdArray(intCtrlCtr).Left = _
                cmdArray(intCtrlCtr - 1).Left + _
                cmdArray(intCtrlCtr - 1).Width + 75
    Next

    For Each varCtrl In cmdArray
        varCtrl.Visible = True
    Next
End Sub
```

Controls belonging to a single control array share the same event handlers. However, their Index property is passed as a parameter to the event handler, allowing you to determine which control fired the event.

Trying to load a control that's already loaded causes an error, so it's a good idea to maintain an instance counter to determine the next index number to use when creating a control.

Note that, unlike previous versions of VB, VB6 supports dynamic control creation. Also note that hosted versions of VBA don't support dynamic control creation.

- Referencing any property or method of a form—or of a control on a form—that isn't already loaded forces the form to be loaded into memory.

- In Visual Basic, the **Form_Initialize** event, followed by the **Form_Load** event (for VBA UserForms, the **UserForm_Initialize** event only) is fired when the **Load** statement is called, or when the form is loaded into memory.

- In these days of VB rapidly becoming a more object-oriented language, a new syntax is emerging for loading and unloading controls and forms. The idea is to create an instance of a form and assign that instance to a local object variable as you would for any another object. The following example shows a comparison of the new and old styles for loading a form:

```
'New Syntax
Dim frmNewForm As Form2
Set frmNewForm = New Form2
frmNewForm.Show vbModal
Set frmNewForm = Nothing

'Old Syntax
Load Form2
Form2.Show vbModal
Unload Form2
```

- Loading a form causes the form's visual interface to be loaded. Whether or not the form is loaded, however, its code remains in memory and continues to be accessible.

See Also

Set Statement, Unload Statement

LoadResData Function

Syntax

```
LoadResData(resID, resType)
resID
```
Use: Required

Data Type: Variant

A numeric or string value specifying the resource ID of the data to load.

resType

Use: Required

Data Type: Variant

A numeric or string value denoting the format of the data to load. See the table below for valid values:

ResType Value	Meaning
1	Cursor resource
2	Bitmap resource
3	Icon resource
6	String resource
10	User-defined resource
12	Group cursor
14	Group icon

Return Value

A Unicode string.

Description

Returns a binary (Unicode) string containing the specified resource from a resource (*.RES*) file included with the project.

Resource files store graphics, strings, and other data inside the application, the contents of the *.RES* file being compiled into the final EXE. The advantage of storing support files in this manner is that they are permanently available to the application, unlike separate support files that can be accidentally deleted or not transferred should the application be moved. You can also store several localized versions of your resources in the *.RES* file that loads depending on the locale of the current machine, thereby easily internationalizing your application.

Rules at a Glance

- You can pass a string value to *restype* if you are loading a custom or user-defined resource. For example:

      sRTFText = LoadResData(102, "CUSTOM")

    This is the only case in which a string value is permitted.

- The maximum string length returned by *LoadResData* is 64KB.

- In Visual Basic, there is no advantage to using *LoadResData* to load a graphic resource because the function returns a Unicode string containing the actual byte data of the resource. When dealing with graphic resources, you should use *LoadResPicture*.

Programming Tips & Gotchas

- String data returned from *LoadResData* is in Unicode format. For the vast majority of current VB controls, you need to convert this string to ANSI before it can be used. The following example shows how to do this.

- Note that *LoadResData* is part of the VB Runtime Library and isn't available in VBA applications.

- Contrary to the documentation for *LoadResData* in both VB5 and VB6, the following resource types aren't supported in Visual Basic and should therefore be ignored: 4 Menu resource, 5 Dialog box, 7 Font directory resource, 8 Font resource, and 9 Accelerator table.

- The VB Runtime Library includes a set of intrinsic constants for specifying resource types, called LoadResConstants. However, these don't match the values of the *LoadResData* resType parameter. The LoadResConstants should be used only with the *LoadResPicture* function.

Example

In the following example, a richtext format document has been stored using the ID 102 as a custom resource within a *.RES* file. The custom RTF resource is displayed in a RichTextBox control. However, because *LoadResData* returns a

Unicode string, the returned string must be converted into an ANSI string before it's used.

```
Private Sub Command1_Click()
    Dim suRTFText As String
    Dim sRTFText  As String
    Dim i         As Integer

    suRTFText = LoadResData(102, "CUSTOM")
    'convert to ANSI
    For i = 1 To LenB(suRTFText)
        sRTFText = sRTFText & _
                   Chr(AscB(MidB(suRTFText, i, 1)))
    Next i

    RichTextBox1.TextRTF = sRTFText

End Sub
```

See Also

LoadResPicture Function, LoadResStringFunction

The VB6 Resource Editor Add-In

Users of VB6 can load a Resource Editor Add-In that greatly simplifies the task of creating and managing *.RES* files within a project. For users of VB5, the add-in is a free download from the Owners Area of the Visual Basic web site. Figure 7-5 shows the resource editor loaded with the resource file used for the *LoadResData*, *LoadResPicture*, and *LoadResString* examples.

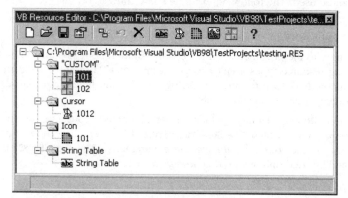

Figure 7-5: The Visual Basic Resource Editor Add-In

LoadResPicture Function

Syntax

```
LoadResPicture(resID, resType)
```

resID

>   Use: Required

>   Data Type: Variant

>   A numeric or string value specifying the resource ID of the picture to load.

resType

>   Use: Required

>   Data Type: Variant

>   A numeric constant denoting the format of the picture to load. See the following table for valid constants and values:

Constant	Value	Description
vbResBitmap	0	Bitmap resource
vbResIcon	1	Icon resource
vbResCursor	2	Cursor resource

Return Value

An IPictureDisp interface.

Description

Assigns a graphic from a resource file (*.RES*) to the Picture property of a form or control.

Rules at a Glance

- The images to be loaded by *LoadResPicture* must be included in a resource (*.RES*) file. Each must be assigned a unique identifier, which is typically represented by a numeric constant.

- The file loaded by *LoadResPicture* can be a Windows bitmap file (*.BMP* or *.RLE*), an icon file (*.ICO*), or a cursor file (*.CUR*).

- The image returned by the *LoadResPicture* function can be assigned to any form or control property that expects an StdPicture object. These include the Picture property of a PictureBox or an Image control, the Icon property of a Form object, or the MouseIcon property of a form.

Programming Tips & Gotchas

- *LoadResPicture* is part of the VB Runtime Library and, as such, isn't available in VBA applications.

- Visual Basic 6 includes an add-in Resource Editor; see the previous sidebar for more information.

Reference

- Using graphics from a *.RES* file speeds up the loading of a form.

Example

In this example, bitmaps that denote the type of employee have been stored in a resource file. A `Select Case` statement then determines which bitmap should be loaded into the Picture property of the current grid cell. The advantage of using this method to load pictures is that the graphic is loaded only as it's needed, as opposed to the traditional method of loading all possible pictures into hidden controls on the form, which slows the loading of the form.

```
Private Function RefreshEmployeeGrid(iEmployeeType _
                                  As Integer)
    Select Case iEmployeeType
        Case Is = MAINT_SERV
            grdEmp.Picture = LoadResPicture(102, vbResBitmap)
        Case Is = PRODUCTION
            grdEmp.Picture = LoadResPicture(103, vbResBitmap)
        Case Is = CLERICAL
            grdEmp.Picture = LoadResPicture(104, vbResBitmap)
    End Select

End Function
```

You could enhance this example by making the ID of each bitmap resource identical to the *iEmployeeType* value, so that you could replace the `Select Case` construct with just one line of code:

```
grdEmp.Picture = LoadResPicture(iEmployeeType, vbResBitmap)
```

See Also

LoadResData Function, LoadResString Function

LoadResString Function

Syntax

```
LoadResString(resID)
resID
```
>   Use: Required
>
>   Data Type: Variant
>
>   A numeric value specifying the resource ID of the string to load.

Return Value

A String.

Description

Retrieves a string from a resource file (*.RES*) that can be assigned to a string variable or to the string property of a control, such as a label caption.

Rules at a Glance

- The strings to be retrieved by *LoadResString* must be included in a resource (*.RES*) file. Each must be assigned a unique identifier, which is typically represented by a numeric constant.

- The identifier 1 is reserved for use by the application icon.

Programming Tips & Gotchas

- *LoadResString* is part of the VB Runtime Library and isn't available in VBA applications.

- Using resource strings is the ideal way to internationalize your application, as the following example demonstrates.

- Unlike the *LoadResData* function, *LoadResString* returns an ANSI string that can be directly assigned to a form or control property.

- VB6 includes an add-in Resource Editor; see the sidebar in the previous entry for more information.

Example

This example demonstrates how to use *LoadResString* in conjunction with the *GetLocaleInfo* API call to internationalize a VB application. This example assumes that a resource file containing menu caption strings in various languages has been created and added to the project. A Form_Load event could call the *getLanguage* function, which in turns calls the relevant API function to return the current language of the machine. This value then passes a code to a function that retrieves the relevant menu caption and assigns it to the menu object. This example uses the language string constant purely to make the code easier to read; however, in a real application, you should return the language ID number from the API call by using the LOCALE_ILANGUAGE constant.

```
Option Explicit

Public Const LOCALE_SLANGUAGE = &H2
Public Const LOCALE_ILANGUAGE = &H1

Declare Function GetLocaleInfo Lib "kernel32" Alias _
        "GetLocaleInfoA" (ByVal Locale As Long, _
        ByVal LCType As Long, ByVal lpLCData As String, _
        ByVal cchData As Long) As Long

Public Function getLanguage() As Boolean

    Dim lReturn    As Long
    Dim lLocID     As Long
    Dim lType      As Long
    Dim sData      As String
    Dim lDataLen   As Long

    lDataLen = 0
    'passing 0 as the data length returns the required
    'size of the string
```

```
        lReturn = GetLocaleInfo(lLID, LOCALE_SLANGUAGE, sData, _
                lDataLen)
        'create a null terminated buffer of the correct length
        sData = String(lReturn, 0) & vbNullChar
        'assign the length
        lDataLen = lReturn
        'call the API funtion again; this time sData will
        'be assigned the Language name
        lReturn = GetLocaleInfo(lLID, LOCALE_SLANGUAGE, sData, _
                lDataLen)


        'determine which language is being used.
        Select Case UCase$(Left$(sData, 6))
    'pass across a code to the SetCaptions function
            Case Is = "ENGLIS"
                SetCaptions 1000
            Case Is = "FRENCH"
                SetCaptions 2000
            Case Is = "GERMAN"
                SetCaptions 3000
            Case Is = "SPANIS"
                SetCaptions 4000
        End Select

End Function

Private Function SetCaptions(iCode As Integer) As Boolean

    'assign strings from the Res file for each caption
    'i.e., The English "Open File" caption will have an
    'ID of 1001
    mnuOpenFile.Caption = LoadResString(iCode + 1)
    mnuCloseFile.Caption = LoadResString(iCode + 2)
    mnuEdit.Caption = LoadResString(iCode + 3)
    mnuCompleteQuestions.Caption = LoadResString(iCode + 4)
    mnuDelete.Caption = LoadResString(iCode + 5)

End Function
```

See Also

LoadResData Function, LoadResPicture Function

Loc Function

Named Arguments

No

Syntax

```
Loc(filenumber)
filenumber
    Use: Required
```

Data Type: Integer

Any valid file number.

Return Value

A Long integer.

Description

Determines the current position of the file read/write pointer.

Rules at a Glance

* If you have opened the file in random mode, *Loc* returns the record number of the last record read or written.

* If you have opened the file in input or output mode (sequential), *Loc* returns the current byte position in the file divided by 128.

* If you have opened the file in binary mode, *Loc* returns the position of the last byte read or written.

Example

```
Dim hFile As Integer
Dim lngPtr As Long, lngFileLen As Long
Dim strBuffer As String

hFile = FreeFile()
Open "loc.bin" For Binary As #hFile
lngFileLen = LOF(hFile)
Do While lngPtr < lngFileLen
    strBuffer = strBuffer & Input(1, hFile)
    lngPtr = Loc(hFile)
Loop
Close #hFile
Text1.Text = strBuffer
```

Programming Tips & Gotchas

For sequential files, the return value of *Loc* isn't required and shouldn't be used.

See Also

Open Statement

Lock Statement

Syntax

```
Lock [#]filenumber[, recordrange]
filenumber
```

Use: Required

Data Type: Integer

Any valid file number.

recordrange
>Use: Optional
>
>Data Type: Long
>
>A range of records.

The syntax for the *recordrange* argument is:

```
recnumber | [start] To end
recnumber
```
>Use: Required
>
>Data Type: Long
>
>The record or byte number at which to commence the lock.

start
>Use: Optional
>
>Data Type: Long
>
>The first record or byte number to lock.

end
>Use: Required
>
>Data Type: Long
>
>The last record or byte number to lock.

Description

Use the Lock statement in situations where multiple programs or more than one instance of your program may need read and write access to the same data file. The Lock statement prevents another process from accessing a record, a section, or the whole file until it's unlocked by the Unlock statement.

Rules at a Glance

* *recnumber* is interpreted as a record number in the case of random files and a byte number in the case of binary files. Records and bytes in a file are always numbered sequentially from 1 onward.

* To lock a particular record, specify its record number, and only that record is locked.

* Use the Lock statement, omitting *recnumber*, to lock the whole file.

* The Lock statement locks an entire file opened in input or output (sequential) mode, regardless of the *recordrange* argument.

* If you omit the *start* argument in the *recnumber* syntax, Lock locks all records from the start of the file to record or byte number *end*.

* Attempting to access a locked file or portion of a file returns runtime error 70, "Permission denied."

Programming Tips & Gotchas

* You must take care to remove all file locks with the Unlock statement before either closing a file or ending the application; otherwise, you can leave the

file in an unstable state. This of course means that, where appropriate, your error-handling routines must be made aware of any locks currently in place so that they may be removed if necessary.

- You use the Lock and Unlock statements in pairs, and the argument lists of both statements must match exactly.

- The Lock statement doesn't guarantee under all circumstances that the locked file will be protected from access by other processes. There are two circumstances under which an apparent access violation can occur:

    - The file has already been opened but has not been locked by a process when the current process locks it. However, the first process can't perform operations on the file once the second file successfully locks it.

    - The block of code responsible for opening the file and then locking it is interrupted by the scheduling policy of the operating system before the file can be locked. If a second process then opens and locks the file, it, not the first process, has sole use of the file.

    Because of this, the Lock statement should immediately follow the Open statement in code. This reduces, but doesn't eliminate, the problems that result from the fact that opening and locking a file isn't an atomic operation.

See Also

Unlock Statement

LOF Function

Named Arguments

No

Syntax

```
LOF(filenumber)
filenumber
```
> Use: Required
>
> Data Type: Integer
>
> Any valid file number.

Return Value

A Long integer.

Description

Returns the size of an open file in bytes.

Rules at a Glance

filenumber must be the number of a file opened using the Open statement.

Example

The following example shows how to use the *LOF* function to determine the length of a data file and to determine the number of records it contains:

```
Open sFileName For Random As #iFile Len = Len(udtCustomer)
iMaxRecs = LOF(iFile) / Len(udtCustomer)
For iRec = 1 To iMaxRecs
    Get #1, iRec, udtCustomers(iRec)
Next iRec
Close #iFile
```

Programming Tips & Gotchas

LOF works only on an open file; if you need to know the size of a file that isn't open, use the *FileLen* function.

See Also

FileLen Function

Log Function

Named Arguments

No

Syntax

```
Log(number)
number
```

Use: Required

Data Type: Double

A numeric expression greater than zero.

Return Value

A Double.

Description

Returns the natural logarithm of a given number.

Rules at a Glance

- The natural logarithm is based on e, a constant whose value is approximately 2.718282. The natural logarithm is expressed by the equation:

```
ez = x
```

where z = Log(x). In other words, the natural logarithm is the inverse of the exponential function.

- *number*, the value whose natural logarithm the function is to return, must be a positive real number. If number is negative or zero, the function generates runtime error 5, "Invalid procedure call or argument."

Programming Tips & Gotchas

- You can calculate base-*n* logarithms for any number, *x*, by dividing the natural logarithm of *x* by the natural logarithm of *n*, as the following expression illustrates:

```
Logn(x) = Log(x) / Log(n)
```

For example, the *Log10* function shows the source code for a custom function that calculates base-10 logarithms:

```
Static Function Log10(X)
    Log10 = Log(X) / Log(10#)
End Function
```

- A number of other mathematical functions that aren't intrinsic to VBA can be computed using the value returned by the *Log* function. The functions and their formulas are:

Inverse Hyperbolic Sine
```
HArcsin(X) = Log(X + Sqr(X * X + 1))
```

Inverse Hyperbolic Cosine
```
HArccos(X) = Log(X + Sqr(X * X - 1))
```

Inverse Hyperbolic Tangent
```
HArctan(X) = Log((1 + X) / (1 - X)) / 2
```

Inverse Hyperbolic Secant
```
HArcsec(X) = Log((Sqr(-X * X + 1) + 1) / X)
```

Inverse Hyperbolic Cosecant
```
HArccosec(X) = Log((Sgn(X) * Sqr(X * X + 1) +1) / X)
```

Inverse Hyperbolic Cotangent
```
HArccotan(X) = Log((X + 1) / (X - 1)) / 2
```

LSet Statement

Syntax

```
LSet stringvar = string
stringvar
```
> Use: Required
>
> Data Type: String
>
> The name of a string variable to receive the string.

```
string
```
> Use: Required
>
> Data Type: String
>
> A string expression to be copied into *stringvar*.

Description

Copies *string* into *stringvar*, left-aligning *string* within *stringvar*.

Rules at a Glance

- *LSet* has meaning only when used with fixed-length strings.

- If the length of **string** is less than that of **stringvar**, the extra characters within **stringvar** are padded with spaces.

- If the length of **string** is greater than that of **stringvar**, **string** is truncated to the length of **stringvar**.

Programming Tips & Gotchas

- *LSet* and *RSet* are legacies from the pre-Visual Basic days of BASIC. *LSet* doesn't really need to be used at all, since the same result can be accomplished with a simple assignment operation to either a fixed-length string or a variable-length string.

- Although its use is unnecessary, *LSet* does appear to yield some performance benefit in comparison to assignment statements. When *LSet* copies a string of approximately 70 characters to a variable-length string, it executes approximately 33% faster than a simple assignment statement. When copying the same string to a fixed-length string, it offers approximately a 25% performance gain.

- According to the Visual Basic documentation, you can also use the *LSet* statement to copy a variable of one user-defined type to a variable of another user-defined type. In fact, the Microsoft VB5 help section goes so far as to include the syntax for this (although the online documentation for VB6 explicitly warns against this practice). However, copying the data from one data type into the memory space of a different data type is a recipe for disaster in any programming language. Basically, what happens behind the scenes is that the raw binary is copied from one memory location to another. This means that the individual data types of the elements within the user-defined types are completely ignored. When you then access the data in the copied user-defined type, the information it holds is, at best, useless. If you must copy (and in the process translate) one user-defined data structure to another, do this using assignment statements on an element-by-element basis.

See Also

RSet Statement

LTrim, LTrim$ Functions

Named Arguments

No

Syntax

```
LTrim(stringexp)
```
stringexp
>   Use: Required
>
>   Data Type: String
>
>   A valid string expression.

Return Value

A Variant of subtype String (in the case of *LTrim*) or a String (in the case of *LTrim$*).

Description

Removes any leading spaces from **stringexp**.

Rules at a Glance

- *LTrim* returns a variant of subtype String.
- *LTrim$* returns a String data type.
- If **stringexp** contains a Null, *LTrim* returns Null.

Programming Tips & Gotchas

- Unless you need to keep trailing spaces, it's best to use the *Trim* function, which is the equivalent of LTrim(RTrim(**string**)). This allows you to remove both leading and trailing spaces in a single function call.
- Although I have seen it done, it's extremely unwise to create data relationships that rely on leading spaces. Most string-based data types in relational database management systems like SQL Server and Access automatically remove leading spaces.

See Also

RTrim Function, Trim Function

Me Operator

Syntax

```
Me
```

Description

The Me operator can represent a class or a form, but only from within that class or form.

Rules at a Glance

- Me is an implicit object reference to the current object module—either a Form, a UserForm, or a Class module.
- The Me operator is particularly useful when passing an instance of the currently executing class as a parameter.

Example

In this example, a class method passes an instance of itself to another class using the Me operator:

```
Public Function ChangeName(NewName As String) As Boolean
    Dim oMain As Main.Utils
    If IsUnique(NewName) Then
        msName = NewName
```

```
            Set oMain = New Main.Utils
                oMain.Save Me
            Set oMain = Nothing
            ChangeName = True
        Else
            ChangeName = False
        End If
    End Function
```

Programming Tips & Gotchas

- Unfortunately, unlike the implementation of the **Me** operator in other languages, the VB/VBA version can't refer to an individual control.

- The **Me** operator can't be used on the left side of an expression.

- Another favorite use of the **Me** keyword is within Form modules, when unloading the Form or UserForm. For example:

```
Private Sub mnuExit
    Unload Me
End Sub
```

Mid, Mid$, MidB, MidB$ Functions

Named Arguments

Yes

Syntax

```
Mid(string, start[, length])
string
```
> Use: Required
>
> Data Type: String
>
> The expression from which to return a substring.

```
start
```
> Use: Required
>
> Data Type: Long
>
> The starting position of the substring.

```
length
```
> Use: Optional
>
> Data Type: Variant (Long)
>
> The length of the substring.

Return Value

A Variant of subtype String or a String data type.

Description

Returns a substring of a specified length from within a given string.

Rules at a Glance

- If *string* contains a Null, *Mid* returns Null.

- If *start* is more than the length of *string*, a zero-length string is returned.

- If *start* is less than zero, runtime error 5, "Invalid procedure call or argument," is generated.

- If *length* is omitted, or *length* is greater than the length of *string*, all characters from *start* to the end of *string* are returned.

- The *MidB* version of the *Mid* function is used with byte data held within a string. When using *MidB*, both *start* and *length* refer to numbers of bytes as opposed to numbers of characters.

Example

The following example parses the contents of a text box control (named *txtString*) and writes each word to a list box (named *lstWord*). Note the use of the *InStr* function to determine the position of either a space or a carriage return/linefeed character combination, the two characters that can terminate a word in this case:

```
Private Sub cmdParse_Click()

Dim strString As String, strWord As String
Dim intStart As Integer, intEnd As Integer
Dim intStrLen As Integer, intCrLf As Integer
Dim blnLines As Boolean

lstWords.Clear

intStart = 1
strString = Trim(txtString.Text)
intStrLen = Len(strString)
intCrLf = InStr(1, strString, vbCrLf)
If intCrLf Then blnLines = True

Do While intStart > 0
    intEnd = InStr(intStart, strString, " ") - 1
    If intEnd <= 0 Then intEnd = intStrLen
    If blnLines And (intCrLf < intEnd) Then
        intEnd = intCrLf - 1
        intCrLf = InStr(intEnd + 2, strString, vbCrLf)
        If intCrLf = 0 Then blnLines = False
        lstWords.AddItem Mid(strString, intStart, _
                        intEnd - intStart + 1)
        intStart = intEnd + 3
    Else
        lstWords.AddItem Mid(strString, intStart, _
                        intEnd - intStart + 1)
        intStart = intEnd + 2
    End If
```

Reference

```
        If intStart > intStrLen Then intStart = 0
    Loop

    End Sub
```

Programming Tips & Gotchas

- Use the *Len* function to determine the total length of **string**.

- Use *InStr* to determine the starting point of a given substring within another string.

See Also

Left, Left$, LeftB, LeftB$ Functions; Len Function; Mid, MidB Statements; Right, Right$, RightB, RightB$ Functions

---

Mid, MidB Statements

Named Arguments

No

Syntax

```
Mid(stringvar, start[, length]) = string
stringvar
```
> Use: Required
>
> Data Type: String
>
> The name of the string variable to be modified.

start
> Use: Required
>
> Data Type: Variant (Long)
>
> The position within **stringvar** at which the replacement commences.

length
> Use: Optional
>
> Data Type: Variant (Long)
>
> The number of characters in **stringvar** to replace.

string
> Use: Required
>
> Required: String
>
> The string that replaces characters within **stringvar**.

Description

Replaces a section of a string with characters from another string.

Rules at a Glance

- If you omit **length**, as many characters of **string** as can be fitted into **stringvar** are used.

- If *start* + *length* is greater then the length of *stringvar*, *string* is truncated to fit in the same space as *stringvar*. This means that the length of *stringvar* isn't altered by the Mid statement.

- If *start* is less than 0, runtime error 5, "Invalid procedure call or argument," occurs.

- The MidB version of the Mid statement is used with byte data held within a string. When using MidB, both *start* and *length* refer to the number of bytes, as opposed to the number of characters.

Programming Tips & Gotchas

- If *string* contains Null, runtime error 94, "Invalid Use of Null," is generated.

- VB6 includes the *Replace* function, which enhances the functionality of the Mid statement by allowing you to specify the number of times the replacement is carried out in the same string.

- Although the documentation refers to *Mid* when it appears on the left side of an assignment statement as a statement and on the right side as a function, you may find it easier to remember their purpose and syntax if you consider both variations as functions. In the second case, *stringvar* is passed to the function by value, and therefore it isn't modified by the function itself, which returns the substring desired. In the first case, *stringvar* is passed to the function by reference, so that, when the function returns, its value is modified accordingly.

See Also

Mid, MidB Functions; Replace Function

Minute Function

Named Arguments

Yes

Syntax

```
Minute(time)
time
```
> Use: Required
>
> Data Type: Date/Time
>
> Any valid date/time expression, or an expression that can be evaluated as a date/time expression.

Description

Returns an integer between 0 and 59 representing the minute of the hour from a given date/time expression.

Rules at a Glance

If *time* is Null, the *Minute* function returns Null.

Programming Tips & Gotchas

If *time* isn't a valid date/time expression, the function generates runtime error 13, "Type mismatch." To prevent this, use the *IsDate* function to check the argument before calling the *Minute* function.

See Also

Hour Function, Second Function

MIRR Function

Named Arguments

Yes

Syntax

```
MIRR(values(), finance_rate, reinvest_rate)
values()
```
Use: Required

Data Type: Array of Double

An array of cash flow values.

```
finance_rate
```
Use: Required

Data Type: Double

The interest rate paid as the cost of financing.

```
reinvest_rate
```
Use: Required

Data Type: Double

The interest rate received on gains from cash investment.

Return Value

A Double representing the modified internal rate of return.

Description

Calculates the modified internal rate of return, which is the internal rate of return when payments and receipts are financed at different rates.

Rules at a Glance

- *values* must be a one-dimensional array that contains at least one negative value (a payment) and one positive value (a receipt). The order of elements within the array should reflect the order in which payments and receipts occur.

- *finance_rate* and *reinvest_rate* are percentages expressed as decimal values. For example, 10% is expressed as 0.10.

Each element of *values* represents a payment or a receipt that occurs at a regular time interval. If this isn't the case, *MIRR* returns erroneous results.

See Also

> IRR Function

MkDir Statement

Named Arguments

No

Syntax

```
MkDir path
path
```
> Use: Required
>
> Data Type: String
>
> The name of the folder to be created.

Description

Creates a new folder.

Rules at a Glance

* If you omit the drive from *path*, a new folder is created on the current drive.

* You can specify the drive using either its local drive letter or its UNC name.

Programming Tips & Gotchas

* If your program is running on Windows NT, ensure that the logged-in user has the rights to create a folder on the specified drive prior to calling the MkDir statement.

* VB doesn't make the new folder the current folder automatically after a call to MkDir. You need to call the ChDir statement to do this.

* To remove a folder, use the RmDir statement.

* Use CurDir to determine the current drive.

* VB6 includes a new File System object model that has a Folders collection object and Folder object. You will find these objects much more flexible and easier to use than the intrinsic VB folder-management functions.

See Also

> ChDir Statement, CurDir Function, File System Objects, RmDir Statement

Reference

Month Function

Named Arguments

No

Syntax

```
Month(date)
date
```
> Use: Required
>
> Date: Variant
>
> Any valid date expression.

Return Value

A variant integer between 1 and 12.

Description

Returns an integer representing the month of the year of a given date expression.

Rules at a Glance

If *date* contains `Null`, *Month* returns `Null`.

Programming Tips & Gotchas

- The validity of the date expression and the position of the month element within the date expression are initially determined by the locale settings of the current Windows system. However, some intelligence has been built into the *Month* function that surpasses the usual comparison of a date expression to the current locale settings. For example, on a Windows machine set to U.S. date format (`mm/dd/yyyy`), the date "13/12/1998" is technically illegal. However, the *Month* function returns 12 when passed this date. The basic rule for the *Month* function is that if the system-defined month element is outside legal bounds (i.e., greater than 12), the system-defined day element is assumed to be the month and is returned by the function.

- Since the *IsDate* function adheres to the same rules and assumptions as *Month*, it determines whether a date is valid before passing it to the *Month* function.

- Visual Basic 6 introduces a new *MonthName* function for returning the name of the month.

See Also

> Day Function, Year Function, IsDate Function, MonthName Function

MonthName Function (VB6)

Named Arguments

No

Syntax

```
MonthName monthnumber [, abbreviate]
monthnumber
```
> Use: Required
>
> Data Type: Long
>
> The ordinal number of the month, from 1 to 12.

```
abbreviate
```
> Use: Optional
>
> Data Type: Boolean
>
> A flag to indicate if an abbreviated month name should be returned.

Return Value

A String.

Description

Returns the month name of a given month. For example, 1 returns January, or if `abbreviate` is `True`, Jan.

Rules at a Glance

The default value for `abbreviate` is `False`.

Programming Tips & Gotchas

- `monthnumber` must be an integer or a long; it can't be a date. Use `DatePart("m", dateval)` to obtain a month number from a date.

- `MonthName` with `abbreviate` set to `False` is the equivalent of `Format (dateval, "mmmm")`.

- `MonthName` with `abbreviate` set to `True` is the equivalent of `Format (dateval, "mmm")`.

See Also

Month Function, WeekdayName Function, DatePart Function

MsgBox Function

Named Arguments

Yes

Syntax

```
MsgBox(prompt[, buttons][, title][, helpfile, context])
prompt
```
> Use: Required
>
> Data Type: String
>
> The text of the message to display in the message box dialog.

buttons

    Use: Optional

    Data Type: Numeric

    The sum of the `Button`, `Icon`, `Default Button`, and `Modality` constant values.

title

    Use: Optional

    Data Type: String

    The title displayed in the titlebar of the message box dialog.

helpfile

    Use: Optional

    Data Type: String

    An expression specifying the help file to provide help functionality for the dialog.

context

    Use: Optional

    Data Type: Numeric

    An expression specifying a context ID within *helpfile*.

Return Value

An Integer value indicating the button clicked by the user.

Description

Displays a dialog box containing a message, buttons, and optional icon to the user. The action taken by the user is returned by the function in the form of an integer value.

Rules at a Glance

- *prompt* can contain approximately 1,000 characters, including carriage return characters such as the built-in **vbCrLf** constant.

- If the *title* parameter is omitted, the name of the current application or project is displayed in the titlebar.

- If the *helpfile* parameter is provided, the context parameter must also be provided, and vice versa.

- In VB5 and VB6 applications, when both *helpfile* and *context* are passed to the *MsgBox* function, a Help button is automatically placed on the *MsgBox* dialog, allowing the user to click and obtain context-sensitive help. However, in VB4, the user was not presented with a Help button and could access help only by pressing the **F1** key. VBA applications such as Excel automatically show a Help button.

- If you omit the *buttons* argument, the default value is 0; that is, VB opens an application modal dialog containing only an OK button.

- The following intrinsic constants can be added together to form a complete *buttons* argument:

```
ButtonDisplayConstant + IconDisplayConstant + _
DefaultButtonConstant + ModalityConstant
```

Only one constant from each group can make up the overall *buttons* value.

Button Display Constants

Constant	Value	Buttons to Display
vbOKOnly	0	OK only
vbOKCancel	1	OK and Cancel
vbAbortRetryIgnore	2	Abort, Retry, and Ignore
vbYesNoCancel	3	Yes, No, and Cancel
vbYesNo	4	Yes and No
vbRetryCancel	5	Retry and Cancel

Icon Display Constants

Constant	Value	Icon To Display
vbCritical	16	Critical Message
vbQuestion	32	Warning Query
vbExclamation	48	Warning Message
vbInformation	64	Information Message

Default Button Constants

Constant	Value	Default Button
vbDefaultButton1	0	First button
vbDefaultButton2	256	Second button
vbDefaultButton3	512	Third button
vbDefaultButton4	768	Fourth button

Modality Constants

Constant	Value	Modality
vbApplicationModal	0	Application
vbSystemModal	4096	System

Reference

- The following intrinsic constants determine the action taken by the user and represent the value returned by the *MsgBox* function:

Return Values

Constant	Value	Button Clicked
vbOK	1	OK
vbCancel	2	Cancel (or Esc key pressed)
vbAbort	3	Abort
vbRetry	4	Retry
vbIgnore	5	Ignore
vbYes	6	Yes
vbNo	7	No

- If the *MsgBox* contains a Cancel button, the user can press the Esc key, and the function's return value is that of the Cancel button.

- The Help button doesn't itself return a value, because it doesn't close the *Msg-Box* dialog. If the user clicks the Help button, a Help window is opened. Once the Help window is closed, the user clicks one of the other buttons on the message box to close the dialog; this then returns a value.

Programming Tips & Gotchas

- *Application modality* means that the user can't access other parts of the application until a response to the message box has been given. In other words, the appearance of the message box prevents the application from performing other tasks or from interacting with the user other than through the message box.

- *System modality* used to mean that all applications were suspended until a response to the message box was given. However, with multitasking operating systems such as Windows 95 and Windows NT, this isn't the case. Basically the message box is defined to be a "Topmost" window that is set to "Stay on Top," which means that the user can switch to another application and use it without responding to the message box, but because the message box is the topmost window, it's positioned on top of all other running applications.

- Unlike its *InputBox* counterpart, *MsgBox* can't be positioned on the screen; it's always displayed in the center of the screen.

- If your application is to run out-of-process on a remote machine, you should remove all *MsgBox* functions, since they won't be displayed to the user, but will instead appear on the monitor of the remote server! For in-process server components, VB now has an option to compile an ActiveX DLL for Unattended Execution, in which case all user interface references are instead written to an event log when the program executes. However, you must decide how your program would execute if this were the case; if you're looking for a particular return value from a *Msgbox* function for your program to continue, your program may not function correctly (if at all) if these references are automatically removed.

See Also

InputBox Function

MTSTransactionMode Property (VB6 only)

Description

Only available when a class is part of an ActiveX DLL project, you should set this property whenever the class is to be registered as a Microsoft Transaction Server (MTS) component. MTS uses this property to determine the level of support a particular component has for transactions. This property is available only at design time.

When MTS components created using VB5 are added to an MTS package, the administrator of the MTS package must manually set the Transaction Support property for the component to operate correctly. VB6 has included the MTSTransactionMode property to ease the burden on MTS administrators either forgetting to set the property or setting the incorrect value. Therefore, developers of MTS components now have more direct control over the way in which their components are registered within MTS.

Values

NotAnMTSObject (Default)

Use this value if the component isn't to be used in Microsoft Transaction Server.

NoTransactions

Use this value if the component is to be a nontransactional part of an MTS package. When the component is installed in MTS, the Transaction property is set to "Does not support Transactions." This value tells MTS that the component shouldn't execute within the context of a transaction regardless of the transactional state of the client.

RequiresTransactions

When the component is installed in MTS, the Transaction property is set to "Requires a Transaction." This means that if the client isn't executing in the context of a transaction, a new transaction is created for this component. However, if the client is executing in the context of a transaction, this component joins in that same transaction.

UsesTransactions

When the component is installed in MTS, the Transaction property is set to "Supports Transactions." There is a subtle yet important difference between a component that supports transactions and one that requires a transaction. A component that supports transactions executes only in the context of a transaction if the client is executing in the context of a transaction, in which case this component will join in that same transaction. If however, the client isn't executing in the context of a transaction, this component won't have a new transaction created for it and won't execute in the context of a transaction.

RequiresNewTransaction

Use this value if the component is to execute in its own transaction. When the component is installed in MTS, the transaction property is set to "Requires a new transaction." This means that regardless of the transactional state of the client, this object is always created in the context of a new transaction.

Programming Tips & Gotchas

For further details about creating Microsoft Transaction Server components using Visual Basic, see my book *Creating MTS Components with VB6*, soon to be published by O'Reilly & Associates.

See Also

Chapter 4

Name Property

Description

Used to name a class, module, or project. This property is only available at design time.

Rules at a Glance

*   Standard VB naming conventions apply.

*   VBA assigns default names (Project1, Class1, etc.) to classes and projects.

Programming Tips & Gotchas

*   You can't use the same name for a class and the project within which the class resides.

*   The Project name for an ActiveX project is used by OLE Automation as the Library name when creating or referring to an object. The object reference takes the form *LibraryName.ClassName*.

*   Since you typically refer to a class, form, or module by its name from outside of that object, it's best to replace the default value of the Name property (unless, of course, that's the name you intend to keep) as soon after adding it to your project as possible.

Name Statement

Syntax

```
Name oldpathname As newpathname
oldpathname
```

Use: Required

Data Type: String

The current filename and optional path.

newpathname
> Use: Required

> Data Type: String

> The new filename and optional path.

Description

Renames a disk file or folder.

Rules at a Glance

* *newpathname* must not already exist or an error is generated.

* *newpathname* and *oldpathname* can't be on different drives.

* Path information included in *newpathname* and *oldpathname* can take the form of the local system's path or the UNC path.

* *newpathname* and *oldpathname* can't include the wildcard characters ? and *.

* You can't use the Name statement with a file that is already open.

Programming Tips & Gotchas

The Name statement can move a file from one folder to another, and optionally, can change the file's name at the same time. If the folder specified in *newname-path* exists and is different from that stated in *oldnamepath*, the file is moved to the folder specified in *newnamepath*. If the filename in *newnamepath* is also different, the file is renamed at the same time. Moving an object in this way, however, only works with files; you can't use the Name statement to move folders.

Now Function

Syntax

Now

Return Value

A Variant of subtype Date.

Description

Returns the current date and time based on the system setting.

Example

The following example returns the date 10 days from today:

```
Dim dFutureDate As Date
dFutureDate = DateAdd("d",10,Now)
```

Programming Tips & Gotchas

* It's often overlooked that workstations in a modern Windows environment are at the mercy of the user! If your application relies on an accurate date and time setting, you should consider including a line in the workstation's logon script to synchronize the time with one of the servers. Many so-called bugs

Reference

have been traced to a workstation that has had its date or time wrongly altered by the user. The following line of code, when added to the logon script of an NT4 machine, synchronizes the machine's clock with that of a server called NTSERV1:

```
net time \\NTSERV1 /set
```

- The date returned by *Now* takes the Windows General Date format based on the locale settings of the local computer. The U.S. setting for General Date is mm/dd/yy hh:mm:ss.

- The *Now* function is often used to generate timestamps. However, for short-term timing and intra-day timestamps, the *Timer* function, which returns the number of milliseconds elapsed since midnight, affords greater accuracy.

See Also

Timer Function

NPer Function

Named Arguments

Yes

Syntax

```
NPer(rate, pmt, pv [, fv [, due]])
```
rate

   Use: Required

   Data Type: Double

   The interest rate per period.

pmt

   Use: Required

   Data Type: Double

   The payment to be made each period.

pv

   Use: Required

   Data Type: Double

   The present value of the series of future payments or receipts.

fv

   Use: Optional

   Data Type: Double

   The future value of the series of payments or receipts. If omitted, the default value is 0.

due

   Use: Optional

   Data Type: Variant

A value indicating when payments are due. 0 indicates that payments are due at the end of the payment period; 1 indicates that payments are due at the end of the period. If omitted, the default value is 0.

Return Value

A Double indicating the number of payments.

Description

Determines the number of payment periods for an annuity based on fixed periodic payments and a fixed interest rate.

Rules at a Glance

- *rate* is a percentage expressed as a decimal. For example, a monthly interest rate of 1% is expressed as 0.01.

- For *pv* and *fv*, cash paid out is represented by negative numbers; cash received is represented by positive numbers.

Example

Typically, the amount of time required to repay credit card debt is never explicitly stated. The following program uses the *NPer* function to determine how much time is required to repay credit card debt.

```
Private Sub HowLongToPay()

On Error GoTo ErrHandler

Dim dblRate As Double, dblPV As Double
Dim dblPmt As Double
Dim lngNPer As Long


dblPV = InputBox("Enter the Credit Card balance: ")
dblPmt = InputBox("Enter the monthly payment: ")
dblRate = InputBox("Enter the interest rate: ")

lngNPer = NPer(dblRate, -dblPmt, dblPV, 0, 1)

MsgBox "Your credit card balance will be paid in " & _
        lngNPer & " months." & vbCrLf & "That's " & _
        Int(lngNPer / 12) & " years and " & _
        Round(lngNPer Mod 12, 2) & " months."

Exit Sub

ErrHandler:

Err.Clear

End Sub
```

Programming Tips & Gotchas

- Both **rate** and *pmt* must be expressed in the same time unit. That is, if *pmt* reflects the monthly payment amount, **rate** must be the monthly interest rate.

- *NPer* is useful in calculating the number of payment periods required to repay a loan when the monthly loan payment is fixed or when the approximate amount of a monthly payment is known. In this case, *pv* reflects the amount of the loan, and **fv** is usually 0, reflecting the fact that the loan is to be entirely repaid.

- *NPer* is useful in determining the length of time required to meet some future financial goal. In this case, *pv* represents the current level of savings, and **fv** represents the desired level of savings.

See Also

IPmt Function, Pmt Function, PPmt Function, Rate Function

NPV Function

Named Arguments

Yes

Syntax

```
NPV(rate, values() )
rate
```
> Use: Required
>
> Data Type: Double
>
> The discount rate over the period, expressed as a decimal.

```
values()
```
> Use: Required
>
> Data Type: Double
>
> An array of cash flow values.

Return Value

A Double specifying the net present value.

Description

Calculates the net present value of an investment based on a series of periodic variable cash flows (payments and receipts) and a discount rate. The *net present value* is the value today of a series of future cash flows discounted at some rate back to the first day of the investment period.

Rules at a Glance

- **rate** must be a percentage expressed as a decimal. For example, 10% is expressed as 0.10.

- **values** is a one-dimensional array that must contain at least one negative value (a payment) and one positive value (a receipt).

- The *NPV* investment begins one period before the date of the first cash flow value and ends with the last cash flow value in the array.

- *NPV* requires future cash flows. If the first cash flow occurs at the beginning of the first period, the first value must be added to the value returned by *NPV* and must not be included in *values*.

Programming Tips & Gotchas

- *rate* and the individual elements of *values* must reflect the same time period. For example, if *values* reflects annual cash flows, *rate* must be the annual discount rate.

- Individual members of *values* are interpreted sequentially. That is, *values(0)* is the first cash flow, *values(1)* is the second, etc.

- *NPV* is like the *PV* function, except that *PV* allows cash flows to begin either at the beginning or the end of a period and requires that cash flows be fixed throughout the investment.

See Also

FV Function, IRR Function, MIRR Function, PV Function

Oct, Oct$ Functions

Named Arguments

No

Syntax

```
Oct(number)
number
```
> Use: Required
>
> Data Type: Numeric or String
>
> Number or string representation of a number to convert.

Return Value

A Variant of subtype String or a String

Description

Returns the octal value of a given number.

Rules at a Glance

- If *number* isn't already a whole number, it's rounded to the nearest whole number before being evaluated.

- If *number* is Null, *Oct* returns Null.

- If *number* is the special Empty variant, *Oct* returns 0 (zero).

- *Oct* returns up to 11 octal characters.

- *Oct* returns a variant string, while *Oct$* returns a string data type.

Programming Tips & Gotchas

You can also use literals in your code to represent octal numbers by appending &O to the relevant octal value. For example, 100 decimal has the octal representation &O144. The following two statements each assign an octal value to a variable:

```
lngOctValue1 = &H200              ' Assigns 128
lngOctValue2 = "&O" & Len(dblNumber)    ' Assigns 8
```

See Also

Hex, Hex$ Function

On Error Statement

Syntax 1

```
On Error GoTo label|0
label
```

> Use: Either *label* or 0 is required
>
> A valid label within the subroutine.

Syntax 2

```
On Error Resume Next
```

Description

Enables or disables error handling within a procedure. If you don't use an **On Error** statement in your procedure, or if you have explicitly switched off error handling, the Visual Basic runtime engine handles the error automatically. First, it displays a dialog containing the standard text of the error message, something many users are likely to find incomprehensible. Second, it terminates the application, so any error that occurs in the procedure produces a fatal runtime error.

Rules at a Glance

Syntax 1

- The 0 argument disables error handling within the procedure until the next **On Error** statement is executed.

- The *label* argument specifies the name of the label defining an error-handling routine within the current procedure that will be branched to should an error occur.

- A subroutine label must be suffixed with a colon; furthermore, you can't use a VB, reserved word for a subroutine label name. For example:

```
someroutine:
```

- *label* must be in the same procedure as the **On Error** statement.

Syntax 2

- When a runtime error occurs, program execution continues with the program line following the line that generated the error.

Programming Tips & Gotchas

- If you have no error handling in your procedure or if error handling is disabled, the VB runtime engine traces back through the call stack until a procedure is reached where error handling is enabled. In that case, the error is
handled by that procedure. However, if no error handler can be found in the
call stack, a runtime error occurs, and program execution is halted.

- On Error Resume Next is useful in situations where you are certain that
errors will occur or where the errors that could occur are minor. The following example shows how you can quickly cycle through the controls on a form
and set the Text property to an empty string without checking what type of
control you're dealing with. Of course, you are aware that many of the controls don't have a Text property, so the attempt to access their Text property
generates an error. By using the On Error Resume Next statement, you force
your program to ignore this error and carry on with the next control.

```
On Error Resume Next
For Each Control In Me.Controls
    Control.Text = ""
Next
```

- Use of the On Error Resume Next statement should be kept to a minimum,
since errors are basically ignored, and their occurrence is silent to the user.
This means that, should an *unexpected* error (that is, an error that you were
not intending to handle when you chose to ignore errors) occur, or should
your application behave unexpectedly, the job of finding and correcting the
cause of the error becomes almost impossible.

- The following is a template for error handling within your procedures:

```
Sub/Function/Property Name ()
    On Error Goto Name_Err
    ... 'procedure code

Name_Exit:
    ... 'tidying up code – such as Set Object = Nothing
    Exit Sub/Function/Property

Name_Err:
    ... 'error handling code e.g. a MsgBox to inform the user
    Resume Name_Exit

End Sub/Function/Property
```

If cleanup code isn't required within the procedure, you can simplify the template by removing the Name_Exit label and removing the Resume Name_
Exit statement.

- If you are writing an error handling routine for use within a class module or a
DLL, you should use the following template, which raises an error back to the client, thereby notifying the client of the error and allowing the client to handle it:

```
Sub/Function/Property Name ()
    On Error Goto Name_Err
    ... 'procedure code
```

```
... 'tidying up code – such as Set Object = Nothing
    Exit Sub/Function/Property
```

```
Name_Err:
    ... 'error handling and tidying up code
    Err.Raise etc...
```

```
End Sub/Function/Property
```

- Errors that occur within an error handler always generate a runtime error.

- The quality of error trapping, error handling, and error reporting within a program often determines the success or failure of the application. Attention to detail in this area can be the difference between a stable, well-behaved, and robust application and one that seems to generate nothing but hassle. Using logs like the NT application log within your error-handling routines can help you track down persistent problems quickly and efficiently. See Chapter 6, which details creating robust VB and VBA error handling routines.

See Also

Resume Statement, Chapter 6

Open Statement

Named Arguments

No

Syntax

```
Open pathname For mode [Access access] [lock] As [#]filenumber
              [Len=reclength]
```

pathname

    Use: Required

    Data Type: String

    The name of the file to open, along with an optional path.

mode

    Use: Required

    Data Type: Keyword

    The file access mode: append, binary, input, output, or random.

access

    Use: Optional

    Data Type: Keyword

    Specifies the allowable operations by the current process.

lock

    Use: Optional

    Type: Keyword

    Specifies the allowable operations by other processes.

---

filenumber
>Use: Required

>Data Type: Integer

>A valid file number between 1 and 511.

reclength
>Use: Optional

>Data Type: Integer

>The length of the record or I/O buffer.

Description

Before reading from and/or writing to a disk file, you must first open the file using the Open statement. The Open statement allocates memory for the I/O buffer and optionally sets access locks on the file.

Rules at a Glance

* *pathname* may include the directory or folder and drive; if these are omitted, the file is assumed to reside in the current working directory. If *pathname* does include drive and path information, this may take the form of a path relative to the local system or a UNC path.

* The default mode for opening a disk file (when *mode* isn't specified) is random.

* If the specified file doesn't exist when opening in input mode, an error occurs.

* A new file is created if the specified file doesn't exist when opening in append, binary, output, or random mode.

* *access* allows you to restrict the actions that can be taken against the file in the current process, by specifying Read, Write, or Read Write. The default is Read Write.

* The *lock* argument allows you to restrict the operations performed on the open file by other processes, as shown in the following table:

Lock Type	Description
Shared	Other processes can open the file for both read and write operations.
Lock Read	Other processes can only write to the file.
Lock Write	Other processes can only read from the file.
Lock Read Write	Other processes can't open the file.

- The `reclength` argument is treated differently, depending upon the open mode, as the following table shows:

Open Mode	Meaning of Len Is...
Random	Length in bytes of each record
Binary	Ignored
Append/input/output	The number of characters to buffer

Example

The following example opens a data file for random access and assigns a record from that file to a user-defined type.

```
Private Function getCustomerData(sFileName As String, _
                                 lCustNo As Long) As Boolean

    Dim iFile As Integer
    iFile = FreeFile

    Open sFileName For Random As #iFile Len = Len(udtCustomer)
    Get #iFile, lCustNo, udtCurrentCustomer
    Close #iFile

End Function
```

Programming Tips & Gotchas

- To avoid using the file number of an already open file and generating an error, use the *FreeFile* function to allocate the next available file number.

- You can open an already opened file using a different file number in binary, input, and random modes. However, you must close a file opened using append or output before you can open it with a different file number.

See Also

FreeFile Function

Option Base Statement

Syntax

```
Option Base {0 | 1}
```

Description

Used at the beginning of a module to specify the default lower bound for arrays dimensioned within the module.

Rules at a Glance

- The default lower bound for arrays created in Visual Basic is 0. Therefore, you should only use **Option Base** 1 to change the default base for arrays to 1.

- The Option Base statement must appear at the start of a module, before any array declarations.

- The Option Base statement affects only those arrays declared in the module in which the Option Base statement appears.

Programming Tips & Gotchas

- Another more flexible method of specifying the lower bound of an array (other than the default) is to use the To clause when dimensioning an array, as the following snippet shows:

```
Dim myArray(1 to 50) As String
```

- Option Base doesn't affect the lower bound of arrays created with the *Array* function or the ParamArray keyword; these are always base 0.

See Also

Dim, Private, Public, ReDim, Static Statements

Option Compare Statement

Syntax

```
Option Compare {Binary | Text | Database}
```

Description

Sets the default method for comparing string data.

Rules at a Glance

- When Option Compare isn't used in a module, the default comparison method is binary.

- When Option Compare is used, it must appear at the start of the module's declarations section, before any procedures.

- *Binary comparison*—the default text comparison method in Visual Basic—uses the internal binary code of each character to determine the sort order of the characters. For example "A" < "a".

- *Text comparison* uses the locale settings of the current system to determine the sort order of the characters. Text comparison is case insensitive. For example "A" = "a".

- *Database comparison* is only for use in Microsoft Access. Strings are compared based on the sort order defined by the international settings stored in the database engine.

Option Explicit Statement

Syntax

```
Option Explicit
```

Description

Use Option Explicit to generate a compile-time error whenever a variable that has not been declared is encountered.

Rules at a Glance

- The Option Explicit statement must appear in the declarations section of a module before any procedures.

- In modules where the Option Explicit statement isn't used, any undeclared variables are automatically cast as variants.

Programming Tips & Gotchas

- It's considered good programming practice to always use the Option Explicit statement. The following example shows why:

```
1:    Dim iVariable As Integer

2:    iVariable = 100
3:    iVariable = iVarable + 50
4:    MsgBox iVariable
```

In this code snippet, an integer variable, *iVariable*, has been declared. However, because the name of the variable has been mistyped in line 3, the message box shows its value as only 50 instead of 150. This is because *iVarable* is assumed to be an undeclared variant whose value is 0. If the Option Explicit statement had been used, the code wouldn't have compiled, and *iVarable* would have been highlighted as the cause.

- You can automatically add the Option Explicit statement to all new modules as follows: Select Options from the Tools menu, select the Editor tab of the Options dialog, then check the "Require Variable Declaration" option in the Code Settings section and click OK.

See Also

DefType Statement

Option Private Module Statement

Syntax

```
Option Private Module
```

Description

Restricts the scope and visibility of the contents of a module (i.e., its variables, classes, functions, and procedures) in VBA-enabled applications that allow references across multiple projects (e.g., Microsoft Office applications) to the module's project. Option Private Module has no effect in the standalone version of Visual Basic.

Rules at a Glance

- The Option Private Module statement must appear in the declarations section of a module before any procedures.

- Publicly declared procedures, variables, and objects contained within a module that has been set as private using the `Option Private Module` statement aren't available to other projects and applications. However, they are still available in the usual way to other members of the same project.

Programming Tips & Gotchas

You should only use the `Option Private Module` statement in applications such as Microsoft Excel that allow you to load multiple projects. In this way, the `Option Private Module` statement restricts visibility of publicly declared items.

Persistable Property (VB6 Only)

Description

Only available when the class is part of an ActiveX DLL project that is both public and createable, this property determines whether the class can be saved to disk. This property is only available at design time.

Values

NotPersistable
> The class properties can't be saved.

Persistable
> The class property values can be saved to a property bag.

Programming Tips & Gotchas

If the property value is set to Persistable, four procedures—the InitProperties, ReadProperties, and WriteProperties events, and the PropertyChanged method—are automatically added to the class module.

See Also

> Chapter 4

Pmt Function

Named Arguments

Yes

Syntax

```
Pmt(rate, nper, pv[, fv[, due]])
rate
```
> Use: Required

> Data Type: Double

> The interest rate per period.

`nper`
> Use: Required

> Data Type: Integer

> The total number of payment periods.

pv

> Use: Required
>
> Data Type: Double
>
> The present value of the series of future payments.

fv

> Use: Optional
>
> Data Type: Double
>
> The future value or cash balance after the final payment.

due

> Use: Optional
>
> Data Type: Variant
>
> A value indicating when payments are due. 0 indicates that payments are due at the beginning of the payment period; 1 indicates that payments are due at the end of the period. If omitted, the default value is 0.

Return Value

A Double representing the monthly payment.

Description

Calculates the payment for an annuity based on periodic fixed payments and a fixed interest rate. An annuity can be either a loan or an investment.

Rules at a Glance

- *rate* is a percentage expressed as a decimal. For example, an interest rate of 1% per month is expressed as 0.01.

- If *fv* is omitted, the default value of 0 (reflecting the complete repayment of a loan) is used.

- For *pv* and *fv*, cash paid out is represented by negative numbers; cash received is represented by positive numbers

- If *due* is omitted, the default value of 0, reflecting payments at the beginning of each period, is used.

Example

See the example for the *IPmt* function.

Programming Tips & Gotchas

- *rate* and *nper* must be calculated using payment periods expressed in the same units. For example, if *nper* reflects the total number of monthly payments, *rate* must be the monthly interest rate.

See Also

IPmt Function, NPer Function, Rate Function

PPmt Function

Named Arguments

Yes

Syntax

```
PPmt(rate, per, nper, pv[, fv[, due]])
```
rate

> Use: Required
>
> Data Type: Double
>
> The interest rate per period.

per

> Use: Double
>
> Data Type: Any valid numeric expression
>
> The period for which a payment is to be computed.

nper

> Use: Double
>
> Data Type: Any valid numeric expression
>
> The total number of payment periods.

pv

> Use: Double
>
> Data Type: Any valid numeric expression
>
> The present value of a series of future payments.

fv

> Use: Optional
>
> Data Type: Variant
>
> The future value or cash balance after the final payment. If omitted, the default value is 0.

due

> Use: Optional
>
> Data Type: Variant
>
> A code indicating whether payments are due at the end (0) or beginning (1) of the payment period.

Return Value

A Double representing the principal paid in a given payment.

Description

Computes the payment of principal for a given period of an annuity based on periodic, fixed payments and a fixed interest rate. An annuity is a series of fixed cash payments made over a period of time. It can be either a loan payment or an investment.

Rules at a Glance

- The value of *per* can range from 1 to *nper*.

- If *pv* and *fv* represent liabilities, their value is negative; if assets, their value is positive.

- If *fv* is omitted, its default value of 0 is used.

- If *due* is omitted, the default value of 0, reflecting payments at the beginning of each period, is used.

Example

See the example for the *IPmt* function.

Programming Tips & Gotchas

- *rate* and *nper* must be expressed in the same time unit. That is, if *nper* reflects the number of monthly payments, *rate* must be the monthly interest rate.

- The interest rate is a percentage expressed as a decimal. For example, if *nper* is the total number of monthly payments, an annual percentage rate (APR) of 12% is equivalent to a monthly percentage rate of 1%. The value of *rate* is therefore .01.

See Also

IPmt Function, NPer Function, Pmt Function, Rate Function

Print # Statement

Named Arguments

No

Syntax

```
Print #filenumber, [outputlist]
filenumber
```
    Use: Required

    Data Type: Integer

    Any valid file number.

```
outputlist
```
    Use: Optional

    A list of expressions to output to a file.

The syntax of *outputlist* is:

```
[{Spc(n) | Tab[(n)]}] [expression] [charpos]
Spc(n)
```
    Use: Optional

    Insert *n* space characters before expression.

Tab(*n*)
    Use: Optional

    Position the insertion point either at the next print zone (by omitting *n*) or at column number (*n*).

expression
    Use: Optional

    The data expression to output.

charpos
    Use: Optional

    Position of the insertion point for the first character of the next expression.

Description

Outputs formatted data to a disk file opened for append or output.

Rules at a Glance

- You can delimit multiple expressions using either a space or a semicolon, both of which have the same effect. In fact, from version 5 of VB, the semicolon is placed automatically in the line of code for you. For example:

```
Print #iFile, sName; sAge
Print #iFile, sName sAge
```

- The semicolon also denotes that the insertion point for the first character of the next expression is immediately after the last character of the current expression.

- The Tab(*n*) argument doesn't actually insert any tab characters (Chr(9)); instead, it fills the space from the end of the last expression to column *n* (or to the start of the next print zone) with space characters.

- Omitting *charpos* forces the next expression to be printed on a new line.

- Using Print # followed by a list separator writes an empty line to the file. For example:

```
Print #iFile,
```

- The Print # statement uses the locale settings of the current system to format dates, times, and numbers using the correct separators.

Programming Tips & Gotchas

- You may find that sequential data files written using the Print # statement don't read back correctly using the Input statement. For heavily structured sequential data, it's recommended that you use the Write # statement, which ensures that all fields are correctly delimited.

- Certain data types may not behave as you may expect. These are listed in the following table:

Output Data Type	Formatted Output to File
Boolean	True or False
Date	Short Format Date based on system locale settings

Output Data Type	Formatted Output to File
Error	Error, followed by the corresponding error code
Null (Variant)	Null

See Also

Write # Statement

Printer Object and Printers Collection

Since it's part of the VB library, the Printer object isn't available to VBA applications. When you write a VBA (as opposed to VB) program, you simply make use of the host application's own built-in printing functionality. For example:

```
Set oWordActiveDoc = oWord.Documents.Add
Set oWordSel = oWord.Selection

oWordSel.TypeText "This is text coming in from the VB app."
oWordSel.WholeStory
oWordSel.Font.Name = "Arial"
oWordSel.Font.Size = 12
oWordSel.Font.Bold = wdToggle

oWordActiveDoc.PrintOut
```

Printer Object

- Visual Basic contains a global printer object, which refers to the default printer for the current system. Because this object is global to all parts of the VB project, you don't need to create an object variable; you can simply use the Printer object directly. For example:

  ```
  If Printer.Duplex Then
  ```

- The global printer object is also a virtual document onto which you place your text output using the Print method and a range of built-in graphics methods. For example:

  ```
  Printer.Print "Private and Confidential"
  Printer.Line (0, 100)-(Printer.ScaleWidth, 100)
  ```

- You can position text and drawings precisely in output by using the Printer object's CurrentX and CurrentY properties. The coordinate system of the printer object is based from the top left corner of the object. The default coordinate unit is a Twip, but this can be changed by using the ScaleHeight, Scale-Width, ScaleLeft, ScaleTop, and ScaleMode properties.

- Because the output of proportional fonts is so hard to predict, two very useful properties are TextWidth and TextHeight. These return the actual size that a given string will occupy when placed on the printer object using the current font, font size, and font style. This allows you to determine at what coordinates to start printing the string on the printer object.

- The Printer object holds a virtual document that can contain any number of pages; you start with page one, can add pages by calling the NewPage method, and can keep count of the number of pages with the Page property. For example:

```
Printer.NewPage
Printer.Print "Page No:" & Printer.Page
```

- When you've finished the document and want to output it to the printer device, simply call the EndDoc method, which dumps the current Printer buffer to the device and resets the Printer object:

```
Printer.EndDoc
```

- A useful tip is that the PictureBox control and the Printer object have identical graphics and print methods. Why is this significant? The following code shows how you can start to create a Print Preview form using the same code to reference either a Printer object or a PictureBox control:

```
Private Sub mnuPrintPreview_Click()

    Dim oPic As PictureBox
    Set oPic = Picture1
    If PrintOutput(oPic) Then
        oPic.Visible = True
    End If

End Sub

Private Sub mnuPrint_Click()
    If PrintOutput(Printer) Then
        Printer.EndDoc
    Else
        Printer.KillDoc
    End If
End Sub

Public Function PrintOutput(oPrintSurface As Object) _
                        As Boolean
    oPrintSurface.Print "Hello World"
    oPrintSurface.Line (100, 300) - (600, 300)
    PrintOutput = True
End Function
```

Printer Object Properties

The Printer object supports the following properties and methods. Note that not all properties are available to all printer devices; some properties depend on the capabilities of the current device driver. In the following synopses, *oPrinter* is an expression that evaluates to a Printer object:

ColorMode

Returns or sets a flag denoting whether a color printer outputs in monochrome or color.

Syntax: *oPrinter*.ColorMode [= *constValue*]

where *constValue* can be **vbPRCMMonochrome** or **vbPRCMColor**.

Copies

Returns or sets the number of copies to be printed.

Syntax: *oPrinter*.Copies [=*intValue*]

CurrentX

Returns or sets the horizontal coordinate for the next print or drawing method.

Syntax: *oPrinter*.CurrentX [= *singValue*]

CurrentY

Returns or sets the vertical coordinate for the next print or drawing method.

Syntax: *oPrinter*.CurrentY [= *singValue*]

DeviceName

Read-only property that returns the name of the current printer device.

DrawMode

Returns or sets a flag denoting the method used to output graphics methods.

Syntax: *oPrinter*.DrawMode [= *constValue*]

constValue can be:

vbBlackness	vbCopyPen *(default)*	vbInvert
vbMaskPen	vbMaskPenNot	vbMaskNotPen
vbMergeNotPen	vbMergePen	vbMergePenNot
vbNop	vbNotCopyPen	vbNotMaskPen
vbNotMergePen	vbNotXorPen	vbXorPen
vbWhiteness		

DrawStyle

Returns or sets a flag denoting the style of lines output in graphics methods.

Syntax: *oPrinter*.DrawStyle [= *constValue*]

constValue can be vbSolid, vbDash, vbDot, vbDashDot, vbDashDotDot, vbInvisible, vbInvisibleSolid.

DrawWidth

Returns or sets the width in pixels of lines output by graphics methods.

Syntax: *oPrinter*.DrawWidth [= *intValue*]

DriverName

Returns the name of the current driver for the current Printer object.

Syntax: *oPrinter*.DriverName

Duplex

Returns or sets a flag denoting whether a page is to be printed on both sides.

Syntax: *oPrinter*.Duplex [= *constValue*]

constValue can be vbPRDPSimplex, vbPRDPHorizontal, vbPRDP-Vertical.

FillColor

Returns or sets the fill color used in graphics methods

Syntax: *oPrinter*.FillColor [= *Value*]

Value can be the result of a call to the *QBColor* function or one of the intrinsic Visual Basic color constants.

FillStyle

Returns or sets the pattern used to fill shapes created with graphics methods.

Syntax: *oPrinter*.FillStyle [= *constValue*]

constValue can be:

vbCross	vbDiagonalCross	vbDownwardDiagonal
vbFSSolid	vbFSTransparent	bHorizontalLine
vbUpwardDiagonal	vbVerticalLine	

Font

Returns a Font object. This is the recommended method of setting font properties for the Printer object.

Syntax: *oPrinter*.Font.*FontProperty* [= *FontPropertyValue*]

FontBold, FontItalic, FontStrikeThru, FontTransparant, FontUnderline

Returns or sets the style of the current font. But it's instead recommended that you use the properties of the Font object; for example, Font.Bold.

Syntax: *oPrinter*.FontBold [= *booleanValue*]

Syntax: *oPrinter*.FontItalic [= *booleanValue*]

Syntax: *oPrinter*.FontStrikethru [= *booleanValue*]

Syntax: *oPrinter*.FontTransparant [= *booleanValue*]

Syntax: *oPrinter*.FontUnderline [= *booleanValue*]

FontCount

Returns the number of fonts available to the current Printer object.

Syntax: *NoOfFonts* = *oPrinter*.FontCount

FontName

Returns or sets the name of the current font. But to retrieve the name of the current font, you should use the Font.Name method instead.

Syntax: *oPrinter*.FontName [= *strVal*]

Fonts

Returns a collection of all fonts available to the current Printer object. An individual font can be accessed by its ordinal position in the collection.

Syntax: *oPrinter*.Fonts(*index*)

FontSize

Returns or sets the font size in points of the current font. The recommended method is to use the Font.Size property instead.

Syntax: *oPrinter*.FontSize [= *sngVal*]

Reference

hDC

Returns a window handle that can be used in a Win32 API call to identify the current Printer object. Don't store hDC property values, since they can change while the application is executing.

Syntax: *oPrinter*.hDC

Height

Returns or sets the height of the current printer object in twips. Setting the height property overrides the current PaperSize property.

Syntax: *oPrinter*.Height [= *sngVal*]

Orientation

Returns or sets the orientation of the printed output.

Syntax: *oPrinter*.Orientation [= *constValue*]

constValue can have these settings: *vbPRORPortrait*, *vbPRORLandscape*.

Page

Returns the number of the current page. Reset to one when the EndDoc or KillDoc methods is called. Incremented when the NewPage method is called or when textual output on the current page overruns onto subsequent pages. Note that graphical output is truncated and never overruns onto subsequent pages.

Syntax: *oPrinter*.Page

PaperBin

Sets or returns the tray from which paper is fed.

Syntax: *oPrinter*.PaperBin [= *constValue*]

constValue can have these settings:

vbPRBNUpper	vbPRBNLower	vbPRBNMiddle
vbPRBNManual	vbPRBNEnvManual	vbPRBNAuto
vbPRBNTractor	vbPRBNSmallFmt	vbPRBNLargeFmt
vbPRBNLargeCapacity	vbPRBN-Cassette	

PaperSize

Sets or returns the paper size.

Syntax: *oPrinter*.PaperSize [= *constValue*]

constValue can have these settings:

vbPRPS10x14	vbPRPS11x17	vbPRPSA3
vbPRPSA4	vbPRPSA4Small	vbPRPSA5
vbPRPSB4	vbPRPSB5	vbPRPSCSheet
vbPRPSDSheet	vbPRPSEnv9	vbPRPSEnv11
vbPRPSEnv14	vbPRPSEnvB4	vbPRPSEnvB5
vbPRPSEnvB6	vbPRPSEnvC3	vbPRPSEnvC4
vbPRPSEnvC5	vbPRPSEnvC6	vbPRPSEnvC65
bPRPSEnv10	vbPRPSEnv12	vbPRPSEnvDL

vbPRPSEnvItaly	vbPRPSEnvMonarch	vbPRPSESheet
vbPRPSExecutive	vbPRPSFanfoldLgl-German	vbPRPSFanfoldStd-German
vbPRPSFanfoldUS	vbPRPSFolio	vbPRPSLedger
vbPRPSLegal	vbPRPSLetter	vbPRPSLetterSmall
vbPRPSNote	vbPRPSStatement	vbPRPSTabloid
vbPRPSQuarto	vbPRPSUser	

Port

Returns the name of the port used by the current printer object.

Syntax: *oPrinter*.Port

PrintQuality

Returns or sets the flag denoting the printer's print quality setting.

Syntax: *oPrinter*.PaperSize [= *constValue*]

constValue can have these settings: vbPRPQDraft, vbPRPQLow, vbPRPQMe-dium, vbPRPQHigh.

RightToLeft (VB6 onward)

Returns a True or False value denoting whether or not text in the current system should appear from right to left, as for example when running Arabic or Hebrew Windows.

Syntax: *oPrinter*.RightToLeft

ScaleHeight, ScaleWidth

Returns or sets the height and width of the print object's print area based on the units defined by ScaleMode.

Syntax: *oPrinter*.ScaleHeight [= *sngVal*]

Syntax: *oPrinter*.ScaleWidth [= *sngVal*]

ScaleLeft, ScaleTop

Returns or sets the virtual top and left of the print object's print area based on the units defined by ScaleMode.

Syntax: *oPrinter*.ScaleLeft [= *sngVal*]

Syntax: *oPrinter*.ScaleTop [= *sngVal*]

ScaleMode

Determines the coordinate system used by the ScaleLeft, ScaleTop, Scale-Width, and ScaleHeight properties. Note: due to a bug in the initial release of VB5, the ScaleMode property had no effect; this was corrected with Service Pack 2.

Syntax: *oPrinter*.ScaleMode [= *constValue*]

constValue can have these settings: vbUser, VbTwips, VbPoints, vbChar-acters, VbInches, VbMillimeters, VbCentimeters.

TrackDefault

Returns or sets a Boolean flag to denote whether the Printer object should refer to the default printer, even when the default printer is changed through

Reference

Control Panel (True), or whether the Printer object should continue to refer to the same printer, regardless of the system default printer setting (False).

Syntax: *oPrinter*.TrackDefault [= *booleanValue*]

TwipsPerPixelX, TwipsPerPixelY

Returns the number of twips per pixel in the horizontal plane (TwipsPerPixelX) or vertical plane (TwipsPerPixelY) of the Printer object.

Syntax: *oPrinter*.TwipsPerPixelX

Syntax: *oPrinter*.TwipsPerPixelY

Width

Returns or sets the width in twips of the current Printer object. Setting the width property overrides the current PaperSize property.

Syntax: *oPrinter*.Width[= *sngVal*]

Zoom

Returns or sets the percentage by which the printer output is scaled up or down.

Syntax: *oPrinter*.Zoom [= *sngVal*]

Printer Object Methods

In the following synopses, *oPrinter* is an expression that evaluates to a Printer object:

EndDoc

Outputs the Printer object's output buffer to the printer driver or spooler.

Syntax: *oPrinter*.EndDoc

KillDoc

Terminates the current job, emptying the Printer object's output buffer and, if possible, deleting the current print job.

Syntax: *oPrinter*.KillDoc

Line

Outputs a line, a box outline, or a filled box.

Syntax: *oPrinter*.Line [Step] (*x1, 1*) [Step] (*x2, y2*), [*color*], [B][F]

NewPage

Adds a page to the Printer object and increments the Page property by 1. CurrentX and CurrentY are set to 0,0 on the new page.

Syntax: *oPrinter*.NewPage

PaintPicture

Introduced with VB5, the method is a wrapper for Win32 API *BitBlt* functions to allow *.bmp, .wmf, .emf, .ico*, or *.dib* images to be transferred from the Picture property of a form or picture box, and to be manipulated and transferred onto the Printer object.

Syntax: *oPrinter*.PaintPicture *picture, x1, y1, width1, height1, x2, y2, width2, height2, opcode*

PSet

Outputs a single pixel of a given color to the Printer object at a given point.

Syntax: *oPrinter*.PSet [Step] (*x, y*), [*color*]

Scale

Sets the coordinate system for the printer object. If no arguments are passed to the method, the scale mode is reset to twips.

Syntax: *oPrinter*.Scale [(*x1, y1*) – (*x2, y2*)]

ScaleX, ScaleY

Converts the width or height of the Printer object from one scale mode to another.

Syntax: *oPrinter*.ScaleX (*width, fromscale, toscale*)

Syntax: *oPrinter*.ScaleY (*height, fromscale, toscale*)

TextHeight

Returns the width in pixels that the given text will take up on the printer object using the current font settings.

Syntax: *oPrinter*.TextHeight (*string*)

TextWidth

Returns the width in pixels that the given text will take up on the printer object using the current font settings. Due to a bug in the initial release of VB5, the TextWidth property gave inconsistent results when run within the VB IDE. This problem was rectified with Service Pack 2.

Syntax: *oPrinter*.TextWidth (*string*)

Printers Collection

- The Printers collection represents all printers installed on the current system. You can iterate through the Printers collection either by ordinal number or by using the **For Each...Next** statement. For example:

```
For i = 0 To Printers.Count - 1
    Debug.Print Printers(i).DeviceName
Next i

For Each oPrinter In Printers
    Debug.Print oPrinter.DeviceName
Next
```

- You can use the Printers collection to find a specific printer that provides particular functionality, then assign that printer to the global Printer object using the **Set** statement. For example, you may need a printer that handles duplex printing:

```
For Each oPrinter In Printers
    If oPrinter.Duplex Then
        Set Printer = oPrinter
    End If
Next
```

Or

```
For i = 0 to Printers.Count -1
```

Reference

```
      If Printers(i).Duplex Then
          Set Printer = Printers(i)
      End If
Next
```

- A bug in VB5 prevented you from assigning a printer from the collection to a locally defined Printer object variable. This was corrected in VB5 Service Pack 1. For example:

```
Dim oPrinter As Printer
Set oPrinter = Printers(2)
```

- If you reference a printer using the Collection object, the properties of that printer are read-only. To access printer properties on a read-write basis, you have to assign the reference to the Printer object, thereby making it the default printer.

- The Printers collection has one property, Count, which returns the number of printers connected to the current machine. Remember, however, that the Printers collection is 0-based, unlike standard collection objects, which are 1-based. Therefore, you iterate through the Printers collection from 0 to Count–1.

- The Printers collection's Item method is its default method and therefore can be used implicitly as shown above.

Private Statement

Named Arguments

No

Syntax

```
Private [WithEvents] varname[([subscripts])] [As [New] _
        type] [, [WithEvents] varname[([subscripts])] _
        [As [New] type]] . . .
```

WithEvents

    Use: Optional

    Type: Keyword

    A keyword that denotes the object variable *varname* can respond to events triggered from within the object to which it refers.

varname

    Use: Required

    Data Type: Any

    The name of the variable, following Visual Basic naming conventions.

subscripts

    Use: Optional

    Data Type: Integer or Long

    Denotes *varname* as an array and specifies the number and extent of array dimensions.

New
> Use: Optional
>
> Type: Keyword
>
> Automatically creates an instance of the object referred to by the object variable *varname*.

type
> Use: Optional
>
> Data type of the variable *varname*.

Description

Used at module level to declare a private variable and allocate the relevant storage space in memory.

Rules at a Glance

- A `Private` variable's scope is limited to the module in which it's created.

- `WithEvents` is only valid when used to declare an object variable. The `With-Events` keyword informs VB that the object being referenced exposes events. When you declare an object variable using `WithEvents`, an entry for the object variable is placed in the code window's object list, and a list of the events available to the object variable is placed in its procedures list. You can then write code in the object variable's event handlers in the same way that you write other more common event handlers like Form_Load.

- There is no limit to the number of object variables that can refer to the same object using the `WithEvents` keyword; they all respond to that object's events. For example:

```
Private WithEvents adrEmployees As ADODB.Recordset
Private WithEvents adrDepartments As ADODB.Recordset

Private Sub adrDepartments_MoveComplete( _
            ByVal adReason As ADODB.EventReasonEnum, _
            ByVal pError As ADODB.Error, _
            adStatus As ADODB.EventStatusEnum, _
            ByVal pRecordset As ADODB.Recordset)
    'code here....
End Sub

Private Sub adrEmployees_MoveComplete( _
            ByVal adReason As ADODB.EventReasonEnum, _
            ByVal pError As ADODB.Error, _
            adStatus As ADODB.EventStatusEnum, _
            ByVal pRecordset As ADODB.Recordset)
    'code here....
End Sub
```

- You can't create an array variable that uses the `WithEvents` keyword.

- The `New` keyword can't be used in the same object variable declaration as `WithEvents`. This is because `WithEvents` is designed to trap event notifications that would ordinarily be inaccessible to a Visual Basic program. Consequently, `WithEvents` can define only an instance of an existing object.

- The *subscripts* argument has the following syntax:

  `[lowerbound To] upperbound [, [lowerbound To] upperbound]`

  For example:

  `Private strNames(10)`

  defines an array of 11 elements (an array whose lower bound is zero, since an explicit *lowerbound* value isn't provided, and whose upper bound is ten). Similarly:

  `Private(lngPrices(1 to 10)`

  defines an array of ten elements whose index values range from 1 through 10.

- Using the *subscripts* argument, you can declare up to 60 multiple dimensions for the array.

- The *lowerbound* argument of the *subscripts* argument is optional; when not used, the lower bound of the array is specified by the `Option Base` statement. If `Option Base` isn't used, the lower bound of the array is 0.

- If the *subscripts* argument isn't used (i.e., the variable name is followed by empty parentheses), the array is declared dynamic. You can change both the number of dimensions and number of elements of a dynamic array using the `ReDim` statement.

- The `New` keyword is used only when declaring an object variable and denotes that a new instance of the object is created when the first reference to the object is made. Use of the `New` keyword therefore eliminates the need to use the `Set` statement to instantiate the object. For example:

  ```
  Private oEmployee As Employee
  Set oEmployee = New Employee
  ```

  or:

  ```
  Private oEmployee As New Employee
  ```

- The `New` keyword can be used only with early bound objects; that is, an object that has a reference added to the project using the References dialog.

- You can't use the `New` keyword to declare variables of any intrinsic data type, instances of dependent objects, or variables that use the `WithEvents` argument.

- If you don't use the `New` keyword with an object variable, you must use the `Set` statement to assign an existing object to the variable before you can use it.

- *datatype* may be Byte, Boolean, Currency, Date, Double, Integer, Long, Object, Single, String, Variant, a user-defined type, or an object type.

- If you don't specify *datatype* and you haven't used a `DefType` statement, the variable is cast as a Variant.

- The following table shows the values held by each data type when a variable is first initialized.

Data Type	Initial Value
Numeric	0
Variable-length string	Zero-length string ("")
Fixed-length string	Filled with zeros
Variant	Empty
Object	Nothing
Date	Saturday 30 December 1899 12:00:00

- The individual elements of a user-defined type are initialized with the value corresponding to their data type.
- To declare a fixed-length string, use the syntax:

```
Private stringvar As String * stringlength
```

Programming Tips & Gotchas

- All variables created at procedure level are `Private` by default. That is, they don't have scope outside the procedure in which they are created.
- In VBA applications, the `WithEvents` keyword is valid only in class modules. However, standalone versions of VB allow the use of `WithEvents` in class, form, and other object modules.
- A new type of scope was introduced in Visual Basic 5.0. The `Friend` scope is halfway between `Public` and `Private`. It's useful in situations where `Private` is too restricting, and `Public` is too open. For more information, refer to the `Friend` statement.
- Note that when you use the `New` keyword to declare an object variable, the Initialize event of the object is fired on the first reference to the object, not when the object variable is declared.
- It's good programming practice to always use `Option Explicit` at the beginning of a module to prevent misnamed variables from causing hard-to-find errors.
- You may have occasion to maintain legacy Visual Basic code that was written prior to Version 4, when the `Private` and `Public` statements came into the language. In this case, those variables declared in the Declarations section at the start of a code or form module that aren't explicitly defined as global are in fact `Private` variables.

See Also

Friend Statement, Public Statement, ReDim Statement, Set Statement, WithEvents Keyword

Property Get Statement

Named Arguments

No

Syntax

```
[Public | Private | Friend] [Static] Property Get name _
                [(arglist)] [As type[()]]
    [statements]
    [name = expression]
    [Exit Property]
    [statements]
    [name = expression]
End Property
```

Public

> Use: Optional
>
> Type: Keyword
>
> Gives the property scope through all procedures in all modules in the project. If used within a createable class module, the property is also accessible from outside the project. Public, Private, and Friend are mutually exclusive.

Private

> Use: Optional
>
> Type: Keyword
>
> Restricts the scope of the property to those procedures within the same module. Public, Private, and Friend are mutually exclusive.

Friend

> Use: Optional
>
> Type: Keyword
>
> Only valid in a class module, it gives the property scope to all modules within a project, but not to modules outside the project. Public, Private, and Friend are mutually exclusive.

Static

> Use: Optional
>
> Type: Keyword
>
> Preserves the value of variables declared inside the property between calls to the property.

name

> Use: Required
>
> The name of the property.

arglist

> Use: Optional
>
> Data Type: Any

A comma-delimited list of variables to be passed to the property as arguments from the calling procedure.

type

Use: Optional

The return data type of the property.

()

Use: Optional

Indicates that the property returns an array. As of VB6, `Property Get` procedures can return arrays.

statements

Optional

Program code to be executed within the property.

expression

Optional

Data Type: Any

The value to return from the property to the calling procedure.

arglist has the following syntax:

```
[Optional] [ByVal | ByRef] [ParamArray] varname[( )] _
          [As type] [= defaultvalue]
```

`Optional`

Use: Optional

Indicates the argument is optional. An optional argument is one that need not be supplied when calling the property. However, all arguments following an optional one must also be optional. A `ParamArray` argument can't be optional.

`ByVal`

Use: Optional

The argument is passed by value; that is, a local copy of the variable is assigned the value of the argument.

`ByRef`

Use: Optional

The argument is passed by reference; that is, the local variable is simply a reference to the argument being passed. All changes made to the local variable are reflected in the calling argument. `ByRef` is the default method of passing variables.

`ParamArray`

Use: Optional

Indicates that the argument is an optional array of variants containing an arbitrary number of elements. It can be used only as the last element of the argument list, and it can't be used with the `ByRef`, `ByVal`, or `Optional` keywords.

Reference

varname
> Use: Required

> The name of the local variable containing either the reference or value of the argument.

type
> Use: Optional

> The data type of the argument.

defaultvalue
> Use: Optional

> For optional arguments, you can specify a constant default value.

Description

Declares the name, arguments, and code for a procedure that reads the value of a property and returns it to the calling procedure.

Rules at a Glance

- Property procedures are Public by default.

- In VBA applications the Option Private Module statement restricts the scope of a procedure defined as public to the project in which it was defined.

- The Friend keyword is only valid within class modules. Friend procedures are accessible to all procedures in all modules and classes within a project, but aren't listed in the class library for that project. Therefore, they can't be accessed from projects or applications outside the defining application.

- Properties and procedures defined using the Friend keyword can't be late-bound.

- The Static keyword only affects variables declared within the Property Get procedure. If you don't use the Static keyword, the values of all local variables are lost between calls.

- Unlike other function and procedure names, the name of the Property Get procedure doesn't have to be unique within its class module. Specifically, the Property Let and Property Set procedures can have the same name as the Property Get procedure. For example:

```
Property Let Name(sVal as String)
    msName = sVal
End Property

Property Get Name() as String
    Name = msName
End Property
```

- The number and data types of the arguments passed to a Property Get statement must match the corresponding Property Let or Property Set statement. For example:

```
Public Property Let MyProperty(sVal As String, iVal As Integer)
    miMyProperty = iVal
End Property
```

```
Public Property Get MyProperty(sVal As String) As Integer
    MyProperty = miMyProperty
End Property
```

Both the **Property Let** and **Property Get** procedures share a common argument, *sVal*. The **Property Let** procedure has one additional argument, *iVal*, which represents the value that is to be assigned to the MyProperty property. (For details, see the next point.)

* In a **Property Let** procedure, the last argument defines the data type for the property. Therefore, the return data type of the **Property Get** procedure must match the last argument of any corresponding **Property Let** or **Property Set** procedure.

* *type* may be Byte, Boolean, Currency, Date, Double, Integer, Long, Object, Single, String, Variant, a user-defined type, or an object type.

* Fixed-length strings can't be used for *type*.

* From VB6 onward, *type* can be an array of any type.

* VB6 introduces the concept of remote user-defined types. Before VB6, *type* could only be a user-defined type if the property was **Private**. Now UDTs can be passed as **Public** variables or as the return values of **Public** properties. However, this requires that either NT Service Pack 4 or the latest DCOM95 patch has been applied. For details, see Chapter 4.

* If an **Exit Property** statement is executed, the property procedure exits and program execution immediately continues with the statement following the call to the property. Any number of **Exit Property** statements can appear in a **Property Get** procedure.

* If the value of the **Property Get** procedure has not been explicitly set when the program execution exits the procedure, its value is the uninitialized value of the return data type, as shown in the following table:

Data Type	Initial Value
Numeric	0
Variable-length string	Zero-length string ("")
Variant	Empty
Object	Nothing
Date	Saturday 30 December 1899 12:00:00

Programming Tips & Gotchas

* You can create a read-only property by defining a **Property Get** procedure without a corresponding **Property Let** or **Property Set** procedure.

* You should protect the values of properties by defining a **Private** variable to hold the internal property value and control the updating of the property by outside applications through the **Property Let** and **Property Get** statements, as the following template describes:

```
'Class Module Declarations Section
'private data member only accessable from within
```

Reference

```
'this code module
Private miMyProperty As Integer

Public Property Let MyProperty(iVal As Integer)
    'procedure to allow the outside world to
    'change the value of private data member
    miMyProperty = iVal
    '(do not use a Property Let when creating a
    'Read-Only Property)
End Property

Public Property Get MyProperty() As Integer
    'procedure to allow the outside world to
    'read the value of private data member
    MyProperty = miMyProperty
End Property
```

Otherwise, if the variable used to store a property value is public, its value can be modified arbitrarily by any application that accesses the class module containing the property.

See Also

Property Let Statement, Property Set Statement, "Implementing Properties" in Chapter 4

Property Let Statement

Named Arguments

No

Syntax

```
[Public | Private | Friend] [Static] Property Let name _
        ([arglist,] value)
    [statements]
    [Exit Property]
    [statements]
End Property
Public
```

Use: Optional

Type: Keyword

Gives the property scope through all procedures in all modules in the project. If used within a createable class module, the property procedure is also accessible from outside the project. Public, Private, and Friend are mutually exclusive.

```
Private
```

Use: Optional

Type: Keyword

Restricts the scope of the property to those procedures within the same module. Public, Private, and Friend are mutually exclusive.

Friend
> Use: Optional
>
> Type: Keyword
>
> Only valid within a class module; gives the property scope to all modules within a project, but not to modules outside the project. `Public`, `Private`, and `Friend` are mutually exclusive.

Static
> Use: Optional
>
> Type: Keyword
>
> Preserves the value of all private variables declared inside the property between calls to the property.

name
> Use: Required
>
> Type: Keyword
>
> The name of the property.

arglist
> Use: Required
>
> Data Type: Any
>
> A comma-delimited list of variables to be passed to the property as arguments from the calling procedure.

value
> Use: Required
>
> Type: Any
>
> The last (or only) argument in *arglist*, being a variable containing the value to be assigned to the property.

statements
> Use: Optional
>
> Program code to be executed within the property.

arglist uses the following syntax and parts:

```
[Optional] [ByVal | ByRef] [ParamArray] varname[( )] [As type] _
          [= defaultvalue]
```

Optional
> Use: Optional
>
> Type: Keyword
>
> An optional argument is one that need not be supplied when calling the property. However, all arguments following an optional one must also be optional. A `ParamArray` argument can't be optional.

ByVal
> Use: Optional
>
> Type: Keyword

The argument is passed by value; that is, a local copy of the variable is assigned the value of the argument.

ByRef

Use: Optional

Type: Keyword

The argument is passed by reference; that is, the local variable is simply a reference to the argument being passed. All changes made to the local variable are reflected in the calling argument when control returns to the calling procedure. ByRef is the default method of passing variables.

ParamArray

Use: Optional

Type: Keyword

Indicates that the argument is an optional array of variants containing an arbitrary number of elements. It can be used only as the last element of the argument list, and it can't be used with the ByRef, ByVal, or Optional keywords.

varname

Use: Required

Type: Any

The name of the local variable containing either the reference or value of the argument.

type

Use: Optional

The data type of the argument.

defaultvalue

Use: Optional

For optional arguments, you can specify a constant default value.

Description

Declares the name, arguments, and code for a procedure which assigns a value to a property.

Rules at a Glance

- A Property Let statement must contain at least one argument in *arglist*. If there is more than one argument, it's the last one that contains the value to be assigned to the property.

- The data type of the last argument in *arglist* must match both the private data member (at least, it should be defined as Private; see the "Programming Tips & Gotchas" section) that holds the property value and the return value of the corresponding Property Get procedure, if there is one.

- Property procedures are Public by default.

- In VBA applications, the Option Private Module statement restricts the scope of procedures defined as public to the project in which they were defined.

- The Friend keyword is only valid within class modules. Friend procedures are accessible to all procedures in all modules and classes within a project, but aren't listed in the type library for that project. Therefore, they can't be accessed from projects or applications outside the defining application.

- Properties and procedures defined using the Friend keyword can't be late bound.

- The Static keyword affects only variables declared within the Property Let procedure. If you don't use the Static keyword, the values of all local variables are lost between calls.

- Unlike other functions and procedures, the name of the Property Let procedure can be repeated within the same module as the name of the Property Get and Property Set procedures.

- The number and data types of the arguments passed to a Property Let statement must match the corresponding Property Get statement. For details, see the section "Rules at a Glance" in the entry for Property Get.

- If an Exit Property statement is executed, program flow continues with the statement following the call to the property. Any number of Exit Property statements can appear in a Property Let procedure.

Programming Tips & Gotchas

You should protect the values of properties by defining a Private variable to hold the internal property value and control the updating of the property by outside applications via Property Let and Property Get statements, as described in the "Programming Tips & Gotchas" section of the Property Get Statement.

See Also

Property Get Statement, Property Set Statement, the section "Implementing Properties" in Chapter 4

Property Set Statement

Named Arguments

No

Syntax

```
[Public | Private | Friend] [Static] Property Set name _
        ([arglist,] reference)
    [statements]
    [Exit Property]
    [statements]
End Property
```

Public

Use: Optional

Type: Keyword

Gives the property scope through all procedures in all modules in the project. If used within a createable class module, the function is also accessible from outside the project. `Public`, `Private`, and `Friend` are mutually exclusive.

Private

Use: Optional

Type: Keyword

Restricts the scope of the property to those procedures in the same module. `Public`, `Private`, and `Friend` are mutually exclusive.

Friend

Use: Optional

Type: Keyword

Only valid within a class module; gives the property scope to all modules within a project, but not to modules outside the project. `Public`, `Private`, and `Friend` are mutually exclusive.

Static

Use: Optional

Type: Keyword

Preserves the value of all private variables declared inside the property between calls to the property.

name

Use: Required

Type: Any

The name of the property.

arglist

Use: Required

A comma-delimited list of variables to be passed to the property as arguments from the calling procedure.

reference

Use: Required

Type: Object

The last (or only) argument in *arglist*, which is a variable containing the object reference to be assigned to the property.

statements

Use: Optional

Program code to be executed within the property.

arglist uses the following syntax and parts:

[Optional] [ByVal | ByRef] [ParamArray] *varname*[( )] _

        [As *type*] [= *defaultvalue*]

Optional

    Use: Optional

    Type: Keyword

    An optional argument is one that need not be supplied when calling the property. However, all arguments following an optional one must also be optional. A **ParamArray** argument can't be optional.

ByVal

    Use: Optional

    Type: Keyword

    The argument is passed by value; that is, a local copy of the variable is assigned the value of the argument.

ByRef

    Use: Optional

    Type: Keyword

    The argument is passed by reference; that is, the local variable is simply a reference to the argument being passed. All changes made to the local variable are reflected in the calling argument when control returns to the calling procedure. **ByRef** is the default method of passing variables.

ParamArray

    Use: Optional

    Type: Keyword

    Indicates that the argument is an optional array of variants containing an arbitrary number of elements. It can be used only as the last element of the argument list, and it can't be used with the **ByRef**, **ByVal**, or **Optional** keywords.

varname

    Use: Required

    Data Type: Any

    The name of the local variable containing either the reference or value of the argument.

type

    Use: Optional

    The data type of the argument.

defaultvalue

    Use: Optional

    For optional arguments, you can specify a constant default value.

Reference

Description

Declares the name, arguments, and code for a procedure that assigns an object reference to a property.

Rules at a Glance

- A Property Set statement must contain at least one argument in *arglist*. If there is more than one argument, it's the last one that contains the object reference to be assigned to the property.

- The data type of the last argument in *arglist* must match both the private data member used to hold the property value and the return value of the corresponding Property Get procedure, if there is one.

- Property procedures are Public by default.

- In VBA applications, the Option Private Module restricts the scope of procedures defined as public to the project in which they were defined.

- The Friend keyword is only valid within class modules. Friend procedures are accessible to all procedures in all modules and classes within a project, but they aren't listed in the type library for that project. Therefore, they can't be accessed from projects or applications outside the defining application.

- Properties and procedures defined using the Friend keyword can't be late bound.

- The Static keyword only affects private variables declared within the Property Set procedure. If you don't use the Static keyword, the values of local variables are lost between calls.

- Unlike other variables and procedures, the name of a Property Set procedure can be repeated within the same module as the name of a Property Get procedure.

- The number and data types of the arguments passed to a Property Set statement must match the corresponding Property Get statement. For example:

```
Public Property Set MyProperty(sVal As String, _
                               oVal As myObject)
    Set miMyProperty = oVal
End Property

Public Property Get MyProperty(sVal As String) As myObject
    Set MyProperty = miMyProperty
End Property
```

- If an Exit Property statement is executed, program execution immediately continues with the statement following the call to the property. Any number of Exit Property statements can appear in a Property Set procedure.

Programming Tips & Gotchas

You should protect the values of properties by defining a Private variable to hold the internal property value and control the updating of the property by outside applications via Property Let and Property Get statements, as described in the "Programming Tips & Gotchas" section of the entry for the **Property Get** statement.

See Also

Property Get Statement, Property Let Statement, the section "Implementing Properties" in Chapter 4

Public Statement

Named Arguments

No

Syntax

```
Public [WithEvents] varname[([subscripts])] _
    [As [New] type] [, [WithEvents] _
    varname[([subscripts])] [As [New] type]] . . .
```

WithEvents

Use: Optional

Type: Keyword

A keyword that denotes the object variable *varname* can respond to events triggered from within the object to which it refers.

varname

Use: Required

Data Type: Any

The name of the variable, which must follow Visual Basic naming conventions.

subscripts

Use: Optional

Denotes *varname* as an array and specifies the dimensions and number of elements of the array.

New

Use: Optional

Type: Keyword

Used to automatically create an instance of the object referred to by the object variable *varname*.

type

Use: Optional

Data type of the variable *varname*.

Description

Used at module level to declare a public variable and allocate the relevant storage space in memory. A **Public** variable has both project-level scope—that is, it can be used by all procedures in all modules in the project—and, when used in a class module, it can have scope outside the project.

Rules at a Glance

- The behavior of a Public variable depends on where it's declared, as the following table shows:

Variable Declared in...	Scope
Any procedure	Illegal; generates a compile-time error.
Code module declarations section	Variable is available to all modules within the project.
Class module declarations section	Variable is available as a property of the class to all modules within the project, and to all other projects referencing the class.
Form module declarations section	Variable is available as a property of the form to all modules within the project.

- In VBA applications, the Option Private Module statement restricts the scope of a public variable to the project in which it was defined.

- WithEvents is only valid when used to declare an object variable.

- There is no limit to the number of variables that can refer to the same object using the WithEvents keyword; they will all respond to that object's events.

- You can't create an array variable that uses the WithEvents keyword.

- The New keyword can't be used in the same object variable declaration as WithEvents.

- The *subscripts* argument has the following syntax:

```
[lowerbound To] upperbound [, _
    [lowerbound To] upperbound]
```

- Using the *subscripts* argument, you can declare up to 60 dimensions for the array.

- The *lowerbound* argument of the *subscripts* argument is optional; when not used, the lower bound of the array is specified by the Option Base statement. If Option Base isn't present, the lower bound of the array is zero.

- If the *subscripts* argument isn't used (i.e., the variable name is followed by empty parentheses), the array is declared as dynamic. You can change both the number of dimensions and number of elements of a dynamic array using the ReDim statement.

- The New keyword denotes that a new instance of the object is created when the first reference to the object is made. Use of the New keyword therefore negates the need to use the Set statement.

- You can't use the New keyword to declare any of the following: variables of any intrinsic data type (the New keyword is for use with object variables only), instances of dependent objects (a dependent object is one that can only be created from a method or property in another object; a dependent object isn't publicly createable), a variable that uses the WithEvents argument.

- If you don't use the New keyword with an object variable, you must use the Set statement to assign an existing object to the variable before you can use it.

- *type* may be Byte, Boolean, Currency, Date, Double, Integer, Long, Object, Single, String, Variant, a user-defined type, or an object type.

- If you don't specify *type*, and you haven't used a DefType statement, the variable is cast as a Variant.

- The following table shows the values held by each data type when a variable is first initialized:

Data Type	Initial Value
Numeric	0
Variable-length string	Zero-length string ("")
Fixed-length string	Filled with zeros
Variant	Empty
Object	Nothing
Date	Saturday 30 December 1899 12:00:00

- The individual elements of a user-defined type are initialized with the value corresponding to their data type.

- To declare a fixed-length string, use the syntax:

```
As String * stringlength
```

where *stringlength* is the number of characters to allocate to the string.

- You can't use the Public statement to declare a fixed-length string variable in a class module.

Programming Tips & Gotchas

- Instead of declaring a variable as Public within either a form or class module, you should create Property Let and Property Get sub procedures that assign and retrieve the value of a private variable, respectively.

- In VBA applications, WithEvents is valid only in class modules; however, standalone versions of VB allow the use of WithEvents all object modules.

- A new type of scope has been introduced in Visual Basic 5.0. The Friend scope is halfway between Public and Private. It's useful in situations where Private is too restricting, and Public is too open. For more information, refer to the Friend statement.

- You should note that when you use the New keyword, the Initialize event of the object is fired on the first reference to the object, not when the object variable is declared.

- It's good programming practice to always use Option Explicit at the beginning of a module to prevent misnamed variables causing hard-to-find errors.

- You may have occasion to maintain legacy Visual Basic code written prior to Version 4, when the Private and Public statements came into the language. In this case, those variables declared in the Declarations section at the start of a code or form module that carry the prefix keyword Global are similar to Public variables.

See Also

Friend Statement, Option Private Module Statement, Private Statement, ReDim Statement, Set Statement

---

Put Statement

Named Arguments

No

Syntax

```
Put [#] filenumber, [recnumber], varname
filenumber
```
    Use: Required

    Data Type: Integer

    Any valid file number.

```
recnumber
```
    Use: Optional

    Data Type: Variant (Long)

    Record or byte number to begin the write operation.

```
varname
```
    Use: Required

    The name of the variable containing the data to be written to the file.

Description

Writes data from a program variable to a disk file.

Rules at a Glance

- If *filenumber* is opened in random access mode, *recnumber* refers to the record number; if the file is opened in binary access mode, *recnumber* refers to a byte number.

- Both bytes and records in a file are numbered from 1 upward.

- If *recnumber* is omitted, the next byte or record to be written is placed at the position immediately after the position pointed to by the last Get or Put statement, or by the last *Seek* function. To omit *recnumber*, you must use the delimiting commas, as the following statement shows:

```
Put #1,,myVar
```

- If you have opened the file in random mode, it's important to ensure that the record length specified in the Len clause of the Open statement matches the actual length of the data being written. If the length of the data being written is less than that specified by the Len clause, the space up to the end of the record is padded with the current contents of the file buffer—whatever that may be. If, on the other hand, the actual data length is more than that specified, an error occurs.

- Certain data types complicate determining the actual data length of a record. These data types need a secondary data element called a *descriptor* to inform VB of either their underlying data type or their physical length. The following table details the descriptors used in VB:

Variable Data Type	Descriptor
Variable-length string	2 bytes containing length of string
Variant (numeric)	2 bytes identifying V*arType*
Variant (string)	2 bytes containing length + 2 bytes identifying vartype
Dynamic array	2 + (8 × number of dimensions)
Any other data types	No descriptor
User-defined type	Each element treated the same as the individual data type

- If the file was opened in random access mode, you can use the Put statement to write a variant array to disk.
- The Put statement can't write objects to disk.
- If you open the file in binary mode, the Len clause has no effect. When you use Put to write data to the disk, the data is written contiguously, and no padding is placed between records.
- When you write arrays to disk using the Put statement with a file opened in binary mode, only arrays contained within a user-defined type have the array descriptor added; all other arrays are written to disk without the descriptor. Individual array elements, however, may have descriptors, depending on their data types.
- Similarly, variable-length strings written to a file opened in binary mode are written without the two-byte descriptor.

Programming Tips & Gotchas

Because of the structured format of data written with the Put statement, it's customary to read the data back from the file using the Get statement.

See Also

Get Statement

PV Function

Named Arguments

Yes

Syntax

```
PV(rate, nper, pmt[, fv [, due]])
```

rate
>   Use: Required
>
>   Data Type: Double
>
>   The interest rate per period.

nper
>   Use: Required
>
>   Data Type: Integer
>
>   The number of payment periods in the annuity.

pmt
>   Use: Required
>
>   Data Type: Double
>
>   The payment made in each period.

fv
>   Use: Optional
>
>   Data Type: Variant
>
>   The future value of the loan or annuity.

type
>   Use: Optional
>
>   Data Type: Variant
>
>   Flag specifying whether payments are due at the start or the end of the period.

Return Value

A Double specifying the present value of an annuity.

Description

Calculates the present value of an annuity (either an investment or loan) based on a regular number of future payments of a fixed value and a fixed interest rate. The *present value* is the current value of a future stream of equal cash flows discounted at some fixed interest rate.

Rules at a Glance

- The time units used for the number of payment periods, the rate of interest, and the payment amount must be the same. In other words, if you state the payment period in months, you must also express the interest rate as a monthly rate and the amount paid per month.

- The rate per period is stated as a fraction of 100. For example, 10% is stated as .10. If you are calculating using monthly periods, you must also divide the rate per period by 12. Therefore, 10% per annum, for example, equates to a rate per period of .00833.

- The *fv* argument indicates the future value or cash balance after the last payment. The default is 0, since that reflects the value of a loan after the final payment.

- Payments made against a loan or added to the value of savings are expressed as negative numbers.

- The *due* argument states whether the payment is made at the start of a period (1) or at the end (0, which is the default value).

Programming Tips & Gotchas

Make sure that *nper*, *rate*, and *pmt* are all reflect values for an identical time period. For example, if *pmt* represents a monthly payment, *rate* should represent the monthly interest rate, rather than an annual interest rate.

See Also

FV Function

QBColor Function

Named Arguments

No

Syntax

```
QBColor(color)
color
```
> Use: Required
>
> Data Type: Integer
>
> A whole number between 0–15.

Return Value

A Long integer.

Description

Returns a long integer representing the RGB system color code.

Rules at a Glance

color has the following settings:

Number	Color
0	Black
1	Blue
2	Green
3	Cyan
4	Red
5	Magenta
6	Yellow
7	White
8	Gray
9	Light Blue

Reference

Number	Color
10	Light Green
11	Light Cyan
12	Light Red
13	Light Magenta
14	Light Yellow
15	Bright White

Programming Tips & Gotchas

- The *RGB* function allows much more flexibility than the older *QBColor* function, which is a remnant of QBasic.

- Visual Basic now contains a wide range of intrinsic color constants that can assign colors directly to color properties of objects.

See Also

RGB Function

RaiseEvent Statement

Named Arguments

No

Syntax

```
RaiseEvent eventName [arglist]
eventName
```

> Use: Required
>
> Data Type: String
>
> The name of the event.

```
arglist
```

> Use: Optional
>
> Data Type: Any (defined by the Event statement)
>
> A comma-delimited list of variables.

Description

Generates a predefined custom event within any procedure of an object module.

Rules at a Glance

- *eventName* must already be defined in the Declarations section of the module using the Event statement.

- *arglist* must match the number and data type of parameters defined in the Event statement.

- The RaiseEvent and Event statements can be used only in object modules—i.e., in form and class modules—and not in code modules.

Example

The following snippet demonstrates how you can use an event to communicate a status message back to the client application, and at the same time use a **ByRef** argument to trap a user response in the client application. This gets around the fact that events can't return values. To take advantage of this functionality, the client must declare a reference to this class using the **WithEvents** keyword.

```
Public Event Status(Message As String, _
                    ByRef Cancel As Boolean)

Private Function UpdateRecords(iVal As Integer) as Boolean
    Dim blnCancel As Boolean
    ...
    If iVal > 1000 Then
        RaiseEvent Status "Is value too high?", blnCancel
        If blnCancel Then
            Exit Function
        End If
    End If
    ...
End Function
```

Programming Tips & Gotchas

- To allow the client application to handle the event being fired, the object variable must be declared using the **WithEvents** keyword.

- VB custom events don't return a value; however, you can use a **ByRef** argument in *arglist* to simulate a return value, as shown in the above example.

- **RaiseEvent** is *not* asynchronous. In other words, when you call the **RaiseEvent** statement in your class code, your class code won't continue executing until the event has been either handled by the client or ignored (if the client isn't handling the events raised by the class). This can have undesirable side effects, and you should bear in mind when planning your application. For example, you may have a recordset open or a transaction pending and have to wait for the user to respond to a message dialog at the client. This could easily turn into a bottleneck adversely affecting the scalability of your application.

- Events can't be raised from within a Microsoft Transaction Server context.

- For more information about implementing your own custom events, see the section "Implementing Custom Events," in Chapter 4.

See Also

Event Statement, WithEvents Keyword

Randomize Statement

Named Arguments

No

Syntax

```
Randomize [number]
number
```

Use: Optional

Data Type: Variant

Any valid numeric expression.

Description

Initializes the random number generator.

Rules at a Glance

- **Randomize** uses *number* as a new seed value to initialize the random number generator used by the *Rnd* function. The seed value is an initial value that generates a sequence of pseudo-random numbers.

- If you don't pass *number* to the **Randomize** statement, the value of the system timer is used as the new seed value.

- Repeatedly passing the same number to **Randomize** doesn't cause *Rnd* to repeat the same sequence of random numbers.

Programming Tips & Gotchas

If you need to repeat a sequence of random numbers, you should call the *Rnd* function with a negative number as an argument immediately prior to using **Randomize** with any numeric argument.

See Also

Rnd Function

Rate Function

Named Arguments

Yes

Syntax

```
Rate(nper, pmt, pv[, fv[, due[, guess]]])
nper
```

Use: Required

Data Type: Double

The total number of periods in the annuity.

```
pmt
```

Use: Required

Data Type: Double

The payment amount per period.

```
pv
```

Use: Required

Data Type: Double

The present value of the payments or future receipts.

fv

Use: Optional

Data Type: Variant

The future value or cash balance after the final payment. If omitted, its value defaults to 0.

due

Use: Optional

Data Type: Variant

A flag indicating whether payments are due at the beginning of the payment period (a value of 0, the default) or at the end of the payment period (a value of 1).

guess

Use: Optional

Data Type: Double

An estimate of the value to be returned by the function. If omitted, its value defaults to .1 (10%).

Return Value

A Double representing the interest rate per period.

Description

Calculates the interest rate for an annuity (a loan or an investment) that consists of fixed payments over a known duration.

Rules at a Glance

- For *pv* and *fv*, cash paid out is expressed as a negative number; cash received is expressed as a positive number.

- The function works using iteration. Starting with *guess*, *Rate* cycles through the calculation until the result is accurate to within 0.00001 percent. If a result can't be found after 20 tries, the function fails.

Programming Tips & Gotchas

- In the case of a loan, *pv* is the loan amount. In the case of an investment, *pv* is the beginning balance.

- In the case of a loan, *fv* is typically 0, reflecting that the entire loan has been paid. In the case of an investment, *fv* is the value of the investment with interest at the end of the investment period.

- If the function fails because it couldn't calculate an accurate interest rate in 20 iterations, try a different value for *guess*.

- The value returned by the function rate is the interest rate for the same time period as payments were made. Typically, this is one month, in which case you must multiply by 12 to derive the annual percentage rate.

Reference

See Also

IPmt Function, NPer Function, Pmt Function, PPmt Function

ReDim Statement

Named Arguments

No

Syntax

```
ReDim [Preserve] varname(subscripts) [As type] _
                 [, varname(subscripts) [As type]] . . .
```

Preserve

Use: Optional

Type: Keyword

Preserves the data within an array when changing the only or last dimension.

varname

Use: Required

Data Type: Any

Name of the variable.

subscripts

Use: Required

Number of elements and dimensions of the array, using the syntax:

```
[lower To] upper [, [lower To] upper] . . .
```

type

Use: Optional

Data type of the array.

Description

Used within a procedure to resize and reallocate storage space for a dynamic array.

Rules at a Glance

- A dynamic array is created using a `Private`, `Public`, or `Dim` statement with empty parentheses. Only dynamic arrays created in this manner can be resized using the `ReDim` statement. There is no limit to the number of times you can redimension a dynamic array.

- Use of the `Preserve` keyword allows you to retain the current values within the array, but it also places several limitations on how the `Redim` statement can be used:

  - The data subtype of elements of an array held within a variant can't be changed.

  - Only the last dimension of an array can be resized.

- The number of dimensions can't be changed.
- Only the upper bound of the array can be changed.

- If you reduce either the number of elements of the array or the number of dimensions in the array, data in the removed elements is permanently lost, irrespective of the use of the **Preserve** keyword.

- If the *lower* argument isn't used within the *subscripts* syntax, the lower bound of the dimension is determined by the **Option Base** statement. If **Option Base** isn't used, the lower bound defaults to zero.

- *type* may be Byte, Boolean, Currency, Date, Double, Integer, Long, Object, Single, String, Variant, a user-defined type, or an object type.

- When the array is held within a variant, *type* refers to the underlying data subtype of the elements.

- The following table shows the values held by each data type when an array is initialized.

Data Type	Initial Value
Numeric	0
Variable-length string	Zero-length string ("")
Fixed-length string	Filled with zeros
Variant	Empty
Object	Nothing
Date	Saturday 30 December 1899 12:00:00

Programming Tips & Gotchas

- Microsoft's documentation for ReDim states that if the array has been passed by reference to a procedure, you can't redimension it within the procedure and return the modified array to the calling procedure. This doesn't appear to be the case, as the following example shows:

```
Private Sub Command1_Click()

    Dim strArray() As String
    Dim strElement As String
    Dim intCtr As Integer

    ReDim strArray(9)

    For intCtr = 0 To UBound(strArray)
        strArray(intCtr) = "Original element"
    Next

    Call ExpandArray(strArray)

    For intCtr = 0 To UBound(strArray)
        Debug.Print strArray(intCtr)
    Next
```

```
    End Sub

    Private Sub ExpandArray(ByRef arrDynamic() As String)

        Dim intBound As Integer, intCtr As Integer

        intBound = UBound(arrDynamic)

        ReDim Preserve arrDynamic(UBound(arrDynamic) * 2)

        For intCtr = intBound + 1 To UBound(arrDynamic)
            arrDynamic(intCtr) = "New element"
        Next

    End Sub
```

When you run this example, both the original elements and new elements are printed to the immediate window, proving that in fact the array was success-fully expanded in the *ExpandArray* procedure.

- It's possible to create a new dynamic array within a procedure using the ReDim statement if the array to which it refers doesn't already exist at either module or level. Typically, this results from an error of omission; the pro-grammer forgets to explicitly define the array using Dim, Public, or Pri-vate. Since this method of creating an array can cause conflicts if a variable or array of the same name is subsequently defined explicitly, ReDim should be used only to redimension an existing array, not to define a new one.

- An array contained within a variant can only be resized if the variable has been explicitly declared as a variant.

See Also

Dim Statement, Private Statement, Public Statement

Rem Statement

Syntax

```
Rem comment
' comment
comment
```

> Use: Optional

> A textual comment to place within the code.

Description

Use the Rem statement or an apostrophe (') to place remarks within the code.

Rules at a Glance

- Text or code commented out using either the Rem statement or an apostro-phe isn't compiled into the final program and therefore doesn't add to the size of the executable.

- If you use the Rem statement on the same line as program code, a colon is required after the program code and before the Rem statement. For example:

```
Set objDoc = MyApp.MyObj : Rem Define the object
                           Rem reference
```

This isn't necessary when using the now more common apostrophe:

```
Set objDoc = MyApp.MyObj    ' Define the object reference
```

- Apostrophes held within quotation marks aren't treated as comment markers, as this code snippet shows:

```
myVar = "'Something'"
```

Programming Tips & Gotchas

- The VB and VBA development environments contain block comment and block uncomment buttons on the Edit toolbar, which allow you to comment out or uncomment a selection of many rows of code at once.

- You can also use the line continuation character (_) with comments, as this snippet shows:

```
'this is _
a comment _
on more than one line
```

Replace Function (VB6)

Named Arguments

No

Syntax

```
Replace(string, stringToReplace, replacementString [, _
        start[, count[, compare]]])
```

string
    Use: Required

    Data Type: String

    The complete string containing the substring to be replaced.

stringToReplace
    Use: Required

    Data Type: String

    The substring to be found by the function.

replacementString
    Use: Required

    Data Type: String

    The new substring to replace *stringToReplace* in *string*.

start
    Use: Optional

Data Type: Long

The character position in *string* at which the search for *stringToReplace* begins.

count

Use: Optional

Data Type: Long

The number of instances of *stringToReplace* to replace.

compare

Use: Optional

Data Type: VbCompareMethod constant

The method that compares *stringToReplace* with *string*; its value can be vbBinaryCompare, vbTextCompare, or vbDatabaseCompare.

Return Value

The return value from *Replace* depends on the parameters you specify in the argument list, as the following table shows:

If	Return Value
string = ""	Zero-length string ("")
string is Null	An error
StringToReplace = ""	Copy of *string*
replacementString = ""	Copy of *string* with all instances of *stringToReplace* removed
start > Len(*string*)	Zero-length string ("")
count = 0	Copy of *string*

Description

Replaces a given number of instances of a specified substring in another string.

Rules at a Glance

- If *start* is omitted, the search begins at the start of the string.

- If *count* is omitted, all instances of the substring after *start* are replaced.

- vbBinaryCompare is case sensitive; that is, *Replace* matches both character and case, whereas vbTextCompare is case insensitive, matching only character, regardless of case.

- The default value for *compare* is vbBinaryCompare.

- *start* not only specifies where the search for *stringToReplace* begins, but also where the new string returned by the *Replace* function commences.

Programming Tips & Gotchas

- If *count* isn't used, be careful when replacing short strings that may form parts of unrelated words. For example, consider the following:

```
Dim sString
sString = "You have to be careful when you do this " _
          & "or you could ruin your string"
Debug.Print Replace(sString, "you", "we")
```

Because we don't specify a value for count, the call to *Replace* replaces every occurrence of "you" in the original string with "we." But the fourth occurrence of "you" is part of the word "your," which is modified to become "wer."

- You must also be aware that if *start* is greater than 1, the returned string starts at that character, and not at the first character of the original string, as you might expect. For example, given the statements:

```
sOld = "This string checks the Replace function"
sNew = Replace(sOld, "check", "test", 5, _
          vbTextCompare)
```

sNew will contain the value

```
"string tests the Replace function"
```

- You can use the *Mid* function on the left side of an argument to replace a part of string, but to replace more than one instance of a substring requires a complicated Do While loop that constantly checks for the position of any remaining instances of the substring to be replaced.

See Also

Mid Function

Reset Statement

Syntax

```
Reset
```

Description

Closes all currently open files.

Rules at a Glance

- Reset only closes those files that were opened using the Open statement.
- The contents of any current file buffers are written to disk by the Reset statement immediately prior to Reset, thereby closing the respective files.

Programming Tips & Gotchas

The Reset statement should be used only as a last resort to clean up if your program is terminating abnormally. Normally, you should write code to close each open file using the Close statement.

See Also

Close Statement, Open Statement

Reference

Resume Statement

Syntax

```
Resume
Resume Next
Resume label
```

Description

Used to continue program execution when an error-handling routine is complete.

Rules at a Glance

Statement	Description
Resume	• If the error-handling routine is in the same procedure as the statement that caused the error, program execution continues with the statement that caused the error.
	• If the error occurred in an external procedure called by the procedure containing the error handler, program execution continues with the statement in the procedure containing the error handler that last called the external procedure.
Resume Next	• If the error-handling routine is in the same procedure as the statement that caused the error, program execution continues with the statement following the statement that caused the error.
	• If the error occurred in an external procedure called by the procedure containing the error handler, program execution continues with the statement in the procedure containing the error handler immediately following the statement that last called the external procedure.
Resume label	• label must be in the same procedure as the error handler.
	• Program execution continues at the specified label.

Programming Tips & Gotchas

*   You can only use the Resume statement in an error-handling routine; otherwise, a runtime error is generated.

*   An error-handling routine doesn't necessarily have to contain a Resume statement. If the error-handling routine is at the end of the procedure, and the result of the error handling would be to exit the procedure, you can simply allow the program to execute the End Sub or End Function statement. This has the effect of both resetting the Err object and exiting the procedure. This is shown in the following simple snippet:

```
Private Sub DoSomething()

    On Error GoTo DoSomething_Err
    ...
DoSomething_Err:
    MsgBox Err.Description
```

```
     End Sub
```

See Also

On Error Statement

Return Statement

Syntax

```
GoSub label
...
label

Return
label
```
Use: Required

A subroutine label within a procedure.

Description

Branches back to a calling GoSub statement after executing a subroutine within a procedure.

Rules at a Glance

* A subroutine can include an number of Return statements.

* Return branches back to the statement immediately following the last executed GoSub statement in the current subroutine.

* A GoSub statement and the subroutine it calls must reside within the same procedure.

Programming Tips & Gotchas

The Return statement is only included in this book for completeness, should you have to maintain legacy code; otherwise, you shouldn't be writing new code using the GoSub...Return statements, since it tends to create "spaghetti" code that is very difficult to read and to maintain. Code should be rewritten using separate procedures.

See Also

GoSub Statement

RGB Function

Named Arguments

Yes

Syntax

```
RGB(red, green, blue)
red
```
Use: Required

Data Type: Variant (Integer)

A number between 0 and 255, inclusive.

green
   Use: Required

Data Type: Variant (Integer)

A number between 0 and 255, inclusive.

blue
   Use: Required

Data type: Variant (Integer)

A number between 0 and 255, inclusive.

Return Value

A long integer representing the RGB color value.

Description

Returns a system color code that can be assigned to object color properties.

Rules at a Glance

* The RGB color value represents the relative intensity of the red, green, and blue components of a pixel that produces a specific color on the display.

* The RGB function assumes any argument greater than 255 is 255.

* The following table demonstrates how the individual color values combine to create certain colors:

Color	Red	Green	Blue
Black	0	0	0
Blue	0	0	255
Green	0	255	0
Red	255	0	0
White	255	255	255

Programming Tips & Gotchas

* The RGB value is derived with the following formula:

```
RGB = red + (green * 256) + (blue * 65536)
```

In other words, the individual color components are stored in the opposite order one would expect. VB stores the red color component in the low-order byte of the long integer's low-order word, the green color in the high-order byte of the low-order word, and the blue color in the low-order byte of the high-order word.

* Visual Basic now contains a wide range of intrinsic color constants that can assign color values directly to color properties of objects.

See Also

QBColor Function

Right, Right$, RightB, RightB$ Functions

Named Arguments

Yes

Syntax

```
Right(string, length)
```
string

> Use: Required

> Data Type: String

> The string to be processed.

length

> Use: Required

> Data Type: Variant (Long)

> The number of characters to return from the right of the string.

Return Value

A string or variant of subtype String.

Description

Returns a string containing the rightmost *length* characters of *string*.

Rules at a Glance

- If *length* is 0, a zero-length string ("") is returned.

- If *length* is greater than the length of *string*, *string* is returned.

- If *length* is less than zero or is Null, an error is generated.

- If *string* contains a Null, *Right* returns Null.

Example

The following function assumes it's passed either a filename or a complete path and filename, and returns the filename from the end of the string:

```
Private Function ParseFileName(strFullPath As String)

Dim lngPos As Long, lngStart As Long
Dim strFilename As String

lngStart = 1
Do
    lngPos = InStr(lngStart, strFullPath, "\")
    If lngPos = 0 Then
        strFilename = Right(strFullPath, Len(strFullPath) -
lngStart + 1)
```

```
        Else
            lngStart = lngPos + 1
        End If
    Loop While lngPos > 0

    ParseFileName = strFilename

End Function
```

Programming Tips & Gotchas

* Use the *Len* function to determine the total length of **string**.

* When you use the *RightB* function with byte data, `length` specifies the number of bytes to return.

See Also

Len Function, Left Function

RmDir Statement

Named Arguments

No

Syntax

```
RmDir path
path
```

> Use: Required
>
> Data Type: String
>
> The path of the folder to be removed.

Description

Removes a folder.

Rules at a Glance

* You may include a drive letter in `path`; if you don't specify a drive letter, the folder is assumed to be on the current drive.

* If the folder contains files or other folders, `RmDir` will generate runtime error 75, "Path/File access error."

Example

The following subroutine deletes all the files in a folder and removes its subfolders. If those contain files or folders, it deletes those too by calling itself recursively until all child folders and their files are removed.

```
Private Sub RemoveFolder(ByVal strFolder As String)

Static blnLowerLevel As Boolean    ' A recursive call - no
                                   '    need to prompt user
Dim blnRepeated As Boolean   ' Use Dir state info on
```

```
                                    ' repeated calls
    Dim strFile As String        ' File/Directory contained in
                                 ' strFolder


    ' Delete all files
    Do
        strFile = Dir(strFolder & "\*.*", _
                      vbNormal Or vbHidden Or vbSystem)
        If strFile <> "" Then
            If Not blnLowerLevel Then
                If MsgBox("Delete files in directory " & _
                          strFolder & "?", _
                          vbQuestion Or vbOKCancel, _
                          "Confirm File Deletion") _
                          = vbCancel Then Exit Sub
            End If
            strFile = strFolder & "\" & strFile
            Kill strFile
        End If
    Loop While strFile <> ""
    ' Delete all directories
    Do
        If Not blnRepeated Then
            strFile = Dir(strFolder & "\*.*", vbDirectory)
            blnRepeated = True
        Else
            strFile = Dir(, vbDirectory)
        End If
        If strFile <> "" And _
            strFile <> "." And strFile <> ".." Then
            If Not blnLowerLevel Then
                blnLowerLevel = True
                If MsgBox("Delete subdirectories of " & _
                          strFolder & "?", _
                          vbQuestion Or vbOKCancel, _
                          "Confirm Directory Deletion") _
                          = vbCancel Then Exit Sub
            End If
            RemoveFolder strFolder & "\" & strFile
            blnRepeated = False
        End If
    Loop While strFile <> ""

    RmDir strFolder

End Sub
```

Programming Tips & Gotchas

- Use the Kill statement to delete any remaining files from the folder prior to removing the folder.

- To remove folders, you can call the *Dir* function recursively to navigate downward into a folder's subfolders. Note that because it saves state information between invocations, the documentation incorrectly indicates that the *Dir* function can't be called recursively. The previous example indicates how this might be done.

- The effects of using Kill and RmDir are irreversible, since these statements don't move deleted files to the Recycle Bin.

- Visual Basic Version 6 introduces the File System object model, which contains Folders and Folder objects and gives much greater control and flexibility that the intrinsic MkDir and RmDir statements. Removing a folder using the FileSystemObject.DeleteFolder method is similar to deleting a folder using the Windows Explorer: i.e., all files, subfolders, and their contents are removed.

See Also

MkDir Statement, ChDir Statement, Kill Statement, File System Object Method

---

Rnd Function

Named Arguments

No

Syntax

```
Rnd[(seed)]
```
seed
>   Use: Optional
>
>   Data Type: Single
>
>   Any valid numeric expression.

Return Value

A Single data type random number.

Description

Returns a random number.

Rules at a Glance

- The behavior of the *Rnd* function is determined by *seed*, as described in this table:

number	Rnd Generates...
< 0	The same number each time, using *seed* as the seed number
> 0	The next random number in the current sequence
0	The most recently generated number
Not supplied	The next random number in the current sequence

- The *Rnd* function always returns a value between 0 and 1.

- If number isn't supplied, the *Rnd* function uses the last number generated as the seed for the next generated number. This means that given an initial seed

---

(*seed*), the same sequence is generated if number isn't supplied on subsequent calls.

Example

The following example uses the `Randomize` statement along with the *Rnd* function to fill 100 cells of an Excel worksheet with random numbers.

```
Public Sub GenerateRandomNumbers()

Dim objSheet As Worksheet
Dim intRow As Integer, intCol As Integer

Set objSheet = Application.ActiveWorkbook.ActiveSheet
Randomize
' Set the color of the input text to blue
objSheet.Cells.Font.ColorIndex = 5
' Loop through first 10 rows & columns,
' filling them with random numbers
For intRow = 1 To 10
    For intCol = 1 To 10
        objSheet.Cells(intRow, intCol).Value = Rnd
    Next
Next
' Resize columns to accommodate random numbers
objSheet.Columns("A:C").AutoFit
Set objSheet = Nothing

End Sub
```

Programming Tips & Gotchas

- Before calling the *Rnd* function, you should use the `Randomize` statement to initialize the random number generator.

- The standard formula for producing numbers in a given range is as follows:

```
Int((highest - lowest + 1) * Rnd + lowest)
```

where *lowest* is the lowest required number in the range, and *highest* is the highest.

See Also

Randomize Statement

Round Function (VB6)

Syntax

```
Round(expression[, numdecimalplaces])
expression
```
    Use: Required

    Data Type: Numeric Expression

    Any numeric expression.

> *numdecimalplaces*
>> Use: Optional
>>
>> Data Type: Long
>>
>> The number of places to include after the decimal point.

Return Value

The same data type as *expression*.

Description

Rounds a given number to a specified number of decimal places.

Rules at a Glance

- *numdecimalplaces* can be any whole number between 0 and 16.

- *Round* follows standard rules for rounding. That is, if the digit in the position to the right of *numdecimalplaces* is 6 or greater, the digit in the *numdecimalplaces* position is incremented by 1; if 5, it becomes the nearest even number; otherwise, the digits to the right of *numdecimalplaces* are dropped.

Programming Tips & Gotchas

- *Round* with a *numdecimalplaces* set to 2 is equivalent to Format (*expression*, "#.##").

- If *expression* is a string representation of a numeric value, *Round* converts it to a numeric value before rounding. However, if *expression* isn't a string representation of a number, *Round* generates runtime error 13, "Type mismatch." The *IsNumeric* function insures that *expression* is a proper numeric representation before calling *Round*.

- If *expression* contains fewer decimal places than *numdecimalplaces*, *Round* doesn't pad the return value with trailing zeros.

See Also

Fix Function, Int Function

RSet Statement

Syntax

```
RSet stringvar = string
```
stringvar
> Use: Required
>
> Data Type: String
>
> The name of a string variable to receive *string*.

string
> Use: Required
>
> Data Type: String
>
> A string expression to be copied into *stringvar*.

Description

Copies *string* into *stringvar*, right-aligning *string* within *stringvar*.

Rules at a Glance

- *RSet* has meaning only when dealing within fixed-length strings.

- If the length of *string* is less than that of *stringvar*, the extra characters within *stringvar* are padded with spaces.

- If the length of *string* is greater than that of *stringvar*, *string* is truncated to the length of *stringvar*.

Programming Tips & Gotchas

- *RSet* can't be used with user-defined types.

- *RSet* overwrites the entire contents of *stringvar*. The last `len(string)` characters are overwritten by the value of *string*, while the remaining characters are replaced with spaces.

See Also

LSet Statement

RTrim, RTrim$ Functions

Named Arguments

No

Syntax

```
RTrim(stringexp)
stringexp
```
   Use: Required

   Data Type: String

   A valid string expression.

Return Value

RTrim returns a variant of subtype String; *RTrim$* returns a string.

Description

Remove any trailing spaces from *stringexp*.

Rules at a Glance

- If *stringexp* contains a Null, *RTrim* returns Null.

- *RTrim* returns a variant of subtype String.

- *RTrim$* returns a String data type.

Programming Tips & Gotchas

Unless you need to keep leading spaces, you should use the *Trim* function, which is the equivalent of `RTrim(LTrim(`*string*`))`, thereby clearing both leading and trailing spaces in a single function call.

See Also

LTrim Function, Trim Function

SaveSetting Statement

Named Arguments

Yes

Syntax

```
SaveSetting appname, section, key, setting
```
appname
> Use: Required
>
> Data Type: String
>
> The name of the application.

section
> Use: Required
>
> Data Type: String
>
> The name of the registry key.

key
> Use: Required
>
> Data Type: String
>
> The name of the value entry whose value is to be saved.

setting
> Use: Required
>
> Data Type: String or numeric
>
> The value to save.

Description

Creates or saves an entry for a VB application in the Windows registry.

Rules at a Glance

- If either the *appname* or *section* subkeys isn't found in the registry, it's automatically created.

- The function writes a value to a subkey of the `KEY_CURRENT_USER\Software\VB and VBA Program Settings` key of the registry.

- *section* need not be an immediate subkey of *appname*; instead, *section* can be a fully qualified path to a nested subkey, with each subkey separated from its parent by a backslash. For example, a value of `Settings\Coordi-`

nates for the *section* argument indicates that the value is to be retrieved from `HKEY_CURRENT_USER\Software\VB` and `VBA Program Settings\ appname\Settings\Coordinates`.

- Visual Basic writes *setting* to the registry as a string (`REG_SZ`) value. If *setting* isn't a string, VB attempts to coerce it into a string in order to write it.

- If the setting can't be saved, a runtime error is generated.

Programming Tips & Gotchas

- Use the App object's EXEName property to pass your application's name to the *GetSetting* function.

- The built-in registry manipulation functions allow you to create professional 32-bit applications that use the registry for holding application-specific data, in the same way *.INI* files were used in the 16-bit environment. You can, for example, store information about the user's desktop settings (i.e., the size and position of forms, for example) the last time the program was run.

- Since it writes to the current user's registry key, `SaveSetting` should be used exclusively for storing user settings; it shouldn't store nonuser information (i.e., hardware information, system-level information, or application information that is independent of the user).

- *GetSetting*, *GetAllSettings*, and *SaveSetting* allow you direct access to only a limited section of the windows registry, that being a special branch created for your application (`HKEY_CURRENT_USER\Software\VB` and `VBA Program Settings\yourappname`). You can't access or change other registry settings without resorting to the Windows API.

- *SaveSetting* doesn't allow you to write to the default value of a registry key. Attempting to do so produces runtime error 5, "Invalid procedure call or argument." This isn't as great a limitation as it may appear, since *GetSetting* also can't retrieve a default value from a registry key.

- It may seem obvious but has been often overlooked: if a user hasn't run the application before, and your application's initialization doesn't set up the registry structure for the application, the key values won't be there.

- The above point is particularly apt when running your application on Windows NT and Windows 95 in a multiuser environment, since Microsoft chose to use the `HKEY_CURRENT_USER` branch of the registry to store entries for VB and VBA applications. This means that your application can be running swimmingly for one user, but when another user logs onto the machine, the registry settings aren't available.

See Also

DeleteSetting Statement, GetSetting Function, GetAllSettings Function

---

Second Function

Named Arguments

No

Syntax

```
Second(time)
time
```
> Use: Required
>
> Data Type: Variant
>
> Any valid expression that can represent a time value.

Return Value

A Variant of subtype Integer in the range 0 to 59.

Description

Extracts the seconds from a given time expression.

Rules at a Glance

If the time expression time is **Null**, the *Second* function returns **Null**.

See Also

> Hour Function, Minute Function

Seek Function

Named Arguments

No

Syntax

```
Seek(filenumber)
filenumber
```
> Use: Required
>
> Data Type: Integer
>
> Any valid file number.

Return Value

A Long integer indicating the current read/write position.

Description

Returns the current position of the read and write marker in the open file `filenumber`.

Rules at a Glance

* The *Seek* function returns a whole number in the range 1 to 2,147,483,647.
* If `filenumber` was opened in random mode, the number returned by the *Seek* function refers to the next record to be written or read.
* In all other file open modes (append, binary, input, and output), the number returned by the *Seek* function is the byte position at which the next read or write operation occurs.

See Also

Get Statement, Open Statement, Print# Statement, Put Statement, Write# Statement

---

Seek Statement

Syntax

```
Seek [#]filenumber, position
```
filenumber
Use: Required

Data Type: Integer

Any valid file number.

position
Use: Required

Data Type: Long Integer

Any whole number between 1 and 2,147,483,647.

Description

Places the read/write marker at a given position where the next read/write operation should occur.

Rules at a Glance

- If the file has been opened in random mode, *position* refers to the next record number that should be read or written.

- In all other file open modes (append, binary, input, and output), *position* is the byte where the next read or write operation will start.

- The use of a record number in any subsequent Get or Put statement overrides the position set by the Seek method.

- The size of a file can be increased as the result of a write operation that is performed after a Seek statement in which *position* is beyond the end of the file.

- If *position* is 0 or negative, a runtime error is generated.

Programming Tips & Gotchas

Unused records in a random access data file aren't necessarily blank. For example, if you open a brand new data file, then perform a seek operation to record 10 and write a new record, the preceding nine records are filled with binary data that was present on the section of the disk used by the new file prior to its creation.

See Also

Get Statement, Open Statement, Print# Statement, Put Statement, Write# Statement

Select Case Statement

Syntax

```
Select Case testexpression
   [Case expressionlist-n
       [statements-n]] ...
   [Case Else
       [elsestatements]]
End Select
```

testexpression

> Use: Required
>
> Data Type: Any
>
> Any numeric or string expression whose value determines which block of code is executed.

expressionlist-n

> Use: Required
>
> Data Type: Any
>
> Comma-delimited list of expressions to compare values with *testexpression.*

statements-n

> Use: Optional
>
> Program statements to execute if a match is found between any section of *expressionlist* and *testexpression.*

elsestatements

> Use: Optional
>
> Program statements to execute if a match between *testexpression* and any *expressionlist* can't be found.

expressionlist can use any (or a combination of any) of the following:

expressionlist Syntax	*Examples*
expression	iVar - iAnotherVar iVar
expression To *expression*	5 To 10 8 To 11, 13 to 15 "A" To "D"
Is *comparisonoperator expression*	Is = 10

Description

Allows for conditional execution of a block of code, typically out of three or more code blocks, based on some condition. Use the Select Case statement as an alternative to complex nested If...Then...Else statements.

Rules at a Glance

- Any number of Case clauses can be included in the Select Case statement.

- If a match between *testexpression* and any part of *expressionlist* is found, the program statements following the matched *expressionlist* are executed. When program execution encounters the next Case clause or the End Select clause, execution continues with the statement immediately following the End Select clause.

- If used, the Case Else clause must be the last Case clause. Program execution encounters the Case Else clause—and thereby executes, the *els-estatements*—only if all other *expressionlist* comparisons fail.

- Use the To keyword to specify a range of values. The lower value must precede the To clause, and the higher value follow it. Failure to do this doesn't generate a syntax error; instead, it causes the comparison of the expression with *testexpression* to always fail, so that program execution falls through to the Case Else code block, if one is present.

- The Is keyword precedes any comparison operators.

- Select Case statements can also be nested, resulting in a successful match between *testexpression* and *expressionlist* being another Select Case statement.

Example

The following example uses Select Case to implement the click event handler for a menu control array—that is, several menu options with the same name and different index numbers.

```
Private Sub mnuOption_Click(Index As Integer)

Select Case Index
    Case Is = 0
        Call ShowAddNewForm
    Case Is = 1
        Call ShowEditForm
    Case Is = 2
        Call ShowDeleteForm
    Case Else
        MsgBox "Not a valid menu option"
End Select

End Sub
```

Programming Tips & Gotchas

- The Select Case statement is the VB equivalent of the Switch construct found in C and C++.

- The Case Else clause is optional. However, as with If...Then...Else statements, it's often good practice to provide a Case Else to catch the exceptional instance where—perhaps unexpectedly—a match can't be found in any of the *expressionlists* you have provided.

- The To clause can specify ranges of character strings. However, it's often difficult to predict the thousands of possible combinations of valid characters between two words that are successfully matched by Select Case.

- The Is keyword used in the Select Case statement isn't the same as the Is comparison operator.

- Multiple conditions in a single Case statement are evaluated separately, not together; that is, they are connected with a logical OR, not a logical AND. For example, the statement

```
Case Is > 20, Is < 40
```

evaluates to True whenever the value of *testexpression* is greater than 20. In this case, the second comparison is never evaluated; it's evaluated only when *testexpression* is under 20. This suggests that if you use anything other than the most straightforward conditions, you should test them thoroughly.

See Also

If...Then Statement

SendKeys Statement

Named Arguments

Yes

Syntax

```
SendKeys string[, wait]
string
```
    Use: Required

    Data Type: String

    The keystrokes to send.

```
wait
```
    Use: Optional

    Data Type: Boolean

    Expression evaluating to True or False denoting the wait mode.

Description

Programmatically simulates specified keys being typed at the keyboard.

Rules at a Glance

- SendKeys sends its keystrokes to the application and application window that has the focus.

- One or more characters represent each key.

- The default setting for *wait* is False. Setting *wait* to True informs the application to wait until the keystrokes have been processed before passing control back to the current procedure. A False setting returns control back to the current procedure as soon as the keys are sent.

- To send normal alphabetical or numeric characters, simply use the character or characters enclosed in quotation marks. For example, "SOME Text 123".

- The following characters represent special keys or have special meaning within the **SendKeys** string:

Character	Special Key Representation
+	Shift
^	Ctrl
%	Alt
~	Enter
[ ]	May be used by Dynamic Data Exchange (DDE)

To use these characters literally, you must surround the character with braces. For example, to specify the percentage key, use {%}.

- Preceding a string with the special characters described in the table above allows you to send a keystroke combination beginning with Shift, Ctrl, or Alt. For example, to specify Ctrl followed by M, use ^M.

- If you need to specify that the Shift, Ctrl, or Alt key is held down while another key is pressed, you should enclose the key or keys in parentheses and precede the parentheses with the special character code. For example to specify the M key being pressed while holding down the Alt key use %(M).

- The following table describes how to specify nondisplaying (action) characters in the **SendKeys** string:

Key	Code
Back Space	{Backspace}, {Bs}, or {Bksp}
Break	{Break}
Caps Lock	{CapsLock}
Del or Delete	{Del} or {Delete}
Down arrow	{Down}
End	{End}
Enter	{Enter} or ~
Esc	{Esc}
Help	{Help}
Home	{Home}
Ins or Insert	{Ins} or {Insert}
Left arrow	{Left}
Num Lock	{Numlock}
Page Down	{Pgdn}
Page Up	{Pgup}
Right arrow	{Right}
Scroll Lock	{Scrolllock}
Tab	{Tab}

Key	Code
Up arrow	{Up}
F1	{F1}
F2	{F2}
F3	{F3}
F4	{F4}
F5	{F5}
F6	{F6}
F7	{F7}
F8	{F8}
F9	{F9}
F10	{F10}
F11	{F11}
F12	{F12}
F13	{F13}
F14	{F14}
F15	{F15}
F16	{F16}

- Special formatting syntax allows you to specify a key being repeatedly pressed. The syntax is:

    {key numberoftimes}

    For example, "{M 3}" represents pressing the M key three times.

Example

The following program launches Notepad, loads a text file whose name is passed as a parameter, gives the focus to Notepad, then uses its File Exit menu option to close the application:

```
Private Sub LaunchNotepad(strFN As String)

Dim lngTaskID As Long
Dim strCmdLine As String

strCmdLine = "C:\windows\notepad.exe " & strFN
lngTaskID = Shell(strCmdLine, vbNormalNoFocus)
' timing delay
DelayLoop 100000

AppActivate lngTaskID, False
DoEvents
' timing delay
DelayLoop 100000

SendKeys "%Fx", False

End Sub
```

Programming Tips & Gotchas

- **SendKeys** works directly only with applications designed to run in Microsoft Windows. To send keystrokes to an MS-DOS application or to the console window, you must use the Clipboard as an intermediary. For example, the following subroutine uses the Clipboard and **SendKeys** to launch a command or program from the DOS window:

```
Private Sub RunDOSCommand(strCmd As String)

Dim lngCtr As Long

Shell "Command.com", vbNormalNoFocus
Clipboard.Clear
Clipboard.SetText strCmd & Chr(13)
AppActivate "MS-DOS Prompt", False
SendKeys "% ep", True
For lngCtr = 0 To 700000
Next

SendKeys "% c", True

AppActivate Me.Name

End Sub
```

- You may find that some keys or key combinations can't be sent successfully. For example, you can't use **SendKeys** to send the Print Screen key to any application. And you can't send the Alt-Tab keys (**%{Tab}**) under Windows 9x.

- Typically, **SendKeys** is used as a "convenience" feature to send an occasional keystroke to its application or to another application. It can also add a keystroke macro capability to an application. In some cases, it's used for remotely controlling an application. In this latter case, **SendKeys** is often combined with the *Shell* function to start an instance of another application and with the **AppActivate** statement to give it the focus before **SendKeys** is used; the previous example illustrates this.

- It's worthwhile mentioning the difficulties of using **SendKeys** as a method for controlling a program remotely. Windows is an event-driven operating system. Direct consequences of this are that the order of events is controlled primarily by the user, and the precise order of events is difficult or even impossible to anticipate in advance. Remote control of an application using **SendKeys**, however, typically makes a number of assumptions about that application, the most basic of which is that it has the focus when **SendKeys** is called. Given that **SendKeys** doesn't offer close control over a remote application in the same way that, for instance, OLE automation does, the event-driven character of Windows can easily intervene to invalidate those assumptions. This makes **SendKeys** a less than optimal tool for remotely controlling an application.

Set Statement

Named Arguments

No

Syntax

```
Set objectvar = {[New] objectexpression | Nothing}
```
objectvar

> Use: Required
>
> Data Type: Object
>
> The name of the object variable or property.

New

> Use: Optional
>
> Type: Keyword
>
> Creates a new instance of the object.

objectexpression

> Use: Required
>
> Data Type: Object
>
> An expression evaluating to an object.

Nothing

> Use: Optional
>
> Type: Keyword
>
> Assigns the special data type Nothing to objectvar, thereby releasing the reference to the object.

Description

Assigns an object reference to a variable or property.

When using Dim, Private, Public, ReDim, or Static to declare an object variable, the variable is assigned a value of Nothing unless the New keyword is used in the statement. The Set statement is then required to assign a reference to an instance of the object referred to in the declarative statement.

Rules at a Glance

- Before the Set statement is used, *objectvar* must have been declared either as a generic object data type or (preferably) using the same object type as *objectexpression*. For example:

```
Dim objVar As Object
Dim objExcel As Excel.Application

Set objVar = Word.Application
Set objExcel = Excel.Application
```

- *objectvar* doesn't hold a copy of the underlying object; it simply holds a reference to the object.

- If the New keyword is used, a new instance of the class is immediately created. This fires that class's Initialize event.

- The New keyword can't be used with intrinsic data types or dependent objects; in other words, objects and classes must be createable.

- If *objectvar* holds a reference to an object when the Set statement is executed, the current reference is released and the new one referred to in *objectexpression* is assigned.

- *objectexpression* can be any of the following:

  - The name of an object.

  - A variable that has been previously declared and instantiated using the Set statement and that refers to the same type of object.

  - A call to a function, method, or property that returns the same type of object.

- By assigning Nothing to *objectvar*, the reference held by *objectvar* to the object is released.

Example

The following example uses the Set statement to create instances of two ActiveX objects.

```
Private Function GetEmployeeName(sEmpNo As String) As String
Dim oEmps As Employees
Dim oEmp As Employee

Set oEmps = New Employees

If oEmps.Exists(sEmpNo) Then
    Set oEmp = oEmps.Employee(sEmpNo)
    GetEmployeeName = oEmp.Name
    Set oEmp = Nothing
End If
Set oEmps = Nothing

End Function
```

Programming Tips & Gotchas

- You can have more than one object variable referring to the same object. However, bear in mind that a change to the underlying object using one object variable is reflected in all the other object variables that reference that object. For example, consider the following code fragment, in which the *obj-ColorCopy* object reference is set equal to the *objColor* object:

```
Dim objColor As CColor, objColorCopy As CColor
Set objColor = New CColor
Set objColorCopy = objColor

objColor.CurrentColor = "Blue"
Debug.Print objColorCopy.CurrentColor
```

Since both *objColor* and *objColorCopy* reference a single object, the value of the CurrentColor property is Blue in both cases.

- If you use the New keyword when declaring an object, you don't have to use the Set statement to instantiate the object. In most cases, this is more a matter of programming style than of programming optimization or performance issues. The following snippets show the two methods of instantiating an early bound object (that is, an object that has had a project-level reference created using the references dialog):

Method 1

```
Dim myObj As New SomeClass
```

Method 2

```
Dim myObj As SomeClass
Set myObj = New SomeClass
```

There are, however, certain instances where you can only use the New keyword with the Set statement, as the next example shows. Here a recordset has been created from a database, and each record is assigned to an object that is held in a collection. With each loop, a new instance of the class has to be created. Therefore, the New keyword is used with the Set statement:

```
Dim oVar As clsNames
Do While Not rsNames.EOF
    Set oVar = New clsNames
    oVar.FirstName = rsNames!FName
    oVar.LastName = rsNames!LName
    mcolNames.Add oVar
    Set oVar = Nothing
Loop
```

- It's often essential (and certainly good programming practice) to set object references to Nothing once the application is finished using them. For example, you *must* set an object to Nothing when you have created one or a number of sub (or dependent) objects from within another object. If you don't release the references to the child objects from the client code when you have finished with them, you can't explicitly release the reference to the main object from the client. This snippet shows how it should be done:

```
Dim myMainObj as MainClass
Dim mySubObj as SomeSubClass

Set myMainObj = New MainClass
    Set mySubObj = MainClass.Item(1)
        'work with the sub object
    Set MySubObj = Nothing
Set MyMainObj = Nothing
```

Each object instance maintains a counter of the number of current references to it. If the object referenced by the object variable has no other references when object variable is set to Nothing (that is, its counter is decremented to zero), the object's Terminate event is fired, and the object unloads from memory.

During the development stage, you should use conditional compilation and the Debug.Print method to check that all references to an object or class are being released correctly. This can be done as shown in the snippet below within the class's Terminate event:

```
#If ccDebug Then
    Debug.Print "Class myClass Terminated"
#End If
```

This is important because although you are prevented from specifying circular object references (where one class references another and—perhaps indirectly—the referenced class also holds a reference to the class referencing it) within the references dialog, you can build in circular object references quite easily without realizing it or even deliberately, as a result of your application design. Classes with circular references don't release from memory until the application terminates. For more details, see Chapter 4.

- When trying to discover whether or not an object reference has been successfully assigned, you should determine if the object variable has been assigned Nothing. However, you can't use the equality comparison operator (=) for this purpose; you must use the Is operator, as the following code snippet shows:

```
If objectvar Is Nothing Then
    ... 'assignment failed
End If
```

- While the Set statement used with the New keyword provides for early binding to an externally createable object, a type library may not be available for a particular automation object, or the precise automation object to be used may not be known at design time. In that case, externally createable objects can be instantiated at runtime (i.e., can be late bound) by using the Set statement along with the *CreateObject* function. For example:

```
Dim oMainObject As MainLib.MainObject
Set oMainObject = CreateObject("MainLib.MainObject")
```

In addition, from VB6 onward, *CreateObject* supports an extra parameter specifying the remote machine on which the object is registered. For example:

```
Dim oRemServ As MainLib.MainObj
If ServerOnLine("NTSERV1") Then
    Set oMainObject = CreateObject("MainLib.MainObj", _
                                   "NTSERV1")
Else
    Set oMainObject = CreateObject("MainLib.MainObj", _
                                   "NTSERV2")
End If
```

See Also

Dim Statement; Friend Statement; Private Statement; Public Statement; Chapter 5, *Automation*

SetAttr Statement

Named Arguments

Yes

Syntax

```
SetAttr pathname, attributes
pathname
```
      Use: Required

      Data Type: String

      The name of the file whose attributes are to be set.

```
attributes
```
      Use: Required

      Data Type: Integer

      Numeric expression or constant specifying the attributes.

Description

Changes the attribute properties of a file.

Rules at a Glance

- Visual Basic now includes the following intrinsic constants for setting file attributes:

Constant	*Value*	*Description*
vbNormal	0	Normal (default)
vbReadOnly	1	Read-only
vbHidden	2	Hidden
vbSystem	4	System file
vbArchive	32	File has changed since last backup

- File attributes' constants can be added together or logically ORed to set more than one attribute at the same time. For example:

```
SetAttr "SysFile.Dat", vbSystem Or vbHidden
SetAttr "MyFile.Txt", vbArchive + vbReadOnly
```

- *pathname* can include a drive letter. If a drive letter isn't included in *pathname*, the current drive is assumed. If a drive letter is used, the fully qualified path is required unless the file is located in the current directory.

- *pathname* can include a folder name. If the folder name isn't included in *pathname*, the current folder is assumed.

- Attempting to set the attributes of an open file will generate a runtime error.

Example

```
Private Sub AddAttributes(strFN As String, _
                          intNewAttrib As Integer)
```

```
Dim intAttrib As Integer

intAttrib = GetAttr(strFN)
SetAttr strFN, intAttrib Or intNewAttrib

End Sub
```

Programming Tips & Gotchas

- Setting file attributes simultaneously *clears* any attributes that aren't set with the `SetAttr` statement. For example, if *SysFile.Dat* is a read-only, hidden system file, the statement:

  ```
  SetAttr "sysfile.dat", vbArchive
  ```

  sets the archive attribute but clears the read-only, hidden, and system attributes. Clearly, this can have disastrous implications. To retain a file's attributes while setting new ones, first retrieve its attributes using the *GetAttr* function, as the previous example illustrates.

- Setting a file's attributes to `vbNormal` clears all file attributes.

See Also

GetAttr Function

Sgn Function

Named Arguments

No

Syntax

```
Sgn(number)
number
```
> Use: Required
>
> Data Type: Numeric
>
> A numeric expression.

Return Value

A Variant of subtype Integer.

Description

Determines the sign of a number.

Rules at a Glance

The return value of the *Sgn* function is determined by the sign of *number*:

If number is...	Sgn Returns
Positive	1
Zero	0
Negative	−1

Programming Tips & Gotchas

- I suppose that someone, somewhere, has found a really good use for the *Sgn* function. However, its usefulness escapes me, because you need to carry out a test on the return value of the function identical to that which you could use on the number to find its sign.

- If you're planning on using the *Sgn* function to evaluate a result to **False** (0) or **True** (any nonzero value), you could also use the *CBool* function.

- The major use for *Sgn*—and a fairly trivial one—is to determine the sign of an expression. It's equivalent to the following code:

```
Public Function Sgn(varNumber as Variant) as Integer

If varNumber > 0 Then
    Sgn = 1
ElseIf varNumber = 0 Then
    Sgn = 0
Else
    Sgn = -1
End If
```

- *Sgn* is useful in cases in which the sign of a quantity defines the sign of an expression. For example:

```
lngResult = lngQty * Sgn(lngValue)
```

See Also

If...Then Statement

Shell Function

Named Arguments

Yes

Syntax

```
Shell(pathname[,windowstyle])
```
pathname

> Use: Required
>
> Data Type: Variant (String)
>
> Name of the program to execute.

windowstyle

> Use: Optional
>
> Data Type: Variant (Integer)
>
> The style of window and whether it receives the focus.

Return Value

A Variant of subtype Double.

Description

Launches another application and, if successful, returns that application's task ID.

Rules at a Glance

- *pathname* can include a drive letter. If a drive letter isn't included in *pathname*, the current drive is assumed. If a drive letter is used, the fully qualified path is required unless the file is located in the current directory.

- *pathname* can include a folder name. If the folder name isn't included in *pathname*, the current folder is assumed.

- *pathname* can include any command-line arguments and switches required by the application.

- Visual Basic includes the following intrinsic constants for setting the *windowstyle* argument:

vbHide
> Value: 0
>
> New application window is: hidden
>
> Focus: New Application

vbNormalFocus
> Value: 1
>
> New application window is: shown in its original position and size
>
> Focus: New Application

vbMinimizedFocus
> Value: 2
>
> New application window is: displayed as an icon
>
> Focus: New Application

vbMaximizedFocus
> Value: 3
>
> New application window is: maximized
>
> Focus: New Application

vbNormalNoFocus
> Value: 4
>
> New application window is: shown in its original position and size
>
> Focus: Current Application

vbMinimizedNoFocus
> Value: 6
>
> New application window is: displayed as an icon
>
> Focus: Current Application

- The default when no *windowstyle* is specified as vbMinimizedFocus (2).

- If the application named in *pathname* executes successfully, *Shell* returns the window's task ID of the program. (The task ID is better known as the process ID (or PID), a unique 32-bit value used to identify each running process.) It can be used as a parameter to the **AppActivate** statement to give the application the focus and possibly control it remotely using the **Send-Keys** statement. The process ID is also required by a number of Win32 API calls.

- If the application named in *pathname* fails to execute, a runtime error is generated.

- The file launched by *Shell* must be executable. That is, it must be a file whose extension is *.EXE* or *.COM* (an executable file), *.BAT* (a batch file), or *.PIF* (a DOS shortcut file).

Programming Tips & Gotchas

- Applications launched by the *Shell* function run asynchronously, which means that the launching application isn't notified when the launched application has finished executing. Therefore, program statements in the launching application may execute before the launched application has completed.

- If you require the *Shell* function to run another program synchronously, you need to use Win32 API calls. The required calls vary depending upon whether you are using Windows 95 or Windows NT. Be aware, though, that the programming required to run another process in Windows NT is quite complex, and I could quite easily take up another book trying to explain it. In fact, certain procedures relating to launching processes in Windows NT aren't possible using VB—or for that matter MFC. In 16-bit Windows, launching applications or processes synchronously and keeping track of them was a relatively painless exercise; you'd simply monitor the *GetModuleUseage* API call. However, 32-bit Windows operates on an entirely different system of launching and monitoring (or not, as the case may be) processes, which doesn't allow you to use *GetModuleUseage*.

- The *Shell* function doesn't use file associations. You can't, for example, supply *MyReport.Doc* as the *pathname* in the hope that VB will load Microsoft Word, which in turn will load *MyReport.Doc*.

Sin Function

Named Arguments

No

Syntax

```
Sin(number)
number
```

> Use: Required
>
> Data Type: Numeric
>
> An angle expressed in radians.

Return Value

A Double containing the sine of an angle.

Description

Returns the ratio of two sides of a right triangle in the range –1 to 1.

Rules at a Glance

The ratio is determined by dividing the length of the side opposite the angle by the length of the hypotenuse.

Programming Tips & Gotchas

- You can convert degrees to radians using the formula:

  ```
  radians = degrees * (pi/180)
  ```

- You can convert degrees to radians using the formula:

  ```
  degrees = radians * (180/pi)
  ```

See Also

The math teacher I wish I'd listened to in school.

SLN Function

Named Arguments

Yes

Syntax

```
SLN(cost, salvage, life)
cost
```
> Use: Required
>
> Data Type: Double
>
> The initial cost of the asset.

```
salvage
```
> Use: Required
>
> Data Type: Double
>
> The value of the asset at the end of its useful life.

```
life
```
> Use: Required
>
> Data Type: Double
>
> The length of the useful life of the asset.

Return Value

A Double representing depreciation per period.

Description

Computes the straight-line depreciation of an asset for a single period.

Rules at a Glance

- The function uses a very simple formula to calculate depreciation:

  `(cost - salvage) / life`

- The depreciation period is determined by the time period of *life*.
- All arguments must be positive numeric values.

See Also

DDB Function, SYD Function

Space, Space$ Functions

Named Arguments

No

Syntax

```
Space(number)
number
```
> Use: Required
>
> Data Type: Integer
>
> An expression evaluating to the number of spaces required.

Return Value

A Variant of subtype String containing *number* spaces (in the case of *Space*) or a String containing *number* spaces (in the case of *Space$*).

Description

Creates a string containing *number* spaces.

Rules at a Glance

While *number* can be zero (in which case the function returns a null string), runtime error 5, "Invalid procedure call or argument," is generated if *number* is negative.

Programming Tips & Gotchas

You can use the *Space* function to both pad and clear data stored in fixed-length strings. For example, the following code fragment fills a fixed-length string with spaces:

```
Dim strFixed As String * 32
...
strFixed = Space(Len(strFixed))
```

See Also

String Function

Spc Function

Syntax

Spc (*n*)

n

> Use: Required
>
> Data Type: Integer
>
> The number of spaces required.

Return Value

A String containing *n* spaces.

Description

Inserts spaces between expressions in a `Print #` statement, Debug.Print method, or Printer.Print method.

Rules at a Glance

- Although *Spc* has more built-in "intelligence" than the *Space* function, it can be used only with the `Print #` statement and the Debug.Print method. For example, it isn't possible to use the *Spc* function to pad a fixed-length string as the *Space* function does. When dealing with the Printer object, far more flexibility is available by setting properties, such as CurrentX, for accurately placing text strings.

- If the width of the device being printed to is greater than *n*, the print position is set to be immediately after the number of spaces printed by the *Spc* function.

- If the width of the device being printed to is less than *n*, the print position is set to the current position plus the result of the formula *n* Mod *devicewidth*.

- If *n* is greater than the difference between the current print position and the width of the device, *Spc* inserts a line break and then inserts spaces in accordance with the following formula:

```
n - (devicewidth - currentposition)
```

- When using a proportional font, the *Spc* function uses the average width of all characters for the particular font to determine the width of the space character to print.

- When the number of fixed-width columns is important, you should use either the *Space* or the *Tab* function, since there isn't necessarily a relationship between the spaces provided by the *Spc* function and fixed-width columns.

Programming Tips & Gotchas

- When placing output on the Printer object, use the TextWidth method to determine the actual width taken up by a given string in a given font and font size.

- While on the surface it appears that *Spc* and *Space* are interchangeable functions that both simply return a given number of spaces, their internal workings are somewhat different. The *Spc* function can be used only in

Reference

conjunction with a *Print* or *Print #* function. For example, you generate a design-time error if you try to write the following code:

```
Dim sStr As String * 20
'no can do
sStr = Spc(20)
```

See Also

Print # Statement, Debug Object, Printer Object

Split Function (VB6)

Named Arguments

No

Syntax

```
Split (expression, [delimiter[, count[, compare]]])
expression
```
    Use: Required

    Data Type: String

    A string to be broken up into multiple strings.

delimiter

    Use: Optional

    Data Type: Variant

    The character used to delimit the substrings in *expression*.

count

    use: Optional

    Data Type: Log

    The number of strings to return.

compare

    Use: Optional

    Data Type: VbCompareMethod constant

    The method of comparison. Possible values are vbBinaryCompare, vbTextCompare, or vbDatabaseCompare.

Return Value

A variant array consisting of the arguments passed into the function.

Description

Parses a single string containing delimited values into an array

Rules at a Glance

•   The returned array is always base 0 regardless of any Option Base setting.

- If *delimiter* isn't found in *expression*, *Split* returns the entire string in element 0 of the return array.

- If *delimiter* is omitted, a space character (" ") is used as the delimiter.

- If *count* is omitted or its value is –1, all strings are returned.

- The default comparison method is vbBinaryCompare.

- Once *count* has been reached, the remainder of the string is placed, unprocessed, into the next element of the returned array.

Programming Tips & Gotchas

- The array you declare to assign the return value of *Filter* must be a dynamic, single-dimension string array, or a variant.

- Strings are written to the returned array in the order in which they appear in *expression*.

See Also

Join Function

Sqr Function

Named Arguments

No

Syntax

```
Sqr(number)
number
```
   Use: Required

   Data Type: Double

   Any numeric expression greater than or equal to 0.

Return Value

A Double containing the square root of *number*.

Description

Calculates the square root of a given number.

Rules at a Glance

number must be equal to or greater than zero or runtime error 5, "Invalid procedure call or argument," occurs.

Static Statement

Syntax

```
Static varname[([subscripts])] [As [New] type] _
      [,varname[([subscripts])] [As [New] type]] . . .
```

varname
> Use: Required
>
> Data Type: Any
>
> The name of the variable, following Visual Basic naming conventions.

subscripts
> Use: Optional
>
> Data Type: Long Integer
>
> Denotes *varname* as an array, and specifies the number and extents of dimensions of the array.

New
> Use: Optional
>
> Type: Keyword
>
> Used to automatically create an instance of the object referred to by the object variable *varname*.

type
> Use: Optional
>
> Type: Keyword
>
> Data type of the variable *varname*.

Description

Used at procedure level to declare a static variable and allocate the relevant storage space in memory. Static variables retain their value between calls to the procedure in which they are declared.

Rules at a Glance

- A static variable's scope is limited to the procedure in which it's created.

- The *subscripts* argument has the following syntax:

  ```
  [lowerbound To] upperbound [, _
  [lowerbound To] upperbound]
  ```

- Using the *subscripts* argument, you can declare up to 60 multiple dimensions for the array.

- The *lowerbound* argument of the *subscripts* argument is optional. When not used, the lower bound of the array is specified by the Option Base statement. If Option Base has not been used, the lower bound of the array is zero.

- If the *subscripts* argument isn't used (i.e., the variable name is followed by empty parentheses), the array is declared as dynamic. You can change both the number of dimensions and number of elements of a dynamic array by using the ReDim statement.

- The New keyword denotes that a new instance of the object is created when the first reference to the object is made. Use of the New keyword in the Static statement therefore eliminates the need to use the Set statement.

- You can't use the New keyword to declare variables of any intrinsic data type or instances of dependent objects.

- If you don't use the New keyword with an object variable, you must use the Set statement to assign an existing object to the variable before you can use the variable.

- *datatype* may be Byte, Boolean, Currency, Date, Double, Integer, Long, Object, Single, String, Variant, a user-defined type, or an object type.

- If you don't specify *datatype* and you haven't used a DefType statement, the variable is cast as a variant.

- The following table shows the values held by each data type when a variable is first initialized:

Data Type	Initial Value
Numeric	0
Variable-length string	Zero-length string ("")
Fixed-length string	Filled with zeros
Variant	Empty
Object	Nothing
Date	Saturday 30 December 1899 12:00:00

- The individual elements of a user-defined type are initialized with the value corresponding to their data types.

- To declare a fixed length string, use the syntax:

```
Static varname As String * stringlength
```

Programming Tips & Gotchas

- It's a recognized programming practice when using the Static statement in a procedure to put the Static statements at the beginning of that procedure.

- Although their value persists between calls to a procedure, static variables don't have scope outside of the procedure in which they are created.

- You should note that when you use the New keyword, the Initialize event of the underlying object is fired on the first reference to the object, not when the object variable is declared.

- It's good programming practice to always use Option Explicit at the beginning of a module to require variable declaration, and thus prevent misnamed variables causing hard-to-find errors.

See Also

Friend Statement, Public Statement, ReDim Statement, Set Statement

Reference

stdDataFormat Object (VB6)

Description

The stdDataFormat object sits silently between the Binding object and the data consumer control. Data coming into the Binding object is reformatted by the stdDataFormat object and made ready for display in the consumer control. Data changed by the user that the Binding object is returning to the database is automatically unformatted as it leaves the data consumer control.

The formatting applied to the data is based on the properties you have set for the particular format object. In the case of complex formatting, you may also be required to unformat the data manually before processing by the database. In all cases, you should set the Type property, which tells the format object which format you require; optionally, you can provide a property value for one or more of the special format properties.

Only one format object can be applied to a Binding object, but there is no limit on how many different format objects your application can contain. If you use multiple format objects, you should contain them within the stdDataFormats collection object and simply pass a reference to the object in the collection to the Binding object. This prevents you from having many stdDataFormat objects all live at the same time. The drawback to this approach, though, is that the collection object stifles the format object's Format and Unformat events, which are vital for custom formatting.

If the purpose of the format object is incompatible with the control being bound, an error is generated by the BindingsCollection.Add method. For example, if you have created a format object that deals with a checkbox format and try to bind this to a Textbox control, an error occurs.

For an overview of data format objects, including the library reference needed to access the object model, see the Data Format Objects entry.

Createable

Yes

Properties

FalseValue

Data Type: Variant

When used in conjunction with a Type value of `fmtBoolean`, the FalseValue is assigned to the consumer control's bound property if the incoming data is `False` (0). For example, in the following snippet, if the value of the bound data field is 0, the string `"No Contract"` is placed in the bound control:

```
Set fmtF2 = New StdDataFormat
    fmtF2.Type = fmtBoolean
    fmtF2.FalseValue = "No Contract"
```

When changed data is read back into the database, if the value of the bound control property matches FalseValue, a `False` (0) is written to the database.

For example, using our snippet above, if the data in the bound control is changed to "No Contract," 0 or `False` is written to the database.

It's advisable to provide both a FalseValue and a TrueValue for a format object whose Type is `fmtBoolean`.

FirstDayOfWeek

Data Type: constant from `FirstDayOfWeek` enumeration

Specifies which day should be treated as the first day of the week. This property can be used for date formatting. The `FirstDayOfWeek` constants used by stdFormatObject differ from the intrinsic ones by their "fmt" (instead of "vb") prefix.

FirstWeekOfYear

Data Type: constant of `FirstWeekOfYear` enumeration

Specifies which week of the year should be treated as the first. This property can be used for date formatting. The `FirstWeekOfYear` constants used by stdFormatObject differ from the intrinsic ones by their "fmt" (instead of "vb") prefix.

Format

Data Type: String

When the value of the Type property is `fmtCustom`, the Type property can provide a formatting string identical to those recognized by the *Format* function; for details, see the entry for the *Format* function.

NullValue

Data Type: Variant

Defines the value to replace a `Null` for all format types. If the data from the data source is `Null`, it's automatically replaced by this value. Beware, though: if the data in the bound control is changed to this value, the Binding object attempts to write a `Null` to the database. For example, in the following snippet, a value of 0 appears in the bound control if the original value in the database is `Null`. However, if the original database value is 1 and the user changes it to 0, then `Null` is written to the database.

```
Set fmtF2 = New StdDataFormat
    fmtF2.Type = fmtGeneral
    fmtF2.NullValue = 0
```

Note that an order of precedence applies when translating the values of bound data controls back to their original values. Typically, the NullValue property has the lowest precedence. For example, if the value of the Type property is `fmtCheckbox`, a data value of 0 sets the checkbox's value to `vbUnchecked`, and a value of 1 sets it to `vbChecked`. If the value of the NullValue property is also 0, a `Null` isn't written to the database when the checkbox control becomes unchecked (i.e., its value changes to 0), since this 0 is interpreted as `vbUnchecked` rather than `Null`. Similarly, for a type of `fmtBoolean`, a 0 is interpreted as `False` rather than `Null`.

TrueValue

Data Type: Variant

Defines the value assigned to the consumer control's bound property for format objects whose Type is `fmtBoolean` and whose incoming data is `True` (1 or –1). For example, in the following code fragment, if the value of the bound data field is 1 or –1, the string `"Contract Signed"` appears in the bound control:

```
Set fmtF2 = New StdDataFormat
    fmtF2.Type = fmtBoolean
    fmtF2.TrueValue = "Contract Signed"
```

Type

Data Type: Constant of `FormatType` enumeration

Defines the type of data to be formatted, which in turn determines which properties are used in formatting a data item. Ensure that the type you set is compatible with both the data you are binding and with the control you are binding to. The `FormatType` constants are as follows:

Constant	Value	Description
fmtGeneral	0	For any type of data. Forces the Format and Unformat events to fire.
fmtCustom	1	For any type of data. The Format property can define a custom format value. Forces the Format and Unformat events to fire.
fmtPicture	2	Format and Unformat events aren't fired.
fmtObject	3	Format and Unformat events aren't fired.
fmtCheckbox	4	For binding to a checkbox control. A data value of 0 equates to vbUnChecked, whereas 1 or –1 equates to vbChecked. Format and Unformat events aren't fired for this type.
fmtBoolean	5	For Boolean data; specifies that the TrueValue and FalseValue properties be used. Format and Unformat events aren't fired.

stdDataFormats Events

Your stdDataFormat object variable must be declared `WithEvents` to receive events. The following events are supported by the stdDataformat object:

Changed

Fired when the formatting properties of the object are changed.

Format

Fired when the bound data is about to be formatted for the `fmtGeneral` and `fmtCustom` format types. The event handler can override the formatting manually. An stdDataValue object is passed to the event, as the following example shows:

```
Private Sub fmtF1_Format(ByVal DataValue As _
                    StdFormat.StdDataValue)
    If DataValue.TargetObject.Name = "txtFirstName" Then
        'force lowercase
        fmtF1.Format = ">"
```

```
        Else
            'force uppercase
            fmtF1.Format = "<"
        End If
End Sub
```

Note that the stdDataValue object isn't createable and only manifests itself as a parameter passed to the Format and Unformat event handlers.

Unformat

Fired for the **fmtGeneral** and **fmtCustom** format types when the bound data is to be unformatted and written back to the database. The event handler can override the unformatting manually. A stdDataValue object is passed into the event, as the following example shows:

```
Private Sub fmtF1_UnFormat(ByVal DataValue As _
                        StdFormat.StdDataValue)
    DataValue.Value = StrConv(DataValue.Value, _
                        vbProperCase)
End Sub
```

Note that the stdDataValue object isn't createable and only manifests itself as a parameter passed to the Format and Unformat event handlers.

Example

See the Data Binding Objects entry for a complete example of how data binding and data formatting is performed.

See Also

stdDataFormats Object

---

stdDataFormats Object (VB6)

Description

Contains a collection of stdDataFormat objects. For an overview of the data format object model, including the library reference needed to access it, see the Data Format Objects entry.

Createable

Yes

stdDataFormats Properties

Count

Data Type: Long

The number of stdDataFormat objects held in the collection.

Item

Data Type: stdDataFormat Object

Allows access to individual stdDataFormat objects in the collection. You can use either the **For...Each...Next** statement or the item's key to specify a member of the collection. For example:

```
Set oFormat = oStdDataFormats.Item("bool")
```
Since the Item property is the stdDataFormat object's default property, you call it implicitly like this:
```
Set oFormat = oStdDataFormats("bool")
```

stdDataFormats Methods

Add

Adds a stdDataFormat object along with its optional variant key to the collection. For example:
```
oStdDataFormats.Add oFormat, "bool"
```

Clear

Removes all stdDataFormat objects from the collection.

Remove

Removes a particular stdDataFormat object from the collection. For example:
```
oStdDataFormats.Remove "bool"
```

Stop Statement

Syntax
```
Stop
```

Description

Halts program execution.

Rules at a Glance

- There is no limit to the number and position of Stop statements within procedures.

- The Stop statement acts like a breakpoint, placing the program in break mode and highlighting the current line in the development environment, allowing you to step through the code line by line.

Programming Tips & Gotchas

- Stop is intended primarily for use in the design-time environment, where it suspends program execution without terminating it. In the runtime environment, however, Stop displays a message box that reads Stop statement encountered before terminating program execution. Needless to say, users are sure to find this type of behavior baffling. Consequently, all Stop statements should be removed (or commented out) before compiling the executable file.

- Care must be taken when using the Stop statement, because unlike the End statement, Stop doesn't explicitly close any open files or clear variables unless running in a compiled EXE.

- These limitations suggest that the Stop statement, which exists primarily to permit a programmatically generated breakpoint, is best replaced by explicit breakpoints in the design-time environment.

End Statement

Str, Str$ Functions

Named Arguments

No

Syntax

```
Str(number)
number
```
   Use: Required

   Data Type: Numeric Variant

   Any numeric expression.

Return Value

A Variant of subtype String (returned by *Str*) or a String (returned by *Str$*) representing *number*.

Description

Converts *number* from a numeric to a string.

Rules at a Glance

If the return value is positive, the *Str* function always includes a leading space in the returned string for the sign of *number*.

Programming Tips & Gotchas

- Use the *LTrim* function to remove the leading space that the *Str* function adds to the start of the returned string.

- Both the *CStr* and *Format* functions have now superseded the *Str* function. The *CStr* function doesn't add a leading space for the sign of a positive number. The *Format* function is internationally aware, being able to recognize decimal delimiters other than the period (.).

See Also

CStr Function, Format Function, LTrim Function

StrComp Function

Named Arguments

Yes

Syntax

```
StrComp(string1, string2[, compare])
string1
```
   Use: Required

Data Type: String

Any string expression

string2
Use: Required

Data Type: String

Any string expression

compare
Use: Optional

Data Type: Integer constant

The type of string comparison to perform.

Return Value

A Variant of subtype Integer.

Description

Determines whether two strings are equal and, if not, which of two strings has the greater value.

Rules at a Glance

- The following intrinsic constants are available to use as the settings for the *compare* argument:

Constant	Value	Comparison to perform
vbBinaryCompare	0	Binary (default)
vbTextCompare	1	Textual
vbDatabase	2	Database (Microsoft Access only)

- If *compare* isn't specified, the setting of Option Compare (if present) determines the type of comparison performed.

- This table describes the possible return values from the *StrComp* function:

Scenario	Return Value
string1 < string2	−1
string1 = string2	0
string1 > string2	1
string1 or string2 is Null	Null

Programming Tips & Gotchas

- If you just need to know if *string1* is greater than *string2* (or vice versa), couldn't you simply use the < or > comparison operators? When you're dealing with strings of characters, Visual Basic sees each character as a number. Simply using the comparison operators therefore compares the numerical value of one string with the other. Take this scenario:

```
Dim sString1 As String
Dim sString2 As String

sString1 = "hello world"
sString2 = "HELLO WORLD"
```

Subjectively, because of the significance of uppercase letters in text, we'd probably say that *sString2* is greater than *sString1*. But Visual Basic sees these strings as a series of Unicode numbers, and because uppercase characters have a lower Unicode number than lowercase numbers, the lowercase string (*sString1*) is greater.

This is exactly how the default *StrComp* option **vbBinaryCompare** operates—comparing the Unicode numbers of each string at binary level. However, the **vbTextCompare** option effectively equalizes the case of both strings prior to conducting the comparison; **vbTextCompare** looks only for differences in the character. You could think of **vbTextCompare** as representing:

```
If UCase(sString1) < UCase(sString2) Then
    '-1
ElseIf UCase(sString1) = UCase(sString2) Then
    '0
Else
    '1
End If
```

- Even performing a simple single comparison like:

```
If UCase(sString1) < UCase(sString2) Then
```

  shows a performance hit of about 30% over the much more elegant and efficient *StrComp* function call:

```
If StrComp(sString1,sString2, vbTextCompare) = -1 Then
```

  The former version, though, is easier to read and makes the code self-documenting.

See Also

Option Compare Statement

StrConv Function

Named Arguments

Yes

Syntax

```
StrConv(string, conversion)
string
```
    Use: Required

    Data Type: String

    The string expression to convert.

conversion
   Use: Required

   Data Type: Integer

   Sum of constant or numeric values denoting the conversion to apply to
   string.

Return Value

A Variant of subtype String converted according to *conversion*.

Description

Performs special conversions on a string.

Rules at a Glance

- The following intrinsic conversion constants specify the type of conversion to
  perform:

Constant	Value	Converts...
vbUpperCase	1	the entire string to uppercase.
vbLowerCase	2	the entire string to lowercase.
vbProperCase	3	the first letter of every word in *string* to an uppercase character.
vbWide	4	narrow (single-byte) characters in *string* to wide (double-byte) characters.
vbNarrow	8	wide (double-byte) characters in *string* to narrow (single-byte) characters.
vbKatakana	16	Hiragana characters in *string* to Katakana characters.
vbHiragana	32	Katakana characters in *string* to Hiragana characters.
vbUnicode	64	the entire string to Unicode using the default code page of the system.
vbFromUnicode	128	the entire string from Unicode to the default code page of the system.

- You can combine most of these constants by adding them together or using a
  logical OR. For example:

```
vbUpperCase + vbUnicode
```

  The only restriction is that the constants must be mutually exclusive. For
  example:

```
vbUpperCase Or vbProperCase    ' Error
```

  is the type of value that's not permitted.

- vbKatakana and vbHiragana apply only to locales in Japan. Use of these
  constants on systems using other locales generates runtime error 5, "Invalid
  procedure call or argument."

- **vbWide** and **vbNarrow** apply only to locales in the Far East. Use of these constants on systems using other locales generates a runtime error.

- When determining the start of a new word to perform a conversion to Proper Case, *StrConv* recognizes the following characters as word separators:

  - Null: **Chr$(0)**
  - Horizontal tab: **Chr$(9)**
  - Linefeed: **Chr$(10)**
  - Vertical tab: **Chr$(11)**
  - Formfeed: **Chr$(12)**
  - Carriage return: **Chr$(13)**
  - Space: **Chr$(32)**

Example

This short example demonstrates how to convert a string to an array of bytes, for use in an API function call.

```
Dim byArray() As Byte
Dim sString As String
sString = "Some stuff"
byArray = StrConv(sSting, vbFromUnicode)
```

Programming Tips & Gotchas

The *StrConv* function is important when using the Win32 API, since many calls require that Unicode strings be passed to them, or they assign Unicode strings to return variables.

See Also

UCase Function, LCase Function

String, String$ Functions

Named Arguments

Yes

Syntax

```
String(number, character)
number
```
> Use: Required
>
> Data Type: Long
>
> The length of the required string.

```
character
```
> Use: Required
>
> Data Type: Variant
>
> Character or character code used to create the required string.

Return Value

A Variant of subtype string made up of *character*, repeated *number* times.

Description

Creates a string comprising a specified single character repeated a specified number of times.

Rules at a Glance

- If *number* contains Null, Null is returned.

- If *character* contains Null, Null is returned.

- *character* can be specified as a string or as an ANSI character code. For example:

```
strBuffer1 = String(128, "=")      ' Fill with "="
strBuffer2 = String(128, 0)        ' Fill with Chr$(0)
```

Programming Tips & Gotchas

- The *String* function is useful for creating long strings of "_" , "-", or "=" characters to create horizontal lines for delimiting sections of a report.

- When calling Win32 API functions that write string values to a buffer, the *String* function is typically used beforehand to create a string variable of the proper length and to fill it with a single character, like *Chr$(0)*. For example, given the following statements in the declarations section of a code module:

```
Private Declare Function GetWindowsDirectory _
        Lib "kernel32" _
        Alias "GetWindowsDirectoryA" _
        (ByVal lpBuffer As String, _
        ByVal nSize As Long) As Long

Private Const MAX_PATH = 260
```

the following code fragment retrieves the drive and path to the Windows directory:

```
Dim strWinDir As String
Dim lngDirLen As Long

strWinDir = String(MAX_PATH + 1, 0)
lngDirLen = GetWindowsDirectory(strWinDir, _
                          Len(strWinDir))
strWinDir = Left(strWinDir, lngDirLen)
```

See Also

Space Function, Str Function

StrReverse Function (VB6)

Named Arguments

No

Syntax

```
StrReverse(str_expression)
str_expression
```
    Use: Required

    Data Type: String

    The string whose characters are to be reversed.

Return Value

A String.

Description

Returns a string that is the reverse of the string passed to it. For example, if the string "and" is passed to it as an argument, *StrReverse* returns the string "dna."

Sub Statement

Named Arguments

No

Syntax

```
[Public | Private | Friend] [Static] Sub name [(arglist)]
    [statements]
    [Exit Sub]
    [statements]
End Sub
```
Public

    Use: Optional

    Type: Keyword

    Gives the sub procedure scope through all procedures in all modules in the project. If used within a createable class module, the sub procedure is also accessible from outside the project. Public, Private, and Friend are mutually exclusive.

Private

    Use: Optional

    Type: Keyword

    Restricts the scope of the sub procedure to those procedures within the same module. Public, Private, and Friend are mutually exclusive.

Friend

    Use: Optional

    Type: Keyword

    Only valid within a class module; gives the sub procedure scope to all modules within a project, but not to modules outside the project. Public, Private, and Friend are mutually exclusive.

Reference

Static

> Use: Optional
>
> Type: Keyword
>
> Preserves the value of variables declared inside the sub procedure between calls to the sub procedure.

name

> Use: Required
>
> The name of the sub procedure.

arglist

> Use: Optional
>
> Data Type: Any
>
> A comma-delimited list of variables to be passed to the sub procedure as arguments from the calling procedure.

statements

> Use: Optional
>
> Program code to be executed within the sub procedure.

arglist uses the following syntax and parts:

```
[Optional] [ByVal | ByRef] [ParamArray] varname[( )] _
      [As type] [= defaultvalue]
```

Optional

> Use: Optional
>
> An optional argument is one that need not be supplied when calling the sub. However, all arguments following an optional one must also be optional. A ParamArray argument can't be optional.

ByVal

> Use: Optional
>
> The argument is passed by value; that is, a local copy of the variable is assigned the value of the argument.

ByRef

> Use: Optional
>
> The argument is passed by reference; that is, the local variable is simply a reference to the argument being passed. All changes made to the local variable are also reflected in the calling argument. ByRef is the default method of passing variables.

ParamArray

> Use: Optional
>
> Indicates that the argument is an optional array of variants containing an arbitrary number of elements. It can be used only as the last element of the argument list, and it can't be used with the ByRef, ByVal or Optional keywords.

varname

> Use: Required

The name of the local variable containing either the reference or value of the argument.

type
Use: Optional

The data type of the argument.

defaultvalue
Use: Optional

For optional arguments, you can specify a constant default value.

Description

Defines a sub procedure.

Rules at a Glance

- If you don't include one of the Public, Private, or Friend keywords, a sub procedure is Public by default.

- If you declare a sub procedure as Public within a module that contains an Option Private directive, the sub procedure is treated as Private.

- Unlike a Function procedure, a sub procedure doesn't return a value to the calling procedure, and therefore can't be used as part of an expression.

- Any number of Exit Sub statements can be placed within the sub procedure. Execution continues with the line of code immediately following the call to the sub procedure.

- A sub procedure can't define a fixed-length string as an argument in *arglist*; this produces the design-time error, "Expected array."

- A user-defined type can be passed as an argument only if the argument is required (i.e., not optional). In addition, if a Public sub procedure accepts a user-defined type as an argument, that user-defined type must also be defined as Public within a code module.

- The default value for an optional object argument can only be Nothing.

Programming Tips & Gotchas

- There is often confusion between the ByRef and ByVal methods of assigning arguments to the sub procedure. ByRef assigns the reference of the variable in the calling procedure to the variable in the sub procedure; that is, it passes a pointer containing the address in memory of the variable in the calling procedure. As a result, any changes made to the variable from within the sub procedure are, in reality, made to the variable in the calling procedure. On the other hand, ByVal assigns the value of the variable in the calling procedure to the variable in the sub procedure; that is, it makes a separate copy of the variable in a separate memory location. Changes made to the variable in the sub procedure have no effect on the variable in the calling procedure. In general, ByRef arguments (Visual Basic's default method of passing parameters) within class modules take longer to perform, since marshalling back and forth between sub procedure and calling module must take place; so

Reference

unless you explicitly need to modify a variable's value within a sub procedure, it's best to pass parameters by value.

- Sub procedures can't return a value, or can they? Look at the following code:

```
Sub testTheReturns()
    Dim iValOne As Integer

    iValOne = 10
    Call testValues(iValOne)
    Debug.Print iValOne
End Sub

Sub testValues(ByRef iVal As Integer)
    iVal = iVal + 5
End Sub
```

Because the argument was passed **ByRef**, the sub procedure acted upon the underlying variable *iValOne*. This means that you can use **ByRef** to obtain a "return" value or values (although they're not strictly return values) from a sub procedure call.

- Optional arguments afford wonderful flexibility, allowing you to create generic sub procedures that can be used in a wide variety of scenarios. Until version 5 of VBA, optional arguments could be only of the Variant data type. With the release of VB 5.0, almost any data type can be cast as an optional argument. However, I would still advocate the use of a variant for optional arguments. Why? The variant has a special state called Missing that makes it easy to check the value of an optional argument using the *IsMissing* sub procedure. If *IsMissing* returns **True**, you know immediately that the optional argument was not supplied in the sub procedure call. Checking to determine whether a strongly typed variable (an integer, for example) is missing is much more difficult, as the following code shows:

```
Sub testMissingInt()
    Dim iVal As Integer
    Dim iValTwo As Integer

    iVal = 10
    iValTwo = 0

    Call testFunc(iVal, iValTwo)
End Sub

Sub testFunc(ByRef iVal As Integer, _
             Optional iValTwo As Integer)
    If iValTwo = 0 Then
        'perform this if iValTwo is missing
        glbTest = iVal + 10
    Else
        'perform this if iValTwo is present
        glbTest = iVal + iValTwo
    End If
End Sub
```

A missing optional integer argument appears within the sub procedure as its initialized value, which is 0. But what happens when you want to pass the value 0 to the sub procedure? It's interpreted as being missing. In other words, in a case such as this, you have no way to tell if the argument is really missing. In this case, it's important to take advantage of the *defaultvalue* argument to replace a missing optional argument either with a meaningful default value or with a value that can be readily identified as missing.

- A `ParamArray` must be declared in the sub procedure as an array of variant. However, the calling procedure doesn't pass the argument explicitly as an array; the individual elements are passed as a comma-delimited list of values or variables, as the following example shows:

```
Sub testParam()

    Call testFunc(10, 500, 60)

End Sub

Sub testFunc(ParamArray someArgs() As Variant)

    Dim iArg As Integer
    Dim i As Integer
    Dim iResult As Integer
    Dim vArg As Variant

    For Each vArg In someArgs
        iResult = iResult + vArg
    Next

End Sub
```

- For reasons that I haven't quite fathomed yet, you can't use `ParamArrays` to pass arguments to sub procedures in remote server applications. It's difficult to describe the results you obtain; suffice it to say that they don't generate errors, but that, quite simply, the results are little more than garbage. However, you can pass an explicit variant array to a sub procedure in a remote server application. The enormous advantage of this is that you can change both the type and number of arguments passed into the sub procedure without changing the COM interface, thereby retaining compatibility with a previous version of the server application.

- One of the most useful additions to VBA (as of Version 5.0) is the `Friend` keyword, which allows you to expose a property, sub procedure, or function in a class module to the other modules within the same project, but at the same time prevent "the outside world" from having access to the interface. This can be seen as halfway between `Private`—which prevents the interface from being seen by any module—and `Public`—which exposes the interface both to modules in the same project and to modules outside the project.

- There are many occasions in which you will run into the dreaded (by some!) recursive sub procedure call. Recursion occurs when you call a sub procedure from within itself. Recursion is a legitimate and often essential part of software development; for example, it's the only reliable method of enumerating or iterating a hierarchical structure. However, you must be aware that Microsoft—while never being specific on this point—indicates that recursion can lead to stack overflow. The extent to which you can get away with recursion really depends upon the complexity of the sub procedure concerned, the amount and type of data being passed in, and an infinite number of other variables and unknowns.

- Fixed-length strings can't be passed as parameters to a sub procedure. You may think that you can get around this by using code similar to the following:

```
Private Sub Command1_Click()

    Dim sFixed As String * 20
    sFixed = "Hello"
    AddSomeStuff sFixed
    MsgBox sFixed

End Sub


Private Sub AddSomeStuff(ByRef sStrFx As String)

    sStrFx = sStrFx & " World"

End Sub
```

In fact, what happens in this case is that the variable *sStrFx* isn't actually a reference to *sFixed* in the calling procedure. It's as though you have passed the string by value—*sStrFx* is a variable-length copy of *sFixed*. So adding to the string affects only *sStrFx*; when control returns to the calling procedure, *sFixed* is unchanged.

See Also

Call Statement, Exit Statement, Function Statement

Switch Function

Named Arguments

No

Syntax

```
Switch(expr-1, value-1[, expr-2, value-2 ... [, _
      expr-n, value-n]])
```

expr

Use: Required

Data Type: Variant

A number of expressions to be evaluated.

value

Use: Required

Data Type: Variant

An expression or value to return if the associated expression evaluates to True.

Return Value

A Variant value or expression.

Description

Evaluates a list of expressions and, on finding the first expression to evaluate to True, returns an associated value or expression.

Rules at a Glance

- A minimum of two expression/value pairs is required; additional pairs are optional.

- Expressions are evaluated from left to right.

- If none of the expressions are True, the *Switch* function returns Null.

- Although *Switch* returns only the first True expression's associated value, all expressions in the list are evaluated. This means that no performance gains result from placing expressions that are more likely to evaluate to True earlier in the list. It also means that any expression is capable of raising a runtime error.

- *value* can be a constant, a variable, or an expression.

Example

The *GetTextColor* function uses the *Switch* function to return a color value that depends on the sign of the long integer passed to it as a parameter.

```
Private Function GetTextColor(lValue As Long) As Long

GetTextColor = Switch(lValue > 0, vbBlue, lValue = 0, _
                      vbBlack, lValue < 0, vbRed)

End Function
```

Programming Tips & Gotchas

The *Switch* function can prove to be an efficient alternative to If...Then...Else statements, but it can't be used in situations where multiple lines of code are required to be executed on finding the first True expression.

See Also

If...Then Statement, Select Case Statement

SYD Function

Named Arguments

Yes

Syntax

```
SYD(cost, salvage, life, period )
```
cost

> Use: Required
>
> Data Type: Double
>
> The initial cost of the asset.

salvage

> Use: Required
>
> Data Type: Double
>
> The value of the asset at the end of its useful life.

life

> Use: Required
>
> Data Type: Double
>
> The length of the useful life of the asset.

period

> Use: Required
>
> Data Type: Double
>
> The period whose depreciation is to be calculated.

Return Value

A Double representing depreciation per period.

Description

Computes the sum-of-years' digits depreciation of an asset for a specified period. The sum-of-years' digits method allocates a larger amount of the depreciation in the earlier years of the asset.

Rules at a Glance

* **life** and **period** must be expressed in the same time unit. For example, if **life** represents the life of the asset in years, **period** must be a particular year for which the depreciation amount is to be computed.

* All arguments must be positive numeric values.

* To calculate the depreciation for a given period, *SYD* uses the formula:

```
(Cost-Salvage)*((Life-Period + 1)/(Life*(Life + 1)/2))
```

See Also

DDB Function, SLN Function

Tab Function

Syntax

```
Tab[(colno)]
```

`colno`

> Use: Optional
>
> Data Type: Integer
>
> A column number to which the insertion point moves before displaying or printing the next expression.

Description

Moves the text insertion point to a given column or the start of the next print zone

Rules at a Glance

- If the `colno` argument is omitted, the text insertion point is moved to the beginning of the next print zone.

- The value of `colno` determines the behavior of the insertion point:

Value of `colno`	Position of Insertion Point
Current column > `colno`	Moves one line down and moves to the `colno` column.
`colno` > Output Width	Uses the formula `colno Mod width`. If the result is less than the current insertion point, the insertion point moves down one line; otherwise, the insertion point remains on the same line.
< 1	Column 1

- The left column is always 1.

- When expressions are output to files using the `Print #` statement, the width of the output is determined by the `Width #` statement.

- When output is sent to either the screen or the printer, the surface is divided into columns, the width of each column being the average width of all characters in the current point size of the current font. This means that the number of columns for tabulation purposes doesn't necessarily relate to the number of characters that can be printed across the width of the output surface.

Programming Tips & Gotchas

- When placing output on the Printer object, use the TextWidth method to determine the actual width of a given string in a given font and font size. Another more flexible (although more complex) method of setting the current print position for the Printer object is to set the CurrentX property.

- The *Tab* function without a `colno` argument is useful when outputting data to a file using the `Print #` statement in locales where the comma would be recognized as a decimal separator.

See Also

> Width # Statement

Reference

Tan Function

Named Arguments

No

Syntax

```
Tan (number)
number
```
   Use: Required

   Data Type: Double

   An angle in radians.

Return Value

A Double containing the tangent of an angle.

Description

Returns the ratio of two sides of a right angle triangle.

Rules at a Glance

The returned ratio is derived by dividing the length of the side opposite the angle by the length of the side adjacent to the angle.

Programming Tips & Gotchas

* You can convert radians to degrees using the following formula:

```
radians = degrees * (pi/180)
```

* You can convert degrees to radians using the following formula:

```
degrees = radians * (180/pi)
```

Terminate Event

Syntax

```
Private Sub object_Terminate( )
Private Sub Class_Terminate( )
object
```
   Use: Required

   Data Type: Object

   A Form, MDIForm, User control, Property Page, or a VBA UserForm.

Description

The Terminate event is fired when the last instance of an object or class is removed from memory.

Rules at a Glance

- Instances of an object or class are removed from memory by explicitly setting the object variable to Nothing or by the object variable going out of scope.

- The Terminate event of a form-based object is fired after the Unload event.

- If an application ends because of a runtime error, a class's Terminate event isn't fired.

Example

The following example shows a typical terminate event in a class object that decrements a global instance counter used to ensure only a single instance of a particular utility object is created. When the counter reaches 0, the global object reference to the utility object is destroyed.

```
Private Sub Class_Terminate()

    glbUtilCount = glbUtilCount - 1
    If glbUtilCount = 0 then
        Set goUtils = Nothing
    End If

End Sub
```

Programming Tips & Gotchas

- If an application is terminated using the End statement prior to removing all instances of a class or form from memory, the Terminate event of that class isn't fired. This is the main reason you shouldn't use the End statement to terminate an application. Instead, you should use a Sub Main procedure. Specify Sub Main as the start-up procedure of your application; when program execution reaches the End Sub statement of the Sub Main procedure, the program terminates cleanly.

- The Terminate event is also fired when the object variable holding a reference to the last instance of an object is re-referenced in a Set statement using the New keyword, or is assigned a reference to a new instance of the same type of object. In the following example, two object variables of the same object type are declared at form level. When the Command1 button is clicked, they are both referenced to new (and different) instances of the same class. When the Command2 button is clicked, the reference held by oTwoObj is assigned to the variable oOneObj; this implicitly releases the reference held by oOneObj, and the Terminate event of that original instance is fired:

```
Option Explicit
Private oOneObj As myClass
Private oTwoObj As myClass

Private Sub Command1_Click()
    Set oOneObj = New myClass
    Set oTwoObj = New myClass
End Sub
Private Sub Command2_Click()
    Set oOneObj = oTwoObj
```

```
End Sub
```

Code for the myClass class:

```
Option Explicit

Private Sub Class_Initialize()
    Debug.Print "My Class Initialized"
End Sub

Private Sub Class_Terminate()
    Debug.Print "My Class Terminated"
End Sub
```

- You should get into the habit of setting object variables to Nothing explicitly. This is good programming practice, and it allows you to follow the life cycle of an object through your code. This should also include setting object variables to Nothing within error-handling routines.

- During the development stage, you should make use of conditional compilation and the Debug.Print method to check that all references to an object or class are being released correctly. This can be done as shown in the snippet below, which is added to the class's Terminate event:

```
#If ccDebug Then
    Debug.Print "Class myClass Terminated"
#End If
```

This is important, because although you are prevented from specifying circular object references (where one class references another and—perhaps indirectly—the referenced class also holds a reference to the class referencing it) within the references dialog, you can quite easily build in circular object references without realizing it or even deliberately. Classes with circular references don't release from memory until the application terminates. For more details, see Chapter 4.

See Also

Initialize Event, Set Statement

TextStream Object

Description

The TextStream object represents a text file. You can open a TextStream object to read, append, or write. The TextStream object provides methods to read, write, and close the text file.

The TextStream object is one of objects in the File System object model; for an overview of the model, including the library reference needed to access it, see the File System object model entry.

Createable

No

Returned by

File.OpenTextStream Method, FileSystemObject.CreateTextFile Method, FileSystem-Object.OpenTextFile Method

Properties

All of the following TextStream object properties are read-only:

AtEndOfLine
> Data Type: Boolean

> A flag denoting when the end of a line marker has been reached. Only relevant when reading a file.

AtEndofStream
> Data Type: Boolean

> A flag denoting when the end of the stream has been reached. Only relevant when reading a file.

Column
> Data Type: Long

> Returns the column number position of the file marker.

Line
> Data Type: Long

> Returns the line number position of the file marker.

Methods

Close	Read	ReadAll
ReadLine	Skip	SkipLine
Write	WriteBlankLines	WriteLine

TextStream.Close Method

Syntax

```
oTextStreamObj.Close
```

Description

Closes the current TextStream object.

Rules at a Glance

You shouldn't try to reference a TextStream object that has been closed.

Programming Tips & Gotchas

After closing the TextStream object, set oTextStreamObj to Nothing.

TextStream.Read Method

Named Arguments

Yes

Syntax

```
oTextStreamObj.Read(Characters)
oTextStreamObj
```
> Use: Required
>
> Data Type: TextStream object
>
> Any object variable returning a TextStream object.

```
Characters
```
> Required
>
> Data Type: Long
>
> The number of characters you want to read from the TextStream.

Return Value

A String.

Description

Reads a given number of characters from a file.

Rules at a Glance

Files opened for writing or appending can't be read; you must first close the file and reopen it using the **ForRead** constant.

See Also

TextStream.ReadAll Method, TextStream.ReadLine Method

TextStream.ReadAll Method

Syntax

```
oTextStreamObj.ReadAll
```

Return Value

A String.

Description

Reads the entire file into memory.

Rules at a Glance

- For large files, use the ReadLine or Read methods to reduce the load on memory resources.

- Files opened for writing or appending can't be read; you must first close the file and reopen it using the **ForRead** constant.

TextStream.Read Method, TextStream.ReadLine Method

TextStream.ReadLine Method

Syntax

```
oTextStreamObj.ReadLine
```

Return Value

A String.

Description

Reads a line of the text file into memory, from the start of the current line up to the character immediately preceding the next end of line marker.

Rules at a Glance

Files opened for writing or appending can't be read; you must first close the file and reopen it using the `ForRead` constant.

See Also

TextStream.ReadAll Method, TextStream.ReadLine Method

TextStream.Skip Method

Named Arguments

Yes

Syntax

```
oTextStreamObj.Skip (Characters)
oTextStreamObj
```
    Use: Required

    Data Type: TextStream object

    Any object variable returning a TextStream object.

```
NoOfChars
```
    Use: Required

    Data Type: Long

    Number of characters to skip when reading.

Description

Ignores the next *Characters* characters when reading from a text file.

Rules at a Glance

The internal file marker is placed at the character immediately following the last skipped character.

Reference

See Also

TextStream.SkipLine Method

TextStream.SkipLine Method

Syntax

```
oTextStreamObj.SkipLine
```

Description

Ignores the current line when reading from a text file.

Rules at a Glance

The internal file marker is placed at the beginning of the line immediately following the skipped line.

TextStream.Write Method

Named Arguments

Yes

Syntax

```
oTextStreamObj.Write(Text)
oTextStreamObj
```
    Use: Required

    Data Type: TextStream object

    Any object variable returning a TextStream object.

Text

    Use: Required

    Data Type: String

    Any string expression to write to the file.

Description

Writes a string to the text file.

Rules at a Glance

The file marker is set at the end of string. As a result, subsequent writes to the file adjoin each other, with no spaces inserted. To write data to the file in a more structured manner, use the WriteLine method.

See Also

TextStream.WriteBlankLines Method, TextStream.WriteLine Method

TextStream.WriteBlankLines Method

Named Arguments

Yes

Syntax

```
oTextStreamObj.WriteBlankLines (Lines)
oTextStreamObj
```
   Use: Required

   Data Type: TextStream object

   Any object variable returning a TextStream object.

`Lines`
   Use: Required

   Data Type: Long

   The number of new line characters to insert.

Description

Inserts one or more newline characters in the file at the current file marker position.

See Also

   TextStream.Write Method, TextStream.WriteLine Method

TextStream.WriteLine Method

Syntax

```
oTextStreamObj.WriteLine (String)
oTextStreamObj
```
   Use: Required

   Data Type: TextStream object

   Any object variable returning a TextStream object.

`String`
   Use: Required

   Data Type: String

   A string expression to write to the file.

Description

Writes a string immediately followed by a new line character to a text file.

See Also

   TextStream.WriteBlankLines Method

Reference

Time, Time$ Functions

Syntax

```
Time
```

Return Value

A Variant of subtype Date.

Description

Returns the current system time.

Rules at a Glance

The *Time* function returns the time in the date format hh:mm:ss AM/PM.

Programming Tips & Gotchas

The *Time* function returns only the system time; you can use the Time statement to set the system time.

See Also

Time Statement, Now Function

Time Statement

Syntax

```
Time = time
time
```
> Use: Required
>
> Data Type: Variant
>
> Any valid time expression.

Description

Sets the current system time.

Rules at a Glance

The Time statement attempts to evaluate the variant you are assigning as a valid time; if it can't be converted to a valid time, a runtime error is generated.

Programming Tips & Gotchas

* It's not a good idea to independently set the date and time in a networked environment. Instead, the log-on script of each workstation should include code to set the date and time of the workstation to be that of the PDC or another centrally used server.

* You can use the *Time* function to return the current system time.

See Also

Time Function

Timer Function

Syntax

```
Timer
```

Return Value

A Single.

Description

Returns the number of seconds since midnight.

Programming Tips & Gotchas

- You can use the *Timer* function as an easy method of passing a seed number to the Randomize statement, as follows:

```
Randomize Timer
```

- The *Timer* function is ideal for measuring the time taken to execute a procedure or program statement, as the following snippet shows:

```
Dim sStartTime As Single
Dim i As Integer

sStartTime = Timer
    For i = 1 To 100
        Debug.Print "Hello"
    Next i
MsgBox "Time Taken = " & Timer - sStartTime & " Seconds"
```

TimeSerial Function

Named Arguments

Yes

Syntax

```
TimeSerial(hour, minute, second)
```
hour
> Use: Required
>
> Data Type: Integer
>
> A number in the range 0 to 23.

minute
> Use: Required
>
> Data Type: Integer
>
> Any valid integer.

second
> Use: Required
>
> Data Type: Integer

Any valid integer.

Return Value

A Variant of subtype Date.

Description

Constructs a valid time given a number of hours, minutes, and seconds.

Rules at a Glance

- Any of the arguments can be specified as relative values or expressions.

- The *hour* argument requires a 24-hour clock format; however, the return value is always in a 12-hour clock format suffixed with A.M. or P.M.

- If any of the values are greater than the normal range for the time unit to which it relates, the next higher time unit is increased accordingly. For example, a second argument of 125 is evaluated as 2 minutes 5 seconds.

- If any of the values are less than zero, the next higher time unit is decreased accordingly. For example, *TimeSerial(2,-1,30)* returns 01:59:30.

Programming Tips & Gotchas

Because *TimeSerial* handles time units outside of their normal limits, it can be used for time calculations. However, because the *DateAdd* function is more flexible and is internationally aware, it should be used instead.

See Also

DateAdd Function

TimeValue Function

Named Arguments

No

Syntax

```
TimeValue(time)
```
time

Use: Required

Data Type: String

Any valid string representation of a time.

Return Value

A Variant of sub data type Date.

Description

Converts a string representation of a time to a Variant Date data type.

Rules at a Glance

- If *time* is invalid, a runtime error is generated.

- If *time* is Null, *TimeValue* returns Null.

- Both 12- and 24-hour clock formats are valid.

- Any date information contained within *time* is ignored by the *TimeValue* function.

Programming Tips & Gotchas

- A time literal can also be assigned to a Variant or Date variable by surrounding the date with hash characters (#), as the following snippet demonstrates:

```
Dim dMyTime As Date
dMyTime = #12:30:00 AM#
```

- The *CDate* function can also cast a time expression contained within a string as a Date variable, with the additional advantage of being internationally aware.

See Also

CDate Function, TimeSerial Function

Trim, Trim$ Functions

Named Arguments

No

Syntax

```
Trim(string)
string
```
       Use: Required

       Data Type: String

       Any string expression.

Return Value

A String (*Trim$*) or Variant of subtype String (*Trim*).

Description

Removes both leading and trailing spaces from a given string.

Rules at a Glance

If string is Null, the *Trim* function returns Null.

Programming Tips & Gotchas

Trim combines into a single function call what would otherwise be separate calls to the *RTrim* and *LTrim* functions.

See Also

LTrim Function, RTrim Function

Type Statement

Named Arguments

No

Syntax

```
[Private | Public] Type varname
    elementname [([subscripts])] As type
    [elementname [([subscripts])] As type]
    . . .
End Type
```

Public

    Use: Optional

    Type: Keyword

    Gives the user-defined type scope through all procedures in all modules
    in the project. Public and Private are mutually exclusive.

Private

    Use: Optional

    Type: Keyword

    Restricts the scope of the user-defined type to those procedures within
    the same module. Public and Private are mutually exclusive.

varname

    Use: Required

    The name of the user-defined type.

elementname

    Use: Required

    Data Type: Any

    The name of an element of the user-defined type.

subscripts

    Use: Optional

    Data Type: Numeric literal or constant

    The dimensions of an array element.

type

    Use: Required

    The data type of the element.

Description

Used at module level to define a user-defined type.

Rules at a Glance

- A user-defined type can contain one or more elements.

- The Type statement can't be used within a procedure; it can be used only
  within the declaration section of a module.

- In form and code modules, user-defined types are `Public` by default. You can reduce the scope and visibility of a user-defined type to the current module by using the `Private` keyword.

- Until Version 6 of VB, publicly declared user-defined types were not permitted in class modules. Now, VB6 has introduced the remote user-defined types, which allow you to declare a property as a user-defined type, or have a class method return a user-defined type. The following snippet shows how to implement a remote user-defined type property within a class module:

```
Public Type udtTestType
    EmployeeNo As Integer
    EmployeeName As String
End Type

Private mudtTestType As udtTestType

Public Property Get TestType() As udtTestType
    TestType = mudtTestType
End Property

Public Property Let TestType(udtVal As udtTestType)
    mudtTestType = udtVal
End Property
```

- A variable can be declared as being of a user-defined type by using the `Dim`, `Private`, `Public`, `ReDim`, or `Static` statements anywhere within the scope of the user-defined type.

- The *subscripts* clause uses the following syntax:

```
[lowerbound To] upperbound [, _
[lowerbound To] upperbound] . . .
```

- When the optional *lowerbound* clause isn't present, the lower bound of the array defaults to that defined by the `Option Base` statement.

- If an `Option Base` statement has not been used in the current module, the lower bound is zero.

- *lowerbound* and *upperbound* must be stated as numeric literals or constants; variables can't be used.

- Contrary to standard variable naming conventions, keywords can be used for the names of the elements of a user-defined type. However, this isn't recommended, since it makes code confusing to read.

- *type* may be Byte, Boolean, Currency, Date, Double, Integer, Long, Object, Single, String, Variant, another user-defined type, or an object type.

- The following table shows the values held by each data type when an element is initialized:

Data Type	Initial Value
Numeric	0
Variable-length string	Zero-length string ("")

Data Type	Initial Value
Fixed-length string	Filled with zeros
Variant	Empty
Object	Nothing
Date	Saturday 3o December 1899 12:00:00

Programming Tips & Gotchas

- Frequently, related items of information in an application are stored to parallel arrays. There is far less coding (and confusion) involved, however, if the elements are stored to a user-defined type instead. Using an array of user-defined types also tends to produce more readable code than using a multidimensional array.

- User-defined types are central to building advanced data structures such as linked lists, stacks, and queues.

- Visual Basic classes and collections of classes have largely taken over from user-defined types. A class module can be thought of as a direct development of the user-defined type. In a class module, properties replace the elements of a user-defined type. Furthermore, class modules contain subroutines and functions and can have scope outside of the current project. However, VB6 has somewhat revived the user-defined type by allowing user-defined types to be passed across process boundaries. For more information, see Chapter 4.

- Using remote user-defined types requires NT 5, NT 4 Service Pack 4, or the latest version of DCOM95. Win98 also support remote user-defined types.

- When using UDTs in an ActiveX Server (in VB6 onwards), a client of the server sees the UDT as an ActiveX object. Proof of this comes from the fact that you can use the **TypeOf** operator (which compares one object with another) with a user-defined type, as the following example demonstrates. This example also shows the use of the new **vbUserDefinedType** vartype constant, and the use of **TypeName** with a remote UDT. The first code snippet comes from an ActiveX server, which is referenced by a standard EXE project (the second code snippet) using the References dialog (this works only with early binding).

Code From Class Module in ActiveX DLL Project

```
Option Explicit

Public Type udtTestType
    Name As String
    Age As Integer
End Type
```

Code From Form Module in Standard EXE Project

```
Option Explicit

Private udtTest As udtTestType
```

```
Private Sub Command1_Click()

    If VarType(udtTest) = vbUserDefinedType Then
        Debug.Print "user defined type"
    End If

    'returns "udtTestType"
    Debug.Print TypeName(udtTest)
    ' returns "Integer"
    Debug.Print TypeName(udtTest.Age)
    'returns "String"
    Debug.Print TypeName(udtTest.Name)

    If TypeOf udtTest Is udtTestType Then
        Debug.Print "this is a udtTestType"
    End If

End Sub
```

See Also

ReDim Statement

TypeName Function

Named Arguments

No

Syntax

TypeName(*varname*)

varname

    Use: Required

    Data Type: Any

    The name of a variable.

Return Value

A String

Description

Returns a string containing the name of the data type of a variable.

Rules at a Glance

- If *varname* is a Variant, *TypeName* returns the variant's data subtype. If the variant has not been assigned a value, *TypeName* returns **Empty**. Therefore, *TypeName* never actually returns the string "Variant."

- *TypeName* can't be used with a user-defined type.

- The following table describes the possible return values and their meaning;

Return Value	Underlying Data Type
Boolean	Boolean
Byte	Byte
classname	An object variable explicitly declared as type *classname*
Currency	Currency
Date	Date
Decimal	Decimal
Double	Double-precision floating-point number
Empty	Uninitialized variant
Error	An error
Integer	Integer
Long	Long integer
Nothing	Unassigned object variable
Null	No valid data
Object	Variable explicitly declared as type Object
Single	Single-precision floating-point number
String	String
Unknown	An object whose type is unknown
Variant()	A variant containing an array created using the *Array* function

- If *varname* contains an array, *TypeName* appends the appropriate data type name with empty parentheses to denote an array. For example, an array of String returns `String()`.

See Also

VarType Function

UBound Function

Syntax

```
UBound(arrayname[, dimension])
arrayname
```
Use: Required

The name of the array.

dimension

Use: Optional

Data Type: Variant (Long)

A number specifying the dimension of the array.

Return Value

UBound returns a Long integer.

Description

Indicates the upper limit of a specified dimension of an array. The upper boundary is the largest subscript you can access within the specified array.

Rules at a Glance

- If *dimension* isn't specified, 1 is assumed. To determine the upper limit of the first dimension of an array, set *dimension* to 1, to 2 for the second dimension, and so on.

- The upper bound of an array dimension can be set using To, Dim, Private, Public, Redim, and Static, and can be set to any integer value.

Programming Tips & Gotchas

- Note that *UBound* returns the actual subscript of the upper bound of a particular array dimension

- *UBound* is especially useful for determining the current upper boundary of a dynamic array.

- The *UBound* function works only with conventional arrays. To determine the upper bound of a collection, retrieve the value of its Count property. To determine the upper bound of a control array or a menu control array, use the array's UBound property.

See Also

LBound Function

UCase, UCase$ Functions

Named Arguments

No

Syntax

```
UCase(string)
string
```
Use: Required

Data Type: String

A valid string expression.

Return Value

A String or Variant of subtype String.

Description

Converts a string to uppercase.

Rules at a Glance

- *UCase* affects only lowercase alphabetical letters; all other characters within *string* remain unaffected.

- *UCase* returns Null if *string* contains a Null.

Programming Tips & Gotchas

As with all string functions in which two variations are available (one suffixed with the $ sign and one without), the $ version returns a String data type; the plain version returns a variant of subtype string.

See Also

LCase Function

Unload Statement

Syntax

```
Unload object
object
```

    Use: Required

    Data Type: Object

    A form or control loaded at runtime.

Description

Removes a form or (in Visual Basic) a dynamically created member of a control array from memory.

Rules at a Glance

- Only controls added to a control array at runtime can be removed from memory using the Unload statement. Those controls added to a form at design time can't be unloaded individually.

- When a form, the form's Query_Unload event is fired. Once its event handler has executed, the form's Form_Unload event is fired.

- When *object* is an MDI form, the following is the order of events:

    a. MDI form QueryUnload event

    b. All loaded child forms' QueryUnload events

    c. All loaded child forms' Form_Unload events

    d. MDI form Form_Unload event

Programming Tips & Gotchas

- You can prevent a form from unloading by setting the *Cancel* argument to True in a QueryUnload or Form_Unload event procedure. Cancel is a parameter passed by reference to both the QueryUnload and the Unload events.

- When you unload a form from within the form's code, you should use the Me keyword to refer to the form. This makes your code more readable, as the following snippet shows:

```
Unload Me
```

- Microsoft recommends that forms should be unloaded only in the Click event of a CommandButton or menu control. Calling the Unload statement in other event handlers can have undesirable side effects and cause *general protection faults* (GPFs).

- You can also bring your code for loading and unloading forms in line with the latest object coding in Visual Basic. The following snippet shows the modern alternative to using the Load and Unload statements for a Form object:

```
Dim frmVar as Form1
Set frmVar = New Form1
...
frmVar.Show vbModal
...
Set frmVar = Nothing
```

This requires, of course, that a form named Form1 be included in the project, and that it not be designated as the startup module.

- When you unload a form from memory, only the form window and controls are unloaded; the code attached to a form and controls within the form module remain in memory.

See Also

Load Statement

Unlock Statement

Syntax

```
Unlock [#]filenumber[, recordrange]
filenumber
```

> Use: Required
>
> Data Type: Integer
>
> Any valid file number.

```
recordrange
```

> Use: Optional
>
> Data Type: Long
>
> A range of records.

The syntax for the *recordrange* argument is:

```
recnumber | [start] To end
recnumber
```

> Use: Required
>
> Data Type: Long

The record or byte number to unlock.

start

Use: Optional

Data Type: Long

The first record or byte number to unlock.

end

Use: Required

Data Type: Long

The last record or byte number to unlock.

Description

Use the Unlock statement in situations where more than one part of your program may need read and write access to the same data file. The Unlock statement removes a lock placed on a section or the whole file that was locked with the Lock statement.

Rules at a Glance

- Records and bytes in a file are always numbered sequentially from 1 onwards.

- To unlock a particular record, specify its record number and only that record is unlocked.

- Use the Unlock statement omitting *recnumber* to unlock the whole file.

- The Unlock statement unlocks an entire file opened in input or output (sequential) mode, regardless of the *recordrange* argument.

- If you omit the *start* argument in the *recnumber* syntax, Unlock unlocks all records from the start of the file to record or byte number *end.*

Programming Tips & Gotchas

- You must take care to remove all file locks using the Unlock statement before either closing a file or ending the application; otherwise, you can leave the file in an unstable state. This, of course, means that, where appropriate, your error handling routines must be made aware of any locks you currently have in place so that they may be removed if necessary.

- You use the Lock and Unlock statements in pairs, and the argument lists of both statements must match exactly.

See Also

Lock Statement

Val Function

Named Arguments

No

Syntax

```
Val(string)
string
```
   Use: Required

   Data Type: String

   Any string representation of a number.

Return Value

A numeric data type able to hold the number contained in *string*.

Description

Converts a string representation of a number into a numeric data type.

Rules at a Glance

- The *Val* function starts reading the string with the leftmost character and stops at the first character it doesn't recognize as being part of a valid number. For example, the statement:

```
iNumber = Val("1A1")
```

   returns 1.

- &O and &H (the octal and hexadecimal prefixes) are recognized by the *Val* function.

- Currency symbols such as $ and £, and delimiters such as commas aren't recognized as numbers by the *Val* function.

- The *Val* function recognizes only the period (.) as a decimal delimiter.

- Prior to processing *string*, *Val* removes spaces, tabs, and linefeed characters.

Programming Tips & Gotchas

If you are developing an international application, you should use the more modern, internationally aware *CDbl* function to convert strings to numbers, since *CDbl* can recognize decimal separators.

See Also

   CCur Function, CDbl Function, CDec Function, CInt Function, CLng Function, CSng Function

---

VarType Function

Named Arguments

No

Syntax

```
VarType(varname)
```

```
varname
```
      Use: Required

The name of a variable.

Return Value

An integer representing the data type of **varname**.

Description

Determines the data type of a specified variable.

Rules at a Glance

• The *VarType* function can't be used with user-defined types.

• The following intrinsic constants can test the return value of the *VarType* function:

Constant	Value	Data Type or Variant Value
vbBoolean	11	Boolean
vbByte	17	Byte
vbCurrency	6	Currency
vbDataObject	13	A data access object variable
vbDate	7	Date
vbDecimal	14	Decimal
vbDouble	5	Double-precision floating-point number
vbEmpty	0	Uninitialized variant
vbError	10	An error
vbInteger	2	Integer
vbLong	3	Long integer
vbNull	1	No valid data
vbObject	9	Variable explicitly declared as type Object
vbSingle	4	Single-precision floating-point number
vbString	8	String
cbUserDefinedType	36	User-defined type
vbVariant	12	Variant—only returned with **vbArray** (8194)

• If **varname** is an array, the *VarType* function returns 8194 (**vbArray**) plus the value of the data type of the array. For example, an array of strings returns 8194 + 8 = 8204. To test for an array, you can use the intrinsic constant **vbArray**. For example:

```
If VarType(myVar) And vbArray Then
    MsgBox "This is an array"
End If
```

Programming Tips & Gotchas

When you use *VarType* with an object variable, you may get what appears to be an incorrect return value. The reason for this is that if the object has a default property, *VarType* returns the data type of the default property.

See Also

TypeName Function

Weekday Function

Named Arguments

Yes

Syntax

```
Weekday(date, [firstdayofweek])
```
date
> Use: Required
>
> Data Type: Variant
>
> Any valid date expression.

firstdayofweek
> Use: Optional
>
> Data Type: Integer
>
> Constant value specifying the first day of the week.

Return Value

A Variant of subtype Integer.

Description

Determines the day of the week of a given date.

Rules at a Glance

- The following intrinsic constants determine the value returned by the *Weekday* function:

Constant	Return Value	Day Represented
vbSunday	1	Sunday
vbMonday	2	Monday
vbTuesday	3	Tuesday
vbWednesday	4	Wednesday
vbThursday	5	Thursday
vbFriday	6	Friday
vbSaturday	7	Saturday

- If *date* is Null, the *Weekday* function also returns Null.

- The following table describes the possible settings for the *firstdayofweek* argument:

Constant	Value	Description
vbUseSystem	0	Use the NLS API setting
vbSunday	1	Sunday (default)
vbMonday	2	Monday
vbTuesday	3	Tuesday
vbWednesday	4	Wednesday
vbThursday	5	Thursday
vbFriday	6	Friday
vbSaturday	7	Saturday

Programming Tips & Gotchas

- If you specify a *firstdayofweek* argument, the function returns the day of the week relative to *firstdayofweek*. For instance, if you set the value of *firstdayofweek* to vbMonday (2), indicating that Monday is the first day of the week, and attempt to determine the day of the week on which October 1, 1996, falls, the function returns a 2. That's because October 1, 1996, is a Tuesday, the second day of a week whose first day is Monday.

- The fact that the function's return value is relative to *firstdayofweek* makes using the day of the week constants to interpret the function's return value confusing, to say the least. If we use our October 1, 1996, example once again, the following expression evaluates to **True** if the day of the week is Tuesday:

```
If vbMonday = WeekDay(CDate("10/1/96"), vbMonday) Then
```

See Also

DatePart Function, Day Function, Month Function, Year Function

---

WeekdayName Function (VB6)

Syntax

```
WeekdayName(WeekdayNo, [abbreviate [, FirstDayOfWeek]])
WeekdayNo
```
    Use: Required

    Data Type: Long

    The ordinal number of the required weekday from 1 to 7.

abbreviate
    Use: Optional

    Data Type: Boolean

    Specifies whether to return the full day name or an abbreviation.

FirstDayOfWeek
> Use: Optional
>
> Data Type: vbDayOfWeek constant
>
> Specifies which day of the week should be first.

Return Value

A String

Description

Returns the real name of the day.

Rules at a Glance

* *WeekDayNo* must be a number between 1 and 7, or the function generates runtime error 5, "Invalid procedure call or argument."

* If *FirstDayOfWeek* is omitted, *WeekdayName* treats Sunday as the first day of the week.

* The default value of *abbreviate* is False.

Programming Tips & Gotchas

* *WeekdayName* with *abbreviate* set to False is the equivalent of Format (*dateval*, "*dddd*").

* *WeekdayName* with *abbreviate* set to True is the equivalent of Format (*dateval*, "*ddd*").

* You'd expect that, given a date, *WeekDayName* would return the name of that date's day. But this isn't how the function works. To determine the name of the day of a particular date, combine *WeekDayName* with a call to the *WeekDay* function, as the following code fragment shows:

```
sDay = WeekDayName(Weekday(dDate, iFirstDay), _
                   bFullName, iFirstDay)
```

Note that the value of the *FirstDayOfWeek* argument must be the same in the calls to both functions for *WeekDayName* to return an accurate result.

See Also

Format Function, WeekDay Function

While...Wend Statement

Named Arguments

No

Syntax

```
While condition
    [statements]
Wend
```

> condition
>> Use: Required
>>
>> Data Type: Numeric or String
>>
>> An expression evaluating to **True** or **False**.
>
> statements
>> Use: Optional
>>
>> Program statements to execute while condition remains **True**.

Description

Repeatedly executes program code while a given condition remains **True**.

Rules at a Glance

- A **Null** condition is evaluated as **False**.

- If *condition* evaluates to **True**, the program code between the **While** and **Wend** statements is executed. After the **Wend** statement is executed, control is passed back up to the **While** statement, where *condition* is evaluated again. When *condition* evaluates to **False**, program execution skips to the first statement following the **Wend** statement.

- You can nest **While...Wend** loops within each other.

Programming Tips & Gotchas

The **While...Wend** statement remains in Visual Basic for backward compatibility only. It has been superseded by the much more flexible **Do...Loop** statement.

See Also

> Do...Loop Statement

Width # Statement

Syntax

```
Width #filenumber, width
```
> filenumber
>> Use: Required
>>
>> Data Type: Integer
>>
>> Any valid file number.
>
> width
>> Use: Required
>>
>> Data Type: Numeric
>>
>> A number between 0 and 255.

Description

Specifies a virtual file width when working with files opened with the **Open** statement.

Rules at a Glance

- *width* defines the number of characters that can be placed on a single output line.

- The default *width* of 0 denotes that there isn't a limit to the number of characters that can be placed on a single output line.

See Also

Input # Statement, Open Statement, Print # Statement, Write # Statement

---

With Statement

Named Arguments

No

Syntax

```
With object
    [statements]
End With
```

object

> Use: Required
>
> Data Type: Object
>
> A previously declared object variable or user-defined type.

statements

> Use: Optional
>
> Program code to execute against object.

Description

Performs a set of property assignments and executes other code against a particular object or user-defined type, thus allowing you to refer to the object only once. Because the object is referred to only once, the "behind the scenes" qualification of that object is also performed only once, leading to improved performance of the code block.

Rules at a Glance

- The single object referred to in the With statement remains the same throughout the code contained within the With...End With block. Therefore, only properties and methods of *object* can be used within the code block without explicitly referencing the object. All other object references within the With...End statement must start with a fully qualified object reference.

- With statements can be nested, as long as the inner With statement refers to a sub object or a dependent object of the outer With statement.

Programming Tips & Gotchas

It's important that you don't include code within the With statement block that forces execution to branch out of the block. Similarly, don't write code that forces program flow to jump into a With block. Both the With and its associated End With statement must be executed or you will generate unpredictable errors and results.

See Also

Do...Loop Statement, Set Statement

WithEvents Keyword

Named Arguments

No

Syntax

```
Dim|Private|Public WithEvents objVarname As objectType
```

objVarName
> Use: Required
>
> Data Type: String
>
> The name of any object variable that refers to an object that exposes events.

objectType
> Use: Required
>
> Data Type: Any object type other than the generic Object
>
> The ProgID of a referenced object.

Description

The WithEvents keyword informs VB that the object being referenced exposes events. When you declare an object variable using WithEvents, an entry for the object variable is placed in the code window's drop-down Object List, and a list of the events available to the object variable is placed in the code window's drop-down Procedures List. You can then write code event handlers for the object variable in the same way that you write other more common event handlers such as Form_Load.

Rules at a Glance

- An object variable declaration using the WithEvents keyword can be used only in an object module such as a Form or Class module.

- An object variable declaration using the WithEvents keyword should be placed only in the Declarations section of the object module.

- Any ActiveX object or class module that exposes events can be used with the WithEvents keyword. WithEvents is valid only when used to declare an object variable.

- You can't use WithEvents when declaring the generic Object type.

- Unlike other variable declarations, the As keyword is mandatory.

- There is no limit to the number of object variables that can refer to the same object using the `WithEvents` keyword; they all respond to that object's events.

- You can't create an array variable that uses the `WithEvents` keyword.

Example

The following example demonstrates how to trap and respond to the events within an ADO recordset. An object variable is declared using the `WithEvents` keyword in the declarations section of a form module. This allows you to write event-handling code for the ADO's built-in events, in this case the FetchProgress event. (The FetchProgress event allows you to implement a Progress Bar control that shows progress in populating the recordset.)

```
Private WithEvents oADo As ADODB.Recordset

Private Sub oADo_FetchProgress(ByVal Progress As Long, _
                ByVal MaxProgress As Long, _
                adStatus As ADODB.EventStatusEnum, _
                ByVal pRecordset As ADODB.Recordset)

    ProgressBar1.Max = MaxProgress
    ProgressBar1.Value = Progress

End Sub
```

Programming Tips & Gotchas

- Placing the object variable declaration that uses the `WithEvents` keyword in a procedure doesn't add the object variable name to the module's Object List. In other words, the events fired from the object would have scope only in the procedure and therefore can't be handled.

- Even if you declare the object variable using the `Public` keyword, the events fired by the object have scope only in the module in which the object variable has been declared.

- Because you can't use `WithEvents` to declare a generic Object type, `WithEvents` can be used only with early bound object references. In other words, objects must have been added to the project using the References dialog. Without this prior knowledge of the object's interface, VB has no chance of knowing how to handle events from the object.

- If the object you are referencing doesn't expose any public events, you will generate a compile-time error, "Object doesn't source Automation Events."

- You can't handle any type of event from within a code module. This isn't really a limitation, because to pass program control to a code module, you can simply call one of its functions or procedures from your event handler, just as you would from a form or control's event handler.

- For information about generating your own custom events in form and class modules, see the "Implementing Custom Events" section in Chapter 4.

Reference

See Also

Dim Statement, Event Statement, Private Statement, Public Statement, RaiseEvent Statement

Write # Statement

Named Arguments

No

Syntax

```
Write #filenumber, [outputlist]
filenumber
```
Use: Required

Data Type: Integer

Any valid file number.

```
outputlist
```
Use: Optional

A comma-delimited list of expressions to be written to the file.

Description

Writes structured data to a sequential file.

Rules at a Glance

* *outputlist* can contain multiple expressions delimited with either a comma, a semicolon, or a space.

* Calling the Write # statement with a single comma in place of *outputlist* forces a blank line to be written to the file.

* Object data can't be written to a file opened with the Open statement.

* The following table describes how the Write # statement handles certain types of data, regardless of the locale, to allow files to be read universally:

Data Type	Data Written to File
Numeric	Decimal separator is always a period (.)
Boolean	#TRUE# or #FALSE#
Date	#yyyy-mm-dd hh:mm:ss# (Hours specified in 24-hour format)
Null	#NULL#
Error	#ERROR errorcode#

* The Write statement automatically does the following:

  - Delimits data fields with a comma.

  - Places quotation marks around string data.

  - Inserts a newline character (Chr(13) + Chr(10)) after the last item in *outputlist* is written to the file.

Programming Tips & Gotchas

The structured data written to a file using the Write # statement is most suited to being read back from the file using the Input # statement.

See Also

Input # Statement, Print # Statement

Year Function

Named Arguments

No

Syntax

```
Year(date)
date
```
> Use: Required
>
> Data Type: Variant
>
> Any valid date expression.

Return Value

A Variant of subtype Integer.

Description

Returns an integer representing the year in a given date expression.

Rules at a Glance

If *date* contains Null, *Year* returns Null.

Programming Tips & Gotchas

- The validity of the date expression and position of the year element within the given date expression are initially determined by the locale settings of the Windows system. However, some extra intelligence relating to two-digit year values (see next item) has been built into the *Year* function that surpasses the usual comparison of a date expression to the current locale settings.

- What happens when you pass a date over to the *Year* function containing a two-digit year? Quite simply, when the *Year* function sees a two-digit year, it assumes that all values equal to or greater than 30 are in the 20th Century (i.e., 30 = 1930, 98 = 1998), and that all values less than 30 are in the 21st Century (i.e., 29 = 2029, 5 = 2005). Of course, if you don't want sleepless nights rewriting your programs in the year 2029, I'd suggest you insist on a four-digit year, which will see your code work perfectly for about the next 8,000 years!

See Also

DatePart Function, Day Function, IsDate Function, Month Function, Weekday Function

PART III

Appendixes

Part III contains four appendixes that supplement the core reference material provided in Part II. These include:

- Appendix A, *Language Elements by Category*, which lists each VBA statement, function, procedure, property, or method in each of a number of categories. You can use it to identify a particular language element so that you can look up its detailed entry in Part II.

- Appendix B, *Language Constants*, which lists the constants that are automatically supported by VBA.

- Appendix C, *Operators*, which lists VBA operators, including a somewhat more detailed treatment of the logical and bitwise operators.

- Appendix D, *What's New in VB6?*, examines the new language features found in the latest release of Microsoft's Visual Basic product.

APPENDIX A

Language Elements by Category

Collection Object

Add Method	Adds a member to the collection
Count Method	Returns the number of members in the collection
Item Method	Returns the member associated with a given key or ordinal position
Remove Method	Removes the member associated with a given key or ordinal position

Conditional Compilation

#Const Statement	Declares a conditional compiler constant
#If...Then Statement	Defines a block of code that will only be compiled into the program if the conditional constant is True

Data Type Conversion Functions

CBool Function	Returns a Boolean data type
CByte Function	Returns a Byte data type
CCur Function	Returns a Currency data type
CDate Function	Returns a Date data type
CDbl Function	Returns a Double data type
CDec Function	Returns a Decimal data subtype
CInt Function	Returns an Integer data type
CLng Function	Returns a Long data type
CSng Function	Returns a Single data type
CStr Function	Returns a String data type
CVar Function	Returns a Variant data type
CVDate Function	Converts expression to Date
CVErr Function	Converts expression to Error
Error Function	Returns an error message as a variant

Error$ Function	Returns an error message as a string
Fix Function	Returns an Integer portion of number
Hex Function	Returns a hexadecimal representation of number as a variant
Hex$ Function	Returns a hexadecimal representation of a number as a string
Int Function	Returns the integer portion of a number
Oct Function	Returns an octal representation of a number as a variant
Oct$ Function	Returns an octal representation of a number as a string
Str Function	Returns a string representation of a value as a variant
Str$ Function	Returns a string representation of a value as a string
Val Function	Returns the Double value of a string representation of a number

Data Bindings Objects (VB6 only)

BindingCollection Object

Add Method	Creates a binding between a control and a data field
Clear Method	Removes all binding objects from the collection
Count Property	Returns the number of Binding objects in the collection
DataMember Property	Returns or sets the data member to provide the data
DataSource Property	Returns or sets the object that will be the source of the data
Item Property	Returns the Binding object associated with a specified key
Remove Method	Removes a single Binding object from the collection
UpdateMode Property	Returns or sets the type of update to be performed

Binding Object

DataChanged Property	Returns **True** if the data has changed
DataField Property	Returns or sets the data field providing the data
DataFormat Property	Returns or sets a DataFormat object to provide formatting for the data
Key Property	Returns the key value used to add the Binding object to the collection
Object Property	Returns or sets a reference to the object providing the data
PropertyName Property	Returns or sets the name of the property within the control that will consume the data

Date and Time Functions

Calendar Property	Returns or sets the system calendar
Date Property	Returns the current system date as a date
Date$ Property	Returns the current system date as a string
Date Statement	Sets the system date

DateAdd Function	Returns the result of a date/time addition or subtraction calculation
DateDiff Function	Returns the difference between two dates
DatePart Function	Returns the part of the date requested
DateSerial Function	Returns a date from an expression containing month, day, and year
DateValue Function	Returns a date from a representation of a date
Day Function	Returns a number representing the day of the week
Hour Function	Returns a number representing the hour of the day
Minute Function	Returns a number representing the minute of the hour
Month Function	Returns a number representing the month of the year
MonthName Function*	Returns the name of the month for a given date
Now Property	Returns the current system time
Second Function	Returns a number representing the second of the time
Time Property	Returns or sets the current system time as a variant
Time$ Property	Returns or sets the current system time as a string
Timer Property	Returns the number of seconds elapsed since midnight
TimeSerial Function	Returns a representation of a given hour, minute, and second
TimeValue Function	Returns a time value from a string representation of a time
Weekday Function	Returns a number representing the day of the week
Year Function	Returns a number representing the year in a date expression

Dictionary Object (VB6 Only)

Add Method	Adds an item to the dictionary against a given key
CompareMode Property	Returns or sets the comparison mode
Count Property	Returns the number of items in the dictionary
Exists Method	Returns True if the key exists
Item Property	Returns or sets the item associated with a given key
Items Method	Returns an array of all items in the dictionary
Key Property	Returns or sets a given key
Keys Method	Returns an array of all keys in the dictionary
Remove Method	Removes an item associated with a given key
RemoveAll Method	Removes all items from the dictionary

Err Object

Clear Method	Resets the current Err object
Description Property	Returns or sets the description of the current error
HelpContext Property	Returns or sets the help file ID for the current error
HelpFile Property	Returns or sets the name and path of the help file relating to the current error
LastDLLError Property	Returns the error number from an error raised with a system API DLL

---

* VB6 only

Number Property	Returns or sets the current error code
Raise Method	Generates a user-defined error
Source Property	Returns or sets the source of an error

FileSystem Objects (VB6 only)

FileSystemObject Object

BuildPath Function	Returns a string containing the full path
CopyFile Method	Copies a file
CopyFolder Method	Copies a folder and its contents
CreateFolder Function	Returns a Folder object for the newly created folder
CreateTextFile Function	Returns a TextStream object for the newly created text file
DeleteFile Method	Removes a file from disk
DeleteFolder Method	Removes the folder and its contents from disk
DriveExists Function	Returns True if the specified drive is found
Drives Property	Returns a Drives object
FileExists Function	Returns True if the specified file is found
FolderExists Function	Returns True if the specified folder is found
GetAbsolutePathName Function	
	Returns the canonical representation of the path
GetBaseName Function	Returns the base name from a path
GetDrive Function	Returns a Drive object for the specified drive
GetDriveName Function	Returns a string representing the name of a drive
GetExtensionName Function	
	Returns a string containing the extension from a given path
GetFile Function	Returns a File object
GetFileName Function	Returns a string containing the name of a file from a given path
GetFolder Function	Returns a Folder object
GetParentFolderName Function	
	Returns the name of the folder immediately above the folder in a given path
GetSpecialFolder Function	Returns a folder object representing one of the special Windows folders
GetTempName Function	Returns a string containing a valid Windows temporary filename
MoveFile Method	Moves a file from one location to another
MoveFolder Method	Moves a folder and all its contents from one location to another
OpenTextFile Function	Returns a TextStream object of the opened file

Drives Collection Object

| Count Property | Returns the number of Drive objects in the collection |
| Item Property | Returns the Drive object associated with the given key (Drive Name) |

Drive Object

AvailableSpace Property	Returns a variant representing the available space on the drive in bytes
DriveLetter Property	Returns a string containing the drive letter
DriveType Property	Returns a `DriveTypeConst` specifying the type of drive
FileSystem Property	Returns a string containing an abbreviation for the file-system type (i.e., FAT)
FreeSpace Property	Returns a variant containing the free space on the drive in bytes
IsReady Property	Returns `True` if the specified drive is ready
Path Property	Returns a string containing the full path of the drive
RootFolder Property	Returns a Folder object representing the root of the drive
SerialNumber Property	Returns a Long containing the serial number of the disk
ShareName Property	Returns a String containing the share name, if any
TotalSize Property	Returns a variant containing the total size of the disk in bytes
VolumeName Property	Returns a string containing the name of the current volume

Folders Collection Object

Add Function	Returns a Folder object for the newly created folder
Count Property	Returns the number of Folder objects in the collection
Item Property	Returns the Folder object associated with the specified key

Folder Object

Attributes Property	Returns a FileAttributes constant value
Copy Method	Copies this folder and its contents to another location
CreateTextFile Function	Returns a TextStream object for the newly created text file
DateCreated Property	Returns the date the folder was created
DateLastAccessed Property	Returns the date the folder was last accessed
DateLastModified Property	Returns the date the folder was last modified
Delete Method	Removes this folder and all its contents
Drive Property	Returns a Drive object representing the drive on which this folder is located
Files Property	Returns a Files collection object representing the files in this folder
IsRootFolder Property	Returns `True` if this folder is the root of the drive
Move Method	Moves this folder and its contents to another location
Name Property	Returns the name of the folder
ParentFolder Property	Returns a Folder object representing the next folder up in hierarchy
Path Property	Returns a string containing the full path of this folder
ShortName Property	Returns a string containing the short name of the folder
ShortPath Property	Returns a string containing the short path of the folder

Size Property	Returns a Variant specifying the total size of all files and all subfolders contained in this folder
SubFolders Property	Returns a Folders collection object representing the subfolders contained in this folder
Type Property	Returns a string detailing the type of folder

Files Collection Object

Count Property	Returns the number of Folder objects in the collection
Item Property	Returns the File object associated with the specified key

File Object

Attributes Property	Returns a FileAttributes constant
Copy Method	Copies this file to another location
DateCreated Property	Returns the date the file was created
DateLastAccessed Property	Returns the date the file was last accessed
DateLastModified Property	Returns the date the file was last modified
Delete Method	Removes this file
Drive Property	Returns a Drive object representing the drive on which this file is located
Move Method	Moves this file to another location
Name Property	Returns the name of this file
OpenAsTextStream Method	
	Opens this file for text manipulation and returns the open file as a TextStream object
ParentFolder Property	Returns a Folder object representing the folder in which this file is contained
Path Property	Returns a string containing the full path of this file
ShortName Property	Returns a string containing the short name of this file
ShortPath Property	Returns a string containing the short path of this file
Size Property	Returns a Variant specifying the size of this file
Type Property	Returns a string detailing the type of this file

TextStreamObject

AtEndOfLine Property	Returns True if the end of the line has been reached
AtEndOfStream Property	Returns True if the end of the text stream has been reached
Close Method	Closes the TextStream object
Column Property	Returns a Long specifying the current column number
Line Property	Returns a Long specifying the current line number
Read Function	Returns a string containing a specified number of characters from the TextStream
ReadAll Function	Returns a string containing the entire contents of the TextStream
ReadLine Function	Returns a string containing the current line within the TextStream
Skip Method	Skips a specified number of characters

SkipLine Method	Skips to the next line
Write Method	Writes a specified string to the TextStream
WriteBlankLines Method	Writes a specified number of blank lines to the TextStream
WriteLine Method	Writes a specified string and a line break to the TextStream

File and Folder Handling

ChDir Statement	Changes the current directory
ChDrive Statement	Changes the current drive
Close Statement	Closes a file opened using the Open statement
CurDir Function	Returns a variant containing the current path
CurDir$ Function	Returns a String containing the current path
Dir Function	Returns the name or names of a matching file or folder
EOF Function	Returns a flag denoting the end of a file
FileAttr Function	Returns a value denoting the attributes of the current file
FileCopy Statement	Copies a file
FileDateTime Function	Returns the date and time a given file was created
FileLen Function	Returns the length of a file in bytes
FreeFile Function	Returns the number of the next available file
Get Statement	Reads from a file opened in random or binary mode
GetAttr Function	Returns the attributes of a given file or folder
Kill Statement	Deletes a file or folder
Loc Function	Returns the position of the current file read or write marker
LOF Function	Returns the length of an open file in bytes
MkDir Statement	Creates a new folder
Open Statement	Opens a file for reading or writing
Print# Statement	Writes to a sequential text file
Put Statement	Writes to a file opened in random or binary mode
Reset Statement	Closes all files opened using the Open statement
RmDir Statement	Deletes a folder
Seek Function	Sets or returns the position of the current file read or write marker
SetAttr Statement	Sets a file's attributes
Write# Statement	Writes to a sequential text file

Financial Functions

DDB Function	Returns double-declining balance depreciation of an asset for a specific period
FV Function	Returns the future value of an annuity
IPmt Function	Returns the interest payment for a given period of an annuity
IRR Function	Returns the internal rate of return for a series of periodic cash flows
MIRR Function	Returns the modified internal rate of return for a series of periodic cash flows

NPer Function	Returns the number of periods for an annuity
NPV Function	Returns the net present value of an investment
Pmt Function	Returns the payment for an annuity
PPmt Function	Returns the principal payment for a given period of an annuity
PV Function	Returns the present value of an annuity
Rate Function	Returns the interest rate per period for an annuity
SLN Function	Returns the straight-line depreciation of an asset for a single period
SYD Function	Returns the sum-of-years' digits depreciation on an asset

Formatting Functions

Format Function	Returns a string variant formatted to a given specification
Format$ Function	Returns a string formatted to a given specification
FormatCurrency Function	Returns a string variant formatted using the currency settings for the current locale
FormatDateTime Function	Returns a string variant formatted using the date settings for the current locale
FormatNumber Function	Returns a numeric variant formatted to a given specification
FormatPercent Function	Returns a numeric variant formatted using the "%" symbol

Information Functions

Err Function	Returns the error code of the last error
IMEStatus Function	Returns the system's current IME mode
IsArray Function	Returns True if a variable is an array
IsDate Function	Returns True if an expression can be converted to a date
IsEmpty Function	Returns True if a variant variable has not been initialized
IsError Function	Returns True if an expression is an error value
IsMissing Function	Returns True if an optional parameter has not been passed
IsNull Function	Returns True if an expression evaluates to Null
IsNumeric Function	Returns True if an expression can be evaluated as a number
IsObject Function	Returns True if a variable contains an object reference
QBColor Function	Returns the RGB color code for a specified color number
RGB Function	Returns a number representing an RGB color value
TypeName Function	Returns the data subtype name of a variant variable
VarType Function	Returns a number representing the data subtype of a variant variable

Interaction Functions

AppActivate Statement	Gives the focus to a specified application
Beep Function	Sounds a note through the computer's speaker
Choose Function	Returns a selected value from a list
Command Function	Returns the argument portion of the command line as a variant
Command$ Function	Returns the argument portion of the command line as a string
CreateObject Function	Returns a reference to an ActiveX component
DeleteSetting Statement	Deletes a given setting in the registry
DoEvents Function	Passes control to Windows to allow the system message queue to be purged
Environ Function	Returns the value assigned to an environment variable as a variant
Environ$ Function	Returns the value assigned to an environment variable as a String
GetAllSettings Function	Returns all values from an applications key within the registry
GetObject Function	Returns a reference to an ActiveX object
GetSettting Function	Returns a specific value from an applications key within the registry
IIf Function	Returns one of two values based on a Boolean expression
InputBox Function	Returns user input from a simple dialog box
MsgBox Function	Returns the user selection of a choice of buttons on a simple message box
Partition Function	Returns a string indicating where a number occurs within a series of ranges
SaveSetting Statement	Saves a value to the registry within the application's key and given section
SendKeys Statement	Replicates a keystroke in the active window
Shell Function	Executes an external application
Switch Function	Returns the first value or expression in a list that is True

Math Functions

Abs Function	Returns the absolute value of a given number
Atn Function	Returns the arctangent of a number
Cos Function	Returns the cosine of an angle
Exp Function	Returns the base of a natural logarithm raised to a power
Log Function	Returns the natural logarithm of a number
Randomize Statement	Initializes the random number generator
Rnd Function	Returns a random number
Sgn Function	Returns an integer indicating the sign of a number
Sin Function	Returns the sine of an angle
Sqr Function	Returns the square root of a number
Tan Function	Returns the tangent of an angle

Programming and ActiveX Programming

AddressOf Operator	Passes the address of a Visual Basic callback function to an API function
CreateObject Function	Returns a reference to an ActiveX component
Declare Statement	Defines a prototype for a call to an external DLL library function
Event Statement	Defines a prototype for a custom event
For Each...Next Statement	Iterates through a collection or array of objects or values, returning a reference to each of the members
GetObject Function	Returns a reference to an ActiveX object
Implements Statement	Denotes that the current module implements all procedures of the specified standard or abstract interface class
RaiseEvent Statement	Fires an event
Set Statement	Assigns an object reference to an object variable
With...End With Statement	Allows the implicit use of an object reference
WithEvents Keyword	Denotes that the current module will handle events fired by the specified object

Printer Object*

Circle Method	Draws a circle, ellipse, or arc on the current object
ColorMode Property	Returns or sets the color mode of a color printer
Copies Property	Returns or sets the number of copies of the current document to print
CurrentX Property	Returns or sets the horizontal coordinates for next print or draw method
CurrentY Property	Returns or sets the vertical coordinates for next print or draw method
DeviceName Property	Returns or sets the name of the device the current printer driver supports
DrawMode Property	Returns or sets the appearance of output from graphics methods or of a Shape or Line control
DrawStyle Property	Returns or sets the line style for output from graphics methods
DrawWidth Property	Returns or sets the line width for output from graphics methods
DriverName Property	Returns or sets the name of the driver for a Printer object
Duplex Property	Returns or sets a value to determine whether a page is printed on both sides
EndDoc Method	Closes the current printer buffer, outputs the buffer to the printer, and resets the printer object
FillColor Property	Returns or sets the color used to fill in shapes, circles, and boxes
FillStyle Property	Returns or sets the fill style of a shape

---

* Not available in hosted versions of VBA

Font Property	Returns a Font object
FontBold Property	Returns or sets the current font to bold
FontCount Property	Returns the number of fonts available to the current printer object
FontItalic Property	Returns or sets the current font to italic
FontName Property	Returns or sets the name of the current font
Fonts Property	Returns the names of all fonts available to the current printer object
FontSize Property	Returns or sets the size in points of the current font
FontStrikethru Property	Returns or sets whether strikethrough is in effect
FontTransparent Property	Returns or sets whether the current font is transparent
FontUnderline Property	Returns or sets whether text is underlined
ForeColor Property	Returns or sets the current foreground color
hDC Property	Returns the Windows handle of the printer object
Height Property	Returns or sets the height of the printer object
KillDoc Method	Ends the current printer operation, empties the printer buffer, and initializes the printer object
Line Method	Draws a line or a box on the printer object
NewPage Method	Creates a new page in the printer object
Orientation Property	Returns or sets the printer object to output either Landscape or Portrait
Page Property	Returns the number of the current printer page
PaintPicture Method	Outputs the contents of a graphic file onto the printer object
PaperBin Property	Returns or sets the paper source on the current printer
PaperSize Property	Returns or sets the size of paper to use for the current print operation
Port Property	Returns the name of the port being used by the current printer
Print Method	Outputs text to the printer object
PrintQuality Property	Returns or sets the printer resolution
PSet Method	Outputs a single point to the printer object
RightToLeft Property	Determines text display direction and controls visual appearance on a bidirectional system
Scale Method	Determines the coordinate system to be used for the current printer object
ScaleHeight Property	Returns or sets the vertical measurement for the current printer object based on the current scale
ScaleLeft Property	Returns or sets the measurement to the left edge of the current printer object based on the current scale
ScaleMode Property	Returns or sets the value indicating measurement units for object coordinates when using graphics methods or positioning controls
ScaleTop Property	Returns or sets the measurement to the top edge of the current printer object based on the current scale
ScaleWidth Property	Returns or sets the horizontal measurement for the current printer object based on the current scale

ScaleX Method	Converts the value for the width of the printer object from one scale mode to another
ScaleY Method	Converts the value for the height of the printer object from one scale mode to another
TextHeight Function	Returns the height that a given string would be if printed with the current font
TextWidth Function	Returns the width that a given string would be if printed with the current font
TrackDefault Property	Returns or sets a value that determines if the current printer object is automatically changed to that set via the Control Panel
TwipsPerPixelX Property	Returns the number of twips per pixel across the width of the printer object
TwipsPerPixelY Property	Returns the number of twips per pixel along the height of the printer object
Width Property	Returns or sets the width of the printer object
Zoom Property	Returns or sets the percentage by which printed output is to be scaled up or down

Program Structure and Flow

CallByName Function*	Calls the procedure specified as a string variable
Declare Statement	Defines a prototype for a call to an external DLL library function
Do...Loop Statement	Repeats a section of code while or until a condition is met
Exit Statement	Branches to the next line of code outside of the currently executing structure
For Each...Next Statement	Iterates through a collection or array of objects or values, returning a reference to each to the members
For...Next Statement	Iterates through a section of code a given number of times
Friend Statement	Declares the procedure or variable to have scope only within the project in which it is defined
Function Statement	Defines a prototype for a procedure that returns a value
If...Then...Else Statement	Defines a conditional block or blocks of code
Private Statement	Declares the procedure or variable to have scope only within the module in which it is defined
Property Get Statement	Defines a prototype for a property procedure that returns a value
Property Let Statement	Defines a prototype for a property procedure that accepts a value
Property Set Statement	Defines a prototype for a property procedure that sets a reference to an object

---

* VB6 only

Public Statement	Declares the procedure or variable to have scope within the module and project in which it is defined and, if declared within an object module, to have scope outside the current project
Select Case...End Select Statement	
	A series of code blocks, only one of which will execute based on a given value
Sub Statement	Declares a prototype for a procedure that does not return a value or an event-handling procedure
While...Wend Statement	Repeats a section of code while or until a condition is met
With...End With Statement	
	Allows the implicit use of an object reference
WithEvents Keyword	Denotes that the current module will handle events fired by the specified object

Registry Functions

DeleteSetting Statement	Deletes a given registry setting
GetAllSettings Function	Returns all values from an application key in the registry
GetSettting Function	Returns a specific value from an application key in the registry
SaveSetting Statement	Saves a value to the application's key in the registry

String Manipulation

Asc Function	Returns a variant number representing the ANSI character of the first character of a string
AscB Function	Returns the value of the first byte in a string
AscW Function	Returns the native character code of the first character in a string (Unicode or ANSI)
Chr Function	Returns a variant string containing the character associated with the specified character code
Chr$ Function	Returns a string containing the character associated with the specified character code
ChrB Function	Returns a variant string containing the specified single byte
ChrB$ Function	Returns a string containing the specified single byte
ChrW Function	Returns a variant string containing the specified native character (Unicode or ANSI)
ChrW$ Function	Returns a string containing the specified native character (Unicode or ANSI)
Filter Function*	Returns an array of strings matching (or not) a specified value
Format Function	Returns a variant string formatted to a given specification

---

* VB6 only

Format$ Function	Returns a string formatted to a given specification
FormatCurrency Function	Returns a string variant formatted using the currency settings for the current locale
FormatDateTime Function	Returns a string variant formatted using the date settings for the current locale
FormatNumber Function	Returns a numeric variant formatted to a specified format
FormatPercent Function	Returns a numeric variant formatted using the "%" symbol
InStr Function	Returns the position of the first occurrence of one string within another
InStrB Function	Returns the byte position of the first occurrence of one string in another
InStrRev Function*	Returns the first occurrence of a string within another string searching from the end of the string
Join Function*	Returns a string constructed by concatenating an array of values with a given separator
LCase Function	Returns a variant string converted to lowercase
LCase$ Function	Returns a string converted to lowercase
Left Function	Returns a variant string containing the leftmost n characters of a string
Left$ Function	Returns a string containing the leftmost n characters of a string
LeftB Function	Returns a variant string containing the leftmost n bytes of a string
LeftB$ Function	Returns a string containing the leftmost n bytes of a string
Len Function	Returns the length of a given string
LenB Function	Returns the number of bytes in a given string or needed to hold a given variable
LTrim Function	Returns a variant string with any leading spaces removed
LTrim$ Function	Returns a string with any leading spaces removed
Mid Function	Returns a variant substring containing a specified number of characters
Mid$ Function	Returns a substring containing a specified number of characters
MidB Function	Returns a variant string containing a specified number of bytes from a string
MidB$ Function	Returns a substring containing a specified number of bytes from a string
Replace Function*	Returns a string where a specified value has been replaced with another given value
Right Function	Returns a variant string containing the rightmost n characters of a string

* VB6 only

Right$ Function	Returns a string containing the rightmost *n* characters of a string
RightB Function	Returns a variant string containing the rightmost *n* bytes of a string
RightB$ Function	Returns a string containing the rightmost *n* bytes of a string
RTrim Function	Returns a variant string with any trailing spaces removed
RTrim$ Function	Returns a string with any trailing spaces removed
Space Function	Returns a variant string consisting of the specified number of spaces
Space$ Function	Returns a string consisting of the specified number of spaces
Split Function*	Returns an array of values derived from a single string and a specified separator
StrComp Function	Returns the result of a comparison of two strings
StrConv Function	Returns the result of converting a string
String Function	Returns a variant string containing a repeated character
String$ Function	Returns a string containing a repeated character
StrReverse Function*	Returns the reverse of a string
Trim Function	Returns a variant string with both leading and trailing spaces removed
Trim$ Function	Returns a string with both leading and trailing spaces removed
UCase Function	Returns a variant string converted to uppercase
UCase$ Function	Returns a string converted to uppercase

Variable Declaration

Const Statement	Declares a constant
Dim Statement	Declares a local variable at procedure level
Friend Statement	Declares the procedure or variable to have scope only in the project in which it is defined
Private Statement	Declares the procedure or variable to have scope only in the module in which it is defined
Public Statement	Declares a procedure or variable to have scope in the module and project in which it is defined and, if declared in an object module, to have scope outside the current project
ReDim Statement	Declares a dynamic array variable
Type...EndType Statement	Declares a user-defined type

* for VB6 only

APPENDIX B

Language Constants

What follows is a series of tables listing the intrinsic enumerated types and their members. While the bulk of constants are defined in the VBA library, several—all of which are preceded by an asterisk—are taken from the Microsoft Scripting Runtime library, and one, the `UpdateMode` enumerated type, is taken from the Microsoft Data Binding Collection. Finally, the logging enumerated constants, `LogEventTypeConstants` and `LogModeConstants`, which are available in the VB runtime library, are also included; note that these may be unavailable to VBA hosted within Office or other applications. Because this book deals solely with the Visual Basic language, constants relating to controls and other nonlanguage UI elements aren't listed.

Application Window Style (VbAppWinStyle)

Constant	Value
vbHide	0
vbMaximizedFocus	3
vbMinimizedFocus	2
vbMinimizedNoFocus	6
vbNormalFocus	1
vbNormalNoFocus	4

Calendar (VbCalendar)

Constant	Value
vbCalGreg	0
vbCalHijri	1

Call Type (VB6 only)
(VbCallType)

Constant	Value
vbGet	2
vbLet	4
vbMethod	1
vbSet	8

Compare Method (VbCompareMethod)

Constant	Value
vbBinaryCompare	0
vbDatabaseCompare	2
vbTextCompare	1

Data Binding Update Mode (VB6 Only)
(UpdateMode)

Constant	Value
vbUpdateWhenPropertyChanges	1
vbUpdateWhenRowChanges	2
vbUsePropertyAttributes	0

Date Time Format Styles (VB6 Only)
(VbDateTimeFormat)

Constant	Value
vbGeneralDate	0
vbLongDate	1
vbLongTime	3
vbShortDate	2
vbShortTime	4

Day of Week (VbDayOfWeek)

Constant	Value
vbSunday	1
vbMonday	2
vbTuesday	3
vbWednesday	4

Constant	Value
vbThurday	5
vbFriday	6
vbSaturday	7
vbUseSystemDayOfWeek	0

Drive Type (VB6 only)
(DriveTypeConst)

Constant	Value
CDRom	4
Fixed	2
RamDisk	5
Remote	3
Removable	1
Unknown	0

File Attributes (VbFileAttribute)

Constant	Value
vbAlias	64
vbArchive	32
vbDirectory	16
vbHidden	2
vbNormal	0
vbReadOnly	1
vbSystem	4
vbVolume	8

File System Objects File Attributes (VB6 Only)
(FileAttribute)

Constant	Value
Alias	64
Archive	32
Compressed	2048
Directory	16
Hidden	2
Normal	0
ReadOnly	1

Constant	Value
System	4
Volume	8

First Week of Year (VbFirstWeekOfYear)

Constant	Value
vbFirstFourDays	2
vbFirstFullWeek	3
vbFirstJan1	1
vbUseSystem	0

IME Status (VbIMEStatus)

Constant	Value
vbIMEAlphaDbl	7
vbIMEAlphaSng	8
vbIMEDisable	3
vbIMEHiragana	4
vbIMEKatakanaDbl	5
vbIMEKatakanaSng	6
vbIMEModeAlpha	8
vbIMEModeAlphaFull	7
vbIMEModeDisable	3
vbIMEModeHangul	10
vbIMEModeHangulFull	9
vbIMEModeHiragana	4
vbIMEModeKatakana	5
vbIMEModeKatakanaHalf	6
vbIMEModeNoControl	0
vbIMEModeOff	2
vbIMEModeOn	1
vbIMENoOp	0
vbIMEOff	2
vbIMEOn	1

Language Constants

Constant	Value
vbBack	Chr$(8)
vbCr	Chr$(13)

Constant	Value
vbCrLf	Chr$(10) & Chr$(13)
vbFormFeed	Chr$(12)
vbLf	Chr$(10)
vbNewLine	Platform-specific
vbNullChar	Chr$(0)
vbNullString	Zero-length string
vbObjectError	−2147221504
vbTab	Chr$(9)
vbVerticalTab	Chr$(11)

Log Event Type Style (LogEventTypeConstants)

Constant	Value
vbLogEventTypeError	1
vbLogEventTypeInformation	4
vbLogEventTypeWarning	2

Log Mode Constants (VB6 only)
(LogModeConstants)

Constant	Value
vbLogAuto	0
vbLogOff	1
vbLogOverwrite	16
vbLogThreadID	32
vbLogToFile	2
vbLogToNT	3

Message Box Result (VbMsgBoxResult)

Constant	Value
vbAbort	3
vbCancel	2
vbIgnore	5
vbNo	7
vbOK	1
vbRetry	4
vbYes	6

Message Box Style (VbMsgBoxStyle)

Constant	Value
vbAbortRetryIgnore	2
vbApplicationModal	0
vbCritical	16
vbDefaultButton1	0
vbDefaultButton2	256
vbDefaultButton3	512
vbDefaultButton4	768
vbExclamation	48
vbInformation	64
vbMsgBoxHelpButton	16384
vbMsgBoxRight	524288
vbMsgBoxRtlReading	1048576
vbMsgBoxSetForeground	65536
vbOKCancel	1
vbOKOnly	0
vbQuestion	32
vbRetryCancel	5
vbSystemModal	4096
vbYesNo	4
vbYesNoCancel	3

Special Folder Types (VB6 only)
(SpecialFolderConst)

Constant	Value
SystemFolder	1
TemporaryFolder	2
WindowsFolder	0

String Conversion (VbStrConv)

Constant	Value
vbFromUnicode	128
vbHiragana	32
vbKatakana	16
vbLowerCase	2
vbNarrow	8
vbProperCase	3

Constant	Value
vbUnicode	64
vbUpperCase	1
vbWide	4

TextStream IOMode (VB6 only)
(IOMode)

Constant	Value
ForAppending	8
ForReading	1
ForWriting	2

Tristate Constants (VB6 Only)
(VbTriState)

Constant	Value
vbFalse	0
vbTrue	−1
vbUseDefault	−2

Variant Type (VbVarType)

Constant	Value
vbArray	8192
vbBoolean	11
vbByte	17
vbCurrency	6
vbDataObject	13
vbDate	7
vbDecimal	14
vbDouble	5
vbEmpty	0
vbError	10
vbInteger	2
vbLong	3
vbNull	1
vbObject	9
vbSingle	4
vbString	8

Constant	Value
vbUserDefinedType (VB6 only)	36
vbVariant	12

APPENDIX C

Operators

There are four groups of operators in VBA: arithmetic, concatenation, comparison, and logical. You'll find some to be instantly recognizable and familiar, while others require a much deeper understanding of mathematics than both the scope of this book and my knowledge of math are able to offer. However, if you have the need to use these types of operators, it is likely that you know the mathematics fundamentals behind them. We will look at each group of operators in turn before discussing the order of precedence VBA uses when it encounters more than one type of operator within an expression.

Arithmetic Operators

+   The addition operator. Used to add numeric expressions, as well as to concatenate (join together) two string variables. However, it's preferable to use the concatenation operator with strings to eliminate ambiguity.

Example: `result = expression1 + expression2`

−   The subtraction operator. Used to find the difference between two numeric values or expressions, as well as to denote a negative value. Unlike the addition operator, it can't be used with string variables.

Example: `result = expression1 - expression2`

/   The division operator. Returns a floating-point number.

Example: `result = expression1 / expression2`

*   The multiplication operator. Used to multiply two numerical values.

Example: `result = expression1 * expression2`

\   The integer division operator. Performs division on two numeric expressions and returns an integer result (no remainder or decimal places).

Example: `result = expression1 \ expression2`

Mod

    The modulo operator. Performs division on two numeric expressions and returns only the remainder. If either of the two numbers is a floating-point number, it's rounded to an integer value prior to the modulo operation.

    Example: `result = expression1 Mod expression2`

^   The exponentiation operator. Raises a number to the power of the exponent.

    Example: `result = number ^ exponent`

String Operator

There is only one operator for strings, the concatenation operator, represented by the ampersand symbol, &. It's used to bind a number of string variables together, creating one string from two or more individual strings. Any nonstring variable or expression is converted to a string prior to concatenation. Its syntax is:

    `result = expression1 & expression2.`

Comparison Operators

There are three main comparison operators: < (or less than), > (or greater than), and = (or equal to). They can be used individually, or any two operators can be combined with each other. Their general syntax is:

    `result = expression1 operator expression2`

The resulting expression is `True` (-1), `False` (0), or `Null`. A `Null` results only if either *expression1* or *expression2* itself is `Null`.

What follows is a list of all the comparison operators supported by VBA, as well as an explanation of the condition required for the comparison to result in `True`:

>   *expression1* greater than and not equal to *expression2*

<   *expression1* less than and not equal to *expression2*

<>   *expression1* not equal to *expression2* (less than or greater than)

>=   *expression1* greater than or equal to *expression2*

<=   *expression1* less than or equal to *expression2*

=   *expression1* equal to *expression2*

Comparison operators can be used with both numeric and string variables. However, if one expression is numeric and the other is a string, the numeric expression is always "less than" the string expression. If both *expression1* and *expression2* are strings, the "greatest" string is the one that is the longest. If the strings are of equal length, the comparison is case sensitive. (Lowercase letters are "greater" than their uppercase counterparts.)

The Is Operator

While not strictly a comparison operator, the `Is` operator determines whether two object reference variables refer to the same object. Thus, it tests, in some sense, for the "equality" of two object references. Its syntax is:

```
result = object1 Is object2
```

If both *object1* and *object2* refer to the same object, the result is True; otherwise, the result is False. You also use the Is operator to determine if an object variable refers to a valid object. This is done by comparing the object variable to the special Nothing data type:

```
If oVar Is Nothing Then
```

The result is True if the object variable does not hold a reference to an object.

Logical and Bitwise Operators

Logical operators allow you to evaluate one or more expressions and return a logical value. VBA supports six logical operators: And, Or, Not, Eqv, Imp, and Xor. These operators also double as bitwise operators. A bitwise comparison examines each bit position in both expressions and sets or clears the corresponding bit in the result depending upon the operator used. The result of a bitwise operation is a numeric value.

And

Performs logical conjunction; that is, it only returns True if both *expression1* and *expression2* evaluate to True. If either expression is False, then the result is False. If either expression is Null, then the result is Null. Its syntax is:

```
result = expression1 And expression2
```

For example:

```
If x = 5 And y < 7 Then
```

In this case, the code after the If statement is executed only if the value of *x* is five and the value of *y* is less than seven.

As a bitwise operator, And returns 1 if the compared bits in both expressions are 1, and returns 0 in all other cases, as shown in the following table:

Bit in expression1	Bit in expression2	Result
0	0	0
0	1	0
1	0	0
1	1	1

For example, the result of 15 And 179 is 3, as the following binary representation shows:

```
00000011 = 00001111 And 10110011
```

Or

Performs logical disjunction; that is, if either *expression1* or *expression2* evaluates to True, or if both *expression1* and *expression2* evaluate to True, the result is True. Only if neither expression is True does the Or operation return False. If either expression is Null, then the result is also Null. The syntax for the Or operator is:

```
result = expression1 Or expression2
```

For example:

```
If x = 5 Or y < 7 Then
```

In this case, the code after the `If` statement is executed if the value of *x* is five or if the value of *y* is less than seven.

As a bitwise operator, Or is the converse of And. Or returns 0 if the compared bits in both expressions are 0, and returns 1 in all other cases, as shown in the following table:

Bit in expression1	Bit in expression2	Result
0	0	0
0	1	1
1	0	1
1	1	1

For example, the result of 15 Or 179 is 191, as the following binary representation shows:

```
10111111 = 00001111 Or 10110011
```

Not

Performs logical negation on a single expression; that is, if the expression is `True`, the Not operator causes it to become `False`, while if it is `False`, the operator causes its value to become `True`. If the expression is `Null`, though, the result of using the Not operator is still a `Null`. Its syntax is:

```
result = Not expression1
```

For example:

```
If Not IsNumeric(x) Then
```

In this example, the code following the `If` statement is executed if *IsNumeric* returns `False`, indicating that x isn't a value capable of being represented by a number.

As a bitwise operator, Not simply reverses the value of the bit, as shown in the following table:

expression1	Result
0	1
1	0

For example, the result of Not 16 is 239, as the following binary representation shows:

```
Not 00010000 = 11101111
```

Eqv

Performs logical equivalence; that is, it determines whether the value of two expressions is the same. Eqv returns `True` when both expressions evaluate to

True or both expressions evaluate to `False`, but it returns `False` if either expression evaluates to `True` while the other evaluates to `False`. Its syntax is:

```
result = expression1 Eqv expression2
```

As a bitwise operator. Eqv returns 1 if the compared bits in both expressions are the same, and it returns 0 if they are different, as shown in the following table:

Bit in expression1	Bit in expression2	Result
0	0	1
0	1	0
1	0	0
1	1	1

For example, the result of 15 Eqv 179 is 67, as the following binary representation shows:

```
01000011 = 00001111 Eqv 10110011
```

Imp

Performs logical implication, as shown in the following table:

expression1	expression2	result
True	True	True
True	False	False
True	Null	Null
False	True	True
False	False	True
False	Null	True
Null	True	True
Null	False	Null
Null	Null	Null

Its syntax is:

```
result = expression1 Imp expression2
```

As a bitwise operator, Imp returns 1 if the compared bits in both expressions are the same or if *expression1* is 1; it returns 0 if the two bits are different and the bit in *expression1* is 1, as shown in the following table:

Bit in expression1	Bit in expression2	Result
0	0	1
0	1	1
1	0	0
1	1	1

For example, the result of 15 Imp 179 is 243, as the following binary representation shows:

```
11110011 = 00001111 Imp 10110011
```

Xor

Performs logical exclusion, which is the converse of Eqv; that is, Xor (an abbreviation for eXclusive OR) determines whether two expressions are different. When both expressions are either `True` or `False`, then the result is `False`. If only one expression is `True`, the result is `True`. If either expression is `Null`, the result is also `Null`. Its syntax is:

```
result = expression1 Xor expression2
```

As a bitwise operator, Xor returns 1 if the bits being compared are different, and returns 0 if they are the same, as shown in the following table:

Bit in expression1	Bit in expression2	Result
0	0	0
0	1	1
1	0	1
1	1	0

For example, the result of 15 Xor 179 is 188, as the following binary representation shows:

```
10111100 = 00001111 Imp 10110011
```

Operator Precedence

If you include more than one operator in a single line of code, you need to know the order in which VBA will evaluate them. Otherwise, the results may be completely different than you intend. The rules that define the order in which a language handles operators are known as the *order of precedence*. If the order of precedence results in operations being evaluated in an order other than the one you intend—and therefore if the value that results from these operations is "wrong" from your point of view—you can explicitly override the order of precedence through the use of parentheses. However, the order of precedence still applies to multiple operators within parentheses.

When a single line of code includes operators from more than one category, they are evaluated in the following order:

- Arithmetic operators
- Concatenation operators
- Comparison operators
- Logical operators

Within each category of operators except for the single concatenation operator, there is also an order of precedence. If multiple comparison operators appear in a single line of code, they are evaluated from left to right. The order of precedence of arithmetic operators is as follows:

- Exponentiation (^)
- Division and multiplication (/, *) (no order of precedence between the two)
- Integer division (\)
- Modulo arithmetic (Mod)
- Addition and subtraction (+, −) (no order of precedence between the two)

If the same arithmetic operator is used multiple times in a single line of code, the operators are evaluated from left to right.

The order of precedence of logical operators is:

- Not
- And
- Or
- Xor
- Eqv
- Imp

If the same arithmetic or logical operator is used multiple times in a single line of code, the operators are evaluated from left to right.

APPENDIX D

What's New in VB6?

At first sight, Visual Basic 6 may not appear to be the revolution of the VB language and development environment that Versions 4 and 5 were. However, when you get under the surface of VB6, you will find some very powerful enhancements and new language features that make the upgrade worthwhile from the viewpoint of productivity and of your ability to create ever more powerful applications that take advantage of new technologies.

Version 6 uses the same development environment as Version 5 and consolidates the major advances made in Versions 4 and 5. This means that you can consolidate your knowledge of and expertise with programming in the new object style of VB without having too much new stuff to learn.

In keeping with the rest of the book, this section details the new language features. Of course there are lots of other new features in VB6 that aren't specifically concerned with the language (like the ability to add new controls to a form at runtime) that are outside the scope of this book.

A final note: VB6 is every bit as stable and well-behaved as VB5—something that's always a worry when it comes time to upgrade. While writing this book, I've used all the prerelease and release candidate versions of VB6, and enjoyed every minute. Unfortunately, I can't say the same for the new VB6 documentation, which—like MSDN—has been moved to a very underdeveloped HTML Help environment.

The major changes in the VB and VBA languages are as follows.

Create DataSource and Data Consumer Classes

A *data source class* is a VB class module that exposes an interface that can be used by the new BindingCollection object to bind data from a property of the class to a property of a form control. A Data Source Class can use any form of external data: a text file, a directory structure, or an ADO recordset are all examples of data that can be accessed via a VB data source class. A number of new properties have been added to VB class modules, one of which is the DataSourceBehavior property, which is set to `vbDataSource` to enable the class to be used as a data source.

A *data consumer class* is a VB class module that is bound to a form control that acts as a data source using the BindingCollection object. Another of the new properties that has been added to VB class modules is the DataBindingBehavior property, which is set to either `vbSimpleBound` or `vbComplexBound` to enable the class to be used as a data consumer.

For information on data source and data consumer classes, see the Data Binding Objects entry in Chapter 7, *The Language Reference.*

Functions Can Return Arrays

Functions and property procedures can now return arrays of any type. Previous versions of VB allowed you to return a variant data type containing an array, but now you can return a strongly typed array. For example:

```
Dim sArray() As String
Dim oCustomers As New Customers
sArray() = oCustomers.Names

Public Property Get Names() As String()
    Dim TempArray() As String
    '...code to get all the names of the customers
        Names = TempArray()
End Function
```

For information, see the entry for the `Function` statement in Chapter 7.

Dynamic Arrays Can Be Assigned

As part of the added functionality to allow functions to return arrays, you can now also place a dynamic array on the left side of an assignment (as shown in the example above). Fixed-size arrays still can't be used on the left side of an assignment.

Remote User-Defined Types

User-defined types (UDTs) have always been a powerful part of VB programming. Their use, however, diminished slightly with the introduction of the Collection object in VB4. VB6 has redressed the balance by allowing you to define a public property or function that returns a UDT, or to use a UDT as an argument in a public function. This means that you can pass around strongly typed complex data structures, as opposed to passing around objects.

To go along with this change, UDTs can now also be used with the *TypeName* function and the *TypeOf* operator, and a new variable type constant, `vbUserDefinedType`, has also been added to the language.

Note that because the use of remote UDTs has required a change to the underlying COM/Automation structure, to use remote UDTs you must apply NT4 service pack 4, the latest version of DCOM95 (DCOM98), or be running on either NT5 or Windows 98.

For information on how to use remote UDTs, see the Type Statement entry in Chapter 7 and the section "Implementing a User-Defined Type Property" in Chapter 4, *Class Modules.*

New Functions

Several new string-manipulation functions have been introduced into VB6 (or rather, they have been borrowed from VBScript). The functions were originally required by the web programming community, and since VB6 extends Visual Basic further into the web programming arena (with DHTML projects, IIS projects, and web classes), these functions are now required in VB6 as well. But even if you're not planning on doing any web work, you'll find loads of uses for these new functions. The new string manipulation functions are:

- Filter
- FormatCurrency
- FormatDateTime
- FormatNumber
- FormatPercent
- InStrRev
- Join
- Replace
- Split
- StrReverse

The *CallByName* function is one of only two really new functions in the VB language. *CallByName* allows you to call a function by using a string variable to specify the name of the function and a `ParamArray` to pass the parameters.

A new function that could possibly be placed in the "miscellaneous improvements" category is *MonthName*, a function that returns the name of the month from a given month number.

For information, see the entry for each new function in Chapter 7.

Enhanced CreateObject Function

The *CreateObject* function has had a major enhancement with an additional string parameter that allows you to specify the name of the server where the object resides. If you're writing client-server applications with remote servers, you should find this a powerful addition to your armory, as this short example demonstrates:

```
Dim sMainServer As String
Dim sBackUpServer As String
```

```
sMainServer = "NTPROD1"
sBackUpServer = "NTPROD2"

If IsOnline(sMainServer) Then
    CreateObject("Sales.Customer",sMainServer)
Else
    CreateObject("Sales.Customer",sBackUpServer)
End If
```

For information, see the *CreateObject* function entry in Chapter 7.

New Object Models

Visual Basic is becoming a more object-oriented language, and much of the new functionality available to VB6 programmers comes in the form of object models that can be referenced and used within VB.

Data binding and formatting

One of the most important additions to VB6 is the data binding functionality provided by the BindingCollection and Binding objects. The data bindings object model allows you to bind a field of a data source to any property of any form control. It's more powerful and affords the developer more control than the previous data controls in Visual Basic.

The new data binding object model includes the Data Format object, which allows you to seamlessly format data from the data source before displaying it in the control, and then unformat the data before it's written to the data source.

For information, see the entries for Data Binding object and Data Format object in Chapter 7.

Dictionary object

A member of the Scripting Runtime Library, the Dictionary object is a much-enhanced version of the Collection object. It's faster in execution and easier to use.

For details, see the Dictionary object entry in Chapter 7.

File System objects

Another member of the Scripting Runtime Library, the File System objects provide a powerful new model representing all connected drives and the folders and files in them. The model is well-designed and is therefore straightforward and intuitive to use. Any drive of any type that is connected to a system, including networked and CD-ROM drives, is included in the Drives collection.

The File System Folders collection and Folder objects give you complete control when moving, adding, and deleting folders and their contents, unlike the built-in VB functions that require you to empty folders prior to deletion. You can also determine and return special Windows folders such as System32.

The Files collection and File objects again allow you to move, copy, and delete files, and provide useful properties to both set and return a file's attributes.

For full details, see the File System object entry in Chapter 7.

Index

Symbols

E

early binding, 48, 76, 78, 89
(see also data binding)
elements, array, 40
concatenating, 396–397
filtering out of arrays, 308–310
parsing strings into, 524–525
resetting values of, 252
email within VB (example), 86–88
Empty subtype (Variant), 34
encapsulation, 54
end of file, 249–252
End... statements, 25, 245–246
ending VB programs, 23–25
Enum statement, 63, 246–248
enumerated constants, 62–63, 246–248
intrinsic (built-in), 598–605
Environ, Environ$ functions, 248–249
environment variables, values of,
248–249
EOF function, 249–252
equal to (=) operator, 607
Eqv operator, 609
Erase statement, 252
Err object, 100, 253–264, 585
Error subtype (Variant), 34
errors, 91–107
in ActiveX servers, 101–104
checklist for handling, 92–95
CVErr function, 183–185
Err object, 100, 253–264, 585
error messages to users, 104
Error statement, 265–266
Error, Error$ functions, 265
handling in ActiveX components, 73
Help to prevent, 104
IsError function, 391–392
logging, 106
On Error statement, 440–442
in procedures, 95–100
for undefined variables, 445
event-driven programs, 11
events, 19
Automation Server, trapping, 84,
576–578
calling functions/methods upon,
20–21
of class modules, 63–68
custom, 66–68, 266–268

DoEvents function, 241–242
errors (see errors)
event handlers, defined, 64
Event statement, 67, 266–268
explicitly creating, 23
firing (see firing events)
keyboard key presses
assigning VB macros to, 15, 17
simulating with SendKeys, 508–511
user actions, launching VB
programs at, 14, 16
Excel (Microsoft), 6
running VBA modules, 15–17
VB output to (example), 88
executables (VB), running, 17
execution flow, 23, 594
EXEs (see out-of-process ActiveX EXEs)
existence check
Dictionary keys, 226–227
drives, 291–292
files, 292–293
folders, 293–294
IsEmpty function, 390–391
IsMissing function, 393
IsNull function, 394
Exists method (Dictionary), 226–227
Exists property, 74
Exit statement, 268–269
Exit Sub statement, 99
Exp function, 269
exponentiation (^) operator, 607
extension, filename, 297–298
externally createable objects, 81

F

FileExists method (FileSystemObject),
292–293
filename extensions, 297–298
files
accessing data from, 350–352,
376–379, 405–406, 552–553
Lock/Unlock statements with,
415–417, 567–568
CopyFile method (FileSystemObject),
283–284
copying (see copying files)
CreateTextFile method
(FileSystemObject), 287–289

About the Author

Paul Lomax is the author of *Learning VBScript* (published by O'Reilly & Associates) and technical director of Mentorweb (*http://www.mentorweb.net/*), a leading web design and hosting company. Over the past two years Paul has created and maintained over 60 commercial websites for Mentorweb's clients. He is also the driving force behind ShopAssistant, a new NT/ASP based high-end shopping cart/web commerce server (*http://www.shopassistant.com/*).

Paul has been a programmer for over 12 years and has been a dedicated fan of Visual Basic since Version 1. He has written systems for financial derivatives forecasting, satellite TV broadcasting, the life insurance industry, and he's written a major materials tracking system for the oil and gas industry. He is also responsible for the concept, design, and programming of the successful "Contact" series of national business databases.

When not sitting in front of a keyboard, Paul can usually be found behind the wheel of a racing car competing in events around the United Kingdom. Paul and his family—wife Deborah and children Russel and Victoria—have recently returned to their home in England after several years spent living in the Arabian gulf.

Colophon

Our look is the result of reader comments, our own experimentation, and feedback from distribution channels. Distinctive covers complement our distinctive approach to technical topics, breathing personality and life into potentially dry subjects.

The animal on the cover of *VB & VBA in a Nutshell: The Language* is a Newfoundland dog, a domesticated breed known for its size and sweet temperament. Newfoundlands, from the island of the same name, are semiaquatic, usually black dogs. They stand about 28 inches tall and weigh around 130–150 pounds.

The Newfoundland, descended from European breeds, has traditionally been used as a working dog, on land and around water, for hunting and fishing. Their large, webbed feet, thick coat, powerful frame, and large lung capacity are well suited for work on ships and around water, as well as for the island's climate. The breed is associated with stories of brave animals making heroic ocean rescues and assisting with shipwrecks. Today, the Newfoundlands' docile nature and calm disposition have made them popular pets.

Mary Anne Weeks Mayo was the copy editor and project manager for *VB & VBA in a Nutshell: The Language*. Melanie Wang, Ellie Fountain Maden, Clairemarie Fisher O'Leary, and Sheryl Avruch provided quality control. Mike Sierra provided FrameMaker support and Seth Maislin wrote the index.

Edie Freedman designed the cover of this book, using a 19th-century engraving from the Dover Pictorial Archive modified in Adobe Photoshop. The cover layout was produced with QuarkXPress 3.32 using the ITC Garamond font. Whenever possible, our books use RepKover™, a durable and flexible lay-flat binding. If the page count exceeds RepKover's limit, perfect binding is used.

The inside layout was designed by Nancy Priest and implemented in FrameMaker 5.5 by Mike Sierra. The text and heading fonts are ITC Garamond Light and Garamond Book. The illustrations that appear in the book were created in Adobe Photoshop 4 and Macromedia FreeHand 7 by Robert Romano. This colophon was written by Nancy Kotary.

More Titles from O'Reilly

Windows Programming

Access Database Design & Programming

By Steven Roman
1st Edition June 1997
270 pages, ISBN 1-56592-297-2

This book provides experienced Access users who are novice programers with frequently overlooked concepts and techniques necessary to create effective database applications. It focuses on designing effective tables in a multi-table application; using the Access interface or Access SQL to construct queries; and programming using the Data Access Object (DAO) and Microsoft Access object models.

Learning VBScript

By Paul Lomax
1st Edition July 1997
616 pages, includes CD-ROM
ISBN 1-56592-247-6

This definitive guide shows web developers how to take full advantage of client-side scripting with the VBScript language. In addition to basic language features, it covers the Internet Explorer object model and discusses techniques for client-side scripting, like adding ActiveX controls to a web page or validating data before sending it to the server. Includes CD-ROM with over 170 code samples.

Developing Visual Basic Add-Ins

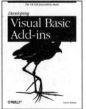

By Steven Roman
1st Edition December 1998)
186 pages, ISBN 1-56592-527-0

A tutorial and reference guide in one, this book covers all the basics of creating useful VB add-ins to extend the IDE, allowing developers to work more productively with Visual Basic. Readers with even a modest acquaintance with VB will be developing add-ins in no time. Includes numerous simple code examples.

Visual Basic Controls in a Nutshell

By Evan S. Dictor
1st Edition July 1999 (est.)
686 pages (est.), ISBN 1-56592-294-8

This quick reference covers one of the crucial elements of Visual Basic: its controls, and their numerous properties, events, and methods. It provides a step-by-step list of procedures for using each major control and contains a detailed reference to all properties, methods, and events. Written by an experienced Visual Basic programmer, it helps to make painless what can sometimes be an arduous job of programming Visual Basic.

Learning Perl on Win32 Systems

By Randal L. Schwartz,
Erik Olson & Tom Christiansen
1st Edition August 1997
306 pages, ISBN 1-56592-324-3

In this carefully paced course, leading Perl trainers and a Windows NT practitioner teach you to program in the language that promises to emerge as the scripting language of choice on NT. Based on the "llama" book, this book features tips for PC users and new, NT-specific examples, along with a foreword by Larry Wall, the creator of Perl, and Dick Hardt, the creator of Perl for Win32.

Learning Word Programming

By Steven Roman
1st Edition October 1998
408 pages, ISBN 1-56592-524-6

This no-nonsense book delves into the core aspects of VBA programming, enabling users to increase their productivity and power over Microsoft Word. It takes the reader step-by-step through writing VBA macros and programs, illustrating how to generate tables of a particular format, manage shortcut keys, create FAX cover sheets, and reformat documents.

Windows Programming

Developing Windows Error Messages

By Ben Ezzell
1st Edition March 1998
254 pages, Includes CD-ROM
ISBN 1-56592-356-1

This book teaches C, C++, and Visual Basic programmers how to write effective error messages that notify the user of an error, clearly explain the error, and most important, offer a solution. The book also discusses methods for preventing and trapping errors before they occur and tells how to create flexible input and response routines to keep unnecessary errors from happening.

Inside the Windows 95 File System

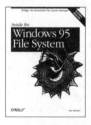

By Stan Mitchell
1st Edition May 1997
378 pages, Includes diskette
ISBN 1-56592-200-X

In this book, Stan Mitchell describes the Windows 95 File System, as well as the new opportunities and challenges it brings for developers. Its "hands-on" approach will help developers become better equipped to make design decisions using the new Win95 File System features. Includes a diskette containing MULTIMON, a general-purpose monitor for examining Windows internals.

Win32 Multithreaded Programming

By Aaron Cohen & Mike Woodring
1st Edition December 1997
724 pages, Includes CD-ROM
ISBN 1-56592-296-4

This book clearly explains the concepts of multithreaded programs and shows developers how to construct efficient and complex applications. An important book for any developer, it illustrates all aspects of Win32 multithreaded programming, including what has previously been undocumented or poorly explained.

Windows NT File System Internals

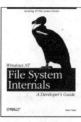

By Rajeev Nagar
1st Edition September 1997
794 pages, Includes diskette
ISBN 1-56592-249-2

Windows NT File System Internals presents the details of the NT I/O Manager, the Cache Manager, and the Memory Manager from the perspective of a software developer writing a file system driver or implementing a kernel-mode filter driver. The book provides numerous code examples included on diskette, as well as the source for a complete, usable filter driver.

Inside the Windows 95 Registry

By Ron Petrusha
1st Edition August 1996
594 pages, Includes diskette
ISBN 1-56592-170-4

An in-depth examination of remote registry access, differences between the Win95 and NT registries, registry backup, undocumented registry services, and the role the registry plays in OLE. Shows programmers how to access the Win95 registry from Win32, Win16, and DOS programs in C and Visual Basic. VxD sample code is also included. Includes diskette.

Windows NT SNMP

By James D. Murray
1st Edition January 1998
464 pages, Includes CD-ROM
ISBN 1-56592-338-3

This book describes the implementation of SNMP (the Simple Network Management Protocol) on Windows NT 3.51 and 4.0 (with a look ahead to NT 5.0) and Windows 95 systems. It covers SNMP and network basics and detailed information on developing SNMP management applications and extension agents. The book comes with a CD-ROM containing a wealth of additional information: standards documents, sample code from the book, and many third-party, SNMP-related software tools, libraries, and demos.

Hand-held Computers

PalmPilot: The Ultimate Guide

By David Pogue
1st Edition June 1998
520 pages, Includes CD-ROM
ISBN 1-56592-420-7

This PalmPilot "bible" covers the
PalmPilot, PalmPilot Professsional,
and the new software and features
of the 1998 PalmPilot model, the
Palm III, as well as OEM models such
as the IBM Workpad. Dense with undocumented information,
it contains hundreds of timesaving tips and surprising tricks
to help both intermediate and advanced users master this
exciting new device. Includes CD-ROM containing 900
PalmPilot programs.

Palm Programming: The Developer's Guide

By Neil Rhodes & Julie McKeehan
1st Edition December 1998
482 pages, Includes CD-ROM
ISBN 1-56592-525-4

Emerging as the bestselling hand-held
computers of all time, PalmPilots
have spawned intense developer
activity and a fanatical following.
Palm Programming, endorsed by
Palm as their official developer's guide, is a tutorial-style
book eagerly awaited by developers and experienced C
programmers. Includes a CD-ROM with source code and
third-party developer tools.

Eliminating Annoyances

Windows 98 Annoyances

By David A. Karp
1st Edition October 1998
464 pages, ISBN 1-56592-417-7

Based on the author's popular
Windows Annoyances Web site
(http://www.annoyances.org), this
book provides an authoritative collection
of techniques for customizing Windows
98. It allows you to quickly identify a
particular annoyance and immediately offers one or more
solutions, making it the definitive resource for customizing
Windows 98. Includes a CD with a trial version of *O'Reilly
Utilities: Quick Solutions for Windows 98 Annoyances*.

Eliminating Annoyances

O'Reilly Utilities: Quick Solutions for Windows 98 Annoyances

Software developed by
Mark Bracewell & David A. Karp
1st Edition October 1998
CD-ROM with full online Help
ISBN 1-56592-549-1

*O'Reilly Utilities: Quick Solutions for
Windows 98 Annoyances* is the stand-alone software companion
to David Karp's *Windows 98 Annoyances* book. This software
provides immediate, automated solutions for many of the key
annoyances described in the book, as well as other important
new enhancements to Windows 98. Developed in cooperation
with David Karp, *O'Reilly Utilities* allows you to immediately
improve your productivity with dozens of Windows extensions
that go beyond Tweak UI and make common tasks easier,
such as group file renaming, file copying, and customizing the
desktop. Even better, we've built programs into this package
that solve some of the most aggravating behaviors of Windows
and other applications.

Excel 97 Annoyances

By Woody Leonhard, Lee Hudspeth & T.J. Lee
1st Edition September 1997
336 pages, ISBN 1-56592-309-X

Excel 97 Annoyances uncovers Excel 97's
hard-to-find features and tells how to
eliminate the annoyances of data analysis.
It shows how to easily retrieve data from
the Web, details step-by-step construction
of a perfect toolbar, includes tips for
working around the most annoying gotchas of auditing, and
shows how to use VBA to control Excel in powerful ways.

Office 97 Annoyances

By Woody Leonhard, Lee Hudspeth & T.J. Lee
1st Edition October 1997
396 pages, ISBN 1-56592-310-3

Office 97 Annoyances illustrates
step-by-step how to get control over
the chaotic settings of Office 97 and
shows how to turn the vast array of
applications into a simplified list of
customized tools. It focuses on the
major components of Office 97, examines their integration
or lack of it, and shows how to use this new Office suite in
the most efficient way.

Eliminating Annoyances

Windows Annoyances

By David A. Karp
1st Edition June 1997
300 pages, ISBN 1-56592-266-2

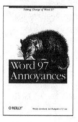

Windows Annoyances is a comprehensive, detailed resource for all intermediate to advanced users of Windows 95 and NT version 4.0. This book shows step-by-step how to customize the Win95/NT operating systems through an extensive collection of tips, tricks, and workarounds. Covers **Registry**, **Plug and Play**, networking, security, multiple-user settings, and third-party software.

Word 97 Annoyances

By Woody Leonhard, Lee Hudspeth & T.J. Lee
1st Edition August 1997
356 pages, ISBN 1-56592-308-1

Word 97 contains hundreds of annoying idiosyncrasies that can be either eliminated or worked around. *Word 97 Annoyances* takes an in-depth look at what makes Word 97 tick and shows you how to transform this software into a powerful, customized tool.

Outlook Annoyances

By Woody Leonhard,
Lee Hudspeth & T. J. Lee
1st Edition June 1998
400 pages, ISBN 1-56592-384-7

Like the other Microsoft Office-related titles in the Annoyances series, this book points out and conquers the annoying features of Microsoft Outlook, the personal information management software included with Office. It is the definitive guide for those who want to take full advantage of Outlook and transform it into the useful tool that it was intended to be.

How to stay in touch with O'Reilly

. Visit Our Award-Winning Site

http://www.oreilly.com/

★ "Top 100 Sites on the Web" —*PC Magazine*
★ "Top 5% Web sites" —*Point Communications*
★ "3-Star site" —*The McKinley Group*

Our web site contains a library of comprehensive product information (including book excerpts and tables of contents), downloadable software, background articles, interviews with technology leaders, links to relevant sites, book cover art, and more. File us in your Bookmarks or Hotlist!

. Join Our Email Mailing Lists

New Product Releases

To receive automatic email with brief descriptions of all new O'Reilly products as they are released, send email to:
listproc@online.oreilly.com
Put the following information in the first line of your message (*not* in the Subject field):
subscribe oreilly-news

O'Reilly Events

If you'd also like us to send information about trade show events, special promotions, and other O'Reilly events, send email to:
listproc@online.oreilly.com
Put the following information in the first line of your message (*not* in the Subject field):
subscribe oreilly-events

. Get Examples from Our Books via FTP

There are two ways to access an archive of example files from our books:

Regular FTP

- ftp to:
  ftp.oreilly.com
  (login: anonymous
  password: your email address)
- Point your web browser to:
  ftp://ftp.oreilly.com/

FTPMAIL

- Send an email message to:
  ftpmail@online.oreilly.com
  (Write "help" in the message body)

4. Contact Us via Email

order@oreilly.com
To place a book or software order online. Good for North American and international customers.

subscriptions@oreilly.com
To place an order for any of our newsletters or periodicals.

books@oreilly.com
General questions about any of our books.

software@oreilly.com
For general questions and product information about our software. Check out O'Reilly Software Online at **http://software.oreilly.com/** for software and technical support information. Registered O'Reilly software users send your questions to:
website-support@oreilly.com

cs@oreilly.com
For answers to problems regarding your order or our products.

booktech@oreilly.com
For book content technical questions or corrections.

proposals@oreilly.com
To submit new book or software proposals to our editors and product managers.

international@oreilly.com
For information about our international distributors or translation queries. For a list of our distributors outside of North America check out:
http://www.oreilly.com/www/order/country.html

O'Reilly & Associates, Inc.
101 Morris Street, Sebastopol, CA 95472 USA
TEL   707-829-0515 or 800-998-9938
        (6am to 5pm PST)
FAX   707-829-0104

O'REILLY®

International Distributors

UK, EUROPE, MIDDLE EAST AND AFRICA (EXCEPT FRANCE, GERMANY, AUSTRIA, SWITZERLAND, LUXEMBOURG, LIECHTENSTEIN, AND EASTERN EUROPE)

INQUIRIES
O'Reilly UK Limited
4 Castle Street
Farnham
Surrey, GU9 7HS
United Kingdom
Telephone: 44-1252-711776
Fax: 44-1252-734211
Email: josette@oreilly.com

ORDERS
Wiley Distribution Services Ltd.
1 Oldlands Way
Bognor Regis
West Sussex PO22 9SA
United Kingdom
Telephone: 44-1243-779777
Fax: 44-1243-820250
Email: cs-books@wiley.co.uk

FRANCE

ORDERS
GEODIF
61, Bd Saint-Germain
75240 Paris Cedex 05, France
Tel: 33-1-44-41-46-16 (French books)
Tel: 33-1-44-41-11-87 (English books)
Fax: 33-1-44-41-11-44
Email: distribution@eyrolles.com

INQUIRIES
Éditions O'Reilly
18 rue Séguier
75006 Paris, France
Tel: 33-1-40-51-52-30
Fax: 33-1-40-51-52-31
Email: france@editions-oreilly.fr

GERMANY, SWITZERLAND, AUSTRIA, EASTERN EUROPE, LUXEMBOURG, AND LIECHTENSTEIN

INQUIRIES & ORDERS
O'Reilly Verlag
Balthasarstr. 81
D-50670 Köln
Germany
Telephone: 49-221-973160-91
Fax: 49-221-973160-8
Email: anfragen@oreilly.de (inquiries)
Email: order@oreilly.de (orders)

CANADA (FRENCH LANGUAGE BOOKS)
Les Éditions Flammarion ltée
375, Avenue Laurier Ouest
Montréal (Québec) H2V 2K3
Tel: 00-1-514-277-8807
Fax: 00-1-514-278-2085
Email: info@flammarion.qc.ca

HONG KONG
City Discount Subscription Service, Ltd.
Unit D, 3rd Floor, Yan's Tower
27 Wong Chuk Hang Road
Aberdeen, Hong Kong
Tel: 852-2580-3539
Fax: 852-2580-6463
Email: citydis@ppn.com.hk

KOREA
Hanbit Media, Inc.
Sonyoung Bldg. 202
Yeksam-dong 736-36
Kangnam-ku
Seoul, Korea
Tel: 822-554-9610
Fax: 822-556-0363
Email: hant93@chollian.dacom.co.kr

PHILIPPINES
Mutual Books, Inc.
429-D Shaw Boulevard
Mandaluyong City, Metro
Manila, Philippines
Tel: 632-725-7538
Fax: 632-721-3056
Email: mbikikog@mnl.sequel.net

TAIWAN
O'Reilly Taiwan
No. 3, Lane 131
Hang-Chow South Road
Section 1, Taipei, Taiwan
Tel: 886-2-23968990
Fax: 886-2-23968916
Email: benh@oreilly.com

CHINA
O'Reilly Beijing
Room 2410
160, FuXingMenNeiDaJie
XiCheng District
Beijing
China PR 100031
Tel: 86-10-86631006
Fax: 86-10-86631007
Email: frederic@oreilly.com

INDIA
Computer Bookshop (India) Pvt. Ltd.
190 Dr. D.N. Road, Fort
Bombay 400 001 India
Tel: 91-22-207-0989
Fax: 91-22-262-3551
Email: cbsbom@giasbm01.vsnl.net.in

JAPAN
O'Reilly Japan, Inc.
Kiyoshige Building 2F
12-Bancho, Sanei-cho
Shinjuku-ku
Tokyo 160-0008 Japan
Tel: 81-3-3356-5227
Fax: 81-3-3356-5261
Email: japan@oreilly.com

ALL OTHER ASIAN COUNTRIES
O'Reilly & Associates, Inc.
101 Morris Street
Sebastopol, CA 95472 USA
Tel: 707-829-0515
Fax: 707-829-0104
Email: order@oreilly.com

AUSTRALIA
WoodsLane Pty., Ltd.
7/5 Vuko Place
Warriewood NSW 2102
Australia
Tel: 61-2-9970-5111
Fax: 61-2-9970-5002
Email: info@woodslane.com.au

NEW ZEALAND
Woodslane New Zealand, Ltd.
21 Cooks Street (P.O. Box 575)
Waganui, New Zealand
Tel: 64-6-347-6543
Fax: 64-6-345-4840
Email: info@woodslane.com.au

LATIN AMERICA
McGraw-Hill Interamericana
Editores, S.A. de C.V.
Cedro No. 512
Col. Atlampa
06450, Mexico, D.F.
Tel: 52-5-547-6777
Fax: 52-5-547-3336
Email: mcgraw-hill@infosel.net.mx

O'REILLY™

O'Reilly & Associates, Inc.
101 Morris Street
Sebastopol, CA 95472-9902
1-800-998-9938

Visit us online at:
http://www.ora.com/
orders@ora.com

O'REILLY WOULD LIKE TO HEAR FROM YOU

Which book did this card come from?

_____

Where did you buy this book?
- ❏ Bookstore   ❏ Computer Store
- ❏ Direct from O'Reilly   ❏ Class/seminar
- ❏ Bundled with hardware/software
- ❏ Other _____

What operating system do you use?
- ❏ UNIX   ❏ Macintosh
- ❏ Windows NT   ❏ PC(Windows/DOS)
- ❏ Other _____

What is your job description?
- ❏ System Administrator   ❏ Programmer
- ❏ Network Administrator ❏ Educator/Teacher
- ❏ Web Developer
- ❏ Other _____

❏ Please send me O'Reilly's catalog, containing
a complete listing of O'Reilly books and
software.

Name _____ Company/Organization _____

Address _____

City _____ State _____ Zip/Postal Code _____ Country _____

Telephone _____ Internet or other email address (specify network) _____

Nineteenth century wood engraving
of a bear from the O'Reilly &
Associates Nutshell Handbook®
Using & Managing UUCP.

PLACE
STAMP
HERE

NO POSTAGE
NECESSARY IF
MAILED IN THE
UNITED STATES

BUSINESS REPLY MAIL

FIRST CLASS MAIL   PERMIT NO. 80   SEBASTOPOL, CA

Postage will be paid by addressee

O'Reilly & Associates, Inc.
101 Morris Street
Sebastopol, CA 95472-9902